Remembering My Good Friends

To Sheridan
in driving enjoyed
the European
[signature]

George Weidenfeld

REMEMBERING
MY GOOD FRIENDS

AN AUTOBIOGRAPHY

HarperCollins*Publishers*

HarperCollins*Publishers*
77–85 Fulham Palace Road,
Hammersmith, London W6 8JB

Published by HarperCollins*Publishers* 1995

1 3 5 7 9 8 6 4 2

Copyright © George Weidenfeld 1994

The Author asserts the moral right to
be identified as the author of this work

A catalogue record for this book
is available from the British Library

ISBN 0 00 215856 6

Photoset in Linotron Sabon by
Rowland Phototypesetting Ltd
Bury St Edmunds, Suffolk

Printed in Great Britain by
HarperCollinsManufacturing Glasgow

To three lovable women:

ANNABELLE, MY WIFE

LAURA, MY DAUGHTER

AND CLARA, MY YOUNGEST GRANDCHILD

CONTENTS

ILLUSTRATIONS

Lally Weymouth in New York.

Barbara Walters and Malcom Forbes.

President L. B. Johnson reminisces about the Six Day War at his Texan ranch, 1969.

Knighted by the Queen. With Sandra and my mother outside Buckingham Palace, 1969.

From a 50th birthday book: drawing by Nabokov; poem and drawing by Paul Johnson; unpublished birthday sketch by Cecil Beaton; montage of regulars at Cleve Lodge by Diana Phipps.

With Moshe Dayan in the 1970s.

With Teddy Kollek. (© *Zev Radovan*)

With Shimon Peres. (*Ita Kaufmann*)

President Chaim Herzog and his wife Aura with Drue Heinz.

Sam Spiegel at his Barbados swimming pool.

Ann Getty and I discussing the Lisbon literary conference of the Wheatland Foundation with President Soares of Portugal, 1988.

George and Barbara Bush at the Dorchester in December 1993 with Annabelle and myself.

With Pope John Paul II and Professor Bernard Lewis at Castel Gandolfo, 1990. (© *Servizio Fotografico*)

The inaugural meeting of the Founders' Council of the Europaeum, 1992. (*Rob Judges/University of Oxford*)

With Helmut Kohl and Edmond de Rothschild in Frankfurt, 1994. (*Deutsche Presse-Agentur GMP*)

Jerusalem wedding, November 1992: Annabelle and myself.

Playing Scrabble on honeymoon, 1992.

The next generation: my daughter Laura and her husband Dr Christopher Barnett with my grandchildren. (© *Times Newspapers Ltd*)

All photographs are from Lord Weidenfeld's own library unless otherwise stated.

ACKNOWLEDGEMENTS

I want to start with an apology to all those whose friendship has meant a great deal to me but whom I have not been able to mention in these memoirs. Some might even prefer it that way.

I must thank those who encouraged me to write the book and subsequently helped me in various and valuable ways. Victoria Glendinning was one of the earliest councillors but I interrupted work on the manuscript for several years. When I resumed, it was Gina Thomas who kept me up to the mark, gave me unstinted support in collating the material, researching and editing it. Her friendship, her Anglo-German background, her knowledge of, and insight into so many themes and ambiances of my life made her effective and indispensable.

I wish to thank Christopher Falkus, my colleague of long standing, for reading the manuscript, filling gaps and clearing my mind on shared experiences.

Two friends, authors and distinguished practitioners of biographical writing, Kenneth Harris and Kenneth Rose, gave me much help. Bud MacLennan kindly dealt for me with my publishers HarperCollins. I am indebted to Simon Cobley, Weidenfeld & Nicolson archivist, for his patient and valuable research. I wish to thank my assistant Pat Kinsman for helping with research and typing the material. I also valued her opinion throughout the process. Sally Strahan and Helen Benckendorff deserve much praise for typing several drafts of the manuscript.

As a fellow publisher I would like to say how much I enjoyed working with my colleagues of HarperCollins, Michael Fishwick, publishing director, and Juliet Van Oss, the editor in charge of my book.

It was important to me that my daughter, Laura, should see the final draft of the earlier chapters and I was pleased that she approved of what she read.

Finally, I owe so much to Annabelle, my wife, who showed her compassionate understanding and her skill at exerting stern but serene discipline on one who has goaded literally hundreds of authors into writing their memoirs, but when attempting the task himself often felt dispirited and cripplingly awed by doubts and dilemmas. To all those men and women, fellow autobiographers, I extend my belated apology.

I count myself in nothing else so happy
As in a soul remembering my good friends

Richard II, Act II, scene iii

REMEMBERING
MY GOOD FRIENDS

Prologue

THE LUGUBRIOUS VOICE of Fred, the Kenyan butler, sounded an octave lower and more sombre than usual: 'Sir, I have bad news. He's dead. Your father has died.'

I ran down the stairs of the building near Oxford Circus where we had our offices, and reached my parents' Edwardian house off Sloane Square some twenty minutes later. My father's study led off the drawing room on the first floor. There the scene was reminiscent of one of those academic paintings of the Victorian era depicting a family tragedy: my mother sobbing disconsolately, the hefty Kenyan staring thoughtfully at the figure slumped over the Biedermeier desk, the head resting on a writing pad; the family doctor, holding a syringe poised for action.

It was a grey and rainy day in the last week of 1967. The doctor pronounced the cause of death. It had been a peaceful, solitary end. It had occurred during the lunch hour whilst my mother was out on an errand. The Irish maid had discovered my father when she brought up a tray with veal goulash and gnocchi. She had rung my house and, in her distress, begged Fred to break the news to me as Sandra, my wife, was abroad.

Though I was numbed by the doctor's needle, a stinging pain broke through my sense of a most unnatural tranquillity, and I knew that I had lost the person that I had loved more deeply than any other being on earth.

There had scarcely been a day in the thirty years since my father's release from a Nazi prison in Austria and his arrival at his English refuge when I did not speak to him at least once on the telephone. He was guardian and confidant, fellow conspirator and sounding-board for dreams and secret ambitions. Yet at the same time, he was also my ward. He had never overcome the pain of disenfranchisement, and suffered from his inability to adapt competitively in a foreign land or master its language, an instrument which he had handled with such virtuosity on his native turf.

I had last seen him a week or so earlier when we celebrated Christmas Eve in Sandra's and my home in Hyde Park Gate. It had been a cordial family reunion. The company assembled in the dining room, where Sandra's Impressionists mixed strangely well with my Italian Mannerists, was as diverse as the paintings on the wall. Sandra, the svelte and statuesque daughter of America's Eastern Seaboard patriciate; her son and daughter, lank and impeccably Long Island; Laura, my daughter from an earlier marriage, reflecting the vivacious good looks of her Anglo-Jewish mother; and my parents, whose appearance, gait and intonation all echoed the vanished world of Imperial Austria.

The evening was a great occasion for us all and one which Sandra, with a gentle touch so typical of her shy and understated thoughtfulness, turned into an ecumenical event. Facing the over-loaded Christmas tree she had discreetly placed a nine-armed Jewish candelabra on the plinth that usually supported an eighteenth-century French rake. Though obviously moved and content, my father had not been himself: he was silent and pensive throughout the meal. We had been worried about his state of health for the last year or so, but not enough to fear the worst. In spite of his seventy-eight years, he was agile and had retained his omniv-orous curiosity. Little did I know when we parted that night that his valedictory gesture, an appreciative semi-circular wave with his right arm, which was meant as a seal of approval, would be his last sign of life to me.

Images of that final evening together ran like film sequences through my mind as I left the room in which he had died to make the necessary arrangements on the telephone next door. Within the hour four men from the Jewish Burial Society, led by the local rabbi, arrived to take my father away. When they left I stared after the car until it had turned into Sloane Square. 'I'm changing places,' I thought, for it was my father who, in a self-imposed ritual, would always stare after me until I was out of sight. I took my mother to her room and went once more into my father's study. Only then did I catch sight of the top sheet on the writing pad which had been covered by his head. It was a letter addressed to me, written in German and in gothic script. It read:

My dearest son,
    Whatever I may have done or failed to do for you, at least I tried to give you a sunny youth . . .

CHAPTER ONE

A Sunny Youth

AUSTRIANS AND JEWS share one illusion: they are convinced that they are the centre of the universe. When the First World War broke out within their imperial boundaries they were confirmed in this belief. The economic crises in Central Europe, forerunners of Black Friday in 1929, the bloody end of democratic government and the rise of right-wing extremism all added to their perception of Austria as the cradle of culture and modernism as well as the 'experimental lab of world destruction', as Karl Kraus put it. Jews have always been concerned with their role as the Chosen People, the conscience, the barometer and the pulse of history. I inherited a combination of these two egocentric attitudes, and they instilled in me a sense, heightened by my being an only child, of destiny and purpose. By the time experience had begun to sow some salutary doubts, my character was formed.

I was born in Vienna in the aftermath of the First World War and the collapse of the Austro-Hungarian monarchy. The world around me had remained largely prewar in character: Houses and street lamps, carpets and curtains, the mouldering fashion magazines in dentists' waiting rooms still bore the stamp of Imperial Austria. It was a time of introspection, poverty and misery; hyper-inflation gnawed at the threads of the social fabric, the upper classes found that their land was devalued, the middle classes were demoralized by unemployment, and universities and technical colleges were disgorging class upon class of graduates without a hope of employment, not least because the huge bureaucracy of the Empire was shrinking into nothingness. The genteel classes and the proletariat shared in the general bitterness.

Whereas the ethnic groups of the dual monarchy formed sovereign nations known as the 'successor states', the German-speaking

Austrians were left to themselves. Prevented from joining the new German Republic by the severe peace treaties of Versailles and St Germain, they settled down to an uneasy statehood, searching for a new identity. Most Austrians, especially those who flocked to the moderate and well-organized Social Democratic Party, thought of themselves as being in a 'waiting room', hoping to board the train of German unification, the Anschluss. A sizeable minority, backed by the Catholic Church, looked further back into history and, longing for the restoration of the multinational monarchy, carved out for themselves an Austrian identity.

The Jews were the one element among the various ethnic communities in the Empire that fitted uneasily. There were of course pockets of assimilation and acceptance. Most Jews felt an overriding sense of loyalty towards the Empire and to its symbol, the Habsburg dynasty, embodied by that incomparable father figure, the Emperor Franz Joseph, whose reign had started in the turmoil of the 1848 revolution and ended in the third year of the First World War. The war had uprooted the large core of Jewish settlements in the outlying provinces of the monarchy, from Austrian Poland (Galicia), the Bukovina, later awarded to Romania, and from the mountainous Carpathian corners of Hungary to the Adriatic littoral. They flocked for shelter to their Imperial city, Vienna, leaving land and property behind. So wartime Vienna was full of Jewish refugees adding to the social discontent already rife in a city which reflected in miniature the complexity and pluralism of the Habsburg Empire.

Vienna had always been the cultural centre of the Empire, the place to which Jews gravitated for their education, for intellectual stimulation or indeed for a career. About three hundred thousand Jews (including a small percentage of converts to Christianity) of a total population of almost two million lived there. The Jewish microcosm was infinitely rich. Its diverse strands were divided by geographical provenance and by a caste system consisting of the old-established families who had been there for generations, those who had divided their lives between their regions of origin and who, having studied or established businesses in the capital, kept in close touch with both, and the flood of the newly arrived who had no Viennese roots whatsoever.

My parents fitted the second mould. My father's family were mainly professional people – doctors, lawyers, businessmen – who had come from the Rhineland and Franconia (Weidenfeld is the name of a Rhenish hamlet) centuries ago and settled in an arc spanning Czechoslovakia, Poland, Romania and the Ukraine. My paternal grandfather was a landowner in the Bukovina, a border district of what is now the Ukraine but which belonged to Romania before the Second World War. The Habsburgs had deliberately created, in centuries past, a multiracial enclave there. The intelligentsia and middle class were made up of Jews and non-Jewish Germans from Swabia, the proletariat was Romanian, and the grindingly poor peasants were Ukrainians who were known as Ruthenians to prevent them from identifying too strongly with their brethren living under the Tsar.

My father was born in the small town of Wiesnitz, near Czernowitz. For two or three generations all the sons of the family had gone to Vienna to study, and most had settled there. Some made good – one of them, a professor of dermatology, was ennobled for curing, as rumour had it, an archduke of an unmentionable disease. But my grandfather stayed behind in the Bukovina and kept the family business. When he was ten years old, my father was sent to school in Vienna, where he lived until he fled the Nazis. His life was torn between the world of action and the world of scholarship. A gifted linguist and a good classical scholar with a passion for archaeology and numismatics, he longed to become an academic. He had spent two years of his youth in Italy studying the remnants of Ancient Rome. At the outbreak of the First World War he had enlisted in the Austrian Army at the Italian front but was invalided out in 1915. Back in Vienna he joined the Academic Legion, which engaged in fire-fighting and similar duties at night. During the day he worked at the university, trying to establish himself in the academic world, eking out a modest existence, but fighting against the odds – it was well nigh impossible to get tenure as there was no money for the establishment of new lectureships or readerships. He was twenty-nine when he met my mother. She was twenty-three. They married in the last few months of the First World War.

Although my father had been educated in Vienna, the first ten years of his life in the cosseted Jewish world of Eastern Europe had had a formative effect on his outlook, instilling in him at an early age an awareness of the Jewish condition and its complex dilemmas. In the small town of Wiesnitz, which was the seat of a legendary Chassidic rabbi, secular enlightenment clashed with fierce religiosity. The study of the Talmud and the strict practice of religion was prescribed for all children from the age of four. The Talmud school, the Cheder, was kindergarten and religious seminary rolled into one. When my father went to Vienna he thought he had left much of this behind. He was never a rigidly practising Jew, but the echoes of childhood, the memories of infant pupils rising at dawn to trudge in sleet and snow single-file behind the crouched figure of the teacher carrying a flickering oil lamp, could never be dislodged.

My father's background – in terms of Jewish self-perception – was dwarfed by that of my mother. She came from one of the great rabbinical dynasties of European Jewry, a family of Levites who traced their descent from a long line of theologians and scholars. The family, variously called Benvenisti and Abulaffia, had originated in Spain in the eleventh century. They lived in Gerona and Barcelona, but left after the Spanish Inquisition and spread out, moving briefly to the Rhine before finding refuge in Horovice, a small town near Prague, where they changed their name to Horowitz. They were distinguished by the prefix *Ish*, meaning 'Man of . . .', as a reward for their long-standing Talmudic prowess. It was a cohesive clan which took enormous pride in its ancestry. The family had produced a large number of chief rabbis of Prague, Krakow, Lvov, Breslau, Glogau and Liegnitz, and many other smaller towns in Poland, Bohemia, Moravia and southern Russia. Some had even ventured into the predominantly Sephardic realms of northern Italy. Colonies of Central and East European Jews in Milan and Trieste summoned various young Horowitzes.

From my earliest youth I was regaled with glorious stories, facts and legends about 'the ancestors'. There was, for instance, a chief rabbi of Prague in the sixteenth century who, at the age of seventy, decided to emigrate to Jerusalem. There he built a synagogue, which still stands today. He was known, as were many distinguished theologians in Jewish history, not by his family name but by the initial letters of the first words of his chief work of scholarship. In his case, the first three words of his thesis were the Hebrew equivalent of 'The Ark of the Covenant'. The Hebrew initials were S.H.L.O., so he was known as 'The Shelo'. Erudite Jews still rank him very highly.

The Shelo started a little community in Jerusalem. Most of his descendants also belonged to the intellectual mainstream of Judaism, the so-called *Misnagdim*, which means 'the followers of the law'. They were, so to speak, the Thomists of Judaism. They did not believe in mysticism, they had a horror of the irrational, the surreal or supernatural. The business of counting angels' heads or wings was anathema to them, and they stood up forcefully for the rational side of Judaism as a code of ethics and as the law triumphant. When in power, they often excommunicated members of the community who indulged in mystical heresies, and in the eighteenth and early nineteenth centuries there were brutal sectarian feuds when the Misnagdim stood up against the Chasidic sect and took their place in the battle against pseudo-messianic deviants.

There were moments in my adolescence when I was assailed by doubts about the authenticity of some of my ancestors' exploits as handed down by my family, but I was agreeably surprised when, much later on in life, Jewish scholars and, indeed, Catholic theologians in places as far apart as Jerusalem and Leyden gave those accounts enthusiastic corroboration. None of these instances was more heart-warming than a Passover evening at the house of Israel's first chief rabbi, whose son, Chaim Herzog, later became president. The rabbi recited a string of my forebears' names and entertained a group of learned men with their *obiter dicta*.

My mother's family kept a detailed genealogical tree which reflected a number of patterns that held good for centuries. The men in the family were carefully married off to rich merchants' daughters whose dowries enabled them to study all day whilst they were trained for the Rabbinate. The females married well-to-do businessmen or landowners to enrich their parvenu strain. The girls were usually educated by private tutors and took piano lessons. They were not unenlightened; in fact the female members of the family received a religious education, albeit scant: they were trained more in ritual than in substance. For the boys, on the other hand, the study of the Talmud was quintessential. By the middle of the nineteenth century, though, things had changed. While retaining their Jewishness, more people went into the professions, and even in my mother's family the secular world began to beckon.

For three generations there had been no male heirs in my mother's branch of the family, but as descent goes through the female line, my great-grandmother and grandmother looked to me to continue the tradition. But circumstances had changed: not only had the ancestral homes disappeared behind the Russian lines, but my mother had married an unalterably 'secular' Jew, so those two strong-willed women sublimated their ambitions for my becoming a learned man in the theological sense into a fierce ambition on my behalf to 'fulfil some great destiny' in the service of the Jewish people.

The fabled past contrasted starkly with drab reality: the sense of being of an intellectual, spiritual elite clashed with our modest material condition. The family had been rich, I was told, before the breakup of the Austrian monarchy, but had lost everything in their flight to Vienna from the Russians. Nonetheless they retained a sense of aristocratic superiority which transcended their discomfort. I remember my great-grandmother, a woman in her late sixties, whose father had been the chief rabbi of Cracow. She was tall, with striking bone structure, and wore prewar clothes made for her by elegant couture establishments. She had several daughters – some still had money, others were penniless – and lived in comfort, selling her jewels to support her siblings.

My mother was brought up on the borders of what is today the Ukraine and Poland. Her father was one of the richest men in the region, with large estates and small wells of oil, *nafta* as it was called. My grandmother lived on the borderline between piety and enlightenment. Strictly observant, she was, nonetheless, not intolerant. Though passionately devoted to me, her only grandchild, she could be critical of my faults. She had given my mother a good education, sending her to a Catholic convent school whilst ensuring that she received Jewish religious instruction at home. The Horowitzses spoke German and not Yiddish in the family, though they were conversant with the language which was, of course, still much used. When, towards the end of the century, the cult of the Hebrew language as a form of modern expression came into fashion, they took a benign interest in emerging Zionism.

My father was a struggling would-be don when he married my mother, working on a thesis on Roman coins and giving private lessons in Latin. I don't think he had a particularly original mind, but he was a gifted teacher. He had an extraordinary capacity for turning the most lethargic student into an enthusiast for his subject. A capacity for make-believe, a combination of pedagogy and salesmanship, and at times an almost hypnotic intensity in conveying and explaining facts, making grammar come alive, searching for the pupil's Achilles heel and encouraging him to overcome it, combined to make him the most impressive teacher I have ever known.

But he was also a romanticist and self-deceiver who could raise false hopes and make unfulfillable promises.

Our first apartment was in the Gumpendorfferstrasse in the sixth district. It was a gloomy house, built in the early nineteenth century, with two inner courtyards. The sixth district was inhabited mainly by the genteel *petite bourgeoisie* – civil servants, small businessmen, pensioners, the very class that had been so harshly hit by hyper-inflation. But it was fairly centrally located, within walking distance of the inner city, the opera and the Kunsthistorisches museum. My maternal grandmother, recently widowed, lived upstairs. A cousin lived on another floor, and we occupied a three-room flat on the ground floor next to the porter's lodge.

There was so little money that one summer, when I was three or four years old, my father went to the railway station to pick up lodgers from the stream of visitors to an international trade fair. My parents vacated their bedroom and slept on the dining-room table. My father tried to hold out as an academic for a while, but family pressure finally prevailed and he was persuaded to accept a job under his uncle who had made a fortune in the insurance business – Uncle Hauptmann, as we called him – a large, ebullient, self-made man who radiated optimism. With his partner, Dr Berliner, who later appeared in a number of Austrian *romans-à-clef* of the 1920s, he built up a chain of insurance companies in the 'successor states' of the monarchy. They took advantage of the discrepancies in insurance law in the various newly formed states and, it was rumoured by their enemies, clandestinely transferred trainloads of share certificates and war loans, which were valueless in Austria, to Czechoslovakia, where they were validated. Their insurance empire was called Phoenix and had headquarters in Vienna with semi-autonomous branches in Prague, Budapest and Trieste.

My father was given a modest job at first and treated by Uncle Hauptmann with a mixture of patriarchal condescension and Victorian severity. When ushered into his presence, my father never knew how Uncle Hauptmann would behave. Once, after my father had come home and reported a particularly humiliating incident, I was incensed. At a grand family party in Uncle Hauptmann's house the same evening, the patriarch asked me benignly what I wished for my sixth birthday. Still seething, I said, in the hearing of the assembled clan, 'From you, Uncle, bugger all!' Uncle Hauptmann stared at me in stunned silence, temples swollen, eyes contracting, with a shocked expression that slowly changed into a broad grin: 'That's my nephew – he'll go very far.' Everyone burst into relieved laughter.

It was not long before my father proved himself in the eyes of my uncle. His income rose steeply, and by the time I left primary school and was accepted at the Piaristen-Gymnasium, we had moved to an elegant flat near the university. We could afford two maids, and my father had a car and a driver. At last he could indulge in his passion for expensive first editions of Latin classics printed in the sixteenth and seventeenth centuries, and build up a notable collection of coins. He rose to the rank of director and had two offices, one in the Herrengasse near the Harrach Palace in the centre, and another in the suburban Zieglergasse, where the more common or garden storm and tempest claims were dealt with. The big deals were done in the Herrengasse.

My father was not a good businessman. He knew little about insurance, and his optimism and self-deceptive enthusiasm caused him, intermittently, deep disappointments. But he had imagination and a gift for salesmanship. His strength lay in recruiting sales forces in unexpected and bizarre quarters, chief among them Austria's impoverished aristocracy. The lingering economic crisis had depreciated the value of land, forests, art treasures and all kinds of property so that innumerable princes, counts, barons or simple 'vons' were unemployed – especially the ranks of the younger sons or daughters. Yet they were well-connected, and still capable of impressing the burgeoning class of *nouveaux riches*, American tourists and other overseas visitors who flocked to the race courses and polo fields of Central Europe. Above all, they still had an entrée to the affluent upper crust among their relations and acquaintances who had not been rocked by the storm. So my father engaged a bevy of blue-blooded insurance agents from the pages of the *Almanach de Gotha*.

His deputy was a Baron Offermann, who still carried on after my father's flight from the Nazis. Count 'Franzi' Vetter von der Lilie opened a branch of 'aristos for aristos' in an old palace, soon spreading his net to the ever-growing number of Indian maharajas or sheikhs who brought their concubines for treatment at Vienna's university clinic where the gynaecological department enjoyed a high reputation. Some of the most sonorous names of mid-European nobility were on the Phoenix payroll and shared their commissions in a very complex way. This meant many trips to outlying feudal castles and country estates, which also brought my father into touch with the monarchist movement of steadfast loyalists to the Habsburg cause who were dreaming of restoring Archduke Otto of Habsburg to the dual thrones of Austria and Hungary.

The monarchist or 'legitimist' cause was not a foolish pipe dream. A large part of the conservative population of Austria – and Austria was as much a country of conservative farmers as of urban socialist workers – yearned for the good old days of the Empire. A number of wealthy farmers in the provinces were prone to financial sacrifice for the monarchist cause, and so my father devised a special insurance scheme whereby Habsburg loyalists, rich or poor, could insure themselves on behalf of the impoverished Imperial family and contribute to the movement. Leaving aside his Jewish origins, this venture made him a hated target of the Nazis and other pan-German nationalists, and he was on their blacklist from an early stage.

My father's chief lieutenant in the alpine shires was a colourful Falstaffian character called Herr Radler, who wore lederhosen and loden coats, carried a silver-topped walking stick and smoked an undulating, oversized pipe. Radler had the gift of the gab, but bordered on the felonious. Addressing a group of Tyrolean peasants in a farmhouse near a snow-capped mountain peak, he gave them glowing descriptions of the benefits of different brands of life insurance. When asked what visible security they might have, he lowered his voice and whispered, 'The vaults! The gold vaults of the Phoenix insurance company.' He proceeded to describe how the cellars of the head office in Vienna held bars of glittering gold on conveyor belts and *Pater Nosters* guarded by armed men. This, Radler told his audience, ensured the unshakeable security of their invested premiums.

One fine day my father was visited by that group of Tyrolean peasants. They had come up to Vienna on a sightseeing tour, the main purpose of which was to inspect the vaults of gold. My father was able to satisfy them of their security by giving a spirited lecture on the essence of the banking system, but though they left reassured, they were inconsolably disappointed. That spelt the end of Herr Radler's career in the insurance world. I believe he became the publisher of an investors' newsletter in Innsbruck and died at a ripe old age.

My father's involvement with the monarchist cause and people of old lineage did not tie him to the conservative camp. He developed many other valuable connections, including those with the leadership of the powerful Austrian Social Democratic Party. Liberal at heart, he sympathized with this party, the most democratic force in the country, and always voted Social Democrat, one reason, of course, being that the party was committed to the fight against anti-Semitism and the levelling of religious barriers.

My father had no social ambitions and did not cultivate the aristos. Among the few blue-blooded friends who came to our house and showed a genuine liking for my family was Countess Vera Fugger, who was statuesque and ravishingly beautiful. She led an adventurous life, later leaving her feudal husband to live with the youthful last prewar chancellor of Austria, Dr Kurt Schuschnigg, a widower who ruled the country for nearly four years. He had been the youngest member of the cabinet when Dollfuss was murdered in a Nazi coup in mid-July 1934, and had taken power, helped by Mussolini's massing of troops at the Brenner frontier. The German-led revolt collapsed and an uneasy peace followed. Many people outside Austria felt the new regime was doomed to failure, for the growth of the illegal Nazi party appeared unstoppable, but most Austrians, optimists by nature, lulled themselves into a false sense of security. Many a foreign visitor, relative or friend warned us to leave our homeland, but my father trusted in the Western powers' strength of arms and purpose. Although I had some offers to go abroad and make my future in a safe haven, the family fiat was that I should stay and study in Vienna, 'centre of the universe'.

The Jewish world in Vienna was a microcosm as varied as the multiracial world outside it. The concentric circles of Jewish snobbery were divided broadly into those who were mindful that they had been in Austria for centuries, and those who came from the backward provinces of the Empire. The former was then divided into, firstly, Jews who had fully 'arrived', reaching the dizzy heights of 'eligibility at court' – they were headed by the Rothschild clan, its blood relations and affiliates, a wafer-thin slice of the community; secondly, those who had entered the ranks of the upper bourgeoisie and often married their daughters to Catholics or converts to the Christian faith (a popular compromise in those circles was to turn

vay house to radical religious change); and,
road-based Jewish bourgeoisie split between
daism and agnosticism, but marked by a fierce
ssimilate, if not identify with, their gentile

wry did not think of themselves as being part
ity or racial minority. All they wanted was to
d and treated as equals. They, of course, nursed
rned love when they were rattled out of their
o face the reality of anti-Semitism. First they
he rubber heels of the creeping Judaea-phobia
horitarian Catholic Party, then came the hob-
ilitant Home Guard, who grew more influen-
d Schuschnigg, and ultimately the jackboots
irts.

Jewish oligarchy, the Rothschilds included,
h, had their traditional pews in the central
ed Jewish charity whilst keeping themselves
mass, or indeed the middle ranks, of the
ey practised the kind of discrimination that
chwarzenberg princes to remark, when he
not receive the Rothschilds in his palace,
Jews to their parties either.' But the larger
was committed to some pattern of Jewish
us and proud of being Jewish, and had its
nd poor, intellectuals and illiterates, pro-
nemployed and the unemployable.

were mixed. My father was a liberal and
knew a great deal about religion. He had
tion, so we went to the synagogue on high
id not adhere strictly to the rituals; we ate
he and in restaurants. Only my maternal
with us, was religious. As a child I spent
. She liked music and went to the theatre,
arly brilliant or cultivated. Nonetheless,
ence, and instilled in me a sense of near
e through the turbulence of adolescence
in cultural environment I experienced

a Sancho Panza to my father's Don

Quixote. She saw things as they were, whilst he could deceive himself into thinking that whatever he touched was magic. When he recounted an incident from work he would embroider it into a heroic tale, and he painted glowing pictures of my future. Temperamentally I aligned myself with the Quixotes, sharing my father's sense of fantasy. I grew up in a sort of hall of mirrors.

The class system in the self-contained Jewish world did not reflect the class system in the gentile world. An Austrian or a German gentile would judge, say, an Ost-Jude or Eastern Jew by his means and the way he lived, and categorize him as middle class, lower middle class or whatever on this basis. In the world of the devout Jews, it was wholly different. The Jewish rabbinical 'aristocracy' was acknowledged by all, even by the richest *nouveau riche* Jew. Whenever such a figure entered the modest flat in which my maternal grandmother lived, he would feel as though he were calling on a great lady who lived in reduced circumstances. He did not go patronizingly; he felt ill at ease, even though he might have made a few millions on the black market.

My parents had no social life in the established sense; they would see only old friends, family or business associates. Among these was a devoted *Hausfreund*, Dr Wiesinger, bachelor son of a well-known flower painter, Olga Wiesinger, who owned the Imperial Pharmacy on the Michaelplatz. He saw me off when I left Austria and kept in touch during the war, and tried to look after my grandmother before she was deported. We also saw my father's brother, Josef, and sister, Mathilde, who was a remarkable woman, unhappily married to a lawyer. As the assistant and close friend of Alfred Adler, the founder of Individual Psychology, she was in the vortex of that movement. Uncle Josef was a distinguished oculist, a passionate Wagnerite and, we all thought, a confirmed bachelor, but late in life he married after all. He was a Freemason and caused something of a scandal by running off with a fellow mason's wife. They were caught in France during the war and killed by the Vichy police.

Relatives and their friends from all over the world often came to visit. Some asked for money, others for advice and help. I remember one occasion when a young rabbi from Palestine came to collect money for the victims of the first big Arab raid on Hebron in 1926. There had been a pogrom and the Arabs had set alight a synagogue and houses in the Jewish settlement. This man described it all in lurid detail, taking off his coat to display the marks left by the lashes and knife wounds. After he left I couldn't sleep for a week.

Then there was the rich uncle from Chicago who would stay at the Imperial Hotel and give me ten dollars, a huge sum at the time, as a birthday present, or some pathetic divorcee, maltreated by her husband, who would come from Brno or Budapest and stay in the guest room. I used to hover, listening feverishly to the family gossip about Tante Ida getting divorced, or Uncle Adolf eloping with a soubrette in Mährisch-Ostrau. The adults would draw me in as a messenger: I became a sort of ombudsman, negotiating between my grandmother, my parents and my cousins. I relished being at the centre of events, and my love of gossip was fed by the multiplicity of family news.

Solitude and conviviality have a special significance in the life of an only child. When you are left alone and surrounded only by adults, mostly a preoccupied parent or grandparent, a sense of isolation is ever present. Although the adults closest to me thought of themselves as generous, supportive and loving, and in practical terms fulfilled all my needs, to me each approach seemed contrived. There was not much small talk in our family: conversations were either abstract discussions or specific interventions on the business of the day or of the moment.

Right up to the time when I was twelve and had passed the first or second form of my secondary school, solitude was the norm, conviviality the form of entertainment I most longed for. Indeed, I passionately believed it to be the highest form of happiness. I dreamt of conviviality and liked reading about it. Amongst my favourites were the *Tales* of E.T.A. Hoffmann upon which Offenbach's great opera is based. Some of the best tales were built around a group of high-minded students and friends who called themselves the Brethren of Serapion and met at a tavern in Leipzig, where each of them would read a story. In between they would eat, drink, make merry and engage in stimulating conversation. I used to imagine myself among them. I was particularly excited by descriptions of food and drink and conversation, and enjoyed reading scenes of wedding breakfasts, wakes, banquets and intimate suppers in Dickens, Balzac and Immermann's *Münchhausen*, where he embroiders the banquet following the nuptials of a rich Westphalian farmer with a graphic description of each and every kind of local sausage.

On festive occasions such as a dinner party at the house of my great-uncle and great-aunt, Uncle Josef Kleinmann and his handsome wife, Helen, being the only child and drawing all the warmth and attention of adults upon my person was having the best of all worlds. I relished family gatherings, festively decorated tables, candlelight, and the predictable and unexpected foods heaped on colourful plates from different periods and countries which had been 'rescued from the Russians'.

Of all the family, my great-uncle and great-aunt were the most generous hosts. He was boisterous and hedonistic, a bit of a cad but warm-hearted all the same. He had a round, pockmarked face, and was prone to great enthusiasms and hard-hitting polemics. A wonderful raconteur, he accompanied his narrative with expressive gesture and with song. He loved the sound of his own voice. When reminiscing about his early life in the Moravian capital, Brno, a few hours east of Vienna, he would describe in vivid detail not only what the coachman who took him to school said but what he sang. Or he would try to render the different voices at the Passover dinner in his father's house, lending each and every one of the voices of his sisters, parents, and guests or visiting business associates a special inflexion. I remember there was a sort of leitmotif, a 'house song', which Uncle Kleinmann intoned on each occasion that he presided over. It ended in the refrain '*Ta ra ra bom bom bom bom*'. Depending on the occasion, his state of mind and the degree of distinction of the guests, he varied this refrain, and elaborated it with a high-pitched coloratura or a castrato touch, sometimes giving it an oriental flavour. On other occasions he made '*Ta ra ra bom bom bom bom*' sound very military. The manner in which he delivered this refrain always betrayed his mood of the night. Since his relations with his wife and his sister-in-law, Ida, who lived with them (a sad woman deserted by her husband who was missing in Australia), were quite stormy, he could also present '*Ta ra ra bom bom*' as a serenading olive branch to his wife or sister-in-law, accompanied by a look of supplication.

Uncle Josef's fierce optimism kept him alive. During the war he hid in an Italian farmer's deserted barn, reached Cuba and landed in America, where he was joined by Aunt Helen. The deserted Aunt Ida waited in vain for her runaway husband. He stayed in Australia and she was killed by the Nazis. These evenings with Uncle Kleinmann provided me with an outlet for my own histrionic ambitions.

At a given moment after the meal, Uncle Kleinmann would call out to me in an imperious voice, 'Turli – Turli, now do your turn.' With feigned reluctance and amid great urgings, I would then leave the table and either stand in a corner on a footstool or sit down, legs crossed, and recite a chunk from the classics. It might be a ballad from Schiller or Heine, but more often it was a scene from the most recent classical play I had seen or read. My favourite turns were from Goethe's *Faust* – Mephisto's playful altercation with God, his Song of the Flea accompanied by a children's lute, or Faust's monologue ending with the Devil's apparition, which enabled me to be Faust and Mephisto at the same time, a feat that invariably brought tears to the eyes of the assembled family and, with equal regularity, yielded a round of cash gifts or promises of future presents.

Theatre and opera had entered my life almost as soon as I could walk. My passion for opera stemmed from smell rather than sound, for on my daily walk to school I passed a vast hoarding onto which men in white overalls were pasting the daily programme of the opera. The smell of fresh paste in the cold wintry air drew me towards the beautiful gothic letters listing long casts of characters from the vast and varied repertory of Vienna's opera house. I memorized the names of characters and singers long before I heard any opera, and amazed my family with recitals of the dramatis personae of both the more popular and the obscurest operatic works.

My first three operas were open-air performances in the Burggarten. The first was Offenbach's *Tales of Hoffmann*, followed by Halévy's *La Juive* and a tatty production of Meyerbeer's *L'Africaine*. It was not until I reached the age of eight, when my father took me into a box with some business friends to hear *Don Giovanni*, that I entered the opera house. From then on, I became a frequent opera-goer.

The summer before I entered the Piaristen-Gymnasium aged ten, my father took me on a sightseeing tour of southern Germany – Munich, Augsburg, Regensburg and, to crown it all, Nuremberg. 1929 was a year in which you could still have an uncontaminated passion for German culture, history, literature, folklore and music – Hitler and his Brown Shirts appeared only as faint specks of dust on the colourful canvas of the Weimar Republic. We raced through museums, lingered in churches, ate in quaint old taverns and sped through those narrow streets right out of Act II of Wagner's *Meister-*

singer. I was overwhelmed by the beauty of the Nuremberg of the German renaissance, city of Albrecht Dürer and Hans Sachs, who was the true hero of Wagner's opera *Die Meistersinger von Nürnberg*, which has always been one of my favourites. Here I learnt that Sachs, the first poet of the burgeoning bourgeoisie at the end of the feudal age of chivalry, artisan and artist, proud burgher and free spirit, was a real person as well as a legend. I remember my father showing me the commemorative plaque on his house:

> Here dwells Hans Sachs, Shoe-
> Maker and Poet too

He wrote in a distinctive verse style, the Knüppelreim, used by Goethe in Part I of his majestic *Faust*. Sachs was revered by the Romantics, appropriated by the liberal bourgeoisie as the first middle-class poet, acknowledged by the radical democrats and, in one fell swoop, hijacked with all of Wagner's operatic heroes by Adolf Hitler.

As I was left alone a great deal, I had the freedom of my father's library which contained an impressive assemblage of books. The ancient Greeks and Romans were well represented, reflecting my father's fascination with the classical world. As a bibliophile he also liked buying the collected works of the great figures of world literature and of the more obscure German and Austrian authors in beautifully bound editions. The library was well stocked with plays, and this gave me a wonderful chance to stage one-man performances of the works of Shakespeare, Goethe, Schiller, Molière, Calderón and Lope de Vega as well as the more modern dramas and comedies of George Bernard Shaw, Arthur Schnitzler, Ibsen or Chekhov. In the middle of the library stood a miniature Victorian roll-top desk which I turned into a stage, using domino sets as scenery and props and chess figures as characters. I would take out a play from the shelves, say Calderón's *Judge of Zalamea*, and read it aloud, following the stage directions and moving the figures about. Over a period of three or four years, I must have put on an enormous number of productions, and though I may have missed many a subtlety, I got my share of exhilaration and dramatic tension. These solitary readings and performances fanned a huge appetite in me for different milieux and ambiances which was to be satisfied only by more reading and more travelling.

One of the highlights of my childhood was the evenings my father regularly devoted to the game of tarok, an Austrian amalgam of whist, bridge and poker which can be played by two, three or four pairs of hands. He played at least twice during the week as well as every weekend. It was more than a mere pastime for him; indeed, I think it was a form of flight from everyday life. He would either go to one of his favourite cafés, or it would be dinner followed by a game of tarok at home. The round of players varied, but over the years they were a reasonably constant group of relatives, friends, business associates or a particular species known as 'tarok partners' who would share no interest or have any role in my father's life away from the card table. My father never lost his passion for the game. Right up to his death when I was nearly fifty, we played *Strohmandl*, the two-handed version. It is very calming.

Every Wednesday night after dinner, my father's younger brother, Uncle Josef, and two close friends – one a lawyer and the other a venerable surgeon – would sit down to a game of special sophistication. None of them would deign to waste their time with amateurs. Although I was not allowed to touch the cards until I was much older, I tried never to miss a Wednesday night game. First by stealth, then by sufferance, and ultimately by right, I hovered on the edge of my chair as an onlooker. The game as such did not have much appeal to me, but the long and often heated conversations during the shuffling of cards, and the long intervals between rubbers and sets when the players lingered over their refreshments, were of burning interest to me. In the intervals they would suddenly argue about the immortality of the soul or religion versus atheism. Was the Jewish religion up to the requirements of the modern world? Quite often the conversation crystallized into polemical debates as to the relative importance of two individuals. Who was the greater genius – Goethe or Shakespeare? Kant or Voltaire? The current Catholic prime minister of Austria or his Socialist opponent? But most frequently the conversation centred on Verdi and Wagner.

My father was a Verdian, whilst my Uncle Josef lived and died for Wagner. He knew all the librettos by heart and used to cite Wagnerian lines to fit every occasion, mingling them deftly with the jargon of the card table: 'Ingratitude is always Loge's wage', the Firegod's complaint in *Rheingold*, when he was dealt a particularly bad hand. 'You are what you are through contracts', another

quote from *Rheingold*, when there was a friendly quarrel about the
score. Lohengrin's admonition, 'Never shalt thou ask me', when he
was overdue in his bidding. Uncle Josef instilled in me an unquenchable curiosity about all things Wagnerian. When at the age of ten
I saw my first Wagner opera, the *Meistersinger*, and the curtain rose
on St Catherine's Church, Nuremberg to the triumphalist sound of
the end of the overture, I entered a new and thrilling world.

Every summer we spent two or three weeks in Salzburg. The
Phoenix Insurance Company had a complex, a sort of holiday village, in Parsch on the Gaisberg near the city, and for more senior
employees they rented villas nearby. I loved promenading up and
down the main streets of Salzburg, passing through the famed Café
Bazar and seeing the great celebrities, prima donnas of stage, opera
and concert hall. Autograph hunting was the great sport, and no
collection could be without at least some hurried squiggles by
Toscanini, Bruno Walter or the great character actors and heroic
leads such as Alexander Moissi, the Albanian-Italian thespian who
played the role of Jedermann in the mediaeval morality play
recreated by Hugo von Hofmannsthal, whose verses, together with
Richard Strauss's music and Max Reinhardt's brilliant stagecraft,
symbolized the spirit and the substance of the Salzburg Festival.

One of the most popular singers, loved for his *bonhomie* and
wit, was the great bass Richard Mayr, whom it was said Richard
Strauss had in mind when he wrote the part of the Falstaffian noble-
man, the Baron Ochs von Lerchenau, who dominates the great
comic opera *Der Rosenkavalier*. I knew my father was acquainted
with Richard Mayr and begged him to get me his autograph. He
said he would do his best if an occasion arose, but Richard Mayr
did not like that kind of chore and, being a man of savage humour,
would often write an insulting line or two so as to discourage
further supplicants.

One evening, my parents had to give up their tickets for *Rosenkavalier* because of some pressing engagement, so I was sent instead
with the local cook-cum-housekeeper. As it was going to be a long
evening, she made up an enormous sandwich of buttered black
bread with thickly cut ham and creamy cheese. The generous
amount of butter was bound to melt in the heat, but she was undeterred. She put this picnic into a striking red bag and off we went.
There I sat in a sailor suit, white-stockinged feet dangling from the
seat, listening to my hero, Richard Mayr. In the interval we joined

the rest of the audience who strolled in pairs, arm in arm, in a circle around the big foyer, a custom still upheld in some German opera houses. I was holding the rather dreadful red bag, which no one could fail to notice, and saw, to my horror, that the butter was beginning to melt and the cheese to smell. I was seized by panic. When the housekeeper went to freshen up and I found myself alone, I decided to drop the bag discreetly and then walk on, hoping that no one would notice. But as soon as I had done so, I could feel burning in the back of my head the disapproving glares of everyone present. People stepped away from the bag, making circles around it, and I nearly fainted with shame. I sat through the rest of the performance nervously and hardly slept that night. In the morning I confessed to my mother, who, after a few stern words, dropped the subject. Next day at breakfast there was the autograph of Richard Mayr addressed to me and wishing me many more pleasurable visits to the *Rosenkavalier* in the future. My father had somehow managed to get this out of him, and ever since *Rosenkavalier* has ranked among my favourite works of music.

Our summer ritual was like a triptych in which Salzburg formed the centrepiece. The holiday ended with a sightseeing tour, but it began with a trip to Italy, usually a fortnight at an Adriatic spa. Riccione was a favourite haunt of the Viennese in the mid-1930s, and my mother and I often stayed there. Through the son of an Italian colleague of my father, I made instant contact with an enterprising group of young Roman and Milanese *signorini*, who hunted in packs picking up pretty girls, organizing soccer and table tennis matches, and roaming as far as Ravenna in the north and Ancona in the south in search of adventure. The cast of characters was quite extensive, and the group also included the two Mussolini sons, Vittorio and Bruno. The Duce's family was and liked to be seen as egalitarian. Vittorio, the eldest, was a fat yet nimble-footed and lively boy who courted the Junoesque wife of a Milanese banker, serenading her on the sandy beaches. But it was the swashbuckling son of one of Italy's best-known surgeons, Nicola Pende, himself a medical student, who influenced my technique of wooing. Over an endless flow of espresso coffee and grappa, he would tutor me on the mysteries of feminine psychology. There was a clinical detachment, an attitude more heartless than callous, which both impressed and disturbed me. It was as if Machiavelli had written a sequel to his masterpiece entitled *The Prince in Bed*. Young Pende introduced me to my first amorous conquest; you might say he prepared the ground for me. She was Mara, the wife of a notary in one of the Lombard cities, a latterday Madame Bovary, unhappy with her fate and surroundings. The love affair did not outlast the summer. It had an unhappy sequel because a few months later her husband discovered a sheaf of letters that she had written to me but not sent off. A mutual friend told me that she and her husband had parted, but I never heard from her again.

During other summers we would go to a spa in Bohemia or in the Austrian provinces. I used to accompany my mother to Franzensbad, which specialized in women's troubles. Looking back, I think my mother must have been having difficulty in conceiving, but her treatment there was to no avail and I remained an only child.

My father would join us for weekends. Although theirs was not a very passionate or physical marriage, my parents had a great deal of affection for one other. There were flare-ups and occasional explosions, but they had a compassionate understanding for each other's weaknesses. My father, it was generally thought, had had a long liaison with one of his assistants, Helene Hoschek, who came from Ottakring, a working-class district of Vienna. She was a good-looking blonde, slavishly devoted to my father, who had not only discovered and promoted her but also helped her family to get jobs. She was loyal and attached to all of us, and generally deferential to my mother. My mother suffered but endured the triangular situation and never showed her feelings; nor did she encourage protestations and emotional eruptions on her behalf by other members of the family. In the harsh period of the Nazi takeover when my father was in prison, Helene Hoschek risked her job and her freedom doing all she could to help my mother after I left the country. Later she joined my parents in England, and lived in the shadow of our family until my parents died. An old and broken woman, she returned to Vienna but remained in constant correspondence with my daughter and my grandchildren.

The Piaristen-Gymnasium, which my father had also attended, was within walking distance of where we lived. It was attended by the sons of professional people and civil servants who tended to be pan-German and Christian conservative, although even at that early time there was already quite a strong Nazi element. Practising Jews were in a small minority. Originally the Piaristen-Gymnasium was a monastic school run by a teaching order founded in Rome in 1617, and was distinguished for its teaching of Latin and Greek. I was there for eight years, which were punctuated by long absences in Switzerland, Italy and France where I was sent to learn languages: my father wanted me to be multilingual. Ironically, the only language nobody bothered to teach me was English – somehow England was not part of our cultural orbit. We looked to Paris and Rome, Zurich and Prague, rather than to London or New York.

My father took an interest in all I studied and read, but his special concern was Latin. He felt that the Latin language and literature and ancient Rome were the keys to all human knowledge, culture and cosmopolitan sophistication. One of his ways of making Latin palatable and interesting was to take me on excursions to Italy and tell me exciting stories about the great men and women of Rome whose images appeared on the coins in his ever-growing collection. He also encouraged me to create new words, to apply Latin to the modern world and relate it to my favourite pastimes. On one occasion he promised me a bonus on my pocket money if I could write a short account of a football match in Latin. We then discussed my report and argued about the proper words for football, referees, half-time, goalkeeper and so on. He would play on my growing interest in politics and together we would write and design election posters in Latin urging the Viennese 'plebs' to vote Social Democrat for the municipal 'senate'. He could talk about grammar in gripping terms, linking the declension of nouns and conjugation of irregular verbs with colourful tales of the youth of great men of the past, the great 'success stories' of the intellect. On the whole he was courteous, appreciative and full of praise when it was due, but he instantly quashed complacency. 'Don't be smug. At your age Mozart composed his loveliest tunes, Spinoza wrote his first treatise, and as for your mother's ancestor, the great rabbi of Breslau . . .' This never failed to bring me down a notch or two and I would slink back to the shelved alcove of my bedsitting room and dutifully read another ode by Horace or a play by Marivaux.

What made my father such an excellent pedagogue was that he used mainly carrots and only a few sticks in making me take my education seriously. If I did well, he painted the future in such rosy colours that I could not wait to reap my rewards. He spurred me on by saying that if I graduated with summa cum laude, I could go on the most wonderful trip around the world. But this was not to be.

I never distinguished myself in science or technology. In fact I have always been at war with the mechanical world, wholly incapable of grasping the universe of gadgets, even the most primitive accoutrements of daily life. The gulf in my understanding grows apace with the gigantic progress in the field of technology. I cannot drive a car, make coffee or tea, boil eggs, work a video machine and can barely manage to play a record or compact disc. In my most ambitious daydreams I am forever looking for the ideal full-time person or robot who could be styled 'the electronic secretary'.

My favourite subjects were history, German literature and Latin. While my father was concentrating his personal efforts on teaching me to love the world of ancient Rome, he also stimulated my interest in all kinds of history – the local history of Vienna, district by district, Jewish history, of course, but also, through sightseeing trips in Germany and Italy, the grand sweep of European history from the late Middle Ages to the present. The Italian Renaissance became my passion at an early age, a passion that was fuelled by popular historical novels, some of them lurid and lewd. The adventures of the Borgias, the lives of the various dynasts of the Italian city states, tales of cruel men, adulterous women, massacres and conspiracies fired my imagination and I longed to visit the scenes of triumph, crime, orgies, heroism and treason. By and by the historical novel was dropped in favour of serious historical accounts. Soon I collected my own small library covering as many cities of northern and central Italy that I could lay my hands on. Later my interest shifted to the history, politics, thought and cultural ferment of the following century when Spain dominated the Italian peninsula and the Counter-Reformation tightened the grip of the Catholic Church on most of southern and Central Europe.

I have retained a preoccupation with the history of the Catholic Church as a temporal as well as spiritual power to this day. After all, I was brought up in a Catholic country, educated in Catholic schools and had an almost schizophrenic emotional relationship with the Roman Church. I saw it, as many Jews did, as the most powerful and implacable adversary. Its claim to universality, its condemnation of the role of Jewry in the life of Christ, the strong anti-Jewish messages from Catholic pulpits and books clashed in my mind with respect for the vast and seemingly unshakeable structure of the Vatican, a structure which had survived for nearly two thousand years – just as long a time as Jewry had survived in isolated cells, clans and clusters, in exile.

Early in life I learned how dangerous it is to deal summarily with a complex, multifaceted organism, political movement or religious community. I always tried to look for congenial interlocutors, partners in debate and compassionate friends. Among my teachers and acquaintances in the Catholic camp there were indeed fierce zealots who would have no truck with an infidel, narrow-minded bigots who would give no ground in what must have been elementary and primitive theological discussions with a Jewish schoolboy. But I also met wonderful, enlightened priests, none more so than the Jesuit Father Jochem, who took me for long walks and explained to me the essence of Christianity in a manner that was both tactful and reassuring, for at no point did he try to lead me to conversion – almost the opposite. He spoke of Jewry as the elder brother of the Church, a phrase which I did not hear again until Cardinal Koenig, the venerable Archbishop of Vienna of the postwar years and architect of Jewish-Catholic understanding, made it the theme of a most moving speech in a private circle of lay and religious leaders of the two faiths at a conference years later for which he and I were among the co-hosts.

Aware of my passion for the subject, my history teacher at the Piaristen-Gymnasium in the upper forms suggested one term that by way of experiment I should take a class on the French Revolution. It was quite a revolutionary concept for this rather conservative school. I threw myself into this assignment, reading Michelet's *History of the French Revolution* in a German bookclub edition as well as a number of French and German sources, and then gave a series of rather purply lectures which to my surprise received much praise.

The following term I was asked to lecture on the Franco-Prussian War of 1870–71, but just before the time came, my teacher went sick and a relief history master from the provinces took over. He was an undisguised Nazi sympathizer who disapproved of the idea that a pupil, let alone a Jewish one, should talk about the Prussian triumph over the French that led to German unity. After giving a fairly sober rendering of the main events, I became more excitable and, quoting a French source, described in graphic, if not bloodthirsty terms the course of the Battle of Sedan and of a particular

skirmish at which the Prussians acted brutally and 'took no prisoners'. Immediately the teacher pounced on me, shouting in a
clipped military voice, 'How dare you utter such atrocious tales?
I'm glad I came to this class just in time to smash a false halo of
specious scholarship. Sit down.'

I was accused of tarnishing the honour of German arms against
the French and was given a bad mark. When the regular history
master returned there was a disciplinary investigation. The relief
master had complained about the idea of asking 'tendentious
subversive aliens' to talk about the honour of the Prussian Army.
I was asked to write a letter apologizing for my 'disproportionate
rendering of a minor incident' in the larger canvas of a great military
campaign. In private, the history master pleaded with me to yield,
which I did, and after a due interval I was asked again to lecture
on the Balkan Wars, where atrocities on all sides were rampant and
where all our antipathies were equally engaged.

CHAPTER TWO

Storm Signals

IN THE EARLY 1930S in Vienna politics loomed large in our lives. I was an avid newspaper reader and listened keenly to the political discussions at the family dinner table, engaging the grown-ups in endless questions. Storm clouds had been gathering ever since the great bank crashes in Central Europe that came in the wake of Black Friday on the New York Stock Exchange in 1929. For Jews the political crises had a special significance because they fuelled latent and overt anti-Semitism in many quarters. Subconsciously one was trained almost intuitively to seek links and relevancies to 'the Jewish problem' in every article and headline. All political speeches – and indeed all news items – were scrutinized for whether they were 'good for Jews' or 'bad for Jews', and any emergent political personality would be screened for their credentials and attitudes towards the Jews. I was not quite eight years old when the Palace of Justice was set alight by workers embittered because of the acquittal of some fascist home guards who had killed socialist workers in a local brawl. When that venerable building went up in flames many Austrians, prominent among them that great intellectual force and incomparable satirist, Karl Kraus, and the novelist, Heimito von Doderer, proclaimed this event as the beginning of the end of Western civilization. Such a notion might easily be regarded as unseemly arrogance – seeing Austria as the epicentre of the world – but it was curiously plausible: the burning of the Palace of Justice did spell the beginning of the end of parliamentary rule in Austria. It undermined political life and civic ethics and enfeebled those very forces which, when greater tests faced Austria a few years later, might have stood up more manfully for the retention of liberty against the Nazi threat.

The Vienna municipality had a large Socialist majority, whose great social and educational achievements in the fifteen years from the birth of the Austrian republic to the fascist putsch of February 1934 stand out in European history as a successful experiment of a mini-welfare state. The flowering of Austrian culture in the period immediately after the First World War, despite economic crisis and the dramatic shrinkage in the size and significance of Austria, was in no mean part due to the inspiration and the support of the arts by the Socialist leaders of Vienna. In one sense cultural life followed the thread that led back to the great Austrian fin de siècle. In another sense, however, it grew new roots. The Austrian Socialists did an enormous amount of good in the field of adult education, broadening mass participation in artistic activity and art appreciation. We schoolchildren benefited greatly. We saw educational films, attended closed performances at the opera and the national theatre, took part in amateur theatricals, and went to concerts preceded by excellent lectures.

At the age of twelve, during my second year at the Piaristen-Gymnasium, I joined the Bund Sozialistischer Mittelschüler Osterreichs (BSMO), the Union of Social Democratic High-School Pupils. An older boy who lived in the same building, a sturdy, thoughtful sixteen-year-old, 'grown-up' in my eyes, engaged me in earnest discussions, treating me like an equal, and enlightening me on the sufferings and wrongs of mankind. A rebel against his pious Catholic, upper-class parents, he was the leader of a section of the BSMO, and invited me to meetings, Sunday outings at the Vienna Woods, the cinema and discussion groups. Everywhere I met with effortless camaraderie and, above all, a general lack of prejudice. The official greeting was 'Friendship', accentuated by the clenched fist. It was a classless society made up of boys from working-class homes, the daughters of professional families and civil servants. We all wore light-blue shirts, red ties on special occasions and, on attaining full membership, a round patch with three parallel black arrows sewn onto the elbow. Twice a week there was a social evening where we sang the hymns of international brotherhood, the *Internationale*, and a few old German ballads of the peasant wars, both menacing and melancholy in tone. We listened to lectures or ran errands – pamphlets had to be distributed, posters glued onto hoardings.

The great 'signature tune' of the league opened with the rousing words, 'Brothers to the sun and freedom, Brothers unto the light!

Out of the sombre past shines a new future!' When we marched
on the first of May or the anniversary of the Austrian Republic,
the twelfth of November, being part of a large movement, bound
by an ideal, a common faith and a sense of fraternity, made me feel
immensely happy and proud. I treasured brotherhood and conviviality more than anything else. Throughout my life, fraternity which
translates into friendship, compassion and genuine understanding
between people has meant at least as much to me as liberty and
equality.

The family doctor, Dr Friedjung, a patrician figure who was also
a Socialist city councillor, exercised a great influence on my political
development. The son of a great Austrian historian of the liberal
school, he was the classic social democratic 'grand old man'. Friedjung wore a flowing black cape, a solemn, knee-length tunic, a
compromise between a bourgeois morning coat and an artist's
smock. The stiff collar with the black slip and white pearl was the
only concession to conventional dress. His black, broad-rimmed
hat on his fine long head with a full white goatee beard, the silver-
topped walking stick and a worn but elegant doctor's satchel lent
him a wonderful appearance. He was a friend of the family, a tender
counsellor on delicate matters. On his visits to my room, he engaged
me in political discourse. Friedjung was a moderate and belonged
to the right wing of the Social Democrats, but he would listen
patiently to my blabbering outbursts of rebellious left-wing talk.
The only witness to these dialogues was Chippy, the parrot,
who delighted in echoing the most frequently used phrase of a discussion. From time to time he would shrill, 'Left wing, left
wing.' 'I see,' said Dr Friedjung, 'Chippy sides with you. You
are two against one. When you get older you too will be on the
right wing.'

During the three years from 1930 to 1933, the period of my
early initiation into politics, Austrian democracy was in a state of
flux. I see the early 1930s as the age of the buttonhole. Wherever
you walked in Vienna – on the way to school, in the vestibule of
the opera house, or on the promenade in the inner city – and whenever you encountered a passer-by, you would instinctively cast your
eye, not at his or her face, but at the lapel, which enabled you to
place the person at a glance. There you might find the emblem of
the Social Democrats, three arrows on a round enamel background,
or the crooked cross of the Catholic People's Party, or the swastika

of the Nazi movement. Occasionally you might find the Star of David worn by the Zionists, or the stylized ploughshare of the Farmers' Party. But that was not all: the trained eye could discern an infinite number of nuances. For instance, a fully fledged Party member wore an enamel-based swastika with a red surround, a sympathizer or fellow traveller would simply wear a tin-stencilled swastika, whilst a member of the SS would have the fulgurous runic letters. Similar emblematic varieties across the whole spectrum of Austrian party politics could be found in brooches, tiepins, cuff links, belt buckles and blazer buttons.

Political allegiance was also expressed in the clothes people wore. Those on the Right tended to put an alpine and generally rustic accent on their choice of clothes – lederhosen, loden coats, felt hats with a feather. White stockings became the trademark of the Nazi Party, especially during the period of 'illegality'. A Socialist activist, on the other hand, stood out because he wore neither hat nor tie and would place the shirt collar neatly over the jacket. On Saturday and Sunday mornings on the Corso, opposite the strip of pavement at the side of the square on which the opera house stands, from the Hotel Bristol down to the Grand Hotel along the prestigious Ringstrasse, young people promenaded in their finery, parading their political affiliations. Unless you were myopic you could spot your political adversary or ally from afar, which gave you enough time to break into a friendly grin, scowl or look the other way, and if you met a fellow sympathizer you would greet him by raising your arm to the prescribed salute of your party.

The Socialists and Communists used the clenched fist, though there were subtle nuances in the angle of your forearm and its distance from your face. The Catholic supporters of Dollfuss and Schuschnigg raised their arm in a gesture of benediction, thumb and fourth finger crooked, index and third finger erect. The home guard, a fascist breed vacillating between Austrian local patriotism and pan-German nationalism, gave the fascist salute – the outstretched arm rising ninety degrees from the body. The Nazi salute varied according to status within the movement. The subordinate would raise his arm quite high – forty-five degrees; the superior, in imitation of the *Führer*, would raise his hand, palm extended slightly above his head. And the salutes on mutual recognition would also be varied. 'Friendship' was the Socialist call sign, 'Austria' was the greeting of the Catholics, 'Red Front' the

Communist salutation, and the Nazis would invariably bellow *'Heil Hitler!'*

The Austrian sense of elaborate politeness was displayed at its extreme a week after the Anschluss in 1938, when I observed a suave old gentleman, most likely a civil servant, shake the right hand of a passing acquaintance, lift his hat with his left hand and say with a deep bow, 'Goodbye, and please convey many Heil Hitlers to your esteemed lady wife.' This bending of the manners of the *ancien régime* to the new order was much to the taste of a customarily courteous society.

Political affiliations determined not only manners, gestures and dress but also speech. People thought, spoke and wrote in similes drawn from the terminology of the barrack or the battlefield. 'To march' was the verb most frequently used in political discourse. We were marching towards a better future, or a grimmer future. We were at the beginning or at the end of the march. The battlefield, the grey columns, the brown columns, the red columns, the jackboot, the uniform, manoeuvres, exercises, battalions, divisions, bands of brothers – this vocabulary of war and revolution dominated editorial articles, political pamphlets, electoral literature, speeches in taverns and concert halls and mass meetings in the great historic squares. The atmosphere in the streets was often quite explosive. On emotive occasions such as the first of May, Labour Day, the Social Democrats and, to a lesser extent, the Communists claimed freedom of the streets. Marching past a raised dais outside Parliament, the national and municipal leaders of the great Austrian labour movement took the salute of the various socialist formations, youth groups, professional associations and even ethnic memberships. Vienna was not only partially a Jewish city – it also had a large Czech population. The Czechs, mainly working class and small traders, had their own sports movement, the Sokol, and voted to a man for socialism.

The political situation in the country was tense in the years leading up to the Nazi takeover, and the alignment of the parties seemed frozen. The cities, with their working-class components, seemed unshakeably Socialist, whilst the countryside remained solidly Catholic Conservative. The Communist Party was tiny and did not count. A middle-ground coalition between small farmers and a pan-German nationalist section of the middle classes usually coalesced with the Conservatives to form the bourgeois camp. The central government was of the Right, the great muncipalities, Vienna foremost among them, were run by the Left. The Nazi Party was a small, though cohesive and visibly growing, fringe movement. Then suddenly things changed. In Germany the great sister party, the National Socialist German Workers' Party, dramatically increased its seats at the fateful Reichstag elections of September 1930 from 12 to 107 and became the second largest party after the Social Democrats. The echoes were soon felt in Vienna.

I will never forget my first encounter with the spirit of Nazism. It was early in 1931, a warm spring evening. From our windows overlooking the main road leading from the centre of Vienna to the suburbs, we were able to gauge any political demonstration – Left, Right or centre – as there were assembly points on little squares near our house. On that particular day I suddenly heard unfamiliar staccato noises and well-rehearsed choruses. Leaning from the balcony, I saw serried ranks of brown-shirted youths in tight black trousers and jackboots, led by officers. No military band, just choruses: 'Germany awake, Judah perish.' The leader of each platoon would cup his hands to his mouth and shout 'Heil Adolf' in a long drawl, and the followers would complete the slogan with a clipped 'Hit-ler'. The leader would continue, legato, with 'Germany', and the crowd would answer: 'Awake'. The leader would resume with 'Judah', the crowd with 'Perish'. And so it went on, slogan after slogan.

After the first thousand or so uniformed and disciplined crack formations had passed our house, an even more frightening sensation was in store. Huge bands of white-shirted and white-stockinged novices of the Nazi Party, who clearly had neither the money nor, as yet, the status to wear the appropriate uniforms and insignia, marched in seemingly endless rows, shaking their fists at passers-by, stopping at corners, jostling and nudging stunned onlookers and singing in growling tones the early songs of the 'Heroic Age' of the Hitler movement: the Horst Wessel song, 'Volk ans Gewehr' ('People to the Rifle') and others. Their performance was not as well rehearsed as that of the Brown Shirts, but its effect was all the more menacing and primaeval. Later, as a specialist in German propaganda at the BBC during the war, I made a closer study of Nazi Party music, but even then I was intuitively aware of the two radically different strands of music that reflected the two poles of the Hitler movement: the nihilistic, destructive, expressionist beat of metal heels on urban pavements, and the romantic, lilting, folkloristic sounds of the countryside, the melancholy ballad, the green forest, the wind, the snow and the sea.

By the time the last few thousand white shirts with their swastika armlets had marched by, dusk had fallen, torches had been lit, voices, hoarse from all the shouting, had become even more threatening until at last, as I stretched my neck to the left in the direction of the suburbs, the crowds seemed to be thinning out. The rearguard was a regiment, again, of uniformed, well-disciplined Brown Shirts and four rows of drummers wearing black jackets over their brown shirts – the SS, the newly created elite formation of Hitler's bodyguard regiment.

Because of the timing of elections, the Nazi Party in Austria never had an occasion to test its parliamentary strength. However, in municipal elections they made tremendous inroads into both the Catholic and the Socialist vote, and at a crucial election for the Vienna City Hall, thirty brown-shirted members, nearly a third of the total membership, entered the 'Citadel of Democratic Socialism'.

When Hitler came to power in Germany in 1933, pressure for recognition and a share in political power by the Austrian Nazis became intolerably strong. But the Catholic Conservatives held out, leaning on Mussolini's Italy for support. In those days the Duce saw Hitler's expansive policies as the prime threat to his country. It was in his interests that Austria, acting as a buffer between Italy and Germany, remain independent, so he vowed support but named his price: a fascist, or at least semi-fascist, evolution of the Austrian political regime.

The spirit of the time in Central Europe was distinctly sceptical of liberal democracy and parliamentary institution. The moderate, democratically-minded Catholic Conservatives were in the minority in their own movement, as the majority sympathized with authoritarian ideas. The Catholic clergy, too, had never been wholly reconciled to the tenets of the liberal order and its accessories, such as free schools and religious tolerance, and so the Catholic movement easily adapted to a political mutation in which parliamentary government was to be eroded, the trade unions and the Social Democratic Party emasculated and the youth trained in a military, patriotic and specifically Austrian nationalist spirit. The Home Guard, a para-military organization which got its arms and money from Mussolini, was incorporated into the conservative movement, vying with the Nazi Party in its pageantry, brutality and initially cryptic but soon overt anti-Semitism.

Instead of making common cause against the Nazi danger, the Catholic Right and the Socialists glowered at each other with uninhibited hatred. The Socialists were on the defensive – they had little support from outside. The German Left was preoccupied with its own fate, and the Western powers were only mildly concerned with Austria's destiny. Czechoslovakia, with its liberal regime and democratic institutions, was the only beacon of support.

During these years, litigious politics entered the classroom. The fifty or so boys of my class in the Piaristen-Gymnasium were neatly divided into three camps. Nazis and Catholics were equal in number and accounted for ninety per cent. The rest were Socialists, but since my fellow pupils' background was largely professional and upper middle class, practically all the remaining five to seven boys who had Socialist sympathies were Jews. We had a class parliament, an obligatory institution in all Viennese schools, and I represented the Socialist Jewish minority, which held the balance between the Nazis and the Catholic patriots. I was spokesman for my group, so from an early age I learnt, often the hard way, how to operate between two evils – by playing off the Blacks against the Browns I was able to get concessions for my diminutive flock. We had a voice in determining the programmes of the twice-yearly concerts, which were politically charged. Nationalist marches or Verdi choruses predominated, whilst the *Magic Flute* was vetoed by the Nazis as Freemason propaganda.

Even skiing or other excursions arranged by the school during the holidays had subtle political undertones. The winter outings have for ever dampened my enthusiasm for skiing. I remember one ordeal which started on the endless train journey to a Tyrolean mountain resort. Ten of us were crammed into one compartment: eight Nazis, another Jewish boy and myself. Feeling free and unfettered, our eight companions played with a miniature football which intermittently landed on my face. They sang nursery songs with improvised texts, of which the most harmless went: 'Jew, Jew, spit in your hat and tell your mummy I like that.' As the journey progressed, the verses became less innocent. References to knifing, shooting, the gallows and the guillotine crept in. Once we had arrived at our godforsaken destination, hardly had the Nazi contingent gulped down a supper consisting of hot lard, potatoes and coarse black bread than they rushed off parading swastikas and singing raucous songs. The Catholic Conservative element imitated these displays with a rather feeble 'patriotic' camp fire, singing old regimental songs and lewd barrack room ditties from Habsburg days. Our little band of Jews and Socialists, which was one and the same thing, huddled together, praying for the time to pass more swiftly.

I had my revenge when it came to nominating the first eleven for the school soccer cup. The Nazi head boy came up to me and declared, 'We won't have a Jew in the team this year.' At the same time he insisted that we refrain from voting for a Catholic majority, warning, 'There'll be trouble for you if you do.'

I stood my ground. 'You won't only have to have one, you'll have to have two Jews on the team, or there'll be trouble for you.'

'Lick my arse. Take it or leave it, you can only have one Jew!'

'Have it your way, but we'll vote for an all-Catholic team and give up our place to the loyal supporters of the Government.'

Silence.

'All right, two Jews it will be.'

We ended up with a 'grand coalition' of Nazis, Catholics and two Jews, one of whom – not myself, I need hardly say – scored the decisive goal in the final.

I had no scruples in playing off one group of political foes against the other, and learnt, through constant dialogue, the idiom and thought processes of my opponents. These early experiences were lessons in the lifelong effort of living with the 'enemy'. I always wanted to find out as much as possible about an adversary, to learn his 'secret language', study his traits, manners and mores and match my perception of the 'other side' with a clinical appraisal of how it sees itself. I have had a lifelong fascination for the history, philosophy and sociology of the movements I most abhor – Nazism, fascism and Communism – and for the behaviour patterns, speech, dress and thought processes of Totalitarian Man. By the same token, I have developed a compassionate understanding of people's actions and behaviour in the face of totalitarian regimes. I have never approved of the Manichean naivety of the moral apostles who, having lived all their lives in open societies, all too readily pass judgement on others who have not been as fortunate. The mindless condemnation of any form of collaboration without regard to the threat of persecution, terror and death by those who have never smelt the stench of repression has often irritated, indeed repelled me. Some fine men and women have been unjustly accused of collaborating with the enemy when in fact they were appeasing him in pursuit of loftier, humanitarian aims. I have sometimes been criticized for publishing the books of such people, most recently when Chief Rabbi Rosen of Rumania wrote his memoirs. He saved some hundred thousand or more Jews by hobnobbing with the horrible Ceauşescu regime, and procuring their exit visas to Israel.

1933 was the watershed. On 31 January, Adolf Hitler became chancellor of Germany. We soon felt the repercussions. The Austrian Nazi Party gathered self-confidence, the Nazis in my school scented victory, and the school masters began to profess colour more overtly. More than half of them sided with Hitler. Quite a few of them, my favourite history teacher among them, were genuinely anti-Nazi, but the majority vacillated. There is a typically Austrian verb of Gallic provenance – 'lavieren' – which means moving in an undulating way, avoiding commitment, bending to the wind. Well, there was plenty of lavieren among the Piarist masters. Yet the attitude to Jews was complex. For instance, a Nazi master who taught German literature continued to treat me as his favourite up to the end. On the other hand, a semi-fascist, anti-Nazi Catholic persecuted me for my alien influence on the spirit of the class. I fell into a trap when, in a mood of reckless impudence, I once exposed him to derision. Professor H. liked to play a game. He used to challenge the class to offer famous quotations for which he would then give us the source – and vice versa. When my turn came, I recited a two-line verse in the style of a classical elegiac distich:

> Just as the rosy dawn appeared on the distant horizon,
> Xerxes reached for his luminous chalice.

Professor H. hesitated and frowned, uncertain as to what to say. Stunned silence reigned in the class. The tension grew until an embarrassed Professor H. finally declared himself defeated, muttering, 'I fear I don't know.'

I replied demurely, 'Weidenfeld's Collected Works.'

He fulminated, 'This is not just an impertinence, it's typical of your race. You will leave the classroom and spend the rest of the day in the "dungeon,"' – a form of solitary confinement in an outhouse of the school building.

Later in my youth, when I became more pronouncedly and consciously Jewish, I grew a tougher skin. I no longer cared or felt spurned when rejected, and learning from the Jesuits, whose spirit pervaded so much of Austrian schooling, I subordinated my feelings and actions to the central purpose of fighting 'for the greater glory of the Church', in my case for the greater glory of the Jewish cause.

By the end of 1933, the government of Dr Dollfuss, the diminutive chancellor, dissolved Parliament, seizing on a technical point of procedure by which the Social Democrats had played into his hands. Democracy was in a state of limbo for the next few months, but meanwhile both political blocs prepared for a showdown. The Austrian Socialists amassed arms and stored them in the cellars of the fortress-like workers' tenement buildings in the outskirts of Vienna, and the Home Guard trained for civil war.

On 12 February 1934, battle-clad soldiers reinforced by Home Guard battalions from the provinces marched past our windows into the working-class suburbs to crush a Social Democratic uprising. The Socialist leaders were rounded up and sent to detention camps. Some managed to flee the country, others went into hiding. Many of them were caught and some were executed, often without trial. Both the Socialist Party and the trade unions were banned.

Dr Friedjung was put under police detention but was soon released because of his age and health. Julian, my platoon leader, hid in a working-class hovel outside Vienna. Some of my friends mourned casualties in their families. A world collapsed. My world collapsed. For days I stared out of the window, could not eat, and cried. My parents were seriously worried.

At school the Home Guard faction was triumphant, the Nazis were sniggering. The class parliament was abolished and the Home Guard leaders appeared in uniform in class, fawned upon by the majority of masters. A new spirit, a new age, a new trend of teaching became immediately apparent. Brand-new patriotic hymns glorying in the spirit of the new Corporate State became obligatory. These were tense months.

In May I had an unexpected visitor. Julian resurfaced, furtive, and fearful of being recognized. He had changed his identity and become an underground militant. I agreed to accompany him to a cell meeting of the new illegal Socialist Youth Movement. What I saw and heard there left me confused, for there were people present who advocated a common underground front of Socialists and

Communists. A rather aggressive Communist with a club foot and thick-lensed spectacles bellowed Communist slogans and called us to action under Communist leadership. He spoke in an affected language, using Russian words and lapsing into party jargon. I thought of the tales of persecution, anti-Semitism, repression and misery relayed by relatives who had fled the Soviet Union and stopped in Vienna on their way to America.

I was not afraid of danger – in fact, by temperament I courted adventure – but I did not like the Communists' ambience, not least because I shied away from their fierce fanaticism. So I hesitated to join the cell. Instead, in reaction to the impact of manifest anti-Semitism and the emergence of National Socialism, I became a militant Zionist and joined a group called the Revisionists. They were the forerunners of the Likud Party in Israel today. I was struck by their passionate belief in the righteousness of their cause and their grand disdain for their persecutors.

At that time something happened which was to change my life. A medical student, distantly related, who was an active Zionist used to visit my family and banter with me about my political views. He drew a sombre picture of the future of Austria and indeed the whole of Eastern and Central Europe, which was overshadowed by the unstoppable advance of German National Socialism, and he spoke of Palestine as the homeland for the Jews. One day he took me to a Zionist meeting in one of the conference halls in the second district, which was the Jewish quarter.

The speaker was Vladimir Jabotinsky, the leader of the intransigent wing of the Zionist movement, which was fighting for a sovereign Jewish State. It was violently opposed to the more moderate line of world Zionism represented by men like Chaim Weizmann, who believed in cooperating with the British Government, which administered Palestine as a mandate from the League of Nations. As we approached the hall, we saw clusters of white-stockinged Nazis shouting anti-Semitic slogans and threatening to smash windows and doors. The hall was filled, and on the platform, flanked by young men in khaki shirts and black shorts, stood the stocky figure of a middle-aged man with a white mane of hair, black eyebrows and hornrimmed spectacles.

Jabotinsky began his speech. He spoke of the glorious past of the Jewish people, of the uninterrupted link with the soil of the Holy Land, the gathering clouds and the need to concentrate all energies, all passion and faith, on the attainment of the one and only goal, a sovereign homeland for the Jews in Palestine. A heckler called out, 'Why do you wear a brown shirt?' Jabotinsky replied defiantly, 'Khaki is the colour of the desert. Our young men wore it in the Jewish Legion which fought alongside the Allies in the war against the Turks to liberate Palestine. They taunt us about the colour of our shirts. We see no reason to change the colour just because Hitler's thugs are dressed alike. We don't imitate, we are the real thing. Who is Hitler? Hitlers come and go, but the Jewish people are eternal.' The audience stiffened with pride and courage. Another heckler mocked, 'Aren't you afraid of being beaten to pulp by the Nazis outside?' Jabotinsky answered, 'We may be bashed, but we will never be beaten. We are a people of princes.' In front of me two timorous young Jewish boys who had entered the hall in fear and trepidation straightened their curved backs at Jabotinsky's words. His speech met with thunderous applause. At the end of the meeting the audience left the building in orderly formation past the Nazi assailants, who made a hasty retreat.

The meeting made a deep impression on me. Seizing on this mood, my cousin introduced me to the Brit Trumpeldor, a militant organization of the Jabotinsky movement. Trumpeldor was an almost legendary figure, an officer in the Tsarist army who had lost his arm in the Russo-Japanese war and then found his way to the Middle East. There he established the Jewish Legion. He died in battle in 1920, defending Jewish settlers against Arab marauders at the village of Tel Chai. The name of that village, Tel Chai, became the salute among members of the Brit Trumpeldor, which is also known as 'Betar'. The word has a double meaning as it not only reflects the main letters of the name of the organization but is also the name of a fortress in the war of the Maccabeans against the Romans.

As a 'soldier' of the Brit Trumpeldor I received some paramilitary training of a rather elementary kind. I had to learn modern Hebrew (in which I did not, alas, excel), and was given lessons in Jewish history and geopolitics, especially the geography, economics and political and ethnic complexities of the Middle East. Political propaganda consisting of leaflets and oratorical training were among the subjects. After a year I became *Mefaked Gdud* – platoon leader.

In his determination to make me an active Zionist, my cousin, Quint, had another plan. He introduced me to the world of student fraternities, which came to absorb much of my enthusiasm and time, and gave new direction to my whole social and intellectual life, right up to the moment when I left my native Austria.

CHAPTER THREE

The Shadow of the Swastika

The black and gold and purple ribbon
On emerald deep green ground,
Rise up sons of Giskala
To fight a second round

IN A DARKENED ROOM lit only by candles, twenty men in coloured ribbons and caps sat around a table, each with a mug of beer. The two top-ranking leaders stood at either end of the table, sabres in hands, a human skull encased in silver in front of them. They were singing the anthem of the Zionist Junior Fraternity, the Giskala, named after Jochanan of Giskala, a freedom fighter who defied the Romans.

The words were of a rather humdrum patriotic kind, the tune was that of the Hatiqvah, the Zionist anthem which was later to become the national anthem of the State of Israel. The men around the table represented both the *Activitas*, that is to say the active young fellows who were still of public school age, and the 'old gentlemen', the alumni who had once served as active fellows and now largely financed the comfortable, even luxurious, style of the fraternity. Their ages ranged from late teens to sixty or more. The Giskala was a *Penalie*, the expression used for a junior student fraternity which prepared future university students for their work in a proper university fraternity and within the wider community of Jews in Vienna, and for leadership in the Zionist movement.

The universe of student fraternities in Germany, Austria and some of the countries that formed the prewar Austro-Hungarian monarchy had wide ramifications. Socially, and indeed politically and culturally, it played an important role in that part of Europe.

Since the Middle Ages the universities in the Holy Roman Empire had prided themselves on their freedom and self-government, and on the close links between students and teachers. They formed a chain of loosely connected yet sovereign centres of learning, in which, for centuries, Latin was the common language. The teaching syllabuses were very similar, and it was customary for students to begin in one alma mater and then move to another. For a student to start in Vienna, then move on to Leipzig and Heidelberg, spend a year in Prague and then graduate in Vienna or Wittenberg was not unusual. Wherever he chose to go, the student would find congenial company by joining a fraternity. He could either choose a group made up of students from his own home region, or he could mix with others from neighbouring or distant lands. The fraternity not only meant conviviality and the possibility of forging friendships; it also served as a forum for intellectual exchange, a rallying point for political struggle and, ultimately, a stepping stone for a future career. For everywhere the young members of the *Activitas* were under the caring and scrutinizing eyes of the 'old gentlemen', those alumni who had made good in 'civilian life' and who looked out for bright and trustworthy recruits to the professions or the higher reaches of public service.

In the late eighteenth century the student movement in Germany and Austria became more structured and there emerged two closely definable types of fraternity: the corps, which were rather snobbish, and the *Burschenschaften* or 'fellowships'. In the corps, elegance of manner and dress was prescribed; membership was largely confined to the aristocracy and upper bourgeoisie, and their politics were rather right wing. They thought of themselves as being 'feudal' – their social gatherings were elaborate and elitist. The other strand of the student movement, the fellowships, were radical, rough, rebellious against the Establishment, thirsting for reform of the social order and attracted by revolutionary ideas of the Left and the Right. Their dress was deliberately casual, their membership devoid of class distinction. Though nationalist, they were contemptuous of all forms of what they termed Philistinism. Anyone who believed in conventional law and order, manners and morals was dismissed as a Philistine.

The history of these two strands of fraternities is rich and varied. Certain university towns prided themselves on a particularly distinct contribution to the student ethos, foremost among them Leipzig and Jena. The names of the fraternities were mostly taken from Latin names of various regions: *Saxo-Borussia* (Saxony-Prussia), *Thuringia*, *Alemannia*, *Rhaetia* (the ancient Roman name for the alpine provinces), *Pannonia* (which stands for the western part of Hungary), and so on. Right or Left, patrician or plebeian, they had certain things in common: duelling, which was the prerogative of officers and gentlemen; defending a code of honour; a way of life; and distinguishing themselves from the lowest ranks of society. Countless Germans of distinction, politicians, military men, writers, philosophers, historians, leaders of business and industry, lawyers and men of medicine and science went through the formative and disciplinarian education of the fraternities.

During the Napoleonic Wars the duelling fraternities played a significant role. Many of the local levies against Napoleon were led by students and celebrated in the rousing patriotic poetry of such romantics as Theodor Koerner and Ludwig Uhland. The great flowering of the student movement came in the period between the Congress of Vienna in 1815 and the two revolutions of 1830 and 1848, when it gained political prominence. During those troubled times student congresses and high-minded pamphleteering, torch-light processions and mass demonstrations roused Germany and German-speaking Austria, giving the leaders of the Holy Alliance, Austria, Prussia and Russia – but especially the Imperial Austrian chancellor, Metternich, regarded by them as the personification of political reaction – cause for concern. A special international convention at Karlsbad in 1823, known as the 'students' laws', enjoined the European powers to keep an eye on and, if need be, suppress the fraternities. Later in the century, when Germany was united, the sting of radicalism grew numb; political controversy took a different turn. It was no longer revolution against reaction – instead the fraternities moved away from politics towards a rather staid, career-oriented and thus opportunist system of organized conviviality, or they became intensely nationalist and increasingly racialist in outlook, with the Jew serving as the prime scapegoat.

In the Austrian Empire the German-speaking nationalist students grew increasingly hostile to the Habsburg monarchy and its essentially multiracial ethos. They wanted to preserve their German distinctiveness and keep out all those elements which detracted from a pan-German view. A large group therefore decided to form a union of fraternities which would exclude Jews from membership and refuse them the right of 'giving satisfaction', that is to say of defending their honour in a duel.

In the small town of Waidhofen an der Ybbs, an hour or so from Vienna, the nationalist fraternities met and proclaimed the notion of racial exclusivity, banning professional and social intercourse with Jews. The other group of fraternities still held on to a policy of non-discrimination and allegiance to the ideals of liberty, equality and fraternity as proclaimed by the French Revolution and the German Enlightenment, and banded together in a union of 'German-libertarian' fraternities. Alas, as German liberalism shrank and foundered with the passing of time, those fraternities became less important, and by the turn of the century, and certainly in the days of my youth, most of their members were Jews yearning to be assimilated and recognized by their fellow students as German Austrians. Many of them had converted to Catholicism or the Protestant 'middle course' between Judaism and Catholicism.

In the last quarter of the nineteenth century the wind of nationalism spread throughout the Austro-Hungarian monarchy. Czechs and Poles, Slovaks, Croats and Slovenians woke up to clamour for ethnic recognition. The young intelligentsia, the university students, imitated the German model and started their own students' unions, though they stopped short of introducing all their conventions, mannerisms and intricate procedures. The Jewish student population was no exception. A Jewish nationalism bent on professing the Jewish way of life, honouring their own past and flaunting their Jewish separateness began to emerge. It was particularly strong among those young academics who came to study in Vienna from the outlying provinces of the Empire from Austrian Poland (Galicia), Bukovina on the Romanian border, from Bohemia and Moravia – only a few hours' train journey from Vienna, but light years removed in terms of social acceptance.

In 1883 a group of such young Jews decided to establish the first Jewish national student fraternity, the Kadimah, the Hebrew word for 'dawn'. They wrote articles and pamphlets, recruited sympathizers and, after heated discussion, decided after all to take a leaf out of the German students' book: to wear the uniform, accept the rules of conduct, sing the same songs and engage in duels to defend Jewish honour. Behind this stood the firm belief that they had to fight their opponents with their own weapons to win respect and recognition.

The Kadimah attracted talented young writers, architects and other free spirits. They were in search of a leader and a concrete programme through which they could join the political struggle of the times. They found both in the magnetic personality of Theodor Herzl. Herzl was a distinguished and rather flamboyant Viennese journalist, essayist and modish dramatist, steeped in Austro-German culture. An assimilated Jew by upbringing, he was a master of the feuilleton of the revered liberal newspaper, the *Neue Freie Presse*, who, after attending the Dreyfus trial in Paris, that famous and indeed sensational miscarriage of justice perpetrated against a French Jewish officer by his anti-Semitic superiors, had turned Paulus from Saulus. With a sacred fire of injured righteousness and a personal charisma unparalleled in the modern annals of Jewish history, Herzl enunciated a clear-cut programme and initiated a political movement: Zionism. At first he seemed to be alone, but as soon as his historic pamphlet, *The Jewish State*, was published, followers flocked to his banner from every quarter, none more enthusiastic and more determined to go into battle than the students of the Kadimah. They sought him out and offered him their unconditional devotion. Together with the other handful of Jewish student fraternities that had sprung up in their wake, the Kadimah belonged to the most faithful of the faithful, and when Herzl died at the age of forty-four, exhausted from a life's work of adventurous, at times Quixotic, yet in the aggregate almost miraculously effective pioneer work in spreading the notion of a Jewish State in Palestine, it was the young men of the Jewish duelling corps of Vienna who lowered his coffin into the earth.

Following the example of the Kadimah, other Jewish fraternities sprang up in quick succession: Ivria, Unitas, Hasmonaea, Zefriah, Maccabaea, Jordania, Robur. Each had a distinctive characteristic, socially and politically, and each took early precautions to look among public school-boys for future members. Giskala was founded by the members of the Maccabaea, but it soon flourished into a self-contained fraternity whose 'old gentlemen' took pride in independence, especially as quite a few of them had become affluent and self-assertive.

Once accepted, I took the lowest rank in the *Activitas*. I became a Fox and had to run errands for the older Fellows, attaining the next rank after a year of probation. I think I was fifteen when I passed my Fellow's exam. Political activity was top of the list. I had to address meetings of young people in the Jewish community, and go from house to house collecting dues and donations stored in blue-and-white tin boxes and destined for the Zionist fund for the early colonies in Palestine. I also had to practise sabre fencing.

Once a week we had an obligatory council meeting followed by a beer evening. That event, the highlight of the week, was ceremoniously divided into three parts: the *officialis*, the *inofficialis* and the 'pig' session. During the official and ceremonial part we sang our fraternity anthem and listened to speeches. At the *inofficialis* we abandoned ourselves to a contest of choral and individual singing drawn from the inexhaustible, centuries-old repertoire of the German student song book. Mostly we sang the same songs as our German nationalist opponents, but here and there we would change emotive words, substituting the Jordan for the Rhine, German for Jewish or some more neutral word. We also observed traditional German student ritual. This, to give an example, involved performing the Pappenheim Rite, named after a famous general of mercenaries in the Thirty Years War whose soldiers had a special way of toasting their commander. Two by two we would stand on our chairs, salute and bow, cross our beer mugs, drink from each other's mug and then sing:

> Long live General Pappenheim,
> Long live General Pappenheim,
> If beer or if wine,
> We are true followers of General Pappenheim,
> If wine or if beer,
> True Pappenheimers are we here.

But we also had a few specially written Zionist texts which we sang to ancient Hebrew melodies. One of the poets in Herzl's entourage, Nathan Birnbaum, wrote a favourite:

> There where the tall cedar
> Kisses the clouds . . .
> That beautiful land
> Is my homeland on Jordan's shore . . .

Once a year we had a gala night to which friends, relations and ladies were invited, where we all had to appear in white tie. The climax of the evening was the 'Beer Opera', a mini-opera usually composed of a musical medley of well-known arias, choruses and marches with satirical texts. The plot had to be topical and spell a provocative, political message.

When my turn came, aged sixteen, to devise a Beer Opera I chose a plot that parodied Wagner's opera *Lohengrin* in which the hero comes as a saviour to a danger-stricken maiden, saves her from her plight and marries her on condition that she never ask his name or provenance. When curiosity compels her to breach her promise on the wedding night, the hero leaves her, not, however, before revealing his royal birth and that of his father, Parsifal, guardian of the Grail. My Beer Opera had as its theme the plight of an imaginary fraternity of liberal assimilated Jews in Austria whose statutes command, under threat of a curse, the fraternity's disbandment unless they can find at least one new member of non-Jewish origin. The last Aryan member having recently died, the brethren sit lugubriously around the table singing desperate songs of self-pity to the melodies of Weber, Verdi and Wagner. Their very roll call exemplifies their failure. They all have Nordic first names and unmistakably Jewish family names. Thus:

Horst Rosenbaum, Sven Rubinstein and Carl Maria Singer
Frank Odin Kohn, Thor Mossinson and Baldur Fritjof Springer

The door opens and a handsome figure of a man, a giant of distinctly Nordic appearance, enters with his hands outstretched, dressed in a flowing robe, announcing that he has heard their laments from far away and is prepared not only to join but to lead them into battle. A long drawn-out duet, followed by a quartet, merging into a chorus ensue, with protestations of undying loyalty as the leitmotif. The melancholy mood of the opening scene turns into a wild bacchanal.

Such is the gratitude of the assembled Austro-liberal Jews that they spontaneously appoint him leader with discretionary powers over their bank account. Suddenly one of the elders, unable to contain himself, exclaims: 'O, leader, saviour from distant lands, tell us your name and provenance.' There is a stunned silence and then, with pained expression, the stranger exclaims in lines adapted from *Lohengrin*: 'Never shall thou ask my name, but since you did, here is my name and provenance. I am Alois Vollgruber and I am Sales Manager of the famous Schwechat brewery. Since you have

given me full powers and a blank cheque, I will now go on fur-
nishing you with beer for evermore.'

Broken and humiliated by the betrayal, they collapse and, in the
manner of Wagnerian victims and villains, all die instantly.

Life with my fraternity comrades was not all singing, carousing
and fencing. I formed friendly ties with some intelligent and
thoughtful young men, and did not neglect my reading, nor did my
passion for theatre and opera abate. The period from 1933 to 1938,
from Hitler's seizure of power in Germany to the rape of Austria,
was an especially exciting chapter of European cultural history on
Viennese soil. Alongside the creeping progress of semi-fascist authoritarianism and subtle censorship, the cream of liberal and progressive German writers, actors, musicians, philosophers, historians
– either of Jewish origin or uncompromisingly hostile towards the
Nazi regime – sought refuge in Austria where they could work and
think in their native language. Among them was Max Reinhardt,
the giant of the German stage, one of the most influential producer-
impresarios of the century, who spent much of his time in his
Theater an der Josefstadt. There I saw some of his most remarkable
productions of German and foreign classics as well as offerings by
recently exiled writers.

A small trickle of German refugees, Jews and non-Jews, enriched
my class at the Piaristen-Gymnasium. A close friendship with a
young Hamburg boy, whose father chose to leave a sure existence
and brave uncertainty because he could not stand the Nazi spirit,
gave me an insight into the dilemma of the German patriot who
has to choose between his country and his leader. Weekend walks
into the Vienna Woods, summer and winter, were occasions to
debate great issues or finer points of literature and history. We
usually went in groups of three, and there were about a dozen
friends from whom to choose. Perhaps the strongest influence on
me was a slightly older boy from my school, Erwin Schajowicz, son
of a prominent lawyer. He was well-read and of an original and
eccentric turn of mind. It was he who introduced me to contemporary philosophy, to the works of Karl Kraus, whilst I converted him
to Wagner, proselytizing with the help of arguments and interpret-
ations handed down to me by Uncle Josef. We would stand through
whole performances of *Parsifal* and *Tristan* in the upper galleries
of the opera house, and then discuss what we had heard in an
all-night café.

I met regularly with another group of dandyish boys in search of sentimental adventure. Usually we returned empty-handed, for courage would fail us as we approached the objects of our desire, who would discourage us with cool stares. But as we reached the age of credibility, our confidence grew. Our beat was the fashionable *thé dansant*, or five o'clock tea, in the city park, where a well-known band played the latest hits. Etiquette commanded that at the first sounds of music the young men should rise and go to other tables and ask young ladies to join them for a dance. Many a liaison or serious attachment started at the first sound of an Argentinean tango or a slow foxtrot. Assignations had to be made on the dance floor in a whispered tone – it would never do to be seen walking away with a new acquaintance. In my last year at school I joined a rather fashionable five o'clock club frequented by eligible boys and girls who would be escorted to the door, left, and later collected by their mothers or other chaperones.

Last, but not least, my Vienna education was greatly influenced by travel in the holidays. From the age of fifteen I was often sent off alone to stay with families and spend a long summer in Italy, France or the Dalmatian coast of Yugoslavia. My father also took me on shorter trips to participate in archaeological digs or on buying trips to see great coin dealers in places as far apart as Augsburg, Rome and Toulouse.

Perhaps the most important and moving of all my travels was a Mediterranean cruise in the summer of 1935, when I was fifteen. It began in Trieste and took us to Greece, Egypt and then Palestine. Our comfortable and old-fashioned Yugoslav ship, the *Krajica Maria*, docked in Alexandria, and we travelled inland to Cairo and raced through mosques and museums before taking the train to Tel Aviv. On arrival we took a taxi to the house where we were to stay, but before we reached our destination the car was forced to stop in the face of a huge and impenetrable crowd, thousands of people, many of them wearing black armbands of mourning. They were attending the funeral of Palestine's chief rabbi, Kook, a fierce and formidable cleric who was especially respected by the intransigent hawkish wing of the Jewish settlers. I noted a few khaki-shirted members of the local Brit Trumpeldor, and made myself known. They asked me to join in the procession. I begged my mother to let me go and said that I would join our hosts an hour or so later. Marching in a crowd of Jews in their own land for the first time gave me a thrilling sense of solidarity and serenity such as I had never experienced before.

We were staying with a distant relative, a venerable old settler from Russia, who was a senior master of the first Jewish public school and taught European history. His name was Sofermann and he had a pretty daughter, a *sabra*, that is to say 'a locally-born Jewish girl', and a son of my age who played centre forward in the Jewish National Youth soccer team. The old man ended every meal and every discussion with the same mournful exhortation: 'Take down your tents and pitch them here in Palestine. Clouds are gathering. Hitler will drive out the Jews. Today it's Berlin. Tomorrow it will be Vienna, then Prague, then Warsaw ...!' The week in Palestine passed as a dream.

There could be no greater contrast to that trip than my last journey with my father before the Nazi invasion – a journey across Hitler's Germany en route for Norway in the late summer of 1937. The year before, my father's career had been hit rather incisively when the Phoenix Insurance Company, built up by his ebullient Uncle Hauptmann and his associate, Dr Berliner, both of whom had died in the meantime, came to grief. The world economic crisis, changes in the insurance laws of various Central European states and the intricate political wrangling due to changes of government in Austria caused the much-exposed organization to go into liquidation and be taken over by a Government-controlled company. For a short time it looked as if my father's career had come to an abrupt halt. His involvement with the Government and intrigues against him and other Jewish top executives by pro-Nazi elements made his life difficult. On occasions the Government coerced the bigger enterprises, my father's company among them, into lending their reserves to the State to pay the wages of the railwaymen or miners because the Exchequer was empty. The illegal Nazi Party had spies in my father's office and accused him of using his influence in favour of the anti-German forces, or indeed allocating financial grants to the fight against Hitler. Thus, when the firm collapsed, an official investigation incriminating ten or twelve Jewish executives, including may father, was initiated.

To our amazement, it was a German insurance group, the Victoria of Berlin, which asked my father to join it. Its president was a conservative and an outspoken anti-Nazi, a *Junker* type who refused to knuckle under to the Nazi Party's edicts and stated that, as far as foreign branches were concerned, he would not brook interference and would employ anyone he saw fit. He pointed out that some of the managing directors of the Victoria abroad were 'non-Aryan', so my father joined up. He acquired an important client in Norway, a ship owner whose imposing merchant fleet needed a worldwide insurance policy, and so he decided to travel by road, taking me and one of my older friends from the Giskala up north.

We drove to Berlin along the newly built *autobahn*. Somewhere near Dresden we met with roadblocks, and giant signs heading cars off to a secondary exit warned us that something unusual was up. Our driver ignored one of the signs and drove on for a mile or two until he came upon another roadblock. Four soldiers appeared out of the mist, led by a second lieutenant, revolver in hand. They stopped the car and literally tore our passports from our hands, bellowing, 'Your presence is unauthorized. This is a restricted area. Don't you know that we are engaged in manoeuvres?' We suddenly realized that we were right in the middle of the much-heralded manoeuvres of the *Wehrmacht*, heightened in their importance on this occasion by an expected state visit by Mussolini.

We were taken to a military command post where we were all interviewed by a uniformed security officer and a plain clothes Gestapo man. My father documented the purpose of his visit and gave the references of his Berlin associates, but my fraternity comrade, 'Cis' Hecht, a swashbuckling dandy of eccentric appearance, fared less well. With a monocle in his left eye and a lock falling over his right eye, he looked the music hall version of a Balkan spy. His answers, clipped, dismissive and mildly ironical, did nothing to ingratiate us with our interrogators. Before long he became embroiled in a political argument, his interview turned into a shouting match and the Gestapo man recommended his *Wehrmacht* colleague to take us to the nearest military jail.

My father pleaded to be allowed to telephone the chairman of the Victoria Insurance Company in Berlin; only then did it dawn on us that it was the weekend and we did not have his private number. So we all drove off in our car, flanked by motorcyclists and preceded by the two investigators, to a higher command post. Mercifully, my father discovered in his wallet a scribbled note of the address and telephone number of his immediate business contact in Berlin. We were allowed to use the telephone. A long and rather cantankerous conversation then took place between the officer and the insurance executive, as a result of which the Germans allowed us, with the utmost reluctance, to go on our way. There was a last exchange of hostile looks between Cis and the Gestapo man, and the horrific episode came to an end. Our Austrian passport saved us from the kind of chicanery and rudeness that might have been meted out to German Jews, but it was an uncomfortable experience nonetheless.

We reached Berlin late on Saturday evening. Despite our Austrian passports, we had been warned that we would not be safe in the better tourist hotels and that it would be more appropriate to take lodgings in one of the few 'Jewish' hostelries in what had become the Berlin ghetto. So we spent the night at the King of Portugal, a sombre place where the shutters were drawn day and night. What we experienced was a grim foretaste of things to come. A spindly young Jewish-looking porter took our luggage up to the only suite left. Cis and I occupied one double room and my father the other. The 'Aryan' chauffeur went to stay in a nearby pension. We were ravenous and thought of going to one of the restaurants or cafés in the city centre, but both porter and concierge warned us against it. 'Don't go near the Kurfürstendamm or Unter Den Linden, because there is a lot of *risches* about.' Risches is a Yiddish word meaning 'unpleasantness', 'viciousness', 'trouble'. So we stayed behind and had a rather frugal kosher meal of stringy boiled beef and undercooked broad beans washed down with lukewarm beer. We spent a miserable Sunday walking about Berlin. The capital of the Third Reich was bedecked with German and Italian flags, and the grinning faces of a helmeted Mussolini alongside a more thoughtful Hitler in grey field uniform stared at us from hoardings and shop windows. Early on Monday morning my father did his business, and by midday we had left Berlin on our way to the frontier and to the ferry which was to take us towards our Nordic destination.

The scene in the King of Portugal and the countenances of broken-spirited and timid Jews left an enduring mark on me. But I was determined to enjoy that summer and both celebrate and displace the memory of the final exams which I had just taken at the Piaristen-Gymnasium. I was now free from school and qualified to enter university, but I had failed to get the expected summa cum laude. On the morning of my mathematics paper and viva voce I had had a blackout. Somehow I could not concentrate and panicked, leaving the classroom halfway through my figure work. When the exam results were discussed by the Committee of Masters, chaired by an outside inspector, my History and German literature mentors, discreetly seconded by the Jewish religion master, who had only an auxillary status in the school hierarchy, pleaded on my behalf, arguing that I had had exemplary marks throughout eight years of study. But their pleading fell on deaf ears. Since the only candidate for the high distinction remaining in the field was another Jewish boy of Hungarian extraction, they felt it inopportune to cast a vote for a second non-Aryan prize pupil. That this was the reason for their decision was confirmed to me years later by the professor of mathematics himself, an amiable man and a staunch Catholic, Dr Rieck, whom I visited when I went to Vienna as a special correspondent for the BBC after the war. 'Things had become very political by then, very political indeed,' was Dr Rieck's laconic verdict.

My failure to reach the top mark in the final exams and the disappointment it caused my father plagued my dreams for weeks. Even in later years these nightmares recurred almost automatically whenever things went wrong. In one dream I saw the sneering face of the presiding school inspector. In another I identified myself with Wagner's hero, Siegfried, the fearless dragon slayer, inviolable until felled from behind by the thrust of a treacherous spear. The Siegfried syndrome of winning all but the last battle has haunted me all my life.

The six months that followed remain engraved on my memory — the beginning of my student life coincided with the end of Austria. I registered as a law student at the University of Vienna and, concurrently, at the Konsularakademie, a diplomatic college which had a solid international reputation. Founded by the Empress Maria Theresia in the middle of the eighteenth century, it was first named 'Oriental Academy', the idea being that young gentlemen of the nobility should be specially trained for serving in the countries of the Oriental infidel. Renamed Konsularakademie, the school was mandatory for all those who wanted to enter Austria's foreign service, but it also attracted a wider group of students, both from other faculties and from abroad, who were anxious to be tutored in subjects that would stand them in good stead in such fields as

international business, banking and the legal profession. It was a
two-year course; there were only about seventy or eighty students
in all, and the teaching staff was either seconded from the university
or were practitioners of diplomacy. Retired ambassadors and resident foreign office staff gave lectures, seminars and held examinations, and we studied diplomatic history, consular practice, public
and private international law, geostrategy and economic geography.
Above all, we had to be trilingual. French was obligatory, English
a secondary language and Italian my optional third.

The law faculty at the university, overcrowded and impersonal,
left me with few distinctive memories. I can recall the undercurrent
of growing tension between the Nazi majority of the student population and the other groupings already familiar to me from my
schooldays, but little else. Nazi professors increasingly used lectures
for ex cathedra pronouncements of National Socialist philosophy
or anti-Semitic jibes. I remember one bearded pan-German hitting
out at the distinguished Jewish-born international lawyer, Kelsen.
'You may from time to time read references in foreign articles and
books about an eminent Swedish jurist, Dr Kelsen. You should bear
in mind that Dr Kelsen, whatever he may be, is not a Swede.' Howls
of laughter from the Nazi students.

On entering university I had ceased to be a member of the *Activitas* of the Giskala and became one of its 'old gentlemen'. The
question arose whether I should join one of the Jewish university
fraternities, and, if so, which? The Kadimah was the obvious choice,
but though I had many friends there, I also had one or two enemies.
Encouraged by Cis Hecht, I decided to join Unitas, which had a
reputation of being worldly, social and militant. Unitas also had a
record of lusty duelling. Among its alumni was Arthur Koestler,
who by the time I joined was already a successful journalist in Berlin
and had left a trail of apocryphal stories of amorous adventure,
intellectual feuds and hard living. Following the custom whereby
members of these fraternities took on special names, Koestler was
nicknamed 'Perkeo' after the legendary dwarf from Tyrol who
became court jester to the Elector Palatine in Heidelberg around
1720, and who was known for his small stature and huge thirst. I
retained my drinking name from the Giskala which was 'D'Abère',
a Frenchified version of the Hebrew word for 'talker'.

The social life of the Unitas was quite worldly, and relations
between active students and the 'old gentlemen' were effortless and

close. We met in cafés or private houses, or, more often, in the premises of the joint club of the duelling fraternities in the centre of town. The political work within the Zionist camp was quite extensive, but before being marked for promotion from Fox, the lowest rung, to Fellow, you had to fight your compulsory duel. Though I had been taking fencing lessons ever since I joined the Giskala and knew my combat strength would one day be tested, I was not looking forward to it because my fencing was less than average. Cis Hecht, who explained the procedure to me, said I had to find myself an opponent, preferably a pronounced Nazi. So one Saturday morning – two weeks before Hitler's surprise invasion of Austria – Cis and I went to the university where, in the large quad, the various student fraternities, some of them centuries old, promenaded in a circle, canes in hand, wearing caps and ribbons in their fraternity colours and white gloves. This weekly promenade was known as the *Bummel*. Cis and I leant against a pillar. He pointed languidly at a giant of a man with a green cap and a band, the colours of which were gold and silver. 'This is the man you should challenge,' he said. 'How do I do it?' I asked. 'That is an intelligence test, my boy. Use your brain.'

The procession of students advanced slowly. Each fraternity was headed by a leader, deputy leader and Fox major (in charge of fencing). They strode solemnly and self-importantly round and round the fountain. I straightened my tie and jacket and approached my prospective opponent. Bowing lightly, I addressed him: 'Herr Kollege, your shoe laces are undone.' He stepped out of line, thanked me, looked down and realized it was a hoax. He was furious and shouted, 'Impertinence! My seconds will meet yours at two-thirty on Monday afternoon at the Café Landmann.' We both bowed stiffly and I returned to Cis.

On Monday Cis and another second met their opponents at the appointed place, right opposite the entrance to the university, and went through the elaborate ritual prescribed by tradition. Matters of honour were governed by a protocol laid down in the Codex Bolgar and the Codex Barbasetti, both in vogue with officers of the late Austro-Hungarian Army. There were three degrees of insult which called for a 'transaction of honour'. The first was a minor offence that could be caused by remarks such as 'You're a cad, Sir' or by a malicious practical joke such as the one I had played on my adversary. An insult of the second degree was an imputation of bad faith or dishonourable behaviour. The third degree could be an accusation of financial impropriety or other felonious behaviour, or a physical attack or a gross insult to a woman close to the insulted party – his sister, mother or sweetheart. Whereas insults of the first and second degree could be settled by an apology, an affront of the third degree had to be settled by weapons. Unlike Imperial officers in the past, who mostly fought with pistols, students used cavalry sabres, weapons with which you hit but did not stab.

My offence was clearly a matter of the first degree. At the Café Landmann the elder of the two seconds solemnly asked the waiter for pen, ink and writing paper and started recording: ' "A protocol in the transaction of honour between Herr Weidenfeld as the offending party and Herr von Stieler as the offended party." Do the gentlemen opposite offer an apology?' Cis shook his head curtly. 'In that case we will discuss procedure.' There followed a complex discussion about the weight of weapons to be used and pulse, neck and eye protection. We were to fight stripped to the waist with pulse protection but no eye protection. They discussed time and venue. Just as they were about to leave, the opponent's elder second asked quite casually:

'A technical point. Is your client Aryan?'

'No.'

'I regret infinitely this transaction cannot take place. Our fraternity does not give "satisfaction" to non-Aryans.'

Of course he had known my racial status all along, but the pretence was kept up for the sake of ritual. Stieler's seconds clicked their heels and left.

When my seconds reported back I felt half relieved, for I considered I had proved my heroism, only to be told that I would have to challenge Stieler once again and try an offence of the second degree. In order to achieve this I was advised that I should do some research, find out where he lived and, if possible, shame him in front of witnesses. I found out that he lived in a students' hostel, was a member of the Swabian German minority in Romania and took his meals in the academic mess, the Mensa Academica. I sought him out and called him a coward in front of the assembled luncheon group. Our seconds met again at the same place and went through the same procedure, but this time, on hearing from Cis that I would not desist from embarrassing Herr von Stieler, his seconds reluctantly agreed to 'give satisfaction' on condition that we would fight as private individuals and not in the colours of our fraternities.

The duel took place about a week before the Anschluss. It was a Saturday in late February during the ball season, the last carnival of free Austria. We assembled on the premises of a non-duelling Catholic students' union which could be rented by the hour for special meetings. Fifteen minutes before the fight my second informed Stieler's second that I was left-handed – this was allowed by the code of honour. It saved the day for me because Stieler was obviously the better fencer, but he did not know how to deal with that contingency and I had been specially prepared to take advantage of my left-handedness. Cis, an accomplished fencer, had advised me to seem smaller than I was and to aim for his ribs, thus preventing him from meting out his superior blows. This went on for a hundred rounds. A round could last for half a second to a minute before the seconds intervened on some point of order which would be resolved by further altercation and sometimes acrimonious dispute. In fact, a high percentage of duels originated on the fencing floor between seconds who had fallen out while intervening on behalf of their comrades.

After the hundredth round, the seconds got bored. They clearly wanted to leave for dinner, so it was arranged that we were to be given another twenty-five rounds. If there was no decision by then, they would call it a draw. And this is what happened. I had a few minor cuts which were dealt with by Dr Tuttnauer, a cosmetic surgeon and one of our 'old gentlemen', who later emigrated to London, became a fashionable Harley Street specialist and treated the Duke and Duchess of Windsor. My parents were told I had been in a car accident. Not being sporty or much of an outdoor type, I had cleared the deck for more congenial work in the smug knowledge that I had satisfied my comrades of the Unitas by passing my 'ordeal by sword'.

But the story had a sequel. Shortly after I left Austria, my mother had a visit from a Brown Shirt. He stood in the doorway, enquiring after me somewhat sheepishly. My mother, frozen by fear, whispered that I had left the country. He sighed with relief and asked if he could do anything for her. Before she was able to answer, he explained who he was and said that he had fought a duel with me. He asked my mother to remember him to me when she next wrote.

She told me about the incident when she and my father joined me in England.

Ten years later, when I returned to Vienna for the first time after the war, I found myself leafing through the telephone directory in the British Officers' Club at the Hotel Sacher looking for the names of people from my past, wondering who was still alive. I looked under Stieler. He was listed as a veterinary surgeon. At a loss for anything better to do, I rang him up and arranged to have breakfast with him the following day. He arrived, an emaciated figure, limping and using a walking stick. He had lost a leg in Russia and had an artificial limb. Before leaving, he wolfed down some huge sausage sandwiches. Two or three years later when I looked him up in the directory again, he was no longer there.

The Konsularakademie opened a new cosmopolitan world of unfamiliar and complex coloration – young men, and quite a few women, mostly self-confident, sure of their place among the future governing classes of Austria, Germany, Hungary and Yugoslavia, but also exotic young mandarins from the Far East and the Indian subcontinent, as well as a few inquisitive Britons and Americans anxious to improve their German at what was considered the top end of the academic marketplace.

The Austrian contingent hailed from the upper bourgeoisie and aristocracy. Time-honoured names from the *Almanac de Gotha* and the Danubian Patriciate shared memories of hunting weekends, country weddings, lavish wakes after family funerals, a one-year stint at Ellmayr, the famous dancing class, and, as often as not, the same school. The girls might have been at Kalksburg, the breeding ground of young Catholic noblewomen, the boys at the Theresianum. Many of the other Central European and Balkan novices had spent their years of puberty in Swiss schools.

For quite a few of them, the Diplomatic College was a finishing school, training for a life of half-hearted estate management or preparation for a glamorous, conventional marriage. But there was a hard core – a minority – of ambitious, industrious young men of modest means to whom a job in the public service was the supreme goal. One such man was Kurt Waldheim. His father was a functionary of the Catholic Patriotic Front, a cog in the wheel of the Schuschnigg establishment, a devout Christian and anti-Nazi. Kurt wanted to become a lawyer and a diplomat. He kept to himself, attended all seminars and made himself agreeable to all and sundry. We sometimes met with a charming Dutch fellow student, Suzanne K., a staunch patriot and hater of the Nazis. Waldheim was known as a pillar of the Catholic regime. He was a second-year student and so we would never meet in class, but might occasionally in a seminar. It was only after the Anschluss that I got to know him better. He was one of the very few who did not change his attitude to the students of Jewish descent. In fact, he rendered me some invaluable services.

During the five months between the Anschluss and my departure from Vienna, a complex compromise between the German Ministry of Education and the Foreign Ministry meant that Jewish students at the Konsularakademie were allowed to sit for examinations but not to attend lectures. Since there were few text books, lecture notes were essential for the exams. This made life for the Jews more difficult. Waldheim brought lecture notes to my house, a favour which required some courage, all the more so since my father was a prisoner of the German Reich. When the Waldheim Affair erupted I gave testimony to the effect that, whilst I could not vouch for anything the Austrian president might or might not have done during his service in the German *Wehrmacht*, he was not to my knowledge a Nazi sympathizer when I first knew him. I was much criticized by Jewish friends for saying that even the minor services which he had rendered me deserved recognition in the light of all the callous and opportunist behaviour of the time. But apart from helping me, he had also kept in close touch with Suzanne K. in occupied Holland. She later related that Waldheim had visited her in military uniform. He had asked her out to dinner, and when she had pointed out that she could not be seen in public with a German officer, he had kept the appointment – in civilian dress, which was against *Wehrmacht* regulations.

I resumed my acquaintance with him many years after the war when he was a member of the Austrian Government and then secretary-general of the United Nations. Waldheim was no hero; he was not the stuff Resistance fighters are made of. But then he shared the challenges and life-saving responses of the vast mass of middle-class Austrians engulfed in that precision instrument that was the German war machine. If the motive behind the attacks on Waldheim were to rouse the world to the Austrians' inadequate sense of responsibility for and compassion for the victims of the Holocaust, then Kurt Waldheim was not the most suitable target. My appraisal of the affair was shared throughout by Simon Wiesenthal, the indefatigable Nazi-hunter, who became a friend and author.

In those final months in Vienna I moved between the scintillating world of my college, the close-knit camaraderie of the Jewish fraternity and a new group of friends in the Bohemian niches of Viennese life. Some of these circles intersected. There were young aristocrats who liked 'slumming' and meeting writers, singers and painters, and there were, among the 'proud Jews' of the Unitas and Giskala, some worldly and dandyish drawing-room lions who had found entry into the salons of the aristocracy, the race meetings at the Freudenau or indeed the weekends and musicales of the Rothschilds and Ehrenfelds.

An older friend, in his early twenties, was Armand Broch-Rothermann, known as 'Piz', son of the writer Hermann Broch, whom he later translated into English. His reputation as a breaker of hearts and arbiter of fashion aroused the curiosity of hostesses and their eligible daughters. Piz, who was madly in love with the daughter of the novelist Jacob Wassermann, told me of the wondrous world of Englishmen's fashions, the glamour of Savile Row, the bootmakers of St James's, the shirt- and tie-makers of Jermyn Street, the subtle differences between a dozen or so eaux de Cologne and their uses according to mood and diverse stages of seduction.

In the winter of 1937 to 1938 the political situation deteriorated dramatically: Hitler escalated his war of nerves against the Austrian regime. Austria's chancellor, Schuschnigg, was summoned to Berchtesgaden and forced to introduce pro-Nazi politicians into his government and loosen his control over the outlawed Nazi Party. Illegal Nazi members resurfaced, strutting about with a new-found self-confidence, and opponents of the Nazis lost heart. The Western democracies seemed only mildly interested in Austria's fate, thus Austria's legions of waverers sat all the more tightly on the fence. Most serious of all, the former stalwart Socialists, still smarting from the deadly blow dealt to them by the ruling semi-fascist Government, remained sullen. They were equally antagonistic towards the Browns and the Blacks.

And yet while Austria began to burn, its youth danced. The winter before the Anschluss was especially gregarious and festive.

The season started in the middle of December, resumed after Christmas and culminated in the great Viennese Carnival just before Lent, the *Wiener Fasching*, consisting of a veritable avalanche of balls – the Opera Ball, the Architects' Ball, the Lawyers' Ball, the ball in the Konzerthaus, the Academicians' Ball, masked balls and costume balls in period attire, balls for all ages and all classes, public balls for charity and private balls so select that exclusion could mean social ostracism for the hapless member of the set in question.

The ball of the Konsularakademie was a special event because members of the diplomatic corps, the leading figures in the Government and Viennese society were invariably present and lent it international distinction. Two things happened which made 18 February 1938 a night to remember. While we waltzed and tangoed, rumba'd and self-consciously partook in rather stilted rural *Laendlers*, polkas and gavottes, a chilling rumour suddenly spread that Chancellor Schuschnigg had been summoned to Hitler's alpine eyrie and could not therefore be present. Instead, at a late hour, a senior minister, Guido Zernatto, appeared in the somewhat operatesque uniform of the Austrian Storm Squadrons, one of the innumerable variants of fascist gala dress. He made an appearance to reassure us. However, foreign diplomats were whispering to one another. The old guard of the Ballhausplatz, the Austrian foreign ministry, who had only minutes earlier admired the graceful spectacle of the young couples on the dance floor, now clustered in corners with long faces and frightened miens.

Yet I danced with imperturbable abandon because I had fallen in love for the first time in my life, and for the last time in Austria. She was Maria Felding, eighteen years old, Junoesque and blonde. I had met her only an hour earlier at the crowded buffet where she was queueing in front of me, engaged in a vicious row with her escort. He was a young foreign diplomat, obviously jealous and possessive, and she had just called off their liaison. Without waiting her turn, she stormed out of the queue in the direction of the door. I followed her and asked her to dance. After a moment's hesitation she agreed, and we never left the dance floor – or indeed each other for the next few months.

It was a love affair in the shadow of mounting political drama. Maria was the stepdaughter of a Jewish businessman and a Catholic mother. An art student, witty and extremely pretty, she had many

friends and admirers among young painters and architects, most of
whom were Nazi sympathizers. Our attachment soon became
known to them, and she came under strong pressure to stop seeing
me. She was followed when she came to meet me, which was usually
in the house of one of the 'old gentlemen' of my fraternity. Anonymous letters and telephone calls and cuttings from Nazi broadsheets
threatened those 'Aryan' maidens who engaged in miscegenations.
She brusquely refused to comply, but soon her stepfather received
similar and even more threatening missives. With heavy heart I
listened to the reasoning of my mentor, Cis Hecht, and he met her
to tell her how it would be best for both of us if we stopped seeing
one another – at least until the present 'crisis' was over. After a
tearful farewell, she left Vienna to resume her studies in a provincial
town, and I have never seen her since. I believe she returned home
a few months after the Anschluss to find that her mother had left
her stepfather, who was to perish in Treblinka.

That month, from mid-February to the 'ides of March' of 1938,
the last act of the tragic end of independent Austria was played
out, but while spectators abroad had an increasingly clear premon-
ition of the final denouement, the crowd, and even quite a few
actors on the stage, were oblivious to the impending doom. We
optimistically believed that if it came to the crunch the Great Powers
would intervene to save Austria. A small contingent of students and
research fellows showed their discreet concern for Austria's future
by warning the handful of Jewish students to think of their safety.
One such cautionary voice was that of Monsieur Savarnargue, a
chain-smoking Frenchman who always wore a Basque beret and
spoke uncommonly good German without an accent. He was destined to become ambassador in Bonn and Moscow, then foreign
minister, and ultimately ambassador in London.

Complacency, stubborn optimism, an ostrich-like conviction that
the world would never tolerate the worst seemed to immobilize
constructive thinking. It was a testing time for the turncoats and
opportunists – attitudes shifted according to the morning's news.
In spite of the warning headlines of the Western press, a degree of
uncertainty prevailed in the Government camp, within the upper
ranks of the Nazi sympathizers and even among active adherents,
as to whether, when and, if so, to what degree and at what pace
the great changes would take their course. After centuries of dealing
with the problem of balancing decisions and choosing options

imposed by the unenviable position of being a nation wedged between rival powers, the Austrian psyche had learned to live in a state of flux.

Besides the almost untranslatable verb *lavieren*, the vocabulary of Austria's bureaucracy has another equally expressive verb, *fortwursteln* – to muddle through. Both attitudes were much in evidence in those uncertain times. There was no greater *Lavierer* than Herr Generalkonsul Hlavac, the director of the Konsular-akademie. He must, as the name suggests, have been of Slavic origin. He affected aristocratic speech and manner, and donned his char-coal-grey office suit, frock coat and striped trousers with pigeon-grey waistcoat on solemn occasions. He wore pince-nez which sat tightly on his nose and were small enough for his eyes to peer either above or below so as to help him indicate either praise or disapproval. Hlavac seemed to be a pillar of the Catholic regime but, by and by, suspicion spread that he would also, however subtly, utter sympathies for the German cause. It could be said that he was fair on the Jewish question, but there were also hints of a fastidious anti-Semitism. He was not disrespectful of the ideals of Western democracy, yet he also had a healthy bias for the mystique of Italian Fascism. The concept of parliamentary debate and freedom of speech could evoke outbursts of enthusiasm, yet on other occasions he would dismiss elected assemblies as institutions which easily degenerate into futile talking shops. This multiplicity of General-konsul Hlavac's views was analysed by the small band of Hlavac-watchers, who evaluated the many face-to-face interviews or meetings in small groups which the worthy director held in his private study. He liked to stop a student in the corridor and spon-taneously invite him for a conversation. After a few minutes of small talk to put his interlocutor at ease, the thrust and purpose of the encounter would gradually emerge.

A week or so before the Anschluss, it was my turn. 'Herr Weiden-feld, we are pleased with your scholastic progress. I hear you have passed the Italian and French interpreters' exams with flying colours. Good, good. Are your career plans fully formed? Could it be that – as Phillip of Macedon said to his son, the future Alexander the Great – Macedonia is too small for you? The wide world could offer so much to someone of your, hmm, intelligent race!' He bent forward and burst into a brisk smile – his smiles were famed for their lightning speed. They always made me think of Max

Reinhardt's dictum that an actor worth his salt must keep his smile well beyond the moment he leaves the stage until he reaches his dressing room in case someone in the fourth gallery of the theatre or a stage hand behind the curtain should detect the slightest whiff of insincerity. 'Yes,' he continued, 'I see a future for you abroad: America, the Far East, even Africa, Madagascar, Rhodesia – but,' he added in a whisper, 'not Palestine. You know there are too many Arabs there and with the coming constellation, you know ... Well I enjoyed our talk. You may go far. You never know.' He rose, dismissing me with that lightning smile and a piercing glance over the pince-nez.

I left in a confused and pensive mood. Two fellow students of vastly different backgrounds had received similarly puzzling messages the same day. Manfred Ragg, son of a Hamburg shipper doing brisk business with the German military establishment, had a peculiar place at the college. He came from a wealthy and well-connected background but had rebelled against his family and the Nazi Reich. Mistrusted by the local Nazi watchdogs in the embassy, Manfred moved in left-wing circles and was a treasure trove of jolly anti-Nazi jokes. That same day Director Hlavac had given him a stern warning not to 'foul his nest'. Tapping his pince-nez against his left hand, he ventured mournfully, 'Opinions may well differ about your fatherland, but Germany is a great country and the, hmm, experiment of vast social change there deserves, objectively speaking, the acknowledgement, dare I say the admiration, of the whole world.' Hardly had the stunned German student left the study of the director when Mr Parry-Jones, the English tutor who was to play a decisive role in my fate, was summoned to the inner sanctum. PJ, a fiery Welshman, easy-going and somewhat bibulous, told me of this interview saying that he was thoroughly heartened by the courageous stand 'old Hlavac' had taken. 'Would you believe it, the old boy has his heart in the right place. He hates the Nazis and urged me to use my influence – my influence, if you please – with our legation to give poor Schuschnigg a helping hand. Well, well, it's nice to know you have staunch allies.'

The kaleidoscope of political colours in Generalkonsul Hlavac's political pronouncements was, of course, a calculated attempt at multiple banking.

Austria's last week of independence ended in a most dramatic way. Out of the blue, Dr Schuschnigg's Government announced a plebiscite for the following Sunday in which the people of Austria would declare themselves either in favour of or against continued independence as a sovereign state. This was a tactical coup, brave and risky, and bound either to call the Nazis' bluff or provoke a lightning response. But the whole machine of Government was geared to winning the visceral plebiscite.

On the morning of Friday 12 March 1938, all students of the Konsularakademie were bidden into the Festive Hall to listen to an emergency address by the director. The front rows were occupied by professors and lecturers, whose almost uniform charcoal colours of their business suits were interspersed with the bright violet uniforms worn by the student leaders of the Government loyalists, the Austrian Storm Squads, chief among them the amiable Helmut Joham.

The caricature of an old Austrian civil servant, Generalkonsul Hlavac rose to the occasion: 'Gentlemen, it is my solemn duty to summon you to a supreme act of loyalty and profession of faith! Later this afternoon, you will be called upon to carry the torch for Austrian independence.' We were to assemble in front of the Akademie and then march in a great torchlight procession on the Balhausplatz to serenade the chancellor on the balcony where Metternich had stood. At the end of his emotional address, which was steeped in patriotic pathos, Hlavac raised his right arm to give the official salute, and uttered the word 'Austria' with a guttural *r*.

At the appointed hour, a hundred or so of us stood before the Akademie ready to march. Most of us were in civilian clothes, though some of the students had recently had some uniforms made. It struck me as something of an anomaly that, while the Schuschnigg Government was trying to stand out for independence, it imitated the fascist and Nazi style by producing its own theatrical uniforms in mauve and purple, colours not yet preempted by other political parties. There were not enough torches for us all. Unsure whether we should march in serried ranks or walk in dignity, and feeling slightly encumbered by the ladies in our midst, some of whom had put on their most elegant racecourse clothes, we set out to cover the distance which would normally take some twenty minutes. Led by half a dozen violet-shirted, black-booted Austrian Storm Squad leaders, we passed silently through the academic quarter of Vienna, past branch buildings of the medical faculty, bleak tenement houses, the spidery neo-Gothic Votivkirche. As we reached the great arterial

junction of the Ringstrasse, where many roads from the Viennese
suburbs converge, more torches and more processions came into
our field of vision. The sound of patriotic songs, a spontaneous
and genuine movement of crowds anxious to give voice to their
passionate faith in freedom, and anti-Hitler slogans filled the air.
But suddenly, as if from nowhere, there was a strange movement
in the air. From the side streets, left and right, of the broad and
majestic Ringstrasse, groups surged forward, at first hesitant, then
increasingly confident: white-stockinged young men in lederhosen,
grey and green two-piece suits, many white shirts and here and
there a brown shirt and black boots – the illegal Nazis. And the
crescendo of voices surged forward: 'Plebiscite cancelled. Plebiscite
cancelled.' The white-stockinged masses seemed to multiply – to
double, to treble and quadruple. From every direction they streamed
forward towards the Balhausplatz, our own destinaton. '*Sieg heil,
Heil Hitler.*' A thunderous chorus of voices intoned the Horst
Wessel song and the song of the Nazi bodyguards, '*Führer*, command and we'll follow thee.'

There we stood, a hundred or so assorted 'proud disciples of
Metternich', feeling encircled and insecure. Then it was as if we
were acting out Haydn's Farewell Symphony, when the various
instruments gradually cease to play and the musicians slip out of
the orchestra pit one by one. I heard some whispers around me:
'It's time to leave! Plebiscite cancelled.' One of the first to disappear
was Joham, a leading torchbearer. Most of my colleagues removed
themselves discreetly, quite a few of them mingling anonymously
with the masses of the white-stockinged winners of the day. For us,
the few real losers, Jews professing or baptized, that option did not
exist, and so each of us found his own furtive route to a temporary
shelter: home.

While we were marching, the penultimate turning point had been
reached: the Austrian Government had bowed to Hitler's ulti-
matum. Schuschnigg had cancelled the plebiscite and resigned. At
home I found the family assembled around the radio. My maternal
grandmother had decided to move in with us; some of my father's
colleagues had joined us for the gloomy hour to hear our fate.
Schuschnigg appeared on the air and in a few brief sentences
entrusted the fate of Austria . . . to God. His closing word was the
salute, 'Austria', and then, turning to the small band of followers
in the studio with, it seemed, his back to the microphone, he was

heard repeating it: 'Austria. Gentlemen, good luck.' Then the Austrian anthem was played for the last time, slowly and languidly, as laid down by Haydn. Silence fell, but after a seemingly endless minute or two another recorded version, with quickening tempo and a triumphalist tone, the same music but with a different text – '*Deutschland, Deutschland, Über Alles*' – began. And, to complete the ritual, the sounds of the Horst Wessel song, the Nazi Party anthem, that blend of political triumphalism and folkloric romanticism signalling the beginning of a new era, rang out: 'The Thousand Year Reich'.

Finis Austriae.

CHAPTER FOUR

Departure and Arrival

WE STOOD IN A SEMICIRCLE around my father's high-backed stool in front of his huge desk, dazed and disconsolate, my mother and grandmother in dressing gowns, myself in a long nightshirt, and the stout Croatian maid absurdly formal in her starched blouse and white apron. On the desk lay a leather-bound copy of one of my father's favourites, Heine's *Book of Lyrics*, and a pile of crossword puzzle magazines with the fountain pen still poised over his latest entries. But my father was not there.

It was six-thirty on the morning of Monday 15 March, 1938, two days after the Anschluss. Everything had happened at lightning speed. The knock on the door had come at six. Four men – two from the regular police force and two Brown Shirt 'auxiliaries' – made their way straight into my parents' bedroom, asked my father to dress, read him charges and searched the flat, the policemen somewhat sheepishly, the Brown Shirts with a newfound imperious self-confidence. My father packed two shirts, shaving gear, toothbrush and a copy of the *Pickwick Papers*. Whilst the three women sobbed, he tried to be calm and reassuring. He wanted to talk to us but they hustled him out of the front door, and now there we stood, around his desk in the library, immobilized by uncertainty, a feeling worse than fear.

It had been a frightening weekend, unreal and yet vivid in my mind. Since I had made my way through the cheering masses in front of the town hall and university on Friday evening, and found the family and a few of my father's friends sitting round the radio at home, staccato communiqués had alternated with military marches and 'outside broadcasts' which reported live the spontaneous popular acclaim of German troops and distinguished visitors from the Reich. Hitler crossing the border! The Führer arriving in Linz! Had all this not been so tragic, the absurd eulogies would have struck one as pure farce. 'Yes, little Adolf was a genius, a prize pupil at ten,' cried the aged school teacher from Braunau, Hitler's birthplace. 'He had the eyes of a prophet.' The radio broadcast improvised doggerel verses mocking Jews, Communists and priests and we heard raucous laughter from the crowd at the burning of effigies and banners of the deposed Catholic Government. We sat as if paralysed all through Saturday, and then on Sunday the telephone never stopped ringing: anxious relations, solicitous friends – and anonymous callers with lewd or threatening messages and ironical wishes of a long life, all in different accents ranging from the heavy working-class drawl of the outer suburbs to the guttural *r* affected at finishing schools for aristocratic girls.

Meanwhile the rumour mill ground furiously. We heard that Jews had been intercepted at the airport, taken away outside the central synagogue, apprehended in restaurants, at bus stations and taxi ranks, and it was said not to be safe to carry a suitcase. We heard that an eminent surgeon had committed suicide and that a Socialist deputy had been found shot with his entire family.

Himmler had arrived with a staff of two hundred and meticulous lists of candidates for Dachau and Buchenwald. My father's name was on a Gestapo list of prominent Viennese Jews, but instead of being deported he was taken to a common or garden prison half a mile away. The Nazis had unearthed the dormant file about the Phoenix Insurance Company, which they used to fabricate a case arguing that shareholders' money had been spent for political purposes to support the Dollfuss-Schuschnigg regime and to combat the illegal Nazi Party. As a former senior executive my father was among those implicated: he was charged with conspiring against the interests of the Reich. Fortunately this meant that he and his eighteen fellow detainees became subject to civil judicial procedures. My father was thus spared the rough justice of the concentration camp. The old family lawyer, a relic of Imperial Austria and a devout supporter of the Emperor in exile, yet – oh so Austrian! – with excellent links to the upper crust of the Nazi underground, came to the house hours after my father's departure. He was soothing and courageous but not very constructive. Nobody knew how hard it would be to lean on legal procedure.

My mother went to the bank, where she was told that all Jewish assets were frozen. My grandmother resolutely went to a pawn shop and returned with a handful of bank notes. The maid professed her loyalty and offered to work for board and lodging only – but this didn't last long as Jews were soon forbidden to have 'Aryan' servants living under the same roof.

While my mother reorganized the household, I tried to find out where I stood with my studies. I went back to the Diplomatic Academy that Monday morning to find that we were all supposed to assemble at lunchtime to hear a speech by Consul General Hlavac. On arriving, I spotted my fellow student, Helmut Joham, torch-bearer of the *jeunesse dorée* of the Austrian Corporate State. His father was a State Counsellor, a banker of renown and a member of successive kitchen cabinets of right-wing governments. He had worn a specially tailored operatic outfit for the procession of loyalty on the previous Friday. Now he was clad in an equally chic uniform which looked as though it had been made to fit his elegant frame – the black double-breasted jacket, breeches and leather boots of the National Socialist Motor Corps. Could it have been bought off the peg? A somewhat flamboyant figure, Joham was impeccably dressed and eloquent in all matters sartorial. He would use such phrases as 'I've just built myself a dress suit and morning coat at Knize [the leading tailor]', or 'My English mail is late: no boots from Lobb's or hats from Locke's in time for the Kinski weekend'. Only a few months later, just after my arrival in England, I came across Joham in yet another guise. Having spent my first Sunday walking along Piccadilly and Park Lane, inhaling the newfound air of freedom, I strode into the Cumberland Hotel at Marble Arch, a meeting point of many refugees. There was Helmut Joham once again, now dressed in an immaculate summer suit. He greeted me exuberantly, 'Servus, Servus! I've come to London to learn banking. I might work with Schroder's or Lazard's.' In the end he stayed in England, and when war broke out he asked for political asylum whilst his father remained head of one of Austria's leading banks, which had been taken over by the Reich. Joham explained that there had been an arrangement with his father who wanted him to stay abroad to exchange telegrams which 'covered' Joham père. The father urged his son to return and fight for the fatherland. The son delayed his reply and pleaded hepatitis so that when war broke out he would not easily be able to return to Vienna. Father and son had clearly made a foolproof mutual reinsurance deal. They were covered for the risks of victory or defeat on either side.

On that day back in Vienna, Helmut Joham, like most of my fellow students and teachers, pretended not to recognize me. I think there were three Jews among the eighty undergraduates, but on that morning quite a few more failed to qualify as Aryans. We all drew naturally together and stood in a corner of the room as the director extolled the 'historic hour' of Austria's 'return to the Reich', speaking in mellifluous terms about the Führer and the mission of Austria in the new Europe. When the students filed out of the room, our little group stayed behind. The director beckoned to me. 'Weidenfeld, you remember our conversation not so long ago? Yours is a resourceful race. Try to get out as soon as possible. Don't go to Palestine: too many Arabs there! I have two tips for you — Madagascar or Paraguay.'

Within a week of Germany's annexation a routine pattern evolved for me. I spent most days indoors, studying for my exams. The telephone was the only link with friends and relatives. In the Jewish district, Leopoldstadt, specifically Jewish cafés and restaurants flourished although they were exposed to occasional raids by the police. But it was not safe to walk in groups or go to public places — there was always the danger of being stopped and asked to show our papers or to scrub graffiti off the walls or pavements.

A group of friends and I banded together 'consulate-hopping' in search of a final safe haven. The United States had a rigid quota system and Austria could only lay claim to a tiny share. Britain was highly selective and Palestine was virtually closed to Jewish immigrants. Adolf Eichmann had taken up his post at the Rossauerlaender police station, seat of the Vienna Gestapo, and the first Zionist transports of illegal emigrants began to form. Many of my friends applied. The official Zionist organization in Jerusalem sent emissaries to make arrangements, among them the young, blue-eyed, blonde Teddy Kollek, and the chubby, suave Ehud Avriel, both Viennese by birth and both kibbutz youth leaders in Palestine who were later to become commanding figures in the State of Israel, and intimate friends. The revisionist Zionists (one of whose underground leaders was the young Menachem Begin) organized their own transport. With the tacit help of the Gestapo, these illegal emigrants would assemble at dawn at the Danube quay and travel all the way down to the Black Sea and thence by unseaworthy boats to the shores of Palestine. My mother would not let me join any of these transports. She wanted me to hang on until my father's release,

and never gave up hope that we would depart as one family –
uncles, grandmothers and all.

My friends and I worked ceaselessly in search of an immigration
target, exchanging news and information. Shanghai was a popular
destination because it was fairly easy to get a visa, and the same
was said to apply to various South American countries. But before
long it became clear that some of the visas were ineffective, and we
heard reports of immigrants being turned away at the border.

I had a distant relative in London – the newly married wife of a
doctor in Battersea. She had already done her best to bring her
closest relations over and reluctantly sent me a carefully phrased
letter stating that, once in England, she and her husband would
look after me for a while so that I would not be a burden on the
country. The letter was not strong enough to get me a British entry
visa. We needed more British-born referees. I thought a few heavy-
weight names would help, so with two friends I went to the reading
room of the British legation to consult *Who's Who*. From there we
copied addresses of those we thought to be eminent British Jews.
There was no point, we agreed, in writing to legendary names like
Rothschild, Montefiore, Bearsted, Reading or Samuel – we assumed
that they must be flooded with requests – so we resolved instead
to find less obvious candidates. We fell on the letter G and found
the name of Viscount Greenwood. Feeling sure that this must be
an Anglicized version of Gruenwald, I wrote him a long letter asking
for support. He replied by return of post, coolly stating that he was
unable to help and that, incidentally, he was a churchgoing Anglican. I also wrote to Lord Robert Cecil, because he was renowned
for his humanitarian and staunch anti-Nazi views, and received a
charming letter back in which he offered his support with the British
passport authorities as well as help with my studies in England.

Even this was not enough. But through the intervention of the
Diplomatic Academy's English tutor, the eccentric Welshman who
wore summer suits throughout the year and looked like Ronald
Colman in the role of a Foreign Legion officer, my mother and I
obtained an interview with Captain Kendrick, the passport officer.
Just as he was about to end the interview with a lugubrious mien
and a shrug of his shoulders, my mother broke down and sobbed.
Captain Kendrick relented and gave me the flimsiest of all visas –
the right to enter England for a period of three months in transit
to a final destination.

I had a month to prepare for my departure. First I finished my exams, and then I embarked on a round of farewell visits. Those of us who were preparing to leave plunged into a febrile social season. Threatened with severance, old friendships and budding romances, deep love affairs and callous flirtations accelerated in pace, and marriages were impulsively arranged. There was a mood of intensity and reckless abandon in which conventional inhibitions suddenly disappeared. Countless bottle parties helped to drown the sense of sadness and despair whilst lubricating a sense of adventure enhanced by the lure of the unknown. The farewells were filled with black humour, 'humour of the gallows', as the German saying goes. We danced to the latest tunes and, when it was thought to be safe, sang biting parodies of the current Nazi anthems. The party given for me by one of my cousins and two female students at the academy ended to the strains of the hit of the moment, 'The Lady is a Tramp'.

A week before my departure I was allowed to see my father in prison. He shuffled to the interview grille, looking haggard and ashen-faced, his clothes smelling of prison detergents. The law pre-scribed that he sign a document 'releasing me from parental auth-ority' to allow me to make proper business decisions. We spoke very little. On parting he held up his right hand, waving and bending it in some vague gesture of benediction. At that moment in the prison I felt I had formally come of age.

One evening after a hot day at the end of July I left for the Western Railway Station with one suitcase, a postal order for six-teen shillings and sixpence in English money, an exam certificate from the Diplomatic Academy, a sheaf of curricula vitae of hapless friends wishing to join me in England and the blessings of many relatives and friends. My mother and grandmother, Uncle Klein-mann, the inveterate optimist, his wife and her spinster sister, my father's secretary and two of his faithful card partners came to see me off. Even that little assembly was risky because the Gestapo especially discouraged Jewish farewell groups at railway stations.

We passed the Swiss border in the morning. Fact and fiction about refugees being hounded out of the train and sent to concen-tration camps abounded, but my train went through unscathed. After the self-important, bellowing Nazi guards the phlegmatism of the Swiss border police came as a relief.

When I arrived in Zürich after breakfast, my first task was to

visit the Jewish refugee centre. All I remember is an endless queue
stretching along the four walls of a courtyard and two female secretaries checking the names and documents before disappearing
behind shuttered doors. They would come back, call out names,
and people would either leave the queue and go in through the
door or go to the exit, dejected. It all seemed quite mysterious.
After an hour's waiting, a bearded man with a black hat suddenly
came out of the office, called out my name and ushered me into
the office with great courtesy. This sudden preferment caused great
dismay in the queue. Someone behind me hissed, '*Luxusemigrant*'
– deluxe refugee.

The bearded old man introduced me to the presiding officer of
the committee. He knew my family. 'They've been generous to
many good causes,' he said, apologizing that his organization was
short of money and could not reciprocate in the same way, but
telling me they would pay for board and lodging and give me a
little pocket money.

I spent my first day of freedom at a lakeside café listening to
Swiss military music. It sounded heavenly after the harsh, synco-
pated tones of the SS anthems or the Prussian military marches
played by Austrian bands with exaggerated zeal.

In Zürich I ran into familiar Viennese faces and we compared
notes about the last days in our former homeland. Each of us had
his own hard luck story to tell, but we all shared a resentment
against the Austrian reaction to our fate. I have never stopped
asking myself how genuine the Austrian people's welcome of their
new National Socialist masters was. This question runs like a thread
through fifty years of debate in Austria and of the world's appraisal
of her. Whilst Austria's supporters regard her as a victim, her
detractors see her as a conniving and enthusiastic ally of the Nazis.
Now that I have come to know a new generation of Austrians and
been able to talk more calmly about the events of that time to my
Austrian contemporaries, I believe that the vast majority of Austrians were passive, listless or hostile to the Anschluss. A determined
minority, no more than a quarter or a third, actively espoused it,
but even small minorities can fill vast arenas and line lengthy
avenues. The Catholic Schuschnigg Government had catastrophi-
cally failed to unchain the outlawed Social Democrats and trade
unionists who, after years of persecution, felt embittered and immo-
bile. What has so often been said of the Jews is also true of

Austrians: they are people like any others, only more so. Thus, when they embraced the new creed of Adolf Hitler, they did so with an exuberance which had no equal in any other part of greater Germany.

I had a fortnight in hand before I was scheduled to arrive in England, and away from the oppressive atmosphere of Vienna I felt temporarily relieved and irresponsible. My next port of call was Ascona in the Italian part of Switzerland where my host was an old friend of my father, Baron Phillipe de Schey. Dandy and dilettante, Anglophile and Good Samaritan with an amorous past, he lived in a charming small villa with his White Russian wife, supported by his daughter who was married to Guy de Rothschild, then the dauphin and now the patriarch of the French branch of the Rothschilds. There my host spent much of his time helping deserving young refugees. When I read Patrick Leigh Fermor's remarkable account of his travels in Europe before the war, I was amused to come across his description of a visit to 'Pipsi' Schey at his Czechoslovak country house.

Schey put me up for a weekend. He was a delightful host, and we made the rounds of the illustrious refugees who had elegant lakeside villas. We visited Erich Maria Remarque, the author of *All Quiet on the Western Front*, and dined at the *Stammtisch* of a group of famous Berlin actors and dramatists in a Ticinese trattoria. Before I left, Schey wrote half a dozen letters of introduction to friends in Paris and London, recommending me for jobs. In the end none of them worked directly, but each of them opened some door or other.

From Switzerland on to Paris. My week's interlude there widened my horizons in more than one way. In Zürich the German and Austrian exiles had been relatively few in number and lived in modest comfort; Paris was the metropolis of the 'sick and poor' among Hitler's victims. The waiting rooms of the refugee committees were vastly overcrowded and all resources exhausted, and the prefecture of the police was harsh and hostile. I stayed in a miserable suburban hotel, and having run out of money I had nowhere to go – it was the summer holidays and the shutters of the apartments I might have called on were firmly closed. I wandered round the city, strolled through museums, browsed in book shops and read the 'free press'. At the Luxembourg Gardens I struck up a chance acquaintance with an Egyptian student, also bound for England.

He was full of ideas and addresses and guided me through the
Sorbonne district; we found free meals at various eccentric student
associations and inevitably landed up in a brothel. I had only visited
one once before, after a drunken celebration of a Zionist duelling
fraternity at Bratislava, across the Danube from Vienna. There was
never to be a third time.

On my third day in Paris I received a letter from my mother
suggesting that I go to the Circle of Exiled Austrian Monarchists
and call on a Herr Martin Fuchs who had been at the Austrian
legation in Paris. A personal friend of Archduke Otto von Habsburg, he had become leader of the Habsburg loyalists in France. I
arrived at a dingy office where half a dozen men in shirtsleeves sat
around a table scrutinizing applications from stranded Austrians in
the waiting room. One of them, testy and deeply bored, was a man
whose work I did not know then, but he has since become one of
my favourite authors. It was Joseph Roth, the author of *Radetzky
March*, one of the greatest novels about the sombre demise of the
Emperor Franz Joseph's Austria.

I handed them a letter of introduction from my father's lawyer.
They had vaguely heard of my father, but there was little they could
do. One young man with an aquiline nose and the biggest Adam's
apple I have ever seen looked at my gold wristwatch: 'Surely, you're
a rich man. I know the finest pawnbroker in the sixth arrondisse-
ment.' He dismissed me with a limp handshake.

As I wandered aimlessly around the ancient Jewish quarter in
the Marais I heard quickening footsteps behind me. A husky voice
called my name and an elderly Jew in a kaftan with a long beard,
sidelocks and an extra large top hat tugged at my sleeve. He knew
my grandmother and recognized me from a visit he had made to
our house in Vienna. 'You're Laura's grandson. Is she still alive?
She was so wonderful to me. She paid my wife's hospital fees. I
would so like to help you. Come along.'

Hobbling alongside me the stranger guided me crisscross through
the narrow streets of the Marais until we reached an imposing
house that seemed entirely uninhabited. We walked up three flights
of stairs and entered an enormous hallway leading to a salon with
a baronial chimneypiece. The blinds were drawn and although it
was the middle of summer a fire was lit. But for two Louis XIII
stools, a brass bed in the corner and two suitcases, the room was
quite empty. The old man explained that the *poretz* – the Yiddish

word for proprietor – was away on holiday and was having the house redecorated in his absence. He said he was a very rich, god-fearing Jew who had allowed him to stay there for the next few weeks. He wanted to give me something to eat and offered to fill a bag of cheese and kosher cold meat. And bread. And fruit. He got quite excited, revelling in his munificence. 'May God reward your grandmother for what she has done.' He tried to persuade me to stay in Paris and wait for his benefactor's return, but I told him that I was on my way to a new life in England.

'England,' he sighed, 'England. But they say that the only job for a foreigner there is to be a butler. Is that what you want?'

Feigning nonchalance and protesting that I had high hopes of continuing my studies, I left the old man. Many years later his grandson called on me in my London office. He had become a prosperous literary agent in France.

On Friday, 8 August 1938 I took the ferry from Calais to Dover. I was met at the pier by a slim, elegant young woman wearing a straw hat. She was my cousin, Eva Golomb. We travelled by train to London, where she took me to dinner at her house. There I met her husband, an elderly, good-natured Russian-born GP. For all their friendliness I detected a slight unease at having to add another distant cousin, uncle or baby niece to the string of responsibilities, but they gave me good advice about first steps in England and periodically checked on my progress. A few weeks later, on another Friday, 13 September, they gave me a surprise birthday party in the course of which my mother and a bevy of relations telephoned from Vienna intoning a choral birthday song.

After dinner I made my way back to Victoria Station to collect my suitcase. In my pocket I had a crumpled note given to me by my Egyptian companion in Paris with the address of a boarding house. I showed it to one of the policemen standing by. 'It looks like Belgrave Square,' he said, 'that's quite near.' I dragged the case to a palatial building in one of London's most exclusive residential squares and rang the bell repeatedly. After a few minutes an impeccably dressed butler opened the door and eyed me suspiciously. In the ensuing pantomime he peered at the crumpled address, pointing out with some relief that it said Belgrove, not Belgrave, and Street, not Square. After a few seconds he added, 'King's Cross – it's quite a distance.' Years later I discovered that I had invaded the privacy of Sir Henry Channon, Member of Parliament, host to royalty, stalwart of the Conservative Party and chronicler of his age. I published the *Channon Diaries* and still think of them as one of the most interesting social chronicles of London life ever written.

In a twenty-minute taxi ride I descended from Dante's Paradise to the Inferno, landing at the humblest of boarding houses in the vicinity of one of London's main railway stations. There I was listlessly received by an Italian caretaker who showed me to an attic room in front of which the previous occupant's half-finished breakfast emitted that, to me, so alien smell of cold bacon, lard, kidneys and rancid butter. The smells of prewar London were the first attack on my mid-European senses – the smell of smog and fog and of local detergents. Until then English cuisine was known to me only through the German translations of *David Copperfield* or *Bleak House*, but soon I became all too familiar with the quaint idea of having milk in one's tea, covered sandwiches with beef and ham, lettuce and tomato or just cucumber, the limp white bread, Indian spices and pickles.

I had an empty weekend in front of me, which I spent exploring the neighbourhoods of King's Cross and Bloomsbury, right up to Piccadilly. I found the strange mixture of metropolitan grandeur and almost village-like modesty baffling. On Monday morning I donned what I thought was the proper city attire and took the underground to Bank to call on a Mr William Freund of Leadenhall Securities, an offshoot of the patrician firm of Hambro's. He was a middle-aged man of Austrian origin with rich connections in Czechoslovakia, a kinsman of the Weiningers and Weinmans, who were involved in the Boothby affair a year or two later. Freund had been forewarned that I might come by my tutor at the Diplomatic Academy, of which he was an alumnus. His firm also managed one of my family's accounts that had been spirited out of Austria and was meant to be the nest egg for my parents and other relatives in case of a great crisis. On bidding farewell to my father in prison, he had whispered to me, 'Give my regards to our London friend.' 'Freund' is of course the German translation of 'friend' and I picked up the hint.

At Leadenhall Securities I was kept waiting for at least an hour before being ushered into the banker's office. Two lugubrious clerks stood on either side of the desk at which Freund was sitting. 'How long is it since you last saw your father?' was his first question. 'Three weeks or so,' I answered. 'Alas, there is no money left. Your father wrote to ask for it to be repatriated and we had to follow his instructions.' Of course he suspected that this request had been made under duress, but Freund explained that his bank was doing daily business on a grand scale with Germany and they could not start querying every signature. He looked at me mournfully, drew two brand-new five pound notes from his pocket and wished me Godspeed. My father told me after his flight from Austria that he had disclosed his foreign holdings at the lawyer's behest. The money in that account was never returned to him.

My second errand was to Woburn House in Bloomsbury, head-quarters of the British Refugee Relief Organization and a monument to the kind-heartedness and solidarity of British Jews towards their expatriate Jewish kinsfolk in Central Europe. To most refugees, Great Britain was but a transit hall – only a very small number of them were permitted to stay for good. Unless explicitly allowed to settle, each entrant had to have made arrangements to go on to another destination. Woburn House and its affiliate, Bloomsbury House, were there to ensure that they reached their ultimate haven safely, if possible reequipped with useful civic and professional qualifications. Of course, many of these transmigrants wanted to settle in Britain. Only the war, the shortage of shipping tonnage and the need for service and auxiliary personnel froze the status of the fugitives. So most of them remained *faute de mieux* and eventually became naturalized.

Woburn House was a highly efficient voluntary organization where money and advice were generously offered. The scions of the great Anglo-Jewish families – the Rothschilds, Bearsteds, Montefiores – gave hours of active service there every day, as did the next echelons in the British Jewish elite, the more recently enriched and accepted Markses and Sieffs, the Gestetners, and the Warburgs and Schiffs of recent German ancestry. At Woburn House they all rubbed shoulders with ordinary public-spirited young Jewish businessmen and energetic matrons and debutantes, working in shifts to cope with a myriad personal problems.

There was a hospitality committee which found personal billets for refugees, and a vocational training advice committee that turned German or Austrian accountants into electricians and café owners into agricultural recruits for a new life in New Zealand. Young businessmen spent the lunch hour interviewing special hardship cases. One such young businessman was Teddy Sieff, younger brother of the revered Israel (later Lord) Sieff, joint managing director, with his brother-in-law, Simon Marks, of Marks & Spencer. It was Teddy Sieff who heard the hard luck story of my morning in the City and assigned to me my first weekly subsistence cheque of thirty-five shillings. By one of those quirks of fate he was to become my father-in-law fourteen years later.

In the summer of 1938 I had no idea what the future would hold for me. Should I continue my studies? Should I learn a trade? Should I try to leave for a distant land, with my parents' fate uncertain? Lord Robert Cecil's long arm of charity facilitated my decision. Through his connection with the International Students' Service I got a scholarship to read Law at London University and enrolled for the autumn term.

The life of the majority of the impermanents followed certain well-structured routines. Central European refugees were recognizable by their clothes – overcoats a trifle too long, hats too large and too jauntily set, ties a little too bright and too large, a peculiar type of blazer of artificial wool in grey, blue or black, the waistline taken in at the back with elastic. In London they assembled in the lobbies of the Cumberland Hotel, the Strand Palace Hotel and the Regent Palace, Piccadilly. Slightly more affluent emigrés stepped up to the first-floor lounge of the Mount Royal of Oxford Street. There was a bustle and a wave of excitement when one discovered a new arrival and heard the latest news from Vienna, Frankfurt or Berlin.

These hotels were stock exchanges for personal information, business tips, and the ratings for small boarding houses, continental grocery shops and private sales outlets for second-hand clothes, pictures and trinkets of each and every kind. But above all they served as a centre for information on job prospects or sudden openings in distant lands. Besides this they were enormous rumour mills, about both fellow refugees and those left behind. Some pretty Viennese girl had found a rich admirer, an ageing actress a bit part on the BBC, a dubious Czech journalist had been unmasked as a Gestapo informer, and so on ad infinitum.

The hotel lobbies were the equivalent of the traditional Viennese café. Indeed, they proved much more all-encompassing. In the Regent Palace, for instance, you could sit at a table from 2.30 p.m. to midnight and consume a glass of hot loganberry juice for tuppence ha'penny, a ha'penny less than tea and a full tuppence cheaper than coffee, while listening to the strains of the band dressed in Hungarian or Romanian constumes. You could have business conferences, flirt with strangers, read or even write. The band played innocuous entertainment music, ranging from 'The Teddy Bears' Picnic' to Gilbert & Sullivan potpourris and occasional snatches of Puccini. A bevy of former Viennese journalists now working as stringers for London gossip columns drew material from their table hoppings. Willi Frischauer, who left a name behind in Vienna and made a fresh one for himself in London, used me as a stringer's stringer and paid me as much as one pound when I once discovered for him the whereabouts of one of Goering's nieces, who had been on a shopping spree in Bond Street. I used the Regent Palace as the place for studying or writing short articles for German language papers in London, Prague and Amsterdam.

Three committee ladies at Woburn House took my life in hand: Mrs Yvonne de Rothschild, the mother of the present head of the Rothschild family bank, Sir Evelyn, reintroduced me to Zionist life by a stroke of the pen; Mrs Ruth Cohen, a charming and thoughtful north London matriarch, saw to it that I was asked to 'decent and serious' families for tea or Sunday meals; and the formidable Mrs Schwab, wife of a Hampstead rabbi and grandmother of Julia Neuberger, herself now an ordained and practising rabbi and British media personality, changed my living arrangements. Boarding house life was demoralizing. The comings and goings at King's Cross could be quite perilous. Drunks would enter my room at night and conjugal tragedies were acted out behind the thin partitions. Mrs Schwab arranged for me to move into the home of a family of Plymouth Brethren in Parliament Hill Fields, Highgate.

So it was that four months after arriving in England I trudged up the snow-covered hill and heard organ music coming from the semidetached house which was to be my new home. Mr Smythe, a civil servant with His Majesty's Customs & Excise, was a benign, almost saintly man. His vivacious, Italian-born wife and two children took me into their family as if I belonged to it. They gave me a comfortable room and full board. Although they were passionate and proselytizing Christians, they soon noticed that I was not one for converting. Instead we revelled in the mutual recognition of the comforting affinity between the Old and the New Testaments. Almost every Sunday I went on a family picnic to the head of the brethren in north London, Mr Jacob, an elderly accountant, gaunt and unmarried, who shared a house with his devoted sister, Miss Jacob, who would prepare cucumber sandwiches for fifty or sixty faithful. We sang hymns, interpreted the Scriptures and basked in the glow of interfaith companionship. Half of the guests were fellow refugees and quite a few of them turned to the new faith. They received professional help and ended up with little shops, professional practices or prepaid passages to the Antipodes.

Among the Plymouth Brethren in north London were Mr and Mrs Crosland, parents of one the most distinguished Labour politicians of postwar Britain and author of perhaps the best theoretical work on democratic socialism. Whenever Tony Crosland and I met decades later we used to exchange reminiscences about that austere but touchingly compassionate sect of Nonconformist English Protestantism.

With Mr Jacob's help and, of course, that of my landlord, my father and mother were brought to safety. My father won his freedom by a happy set of circumstances. Since he was destined to be part of a show trial of influential Jews in Vienna who were accused of conspiring against the interests of the Nazi movement in the days before the Anschluss, he was involved in lengthy cross-examinations. His skill in parrying questions and in not disclosing the identity of a number of prominent Austrian politicians and bankers who, while acting as undercover agents of the Nazis, had played both sides of the political game, earned him the gratitude of one particular man who had meanwhile risen to eminence in the Third Reich. He saw to it that my father was released and, indeed, that the whole trial never took place. On the day of his release in June 1939, my father received a message from that same source urging him to pack his bags and run without delay because, now that he stood outside even the most tenuous framework of the law, he risked being thrown into a concentration camp. My parents fled to Italy over the Brenner Pass, where they waited for visas for England. Mr Jacob and Mr Smythe provided full financial guarantees for their British sojourn.

Another contact helped satisfy the British Home Office that they would not stay in England for longer than necessary. This was the result of a strange encounter at the Regent Palace. One night a little man in an enormous fur coat, flanked by a platinum blonde, French-speaking wife and a lascivious-looking female companion, addressed me brusquely: 'I've been watching you. You speak good French and Italian and of course you are an Austrian, judging by your accent. I have a job for you. I need a translator and correspondent. Here is my visiting card. Telephone me in the morning.'

Next day I called on him at the Consulate of Honduras of which he was the honorary consul general. His name was Andrei Rubinstein and he was the son of a famous Tsarist banker in St Petersburg, rumoured to have been the financial counsellor to Rasputin. He was also the brother of Sergei Rubinstein, who figured in a notorious financial scandal in the New World and came to a sticky end in a Mafia shoot-out.

The consul general offered me two pounds a week to translate business letters and to interpret business conversations in his office. He knew full well that I had no work permit, but this created a secure bond between us. After working for four or five weeks I found the substance of the correspondence more than puzzling: it seemed to consist of strings of meaningless codewords. By and by I realized what Rubinstein was up to. He bought supplies for the Spanish Republic, and subsequently informed an office in Geneva what their destination was and where they could be picked up in transit. Through an oversight of his I easily deduced that he was buying and selling arms to both sides in the Spanish civil war. I took fright and wondered how to disentangle myself. I told him that my studies were taking more time than I had bargained for and also hinted that it was unseemly for me to be seen so often in the company of his wife during his many long absences. But before leaving I asked him for one last favour. Could he procure Honduras visas for my parents so that they would be accepted in Britain as temporary visitors? Rubinstein pleaded that this was very difficult and costly. 'You see,' he said, 'I would have to pay money to a Mr Gomez and a Mr Hernandez and other officials back in Tegucigalpa and all that costs money: thirty pounds.' Of course I did not have thirty pounds, and said so. 'No,' he said 'but you still have your father's fur coat – I'll take that as payment instead.' And so my parents received their Honduran visas and *laissez passer* to Britain.

In spite of my settled habitat, I still frequented the Regent Palace Hotel, made friends with pretty Scandinavian au pair girls who came there on their days off and fell in love with a young Swedish student. She was part-time companion to one of the children of the Swedish ambassador, Bjoern Prytz, who later rose to wartime fame for trying to mediate a negotiated peace with Britain and Germany. Only the outbreak of war spared us the risky fate of formal engagement and marriage.

After Mrs de Rothschild had interviewed me at the refugee committee about my political views and heard that I had served in the Zionist youth movement in Vienna, she had sent a note on my behalf to Arthur Lourie, who was then political secretary to Dr Weizmann, the president of the World Zionist Organization at 77 Great Russell Street. Though anything but a Zionist sympathizer, she asked whether they might have a job to suit my talents.

Arthur Lourie was a sophisticated, Cambridge-educated South African of a prominent Jewish family. He ran Dr Weizmann's political office together with a devout non-Jewish Zionist, Miss Doris May, who was emotionally attached to Dr Weizmann and later, unexpectetdly, became an equally devoted assistant to Ben-Gurion. I was interviewed by Arthur Lourie and Miss May. They seemed quite interested in my Diplomatic Academy training. 'If only you knew Arabic,' they said, 'we'd have a job for you.' That was the most diplomatic brushoff I had ever had. But happily at that moment Lourie's brother, Norman, entered the room. A film producer, business entrepreneur, powerful enthusiast and pioneer of many hazardous causes, he announced: 'I need a young man, part-time, to help me in a lobbying campaign for an independent Jewish brigade in the British Army. There will soon be a war and we've got to prepare now.' He took me on there and then. I had to write articles or translate English pamphlets into French and German – for Switzerland – and although I was not actually paid, I was constantly taken out for opulent meals, fund-raising parties and dinners where I met the Zionist hierarchy.

Norman Lourie remained a friend until his death. In 1950 he married Alena, one of a stunning pair of Czech twins whom he had met while filming in an immigrant camp in Israel. The two sisters and their family had recently arrived from Prague having spent part of the war in Auschwitz and Teresienstadt. They were remarkable girls, highly intelligent and active in philanthropy and politics, and they have become life-long friends. Alena Lourie now lives in Geneva. Irena found happiness in her marriage to Lane Kirkland, for many years the head of the American Federation of Labour and the Congress of Industrial Organization, the American labour union. His ceaseless work against Communism in Eastern Europe and moral and material support for Solidarnosc in Poland earned him great respect.

77 Great Russell Street was a hive of political activity in the period before Munich and the outbreak of war. The sombre future of European Jewry in a conflagration with Hitler was nowhere more viscerally felt than in that corner house in Bloomsbury. If you were a familiar face, you could walk into any of the senior people's rooms – except one, that of Weizmann. Lewis Namier, the historian, was among those I met there. An ardent Zionist, he might have been the first foreign minister of the new State of Israel but for his conversion to Chistianity in the wake of his marriage to a Greek Orthodox. He fell out with Weizmann and became the fallen angel of Zionism.

Selig Brodetzky, Professor of Mathematics at Leeds University, also worked in the political office. A staunch Weizmannite, he lost out in the power struggle with Ben-Gurion at the end of the war. My first meeting with two other hallowed names in the history of Zionism, the organizer, Berl Locker, and Berl Katzenelson, the great theorist of the Zionist Labour Movement, was very unconventional. I burst into their room with the proofs of some inflammatory article on the Negev to find them crouched on the floor trying to light a fire in an awkward chimney. 'Did you know that we are trained plumbers, Weidenfeld?' cried Locker. 'Liar,' countered the puckish Ketzenelson, 'you've never done a day's work with your hands. You're a desk man, a *luftmensch*.' What started as an amiable banter ended as a serious altercation between the two Berls and I tiptoed silently out of the room.

Two other men I got to know during this period impressed me in different ways. One was Orde Wingate, a captain in the British Army who had embraced Zionism with fierce fervour. He had been one of the people responsible for the whole concept and organization of Jewish self-defence in Palestine. His Night Raiders trained young Jewish settlers such as Moshe Dayan and Yigal Allon during the Arab Revolt and the Jewish counterattack on Arab irregulars and, up to his death in the Burmese jungles, where he was the leader of the famous Chindits, he kept his faith with the Jewish cause. Orde Wingate came to several meetings campaigning for a Jewish brigade and earned the passionate disapproval of both the British War Office and the Colonial Office, which had a distinct bias in favour of the Arab majority in Palestine.

The second man was Theodore Zissiu, the son of a rich

Romanian businessman. A Cambridge-educated dilettante, Zissiu devoted his private fortune and all his time and energy to the cause of the Negev, that large strip of desert in the south of Palestine which today represents nearly forty per cent of Israel's territory but less than ten per cent of its population. Zionist leaders had never paid much attention to that largely uninhabited land, not realizing that it could be turned into fertile soil and provide a prosperous homeland for more than a million settlers. Strategically the Negev was the land link between Egypt and the northern tier of the Arab world and it did not have a large indigenous Arab population. Zissiu spent thousands of pounds financing cartographers, geologists and economists, sending them to the Negev and working up a case for adding a claim to that area to the Zionist programme of future statehood. I became infected by his enthusiasm and spent a good deal of time helping to draft speeches and memoranda urging the Jewish leadership to persuade the British authorities to grant concessions in the Negev. Unfortunately Zissiu died early in the war fighting with the Free French Army. Had he survived, he could have played a significant role in Israel. His name is virtually forgotten now, but every time I visit Beersheva, the flourishing and sprawling capital of the Negev, I try to urge the city fathers to erect a monument or name a street in honour of that Romanian eccentric, who was one of the first people in London to befriend me and who shared his dreams with me.

While freelancing and meddling in the Zionist camp, I looked for something more permanent and solid. An absurd suggestion that I become a stockbroker and cultivate the more affluent refugees to make them invest in British shares came from a slightly exasperated but well-meaning City mandarin, Captain Eric Waley, who was related to the Rothschilds and had Austrian connections. He sent me on to a very grand and social courtier, Bob Maurice, of the firm of Schweder & Company, whose clientele included dowager duchesses and an elderly spinster of the British reigning house, Princess Helen Victoria and her younger sister, Princess Marie Louise.

He took me in as a trainee. I duly went to the fifty shilling tailor to equip myself with a three-piece suit with double-breasted waistcoat, a dark grey homburg hat and an umbrella. In the office I sat on a high stool flanked by a young clerk whose cockney English sounded more like Basque or Berber to my wholly unfamiliarized ear, and by a rather dissolute and wholly uninterested young scion of one of the Anglo-Jewish banking dynasties who had been sent to an outside firm to learn the ropes the hard way. For six weeks I was broken into the per cent and per mille fractions of commissions and the basic elements of the stock market. Mr Maurice, the senior chief, took an interest in me and even allowed me to walk with him around the City. When he tipped his top hat to fellow brokers, his demeanour and the volume of his voice revealed the ratings he gave the social standing of whomever he greeted. Mr Maurice also took me along to dine with his aged female clients. On one occasion I was invited to spend an evening dining and dancing with Princess Marie Louise and her lady-in-waiting at the Hungaria Restaurant in Lower Regent Street.

The social microcosm of the Jewish and refugee community engaged much of my attention. Through Mrs Ruth Cohen I moved in the tea-party circuit of the patrician Hampstead set. At the house of Sir Leon Simon, head of the Post Office and a great Hebrew scholar, I disgraced myself by breaking a gilt chair and was banished by Lady Simon from her immediate circle. The historian Cecil Roth asked me to family lunches followed by long walks on Hampstead Heath. Free Austria's last envoy at the Court of St James, Baron Frankenstein, to whom I had an especially warm introduction from 'Pipsi' Schey, told me quite candidly, 'In some ways your position is so typically Austrian. It's hopeless but not serious. I can't get you a job but I can get you invitations. You're musical, aren't you? Well, there's a shortage of guests for private chamber music and there are quite good dinners after the concerts.' His guiding hand led me to innumerable dinners with soulful recitals before or after the meal.

At the apex of Central European refugee society stood those who had for a decade or more wisely spirited most of their money to England, bought farms and town houses and mingled with the hunting gentry or the Kensington and Mayfair patriciate. Labelled refugees by their peers, they themselves looked down on newcomers. They treasured their acquaintance with and friendships among the bearers of great English titles, with some of whom they were on Christian name terms. They looked at one's credentials, one's speech and dress with cold, scrutinizing eyes. 'Don't waste your time on him, he's an *Emigrant*,' hissed the imperious banker's wife, Frau E., into her daughter's ear when she asked about me.

The kindliest among them was Vera Reiss, a majestic figure of a

woman married to a Viennese doctor, the first 'commoner' after
three aristocratic marriages. Far from being Jewish, her father's
family were among the founders of the mighty German I.G. Farben
Industrie, but she had followed her Jewish husband into exile. Vera
entertained generously, mixing British notables and important
guests from abroad with her own lame ducks and refugee protegés
of every age and condition. She loved matchmaking and scored
many successes, finding suitable husbands for her mixed troupe of
Viennese debutantes, street-smart adventuresses or budding artists.
One of her protegées, a buxom blonde who hailed from much
farther down the Danube than Vienna, was sent off by Vera to a
charity ball at the Dorchester to sell flags and programmes. One
customer bought a flag and a programme and ended up marrying
her. He was the Sultan of Johor, one of the world's richest men,
and, as Sultana, Marcella Mendel spent the war on her exotic throne
a virtual captive of the Japanese.

The most tragic of all the matches poor Vera carried off at her
domestic hearth involved a young actress, Gerd Marburg, who
started a clandestine affair with her husband whilst living in their
house. When she discovered the strength and sincerity of the two
lovers' feelings, Vera committed suicide. In her last message she
wished them both well. The stricken doctor, who was to be my GP
for over thirty years, did not find the happiness that he had hoped
for, and his last marriage ended in tragedy.

The life of a young exile, with its constant novelty, its dashed
hopes and furtive adventures, was, of course, set against the worsening scene in Europe. We Austrians, Germans and Czechs yearned
for a decisive settlement with Nazi Germany and looked to the
Western powers to stop Hitler, by force if necessary. Yet at the
same time we lived in anguish, fearing for our relatives and friends.
Each of us was waiting for a parent, a brother, a sweetheart to
extricate himself from the vast Hitlerite prison. In the days before
Munich I remember returning to my room in the boarding house
and praying, prostrate on the floor, for my parents' survival and
for some divine blow to fall on Hitler's head. We grabbed successive
editions of the *Evening Standard* to read beyond the banner headlines about every new Nazi coup. It was August 1938, and a few
fellow refugees and I went to explore the wonders of Speakers'
Corner, still dazed by the almost orgiastic freedom of expression.
There we stumbled on a group of Mosley's Union of Fascists. We

stood out clearly and were soon surrounded. There were jeers, curses, raised fists. Then, suddenly, two archetypal British bobbies, six feet tall, their arms folded behind their backs, appeared from nowhere. They stood firm and the menacing crowd dispersed. We walked away, shaken and relieved, but, above all, impressed. For at least half an hour afterwards we sat in silence over our coffee – we were not tea drinkers yet – at the nearby Lyons Corner House.

When Hitler marched into Prague in March 1939, at which time Neville Chamberlain was beginning to see the light, the mood of the country changed almost overnight. War seemed more and more inevitable, and preparations for a National Emergency began on a massive scale. At breakfast one morning during the last stages of the Czech crisis, my host opened *The Times*, as was his wont. He always read the quotation from the Scriptures and then turned to 'Appointments Vacant'. That day a large advertisement caught his eye. The BBC was looking for foreign linguists to man a new monitoring service. Mr Smythe exclaimed, 'Turli, this is your chance.' I was sure I would not be up to the job, given my age and lack of experience, and I reasoned that there must be a legion of distinguished experts of all sorts among the flood of refugees. But Mr Smythe insisted I apply, adding, 'Today's quote from the Bible is very encouraging.'

That afternoon I went to the Regent Palace Hotel, vaguely aware that there was a typing service for foreign salesmen on the first floor. There I found a woman with dark, sleek hair, thick eyelashes and long fingernails. For two shillings and sixpence she drafted letters for clients who told her in pidgin English what they wanted to say. I showed her the advertisement and gave her a summary of my qualifications, and she put it all into a neat letter. Within two weeks I got a letter from the General Establishment Officer of the BBC inviting me to a French test. At the test I felt as if I was joining the Foreign Legion. There was a White Russian prince, a Portuguese colonial doctor, a Maltese impresario of circus acts and a bevy of bespectacled Central European intellectuals, some clutching dictionaries. We all sat at long benches transcribing English summaries of a long-winded French radio talk on military manoeuvres in the Alps, followed by a short news bulletin from Radio Paris featuring press comments on Hitler's rape of what was left of Czechoslovakia.

Three weeks later I got a second letter asking me to come to Broadcasting House for an appointment. A stocky bureaucrat and a languid, informally attired producer asked me some searching questions. Had I ever belonged to an extremist organization – Nazi or Communist? What were my hobbies? What did I think of the English? Was I emotionally stable? What did I feel for my native land? I steered through the questions as best I could and was told to wait for a decision. In mid-June I received a letter telling me that on a date yet to be announced the BBC would employ me for three months or the duration of a National Emergency, whichever was the shorter.

So by the time my parents finally arrived at the end of June I was able to announce to them that I was on the point of getting a job with the BBC. At Victoria Station I was seized by the double excitement of seeing them again and my desire to show them the splendours of London. Though anxious to get to Parliament Hill Fields after their long journey, they were too kind to dampen my enthusiasm and I dragged them on foot all the way from Victoria to Highgate. They had had their own share of adventures in transit. In Italy they had been robbed by a guide who had taken them over the frontier, and by the time they reached Paris they had run out of money. Mr Smythe had sent them the wherewithal for the last stretch to London.

My parents stayed with Mr and Mrs Smythe for some months, and when eventually I joined the BBC I rented them rooms at a farm near Stroud, an hour or so away from my workplace in the West Country. My mother's asthma and my father's strained nerves would have made life in wartime London difficult. Although my father, at barely fifty, was still a relatively young man, he never made it again in his profession. Instead he reverted to his early passion, teaching Greek and Latin at grammar schools and private crammers, where he built quite a reputation for himself. For many years he was a much sought-after coach for entrants to Oxford, took private pupils and genuinely enjoyed a life of reading and teaching. But England remained for him a quaint, strange world that he admired but never quite understood. Imperceptibly our roles were reversed – not that I did not continue getting shrewd advice and unconditional love, but my parents were now the innocent babes in the wood and I became their guardian and provider, a role I cherished for the rest of their lives.

My mother died in 1983 at the age of eighty-nine. My father, who had followed my career with blind faith, punctuated by intermittent bursts of highly articulate condemnation of my failings, died in 1967, a disappointed but not an unhappy man. Sustained by many inner resources, he had, however, invested all his emotional energies in love and concern for his only son.

CHAPTER FIVE

The BBC at War

AT THE END OF JULY I got the summons from the BBC, and ten days before the outbreak of war I boarded a bus outside Broadcasting House with twenty-five others. None of us knew the destination. This trip was known in BBC folklore as the Mayflower Bus because the little pioneer band of monitors ultimately swelled to 184. We were part of the new BBC Overseas Intelligence Department and our place of work was Wood Norton, a large manor house near Evesham in Worcestershire which had been the residence of Louis Philippe of Orleans, the exiled king of France, in the mid-nineteenth century. The fleur-de-lys was emblazoned everywhere. We were billeted in Evesham, a pleasant market garden town on the Avon. I was assigned a room with an elderly couple where the husband never ceased to wonder at the polyglot influx and the wife never ceased to puzzle me with her flood of malapropisms. She said she thought me morose when she meant thoughtful, used resilient for responsive and cataract for catastrophe.

At weekends a well-known landed family prominent in the City used to invite foreign monitors for tea. On one such occasion our hostess, who looked like a younger version of Barbara Cartland, turned to me and said, 'I hear you come from Germany. Did you know the Goerings?' I only just managed to conceal my amazement at the blatant mixture of insouciance and naivety by spluttering something about having lived in Vienna, while the Goerings were busy in Berlin.

We worked in three shifts, listening to enemy broadcasts eight hours at a time. After each transmission we had to report the gist to two supervisors, one for general information and the other, who was known as the 'flash' supervisor, for immediate news value. Then we would go into small cubicles and dictate a summary of what we had heard to carefully picked secretaries. The BBC recruitment policy eschewed what were internally described as CTs (commercial types), products of large city typing pools. I owe a great deal to the Unknown Secretary of Wood Norton because she was editor and language teacher all in one. They were all patient, dedicated and highly efficient. Our summaries of world broadcasting were collated in a document called 'Daily Digest' which was sent off to the BBC output services and government and services departments.

Wood Norton soon outgrew its capacity so that only senior administrative personnel had their offices in the main building, and we were housed in improvised huts. A few hundred yards away from where my group worked lay another cluster of huts separated by barbed wire. This was the mysterious 'Y' unit, a different assemblage of monitors who were forbidden to talk about their work, about which rumours abounded. In fact their task was to listen to unintelligible noises, distress signals of ships and aircraft, strange atmospheric sounds and codes which they recorded and transcribed. But in the Evesham club house, the local hotels and pubs, monitors and supervisors mixed freely and grew into a jolly, convivial community. More and more of the BBC's programme departments were moved to the area and soon we had orchestras, the BBC Repertory Company and a large part of the music department settling in the neighbourhood. With them came a very stimulating variety of talented men and women, who included Gilbert Harding, a former schoolmaster who became a famous television personality after the war, Archie Gordon, a BBC talks producer, the future Marquess of Aberdeen, and Leonard Schapiro, a struggling barrister who later achieved renown as a Kremlinologist and professor at the London School of Economics.

As the foreign language output of Britain's war effort grew, groups of national contingents also moved in – the BBC Middle East service with its British orientalist supervisors from Cambridge and London, Arabs and Turks, and the whole of the Latin American service with nationals from each and every Luzo-Hispanic country. Our own unit contained a colourful mixture of people. My fellow Austrians included Ernst Gombrich, the art historian, Ilse Barea, the Viennese-born wife of the distinguished Spanish republican novelist, and Ernst Buschbeck, another art historian, who become director of Vienna's Kunsthistorisches Museum after the war. Buschbeck was eloquent and at times almost garrulous, but he had a secret: though not a Jew himself, he had left his family in Austria and followed his mistress, a Viennese Jewess, into exile – he had two sons serving in the German Army. Besides academics and journalists from Eastern Europe, we also had stockbrockers and businessmen, not to mention a number of dark horses like myself.

I loved the work and plunged into it with great zest, intent on mastering my job and on improving my English by concentrated reading. I was particularly attracted by eighteenth-century oratory and the lofty prose of the nineteenth-century historians, Macaulay and Trevelyan, Roscoe and John Addington Symonds. The last two enabled me to combine my interest in language with my fascination for the Italian Renaissance. Country picnics and cycling parties, polyglot birthday celebrations and amateur theatricals made time fly. I developed a passion for mimicry, impersonating not only my immediate colleagues and superiors but also heroes and villains of the war in Europe whose voices it was our job to study. My favourite turns were Hitler and Mussolini and, as a *pièce de résistance*, I would often perform a meeting between them steered by the Führer's famous interpreter, Dr Schmidt. The fictitious dialogue was based on a well-known account of the first meeting between Hitler and Mussolini in Venice on a rainy day in 1934 which proved to be a disaster. At that time Mussolini was still being wooed by the Western powers, and Hitler tried to break out of diplomatic isolation and gain the Duce's sympathy. Mussolini's German was far worse than he professed and Hitler's Italian was nonexistent. They both became increasingly suspicious and ill-tempered, and poor Schmidt tried to calm them down by deliberate mistranslation. In my rendition Mussolini cried:

> – Schmidt, tell the Führer that when the ancient Teutons were still no better than ordinary cannibals, Rome already ruled the world.
> HITLER: What did the Duce say? Germans . . . Kannibal?
> SCHMIDT: Not Kannibal, *mein Führer*, Hannibal, Hannibal! You must realize the Duce comes from a part of Italy where the *K* is pronounced as *H*. Hannibal, Hannibal.

In the club house I was often asked to improvise a Hitler speech on the most preposterous topics. As I had read most of his speeches

before and after his seizure of power I found it easy to comply.
These imitations had an unexpected consequence. One of the most
popular features broadcasts was a weekly programme which went
out at prime time after the evening news. Called *The Shadow of
the Swastika*, it consisted of dramatic reconstructions of episodes
in the history of the Third Reich culminating in recorded extracts
from authentic Hitler speeches superimposed on the voices of the
English actors. The department responsible for features and drama
had been evacuated to a place nearby, and the Hitler records were
always brought from London headquarters. On one occasion heavy
air raids prevented the record from arriving. The programme was
threatened and the producer, Laurence Gilliam, was at his wits' end
until one of his assistants told him that there was this young Austrian who did a pretty good imitation of the Führer's voice as an
occasional party turn. Gilliam gave me an audition and said reluctantly, 'I suppose this will have to do.' And so for thirty seconds I
was Germany's warlord, bellowing about a dozen cadences from
Hitler's speech after the Night of the Long Knives in 1934 to an
audience of millions: 'On that night I was the supreme judge of the
German nation.' It was my debut as a broadcaster.

This incident improved my standing with the programme producers and news talks editors who beamed their programmes to
North America and the Commonwealth from nearby Abbey
Manor. They needed commentaries on the latest news events at a
moment's notice and, hampered by wartime difficulties in communication, sometimes had trouble bringing in broadcasters from
London. I was used more and more frequently as a commentator
on people and events in Nazi Germany. But most of my time was
still spent monitoring broadcasts in German, Italian and French.
As I became more skilled I was chosen to be part of the small team
of flash monitors who were quick enough to translate an important
unscheduled broadcast, say a special communiqué from high command or a Hitler speech, straight onto the teleprinter to London
so that the service departments or the foreign office could get the
gist within minutes.

After a year or so I grew increasingly interested in the uses to
which all this material was put. Early in 1941 I put a plan before
my superiors for a new venture. It entailed selecting nuggets from
German propaganda which the BBC's output services could beam
back to Germany on the same day. I criticized the rather wooden

style of our broadcasts to Germany, arguing that the German language had been changing during the war and that the BBC German service missed some of the flavour of the new idiom. I pointed out that something of the mood and morale could be gleaned from unsuspected sources such as the letters of German soldiers to their wives, the choice of music in the daily request concerts, and the growing sentimentality and melancholy pervading the *Wehrmacht*. My proposal was accepted and I became head of a special German section that produced a daily digest entitled *Deutschlandspiegel* – *Germany Day by Day*. My digest became more ambitious, and by juxtaposing various items I tried to put across arguments with which to score propaganda points and inspire ideas for talks or feature programmes.

Deutschlandspiegel proved a success and brought me to the notice of Richard Crossman, the Oxford philosopher and Labour politician who was the supremo of British 'black' and 'white' propaganda to Germany. White propaganda was that broadcast on the official channels of the BBC. Black propaganda meant covert radio stations purporting to broadcast from inside Germany. The latter were directed by secret departments manned by a mixture of refugees, willing prisoners of war and 'turned' Nazis in our power. Crossman asked me to come and see him in London and invited me to take part in regular directive meetings at BBC headquarters in Bush House, where I met the members of his remarkable team. It included Lindley Fraser, a bibulous don from Aberdeen and a German scholar, and the eager young Yorkshire historian, Alan Bullock, who had also taught at Oxford, and was to go on to found a college, rise to the vice chancellorship of that university and write the best biography of Hitler next to Joachim Fest's. Marius Goring, the actor, ran a programme for the German forces and Patrick Gordon Walker, another Oxford Labour politician, addressed himself to the German workers. Since it was held that German workers might secretly listen before their morning shift, he was condemned to permanent night duty.

Richard Crossman had a powerful personality and a quick mind which enabled him to make his arguments seem instantly plausible. But with his mercurial temperament he could turn devotees into detractors at lightning speed. Intellectually, he was a self-intoxicating mechanism. He would get excited about a particular propaganda theme, and our meetings followed a set pattern which

went something like this. 'Forget the German *Junkers*, the aristocrats, the *Wehrmacht* generals!' Crossman would exclaim. 'We have
to concentrate on the German proletariat! Patrick [Gordon
Walker], prepare a new series, be as inflammatory as you can. I
want a brief for all departments by next Monday.' Poor Gordon
Walker would add six sleepless days to his night duty and produce
an elaborate and well-argued brief. By that time, Crossman would
have changed his mind: 'You can't trust the German worker! Latest
intelligence reports show that they are still behind the Party. We
need a structured brief to appeal to the Protestant conscience of
the *Wehrmacht* upper crust. Who here has good contacts with the
churches? We need a few German-speaking army chaplains. Marius
[Goring], get cracking. We want a brand new series of talks to start
next Sunday.'

Both Crossman and Gordon Walker were destined to become
cabinet ministers, and it may well be that the roots of the political
enmity between them which surfaced in future Labour governments
lay in those Bush House directive meetings.

Back in Evesham my special German section expanded and
became the kernel of similar daily propaganda digests in Italian –
Specchio d'Italia : Italy Day by Day – and in French – *France à
L'Ecoute: France Day by Day*. My closest collaborator was Otto
Giles. Of German extraction, he had been a law don at London
University. He was an excellent organizer and left me to think up
ideas for propaganda and news exploitation. My workload
expanded too. Besides the daily digests, I did more and more broadcasting, scriptwriting and feature writing for BBC publications and
the national press.

In 1942 I was transferred to London and given a job specially
created for me by Tony Rendell, assistant controller of overseas
services: I became a one-man script factory producing talks and
features on Occupied Europe. After a certain amount of interdepart-
mental haggling, I was released from the monitoring service and
joined the news department at 200 Oxford Street, site of the old
department store Peter Robinson, which had been taken over by
the BBC for the duration of the war. The building housed *Radio
Newsreel*, the longest-running news and features programme on the
British airwaves and only quite recently subsumed into the BBC
World Service. The building also housed such eminent writers as
George Orwell, Edmund Blunden, William Empson and Norman

Collins, all of whom worked in the Overseas Service as part of the war effort. The studios, hospitality rooms and canteens of 200 Oxford Steet welcomed all the Allied war leaders, statesmen and politicians in London.

I was assigned a large office with a desk for myself and one for a secretary. A large partner's desk at the other end of the room was occupied by two colleagues, James Fergusson, a Scottish laird whose mood alternated between dourness and sentimentality, and Edgar Lustgarten, with whom I had an uneasy relationship. Fergusson broadcast a programme called *Listening Post* which showed up the evils and hypocrisies of Nazi propaganda and was directed at listeners in the Commonwealth. One of my many jobs was to feed him with suitable items. He was a generous soul, and though he found me a bewildering intruder at first, he opened up and intro-duced me to his family and to his mother-in-law, Mrs 'Baffy' Dugdale, a niece of Lord Balfour and close freind of Chaim Weizmann. His brother was the famous Bernard Fergusson, second-in-command Orde Wingate in Burma.

No more contrasting figure could have been invented than the dapper, nervy Edgar Lustgarten, a talented, stage-struck lawyer from Manchester who made his career as a broadcaster, thriller writer and, after the war, illustrious television performer in real-life criminal cases. His telephone line never ceased to ring, and 'dar-lings', 'sweethearts' and 'pets' preceded the names of the stars of stage, screen and music hall. He held court in the canteen and ingratiated himself with free tickets for first nights. Once in a while he received the great and feared James Agate, drama critic of the *Daily Express*. Lustgarten did not like me one bit. He hardly ever addressed a word to me, let alone graced me with a look, but once he felt obliged to ask for my support when James Agate telephoned him to ask for the full name and spelling of a contemporary Nazi playwright. My ability instantly to oblige granted me a temporary patent of tolerance.

The three years I had spent in the highly structured, subtly idio-syncratic and yet quintessentially English organizational environ-ment of the BBC had already made their mark. Anyone who, like me, had burst in from an alien scene came to identify the BBC with Britain. I felt that the world outside the corporation was but an enlarged model of the BBC universe. There were indeed subtle hier-archies, patterns of Byzantine absolutism and class distinction in the prewar BBC, but they were markedly different from those prevailing beyond its portals. In some cases they were even an inversion of the established order.

The Corporation bore the stamp of its founder, Sir John (later Lord) Reith. One of the secrets of his success was that he instilled a sense of belonging to an elite without necessarily conforming to the canons of the established elite in English society. The BBC was like a private chapter, a monastic order with its own rules and criteria. One of Reith's great achievements was in bridging the gap between the engineers and the creative programme makers – intellectuals and, more often than not, products of the major public schools and Oxbridge. Reith gave the two groups equal standing. The engineering division was an elitist formation of its own, a priesthood of self-confident, proud technocrats. When I arrived on my bicycle in the early morning to start the day shift in Evesham, I would run into a platoon of solemn, pipe-smoking men returning from the night shift and boarding their buses with an almost lofty sense of tired satisfaction about a job well done, and the quiet feeling that they were the masters of their little universe, but for whom the airwaves would remain silent. The technicians did not have to look up to the programme makers, or vice versa. This was one of the factors which contributed to the special atmosphere of the BBC.

Just as any imperial society leaves its most distinctive traces in outlying garrisons rather than in the metropolis, the BBC's imperial ambiance could be more strongly felt in provincial Evesham than in London, W.1, where I now moved. I was twenty-two years old and a news commentator with the title 'our European correspondent', who broadcast in English for the North American, African and Pacific services. My output was prodigious. I churned out something like twenty programmes a week, mainly news talks of no more than five minutes in length, but also longer commentaries and documentary features with a fictitious plot built around an authentic event or person. Though my real name was Arthur Weidenfeld, the programme director told me bluntly that my surname was too long and my first name did not transmit well on short wave because of the diphthong. He asked me whether I had a middle name and I said, 'George.' He said, 'Drop the Arthur, drop the feld,' so I broadcast under the name George Weiden. When I returned to civilian life I resumed my real surname, but by that time so many people knew me as George that I stuck to it.

Besides a full-time secretary I was given a research assistant and an expense account which allowed me to take my 'sources' out to an ever-widening range of eating places. Wartime austerity levelled the prices of all meals to five shillings per head. Drink was not uniformly priced – you paid more for it at the Ritz, the Coq d'Or or Les Ambassadeurs in Mayfair than at Bertorelli, Kettner or the White Tower in Soho. Since I am a teetotaller, I naturally chose to lunch at the Ritz and Claridge's, where I could inhale the cosmopolitan air filled with whiffs of tobacco from every segment of the Atlantic Alliance and watch the Allied parade go by, rather than stand queueing behind the bar in a crowded Fitzrovian pub. My preference for the sedentary life has not always been so overwhelming, but I eschew cocktail parties and arrive late at any gathering where standing or milling around is part of the ritual.

One of my favourite BBC assignments was *The Axis Conversation*, broadcast on the Italian Forces programme which was launched in the spring of 1941. It was a weekly dialogue scripted by Leo Shepley, a bilingual English journalist, about the fortunes of the war between Signor Mancini, played by Uberto Limentani, and a beastly, blustering German industrialist called Herr Bacher – myself. As Herr Bacher I had to speak Italian with a strong German accent and make myself as obnoxious to the Italian public as I could. Our weekly routine was to meet and have a good lunch where we agreed on the most topical items of the week for our broadcast to the Italian people. We made use of intelligence material that had reached us about Italian morale, food shortages, incidents between German soldiers and local girls and whatever else we could find that would, coming from an arrogant German, offend the pride of the Italian public. There were no holds barred. I would growl a Verdi aria and then belittle its musical quality before launching into a few triumphalist bars of Wagner. I would compare the fighting quality of the *Wehrmacht* with the inadequacies of the Bersaglieri. Or we would quarrel about the relative qualities of Italian and German food.

At the outset of the programme's life, Mancini was meek and Bacher overbearing. Gradually, as the fortunes of war changed, Mancini gained confidence and Bacher started to lose his. Towards the end of the war our roles had completely reversed: Bacher became self-pitying and almost suicidal. In one of the last programmes the generous Mancini even promised to see what he could do to get Herr Bacher a certificate of good behaviour and, failing that, make sure he received parcels of special rations in his detention camp. According to BBC listeners' research in neutral countries, *The Axis Conversation* enjoyed great popularity in Italy. After the war, whenever I revealed my identity as Herr Bacher to Italians, I found I was quite a well-known personality.

As the war took a more happy turn towards an Allied victory and preparations for a second front intensified, the BBC expanded accordingly. More theatres of war meant a greater volume of news, heavier traffic in the news department and a need for more experts. In the two years between 1942 and 1944 my journalistic output nearly quadrupled. Besides my daily commentaries and fictionalized documentaries, I branched out into newspaper journalism. For eighteen months or so I wrote a weekly column for the *News Chronicle*, the Liberal daily newspaper edited by Gerald Barry, a friend at the time. He asked me to comment on long-term trends emerging in Occupied Europe. The column had the byline George Weiden and was entitled 'Subject Europe'.

With the help of Derek Sington, a shy, self-effacing BBC news editor who had been on the *Manchester Guardian*, I also wrote a book. *The Goebbels Experiment* set out to explain the techniques and dissect the organization of the Nazi propaganda machine. Although most of the research was based on the vast outpourings of the Nazi propaganda machine – newspaper cuttings, films and all the broadcast material stored up in the reports of the BBC monitoring service – I was fortunate in meeting two refugees with considerable first-hand experience of Goebbels, Dr Weiss and Alfred Kerr.

Dr Ignaz Weiss had served as the Berlin police commissioner under the Socialist Government of Prussia headed by Prime Minister Otto Braun and Interior Minister Severing. He had been a principal butt of *Der Angriff*, the Nazi daily in Berlin, which regularly published cartoons of 'Isidor' Weiss. Marked by a long, bulbous nose, a curly forelock and large hornrimmed spectacles, this figure became a favourite totem of Goebbels' denigration campaign against Jews, socialists and democrats. Dr Weiss was living quietly in London when I went to see him. In a rather flat and deadpan tone he gave me a better picture of the ordeal that officials of the dying Weimar system underwent at the hands of the Nazis than any other source. Alfred Kerr was the famous dramatic and literary critic of Berlin, whose aphorisms and trenchant studies of German cultural life had made him one of the most respected of Weimar's cultural arbiters. He was neatly dressed with a high collar and bow tie, with eyes sunk below a domed forehead, and had a caustic wit which he applied to the literary gossip of wartime London – which alas found no outlet in print.

The Goebbels Experiment was published by John Murray in the autumn of 1943. It was translated into Swedish and accepted by the Yale University Press. I came to be regarded as something of a propaganda expert, and during the Nuremberg Trials I was often asked for depositions and opinions on various members of the Nazi propaganda ministry. There was the case of one official, Hinkel, who pleaded innocence although his section had furnished a large amount of viciously anti-Semitic material, all destined for one particular area in Germany, within a short space of time. I was able to prove that this concentration of propaganda material was typical of an operation codenamed 'Propagandawave'. It was usually undertaken to prepare the local population for massive deportations of Jews in their particular area.

One of my first assignments when I arrived at 200 Oxford Street was to secure my sources of information. There were of course the many BBC digests of daily monitoring reports, a digest of the German and European press, confidential briefs and position papers. Through Richard Crossman I got an insight into the morale reports delivered by prisoners of war, but the greatest live sources of what went on behind the Atlantic wall were the Allied governments in exile in London and the various freedom movements of nationals of enemy countries who drew on their own sources of information from the underground. I made the round of the Allied governments, cultivated diplomatic information officers and tasted rather than sipped or drank Yugoslav slivovitz, Czech brandy, Norwegian aquavit, Dutch kummel and of course a wide variety of French wines. And before long I became involved in such cabals as the Mihailovich versus Tito struggle.

The Allies were all eager to get their subtly differentiated point of view put across by the BBC. Soon I had hundreds of new acquaintances, but the Free French and the Czechs were my clear favourites. The Free French were a picturesque and civilized lot. General de Gaulle had assembled a number of outstanding men in his entourage, who included Jacques Soustelle and Raymond Aron, by far the most brilliant exile in London, who was not uncritically devoted to the General. He worked on *La France Libre* with André Labarthe, a scientist turned journalist and colleague of André Malraux at the Musée de L'Homme in Paris before the war. He had been in de Gaulle's first team of commissioners, but they had soon fallen out as Labarthe opposed the General's authoritarian tendencies. The friendship of these people was invaluable to me, for they opened my mind to the complexities of de Gaulle's position not only with the Allies, but also within his own camp. The crew that ran the BBC French service was headed by Michel St Denis, pioneer of the modern French theatre and broadcaster of *Les Français Parlent Aux Français*, who later did much to encourage me to become a publisher. Besides imparting news of the French underground, Maurice Schumann, a future foreign minister of France, dispensed some good black humour. The writer, Romain Gary, a Free French air-force officer, often joined the circle. He introduced me to the Polish painter and graphic chronicler of his age, Feliks Topolski.

For two decades Feliks, an irrepressible womanizer and, like myself, a teetotaller, was one of my great friends. We laughed at the same absurdities and cared about the same slights or setbacks. He was generous and tough, unpredictably kind to some and unfeeling towards others. As an artist Feliks suffered from lack of recognition by those he really admired while being suffocated with praise from those he half despised. His war reporting and his sketches of London high life and low life will one day be much better appreciated by serious critics than they were at the time.

Each Allied government in exile had its own quarter in London. The Norwegians and Dutch were in Kensington, the Free French in Carlton Terrace and St James's, the Poles between Knightsbridge and Kensington and the Czechs west of Marble Arch in Bayswater. They still maintained their proper embassies and made use of their prewar palatial quarters, but some of their leaders preferred suites in hotels – the Rembrandt and the Rubens in Buckingham Palace Road were reserved for the French, whilst Hampstead and Putney, with their suburban cosiness, were chosen by the more bourgeois-minded Central and East European Allies. Some of the exiled monarchs had country houses assigned to them. Each quarter and each government had its favourite pubs and restaurants, or even exclusive dining clubs. Rumour had it that the Free French kept a dining club in St James's, below which Colonel Passy's feared counterintelligence service debriefed recent arrivals from inside France using methods which would not have shocked their colleagues in the Levant forty years later.

I loved Czech food and liked listening to the internal intrigues of the Czechoslovak Government from the information minister, Hubert Ripka, or Benes' press counsellor, Ambassador Kraus, who spoke and moved like an old Habsburg bureaucrat. I often saw the Foreign Minister Jan Masaryk, the debonair and wisecracking son of the founder of modern Czechoslovakia. He moved by preference in Jewish circles and was a great friend of the Marks and Sieff families.

The Poles frequented special restaurants in Kensington, though one of their leaders, the bearded and ponderous Mr Grabski, who represented a traditionally anti-Semitic party in the exiled coalition, was addicted to kosher food and was seen lunching and dining as often as he could in a special restaurant in Maida Vale where the *gefilte Fisch* and chopped egg and goose liver had kept their authentic flavours.

The Milroy nightclub and Les Ambassadeurs in Mayfair were the most elegant nightspots. The quality of the food owed something to the presence of the former chef from the Polonia Hotel in Warsaw. They were located in Stratton Street, with the restaurant downstairs and the nightclub on the first floor. The guiding spirit was one John Mills who looked the picturesque villain some people thought he was – huge, moustached, with a deep, booming voice. Mills managed to get all the food and drink a five-star establishment might well provide in deepest peace. Malicious tongues suggested that he had the tacit backing of every secret service among London's guest governments and a special line to British Intelligence. In Stratton Street you could eavesdrop on what ally said to ally in their cups, and, it was whispered, there may have been some Mata Haris among the uniformed debutantes dining or dancing.

I was often entertained by Allied politicians and journalists, and by frequenting Les Ambassadeurs and the Milroy I met beautiful and sophisticated women diplomats and intelligence officers. The Allies were anxious to know what Britain thought about postwar aims and frontiers in Europe. They were jealous of one another, and each had their own pet ideas about the configuration of the future Continent. The Czechs were on their guard against the slightest hint of an inclination within the British Foreign Office or the

British press to let the Germans keep any part of its post 1937 loot. They felt Austria had to be resurrected and insisted that no part of the Sudetenland was to be left within the Reich. The Poles were far more ambitious. The notion of the Oder-Neisse line as Poland's western frontier was mooted early in the war. At first it had few supporters anywhere, but when Stalin made it clear that he intended to hang on to all his gains in eastern Poland, it was – very reluctantly – accepted that Poland had to be compensated by wholesale amputation of Germany's eastern limbs.

The eager debates about the future were not confined to journalists and exiled government officials; it was a war fought out also between British dons who had temporarily become civil servants and were housed in Oxford colleges or requisitioned country houses up and down the Home Counties. Each Central European country had its devoted partisans and bitter enemies. It seemed as if female specialists felt much more passionately about their ethnic pets. Shiela Grant Duff stood up for the Czechs. The Hon. Marjorie Lambert threw herself wholeheartedly into the struggle between the Serb royalist-Chetniks and the Croat-led Tito Communists. Claire Hollingworth and her husband, Vandelareur Robinson, held up their torches for the Albanians, and the venerable Professor McCarthy broke lances for the Magyars. The war of the dons for the ears and hearts of the British Foreign Office and the Political Warfare Executive, which coordinated policies, directed propaganda and issued directives and guidance notes to the BBC, raged unabated. Although few of my scripts were ever censored, I did engage in many heated debates with various political duty officers.

Each foreign group had one or more Lady Bountifuls in the British aristocracy who liked to entertain their leaders and blue-blooded warriors. The Hon. Mrs Phillimore, a gaunt Irish woman of Fabian sympathies, had a regular luncheon in a private room at the Ritz where she introduced Labour members of the British Government to leading Europeans. I had gained only occasional entrance to the grand political salons, but the Hon. Mrs Phillimore invited me to these functions. It was there that, when asked why he was so persistently hypersensitive about the British, and especially Churchill, General de Gaulle uttered the memorable phrase, 'Ah, Madame, I admire your country and I respect your prime minister, but with France's delicate position in the Alliance, I must use as a weapon my philosophy of calculated bloody-mindedness.' (This is my rather free translation of the phrase *la philosophie de la suscépti-bilité payante*.)

Another frequent guest was Hugh Dalton, the booming sacer-dotal Labour Minister of Economic Warfare who had his hands in both the propaganda and intelligence pies. He asked me what I thought should happen to Austria after the war. 'When Hitler's gone,' I said, 'we should let Austrians determine their own fate.' 'Ah,' boomed Dalton, 'as long as we know beforehand how they will self-determine. We must never let them join up with Germany.' That was quite a daring remark in 1942 or 1943, because both the British Labour Party and the exiled Austrian socialists were still in favour of a democratic Austria becoming part of a politically cleansed democratic Germany. It was one of those contentious issues hotly debated both in the Hampstead boarding houses of the emigrés and in the council rooms of Allied governments. Dalton foreshadowed the fateful decision at the Moscow Conference in December 1943 which declared Austria an independent country and the first 'innocent victim' of Nazi aggression. This decision allowed successive Austrian governments to sweep under the carpet the largely enthusiastic reception accorded to Hitler by the Austrian people. It was to create much bitterness among Jews all over the world about Austria's lack of compassion and compensation of Jewish victims which, in my view, led to the explosion over the Waldheim case more than forty years later, and was only partly laid to rest by the Socialist chancellor Vranitsky's public apology in the spring of 1991.

I had first met Mrs Phillimore through Tangye Lean, brother of the film director David Lean. Before the war Tangye had been deputy literary editor of the *News Chronicle*, and during the war worked at Bush House as one of the foreign language editors. Later he made a career as head of overseas services. A fastidious and complex character, he considered me something of a freak figure. Throughout our friendship he vacillated between hesitant approval and vague distrust of my abilities. Half afraid of me and half affec-tionate, he was one of the people who tutored me in such refine-ments of English life as not being too punctual for lunch appointments: 'Be three minutes late. Your host might still want to read the headlines in the early edition of the evening newspaper.' Tangye's praise was oblique and double-edged but his censure forth-right. He was a gifted man, but although he reached great heights in his postwar BBC career, he never fulfilled his aspirations as a writer in spite of early promise. He was a perfectionist who was loath to commit what he wrote to print. Tangye intrduced me to Trollope and Proust, and during those endless nights of air raids I devoured both. He also introduced me to the literary and intellectual coterie of Fleet Street which did not mix with rough reporters and hard-drinking journalists.

His friends met in the Café Royal, either downstairs or in the gallery. Literary and drama critics kept up with those who regarded themselves as artists of vocation and not profession. The elite of foreign correspondents who cared for style as well as scoops were also admitted to the group. Alan Morehead, Alexander Clifford and some of the high-living stars of the American foreign correspondents corps had entry into any circle they wished, including Downing Street. The formidable Ed Murrow, his junior Howard K. Smith, Quentin Reynolds, whose Sunday night pep talks after the news boosted British morale in the darkest hours, William Shirer and Raymond Gram Swing were national heroes, and when they appeared at the Café Royal they were greeted by all and sundry like toreros after a bullfight.

The only Canadian to have achieved similar fame was Matthew Halton. He became a boon companion of mine because at one point I shared digs with the local head of the Canadian Broadcasting Company, Andy Cowan. Matthew Halton had a long love affair with a pretty librarian at the Ministry of Information. On his desk he kept a photograph of his beautiful blonde baby girl Kathleen, who later married Kenneth Tynan.

I also met Alistair Forbes through Tangye Lean. Then in his twenties, he was already the 'golden boy' of men and women of great influence. A Bostonian of many European connections, he threw himself into wartime England as a passionate observer and budding agent of influence. He was a friend of the Churchill family, especially of Mary Churchill, and was often interrogated by the Prime Minister about his views as a representative of the younger generation. He had a cruel wit, and with his startling self-assurance was intermittently aggressive and courteous in conduct. At our first threesome lunch with Tanyge Lean he did not address a word to me, but over the years we became friends: fate gave us ringside seats in each other's lives.

Ali Forbes was probably spoilt by premature social success. His friendship with the great and the powerful made him lose his sense of perspective. Randolph Churchill was a close companion and he became a pillar of White's Club. Lady Rothermere (later Mrs Ian Fleming) took him up, and Ali was an extra man for all occasions including the most exalted. He wrote a weekly political column in the Rothermere-owned *Sunday Dispatch* which was extremely well informed but, as time went on, grew more and more obscure, except to the initiated who could decipher his coded allusions to people and events. The professionals at the receiving end in Fleet Street resented his powerful connections. He sent his copy by taxi to the editor and almost never set foot in Carmelite House. Small wonder that soon after the Rothermeres split up and Ann married Ian Fleming, the handsome creator of James Bond, Ali's column ceased to appear. But through Mary Churchill and other loyal supporters, Ali Forbes did much talent scouting, bringing deserving people to the notice of the decision-makers.

In addition to the world of the 'legitimate Allies' with their government offices, social hangouts and political salons, there was a different layer of impassioned political lobbying, intrigues and sectional in-fighting: the world of the independent 'freedom movements'. Whitehall barely recognized them; in fact they were largely dismissed by official circles. Many of them were fostered and sheltered by Kingsley Martin, editor of the *New Statesman*, and his common-law wife, Dorothy Woodman. Kingsley and Dorothy made an unconventionally conventional couple. He, conscious of the influence his weekly editorials would have on the left-wing intelligentsia, was eternally tortured by ideological dilemma and she, his determinedly radical conscience, was staunchly pro-Russian and above all concerned with the Third World. In her embroidered coat and fur hat and with her rosy cheeks she looked like an overblown Russian doll. At their flat in Buckingham Gate by the Strand they entertained the Afro-Asian fighters for decolonization and independence. There were the Free Burmese and the Free Indonesians, and there was Kwame Nkrumah from the Gold Coast, then a student in London. He had been taught by Professor 'Freddie' Ayer and was nicknamed 'the Hegelian' because he would frequently get up and ask what Hegel would have thought about this or that current political issue. Abdul Karim Kassem, later to lead a revolution that murdered the King of Iraq before himself being executed after a coup, rubbed shoulders with Krishna Menon who cut a dash in

Bohemian circles. He was one of the founder editors of the Pelican series of Penguin books and was destined to make a career in Nehru's India.

Dorothy Woodman ran the Union of Democratic Control, a philo-Communist organization which included a number of left-wing Labour MPs, notably Tom Driberg. Tom covered many fronts. As the diarist of the *Daily Express* and friend of Lord Beaverbrook, he knew his way through London's labyrinth of sets and clans, provoking, fascinating and repelling people according to their temperament. He became one of my most controversial authors.

The first emissary from Tito's Yugoslavia to arrive in London was General Velebit, son of a pre-First World War Austrian general and later to be deputy foreign minister and leading spokesman for the Communist regime. I had a special interview with him in which he spoke highly of Fitzroy Maclean and Bill Deakin, the two grand apologists of Marshal Tito who had been the first to enter the partisan territory, at Churchill's behest. Later, when I established my publishing firm, he helped me to get to Tito and publish *Tito Speaks*, the partly autobiographical and partly biographical work he produced with the help of Vladimir Dedijer, one of the Marshal's lieutenants.

Tito's memoirs were one of my first coups in my quest for authors on the Continent. In 1952 I followed the lead of the *Life* photographer John Phillips who had taken some remarkable pictures of the Yugoslav partisans and made friends with Dedijer. Through him he obtained the agent's rights for a book of Tito's war memoirs as told to his lieutenant. Phillips and I met in Venice, and over dinner at Countess Anna Maria Volpi Cicogna's in a brand new palazzo on the Giudecca we discussed the strategy for negotiating the world rights. We drafted a contract and the suggested structure of the book. Next morning we drove to Belgrade. I was only allowed to shake the Marshal's hand once. During our brief encounter I was struck by how small he was. He wore a linen suit and a sombre tie. All he said to me was, 'I don't like fat books.' Dedijer was helped by Milovan Djilas, Tito's closest associate until he broke with him in 1954, who contributed a remarkable account of his famous meetings with Stalin in the Kremlin and the acrimonious exchange which preceded the offical break between the Soviets and Tito in 1948. *Tito Speaks* was Weidenfeld & Nicolson's first international bestseller. It launched me into the field of memoirs, where we controlled either all the world rights or a stake in them, enabling us to sell newspaper serialization and other rights in many different countries, something I tried to make a speciality of in my publishing career.

One of my last interesting journalistic assignments during the war was an interview with President Benes of Czechoslovakia on the occasion of his sixtieth birthday in 1944. We lunched at his home in Putney. By that time the Red Army had already entered the easternmost part of his country, Sub Carpathian Russia, and he was in ebullient mood. 'You will see,' he said, 'my country will be the first one to stand on its own feet, to thrive and prosper.' He felt sure that Communists would play a constructive part in a broad-based coalition. 'I know that my own party will win and I will give the lie to those who think you can't have Communists as loyal partners in a parliamentary system.' I pointed out to him that the Poles felt very differently – they were afraid of being overrun and oppressed. 'But there's a difference,' said Benes, and winked. 'Marshal Stalin owes me a thing or two. I've rendered him great services.'

Benes, a sad victim of his self-deceiving confidence, may well have been referring to the bizarre story of the execution of the Russian Marshal Tukachevsky and other leading Red Army officers, which was carried out in collusion with the Gestapo and in which the Czech Intelligence Service had been cynically used by both sides as a conduit.

CHAPTER SIX

The Birth of Contact

DESPITE MY FAR-FLUNG connections and my involvement with the BBC and Fleet Street, I felt very insecure about my future in journalism. I had enjoyed a certain degree of success holding ad hoc seminars and a lecture at the Royal Institute for International Affairs, but I knew that I was regarded as a foreign maverick in a world still dominated by wartime restrictions. As soon as communications opened up the foreign correspondent would take over from the armchair pundit in London: hundreds of prewar staff would return from the fighting services to take up commanding posts in Broadcasting House or Bush House.

I yearned to start something myself and turn my condition of being with the English but not of the English into an advantage. I admired the military record of the British people and their instinctive courage in standing up to the Germans alone – the same courage they have showed since in the face of provocation from Nasser, the Argentine generals and Saddam Hussein. Even though governments and the Establishment might have had their doubts and disagreements, the ordinary people always knew where they stood on what they perceived to be a moral issue – the fight against an evil tyranny. I thought that Britain was the most temperate and tolerant of all societies and that her example could help postwar Europe return to democratic government.

Culturally, I felt that a great deal had happened on British soil during the war that was admirable and fresh: the rise of opera and ballet, the proliferation of literary reviews, the exploding interest in poetry and the short story and a hunger for information about what had happened meanwhile on the Occupied Continent. The Free French had brought fragments of Resistance literature to London, and, though it was hidden in allegory and often expressed in cryptic form, we had also read some of the writings of German opponents of the Nazi regime. A flood of brilliant and moving narrative writing had also come out of Italy as soon as the military coup of the King and General Badoglio drove Mussolini out of power. All this led me to conceive the idea of starting a magazine that would capture and perpetuate this European spirit of wartime London. I thought I would call it *Contact*.

My plan was inordinately ambitious, but in my mind the magazine took on a crystal-clear shape. I dreamt of a lavishly produced monthly that would be investigative, analytical and reflective. It would emulate the best reportage of the *New Yorker* with an occasional dash of *Fortune*; it would try to give comment and interpretation on the lines of what I held to be the high point of critical journalism of the day – somewhere between Kingsley Martin's *New Statesman* and the *New Republic* under Freda Kirchway; and in a third section I wanted to allow the great minds of the day to write idiosyncratic essays on the important issues of our time. Even more ambitiously, I dreamt that *Contact* should eventually be published in several languages in various European capitals by local publishers, with London acting as the coordinating editorial headquarters.

This idea had germinated in my mind as early as 1943. I had no idea where to begin, but I thought of nothing else. I talked to all and sundry, meeting with stunned disbelief, polite interest and obvious scepticism. But I persevered. I had no publishing experience whatsoever, and of course I needed money. Moreover I had to find a way of getting paper, because there was strict rationing and an absolute ban on new periodicals.

Yet here and there I met with some positive responses. Among the Czech Government in exile was a former printer-publisher, Jiri Firt, once boss of the big Melantrich works in Prague and an experienced periodical publisher. He was the first to recognize the merit of the scheme, and we signed an agreement in the BBC canteen that, should he resume his old job on returning to Prague after the war, he would set up a Czech *Contact* and cofinance my British venture. Jiri Firt authorized me to use this 'agreement' in any future negotiations with British financiers. The German Army was still in Stalingrad when we toasted this first publishing contract of my life, but I felt exhilarated.

It so happened that the resident librarian of the BBC branch at

200 Oxford Street, Diana Van Oss, had a young Hungarian friend who worked as sales manager of the publishing firm Nicholson & Watson. His name was André Deutsch, and he too dreamt of starting his own book publishing firm. His employer was a mercurial, self-taught Welshman called John Roberts who wanted to turn Nicholson & Watson into a major literary force. The firm was owned by a wealthy printer, Mr Duncan Mackintosh of Redhill, Surrey, who had a vast paper quota. Wartime quotas of paper were based on the median volume of paper used by a firm during the last two or three years before the war, thus any printer lucky enough to have had a large turnover during that period could wield enormous power in those restricted times: it was tantamount to having gold reserves. Printers or publishers who had gone through a lean prewar period were condemned to a more modest existence.

When I laid my vastly ambitious plans before André Deutsch, I found a receptive listener. He promised to introduce me to the fountainhead of money and paper, but he pointed out that I was not sufficiently well-known to unlock large funds – I needed names that would inspire confidence. I found two men to whom, among so many others, I had confided my plans. One was Tangye Lean and the other the redoubtable Gerald Barry, editor of the *News Chronicle* and a glamorous figure in the worlds of journalism, the arts and Left-to-middle-of-the-road politics. He was at that time involved in a power struggle with Sir Walter Layton, chairman of the *News Chronicle*, and Tangye Lean was also uncertain about his postwar plans, so it suited them to lend their names to a venture of this kind, provided it had the necessary financial backing. They agreed to become coeditors of the embryonic magazine.

We had everything mapped out: Gerald Barry was to be the general leader, Tangye Lean was to look after the cultural and graphic side, and I was to be the editor concerned with European affairs. So towards the end of 1943 the three of us went to a decisive lunch at Claridge's with Duncan Mackintosh, John Roberts and André Deutsch. The meeting went very well. Duncan Mackintosh had until then produced rather meaningless mass paperbacks under imprints which have long since disappeared and was looking for something more prestigious to do. He was hazy about the tone and content of the literary product we had in mind, but was inspired by the prospect of printing millions of copies in various languages. John Roberts sensed an opportunity for fame and glory in the range of brilliant books that he envisaged might emerge as by-products of the magazine. André Deutsch saw himself as the catalyst and sales genius. Tangye and Gerald thought that a foothold in the new venture might at least give them a bargaining ploy for future negotiations in Fleet Street or elsewhere, whilst I saw new worlds opening themselves up to me and a career that could turn into a life mission.

As a result, Contact Publications was registered as a company early in 1944. Harold Rubinstein, senior partner of Rubinstein & Nash and founder of a dynasty of literary agents and publishers, prepared the contract. The three editors were each to receive ten per cent of the shares and the balance would be held by Duncan Mackintosh. With the BBC's consent I signed a service agreement which allowed me to continue with my broadcasting job.

The plan was to start publishing the monthly magazine with the first rays of peace. Our congenital optimism had been heightened by D-Day, and we thought we might have to be ready by the end of the year. The first issue of *Contact* was to be subtitled 'First Spring of Peace', and I asked Richard Crossman to write a long article – fifteen thousand words – about the British Foreign Office. His brief was to be informative and critical and, at the same time, exhortative. His survey, written in American style with the help of research assistants, came out in the first issue. Another feature was to be a scripted discussion, the first of many, between a British political commentator and a distinguished foreign counterpart. We set up such an encounter between Kingsley Martin and Ed Murrow in the White Tower restaurant in Soho, a famous literary haunt. The title of the feature was 'Talking to Neighbours'. A further article in the series brought Michel St Denis and Harold Nicolson together on the subject of Franco-British relations in the future. We laid in a stock of articles which we thought might last to be ready for our own D-day.

Then, in September 1944, I suffered a tremendous blow. Tangye Lean and Gerald Barry resigned without warning. They simply wrote to Messrs Mackintosh and Roberts to say that they had other plans and felt they could not give the time – Gerald Barry had renogotiated his contract with the *News Chronicle*, and Tangye Lean was being successfully wooed by the hierarchy of the BBC. So I was left in the lurch. Thanks to André Deutsch's loyalty and continued faith in me, the project was not dropped. He used his

influence with Mackintosh and Roberts to make them abide by
their agreement, but I was asked to produce substitutes to add to
my credibility. By then the backers believed that I was worthy of
their support, and they gave me a free hand to choose the new
coeditors.

One was H.L. Beales, a Falstaffian Fabian Socialist and friend of
Sidney and Beatrice Webb and Harold Laski, whom I had met at
the Fabian summer school during the war. Lance Beales taught
economic history at the London School of Economics and, together
with Krishna Menon, had been the first editorial advisor to Allen
Lane, the founder of Penguin, and was a figure in the world of the
Hampstead Labour intelligentsia. Wistfully cynical and always very
relaxed, Beales struck me as a rather lazy man. He could be discursive and long-winded when I was burning with impatience to get
on, but he was full of ideas and proved a useful ally.

The other man I found played a more constructive role. I persuaded the brother-in-law of a devoted friend from BBC monitoring
days, Hubert de Cronin Hastings, coproprietor and publisher of
the famous *Architectural Review*, to join me as coeditor. H. de C.
Hastings, as he was known, was an eccentric genius in his field.
The 'Archi Rev', as the paper founded by his father was affectionately called, was the pioneer of the Victorian revival. It employed
and discovered such men as John Betjeman, Osbert Lancaster, Hugh
Casson, J. M. Richards, Gordon Cullen, Nikolaus Pevsner and a
whole bevy of architectural writers, aesthetes and evangelists. It
was not only the bible for a certain school of architects, but with
its daring and distinctive appearance it also served as a fountainhead
of innovation in typography and design. H. de C. was reclusive.
He shunned human company if he could, hated to look people in the
eye, wore Edwardian country clothes and avoided the metropolis as
much as possible. Legend had it that when unwelcome visitors
called on his family in the country, H. de C. would hide in his
elaborately decorated Victorian WC.

There could not have been two more diverse personalities than
the introverted Victorian eccentric and the excitable flamboyant
Austrian emigré, but somehow our chemistry worked from the first
day. H. de C. was a caring, loyal and generous partner. He took a
year of absence from his paper, christened one of his horses *Contact*
and insisted on coming second of the two coeditors on the masthead
of the magazine. He saw it as a platform for doing something he

could not do in his well-established family journal, and that was to create a new style. He was responsible for the brilliant and bizarre design of the first issues.

The pace of preparation quickened. The three-room offices on the top floor of 26 Manchester Square, a beautiful Georgian building, hummed with hyperactivity. H. de C. employed some of his best designers, typographers and pictorial artists, and I reigned unopposed as the procurer of articles. I realized that, since my interests were heavily weighted towards politics and foreign affairs, we needed a link to the world of arts and letters. Through Raymond Klibanski, a Hegelian philosopher at London University involved in wartime propaganda and psychological warfare against Fascist Italy, I met Stephen Spender and offered him the job as literary editor. He declined, because he was off to lecture in the United States, but recommended Philip Toynbee, who accepted.

Philip became a seminal figure in my life, for he not only filled the wide gap in the magazine but opened the gates to wholly new worlds for me. Grandson of the humanist liberal Gilbert Murray and son of Arnold Toynbee, the universal historian, he was a rebel against authority of all kinds, a brilliant conversationalist and social magnet. Tall, stooping, with a large domed forehead and a booming voice, lively in argument, and a lover of paradox, hard drinking and impulsive womanizing he was passionately convivial and clannish. He had been the first Communist president of the Oxford Union but very soon became disillusioned with Stalinism and joined the band of Arthur Koestler and Humphrey Slater, who was a former International Brigade volunteer and editor of a successful, though short-lived, highbrow magazine called *Polemic*. Slater was an intellectual buccaneer, fiercely ideological but receptive rather than original in his thinking. He cultivated George Orwell and Freddie Ayer and worshipped Koestler. A regular patron of the Gargoyle Club, Slater entertained his contributors there for as long as a wealthy Australian playboy-turned-publisher footed his bills, but, to his credit, the pages of *Polemic* contained some fine essays.

Philip assembled around him a group of talented, like-minded friends. Early in my acquaintance with his circle, I realized that although most of the people he mixed with tended to have left-wing views and tastes, they all came from distinguished backgrounds, had been to the best public schools and had studied mostly at Oxford and less frequently at Cambridge. Yet they rebelled against the spirit of their provenance, even though in speech, habit and recourse to its facilities – country-house weekends, fashionable clubs – they were tied to it by an umbilical cord which was very seldom severed. Never in my long friendship with Philip and his companions do I remember having met a member of the working classes or a self-confessed offspring of the petite bourgeoisie – unless they were the temporary bedfellows of its homosexual wing.

It was through Philip that I became involved with the Nicolsons, for Benedict Nicolson, elder son of Harold Nicolson and Vita Sack-ville-West, was his closest friend. Ben had the lugubrious charm and the melancholy countenance of the Sackvilles enlivened by bursts of enthusiasm for many causes. He was fiercely loyal to his friends and to his beliefs. He worked as assistant keeper of the King's pictures under Anthony Blunt and became art critic of *Contact*. It was not until later that he brought me together with his younger brother Nigel, who was to become my partner.

There seemed no end yet to the war, but more ominously there were broad hints from the Government that it would continue paper rationing after the war and not grant permission to start a new periodical. Our printers grew nervous and said they would continue financing us as long as we could find additional monies elsewhere, so we were faced by the double uncertainty of how to raise money and when to announce the first issue. V-E Day found us still planning and plotting future issues. A disturbing letter from the paper controller warned us not to embark on a new magazine without the official licence, and we began to wonder whether all the work and expenditure had been in vain.

As we accumulated articles and extended the network of foreign correspondents, many of whom were drawn from the exiled governments, the prospects of getting our paper licence seemed to get worse rather than better, and the Attlee administration warned all prospective magazine ventures that circumvention of the law would be particularly harshly punished. I was distraught and found no encouragement in Crossman's wry remark, 'You've always got monitoring to fall back on.'

The printers and financial supporters of *Contact* grew more and more restless with the delay, and on learning that it might take years decided they would prefer to sell some of their shareholding. For all the material we had accumulated for *Contact*, we were at a loss as to how to overcome the ban on new publications imposed by the Attlee Government. I was sent to consult John Foster, a barrister and fellow of All Souls who had been a brigadier at the War Office and legal counsellor to the British Embassy in Washington. Foster saw a way out of our dilemma. His idea was to call the magazine *Contact Books*, produce it in hardcover at irregular intervals, give each issue a special theme and create a serious book imprint rather than a magazine. To confuse the paper controller even further, Foster suggested we publish three or four bona fide books a year so as to be able to prove we were not merely producing a single series of camouflaged magazines.

And this is what we did. We planned to have six issues a year with three main sections called 'Action', 'Relations' and 'Reflections'. Of course this ruse complicated the ecomomics of the project. The fact that we carried advertisements was not apparently decisive in differentiating between a book and a magazine, but in our promotion we had to play down the magazine aspect and emphasize that we were a hardcover series. The nearest equivalent to this formula was *American Heritage*, which for a long time came out six times a year, carrying advertisements, and yet kept a definite continuity.

Following Foster's advice we also decided to bring out a few 'ordinary' books on topical subjects in the hope that, when paper control was abolished, we would be able to transform *Contact* into a larger periodical. I asked Lance Beales to find some manuscripts from among his students or friends for a series of books on the postwar world. Time was short, as they had to be published alongside *Contact* until such time as we could shed the hardcover camouflage. Lance Beales told me he happened to have a manuscript on the future of British coal mining. He explained that it was by a bright young statistician from the Ministry of Fuel and Power who had been adopted as a Labour candidate for Ormskirk in Lancashire and so wanted to have the book out by polling day on 5 July. His name was Harold Wilson. Beales handed me a dog-eared manuscript which still bore the rejection slip from Victor Gollancz. *New Deal for Coal* by Harold Wilson became the first *Contact* book. We paid him an advance of fifty pounds, half of which he received on signing the contract, the other half on publication.

I remember him racing up the stairs to our offices in Manchester Square on a hot spring afternoon in his shirtsleeves, perspiring, to collect the galley proofs. As the book had to be produced at breakneck speed, all of us worked on it with great dedication. We saw quite a lot of him, and in his dealings with us he displayed his characteristic blend of donnish pedantry and sense of adventure. He read the proofs with rigorous attention to detail and would talk volubly about his past life and future plans. His Huddersfield accent was much stronger then, but he was self-assured and extremely courteous. The book, which featured a coal miner with his glaring lamplight on the jacket, was well reviewed, and *The Times* made it the subject of a leader. It clearly stood him in good stead, reinforcing his standing as an up-and-coming Labour Party intellectual.

The book's success helped him to junior office. Labour's landslide victory in the 1945 election came as a great surprise to the leadership of the party. Clement Attlee was ushered in just in time to go to the Potsdam Conference instead of the veteran Winston Churchill. The new prime minister was faced with choosing a government, yet he did not know where to look for talent to fill the junior offices – the Labour contingent in the wartime House of Commons had consisted of a mere fifty-odd. Attlee knew few of the younger members, for it was a 'khaki' election in which most of the new candidates had come from the services or far-flung war jobs, so he depended on Transport House, headquarters of the Labour movement, and a number of reliable talent scouts. One such figure was George Tomlinson, a trade unionist and Party stalwart. When on the morrow of victory Clem Attlee asked George Tomlinson, whom he appointed Minister of Works, if he had anyone in mind who had donnish credentials and was a reliable socialist and practised administrator, Tomlinson, as he later told me, had a ready answer. He had just given a young man from the Ministry of Fuel and Power a lift into town from Ormskirk in Lancashire. He was a statistician who had done a spot of work in the cabinet office and had just written a book on the future of the coal industry. Attlee asked to see him. The young Harold Wilson went along. During the ten-minute interview Attlee continued scribbling furiously at his desk. He hardly looked up except to say, 'Wilson, you're going to the Ministry of Works. Parliamentary Secretary. Good luck.' That is how Harold Wilson started his steep ascent to the pinnacles of political power.

Our efforts to meet the March deadline we had set ourselves for the first edition of *Contact* were foiled. Publication had to be postponed more than once. The first version of our elaborate brochure was marred by a Freudian slip. 'Contact,' it should have heralded, 'fulfils an urgent, widely felt need.' Instead it said 'an urgent Weidenfeld need'. Mercifully this version did not reach the fifty thousand addressees in Britain, Europe and overseas.

The much delayed launch of *Contact Books* in 1946 was marked in style with a luncheon at the Savoy. About a hundred guests assembled, half of them advertisers, the rest contributors sprinkled with well-known social figures and members of the diplomatic corps. I sat between Harold Nicolson and Lady Violet Bonham-Carter, who showed a benign interest in the venture. Harold Nicolson made a measured speech, and I launched forth into my first public oration. The occasion was slightly marred by a lapse of etiquette. The Brazilian, Chilean and Peruvian ambassadors were not placed according to their seniority, and, on noticing the faux pas, all three of them turned from the seating plan to their allotted places, smartly turned the plates over and marched out in single file.

On the whole, the magazine had a very good reception. The contents were praised, and the 'radicals' in the world of typography acclaimed the layout and design, but these were panned by the conventional critics. H. de C. Hastings had acted out all his hidden desires and inhibitions by using a panoply of old and ultra-modern typefaces, blow-ups and varying screens and tints. The cover was an enlarged section of Ernest Bevin's face showing an eye and his bulbous nose.

The advertisers responded in different ways. A new influx of clients, persuaded by modernist advertising agents, more or less made up for the loss of safe, traditional sponsors who felt more comfortable with *Punch* or *Country Life*, but the left-of-centre content met with the disapproval of producers or purveyors of luxury goods. Nonetheless, the magazine might have flourished but for the fact that we had to pay for hard covers and play down the name *Contact*. Our competitor, *Future*, which came out at the same time, had a conventional appearance with a cleaner layout, but the content was more pedestrian. It was well backed financially and much better connected in the business world, but both publications suffered from the postwar prohibition.

Now that we had finally got off the ground we needed to stengthen our editorial staff. When I mentioned this to Ben Nicolson one day, he suggested his brother Nigel, who wanted to go into politics but was looking for a job meanwhile. The three of us met at the White Tower in the summer of 1946 and had an instant rapport. Nigel agreed in principle to join *Contact* as Assistant Editor and invest some money in the venture. He gallantly came through with his investment, but not before receiving his parental consent, which was given in a rather unorthodox way. Harold Nicolson was in Paris at the time, covering the peace conference for BBC Radio. Nigel had written to his father asking him to signal his opinion in his broadcast the following Wednesday by means of a prearranged code. Depending on how he viewed the matter he was to let drop the word approval or disapproval somewhere near the beginning of the programme. If he had doubts and wished the matter to rest until his return he was to use the word ambiguous. Vita Sackville-West and her two sons listened eagerly for the verdict. Harold began by saying, 'I have just received a letter from a lady in Eastbourne.' Not long afterwards he slipped in the word approval. Thus was born the partnership of Weidenfeld & Nicolson.

Nigel took up his position at *Contact* on 1 January 1947, bringing a fresh enthusiasm pent up by serving in the Brigade of Guards in Italy. He had a romantic vision of what a magazine could be, and was uncompromising in his desire to have only the best writing, always seeking a relationship of 'exaggerated honesty' with writers and contributors. Neither of us had any business training, but while I considered it a regrettable shortcoming, Nigel was secretly proud of it. We had confidence in each other and in our venture, hoping to establish it as a fearless and constructive forum connecting the worlds of action, imagination and thought in a new age.

The company was fraught with financial worries and veered from one crisis to the next. We were forever teetering on the verge of bankruptcy. Shareholders came and went; Nigel increased his stake and also persuaded his mother and Ben to put some money into the firm. They were eventually reimbursed, but Nigel himself nobly forsook his investment when the company was restructured in 1956. One of our early investors had been George Lowther, a young dilettante with interests in publishing who had edited a monthly magazine for Sir Edward Hulton, proprietor of the trendy *Picture Post* and other pools of talent. Lowther had been recommended to me during the planning stage of *Contact* by David Astor, then an officer in the Royal Marines and preparing to take over the family-owned *Observer*. Astor asked me to dinner at his flat and we talked until the early hours about postwar Europe.

Under his stewardship the *Observer* was without a doubt the flagship of a new European spirit. It employed foreigners, especially 'enemy aliens', on a reckless scale. Most of them had pseudonyms. 'Student of Europe' was Sebastian Haffner, one of the most gifted political journalists of this century and a reticent, aloof and difficult personality who shunned familiarity and hated self-advertisement of any kind. As a non-Jewish German refugee who arrived just before the war, Haffner published a book, *Germany: Jekyll and Hyde*, that electrified the British public. His articles in the *Observer* were of a conservative bent, yet very innovative and revolutionary in concept. He was Cassandra rather than Micawber. His visions and his views were by no means always sound, but they were brilliantly formulated. He contributed a magisterial and provocative essay called 'The End of Europe?' to the first issue of *Contact*. In the 1950s Sebastian Haffner returned to Germany, where he rebuilt a formidable career as journalist and author. In the opinion of many experts his succinct and unconventionally structured book *The Meaning of Hitler*, which I published in 1979, is among the most thoughtful contributions to the literature on the Third Reich.

Isaac Deutscher was another *Observer* contributor, who hid under the pseudonym of 'Peregrine'. He was the author of *Trotsky* – despite his disenchantment with Communism he somehow or other remained a Trotskyist at heart – and he and his wife, Tamar, both Polish Jews though anti-Zionist, had me over at their flat on many occasions. 'You know, Tamar,' he once said, 'George looks the spitting image of Enver Hoxha.' I was not at all pleased by this comparison with the Albanian Communist leader, particularly since I feared it might stick as a codename. The Deutschers had secret nicknames for their friends whom they compared with rather obscure members of the international Communist hierarchy. Thus they referred to Koestler as 'Radek', after the Soviet politician.

David Astor's exponent of military affairs and higher strategy was John Kimche, who had the *Observer* pseudonym of 'Liberator'. He also contributed to the left-wing *Tribune* and the *Evening Standard*. Proficient, secretive and extremely well-informed, Kimche was a Swiss Jew with a strong tie to Israel, whose cause he spent his long life analysing, criticizing and evangelizing. His younger brother, David Kimche, served for years in the Mossad, where

Yitzhak Shamir worked under him before entering politics. When Shamir eventually became foreign minister he appointed his former superior director-general of the Foreign Office.

Finally there was 'Rix' Loewenthal, a prominent member of the left-wing German underground *Neu Beginnen* movement, who emigrated to Britain in 1935. He wrote under the title of 'our diplomatic correspondent'.

David Astor jealously guarded the official anonymity of his key contributors, partly because he did not want attention drawn to the fact that the *Observer*, which had under its previous editor, Garvin, reflected the appeasement policies of the Astor family, was now in the hands of foreign and largely Jewish firebrands, and partly because he wanted his paper to be a cabinet of unnamed talent rather than a showcase for journalistic egos. David Astor had complex relations with his favourites. Many of them, having risen to great familiarity, suddenly fell from favour and were dropped or ended up as enemies. He could become fascinated by or grow dependent on the people he worked with, be generous to a fault, help them with their private problems and look after their families. But then suddenly relations would either cool or end abruptly. The list of those who experienced this treatment is long. It includes Arthur Koestler, George Orwell and Sebastian Haffner, all of whom endured the same pattern of exultant affection, adoration and disenchantment.

David Astor and I were never close. Initially he helped me and encouraged me to use some of his star contributors. On one occasion he even sent me to Prague to cover the first postwar elections for the *Observer*. But then he abruptly broke off relations. I can only surmise that this happened because in an early issue of *Contact* an assistant had inadvertently revealed the real identities behind the pseudonyms of Sebastian Haffner and Isaac Deutscher in the editorial blurb on the list of contributors. Through the good offices of his literary editor, Terence Kilmartin, we restored relations twenty years later. They even reached a certain warmth when I was married to Sandra Whitney Payson, for whom David Astor seemed to have a certain compassionate affection, sensing a lost American soul erring in the British maze.

Besides myself, the small team behind *Contact* consisted of Nigel Nicolson as deputy editor, Philip Toynbee as literary editor, and the young poet Den Newton, a protégé of Lance Beales, as assistant at large and writer of our advertising copy. We shared the offices at Manchester Square with another offshoot of the Duncan Mackintosh printing and publishing concern, a literary review and book publishing imprint called Poetry London. It was run by Tambimuttu, a Sinhalese poet and deft critic who was Pied Piper to a group of young poets and critics. He was also on close terms with T.S. Eliot, Day Lewis and others at the apex of literary London. *Contact* contributors, mainly journalists, politicians or historians, were quite excited to meet the world of Tambimuttu in the corridor or the nearby pubs.

Our offices were rather beautiful. On the ground and first floor were the headquarters of Nicholson & Watson. We had our offices on the second floor, which was big enough to house the small staff, but when Nigel and I and our business manager, Peter Dudley Rider, wanted to talk privately or hold emergency meetings, we had to go round the corner to a Scandinavian café restaurant where we debated, in hushed tones, the strategy of survival. During London's coldest winter this century in 1946/47, we held critical meetings at the café, Nigel in his military greatcoat and I equally well wrapped up. Or we might go to the nearby Mandeville Hotel where the amiable owner, who had bought the hotel with his war gratuity, would serve us drinks. It was his first but certainly not his last venture: Maxwell Joseph rose to become one of the world's largest hoteliers and the founder of Grand Metropolitan Hotels.

Frame Smith Hastings, an old friend from BBC monitoring days and the sister-in-law of Hubert de C. Hastings, whose coeditorship lasted through his sabbatical year from the *Architectural Review*, joined us later as subeditor and became a mother figure in all our lives, but especially Philip Toynbee's. She was the much-needed wet nurse who curbed his excesses and swept up the debris of his disorderly life.

And then there was the advisory board of associates, some of whom spent a day or two a week at our offices. They included Richard Crossman, by then a prolific freelance journalist and backbencher, the economist Ernst Schumacher, prophet of the Green ideology and author of the famous tract *Small Is Beautiful*, Kenneth Clark, director of the National Gallery, and the zoologist, Professor Zuckermann. Benedict Nicolson was responsible for the visual arts section and Hugh Casson was the architectural correspondent.

Arthur Koestler contributed an article in defence of the Jewish underground, William Sansom wrote a series of sociological reports on the new craze of jiving illustrated in colour by the painter Leonard Rosoman, and, with the help of an Italian contact, I procured an essay by Benedetto Croce explaining his philosophy in autobiographical terms.

In a similar vein, Philip Toynbee persuaded his father to write 'My View of History', which explained how the historian evolved his universal vision of the story of mankind. Arnold Toynbee talked it through at a lunch with Philip and myself at the White Tower. He described one of his most vivid memories which he felt personalized the sweep of history most compellingly. It was when, as an undergraduate at Balliol, Oxford, his fellow student Lewis Namier stormed into the junior common room during the Bosnian crisis of 1908–9. He had returned from spending a vacation at his family home just inside the Galician frontier of Austria, and told the other Balliol men with, it seemed to Toynbee, a portentous air: 'Well, the Austrian Army is mobilized on my father's estate and the Russian Army is just across the frontier, half an hour away.' Toynbee recalled the incident in his essay for *Contact*, writing that Namier's statement 'sounded to us like a scene from *The Chocolate Soldier*, but the lack of comprehension was mutual, for a lynx-eyed Central European observer of international affairs found it hardly credible that these English undergraduates should not realize that a stone's throw away, in Galicia, their own goose, too, was being cooked.' Another striking article in the series came from Reinhold Niebuhr, the eminent American Protestant philosopher, who contributed 'My View of Religion'.

It may have been high-handed, but I turned down an essay of George Orwell's on 'Politics and the English Language' which later became famous. My decision had nothing to do with the intrinsic excellence of the article; I just felt that it did not fit in with the purist formula which I had evolved for the magazine. Philip Toynbee agreed with me and wrote the letter of rejection in that vein. Orwell took his revenge when *Contact* came out. In his 'Letter from London' for the *Partisan Review* he wrote about this new hybrid publication about which people had their suspicions because they could not figure out whose money was behind it. It was thought, he wrote, that *Contact* might be financed by the felonious tycoon Clarence Hatry. But I had never heard of, let alone met, the man.

One day a young man with curly hair came into the office and offered his services as an unpaid draughtsman. He wore shorts and spoke in a clipped voice. It was Gerard Hoffnung, a refugee from Nazi Berlin, who was to achieve fame as a cartoonist and musical humorist. The drawings he showed us had a haunting originality echoing Bosch and Breughel with a dash of George Grosz. We took him on as a junior assistant and used some of his work. He only lived to the age of thirty-four, but the recordings of his symphonic caricatures of new music on ludicrous instruments such as road rammers and vacuum cleaners have survived along with other broadcasts, and have made him something of a cult figure.

One edition of *Contact Books* after the other appeared without us making headway with the paper licence. At one point the Government, prompted by the Ministry of Information, had announced that it would license one periodical so that a large proportion of copies should be sent abroad to spread the story of Britain's phoenix-like revival after the war. There was a public tender and *Contact* went into the arena together with *Future* and a number of other candidates. Meanwhile H. de C. Hastings, shocked by the harsh criticism of his work, had resigned, so I approached the dean of neoclassical design, Sir Francis Meynell, who laid out the dummy for presentation. I assembled a star-studded cast of contributors who wrote half a dozen articles, possibly the best of them being Peter Quennell's summary of the current literary situation in Britain, and submitted our product. After weeks of silence the Government announced, in reply to a parliamentary question, that it would desist from the scheme after all in view of the continuing paper shortage. This was a terrible blow, somewhat softened by a message from Harold Wilson letting us know that we would have won the contest had the relevant ministry not backtracked just before the result was due to be announced.

Despite all this I refused to give up – but the final ruse we tried sadly misfired. A number of foreign language periodicals on British soil which had generous paper quotas were winding up as their staff returned to their native European homes, but there was one that survived for a few years – *La France Libre*, edited by André Labarthe aided by Raymond Aron. In its desire to 'double bank', the British Ministry of Information had lent support to voices outside the Gaullist camp and had done much for *La France Libre*.

Working as social hostess for the paper was the ubiquitous and resourceful Moura Budberg, whose adventurous life generated many legends. She was the daughter of a Ukrainian boyar, and was married first to a Baltic count, Ioann von Benckendorff, who was shot by the Bolsheviks, and then to a Baltic baron, Nicolai Budberg. She became involved with the British agent Robert Bruce-Lockhart and helped him escape from prison in St Petersburg; indeed she figured as the heroine of his book *The Secret Agent*. She was the mistress of Maxim Gorky and of H.G. Wells, whose hand she spurned, preferring penury to commitment.

Saved from the horrors of the Russian Revolution by Gorky's intervention, Moura had for a short time acted as hostess to the illustrious Union of Soviet Writers' Club and was said to have met Lenin, Trotsky and Stalin, and had been Gorky's literary secretary. In the early 1920s she left Russia and joined Gorky and his family in Germany. The whole ménage moved to Sorrento in 1924, where the climate was better suited to Gorky's health. In the late 1920s he began making regular visits to Russia again and eventually decided to return for good. Moura chose to stay in the West. She lived in Berlin for a while until the Nazis tightened their grip, and then settled in London, where she led the life of a White Russian exile, churchgoing and associating with the scions of the great princely families of Imperial Russia. She became a much-loved figure, especially in the Nicolson family. I remember a group of us musing in Harold Nicolson's house on the subject of the ideal dinner guest list, and ranking Moura topmost.

Moura was large and usually wore a shapeless tunic, either black or blue, with a large flower design. She had broad shoulders, silvery-white, wavy hair and beautiful hands. An early photograph of her in riding breeches, black boots and top hat recalled the young Marlene Dietrich. Although she radiated geniality and affection, Moura was highly sensitive and could be vindictive. But she was a gallant woman. She had to keep an ailing son and find money for various Baltic relations whom she managed, surprisingly, to 'bring in from the cold'.

Her life spanned many worlds. She moved among the stars of literature, film and theatre, and counted Laurence Olivier, Vivien Leigh and Alexander Korda, who employed her as a reader, among her intimates. She herself was a wonderful mimic. With the help of an improvised moustache and a fierce contraction of her eyes, she could impersonate Peter the Great. Young Peter Ustinov was her protégé, his father having been in the British secret service, and it was in Moura's sitting room that I first experienced Peter's unsurpassable imitations. He had attended a private screening of the Nazi war film, *Ohm Krüger*, which depicted the apotheosis of the Boer leader fighting the vicious British imperialists. Ustinov mimicked a sequence contrasting Queen Victoria on her knees praying for victory and Ohm Krüger invoking the God of his Dutch Reformed Church.

Despite her Bohemian ways, Moura was at home in the most elegant drawing rooms even when she was old, unwell and poor. Dashing military men and British intelligence colonels frequented her Kensington flat, which she shared with a friend. The salt of the English earth came to drink vodka and gin in Moura's dark sitting room with its low sofas and icons on the wall. She was a port of call for Third World ambassadors and East European painters and writers, and had that uncanny gift of drawing confidences from the most bottled-up visitors. She held regular soirées, usually open-ended sessions with twelve to fifteen people. Moura tended to apportion her friends to certain days of the week – I was usually bidden with writers, publishers, journalists and artists, but on one occasion I came on the wrong day and stumbled on a group of greying men of military bearing, many of them with moustaches and monocles. Moura was obviously embarrassed by my presence and told me, 'Darling, you have come a day early.' When I returned the next day I found a completely different gathering, where the Indian nationalist Krishna Menon vied with Feliks Topolski in berating the bellicosity of the British Government and its American paymasters.

Moura understood the art of innuendo to a disquieting degree, applying it with a dismissive smile or an amused giggle. She was part of the secret world of London, and when the Burgess and Maclean scandal broke, she was whispered to be one who perhaps knew too much. It was rumoured that Moura had returned to Moscow during the Stalinist purges to visit Gorky. She was there in June 1936 when Gorky fell ill. It was clear that he was dying and Moura managed to prolong her visa. She stayed on for the funeral, which she was said to have attended in the cortège of the family, accepting the condolences of Stalin himself. In fact, a circumstantial description of that episode had it that her friend Ambassador Maisky in London sent a black limousine to collect her in Kensington and put her on a plane to Helsinki and then on to Moscow, from where she was taken straight to Gorky's datcha, and that the procedure was repeated on her return – without an entry in her passport.

With the first signs of liberalization during the Khrushchev era she started travelling to Russia with unusual frequency. She stayed in the house of Gorky's widow, which was run by her ebullient daughter-in-law, Nadezhda Alexéevna. There Moura received the cream of the Soviet intelligentsia.

She tried to interest British publishers in Russian writers, and it was under her auspices that I made my first trip to Moscow in December 1959. I stayed at the Metropole Hotel for ten days but had my meals at the Gorky house, much to the astonishment of my friends at the British Embassy and of visiting American publishers, who saw me escorting one of Gorky's granddaughters to the Bolshoi opera. The Gorky family belonged to the privileged 'museum set', so called because they were the descendants of intellectual heroes of the Revolution whose houses or flats were open to the public at certain times. At the Gorkys', reverential Red Army soldiers and students from the provinces came to gaze at the reception room and study of the great writer during opening hours, when the family withdrew to the living quarters on the upper floors. But after closing time the samovar was moved downstairs, and the Gorkys entertained generously. There was a large table laden with zakuski, Armenian brandy and Georgian wine. People dropped in from eight o'clock onwards, and the last wave turned up after the theatre. They would play the piano, dance, sing and engage in endless discussion. It was all very Russian and very elitist.

In Madame Gorky's house, writers mingled with high-ranking party officials concerned with culture and other members of the *nomenklatura*. Many of the guests went out of their way to be cordial. 'An off-the-record tip,' whispered a trade minister. 'Why don't you publish books in Latvian and Lithuanian. You would find plenty of readers in America, eh!' A corpulent functionary took me aside, felt the worsted of my coat, and confessed that he had all his suits made in Prague 'because they have the best material there'. But he said that some of his superiors had their tailoring arranged through the Soviet Embassy in Rome. He himself thought that Italian tailors were the best.

I also met Ilya Ehrenburg there. He was condescending and

sardonic. I told him I had just had lunch with Leonov, a conformist novelist, and talked of the difficulty of publishing him in the West because of the translation problem.

'Don't for goodness sake try your hand at Leonov,' snarled Ehrenburg. 'It's hard enough to translate him into decent Russian.'

Ehrenburg spoke about his youth in Paris where he had known Picasso and Aragon. Louis Aragon seemed to be the one foreign Communist writer who was treated like a Russian because his wife, Elsa Triolet, was the sister of Mayakovsky's widow and Mayakovsky, the great national poet of the Soviet Union, was deemed beyond criticism.

I was asked who else I wanted to meet. Having heard that Pjotr Kapitza, the atomic physicist who had worked in Rutherford's Cambridge laboratory but had been spirited away from Britain before the war, was part of the 'museum set', I mentioned his name. I had conceived the perhaps somewhat naive idea that I might get him to write a book about his life in England where he had left many friends. To my amazement I was allowed to go and see him outside Moscow. It proved a barren meeting, for Kapitza pleaded a bad memory, but I remember he asked after Victor Gollancz, the left-wing British publisher.

Moura Budberg was a Russian patriot. To her, the Romanov escutcheon, the Orthodox icon and possibly even the hammer and sickle were emblems of respect. This may explain her ambivalence and her evasive silences when tragic news from the fronts of the Cold War was discussed in her presence. Her detractors thought she might have spied for the Soviets, her friends denied it passionately; but those among her social circle who were politically tolerant and benevolently inclined towards her might have conceded that she could have been a double agent, leaving to individual guesswork the question as to which side Moura was more likely to have favoured.

It was not until Glasnost triumphed under Gorbachev that more information about Moura's past emerged. On one of my visits to Russia in the late 1980s I heard compatible versions from various sources. Apparently Maxim Gorky had already been disturbed by the turn of events during his last visit to Sorrento. He had lost many friends in the purges and had received letters from leading Bolsheviks posted to him from letter boxes outside the Soviet Union complaining of Stalin and his secret service henchmen. Gorky gave

Moura these letters for safekeeping in case anything happened to him – some of them were recently discovered in the Gorky archives. It has since been assumed that Moura handed these documents over to the Soviets and that in return for this service she was allowed to travel freely and negotiate the exit of relatives and friends. Moura has been savagely attacked in Russian exile literature published in the United States, but she is still held in great affection by many who knew her. Whatever her involvements, she was a warm and caring friend, generous to a fault and touching in her anxious and fumbling efforts to remain *à la page* with all worlds and generations until her death in 1974, not long after her eightieth birthday. I feel sure that she could not have harmed either her native or her adopted country, for although she was the bearer of many confidences, she had little to betray that was of a subversive nature.

Moura was always short of money. She found one source of income in translating books from Russian and French for British publishers, but the quality of her work gradually declined, and word got around that she was farming much of her work out to her Baltic nieces. She did a lot of odd jobs. It was when I first knew Moura shortly after the war that she was playing official hostess for the rather clannish and unworldly équipe of *La France Libre*, and it was in the midst of our troubles with *Contact* that Moura suggested merging with *La France Libre*, thereby laying claim to its paper quota. First we had to get the consent of its shareholders, which required a trip to various people who were by then once again resident in France. I set out on this mission accompanied by an extraordinary couple, Stanislas (Stas) Szymanczyk and Marthe Lecoutre.

Szymanczyk was the back-room boy of *La France Libre*. Techically a Pole but born and bred in Teschen, a town inhabited by Poles, Czechs and Austrians, he spoke three languages with a bewildering mêlée of changing accents. One day it was guttural and deep German, the next day his English had a Czech intonation and the day after he would converse in any language he chose with a nasal Polish accent. He had been a courier for the Communist International, but soon became disenchanted with Leninism and became a conservative. However, horrified by Chamberlain's Munich policy, he ended up as an intellectual anarchist, cynic and nihilist. Szymanczyk had an almost morbid preoccupation with *faits divers*, and over many decades collected accounts of murder cases, rapes,

bank robberies, felonies of all kinds and crime trials in every
country. They were all carefully filed in dossiers which filled a spare
room in the flat which he shared with his ex-wife, a Polish woman
called Marthe Lecoutre who, though far from good-looking, exuded
sexuality. Marthe had a past similar to his: she also had been a
Communist courier who had reneged her political faith and focused
her ambitions on making money. Stas and Marthe lived à trois with
André Labarthe, shielding him from the vicissitudes of the outer
world so that he could edit, write and drink in comfort.

Our first port of call was the home of one of the shareholders,
Admiral Muselier, near Toulon. Muselier, the only French naval
officer of flag rank in British exile, had plotted to overthrow de
Gaulle as head of the Free French and had failed in his attempt.
There was no love lost between the two men. While in command
of the Isle of St Pierre de Miquelon, he had dared once again to
rebel against General de Gaulle and now lived in the shade in the
manner of a Lebanese territorial magnate. Muselier was known to
take drugs and to indulge in all kinds of strange practices, and
seemed to have organized his familiars and retainers to cater for
his various vices. He spoke in riddles and spent most of the twenty-
four hours we spent with him polemicizing against General de
Gaulle. But we succeeded in our mission. Muselier was prepared
to relinquish his shares for a small percentage in the new company.

We sought out two other shareholders in the Midi who were far
less colourful, and returned to London with the necessary powers
of attorney. When we proposed the merger to the Ministry of Information we were given a cool hearing, and after a week or so we
received a formal rejection.

When the KGB archives became accessible to Western researchers
with Glasnost, I was gripped to learn more about that strange trio
consisting of André Labarthe, Marthe Lecoutre and Stas Szymanczyk. According to Thierry Wolton's book Le Grand Recrutement,
a study of KGB penetration of the French intelligentsia and techno-
cratic elite, Labarthe was a leading star in the so-called Robinson
network of Soviet agents recruited by one Henri Robinson to infiltrate the corridors of power in France, and Marthe Lecoutre one
of Robinson's most valued agents. It is clear to me now that Labarthe and Lecoutre used Moura Budberg as an entry point into the
most varied layers of British society. They also exploited Admiral
Muselier's passionate hatred of de Gaulle for their purposes.

Though *Contact* was not economically viable, we did, at one point, have about three thousand subscribers, and sales fluctuated between ten thousand and twenty-five thousand copies. Despite the restrictions and our financial difficulties, we continued producing a series of hardcover magazines as well as publishing 'ordinary' books in a somewhat desultory fashion while searching for other means of survival. Mercifully, I eventually found two roads to salvation.

Among the subscribers to *Contact* were the two heads of Lever Brothers and Unilever, Geoffrey Hayworth and Paul Rykens. Rykens was looking for someone to turn the Unilever house magazine into a more widely read and serious publication, while still preserving its role as a superior public relations organ. *Contact* was commissioned to handle this transformation, and so we became the publisher of the quarterly *Progress*. This helped to pay the rent for a few years and staunched our losses. Other house magazines followed: we published the *Steel Review*, the quarterly journal of the British Iron and Steel Federation, up to the point when the Labour Government nationalized the whole industry, and a sprawling department of house magazines and industrial publications produced for outside sponsors carried most of the overheads. But it was bound to be transitory business because we did not have the funds to expand into indigenous technical publishing nor, frankly, could we muster the necessary enthusiasm. Nigel and I wanted to be literary and political publishers.

The other lifeline came from Israel Sieff, who with Simon Marks ran the powerful chainstore Marks & Spencer. I knew him slightly through Flora Solomon, that remarkable Russian-Jewish *grande dame* who ran the staff welfare department at Marks & Spencer, and he was, of course, a legend to me because of his involvement with Zionism and other philanthropic causes. Israel Sieff had seen *Contact*, and shortly before Christmas 1947 he asked me to lunch in his office.

He was round-headed and balding, with a grey moustache. His eyes would occasionally stray as if in pain or anguish and then suddenly turn very benign. He came to the point very quickly. Using a Marks & Spencer in-house term to denote a supplier's distinctive characteristic, he said, 'Young man, I like your handwriting. *Contact* is original, but you'll never make any money. You'd better turn to other things as well. I've an idea for you.'

Without further ado he motioned me out of the room. We descended in the lift, climbed into his Bentley and drove to the Marble Arch store where crowds of people were milling around buying Christmas presents. We made our way to a counter covered with garishly presented children's classics which had been imported from America. 'They're selling like hot cakes,' Sieff explained, 'and we can't get enough of them, but we can't get the dollars from the Treasury either.' He turned to me and said, 'Why don't you do books like that for us?'

I was stunned, as we had no experience of this kind of book production. Next day Mr Ratcliffe, the buyer, came to see me. He looked patronizingly at the somewhat amateurish surroundings but gave me a trial order for half a dozen 'hardy perennials' at fifty thousand copies per title. The series proved a great success and more orders were placed. Robert Harling, the typographer and designer who did much to revolutionize the layout of British newspapers and books, found some of the best illustrators in the country to create the series of low-priced children's classics. Mervyn Peake, Edward Ardizzone, the Zinkeisen sisters, Charles Mozley and Philip Gough were among those who illustrated *Treasure Island, Grimms' Fairy Tales, Arabian Nights, Heidi, Black Beauty* and many other books. We grew more ambitious and asked other publishers to give us the copyright for contemporary children's classics. Jonathan Cape, a generous rival, and one of the few who treated newcomers kindly, allowed me to include *Bambi* and *Emil and the Detectives*. We also added to the list by publishing a whole range of children's annuals, and we paid the BBC the then princely sum of five thousand pounds for their popular series *Dick Barton, Special Agent*.

All this meant that we could no longer regard books as a sideshow with which to prop up the magazine. Nigel Nicolson and I felt that turning ourselves into a proper book publishing outfit might give us more satisfaction as we would be better placed to realize our ideals and ambitions, so in 1948 we decided to formalize our partnership and establish the publishing firm of Weidenfeld & Nicolson. We set out to launch our first list the following autumn. *Contact* survived until 1951. Then we buried it and became book publishers.

CHAPTER SEVEN

Return to Vienna

AS THE GOVERNMENTS in exile and their camp followers left for home and Allied London gradually emptied, quite a few of my friends were faced with the dilemma of whether to stay or whether to return and build new lives in their country of origin.

Manfred Lachs, a Polish lawyer with whom I had spent many hours discussing the postwar world and who had original ideas about a new code of human rights, tried hard to find a permanent job in London. He failed and went back to Warsaw, where he succeeded in navigating the political straits in the most dexterous manner. While never either joining or disowning Communism, he made a spectacular career, first as a professor at the university and legal advisor to the Government, then as a judge at the international court at the Hague, ending up as its president.

All my Czech friends returned home with alacrity, encouraged by President Benes' optimism. The Czechs invited me to Prague, and in 1946 I went to cover the first democratic elections in Czechoslovakia for the BBC and the *Observer*. Travelling in a small Czech service aircraft and unused to air travel, I was sick throughout the journey. It took a good two years to make me a seasoned voyager.

Prague was almost wholly unspoilt by war. Food was plentiful, and the people seemed quite well-clad and in good spirits. There was optimism in the air, and each of the four political parties standing for election appeared confident of the future. I met President Benes again and he predicted a grand coalition government in which the Communists would play their part. He wanted to show the world how, in spite of transient signs of turbulence in relations between East and West, his country would be a model of the grand war alliance surviving in peace.

I looked up my friend Jiri Firt, now back in his palatial offices and once again the largest printer publisher in Czechoslovakia, and we arranged to publish a pocket edition of the best pieces of the first three editions of *Contact* in Czech later in the year. He gave a dinner party at a restaurant near the Hradcany Castle with writers, politicians and beautiful film actresses. I had a turbulent affair with a Czech actress I met during a visit to Prague's Film City, a noted tragedienne whose husband had been killed in the Resistance. Even as early as then the budding Czech film industry had high hopes of gaining international recognition, and the Prague film festivals had already begun.

But amid all the optimism there were voices of doubt and fear. The Communist Party had placed its agents and servile sympathizers everywhere and was beginning to intimidate its rivals. As so often happens, a junior member of the British Embassy seemed better informed than his superiors, and told me of the deep concern many Czechs felt. They feared that they would once again sink into serfdom because this time their leaders, obedient to Moscow, spoke the same language and knew every twist and trick of active and passive resistance.

When I visited the Stranskys, father and son, who were both pro-West politicians, they hinted that difficult times lay ahead. I took a dim view of the prime minister, Zdenek Fierlinger, who, though a titular social democrat, echoed the Communist line, which was critical of the United States and Britain, and warned that there would be drastic changes after the elections. The moving and prophetic prediction of the rector of Prague University, Professor Bielohlavek, also stuck in my mind. Taking me round the venerable Charles University, the oldest in Central Europe, he said to me, 'We may meet in London sooner than you think. I'm afraid that one day soon I might go into my second exile.' Benes' London press secretary, Ambassador Kraus, took me to the opera and mumbled, 'I'm not sure if the old man is not too optimistic. The Russians are leaning very heavily on him.'

I paid my last visit to Clementis, the deputy foreign minister, who was to be one of the victims of the Stalinist terror in Prague and was hanged after a political show trial. I also had a last meeting with Jan Masaryk at a small tea party at the Alcron Hotel. He had come to bid farewell to an Italian diplomat. I thought his indiscreet wisecracks about the Soviets betrayed a 'humour of the gallows' that was out of character. He asked me to send greetings to Lady

Jowett, the wife of the Labour Lord Chancellor, and to Hector MacNeil of the Foreign Office. 'Remember me to London. I don't think I'll have happier years ahead than those I spent in your town.' Less than two years later he fell to his death from a window of the foreign ministry. But unlike that earlier famous defenestration in Prague which triggered off the start of the Thirty Years War, the victim did not land safely in a rubbish heap.

In January 1948 I returned to Vienna. It was a little over ten years since I had left. I went in search of material for *Contact* and to produce a series of commentaries for the BBC. As I was still ranked as a war correspondent, I stayed at the Sacher Hotel, which had been turned into the British Officers' Club.

During the two weeks I spent there I ran through the whole gamut of emotions. The city was drab, ravaged by destruction, and had a sinister aura; the people were cowed and nervous. One could actually sense the Cold War, for although Vienna itself was subject to quadripartite rule, the Russian zone at the very outskirts of the city provided grist for the rumour mill as well as evidence of arbitrary cruelty. Many a repatriated refugee was fawned upon by opportunist aristocrats or other local grandees for as long as he wore the King's uniform. But on demobilization he was made to feel the cold shoulder, the whiplash of derision and social humiliation.

My friends in the Austrian Social Democratic Party were the most outspoken critics of Russian rule. Oskar Pollak, theorist and chief publicist of the party and editor of the *Arbeiterzeitung*, introduced me to some courageous cub reporters who had strayed into the Russian zone and brought back tales of terror, abductions and persecution, chiefly of socialists. Having failed to make a mark on the electorate, the Communists were trying to infiltrate the organized workers' ranks, as in neighbouring Czechoslovakia. But in Austria they failed signally.

I spent a long afternoon with 'General' Deutsch, who had been one of the leaders of the socialist rising against the Dollfuss Government in 1934. He lived in true Jacobin tradition with a lifelong companion, but spurned the bourgeois state of marriage. He told me that this time the socialists would die to the last man before surrendering to the authoritarians of the East. 'We might have war before long,' he warned. 'Potsdam has solved nothing.' His flat was filled with memorabilia and photographs of the great names of Austrian social democracy.

A feeling of utter desolation came over me when I realized that none of my Jewish friends or family were to be found. A cursory look at the telephone book yielded few names that I might contact. I looked up Count Vetter von der Lilie, the man who helped to get my father out of prison. He lived in a grand but half empty flat in which he sublet rooms to foreign diplomats, and in which the tables were crammed with fading photographs of grand house parties, safaris and masked balls on the Riviera straddling two generations. He was delighted to see me again and even more pleased when I took him and Wolly Seibel, an aristocratic boulevardier, to a meal at the Sacher and to the opera, where we saw Johann Strauss's *A Night in Venice*.

Seibel was a cosmopolitan figure, a professional charmer who, when asked what he was doing, would answer, 'I'm much in demand.' Still immaculately dressed and well-groomed, with that distinctive matt nail polish, a buttonhole and a whiff of eau de Portugal, he was a timeless representative of the Austrian gentleman. He drew the social map of Vienna, regaling me with stories of the political tergiversations and genuflexions of his fellow aristocrats throughout the war, and pointing to the first postwar millionaires who had profited from the great 'turning'.

I had a romantic adventure with the Austrian wife of a British defector who had joined the Communists and gone to East Berlin. Years later I met her at a publishing party in Barcelona. Meanwhile she had married a Spanish architect and was the mother of four children. She blanched on seeing me and cried, 'Please don't remind me of my youthful sins.'

My father's deputy at the insurance company, Baron Offermann, received me nervously. He enquired after my father and protested that he had remained loyal during my father's stay in prison and had not added to the prosecutor's dossier. He did, however, say that the man who did most to blacken his name with the Gestapo was a Ukrainian cashier, Ilczinski, who, he whispered, had worked as an informer for the Gestapo throughout the war and was still around.

One night, as I was wandering through the ill-lit streets of the city centre, I saw a haggard figure, manifestly drunk, his tatty collar turned up, limping along the Annagasse where my maternal grandmother had lived. There was a shock of mutual recognition. Ilczinski looked as though he were at death's door, but I was too numbed to stop, let alone to pursue him. We walked past each other.

For one day I walked the streets and squares of my childhood and youth. Our house in the Alserstrasse showed signs of war damage, but even before that it had been rebuilt almost beyond recognition. I could not face ringing the bell of the apartment. The concierge and the grocer, the tobacconist and the nearby café were all still there. Faintly familiar faces appeared to feign nonrecognition. It had been a Nazi neighbourhood inhabited by upper-middle-class professionals and businessmen.

I revisited the Piaristen-Gymnasium in its beautiful Baroque square with a column commemorating the plague. Inside the school I smelled the same old disinfectant. The routine seemed unchanged – youngsters streamed out of the classrooms at the ring of the school bell, and masters flanked by obsequious 'favourites' paced the corridors during the breaks.

I had an instructive talk with the new head of the Vienna opera. The building itself was heavily damaged by the air raids and the opera was temporarily housed at the old Theater an der Wien. Herr Hilbert was in a powerful position – as a victim of Nazi persecution he could take political liberties. He told me proudly that quality of performance and hard currency were his two priorities. To satisfy both ends he hired the best singers in Germany, irrespective of their Nazi past. Those who were politically acceptable would stay mainly in Vienna. The other category was sent to sing abroad and remit dollars and sterling to the hard-pressed State Opera exchequer. In exchange they received an Austrian passport. I asked Hilbert why so many female singers came from the Balkans and he replied, 'You see, we have a problem. Most young German women had their voices spoiled in the BDM (German Maidens' League), the sister organization of the Hitler Youth. But there is plenty of vocal talent in Yugoslavia, Bulgaria and so on.'

Artistic life in Vienna prospered amid the ruins and the political uncertainty. The cultural officers of the Occupation forces vied with one another to introduce their own culture, and the Austrians reciprocated by producing plays, concerts and exhibitions, catching up with the West's intellectual output. The city was abuzz with refugee conductors, soloists, actors and producers like Ernst Lothar who ran the the Theater an der Josefstadt where Max Reinhardt had once ruled. Most of them went through agonies of ambivalence, memories of spurned love and past slights. In Vienna they met with a half cynical, half deferential reserve, and they felt alternately accepted on sufferance and ecstatically acclaimed.

A great figure in artistic Vienna at this time was the Hon. Elizabeth Montagu, the sister of Lord Montagu of Beaulieu. 'Lady Elizabeth' was a passe-partout to a last-minute seat at a theatre premiere, a restaurant table or a fashionable private view. She was also the close friend of Ernst Lothar, but her business in Vienna was to be the representative of Sir Alexander Korda, who, with his uncanny flair, wanted to set a film in the city on the Danube and was looking for a plot. He had sent out a reconnaissance team headed by Carol Reed with Graham Greene as scriptwriter at large.

I had met Graham Greene before, and now came across him again at a cocktail party organized by Charles Beauclerk, the future Duke of St Albans, who was the British Army's chief public relations officer. His parties were sought after because he mixed Allied uniforms with eager young Gräfinnen, Austrian politicos, stray artists and unclassifiable regulars who might have been secret agents or useful tipsters.

Greene was the celebrity of the moment, and people queued to meet him. On one occasion I saw him warding off a throng of admirers and concentrating for the best part of the evening on a pale, slightly seedy-looking British major with a handlebar moustache and a soiled handkerchief sticking out of his sleeve. He became increasingly fascinated by the conversation, and instead of going on to dinner slunk off with the major for the evening. The following day I saw him again. He said he had met this British officer in counterintelligence who had taken him to the sewers of Vienna and told him of the great East–West trade in smuggled drugs, jewels, arms – and human lives. He had gained an insight into that channel of greed, corruption and political intrigue that flowed beneath the city. I detected a glint in his eye, the ferment of an idea for a plot. In fact, the setting for *The Third Man* was born then and there.

One day I ran into a Canadian war correspondent from BBC days who invited me to come and meet his grandfather. He had never boasted about his family and I was not aware that he was the grandson of Karl Renner, the aged socialist who had been a leading light in Austria between the wars and had become the first postwar president in December 1945. We had lunch with the presidential couple and listened to a typically Viennese soliloquy of pessimism lightened with irony. Renner was quite dismissive of his fellow politicians. As his pampered bull mastiff approached the dining table, the president turned to me and exclaimed, 'Look at him, he's as reddish blonde as my federal chancellor – only infinitely more perceptive.'

Another London acquaintance who had settled back in his native Vienna was the ebullient, buccaneering Harry Peter Smollett – Smollett being an anglicized version of his original family name of Smolka. He had become Central European correspondent of *The Times* in London, which was then going through a period of acute Russophilia. Under the aegis of E.H. Carr it employed pro-Soviet correspondents in Budapest and Moscow who doggedly wrote apologias for Soviet foreign policy. During the war Smollett had been head of the powerful Soviet Department of the Ministry of Information and a grand orchestrator of Anglo-Soviet relations. He had been a friend of Britain's Communist leader, Harry Pollitt. This gave rise to the interoffice ditty:

> If Smollett can turn into Smolka,
> Why can't Pollitt turn into Polka?

Peter gave me his interpretation of Austrian politics. He seemed optimistic about the Russians and saw the future of Austria as a political neutral run by a permanent coalition of progressive Catholics and urbane and conciliatory Communists. To prove his point he agreed to stage a discussion to be published as part of a series of conversations in *Contact*. He arranged a dinner party at his house and invited Ernst Fischer, the head of the Austrian Communist Party, a gifted writer and brilliant orator, and Professor Knoll, who taught at the university and was a left-wing Catholic. Professor Knoll was sufficiently Catholic to be tolerated by the emerging Catholic People's Party and sufficiently left-wing to be courted by the Communists. It was a spirited debate between these two people and an intelligently intervening host, all three of whom changed their views in the course of time.

Peter Smollett later left *The Times*'s employ. He regained his family business, which he expanded with enormous success. His political views mellowed and he eventually became a friend and confidant of the social democratic chancellor Bruno Kreisky, that shrewd *enfant terrible* for whom, like Alexander the Great of Macedon, his country, Austria, was far too small.

I caught glimpses of a younger and more optimistic Austrian generation, a circle of young men and women who had risked their lives for Austrian freedom. My schoolmate George Zimmer Lehman took me to a meeting of former Resistance workers, Georg Fürstenberg among them. They were students and young professionals – local patriots who eschewed ideological commitment and yearned for human contact after years of separation from the West. They reflected the kind of atmosphere and language that you could feel in Italy, France and Holland at the time – it was informed by a high-minded but somewhat vague belief in a libertarian society. They were all decent and genuine people, dignified in their bearing towards the occupying forces, among whom they made permanent friendships and whom they spared much iniquity and disappointment. The brothers Otto and Fritz Molden stood at the centre of this circle. They built up a European college at Alpbach in Tyrol as a meeting ground for intellectuals and budding politicians from all over Europe. Fritz, who went into publishing, became a close colleague and friend. He was the only Austrian publisher who made a real impression on the far bigger, dominant West German market.

The last day of my visit turned out to be the most sombre. I had finally tracked down the old family solicitor and he had come into town from his provincial retreat. He revealed to me the fate of my two grandmothers. My maternal grandmother, eldest of the three sisters, had stayed behind in Vienna. She could not get a visa in time, and had been taken to an extermination camp in Riga at the end of 1942 where she perished and was thrown into a mass grave. My father's mother had waited for my uncle Josef, the Wagner enthusiast. She ended up in Teresienstadt, which held her, a headstrong and healthy woman, for a year before she was deported to a Polish extermination centre, where she died.

During this, my first visit to Vienna after the war, my encounters with Austrians left me with a sense of chill and at times even revulsion over their behaviour during the Third Reich. I felt self-conscious and ambivalent, though I had certainly distanced myself irreparably, or so I thought, from my roots. Later, when I began visiting Vienna with increasing frequency, I felt much less affected by all the memories. As I returned again and again to the city of my birth, I felt more compassionate and understanding of other people's dilemmas and motives. In the meantime I had gained a new strength through my involvement with Zionism. It was as if I had heard those words of Jabotinsky humming in my ears as he harangued the crowd and silenced the Nazi hecklers: 'Hitlers come and go. We are indestructible. The Jewish people will live.'

CHAPTER EIGHT

English Life:
The Learning Process

THE PROCESS OF LEARNING about English life, manners and morals took a long time and was not always easy. The move from refugee life in prewar London to the sheltered BBC enclave of Evesham followed by the sudden return to London was like a sequence of Turkish baths. But, for all the different milieux I had encountered, I had seen only a segment of the baffling universe of English society.

When I first moved back to London from Evesham I lived in upmarket boarding and apartment houses. At one point I shared a bachelor flat behind Broadcasting House with Henry Swanzy, who, perhaps more than anyone since, intuitively grasped my failings and appraised such virtues as I might have.

Henry was a stern but well-meaning critic. He had a double first from Oxford, was a good athlete and was widely read, but he was anything but a conformist. He worked as a talks producer, and I had to deliver much day-to-day comment on European politics to him. He later became a widely acknowledged expert on colonial Africa. Earlier than most students of Britain's African colonial burden, he warned the British Government about the deep flaws in its colonial policy. Henry Swanzy was an underrated genius – for decades he cried in the wilderness. Many of his good ideas for reform were tacitly adopted, but he never got enough credit for what he did. Diverging career priorities, marriages and divorces drove us apart, but I will always think of him as one of the most thoughtful and caring guides.

On my first day at 200 Oxford Street I had beheld an unusual sight. It was of an elegant man with his long legs spread out on the desk in front of him, a carnation in his buttonhole and a telephone

Three generations: my father, mother and paternal grandfather.

As a schoolboy, dressed for a play rehearsal.

The lure of Venice: my mother and myself aged 7. . .

. . . and my daughter Laura at the same age.

Family reunion, June 1939. My father (*centre*), just released from Nazi captivity, and my mother (*on his right*), flanked by the Smythe family, who gave us shelter, and myself.

Joining the BBC: with a group of polyglot BBC monitors.

Right: The last carnival in Vienna, February 1938.

Below: A guiding spirit in my life: Flora Solomon, with Simon Marks.

Moura Budberg: a mysterious mother figure.

Introducing the new Yugoslav ambassador (*right*)
to President Weizmann. Foreign Minister Sharett
(*left*) looks on.

Right: With President Weizmann at his 'White
House', 1950.

Below: With Clarissa Churchill (Countess of
Avon), who worked for *Contact* until she married
Anthony Eden, and Mr Hyman Kreitman.

In the library with Nigel Nicolson on the occasion of my 50th birthday party at Cleve Lodge.

Below: Antonia Fraser and Elizabeth Longford, the two celebrated biographers and my best foul-weather friends.

Vladimir Nabokov, the most distinguished writer I have known.

Marriage to Jane Sieff, 1952. *l to r*: Edward Sieff, my father-in-law; Lady Marks, his sister; Sally Sieff, Jane's sister; Jane; myself; Nigel Nicolson, my best man; my mother and father.

Right: Marcus (now Lord) Sieff, one of the most distinguished leaders of Anglo-Jewry and a lifelong friend.

Myself and the infant Laura, 1954.

Right: Barbara Skelton in the south of France.

Konrad Adenauer entertains at Lake Como, 1964. Lady Pamela Berry (*centre*) represents the *Daily Telegraph*, our co-publisher of his memoirs.

Right: Siesta at Portofino: Maurice Bowra and Isaiah Berlin, August 1966.

Jennie Lee, Minister of the Arts, launches the first of the 80 volumes of the World University Library. Author Richard Gregory sits on her right.

Below right: On the platform with Harold Wilson for the Balfour lecture.

Below: A towering figure of the Harold Wilson years, to whom I am devoted: Marcia Williams (later Lady Falkender), with Tommy Balogh.

An evening in Chelsea:
(*l to r:*) Diana Phipps,
Karl Lagerfeld,
Ira von Fürstenberg.

Above: Placido
Domingo, in between
acts, discussing his
forthcoming memoirs.

Left: Daniel
Barenboim and his
wife, the pianist
Elena Bashkirova,
relaxing after
Götterdämmerung
in Bayreuth, 1991.

in his left hand. He had a striking angular profile and was speaking languidly: 'Hello Davidson, will you tell Her Grace that I will be delighted to come to luncheon and that I shall be bringing Princess Callimachi.' This was the first time I set eyes on Peter Quennell, though we did not meet until later. Quennell was not only the biographer of Lord Byron but much in his life and nature was Byronic. He loved women and was in turn loved by women. He wrote fine poetry and excellent prose. He struck poses and affected arrogance and intolerance of the humdrum and the tawdry, yet underneath the unapproachable gentleman and rake was a generous and sentimental middle-class Englishman. We became friends and shared a Nash cottage in Park Village East for a time.

Peter and I went out of our way to respect each other's privacy. We had an understanding that we would only enter each other's rooms by invitation, preferably by appointment made on the telephone from the office the day before. This discretion had an absurd consequence. One night I was woken by what sounded like the faint crying of a very young child. I thought Peter must be putting up a mother and her infant in his part of the house and tried to get back to sleep again. Peter, as it turned out, had assumed the same about me, but in the morning a policeman called at the house and told us that a baby had been left on the doorstep. From thereon we resolved to have a more flexible system of communication and started cohabiting in a less formal way.

Peter tended to compartmentalize his friends. He did not like to be encumbered with social obstacles and he never took risks, but he warmed to me as he thought I became more socially acceptable. My stock rose when I had the Brazilian ambassador to lunch at our cottage one day. It only came about because the ambassador was the unsuccessful suitor of a girl I was involved with at the time and she just brought him along, but Peter was not to know and he now felt confident enough to introduce me to people like Harold Macmillan's daughter, Catherine, who married the MP Julian Amery and to June Churchill, Randolph's second wife. Although Randolph had a reputation for calculated rudeness, he always made me feel extremely comfortable and I realized that the more established and socially secure people felt, the more likely they were to admit outsiders. The less secure, particularly among the indeterminate middle-to-upper classes, tended to exclude new faces.

Although he might still confide to Philip Toynbee that 'our friend,

George, is a bit of a Hebrew', Peter Quennell introduced me to a wide circle of his own friends, to the Gargoyle Club and to the Gargoyle girls, named after the Gargoyle Club in Soho, a group who shared causes and customs much like the 'Liberal girls', daughters of distinguished families who rebelled against convention. The Liberal girls, so aptly characterized in Philip Toynbee's book *Friends Apart*, joined left-wing causes in protest against the political mores of their elders, finding young men of similar inclinations – like Philip Toynbee and Esmond Romilly, Churchill's nephew – with whom they had love affairs or whom they married. Anti-fascist in their views, anti-appeasement, egalitarian, yet unconsciously snobbish.

The Gargoyle girls were recognizable by their slurred and snarling speech, husky voices and a particular way of pursing their lips. They were moody, acerbic, initially difficult to approach and mainly blonde. Their type was a recent creation and it took me a while to get to the root of the ancestry of their mannerisms. I traced them to Ivan Moffat, the son of Curtis Moffat, a Bostonian boulevardier who spent much of his life in London's upper Bohemia, and of Iris Tree of the great theatrical family. Ivan Moffat was, like Alastair Forbes, a young meteor in wartime England. Good-looking, witty and a superb mimic, a whole bevy of beauties succumbed to his charm and adopted his idiosyncratic speech and manner. He had a mid-Atlantic drawl and a slight sneer, and tossed his head or jerked it to the left or right to underpin the point in a story or to strengthen a critical epithet. He was well-read and immensely sensitive to the moods of others. Unlike certain White's Club bullies like Randolph Churchill or Ed Stanley who, seizing on the soft spot in a conversational opponent, would charge at it mercilessly and widen the wound, Ivan launched his attacks in a more feline and oblique way. His method could also be lethal. The worst combination of the two techniques could be found in the notorious Brian Howard, hero or villain of many *romans à clef* and a tragic victim of his desperate sense of futility.

I drifted into the Gargoyle world. Situated at the top of a tall building in Dean Street, the Gargoyle Club was founded by David Tennant, a somewhat dissolute younger son who had married first Hermione Baddeley and then Virginia Tree, now Marchioness of Bath. This confluence of birth, wealth, talent and eccentricity set the tone. The club had private rooms for parties, one could lunch and dine there, a band played in the evening and one could stay on until the early hours of the morning. The décor was curious and the atmosphere relaxed. In fact, the Gargoyle was grand enough for relatively conventional people to feel they would not lose caste if they treated it as their club and Bohemian enough for them to think that they were not at all conventional. During the war it also served as the place where those on leave from the armed forces could find each other without much effort. The club kept its social role in the five years immediately after the war, but with the declining interest of David Tennant it gradually changed in character, lost its membership and eventually disappeared.

Nigel Nicolson, Philip Toynbee and I made frequent use of it. We often entertained our authors or gave parties there, and a regular dining group known as 'Ben's ordinary', of which Ben Nicolson and I were co-hosts, also sometimes met at the Gargoyle. There were other 'ordinaries' in London at that time. Lady Cunard mixed government, politics, the arts – the emphasis being on music, for Sir Thomas Beecham was her lover – with a ration of elegant women and amusing young men. Lady Colefax's ordinary concentrated on celebrities. She had her own technique of locating distinguished visitors while they were still on a transatlantic liner and booking them far in advance. Her trusted assistant was Cynthia Jebb, the effusively efficient wife of Gladwyn, then a rising star in British diplomacy. At Lady Colefax's ordinaries you paid seven shillings and sixpence for the meal – usually held at the Dorchester – and another seven-and-six for a companion. There was a hard core of regulars and an outer circle of occasionals. I joined the outer circle and stayed in it to the end.

Ben's ordinary took a different form. We invited up to twenty people, half of them regular members who paid for their guests. We established a ritual whereby one of the guests would read a paper or make a speech and most of the evening would then be spent in discussion. Philip Toynbee read the first paper, and among those who followed were Richard Crossman, Howard K. Smith of CBS, and Elizabeth Bowen. The regular attendants included Frank Pakenham, then a Labour don at Christ Church, Oxford, Robert Kee, Nicholas Henderson of the foreign office, Father D'Arcy, the legendary head of the Jesuits in Farm Street, various members of the Nicolson family and a changing cast of camp followers.

One such ordinary was immortalized by Evelyn Waugh in an

ill-tempered letter to Penelope Betjeman dated 13 June 1947. He wrote:

> Talking of low company, I was commanded by The Very Rev D'Arcy to accept an invitation from Ben Nicolson to an intellectual dinner, African wine in a South Kensington basement, to discuss 'religion'. P. Toynbee spoke for 20 minutes – absolute balls. I had never seen him sober before & greatly preferred him being sick in Ann Rothermere's lap. He is a pretentious ass. Then a seedy kind of clergyman piped up and I said Who is this and they say Pastor Niemöller and he talked balls too, but not so pretentiously – just flat stupid & boring. There was a young yid who kept snorting contemptuously and they say it is Mr. Ayer but his heart is broken by D. Fellowes' girl and it is tears not derision makes him snort. There was another clergyman there & he never spoke but as we went to pee he said 'perhaps I am best known as the Vicar of Nottingham (?Northampton?) who has John Betjeman to preach in my church'. Two revolting Socialist Members of Parliament called Crossman who is famous but not to me and Woodrow Williams who is famous to no one talked most. I hardly at all. God it was hell.

My recollection is quite different. We heard a moving talk from Pastor Niemöller, a hero of the German Resistance and fellow inmate at Dachau of the charming Colonel Stevens, whom we employed at *Contact* as advertising manager. Stevens had served in the British secret service before the war and became victim of the famous Venloo incident at the outset of the war when he and his colleague Major Best were kidnapped by the Gestapo and taken across the Dutch frontier, having been duped into believing that they were coming to a conspiratorial rendezvous with German opponents of the Nazi regime. With his cover blown, he was looking, after the war, for a job and we gave him one. He felt great pride in being able to bring his fellow inmate, the great Niemöller, to our dinner and Evelyn Waugh's comments were savagely perverse. He attended Ben's ordinary once and never again.

Arthur Koestler also came to the ordinaries but did not feel too comfortable. He preferred small groups of four to six where he could hold forth. Equally, he liked intellectual cockfights with people he deemed his dialectical equals. Koestler and Crossman were great friends for a time, and when they were not playing chess they would sit down and say, 'What are we going to fight about today?' Topics would range from the future of Russia to the moral justification of the Stern gang in Palestine.

I never had particularly friendly relations with Arthur Koestler. At first he took me up in a minor way when he was going through his Zionist phase and I was just beginning my involvement with Israel. I remember him telling me that I should give up *Contact* and devote myself entirely to 'our cause', as he put it. 'We should form a committee,' he suggested, 'and you should run it.' Koestler sent me to Victor Gollancz, the Dean of left-wing publishers, who looked at me with some suspicion. He did not like young rivals. Gollancz had an incisive mind and an abrasive manner, and, like many world reformers of the Left, combined a passion for humanity in the abstract with an insensitive disdain of individual people.

The worlds of Philip Toynbee and Ben Nicolson on the one hand and of Nigel Nicolson on the other converged but also spread in different directions. Philip befriended a world of writers and painters in Fitzrovia, the universe of pubs and drinking clubs in Soho. Although they dipped into the Gargoyle, they felt more at home in the classless taverns. Dylan Thomas was one of Philip's boon companions and he sometimes brought him to the cottage in Regent's Park. Maclaren Ross and Ruthven Todd would join them, and when, late at night, they arrived at the Gargoyle they would be in such a state of intoxication that even its debonair owner and tolerant staff had to insulate them from the rest of the guests.

The Nicolson brothers became an anchor in my life. I had only a slight acquaintance with Harold Nicolson, who had been a governor of the BBC. We were never close friends, but he was generous in his advice. I barely knew Vita Sackville-West, although as Nigel's partner I was a frequent topic of conversation when the family assembled for weekends at Sissinghurst. Vita thought of me as a dark invader of her sons' lives. She rarely came to London, and over a dozen years we had less than a dozen desultory conversations. With her passion for gardening she clearly dubbed me an 'urban' character, and to one who lived with nature as she did I must indeed have seemed alien. She lumped me with the restless intellectuals in the circle of Ben, her elder son.

Ben was deputy to Sir Anthony Blunt, Keeper of the King's Pictures, and later edited the renowned *Burlington Magazine*. In his attic flat near Victoria, the spartan décor, which matched his own careless dress and frugal habits, was in sharp contrast to the harsh beauty of the Italian Mannerist paintings on the walls. Ben belonged to the small band of enthusiasts for that then unfashionable school of Italian and Flemish paintings which bridged the gap between the late Renaissance and the Baroque period. Besides Anthony Blunt, Denis Mahon and the ballet critic Richard Buckle, he was one of the most eager collectors and evangelists of Mannerism. I owe my own passion for that school to him. Prices were still very low and I was able to start my own collection in the late 1940s. The Arcade Gallery, run by an elderly Austrian art dealer, Paul Wengraf, was the most yielding source of supply.

Ben hated anything that he felt smacked of upper-class snobbery and intolerance, and he spurned the grand life. His circle of friends included the last survivors of Bloomsbury and the largely Continental colony of *Kunstforscher*, or art historians, who gathered around the Warburg Institute and the Courtauld. He had a passion for friendship and was fiercely loyal. Ben had an unhappy love affair with a young art historian, David Carritt, who was endowed with an uncanny genius for discovering great paintings. Ben introduced him to the luminaries in the world of art, took him to meet Bernard Berenson at I Tatti near Florence and paved the way for his enormous professional success. But David Carritt did not reciprocate his passion and Ben was miserable. Ben eventually married Luisa Vertova, one of Berenson's assistants, but the marriage ended in divorce.

Nigel Nicolson may have inherited his love for solitude from his mother – he bought a small island in the Hebrides where each year he spent a Trappist holiday – but I think he was more a Nicolson than a Sackville. If Ben had a sense of duty towards art, Nigel felt an obligation to an idealized version of the Establishment. He stood as a Conservative and served his party loyally, though he was really a Liberal at heart. He hated brutality and intemperance, yet had a romantic vision of men at war for a just cause. He demonized public school bullies, the gruff military mind, the elitism of the Brigade of Guards, and yet was not in any way a left-wing intellectual. His heroes were more those like Rupert Brooke than Evelyn Waugh. He admired intellectual achievement, good conversation and 'high gossip', but winced at manifest malice. He often allowed himself to be exploited by friends whose values were anathema to him. James Pope-Hennessy, that talented, moody, unscrupulous seducer of many young men who led a proverbially dissolute life and ended up being murdered by a vengeful homosexual thug, preyed on Nigel's conscience. James borrowed money from him and undermined his self-confidence, ever sure of Nigel's boundless generosity.

The Nicolson brothers loved one another though they were so different. They shared a house in Neville Terrace, Kensington with their father. The three would meet at breakfast, open their mail and comment on the daily intake with caustic remarks and indiscretions.

Harold Nicolson was a club man, excessively convivial during the week and uxorial at his Kentish weekends. He was a mixture of free-thinking Francophile and upper-middle-class bureaucrat who had a sneaking reverence for the grand life. He wanted to be a man of letters and a man of the world, but at the same time he was careful not to burn his bridges with left-wing Bohemia. He also had a roughish side. This created tensions and contradictions within himself.

Although Nigel was rather shy and had a melancholy side, he also had a diffident liking for the beau monde and enjoyed the company of intelligent debutantes and ambitious young men, most of whom were born with silver spoons in their mouths and were on the first rungs of a successful career ladder. He took ascetic pride in declaring that he had refused three invitations in one week while also relishing the life of grand parties, debutante dances and men's dinners at the Travellers' or the Beefsteak. He would describe them to me the next morning in a rather romanticized way, extolling the beauties of the hostesses, the glitter of the dresses and the esprit of the after-dinner conversation when the port and brandy were passed round the table. I noticed a touching desire to instruct me and introduce me to new worlds. By and by I met the people whom I first got to know through Nigel's vivid descriptions.

Nigel's great love was Shirley Morgan, the daughter of Charles Morgan, the bestselling novelist, who was then at the height of his fame but, despite his success in England, more admired abroad. In France there was a *Societé des Amis de Charles Morgan*, but fastidious British intellectuals tended to dismiss him as middlebrow. The question of 'brow' was one of the most hotly contested topics of the 1940s and '50s and a favourite game at dinner tables. Was Maugham a high- or middlebrow? Kate O'Brien was surely middlebrow and so was H.E. Bates? Oh no! Bates was distinctly Lawrencian, he was very high. Cyril Connolly was the most sought-after classifier, and in his *Horizon* magazine would cast his decisive vote for or against a writer.

Shirley worked in the Foreign Office as secretary to Gladwyn Jebb. Whenever any of us came to fetch her for an evening out, Charles Morgan would treat us to a glass of sherry and a brief talk. He was a handsome man. I remember him standing in a picturesque pose, turning his romantic profile to the sunset beyond the open window and intoning a lofty paean on the spirit of France or the virtues of military life. When, years later, Shirley was rumoured to be on the way to becoming officially engaged to Henry Anglesey, the 7th Marquess, he sermonized about the unique distinction of Britain's aristocracy compared with any other nation's. Shirley was good-humouredly loyal to her sacerdotal father and her excitable mother, herself a talented Welsh novelist. Charles Morgan was proud of his daughter and indeed made her the heroine of one of his novels.

But she was not only her father's heroine. Shirley was the Zuleika Dobson of her generation. Though modest by nature she was self-assured, lively, attractive and eminently sensible. She had a resolute charm, was a good listener and had a healthy respect for intellectual conversation. Many brilliant and promising young men – from the Foreign Office, Oxford dons, budding bankers – were in love with Shirley, but, though she was flirtatious, she remained inaccessible. Nigel was deeply smitten with her and wanted to marry her, but his timid, romantic approach was not destined to conquer a much-wooed young woman.

Shirley's suitors included well-known roués and legendary seducers, notably Freddie Ayer, who had achieved fame at the age of twenty-six with his *Language, Truth and Logic*, held to be the seminal introduction of the Vienna school of philosophy to the Anglo-Saxon world. That wiry, mercurial philosopher had something of the looks of Jean-Louis Barrault and spoke and courted fast. It was from that kind of threat to Shirley's virtue and peace of mind that one of her admirers, Isaiah Berlin, tried to protect her – one of many instances in which he saw himself as guide and protector of innocent womanhood against dangerous demon lovers. Isaiah saw Shirley as an English Natasha, the heroine of *War and Peace*, and interposed himself with friendly warnings between the assailant and his intended victim. She helped him with his translation of Turgenev's *First Love* which, with a suitable dedication,

he published in Hamish Hamilton's charming European Novel
Library.

Shirley's closest girlfriend was Vivien Mosley, daughter of Sir
Oswald, a majestic brunette with a cultivated mezzo-soprano, who
remained loyal to her father through scandal and tribulation. She
had been brought up by her maternal aunt, Irene Ravensdale. A
peeress in her own right, handsome and imperious, the Baroness
Ravensdale was hyperactive and public-spirited. She looked after
the three children of her sister Lady Cynthia Curzon's marriage to
Mosley – Vivien (Viv), Nicholas, the novelist, who succeeded to
her title, and Michael. She was the greatest musical hostess of the
time and held court in a large house at the Vale in Chelsea where
Chippendale furniture and Oriental art blended harmoniously.
There Lady Ravensdale reigned in the proconsular tradition of her
father, the first Marquess of Curzon and Viceroy of India. She had
an omnivorous curiosity and cultivated people in different worlds.
Had she been born a man, she would no doubt have been an even
more forceful public figure.

I was rather keen on Viv and we went to the theatre and opera
in a group that included Shirley, sometimes Nigel and, more often,
Fred Warner, the most talked-about young bachelor on several circuits. He was half American on his mother's side, of independent
means and highly intelligent. Sophisticated debutantes enjoyed his
conversation, and ambitious young men, just out of the war and
catching up with their education or rushing headlong into a professional career, all agreed that Fred would go far. He spent the
war in the Navy – in fact at one time he considered pursuing a
naval career before opting for the Foreign Office. He was socially
so much in demand that people had to draw lots to get him for
dinner parties or grand weekends. But in spite of all his graces he
had an introspective side.

Fred worked for Hector McNeil, Ernest Bevin's second-in-
command at the Foreign Office. Working alongside him as a temporary civil servant was Guy Burgess, who, dissolute, ebulliently
eloquent, socially ubiquitous, hero-worshipped Fred and attached
himself to him. Burgess and I did not hit it off. We would meet at
the Gargoyle and with the Nicolsons. He had an unpleasant habit
of breaking into a conversation, sitting down, and bursting into a
soliloquy without regard to the people present. On one occasion
we crossed swords at a cocktail party held by Sir Edward Marsh,

littérateur and former secretary of Winston Churchill. It was an absurd argument about the future of China. He held forth about China dominating the future of mankind before the end of the century, and I dared object that it had no economic infrastructure and would not be effective for at least a hundred years. Burgess turned to Clarissa Churchill, who was already known to be close to Anthony Eden, and urged her to tell Anthony and 'all his Tory friends to pay more attention to the Chinese'. On another occasion, at one of Baroness Budberg's *jours fixes*, Burgess accused me of sitting on the fence by supporting a pro-European policy for Britain. 'There is no such thing as a European policy,' he pontificated. 'You've either got to choose America or Russia. People may have their own view which to choose, but Europe is something wishy-washy that simply does not exist.'

Burgess's friendship might have proved harmful to Fred Warner. But he stuck it out at the Foreign Office on the advice of three wise men, Harold Nicolson, the eccentric banker Leo d'Erlanger, and his uncle, Sir Christopher Warner. In each successive diplomatic post – Moscow, Rangoon, Athens, Laos – he made a name for himself. He shone as ambassador to the United Nations, and later in Tokyo. His marriage to the fiery Simone de Ferranti in 1971 when he was at the United Nations allowed him to lead a settled and indeed patriarchal life. Fred has been a lifelong friend – he was best man at my wedding to Sandra Payson, and I am godfather to his son Valentine.

Another boon companion of Vivien Mosley and Shirley Morgan was Raymond Carr, perhaps the most unconventional fellow of All Souls in the history of the college. At that time he was a historian of seventeenth-century Sweden. Original and intellectually brilliant, he burnt the candle at both ends, nightclubbing, womanizing and fox hunting. He climbed the social ladder to become the confidant of blue-blooded undergraduates and seducer of the most desirable undergraduettes. His friends tried to protect him from his academic detractors. Paradoxically, one of them was the lawyer John Foster, himself a lovable reprobate with lax sexual mores.

Raymond became engaged to the beautiful Rosamund, daughter of Daisy Fellowes, a 'sacred monster' of the 1930s and '40s who owned a yacht and palatial villa on the Riviera. She carpeted her boudoir with tiger skins and revelled in her notoriety. One Friday evening, Raymond and Rosamund arranged a pre-engagement party at the Gargoyle. He had to leave on the milk train back to Oxford, and she was to follow him next morning to look for a house. Rosamund never went – she ran off with a young documentary film producer who had gatecrashed the party. Raymond was devastated. He found temporary solace in the arms of a German courtesan famed for her charms as well as her intellectual curiosity. After a short period of reckless bachelordom spiced with episodes which earned him a place in Nicholas Mosley's novel *Accident* (later filmed by Joseph Losey), Raymond switched from Swedish to Spanish and South American history, married a charming girl and settled down. He became an illustrious and most effective warden of St Antony's College, training and inspiring many future political leaders in Europe and overseas. He was a staunch supporter of Israel. I think of him as one of the most brilliant and independent minds of my generation and treasure him as a close friend.

Lady Ravensdale liked to mix generations as well as worlds, and she took up a small circle of Viv's friends. She frequently invited me to the opera. The first postwar years at Covent Garden under the musical direction of Karl Rankl were thrilling, and opera and ballet reached new heights of popularity. After years of separation, Continental, especially German and Austrian, singers and conductors flocked to London. My dormant passion for opera was reawakened by wonderful performances conducted by Furtwängler and Klemperer with Flagstad and Tito Gobbi. But I was particularly excited by that crop of young German voices that included Hans Hotter and Elisabeth Schwarzkopf. I remember Elisabeth Schwarzkopf making her social debut in the drawing room of her house in the Vale as a plump, pretty ingénue whose rich blonde hair literally stood up on end, testifying to years of lack of shampoo. When I next saw her a year or so later, well-groomed, lithe and luminous, her transformation was complete.

Irene Ravensdale channelled her passions into music. Once, when I was sitting next to her at a performance of *Tristan and Isolde*, she dug her fingernails into my right hand during Flagstad's Liebestod. Luckily my muted groan was lost in the high notes of the Norwegian diva. Hans Hotter, probably the best Wotan I have heard, dominated the first *Ring* to be heard in London since the war. He and his attractive wife were frequent guests at Lady Ravensdale's, and after her formal supper parties the younger set would take the Hotters to a nightclub. Hotter was a great flirt and so was his wife.

In the dark privacy of the Stork Club or The 400, Frau Hotter, flanked by Raymond Carr and myself, would tell us extraordinary stories about daily life in wartime Germany, daredevil adventures involving French prisoners of war, or gruesome tales of Gestapo interventions.

Among Irene Ravensdale's regular guests was Malcolm Sargent, who often played the piano in her house. I found him vain and haughty, not least because he was so dismissive of his Continental rivals. Joseph Cooper, famous as an accompanist, and his pretty wife were regular courtiers, and it was at one of these parties that I first met Lady Ravensdale's beautiful sister, Lady Alexandra Metcalfe, and her schoolboy son, David, who made himself useful by standing gallantly in the rain outside the door regulating the traffic. David grew into a formidable social figure. An enthusiastic host and a warm, loyal friend, he built up a vast international superstructure of convivial contacts that meshed in with his career as an insurance broker and gave him serious alibis for hopping across the Atlantic and engaging in countless flirtations. Having raced through two marriages, one to the widow of Sir Alexander Korda, the other to a French countess, now firmly nesting in the Pearson family, he settled down with a lovable American decorator.

The great English country weekend, never wholly dead during the war, flourished again with the first rays of peace. I was thrown into it at two ends: high Bohemia and grand aristocracy. Two neighbours in Oxfordshire who cohabited in friendly rivalry encompassed a spectrum ranging from fellow travelling socialists to moderate members of the Labour establishment and left-wing intelligentsia, including the odd Liberal or renegade Tory. Gavin, second Lord Faringdon, entertained formally and stylishly at Buscot Park. Among his regular guests were Aneurin Bevan and his wife Jennie Lee, the Crossmans, the Earl of Huntingdon and his novelist wife, Margaret Lane, and the two Hungarian-born Labour economists, Thomas Balogh and Nicholas Kaldor. He mixed them with writers, actors, architects and a resident muralist who embellished or, some thought, defaced, cornices and walls. There was much heated debate about the future of socialism when Labour was in opposition, and the betrayal of socialism when it was in power.

Gavin was hospitable, slightly condescending, secretly a snob but overtly egalitarian. His manner smacked more of Michael Arlen's

Mayfair than of the barricades, but he was good-natured and kind to a young newcomer like myself. Black tie was obligatory – only the Bevans were excused from formal attire. One night after dinner, when the ladies trooped into the drawing room to leave the men to their brandy and debate, I witnessed Jennie Lee storming out of the house into torrential rain. Nye and the host ran after her and brought her back amid protests. This English habit of separating the sexes after the meal, while still in use in conventional London society and British embassies abroad, causes much dismay. Many years later, at a British Embassy dinner in Washington hosted by Lady Ramsbotham, the powerful publisher-owner of The Washington Post, Kay Graham, was torn away from a promising discussion between distinguished foreign guests and American cabinet ministers and made to inspect the newly refurbished guest bedrooms on the second floor. She never forgave her hostess.

Not many minutes away from Buscot Park was the Jacobite domain of Nicholas Davenport, a Fabian and Shavian stockbroker, economist and bon viveur who was close to the Labour Party leadership and stood out as one of the very few supporters of the Left in the City of London. He was also an 'angel' of plays and friend of many stage and film people. His second wife, Olga, South African by birth, was a great beauty and a talented actress. She was the widow of an RAF pilot and much younger than Nicholas, and loved intellectuals and intellectual discourse.

The Davenports entertained generously and widely. Their guest list overlapped agreeably with that of Gavin Faringdon, except that there were more writers and philosophers staying at the house and much Oxford talent came over for meals. Hugh Dalton was Nicholas's great friend. Had he been made chancellor of the exchequer, as he nearly was, Nicholas might well have become governor of the Bank of England. Hugh Dalton also had a great, unconsummated passion for Olga. The Crossmans and the Gaitskells, the philosopher C.E.M. Joad, a goatee-bearded, faun-like man of radio and television fame, and Arthur Koestler were regular guests.

I introduced Nigel Nicolson to the Davenports. Although he was a liberal Tory, he signified in Olga's eyes the legacy of Bloomsbury, and so Nigel and Ben were cordially accepted in the circle. Nigel and Olga became very close friends. On one occasion, when he visited Olga at night, there was a knock at her bedroom door and Hugh Dalton asked to be let in for a goodnight kiss. Poor Nigel had to hide under the Jacobean four-poster while Olga, with elegant sang-froid, engaged the visitor in a brief friendly chat.

In 1948 Shirley Morgan married Henry Anglesey. The wedding was a splendid cavalcade of England's grand families, talents and intellects – Henry's aunt, Lady Diana Cooper, and her husband, Duff, Shirley's large number of friends, admirers and former suitors and, above all, Henry's sisters, the beautiful Paget girls. Each of them was good-looking and known for eccentricity or a passionate interest in one of the arts, especially ballet, but one, Liz, was renowned as one of the most beautiful women in England. Liz Paget, who had been a train bearer at the coronation of King George VI, and had been adored by many famous men, was married to an Austrian, Raimund von Hofmannsthal.

Raimund was a pampered pet of grand ladies and beautiful heiresses who lived largely on his wit. He was son of the famous poet and librettist of Richard Strauss, Hugo von Hofmannsthal, and had been something of a 'Rosenkavalier' in his youth. He moved in the circle of Max Reinhardt, the great Berlin impresario and creator of the Salzburg Festival, and joined the troupe that Reinhardt took to America when he toured the grandiose morality play *The Miracle*. He became a captive and protegé of Diana Cooper, who mimed the Nun in the play. Raimund cut a dash wherever he went. One of the richest women in the United States, Alice, sister of Vincent Astor, had fallen in love with him. They had married, and during the war he had served in the American Army.

He and Liz met in the Salzkammergut where Alice and Raimund rented Schloss Kammer every year. It was the meeting ground of the European and American *jeunesse d'orée* who came to floating dinners on the lake, fireworks and masked balls. The young Bill Paley, the Napoleon of American radio and television, was a frequent visitor, and so was a legendary matchmaker Rudolph Kommer, who managed Max Reinhardt's affairs and always kept an eager eye on marriagable blue-blooded girls whose lives he could steer and control. Raimund fell in love with Liz, and eventually divorced to marry her.

Raimund and Liz von Hofmannsthal played a distinctive role in London social life after the war. His cosmopolitan manner and her looks and provenance radiated an aura of elegance and sophistication. He worked for Time Life and acted as a kind of ambassador at large for the proprietors Henry and Clare Luce. He earned his daily bread by selling advertising space, but hid his humdrum work in a silvery shell worthy of Fabergé. The Hofmannsthals' dinner parties included ducal relations, politicians, dons and artists. Strewn among the glitter one would find a few travelling Time Life executives or powerful advertisers whom their host described in glamorous terms to his fastidious guests.

Raimund was fascinated by his life and had a romantic vision of it. He worshipped the English upper classes and saw himself as a bridge between them and Europe. He introduced interesting people from all over Europe, though he took care to leave out the scions of much of the aristocracy of Central Europe, for the haughty Austrians still considered him an upstart with some Jewish blood in his veins. Conversely, he loved to talk to foreigners or neophytes like myself about the subtle ways of the British upper classes. Very early in my publishing career he took me out to lunch at White's to give me some advice. 'You must get to know more people, George,' he said, and admonished me to employ someone especially to help me widen my circle. I was rather shaken, but he continued, 'Look, there is a man here at the bar who is just between jobs. He's the right person for you.' Raimund beckoned the gaunt gentleman to join us. I discovered he had just been divorced by a rich wife and was looking for work. I remember him summing up his recent life by making the most effective use of the impersonal pronoun I have ever heard: 'Yes, I'm afraid one was a bad husband, but one did have taste.'

I stayed quite frequently at Plas Newydd, the Paget house in North Wales. Though Henry resided there, his sisters and their husbands, surrounding him protectively, dominated the scene until he married. It was a house of much laughter, grace and elegance beneath which lay many undercurrents of competing and conflicting personalities and hidden or overt passions.

The eldest sister, Caroline, was the strongest personality. Ruggedly independent, enigmatic, wayward and melancholy, she was quite irresistible. She loved her Uncle Duff (Cooper) and was revered by a land-owning neighbour, Sir Michael Duff, whom she later married. There was a great deal of mystery about her private life and she fanned it by giving oracular answers to even the most oblique questions. She was not a conventional beauty but had an aura of invincible femininity. I was one of the many who fell for her, though I received no encouragement. Her younger sister Rose had something Wagnerian about her. She was assertive like a Valkyrie and held emphatic views. Her husband, a younger son of Lord Aberconway, was unhappily in love with an American beauty whose suicide caused him to take his own life in despair.

Staying at Plas Newydd was like attending a wholly improvised and yet superbly choreographed ballet premiere. The spirit of Rex Whistler, who painted his famous murals there, still hovered over the place, and Oliver Messel and Cecil Beaton belonged to the charmed circle. House parties of the Pagets would go *en bloc* to visit the neighbouring Aberconways at Bodnant, famous for its gardens. Lady Aberconway amazed and amused me with her stilted speech and her hundred affectations. She was a *grande dame à l'Anglaise* who had been the mistress of Sam Courtauld, the great art collector, and still showed traces of beauty. In her Mayfair townhouse she received musicians, fashionable folk and stray intellectual mavericks.

That great English country house pastime, charades, always referred to as 'The Game', was traditionally played at least once during a long weekend. The company divided into two teams which had to act out a name, an episode, an event or a complicated situation by collective miming. The family and the regulars were extremely good at it and one's performance at 'The Game' contributed significantly to one's social rating.

Raimund acted as impresario and ringmaster in the Paget world and he loved this sense of belonging. When Henry married Shirley the inevitable happened, and the now fully emancipated young head of the family and his new chatelaine began to assert themselves by introducing a great change of style. There was a more stern and austere direction to their lives – above all, there was a decided rejection of the 'grand', the 'smart' and the 'worldly'.

These words – grand, smart and worldly – were much in use at this time among the upper classes. There was a great divide (which still persists) between those who unashamedly enjoyed their inherited wealth and prestige, and the rustic, though no less class-conscious and often even richer, clans who flaunted austerity, dowdiness and lack of ostentation. Whereas the former made conscious use of privilege at home and abroad, notably in the United States, where these English aristocratic ways were aped by 'old money' and, still more eagerly, by the new rich, those belonging to the second category were often demonstratively shabby. The men wore old suits and the women used local seamstresses, bought evening clothes off the peg, drove old cars and hated the 'smart circuits' of London. They subdivided on the question of intellectual pursuits — some of them were aggressively immune to cultural currents while others showed great dedication to the arts, letters and music.

There was a third category which was perhaps the most self-consciously proud of its manners and morals. It consisted of those who blended worldliness with distaste for conspicuous waste. They lived in castles or great country houses surrounded by the world's finest art and libraries and made a point of banishing decorators or plumbers so that old Chippendale chairs had fraying coverings, bathrooms had antediluvian tubs and the food, except for the wholesome breakfast fare, was atrocious. All that was deliberate.

To the first category belonged such figures as the last three Edwardian rakes, the Duke of Marlborough (Bert), the Earl of Carnarvon (Porchie) and Eric, Earl of Dudley. They married Americans, Greek and Yugoslav shipping heiresses or Austrian dancers, alternating with English beauties of long lineage. They flaunted their wealth, lived it up on the Riviera, shot (rather than hunted) in Tallahassee, Florida and loved to mingle with Hollywood glitz and glamour. While holding onto their prejudices they also opened themselves up to, indeed secretly respected, new wealth. American millionaires of recent provenance and British property developers of postwar vintage entered their lives with gusto and entertained them sumptuously in their London townhouses and brand-new country seats.

The social rise of Charles Clore, the self-made Jewish businessman from the East End, was largely helped by the grand, worldly and smart territorial magnates. They liked 'Charlie boy' for his malapropisms and social gaffes and they liked him even more when his French wife, a cousin of the Rothschilds with a craving for conventional success, left him to stand on his own unsteady social feet. I watched the interplay between the newly risen tycoon and his socially unassailable mentors with fascination and amusement. I loved Charlie Clore for himself and because he provided priceless anthropological source material. Uncouth and abrasive yet warm-hearted, he became a munificent philanthropist. He loved the company of beautiful women of every kind and mixed marchionesses with starlets, voluptuous Israeli or South American divorcees with young ingénues and spoke his mind without a censoring inner voice. At one of his dinner parties for twelve I found myself sitting one removed from the host. He addressed me in a loud voice:

'What do you think of this dinner, George?'

'Wonderful, Charles.'

'How do you find the food?'

'Delicious.'

'The wine?'

I feigned approval since I am a teetotaller.

'The women?'

'Irresistible.'

'This is nothing – you should have been here last Tuesday! Then you would have seen some really stunning girls!'

On other occasions Charles would take me aside after dinner and ask, 'What do you really think of all these people I've got here? What do they think of me in the West End?'

'Well, Charles,' I would say cautiously, 'there are two schools of thought: those who see you as you really are and admire you for what you have achieved, and those who can't overcome their prejudices and still keep aloof.'

'I see. Well, to hell with them! Who needs them?' And raising his voice so that bystanders must have heard, he would pronounce, 'I don't need the whole lot of them. They're all bastards and bitches.'

The second category, those who disapproved of false elegance and worldliness and used 'smart' and 'grand' as terms of opprobrium while sticking to all the appurtenances of aristocratic life, counted the newly-wed Angleseys among their number. Viv Mosley married an ebullient Yorkshireman, Desmond Forbes Adam, and after his early death retreated to the shires. There were many earnest young couples who led quiet lives, moved in narrow spheres and would rather go to Glyndebourne than to Covent Garden, and sponsored chamber music and amateur theatricals rather than be seen at the London balls or gala premieres.

The Nicolsons were a class apart. Sissinghurst Castle, where Vita Sackville-West reigned supreme, was austere inside, and Harold's townhouse in Kensington spartan and uncomfortable. A beautiful commode nested between unsprung armchairs. Though shabby, it was not genteel.

Through Raimund von Hofmannsthal I met one of his close friends, Clarissa Churchill. She was a great beauty and became a friend and influence in my life. I was in awe of her, secretly in love but conscious of an unbridgeable distance. What probably cemented our friendship was contrast – her reserve and my ebullience, her hidden ambitions and my overt enthusiasm. Clarissa was a rebel and a tacit conformist all in one. She combined a life of glamorous dinners, weekends and fashionable acquaintances with intimate friendships with musicians, actors and writers. Of course, she often found worldliness and the ivory tower in the same people, as with James Pope-Hennessy, who influenced many of his contemporaries because he was spontaneous and amusing as well as intellectually and sexually seductive.

Clarissa was a working girl. She wrote cultural articles for *Vogue* and later had a job with London Films, the company of that renaissance figure Sir Alexander Korda. I asked her to contribute to *Contact*, which she did by reporting the Edinburgh Festival, and we saw a great deal of each other for several years. I found her laconic and precise descriptions of the people she knew and the human and social crosscurrents of the worlds she frequented fascinating. By and by she took me along, not without hesitation and certainly without my prompting, to meet some of the pivotal people in her life. It was she who first introduced me to Cyril Connolly. Philip Toynbee and the Nicolsons must have delayed this encounter because it was known that Cyril spoke disparagingly of *Contact* even when it was still in its project stage.

Our first meeting was not propitious. I had spent the day at a printing works in Manchester and went directly from the railway station to Cyril's house in Sussex Place wearing a double-breasted brown suit. I had not yet been initiated into the tacit rite whereby gentleman only wear brown in the country and definitely not at a London dinner party. All the others were in evening dress and I arrived just as they were moving from the dining room to the drawing room on the first floor. Cyril greeted me with a limp handshake, raising his eyebrows at the brown suit. His measuring glance made me most uncomfortable and I felt that terrible English freeze which exudes when an unwelcome visitor joins a congenial circle. Although many of the people there were writers, publishers and hostesses whom I knew, they showed little sign of recognition. There was no chair for me and I felt awkward joining groups, kneeling or sitting on the floor.

Clarissa was obviously embarrassed. The only person who took pity was the author and broadcaster Robert Kee. He engaged me in a polemical discourse on the worsening situation in Palestine and, although we disagreed about Arabs and Jews, I was deeply relieved that I was not seen to be standing by myself.

Amid the pretty literary girls with double-barrelled names, the dons and the dowagers, I remember Osbert Lancaster talking to Lady Rothermere and Alan Pryce-Jones, the fashionable editor of the *Times Literary Supplement*, sitting legs akimbo at the feet of a duchess. Alan, unkindly described by some as being lighter than air, was a master of spontaneous familiarity and cold rebuff, a social barometer and the victim of a sophisticated snobbery that eroded his talent and diluted his intellectual strength.

While employed as tutor to a wealthy young Austrian woman, a relation of the Rothschilds, in Vienna, Alan translated the libretto of *Der Rosenkavalier*, and wrote promising verse and perceptive essays. He married his pupil and lived the life of a man of letters, inhaling the scent of Continental and English aristocracy. This over-shadowed his genuine passion for the intellectual world. For some time he succeeded in bridging these two forms of life. He earned respect and was offered many important posts in public life, but he succumbed to the easier option of being a social and intellectual butterfly. Alan emigrated to New York and later to Newport, and lost such grit or purpose as he might have had. His long-expected autobiography was a tragic demonstration of his decay.

It is perhaps because of that warning example that his son, David, who became one of my closest friends, was spurred on to a life of earnest achievement, hard work and principled consistency. Though only half Jewish, he espoused the Zionist cause, wrote excellent books on the Middle East and filled his life with serious journalistic assignments, strongly supported by his wife, Clarissa. The daughter of Lord Caccia, a British ambassador in Washington, head of the Foreign Office and Provost of Eton, she was herself a critic of her background. In her youth she went to school in Vienna where her father was then ambassador. There she not only learnt the German language but, being an excellent mimic, mastered the nuances of the Viennese dialect.

Undeterred by the Connolly incident, Clarissa Churchill intro-duced me to the Rothermere world. At Warwick House, which faced St James's Palace, Ann Rothermere presided over a salon of concentric circles. As the wife of the most powerful newspaper proprietor, owner of the *Daily Mail*, the *Sunday Dispatch* and a cluster of provincial newspapers, she stood at the vortex of politics and glittering diplomatic life. As a member of the Charteris family she was connected with the great and famous families of the land. Yet she was happiest with a small but diverse circle of intimates. She had a gift for friendship, and cosseted her favourites, intervening in their lives, inspiring and above all amusing them with unparalleled vigour, acerbic charm and meticulous interest. There were the courtiers like Peter Quennell, James Pope-Hennessy and Ali Forbes; the protégés like Lucian Freud and Robin Ironside, an art critic and a reasonably good painter himself; there were the sacred monsters whom she alone might hope to tame, like the intemperate Randolph Churchill or Lord Stanley of Alderley; there were the countless exciting and flamboyant visitors from France or America – film moguls, star reporters or dress designers; and there were some lame ducks, usually black sheep of aristocratic families. Ann's curiosity was easily aroused and there were frequent 'experimental' guests who would be asked once or twice and never again. Evelyn Waugh was an intimate, and she was one of the few people he could not only suffer but admire. He beheld in her that quintessence of aristocratic womanhood, an image that she probably shared only with the redoubtable Lady Diana Cooper.

My first appearance at Warwick House was at a grand dinner for Spiro Skouros, the head of 20th-Century Fox. Peter Quennell, who seemed very much at home, slipped unnoticed into the dining room to look at the table plan and moved me from a good seat between Vivien Leigh and a titled Italian lady to a place below the salt between a maiden aunt and a fox-hunting dowager. But what struck me more was seeing Ann Rothermere rush into the room and remove the place card of her stepson, Vere Harmsworth, the present Lord Rothermere, when she discovered she had an extra male guest: 'Poor Vere will have to have dinner upstairs.' She despised her stepson and clearly underestimated his worth. Seemingly ungifted and unambitious, Vere was always brushed aside. His marriage to a young actress who blossomed into the eccentric Bubbles, capricious but street-smart, kind and unsure, was much resented by the Rothermere clan.

Vere fooled everybody. Like the hero of *I Claudius*, he feigned an easy-going, unworldly and unbusinesslike disposition, but when he took the reins of Associated Newspapers he turned out to be one of the most successful press lords of Britain. He was a shrewd and cunning decision-maker and one of the most generous and loyal employers, who survived the decline of Fleet Street and proved a bastion of stability and continuity. I spent quite a few weekends with the Harmsworths in England and at their villa in Cap d'Ail which once housed Greta Garbo, and I found Vere amusing and uncannily accurate in his judgement of people.

I was often asked to Ann Rothermere's dinners and small lunches for four or six people, but we never really hit it off. I found her brittle and restless and I think she was bemused by me. Once, at luncheon, just after the State of Israel was born, she seemed quite impressed by my defence of the new State against the barbs of four ingrained Arabophiles. Next day, Frank Owen, the editor of the *Daily Mail*, whom I knew quite well, rang me to ask if I would go to Tel Aviv and file two articles from there. It was in the spring of 1949 and the commission proved important for me, because it was then that I paid President Weizmann a visit which led him to summon me as his Chief of Staff not long afterwards.

At the height of her social rule as the first lady of the press, Ann Rothermere's life was dominated by her love affair with Ian Fleming, then working for the *Sunday Times*, which was owned by her husband's pedestrian rival, Lord Kemsley. She grew less interested in her role as hostess and retreated to her circle of intimates. When her marriage to Esmond Harmsworth broke up, she resumed her convivial existence, albeit on a different scale, becoming less representational but even more appreciated by her favourites. She surrounded herself with the old courtiers and protégés, and a very select circle was bidden to spend some of the winter months at Golden Eye, Jamaica, where Ian Fleming produced a novel a year with military precision.

I was on lunching terms with Ian and saw a good deal of him when he was embarking on the James Bond series. His two closest friends were also friends of mine. Ivar Bryce, married to the ultra-rich American Jo Huntingdon Hartford, was a dilettante, a fastidious dresser and a touchingly generous host who became, for a time, a sleeping partner in Weidenfeld & Nicolson. His villa in Nassau, Xanadu, was a paragon of comfort and luxury. I stayed with him quite often, once in the company of Margaret Ann du Cane, a great love of mine, who had a mordant wit and tempestuous character. Marriage between us was often discussed but, alas, when she was hesitant I was ardent, and when she warmed to the idea I shuddered with fear. She did much to 'explain' me to her conventional contemporaries.

The other friend I shared with Ian Fleming was Robert Harling, the innovative typographer and designer who helped me with the layout of *Contact* and the children's classics for Marks & Spencer. He was a former naval officer, merciless with the enemy and equally merciless with the bevy of beautiful ladies whom he seduced. At least two of them later confided in me about their stormy liaisons. Outwardly brusque, taciturn and censorious, he was a warm and caring friend. For decades he was editor of *House & Garden*, spurning bigger offers, a living proof of Goethe's verdict that 'only in limitation doth the master show himself'.

Ian Fleming worked on the first Bond book with admirable concentration and laid down a schedule for himself which he followed religiously. While working at the *Sunday Times* he would sketch a plot and discuss it with his old friend William Plomer, editor at Jonathan Cape. Then, during the winter months, he would take unpaid leave and type the manuscript in Jamaica. Before sending it to the publishers he would send a copy to Ivar Bryce, who checked the worldy details, and Robert Harling, who advised him on gadgets or naval drill. Ivar Bryce loved his role. He corresponded with Fleming in the brisk service style so aptly enunciated by Noel Coward, another great friend of theirs. There would be such exchanges as, 'Ian, loved your yarn but vintage of the Widow [Veuve Cliquot] quite wrong. Also black pearl cufflinks at luncheon – very common indeed.'

Ivar and Ian shared a secret service past and revelled in reminiscences. The legendary exploits of Ian Fleming in the secret service, where he had a seat near the centre and knew the 'Ms' or 'Cs' intimately, followed him beyond his grave. Only recently a well-known journalist approached me with the outline of a book which seriously claimed that Ian Fleming and two associates kidnapped Martin Bormann from the Führer's bunker during the last battle for Berlin and brought him back to London where, after cosmetic surgery, he lived in a small house in Hampstead until well into the 1970s.

Ian Fleming designed the covers of his books, chose the typeface, wrote his own blurbs and supervised each detail of the promotion himself. He was determined to be a success and not to be known either as the brother of the eminent travel writer, Peter Fleming, or as the husband of the extraordinary Ann. In terms of universal recognition, he fulfilled his ambition. The launch party of *Casino Royale*, the first of the Bond films, was a great social event, though Ian, increasingly shy of parties and wary of the extent of Ann's entertaining, kept more and more to himself. He felt Ann's intellectual friends regarded him as a potboiler, and as his success exploded into world fame she added to his unease. She had a mocking habit of talking him down, and derided his work and habits. This accelerated their estrangement. It got back to him that the habitués of Victoria Square openly made fun of 'the commander'. A furtive love affair with an American lady in the fashion world that was inadvertently revealed to Ann by a porter at Ian's club, where her love letters to him were sent, critically affected the marriage.

Ann found some solace in her long relationship with Hugh Gaitskell, which brought her into touch with the young lions of the Labour Party. From Hugh's circle of friends she selected two who were to become her intimates: Roy Jenkins, whom she liked for his urbane conversation and slightly deferential affection, and Tony Crosland, whose acerbic intellect and sheer good looks she cherished. She also liked their wives, which was rare.

Hugh Gaitskell fell madly in love with Ann and her world. Though he was usually aloof and not easily impressed, his eyes lit up whenever he discovered a point of contact with Ann. I once lunched with him at the Ritz, and, half a dozen tables away, a group of men and women, obviously just back from an elegant wedding or christening, were celebrating boisterously. They included a few habitués of Victoria Square, and Hugh Gaitskell was transformed. He lost interest in the topic we were discussing, which might have been Labour Party propaganda or the Cold War, and wrote notes and blew kisses to the beautiful Lady Bridget Parsons.

Ann Fleming could not help hurting what she loved. She was full of mildly malicious stories about Hugh's middle-class habits. Once I heard her describe how she had rung him up to invite him to a dance. He came, bringing with him a selection of gramophone records of his favourite tunes. 'I didn't have the heart to tell him there'd be a live band playing.'

Cecil Beaton was another friend Clarissa Churchill brought into my life. Over the years we published a dozen or so books of photographs, autobiographical writings and a spoof novel. We saw a great deal of one another. He circulated in the most diverse milieux and had a great gift for friendship. He was a curious mixture of hard-nosed professional, romantic lover of elegance, fastidious snob and merciless diagnostician of human foibles. His prejudices lacked consistency: he retained a certain degree of the anti-Semitism of his middle-class origins, but had a passion for coloured people. He was a worshipper of tradition, and yet eager for each new signal of innovation, and always on the look out for the 'big names' of tomorrow. He was hypersensitive, and his judgements of people could often reflect the seesaw of reactions he thought he provoked in them. He was easily offended, but did not always show it. A hostile critic of his work could be lulled into a false sense of security and then suddenly feel the lash of his wit or the sting of his revenge.

I felt like a student of anthropology observing a miscellany of contiguous tribes and clans, each with its secret language, mannerisms, rites and tenets of faith. I have always studied them with voracious curiosity. What has interested me particularly is not so much my perception of them but how they perceive each other. I have tried to decipher their codes of behaviour in order to understand what they are about.

CHAPTER NINE

The Wroclaw Congress:
A Watershed

IN THE EARLY SUMMER of 1948 Moura Budberg asked me to lunch with the cultural attaché of the Polish Embassy in London, Antoni Slonimsky. He was a well-known poet and critic, an old-fashioned liberal who, being Jewish and anti-fascist, had thrown in his lot with the Communist regime. He later accepted an invitation to return to Poland and become head of the Writers' Union, but after a few years he became disenchanted and ended up as an important opposition figure.

At Moura's, Slonimsky told us about a 'conference in defence of culture' at which the Polish Government was planning to unite intellectuals from all over the world in the Silesian town of Wroclaw. He described the event in grandiose terms as the first great world congress of peace-loving intellectuals. It was to mark the start of a peace movement in which writers, artists and scholars set out to bring East and West together to avoid any future wars, at a time when the Cold War was just beginning. 1948 was the year of the Berlin airlift and the Czech defenestration. It also marked a political turning point in my life.

Slonimsky showed me the dazzling list of participants. It included legions of great men and women who were living legends. From France there were Picasso, Léger, Paul Éluard, Vercors, Julien Benda, the aged author of the classic *The Treason of the Intellectuals*; from Italy Alberto Moravia, Renato Guttuso, Elio Vittorini, Natalia Ginzburg and the poet and future Nobel prizewinner Salvatore Quasimodo; from Britain Julian Huxley, then head of UNESCO, who was voted onto the presiding committtee at Wroclaw, J.B.S. Haldane, the Communist scientist, A.J.P. Taylor, Kingsley Martin, Ronald Searle, Edward Crankshaw, the architect

Bernard Lubetkin and Feliks Topolski; and hosts of representatives from countries as far afield as Uruguay and Indonesia. The Russians led off with the writers Ilya Ehrenburg and Alexander Fadeyev, the head of the Soviet Writers' Union. Their list included the film directors Eisenstein and Pudovkin and the composers Shostakovitch and Prokofiev, though I can remember only Pudovkin actually being there. Of course there were pronouncedly Communist household names like Hewlett Johnson, known as the 'Red Dean' of Canterbury, and the British Communist Party organizer Ivor Montagu, but they were balanced by many other partisans of the moderate Left.

The only two nationalities that seemed one-sidedly represented were the Germans and the Americans. Well-known Communist novelists and playwrights such as Anna Seghers, Friedrich Wolf, the father of the East German spymaster Markus Wolf and author of the anti-Hitler play *Professor Mamlock*, and Alexander Abusch came from the Soviet sector of divided Germany. But the painter Max Pechstein and the architect Hans Scharoun, who were not Communist, also took part. The American side was the weakest, not least because the Left feared McCarthyite recriminations. It included Ella Winter, Donald Ogden Stuart, Clifford Odets and a New York attorney who was campaign manager for Henry Wallace, the Third Party candidate in the contest against Harry Truman and Thomas Dewey later that year. Several representatives of the New York School of Social Research had also been invited. The young Flora Lewis, who later became the doyenne of American journalists, happened to be in Poland and covered the conference for the *New York Times*.

When Slonimsky asked me to join this illustrious line-up I could hardly believe my ears. My inclusion seemed almost farcically unjustified. 'Ah yes,' he smiled, 'but we also want to invest in the future.'

Although the tenor was unmistakedly left-wing, outspoken Communists and fellow travellers seemed evenly matched by *bien-pensant* social democrats and liberals. As I later found out, this was already a second version of the list of participants who were to be invited, and it omitted the more conservative names. I still remember seeing Graham Greene and T.S. Eliot listed as 'will probably come'.

I accepted Slonimsky's invitation with alacrity and proudly

turned up at London airport in the last week of August to catch the chartered plane which was to take the British contingent to Wroclaw. Simultaneously a dozen or more charters from all over the world unloaded their passengers at the airstrip which the last *Gauleiter* had had built when the town was already under siege. Wroclaw had been as good as razed to the ground by bombs.

Poland was keen to renew its ties with the West and cherished hopes of being that bridge between East and West that so many a country in Central or Eastern Europe before and after the war has eagerly aspired to, without realizing that when a big power in the East and a big power in the West want to communicate in earnest they do not need intermediaries. The Polish Government was anxious to get the credit for this initiative, though it was of course acting in unison with its Soviet masters. Wroclaw, the ancient German town of Breslau, had been chosen in order to draw the world's attention to the new Polish border: the town stood as a symbol of the much-contested Oder-Neisse frontier between Germany and Poland, and to demonstrate the legitimacy of their claim the Poles had staged an exhibition about these newly acquired territories. The Poles were colonizing the city – many came from the Polish Ukraine after it reverted to the Soviet Union, and the population felt alien in these new surroundings. As we drove into the battered town I saw Nissan huts and Polish workers eating sausages and dumplings. People moved around aimlessly and a somewhat ghoulish atmosphere hung over the city.

But among the foreign guests who had followed the call of 'peace and culture' there was an electric feeling. In the medieval town hall, with its statues and green, red and gold ceiling newly restored, old friends who had not seen each other since the war embraced, and men and women who had only heard of one another embraced like old friends. There was laughter and crying as the delegates shared in the excitement of a new-found camaraderie. The mood was impressive and contagious. One had the feeling of suddenly being welcomed into a huge clan.

The British delegation was driven to a hotel with modest cell-like bedrooms and a communal breakfast room. I was struck by the unusual courtesy and warmth with which I was treated by my fellow delegates, most of whom I had never met. The conference itself was held on the bank of the Oder at the College of Technology, though the final session took place in the circular Jahrhunderthalle built in

1913, where Hitler had also spoken. Five hundred or so of us sat in the college hall on benches at rough, refectory-style tables. The various nationalities were placed in alphabetical order, so Great Britain ran alongside France and I was able to observe the reaction of French delegates at close quarters.

The conference organizer, Poland's chief propagandist, Jerzy Borejsza, extended a gracious and on the whole non-political welcome. As soon as he sat down the Russian novelist Alexander Fadeyev, a particular favourite of Stalin, took the floor and delivered a stunning indictment of the United States and their Western allies. It was a crude appeal to 'intellectuals of the world to unite' and prevent the resurgence of fascism which, he claimed, threatened to come from 'imperialist' America and her sinister plans to rearm against the peace-loving Soviet Union. He declared that the Soviet Union had defeated the Nazis single-handed, and denounced American culture as trite and trashy. In his thumping peroration, Fadeyev condemned Western writers who failed to see the light and helped the enemy of peace by their lack of commitment. Everyone knew he meant the political trend of writers like T.S. Eliot, Eugene O'Neill and Jean Paul Sartre when he delivered the stinging remark: 'If hyenas could type and jackals use a fountain pen, they would write such things.' There was a rather slow and patchy simultaneous translation which meant that when a speaker paused after a phrase or left the podium people applauded out of politeness before they had quite absorbed the meaning. Hence ten seconds or so after Fadeyev's speech a few muted boos and hisses could be heard over the crushing applause.

The bell rang and the conference adjourned for a cold midday buffet. Throughout the speech I had watched Vercors, the author of *Le Silence de la Mer*, possibly the best novel that sprang from the French Resistance. Of the French contingent Vercors was the one sitting closest to me. Though a sympathizer, he was not a Communist at the time, but as Fadeyev spoke I saw Vercors grow pale, mumble in disbelief and shake his head. When the Russian stopped speaking, Vercors put his head in his hands and sobbed. All the while I noticed the 'minder' of the French team, Laurent Casanova, a Communist deputy in the French parliament and for many years one of the most influential figures of the French Central Committee, eyeing his faltering recruit from the other end of the table. As soon as the bell rang he jumped out of his seat, made a dash for Vercors and took him into a corner. Throughout the lunch break he plied him with Polish vodka and talked at him, gesticulating wildly. I could see Vercors' depression lifting, and when the bell rang again he returned to his corner seat with straightened back.

Ilya Ehrenburg mounted the dais and delivered the Soviet star turn. Though couched in less brutal terms and much more caustic and witty, his speech was even more devastatingly anti-American and pro-Soviet. When Ehrenburg finished, the first to rise and lead the cheers of the French delegation was Vercors.

These two speeches set the tone of the congress – they were followed by infinite variations on the same theme. There was much local colour. Delegates had been flown in from the battle stations of the Greek civil war. Bearded guerrilla intellectuals in their fatigues brought fraternal messages from 'the firing line against fascism'. Guests from Tito's Yugoslavia moved uncomfortably among the delegates – they had been invited before the official break between the Marshal and Stalin in June of that year and were never mentioned in the recital of 'freedom-loving' peoples; but there was one voice that came out loud and clear in their defence.

A.J.P. Taylor, that dogged free spirit, was the first and, as it turned out, the only truly dissenting voice at Wroclaw. He sat next to me on the British benches with hunched shoulders and a grim face. Indignant at Fadeyev's portrayal of Soviet Russia as the sole liberator of Europe from the Nazi war machine, Alan Taylor asked for the floor. He launched into a brilliant extempore denunciation of the congress. The delegates had come to Wroclaw, he said, to exchange ideas with intellectuals from all over the world and to consider practical ways of securing agreement. But he could see that common standards were lacking. 'This has been a congress preaching war and not a congress preaching peace,' he declared. 'We cannot work together on the basis of claptrap and phrases.' Speaker after speaker had listed the nations who resisted Hitlerism, but Yugoslavia, which had lost two million men, had been conveniently omitted, her people's heroic effort 'blotted out' to suit the Soviet-led Communist parties. Taylor pointed out that far from defeating Hitler single-handedly, the Soviet Union had only joined battle after it had been attacked by Germany, while Britain had gone to war to defend Poland. He spoke of the duty of intellectuals to be critical of the Great Powers and of his hatred for any form of authoritarianism, whether it be American or Soviet. He had come to the conference to look for ways of peaceful cooperation, but concluded that he could not march under this 'banner of dishonesty'.

Again, the short pause in the simultaneous translation meant that there was an automatic round of loud cheering, but as soon as the meaning became clear a sepulchral silence fell on the assembly. There was some desultory clapping and some muted booing. When Taylor sat down I heard him whisper to himself: 'Now I understand what Martin Luther must have felt at the Diet of Worms.'

In a way, Alan Taylor's intervention was a turning point. It broke the Communist ranks and confused the organizers who had, perhaps all too naively, thought they could preserve unanimity through a show of sentimental solidarity, epitomized by the dove of peace specially designed by Pablo Picasso for the occasion. I witnessed the powerful magnetism of an idea that could envelop you in a cocoon of camaraderie – as long as you conformed. But I also saw the brutal and uncompromising dictate of conformism, the sudden switch to impersonal attitudes and instant hostility. On my return to the British billet I spoke warmly of Alan Taylor's remarks. Within seconds I became an outcast. Suddenly, I was the cuckoo in the nest of doves. At breakfast I was cut dead. However, the members of our small group who were either apolitical, like Feliks Topolski, or just benevolently neutral towards the Russians, like Kingsley Martin, continued to be friendly. Ivor Montagu, the British 'minder', realized that I was not pliable.

After hours the congress danced every night. In the large café and adjacent nightclub, people talked eagerly. They exchanged plans for lecture tours, they commissioned articles and books. The central attraction was Picasso. I will never forget him dancing bare-chested with a succession of voluptuous Polish girls, chanting in his Basque-accented French, 'I want to leave a child in Poland.'

I have another unforgettable memory. The Jewish Day of Atonement fell on the Friday of the conference. The day before and on the morning itself, a few men who were not participants of the congress posted themselves in the entrance hall between proceedings, furtively scanning faces and consulting the lists of delegates. They were members of the minuscule Jewish community of Wroclaw, recently repatriated from camps in Soviet Russia or survivors of the Polish holocaust. A little hunchback, who introduced himself as the beadle of the local synagogue, said he was looking for Jews to come and celebrate the end of the Yom Kippur fast on Saturday night and invited me to come.

When I arrived at the appointed place, a large workmen's hut converted into a synagogue and clubhouse, I was amazed at the stream of polyglot intellectuals from all continents arriving for the celebration. The State of Israel had come into existence only three months earlier. At that time the Soviet Union was well disposed towards the fledgling State, seeing British colonialism and its Arab allies ruled by reactionary monarchs as its main enemy in the Middle East. Thus Soviet, Czech and Bulgarian arms made up of army surplus flowed freely into Israel and probably saved the Jewish State from being strangled at birth. Their bitter experiences in Stalin's Russia had left the surviving East European Jews with little sympathy for the Soviet Union or Communism, but the official line was one of undying friendship between the Soviet liberators and the victims of Nazism.

That official sentiment prevailed during the first part of that Sabbath night. About a hundred members of the congress, Jews and non-Jews, put in an appearance. Some of them made lengthy speeches. Zaslavsky, the editor of *Pravda*, and the omnipresent Ehrenburg both spoke. Jorge Amado, the leading writer of Brazil, brought greetings from the peoples of Latin America and compared the Jews with the American Indians. The star guests left after the speeches and a hard core stayed behind with the local community. A lovable old grandmother plied me with gefilte fish and beef and bean stew, telling me in a whisper that the whole lot of them dreamt of leaving their horrible surroundings for Israel.

The second half of the congress was dominated by the battle over the final communiqué. All those invited had accepted on the assumption that it would be a congress of peace and conciliation. Some had hoped that at least it would wish 'a plague on both your houses', condemning extremist policies in East and West. But the first draft of the resolution was unilateral and contained the usual denunciation of Anglo-American imperialism. Not even the few bedraggled Henry Wallace supporters could happily conform. There was much discussion in the wings as the resolution was amended to win over as many signatories as possible – the Communists were intent on avoiding a split. In some delegations dissenting voices were silenced by iron discipline and the manipulative skills

of the 'minders'. In many cases members were urged not to spoil
the total effect of a unanimous declaration of the world's intellectuals just for the sake of a few 'minor nuances'. Alberto Moravia,
whom I had met before Wroclaw, convinced himself that '*grosso
modo*, the East is wrong and the West is wrong. But the West is
more wrong than the East. That's why we have to sign'.

At one point I stumbled on an odd scene in the anteroom. There
the eminent Communist geneticist, J.B.S. Haldane, hard of hearing
and suffering from a bad back, lay on a bench. Cupping his ear
with one hand and waving the text of a declaration in the other,
he cried, 'We can't have those doubters and waverers in our midst.
They're worse than the enemy.' 'But Prof.,' a young female acolyte
pleaded, 'you can't put that in writing. That's bad tactics. That
would drive Kingsley [Martin] away. He loves to agonize. We need
such men.'

Members of the British and American Embassy staffs had kept
a discreet distance from the congress. They were not excluded,
because that would have run counter to the propagandist interests
of the organizers – they made contact with some of their conationals
to put the Western point of view in some perspective. Edward
Crankshaw, Topolski, Denis Saurat, who as head of the French
Cultural Institute in London was included in the British quota of
guests, and, of course, A.J.P. Taylor huddled together and decided
on a counter-resolution to which I also put my name. After a sleepless night, Kingsley Martin compromised by signing the official
resolution while agreeing to add his signature to a letter of protest
in the *Manchester Guardian*. This letter appeared on the last day
of the congress and bore the additional signatures of Richard
Hughes, the author of *High Wind in Jamaica*, and Olaf Stapleton.
It read as follows:

> We, members of the British Group at the Wroclaw Congress, regret
> that we are not able to accept the resolution passed by the Congress
> as the whole truth. We deplore its over-simplification. The first duty
> of intellectuals is to be intelligent, and the duty of this Congress
> should have been to examine impartially the germs of a future war
> rather than to recapitulate the causes of the war which is finished.
> Two ways of life and of thought are in conflict throughout the world,
> and it should be the task of intellectuals to resolve that conflict by
> peaceful means.
> We feel the implication of the resolution that one side alone is to

blame to be a waste of a great opportunity. We believe that, though we were in a minority at the Congress, we represent the majority of men and women throughout the world.

On returning to London, we, the 'counter-revolutionaries', gave the British Embassy an account of the congress. Little did I know that being one of the signatories of the counter-declaration would spare me a great deal of trouble later on. When the McCarthyite immigration laws were in force in the United States, any visa applicant who had either been born or travelled behind the Iron Curtain had difficulties entering the country unless there were mitigating reasons. The first few times I applied for an American visa I had to argue my case, because having taken part in Wroclaw I was put on a blacklist. To prove my credentials I presented the letter in the *Manchester Guardian*. In addition, two friends in the Labour Government, Frank Longford and Woodrow Wyatt, wrote supportive letters to the American ambassador in London.

For a long time I was haunted by my experience of world Communism in action. Particular incidents left their mark: I remember Friedrich Wolf telling me that he already felt let down by developments in the German Democratic Republic, while Anna Seghers, who was hysterically anti-American, hissed abuse at people passing her table. I had never had Communist sympathies, but during the BBC period when I was evaluating news from inside Europe one was drawn into the maelstrom of rival factions and often succumbed to the temptation of seeing events in Manichean terms. War propaganda encourages that approach. So I was on Tito's side against Mihailovich, and sided with the radical French Resistance rather than the conservative forces, who were at times indistinguishable from Vichy.

We used to agonize about whom to support in the pitched battles between factions in Albania and Bulgaria. Often our stance was influenced by an inherent distrust of 'them' – the people behind the directives issued by the Foreign Office and the Political Warfare Executive which controlled all foreign broadcasting. We tried to deduce what line the Foreign Office camarilla were taking on the governments in exile and the postwar order by reading between the lines of these directives. In the journalistic milieu which I frequented, 'they' were regarded as snobbish, xenophobic and reactionary. They were seen as the people who were for Admiral Horthy in Hungary, who disliked Czechoslovakia because they regarded the Czechs as solid, middle-class plodders. These latterday Caruthers would consider Prague as opposed to Budapest a hardship post – in Hungary you could hunt and shoot on grand estates, while in Czechoslovakia you would have to content yourself with conversation or bridge.

But since then I had grown increasingly sceptical, and Wroclaw confirmed my opposition to men and movements of intolerance. Years later, when I discoverd more about the undercover activities of Martha Lecoutre and Stas Szymanczyk, everything fell into place. They had used Polish Communist channels to find suitable recruits among British intellectuals, writers and publishers. It was the Polish Embassy that had invited me to the Wroclaw conference. Of course I had proved a hopeless investment. At Wroclaw I had remarked to a colourless young geneticist that the first congress of world peace seemed to be something of a charade. That must have rung the first alarm bell. After I added my name to the counter-declaration it was obvious that I was a lost cause and I was dropped once and for all.

In the late 1960s, during what became known as the 'Encounter affair', I got another taste of the hypocrisy and intolerance I had witnessed at Wroclaw. A furious row broke out when it transpired that the British monthly periodical *Encounter* and a series of similar publications in France, Germany and elsewhere, all of which were being run on a deficit budget, had been funded by the CIA via real and dummy foundations. Suspicion fell on the Congress of Cultural Freedom, an umbrella organization which funded conferences, international lecture circuits and artistic festivals, subsidized books and gave bursaries to writers. It was thought to be part of an elaborate network run by American intelligence. This was largely true.

The Soviet Union was masterminding a peace movement which set out to win the heart and soul of progressive intellectuals the world over – the Wroclaw conference had, after all, been the grand opening of that battle for the moral high ground. Under the Truman and Eisenhower administrations talented young men at the CIA such as Corde Meyer, and political activists at the American Federation of Labour such as Irving Brown, were convinced of the need to counter the intellectual advance of Communism. Those who were prominent in this struggle regarded it as a crusade: their seriousness and commitment was without question. Mike Josselson, a Russian by birth and a passionate music-lover who worked for US Information Services in occupied Berlin and was responsible for forging cultural links with the Germans, was one of the luminaries of the Congress for Cultural Freedom. But the most colourful figure connected with that organization was Nicolas Nabokov, a cousin of the writer.

A composer, impresario and heartless seducer of men and women, Nicolas Nabokov had a jovial bass tone and a Rabelaisian gift for narrative. He understood intellectual milieux and had a good sense of politics in a wider context as well as a fine instinct for local issues in New York, Paris or London. As a senior officer in the Cultural Department of the American Forces in Berlin, he liaised with the Russians and showed enormous talent for bringing people together socially as well as professionally. Arthur Koestler and Ignazio Silone, two champions of the anti-Communist cause, were among Nabokov's closest friends.

Irving Brown and Mike Josselson, one of his main collaborators, appointed Nabokov secretary-general of the Congress of Cultural Freedom and gave him funds for the first of a series of intellectual conferences organized by Melvyn Laski and the American philosopher, Sidney Hook, in Berlin in 1950. Isaiah Berlin introduced Nabokov to Stephen Spender, who subsequently became coeditor of *Encounter*, presiding over the literary side. Spender deserves a great deal of credit for the early success of the magazine, as does the American journalist Irving Kristol, the original coeditor.

When Kristol left he was replaced by Laski, an American who had been in Berlin as a soldier with the US Forces in the immediate aftermath of the war when the Russians were consolidating their hold on the Eastern Zone. Laski nurtured a deep hatred for Communism and those 'treacherous clerks' who had abandoned libertarian views and become the handmaidens of the Soviets.

When news began to percolate that *Encounter* and other publications and activities were financed by an arm of the American Government, a hue and cry broke out which reached a hysterical pitch. Stephen Spender resigned. He and his wife Natasha joined in the shrill condemnation of Laski and to a lesser extent of Josselson, immediately distanced themselves from the congress and fell into the arms of those left-wing intellectuals who had from the outset seen America as the greater rather than the lesser enemy of peace in the struggle between the superpowers. So violent was the condemnation of Laski and his band of 'cold warriors' that it spilled over into many different spheres of intellectual life. The battle was waged at the dinner tables in New York's Village and Riverside Drive, London's Hampstead and the high tables of Oxford and Cambridge. It assumed Homeric proportions and opened wounds which have still not healed. Even today, mention of an *Encounter* stalwart like the Kremlinologist Robert Conquest, who was triumphantly vindicated by KGB statistics and found, if anything, to have underestimated the victims of Stalinist terror, causes a faint shudder in *bien-pensant* liberals who would by now consider themselves wholly reformed.

I find it hard to believe that Stephen Spender, though in many ways naive and trusting, never suspected that there was official money behind the activities of the Congress for Cultural Freedom. In fact, I remember Malcolm Muggeridge, a great supporter of the idea of starting an intellectual journal to back the anti-Communist cause, reassuring the guests at a small dinner, which included Stephen and myself, as far back as the winter of 1951 to 1952 that although the main funding would come from America, 'his friends in the War Office' had told him that they could help as well. Like Koestler, Muggeridge was a Communist who had turned passionately anti-Soviet. He had worked in British Intelligence during the war and was obviously alluding to his contacts there.

Laski undoubtedly knew the truth. He was the one most shunned and pilloried, not least because he is a loner by temperament, a zealot and an intellectual vigilante. Josselson was only mildly ostracized. Nicolas Nabokov who, though he denied any knowledge of the source of the funding, was in my view well aware of the circumstances. He disarmed all those who might have suspected otherwise with his devastating charm and sense of humour.

CHAPTER TEN

'The Family':
The Marks & Spencer Clan

OF ALL THE MENTORS and mother figures in my life, I doubt whether any has influenced me as much as Flora Solomon. She used to call me Georgek. 'Georgek,' she announced, 'I'm going to take you over, you need a lot of looking after.' I have never looked back. Flora taught me maxims of business, guided my personal affairs and brought me back into the Jewish fold, introducing me to the Marks & Spencer clan and to Chaim Weizmann. She proved an invaluable friend, listened endlessly to my problems and was always ready with sound advice. When she felt that I might be getting too carried away by some new venture, she would say, 'Georgek, don't count your chickens before they hatch.'

Flora was one of three remarkable sisters who were brought up as privileged Jews in St Petersburg. Her father, Grigori Benenson, made his fortune in the oil fields of Baku and wielded considerable economic influence in prerevolutionary Russia. He was banker to the Tsar and had had dealings with Rasputin, who approached him for money to found a newspaper. Benenson had many mistresses, one of whom threw vitriol in his face when he refused to marry her and permanently disfigured him. The family came to England in 1915. Some of their wealth survived the Bolshevik Revolution, but Benenson, who later moved on to New York and founded a new empire there, lost everything in 1931 when the Manufacturers Trust Company foreclosed on him.

The three Benenson girls, sometimes described as the Sisters Karamasov, were close, but very different. Fira, the middle sister, made a career as a fashionable couturière in New York and married a Polish count, Janusz Ilinksi, who managed the Carlyle Hotel. Manya, the youngest, was married to Ralph Harari, the aesthete son of Sir Victor Harari Pasha, governor of the Bank of Egypt. The Hararis and their cousins, the de Menasces, were the two great Alexandrine Jewish families, the Egyptian equivalent of the Rothschilds. Their milieu, transposed from Jewish to Coptic, is portrayed in Lawrence Durrell's *Alexandria Quartet*. Manya converted to Catholicism, as Flora's son Peter Benenson was to do years later. Together with Marjorie Villiers, with whom she had served in the political intelligence department at the Foreign Office during the war, Manya started the distinguished Harvill Press in 1947, backed by Ralph Harari. When he grew tired of financing his wife's venture, William Collins stepped in. The Harvill imprint published some of the greatest contemporary Russian works, among them Pasternak's *Doctor Zhivago*, which Manya herself helped translate, Ilya Ehrenburg's *The Thaw* and Solzhenitsyn's *First Circle*. Other titles included Lampedusa's *The Leopard* and Joy Adamson's *Born Free*.

Flora, the eldest, had been sent to be educated at an establishment for young Jewish girls in Wiesbaden. In 1919 she married Colonel Harold Solomon, an assimilated Anglo-Jew who served in the mandatory British administration of Palestine under Sir Herbert Samuel. As a young bride, rich and socially adept, Flora kept open house in Jerusalem, where the early leaders of the Jewish colony mingled with Arabs and British officials, such as the high commissioner, Herbert Samuel, and the Orientalist Ronald Storrs, who was governor of Jerusalem. She had known Chaim and Vera Weizmann before she married, and whenever the Weizmanns visited Palestine she assembled all the local dignitaries in their honour. Jerusalem made her an even more ardent Zionist than she had been before, though one subtly aware of the nuances in relations between the British authorities, the feuding Jewish factions and the leading Arab families.

Harold Solomon had to resign his post after a riding accident left him paralysed from the waist down. The couple returned to London and set up house in Hornton Street, Kensington, where they began to lead increasingly separate lives. The invalid Colonel was entertained by companions, one of whom was the young pianist Joan Carr, later Lady Drogheda, and Flora began a long liaison with Alexander Kerensky, the hero of the Russian Revolution, whom she met in New York in 1927.

The Solomons lived in great style – Flora kept eleven servants. Their son Peter was tutored by the young Wystan Auden. After

Eton, Peter trained as a barrister and went on to found Amnesty International, complying with his maternal grandfather's wish to call himself Benenson to keep the name alive. Peter grew up in a somewhat unreal milieu, and for all his talents never really found his feet. He became a passionate convert to Catholicism while remaining deeply conscious of his Jewishness. He fell victim to in-fighting at Amnesty International and left in protest against takeover bids from the Communisant Left, who tried to politicize the organization, concentrating on the abuse of human rights by right-wing regimes while condoning injustices in the Communist world.

Flora Solomon's grand life came to an abrupt end when, in the wake of the Wall Street Crash of 1929, her father lost his fortune overnight and her drafts from New York stopped coming. Now a widow with a son whose school fees had to be paid, she had to find a job.

One day, she found herself sitting next to Simon Marks, the chairman of Marks & Spencer, at dinner. She challenged him on labour conditions, which were said to be notoriously bad in his business. Simon Marks charged her there and then with looking into the matter. From this unpaid assignment was born the Marks & Spencer social welfare department, of which Flora was given charge. She introduced subsidized staff canteens in every store and a miniature national health service, and improved working conditions and staff welfare. Within a short space of time she helped turn Marks & Spencer into a model of worker–employer relations. As head of social welfare she earned herself an international reputation, and spoke at many conferences on industrial relations.

It was one such occasion that brought us together in the summer of 1947. *Contact* had an industrial consultant called F.S. Button. A charming old trade union leader with a slighty unctuous manner, he liaised between Transport House and Buckingham Palace, and provided me with useful contacts for contributors from the trade union movement and the Labour party. Button was a close friend of Dame Caroline Haslett, a distinguished figure in the world of social welfare and labour relations, who ran a huge organization of women employees in the electrical industry and was the statutory woman on many public boards. When we were struggling with *Contact*, Dame Caroline had helped me with introductions to advertisers, and on her recommendation I was invited by Sir Stafford

Cripps, then president of the Board of Trade, to join the British delegation at a conference in Stockholm. Our mission was to demonstrate the postwar revival of British industry. I was an odd choice, for I knew nothing about industrial management, and the number of industrialists or businessmen I had met could be counted on the fingers of one hand.

On the boat, among many glittering names – chairmen and managing directors of Britain's premier industries – was Flora Solomon, who was to deliver a paper on human relations in business. We struck an instant rapport. She questioned me about every aspect of my life. She wanted to know exactly how I organized my time, what my household arrangements were, what ambitions I had. At the end of that week in Stockholm I felt that I had acquired a third parent.

Flora looked like something out of Toulouse Lautrec's *Moulin Rouge*. Then in her late forties, she was dumpy but elegantly and simply dressed. She had a distinctive, rather ugly face with a pointed nose and flaming red hair and she spoke with a strong, lisping Russian accent in a soft voice full of quiet assurance. She had a Russian soul and could be quite excitable, but never lost her poise.

Flora graded her favours scrupulously, but when she took you into her closest circle you felt cosseted and cocooned from all outside dangers. She had a capacity for friendship that I have never encountered since. You could burden her with every little detail, be it an affair of the heart or business. She had a sharp, analytical mind. First she listened to your problem, then came the diagnostic stage, and invariably she would come up with a therapeutic solution. Her philosophy of friendship was based on the concept of sustained involvement. She had a legion of lame ducks for whom she found jobs or pensions or husbands or wives. She was tireless in her endeavours on their behalf and would not allow herself to be discouraged by setbacks. Once she had taken somebody on, she monitored their progess or regress. She was the ultimate in loyalty. I owe her more than favours or affection: she changed my life by making me rethink where I was going.

The plight of the Jews and the struggle for Palestine were leitmotifs in Flora Solomon's Mayfair drawing room. She had a small but elegant apartment in Carrington House, off Curzon Street, where she kept open house. People dropped in for tea, dinner and drinks, and Marks & Spencer employees mingled with Labour politicians, Zionist officials, society figures and intellectuals. Flora would prose-lytize whenever she could, but she enjoyed argument and had a jolly way of agreeing to disagree. She introduced me to the British *haute Juiverie* and the top echelon of Zionist leadership, but her circle ranged far beyond the Jewish world; to some extent it over-lapped with Moura Budberg's. Peter Ustinov was as much at home doing his 'Ohm Krüger' star turn in Flora's drawing room as he was in Moura's, and there were many others one would meet in both salons. The two women were rivals, not only out of social jealousy, but because they distrusted each other.

By the time I met Flora in 1947 she had broken off her affair with Kerensky, but he often appeared in her flat, a stocky, cour-teous and talkative man with a round face and cropped hair. Chain-smoking through his crooked cigarette holder, the hero of the Russian Revolution would pace the room and tell stories of the great days gone by. Once I asked him what he thought of Lenin. He stopped short and said, 'I never met him. The Russian Revolution was acted out on a very large stage.'

During the war, Flora had been one of the leading lights of the Churchill Club, where titled ladies entertained American officers. Among her friends in upper-class London she counted Pamela Chur-chill, later Harriman, now President Clinton's ambassadress in Paris, who had just left her first husband, Randolph Churchill, and Nancy Lancaster Tree, founder of Colefax and Fowler, the fashion-setting firm of interior design.

Flora's closest friend in that circle was probably Barbie Agar, the tall and elegant daughter of the architect Edwin Lutyens. She was a hostess and philanthropist who married Herbert Agar after the death of her first husband, Euan Wallace, a member of Chamber-lain's Government. Herbert Agar was an American liberal democrat and Pulitzer Prize-winner much admired for his lofty writings on politics. An archetypal club man, somewhat given to drink, he was a slow teller of long stories and took pride in his far-flung connec-tions. He played a useful part in the distinguished but short-lived publishing house of Rupert Hart-Davis. Of her three sons and two stepsons Barbie lost three during the war, and another died shortly after demobilization. She also outlived her youngest son, Billy Wallace, an intimate of Princess Margaret and a leader of the gilded youth in the immediate postwar period.

Flora also maintained French connections. Once, during a brief visit to Paris together, we called on Misia Sert, the widow of the Catalan ornamentalist José-Maria Sert whose murals adorn the town hall in Barcelona and the Waldorf-Astoria in New York. A friend of Diaghilev, Cocteau and Stravinsky, creator of the Chanel legend and model of Bonnard and Renoir, Misia was famed for her beauty and her artistic salon. She knew Marcel Proust well and rather flaunted his unrequited affection by showing me a box full of letters he had written to her, neatly stacked in their opened envelopes. She appears in his magnum opus as Princess Yourbeleti-eff and as Madame Verdurin. Princess Marthe Bibesco, another salonière in Flora's circle, told me a similar tale. We published a little book of hers, *At the Ball with Marcel Proust*, telling the story of how she avoided his attentions throughout an evening of grand entertainment.

Being the ideal confidante, with a genuine concern for other people's private problems and pipe dreams, Flora's advice was sought by a variety of protégés. Among them were Richard Crossman and Frank Pakenham, later Lord Longford, with whom she had worked in social welfare during the war and who lodged with her for a time. Kim Philby was also part of her circle. She had first met him when his father, the explorer, Orientalist and confidant of Ibn Abdul Saud, Harry St. John Bridger Philby, brought his stammering boy to her house in Jerusalem. Years later he was to meet his second wife, Aileen Furse, a staff manageress at Marks & Spencer, in her flat.

Just before he went to Spain in 1937 Philby called on Flora. Though usually distant and loath to talk of himself, he confessed that he was going through a tremendous psychological turbulence. He told her he had a cause and was doing important work for peace. At that time Flora thought little more of it, though she was surprised that the man she knew as a left-winger was reporting the civil war from the Franco side.

Much later, during a visit to Israel in 1962, I was witness to an incident that was to have grave consequences. Philby, then the *Observer* correspondent in Beirut, was filing particularly hostile stories about Israel which enraged Flora, all the more because she was familiar with his neuroses and political tergiversations. At the Weizmann Institute in Rehovot she bumped into Victor Rothschild, an old friend who also knew Philby well. She asked Victor how it was that the *Observer* could employ him. Did they not know he was a Communist? Shortly thereafter Victor Rothschild asked her whether she would consent to a meeting with a security official in his London flat. Flora agreed to tell all she knew. Unwittingly she provided one of the missing links that led to the confrontation between Philby and Nicholas Elliott in Beirut, whereafter Philby took flight and resurfaced in Moscow.

In the heroic days leading up to the birth of Israel in 1948, Flora was a port of call for Zionist leaders from all over the world. No figure relevant to the cause did not pass through her Mayfair drawing room. It was the backdrop for feverish discussions about what the new State should be called, whether New Judea, Israel or the Jewish Republic; who would be in the first government; would Nahum Goldmann give up his Nicaraguan passport and become an Israeli?

Nahum Goldmann was a frequent visitor. Short and stocky, he had an ebullient personality and was the finest brain and the nimblest international envoy of Zionism. As a young man he had already been a leading force in German Jewry: during the First World War he lobbied the Kaiser's Government, working his way up and down the Wilhelmstrasse on behalf of Jewish Palestine at a time when Chaim Weizmann had long been convinced that a Jewish State could only be achieved through Britain. But in Germany the constellation did not look unfavourable. Berlin was allied to the Ottoman guardian of the Holy Places, and the starkly anti-Semitic government of the Tsar led many American Jews, especially the descendants of fugitives from the Russian pogroms, to show sympathy for the German cause in the war. Whilst Anglo-Jewry fought on the Allied side, Austro-Hungarian and German Jewry rallied to the flag and served in the armies of their fatherlands. Goldmann wrote patriotic articles and pamphlets attacking 'Perfidious Albion'. When Hitler seized power, Goldmann and his wealthy wife emigrated. They led a cosmopolitan life on both sides of the Atlantic, collecting Impressionist paintings, and befriending world leaders and business titans.

Goldmann was close to Weizmann, and founded the World Jewish Congress which looked after the interests of Jews in the Diaspora. He could easily have secured senior office in Israel had he not stuck to his Nicaraguan passport, preferring the luxury of the Avenue Montaigne to the austerity of a public servant's home in Israel. In fact he had one of the most elegant flats in Jerusalem, and until his death in 1982 he entertained European prime ministers, American senators and other grandees there.

As a roving interlocutor, Goldmann rendered Israel and world Jewry enormous services. With his moderate views about the Arabs and the Soviet Empire he unlocked doors that were closed to Israeli officialdom. After 1967, when most of the Third World and the whole Communist bloc broke off relations with Israel, the World Jewish Congress acted as a discreet intermediary. Goldmann fiercely contested Ben-Gurion's and Golda Meir's intransigence and did much to alleviate the lot of Russian Jews during the last years of his life. It was largely due to his efforts that Israel established relations with Germany, thus bringing about the recognition of the Jewish State as legatee of all Jewish heirless property in the Federal Republic and paving the way for the huge reparation payments. He prepared the secret meeting between Konrad Adenauer and Ben-Gurion in the Waldorf Astoria, which Teddy Kollek attended as the head of the Israeli prime minister's office. Goldmann loved opera and women; indeed, a story of his life might well be entitled *Jews, Women and Song*. We often met at the Salzburg Festival, where he invariably had an attractive young companion in tow.

The most colourful of Flora's itinerant friends with whom I had close bonds was Meyer Weisgal. He was a self-made Jew of Russian-Polish origin, small in stature, with a mane of white hair. He made his career as a press agent and impresario before turning fundraiser and science administrator. He came from the lower east side of New York and spoke the most vulgar English laced with four-letter words. Brisk and overflowing with sentimentality, crass and yet noble, an idealist and at the same time a supreme operator, he struck me as a dynamo of irrepressible enthusiasm and was without doubt the greatest fundraiser I have ever encountered – a rainmaker who produced rain. Weisgal could be over-voluble, but he had a big heart and great integrity. He was a father figure, always supportive of me, particularly in difficult periods of my life, for instance when my first marriage broke up.

Weisgal never looked after his own interests. He was born to serve a cause, and this was crystallized through serving a person. He needed someone to worship, and his first idol was Max Reinhardt, the German theatrical genius. When Reinhardt had to leave Nazi Germany, Weisgal offered to rebuild his life in America. A talented showman as well as an impresario, he persuaded Reinhardt to direct a production of a mammoth show called *The Eternal Road*, which was to be a staged cavalcade of the whole of Jewish history from the patriarchs to the present. Weisgal collected money from big sponsors like Bill Paley, the head of Columbia Broadcasting, and from legions of ordinary people who contributed a share. Franz Werfel helped write the text for a cast of hundreds. The show opened in Madison Square Garden and was an instant flop.

Weisgal's first meeting with Chaim Weizmann changed his life. It also marked a turning point in the affairs of his new idol, whose confidant and devoted aide he became. The two men conversed in Yiddish, much to Vera Weizmann's irritation. With his genius for fundraising, Weisgal brought to fruition plans to expand the great scientific complex in Rehovot, officially inaugurated in 1949, which originated as the Daniel Sieff Institute founded in memory of Israel Sieff's son who had committed suicide in 1933. After Weizmann's death Weisgal was appointed president and subsequently chancellor of the Institute which he had helped create with such charm and chutzpah.

Weisgal had an intuitive understanding of the rich, whom he coaxed into opening their pockets by playing on their aspirations of social advancement and prestige. 'My boy,' he once revealed to me, 'when you talk to a self-made man you must realize that there are three stages in his life: the acquisitive stage, the contemplative stage and the distributive stage. The art of fundraising is to get the man just as he enters the contemplative stage and be at the ready when he moves into the distributive stage.'

In the initial stage Weisgal's strategy was deliberately low-key. He would approach a potential donor by telling him of a big new project and showing him a list with a dozen or so names of people who might each give a million. The name of his latest victim would be missing, implying that he was not up to financing such a venture. This was calculated to make the person in question ask why he was not on the list. Weisgal would tell him that he was in a different category: 'I'll come to you when you reach that stage.' 'What do you mean?' the person would ask. 'Are you saying I'm not worth half of so-and-so? This man isn't even worth a quarter of me. I'll tell you what, I'll pay for the whole thing.'

Weisgal was very jealous of his foremost donors and was careful to cultivate them by keeping in constant touch. One of his friends and clients was Sir Isaac Wolfson, himself a great salesman and enthusiast, who founded a British business empire, Great Universal Stores. Weisgal turned him into one of the most munificent donors to the Institute. Legend has it that during his early rise Wolfson confronted Israel Sieff and complained that 'The Family' was cold-shouldering him. Sieff is said to have replied, 'We are very busy people, Ike. We see our relations and those friends with whom we share an interest in the Jewish cause.' This remark ignited a new enthusiasm in Wolfson which yielded millions of pounds.

Only once did Weisgal find himself outclassed. Wolfson had built himself a handsome Californian-style house next door to the Weizmann Institute. One day a delegation of Orthodox Jews called on him there. It was led by a wizened rabbi who claimed to have known Wolfson's father and grandfather. The rabbi managed to make him pledge that he would finance a building in Jerusalem to house offices of the chief rabbinate. The undertaking cost Sir Isaac steadily growing sums of money, and Weisgal never forgave himself for not being there at the same time.

Weisgal was a great storyteller and full of wisecracks. He once explained to me the subtle nuances of busybodiness, pointing out that only Yiddish, which came most naturally to him, has precise definitions. At the apex of the pyramid is the *macher*, the dedicated busybody. He is aided by a *mitmacher*. Both types are full of purpose, whereas the *schwitzer* is an aimless busybody who has no clear objective but just likes officious activity as an end in itself, like the sargeant at the law in Chaucer's *Canterbury Tales*: 'Though there was nowhere one so busy as he, he was less busy than he seemed to be.' Lying athwart is the *kuhler*, who is an unstoppable namedropper. Related archetypes are the *nudnik*, who is a common or garden bore and good for nothing, and the *phudnik*, who is a *nudnik* with a PhD. Once I learnt these subtle distinctions I was able to follow Weisgal's descriptions of people without needing further elucidation.

He also mastered the technique of the universally applicable joke. This consists of using one of the main Yiddish jokes as a matrix which can be transferred to different milieux and situations appropriate to the occasion. There is, for instance, the story of the obnoxious Jewish miser upon whose death no one in the Jewish *shtetl* is willing to give the funeral oration. Eventually a sage from out of town reluctantly agrees to do so. He ends his panegyric by saying,

'The deceased had every disagreeable quality man can imagine, but his late father was much worse.' Weisgal would tell the same story about an American college president and his predecessor, a French duke, and a Bronx union leader.

The Marks & Spencer clan, known in the Jewish world simply as 'The Family', also belonged to Flora's intimate circle. Simon Marks and Israel Sieff, two childhood friends from Manchester, had married each other's sisters. The husbands of the other two Marks sisters were also in the business, and so were some of their children. The clan centred on three men and their wives, Simon Marks, Israel Sieff and Harry Sacher. Harry Sacher, a barrister who had been leader writer on the *Manchester Guardian* in the days of C.P. Scott, that great prewar editor known as 'the Thunderer of the North', had married Simon's sister Miriam. A close collaborator of Chaim Weizmann, Sacher had been instrumental in committing the *Manchester Guardian* to a pro-Zionist line. He was the intellectual of the Family. Caustic, sharp-witted and ultra-cautious, he sat in his book-lined office in Baker Street and acted as a dam to the revolutionary business ideas of the two brothers-in-law, Simon and Israel. He was an active member of the Jewish Agency for Palestine.

The youngest of the four Marks sisters, Elaine, first married Norman Laski, one of the distinguished family of Manchester Jews which produced a top lawyer, Neville, the Labour Party's theoretician, Harold (who was Norman's uncle), and the writer Marganita. Norman also worked in the firm, but Elaine's second husband, Neville Blond, did not. He was a textile magnate with a bulldog face who supplied Marks & Spencer and was one of the founders of the Royal Court Theatre. His son is Anthony Blond, a gifted rebel who turned his hand to publishing and wrote a *roman à clef* about the Family which caused much discomfort.

Simon Marks was a business genius. Sensitive to a fault, he was incapable of articulating himself explicitly and functioned intuitively. He was a master of the worm's-eye view. He would enter a suburban store, see a speck of dust on the counter and launch a hygiene campaign. He would detect a momentary hesitation on the part of a salesgirl in Leeds and decide that the whole system needed a time and motion study.

Israel Sieff was just the opposite. He had a degree from Manchester University and thought in categories and concepts. Like the Markses he came from a family of Russian-Jewish merchants, but the Sieffs were higher up in the social structure of the ghetto. Israel was cultivated and benign. He had cofounded PEP, Political and Economic Planning, an early think-tank of mildly left-of-centre bearing, and represented all that was *bien-pensant* in the world of business and philanthropy.

When his father, the original founder of the Penny Bazaar, died, Simon won a High Court case against the Spencer interest and persuaded Israel, who was already a successful businessman in his own right, to become his main partner. The Marks and Sieff partnership was not only crucial to the making of Marks & Spencer, it also made a major contribution to the creation of the State of Israel. They had a deep faith in Zionism which was inspired by their friendship with Chaim Weizmann, whom they had known from the days when he had taught at Manchester University. They were his disciples and his benefactors. His thoughts on scientific method in industry and the importance of science to any future colonization of Palestine made a deep impression, and they were tireless in their commitment to Zionism. During the First World War, Simon Marks organized a London Zionist office for Weizmann and went with him to the Versailles Peace Conference, while Israel Sieff was appointed to the Palestine Commission which Weizmann set up after the Balfour Declaration to advise the British authorities on the establishment of the Jewish National Home.

Very much in keeping with Tawney's *Rise of Capitalism*, Simon Marks and Israel Sieff became enlightened businessmen rather than narrow-minded traders. Weizmann's scientific input, for which they felt indebted, and their passionate desire to combine merchandizing with science were the real secrets of the firm's success. Simon Marks often said that, but for Weizmann's belief in combining politics and science, or, as he put it, 'his philosophy combined with our commercial flair', he and Israel Sieff would never have gone beyond being conventional businessmen in Manchester.

The Family was a highly structured clan with its own social ceremonial governed by unwritten laws. There were four solar systems: the Markses, the Sieffs, the Sachers and the Blonds. The various strands formed a powerful framework within which the professional and social lives of its members prospered and proliferated. They all lived in or around Grosvenor Square, having moved collectively from the Addison Road area in the 1930s and from

Hampstead before that. Their houses were done up in the same conventional way, with eighteenth-century English furniture and Impressionist paintings. Their style of entertaining was similar and they all had country houses with adjacent farms which they kept partly for tax reasons. They had a collective identity and a common body of friends whom they invited to luncheons, dinners and week-end parties. These included rich Anglo-Jews, but also the big suppliers, the nouveaux riches and some recent immigrants. Besides them there were certain *hausfreunde*, like Robin and Angela Fox, the parents of the actors Edward and James Fox, and the plastic surgeon Sir Archibald McIndoe and his daughters, who enjoyed near-Family status. Years later I overheard a conversation in the house of Nigel Lawson, then married to his Lyons heiress wife Vanessa, at one of their parties in Hyde Park Gate. In the queue for the buffet I found myself standing behind Alun Chalfont, who was talking to one of the McIndoe daughters. She was married to Dennis Walters, a pro-Arab Tory, and Alun asked her: 'Tell me, Vanora, why are you so passionately anti-Israel?' She replied, 'If you had spent every weekend as a child at the Markses in Sunningdale hearing about the kibbutzim, you would feel the same.'

There was also a group of courtiers, self-seeking adventurers and hangers-on. Some found only temporary favour and, once banished from one of the major courts, would automatically be dropped by the whole clan. Others were regularly in attendance. They were a mixed bunch, encompassing lawyers, accountants, a former tennis champion, a Scottish laird who had run into debt and lived on favours, aristocrats who traded on their wits, interior decorators and a florist. In his sardonic way, Chaim Weizmann referred to them as the 'Ps and Ws', short for Pimps and Whores.

Lajos Lederer, a dashing Hungarian who worked on the *Observer*, was part of the family entourage. He had come to England in the 1920s with a delegation of Hungarian monarchists who wanted to offer Lord Rothermere's son, Esmond Harmsworth, the Hungarian crown because of the former's passionate advocacy of their cause in his *Daily Mail*. Rothermere had turned it down after some reflection. Lederer never went back to Hungary and finally persuaded David Astor to give him a job on the *Observer*. Jan Gehrke was also taken into the fold. He had been number two at the Czechoslovak Embassy when Jan Masaryk was ambassador. Munich left him a penniless refugee and the Family appointed him transport officer of Marks & Spencer. He was said to be the lover of Daphne Sieff, the wife of Israel's elder son, Michael.

All the senior members of the clan had their favourite segment in British society, and the various families formed subclans. Simon and Miriam Marks sought the company of politicians, fashionable journalists and big business celebrities, but they also entertained titled decorators, brokers and favourites from the worlds of sport, film and theatre. Miriam had a lively, seemingly dotty manner, but was shrewd and very generous. Israel and Rebecca (Becky) Sieff preferred intellectuals to the social crowd. Most of the 'court intellectuals' had a limited life span with the Family. Some of them were given a temporary office in Baker Street and were commissioned to write papers, or indeed the history of Marks & Spencer. Simon Marks was never happy with the result. He did not realize that if a flourishing business made for spectacular balance sheets, it was not necessarily the stuff of a breathtaking narrative. So the hapless authors would be dismissed with Simon's chilling epitaph: 'Alas, he did not grasp the essential philosophy of our business.'

Newcomers were treated with benign curiosity. Once they had been suitably vetted they would make the circuit. As a friend and protégé of Flora, I was taken up by the Family and spent many weekends in a Marks, Sieff, Sacher, Blond or Laski house in the years before I married Jane, the daughter of Israel's younger brother Edward (Teddy). It was quite an adventure for me to move in this world with its own hierarchy and codes, conversational patterns, interests and prejudices. I saw a great deal of Marcus Sieff, Israel's son, who became my closest friend in the Family. A rugger blue at Cambridge, he was very good-looking and something of a ladies' man. Marcus had a distinguished war record. He inherited his father's dedication to Zionism and contributed more than anyone else in this country towards smoothing the transition from turmoil in Palestine to a functioning State of Israel, engaging a circle of able people to develop a new infrastructure.

For the Jewish community in Britain it was a time fraught with tension and problems. The Attlee-Bevin Government was adopting an increasingly pro-Arab, anti-Zionist course, and prominent Jews were torn in their loyalties between Britain and Zionism. Men like Simon Marks, Israel Sieff, his son Marcus and Sigmund Gestetner, a blunt but warm-hearted businessman who was one of Flora's admirers, took considerable personal risks in financing the purchase and transport of arms to support the Zionist cause. They also helped finance the illegal immigration of Jews from displaced-persons camps all over Europe.

A whole floor of Marks & Spencer was given over to the cause. The headquarters in Baker Street became the brain centre of a Jewish State-to-be, a sort of government-in-exile. Drawing on their retailing and management experience, the directors and senior executives were detailed to help set up systems for procuring supplies, training future civil servants and coordinating a forceful political lobby in Westminster. Marcus was responsible for influencing public opinion. He met with leading members of all parties to lobby for the cause and I used whatever contacts I had to help.

It would be difficult to exaggerate the enthusiasm that swept the Jewish community in Britain and elsewhere during that period from November 1947, when the United Nations decided to partition Palestine into a Jewish and Arab State, through the War of Independence up to the early stages of statehood. Even hitherto uncommitted people wanted to contribute to the cause. Flora undertook an important and consuming mission at the behest of Golda Meir, then Minister of Labour and in charge of absorbing the survivors from Hitler's death camps who were streaming into Israel from Europe. Most of the immigrants arrived without any possessions and had to be put up in makeshift camps. Conditions were appalling, and the local population could not cope with the influx. Flora was famed for her organizational skills – during the Second World War she had applied her Marks & Spencer reforms on a far larger scale, organizing soup kitchens and medical services for those who had lost their homes in the Blitz. She applied the same Marks & Spencer techniques in helping suppliers develop standards and efficiency in Israel. She also introduced cottage industries in the camps. The immigrants wove rugs and made pottery which they sold to buyers whom Flora brought in from all over the world. Her efforts did much to raise morale.

It was around this time that Flora turned to me one day and said, 'Georgek, it's time you did your bit.'

CHAPTER ELEVEN

A State Is Born:
A Year with President Weizmann

EVER SINCE MY CHILDHOOD in Vienna, when I had seen him on a newsreel, I had regarded Chaim Weizmann as a towering figure. The head of the World Zionist Organization had been the cause of a tumultuous anti-Semitic demonstration outside the concert hall, and my parents and I were very excited to see him on the screen. I thought him the most important Jewish leader of the twentieth century, since Herzl's death in 1904, a mixture of the prophet Isaiah and Dr Pasteur. Weizmann was then in his prime. By the time I met him he was a broken man.

It happened towards the end of 1947 at a small dinner in Flora Solomon's flat. The Weizmanns had arrived from New York and settled into the Dorchester, where they always took a suite once they had given up their Kensington home. He was still smarting from the crushing blow of being ousted from the presidency of the World Zionist Movement by David Ben-Gurion, almost fifty years to the day after the first Zionist congress in Basle. In December 1946 the congress had had to decide between peaceful or armed resistance to British colonial rule. At the root of this passionate controversy lay the British Government's White Paper, which virtually put an end to mass immigration.

It was the old story of 'dove' versus 'hawk'. Ben-Gurion, the 'hawk', stood for the unequivocal claim to statehood and militancy, and for convincing the British mandatory Government to lift wartime restrictions on Jewish immigration. Throughout the war Ben-Gurion had proclaimed: 'We must fight Hitler as if there were no White Paper, but simultaneously we must fight the White Paper as if there were no Hitler.' He had come to stand for the frustrated masses, for the people in the displaced persons camps, and also for the more radical mood of the Jewish population within Palestine. He relied increasingly on the United States and the power of American Jewry.

Weizmann was tainted by the British brush – the acute animosity that Ernest Bevin, supported by Attlee, felt for the Zionist cause was becoming more and more apparent. He was too much the statesman-philosopher, the old-fashioned liberal and would ideally have liked a Jewish State to be the seventh dominion, part of the British Commonwealth. Weizmann perceived Zionism as an organic, cultural and societal movement. He was more concerned with what sort of society the Jews could create than with the form of government they would have.

Weizmann had a vision of Israel as the Switzerland of the Middle East, with all the components of the Alpine state: high technology, civilized cantonization, tourism and neutrality. He believed in developing the country 'acre by acre and ox by ox', whereas 'political' Zionists like Herzl, and later Jabotinsky, who represented the opposite pole of Zionism, would argue: 'Let us first have a charter and create our sovereign homeland. Then we will be able to shape the society we want.' Ben-Gurion stood in the middle. He was a pioneer who belonged to the kibbutz movement and knew what it meant to till the soil or turn a marsh into arable land. At the same time he had a political vision.

Weizmann was Moses rather than Joshua. He saw the Promised Land and feared he would never be able to enter it. He was a negotiator, a mediator and a pacifist at heart. Ben-Gurion was a fighter. The struggle between Weizmann and Ben-Gurion had dominated the history of Zionism between the two wars and continued to reverberate long afterwards.

At the Congress in Basle a vote of censure was taken against Weizmann. Many of his protégés, acolytes and aides deserted him. It was a trauma which haunted him to his death. The chilly silence of the majority when he made his last plea for Gandhi-like passive resistance nearly deafened him. Old friends who sided with Ben-Gurion were banished from his life for ever. Reuven Shiloa, later to become one of the founders of Israel's secret service, and Teddy Kollek were among those who were kept at a distance. Later, during my time with Weizmann in Israel, Teddy often gave me a lift from Tel Aviv to the presidential house in Rehovot, but he had to drop me off at the gate.

Weizmann came to London thinking his political life had come to an end. He was in his early seventies and his health was not good. I found him dejected, but also eminently accessible, and a friendship developed. We went for walks in Hyde Park or I would call on him at the Dorchester at the end of my working day. There I would find him alone or with Isaiah Berlin or the faithful George Backer, an American newspaper editor and charming dilettante who was one of Weizmann's closest friends. There would be the odd American senator, or a British Member of Parliament, a member of the shadow cabinet, or the irrepressible Blanche Dugdale ('Baffy'), Balfour's niece and one of Weizmann's closest confidantes. She had a Zionist lunching salon in the private room of a Soho restaurant to which I was often bid.

I was gradually accepted into the narrower family circle. The Weizmanns had suffered the grievous loss of their youngest son, Michael, in 1942. He never returned from an RAF mission over the Bay of Biscay. Michael had obviously been the apple of his parents' eye and they never quite got over his death. The other son, Benji, was something of a maverick. Contrary and sardonic, he had a stormy relationship with his parents, half-revering, half-renouncing his father and positively loathing his mother. He was a lost soul and never really managed to find his feet. Marriage to the delightful and headstrong Maidie, a doctor, gave him some stability, but he divorced her and ended up farming in Ireland and the Channel Islands. Maidie was close to Flora Solomon and also became a good friend of mine.

Chaim Weizmann's self-pity was wholly inappropriate. He did not cease to be a pivotal figure, and in New York, where he had returned after his stay in London, he remained at the centre of the political struggle, valued not least because of his special relationship with President Truman.

In November 1947 the United Nations had voted for the partition of Palestine into a Jewish and an Arab State. The Attlee-Bevin Government had contested the decision and tried to nullify it by finding new solutions, such as a UN trusteeship or some sort of cantonal commonwealth with Jerusalem as an international city. Intense political activity took place in the Jewish camp to achieve the status of nationhood. On 15 May 1948 the Jewish State was proclaimed from an improvised dais at the Mughrabi cinema in Tel Aviv by David Ben-Gurion. On that day in London I stood with hundreds of other people, Jews and Gentiles, in Manchester Square, looking up at the balcony on which there stood the first diplomatic envoy, a distinguished Jerusalem lawyer, Dr Mordechai Eliash, flanked by Simon Marks, Israel Sieff and Richard Crossman, Labour's stormy petrel who had done so much to canvas the cause of Israel, even risking his political career. Ernest Bevin never forgave Crossman, whom he had sent as a senior member of an Anglo-American commission on the future of Palestine, his support for a Jewish State.

On the following day Weizmann, anxiously following events from his suite in the Waldorf Astoria, received news that the provisional council had elected him President of Israel. The next few months were tumultuous. Palestinian Arabs linked forces with Egypt, Syria, Lebanon, Iraq and Saudi Arabia, and, the most effective army of all, the Arab legion of Emir, later King, Abdullah of Jordan, trained by British officers. They attacked Jewish settlers, quite literally attempting to drive them into the sea. The first Jewish-Arab war, named the War of Independence, dominated that fateful Year One of the State of Israel. I played my modest part by broadcasting, writing and lobbying for Israel's survival. Marcus Sieff offered advice and technical expertise, and it was at this time that he turned the Baker Street head office of Marks & Spencer into a headquarters for the war effort, procuring food and money for what was most urgently needed – arms. The Arab armies had been left most of the stores and supplies of the retreating British forces, whilst the Jews had to fend for themselves. Surplus material came from every corner of the world, especially from Soviet and Eastern European sources. Men like Teddy Kollek and Ehud Avriel between them divided the globe in search of equipment, Teddy running guns and munitions from the Hotel Fourteen on New York's Fifth Avenue, and Avriel scouring the depots of Prague, Bucharest and Budapest. At one point he found himself lodging under an assumed name in a suburban Prague hotel whilst his Syrian opposite number was pursuing the same goal for a different cause on the floor above.

Zionist leaders from abroad, Israeli fundraisers and arms merchants came to London, and amid the flurry of activity Weizmann's devoted 'man of affairs', Meyer Weisgal, brought the latest news from the Weizmanns. It was far from reassuring. The Weizmanns were leading an isolated life in their Bauhaus mansion in Rehovot, nicknamed the 'White House' by Israelis. Once settled in the president's residence, Weizmann was ignored by Ben-Gurion and given no share in decision-making. In the President's, and particularly in Mrs Weizmann's, eyes, he was being belittled, slighted and underused. Since Ben-Gurion's office was a powerhouse of many mansions, all key positions in the prime minister's department and the foreign office – the two departments of state which interested Weizmann – were staffed with faithful Ben-Gurionites, and the old guard of Weizmannites, while represented, were distancing themselves from their erstwhile chief. But those who had Weizmann's wellbeing at heart felt he still had a moral and political role to play, especially because leaders like Churchill and Truman held him in high esteem, and complained that the President did not have his own staff who could keep him in touch with what was going on in the *kiryah*, the barbed-wired government enclave on the outskirts of Tel Aviv. The 'Chief' – Weizmann was always known as the Chief – was suffering.

Flora Solomon was particularly concerned, and in her mind was born the idea that someone from outside, someone untainted by Zionist politics, should go out and work for the President. She was not necessarily thinking of a permanent appointment, but one that would see the ailing President out. On one of her frequent visits to Israel she suggested to Weizmann and Moshe Sharett, the foreign minister, that I be considered for the job.

Sharett had been close to Weizmann in the past and had suffered most from the breach between the old man and Ben-Gurion. When my friend Frank Owen, then editor of the *Daily Mail*, sent me to Israel in May 1949 to write a series of articles, I went to stay with the Weizmanns. Flora accompanied me, and Weisgal and Sharett were also there. By the end of my stay I had been offered the position of liaison officer. My title was to be '*chef de cabinet*', head of the President's office and simultaneously senior counsellor in the foreign ministry, entrusted with writing speeches, receiving foreign heads of mission and, most importantly, briefing Weizmann on Israel's relations with the world.

On my return to London I consulted Harold Nicolson. Nigel and I had only just started Weidenfeld & Nicolson and I was in two minds as to whether I could leave the fledgling enterprise at such a crucial moment. As Balfour's secretary, Harold Nicolson had been at hand during the fateful cabinet meeting of October 1917 which finally decided that Britain would endorse the Declaration, demanding the establishment of a national home for the Jewish people in Palestine. Whilst the cabinet was in session Weizmann had been pacing up and down in the anteroom; his anxious wait was brought to an end by Sir Mark Sykes's announcement: 'Dr Weizmann, it's a boy.' Harold Nicolson understood diplomacy and thought that I was not really cut out to be a civil servant, but he wisely said that I would never forgive myself and would therefore always resent Nigel and him if I let the oppotunity go. So he advised me to take the job, making me promise that I would return after a year.

I entered Weizmann's services informally in the summer of 1949 and spent most of it commuting between London and the Bürgen-stock Hotel near Lucerne, where he had gone to rest. There I met other members of his family and his far-flung circle of friends, who hectored him and advised him on how to deal with the Government and Ben-Gurion. I sometimes travelled to Paris, Geneva and Amster-dam to make contacts with Israeli missions, local politicians and Zionist supporters. On my visits to London I had to make arrange-ments for my long absences, but I also fulfilled assignments on Weizmann's behalf and assembled information. Israel's relations with the Labour Government were of vital importance, and although the official policy was cool, there were sympathizers in the cabinet, such as Herbert Morrison and Arthur Creech-Jones, and there were friends in the TUC and on the backbenches.

Before officially taking my post I had to be vetted. Being a new country, Israel had only an embryonic security service which sprang from the underground movement Haganah. One of the heads of Haganah intelligence was an extraordinary man whose Hebrew name was Reuven Shiloa – Shiloa is a biblical mountain – but he had been born Zaslany, the son of a Russian rabbi. He had taught English and Hebrew at a Jewish school in Bagdad run by the Alli-ance Israelite, a French organization which catered for the education of well-to-do Jewish families in the Levant, so he spoke good Arabic and Russian. Shiloa had become a passionate Zionist. During the war he was recruited by Ben-Gurion and worked first in Jerusalem and then in Istanbul, where the Haganah and the Jewish Agency collaborated with the Allies by sending Jews behind Nazi lines and establishing contact with the ghettos in Europe. After the war he set up the secret service. He belonged to the Ben-Gurion faction and was naturally suspicious about the appointment of an unknown

Jew from England to a highly sensitive position where he would be privy to classified information. For all he knew, this stranger could, after all, have been 'planted'. Shiloa therefore insisted on screening me himself.

He was spending a week in Lausanne whilst I was in Bürgenstock and asked me to breakfast. The roads were not very good in those days, and it seemed to me as though we travelled all night in Weizmann's chauffeur-driven Bentley, arriving at the Hotel Beau Rivage at six o'clock in the morning. Shiloa was already up and waiting for me. It was a summery day and we had breakfast on the terrace. Shiloa looked like a mixture of a James Bond villain and the benign Samuel Pickwick. He was bald and squat, his face was scarred, he wore rimmed spectacles and dressed in an oversized American suit. He had a Peter Lorre-like smile and was reputed to be a great ladies' man. His brilliantly capacious mind was a walking enyclopaedia of names and careers of members of the political establishment in the West. Shiloa gave me a grilling which lasted all day. Towards the end he relaxed. He shook my hand impulsively and we became friends. I saw a great deal of him during my stint with Weizmann.

After my vetting I returned to Bürgenstock and later accompanied Dr Weizmann to Israel. Throughout the autumn I did a great deal of commuting, chiefly to help get Weidenfeld & Nicolson's first list off the ground. It was launched in November 1949 at a cocktail party in Brown's hotel where a hundred and fifty guests consumed more than a hundred bottles of the cheap champagne we offered them. Somerset Maugham was there and so were George Orwell, Peter Ustinov, Lady Violet Bonham-Carter, Sibyl Colefax, Simon Marks, Israel Sieff, James Pope-Hennessy, Stuart Hampshire, Dick Crossman and John Sparrow, to name but a few. But my mind was already on the other job. In December 1949 I left for Israel. Ten minutes before landing, the President's aide-de-camp, Major Arnon, greeted me over the radio with this exhilarating message: 'Welcome to Israel's air space.'

As soon as I arrived in Israel my rank became an object of dispute between various government departments. Vera Weizmann made it quite clear that since I was serving the head of state I had to be given a rank on a par with the head of the prime minister's office, which provoked a certain amount of jealousy. Like many others, the director-general of the foreign office, Walter Eytan, initially saw me as an intruder, but he came round to me. Born Ettinghaus, he had been a don at Magdalen College, Oxford and had worked for the British secret service at Bletchley during the Second World War before starting the Israeli Foreign Office. Later, he spent twelve years as ambassador in Paris and became quite close to de Gaulle.

The British Embassy was very puzzled as to who I was and what I was doing. I remember a curious man called Balfour, who ended up as a Greek Orthodox monk, eyeing me with suspicion. He was obviously the local spook. In those days one could take on such duties as I did on a British passport – the Israeli citizenship law was not ratified until 1952, by which time I had left.

My new life was divided between three different places. I had two rooms in a house on the Boulevard Rothschild in Tel Aviv which belonged to the parents of Dan Tolkovsky, later to become chief of the air force; I kept a room at the King David Hotel in Jerusalem; and I had a weekend sanctuary at Weizmann's residence in Rehovot, a serene market-garden town set in hilly surroundings about forty minutes from Tel Aviv. There, in the house the famous Bauhaus architect Eric Mendelsohn had built, the Weizmanns led a highly disciplined life in an atmosphere that blended the lifestyle of the upper-middle-class Kensington professional with a dose of luxury. Weizmann was well-off, thanks largely to Simon Marks and Israel Sieff who had given him founder shares in Marks & Spencer. Early on in their rise to wealth and power they had shrewdly assessed that the leader of Zionism should meet the 'Great and the Good' of Britain on reasonably equal terms. As a result Weizmann stood out among the other Zionist leaders, not only because of his formidable intellect but also because he felt independent. Thanks to his benefactors he was a dollar-a-year man who paid his own expenses and never drew a salary from the Zionist Organization, so he could afford to threaten with resignation. His wealth allowed him to adopt the aristocratic posture of the great Marquess of Salisbury, who could retire to his estate if he was not in sympathy with official policy.

Weizmann was a renowned chemist who had worked for the British Government and private companies between the wars and had kept his oar in research even when politics became all-consuming. His belief in the importance of scholarship to national renaissance lay at the heart of the Scientific Research Institute in Rehovot. It was founded at his suggestion and was endowed by the

Marks-Sieff-Sacher trio. First named after Israel Sieff's son, Daniel, and later renamed and vastly expanded as the Weizmann Institute of Science, it became one of the leading scientific research centres in the world. His involvement with the Institute had led Weizmann to spend more and more time in Palestine during the 1930s, and in order 'to have things like in London' his wife had commissioned Mendelsohn to build the new house nearby. Now a national museum, it is probably one of the best domestic specimens of the Bauhaus period. It had a beautiful garden and a spacious swimming pool with a magnificent view onto the plain of Judea.

Every celebrity, Jewish or non-Jewish, wanted to call on the old man and the Weizmanns did a great deal of entertaining. Life in Rehovot was rather grand by Israeli standards. The untrained servants were recent immigrants from Yemen or Hungary who spoke no languages other than their own, and there was an old English butler, but he was on his last legs. We lunched by the pool, depending on the Chief's state of health. Dinners often had to be cancelled at the last moment.

Weizmann wanted to be informed about international politics and the attitudes of other countries towards the Middle East. I made it my business to introduce him to interesting members of the diplomatic corps. At the lunches or dinners I organized for him I tried to mix politicians, cultural figures and distinguished visitors who were in large supply. Many foreign guests were put up in the White House. Jascha Heifetz and Leonard Bernstein came to stay whilst I was there. I found Bernstein very show-offy. I remember him playing football with Weizmann's grandson and was amused by the provocative way in which he wiggled his bottom as he conducted the Israel Philharmonic in a sleeveless shirt. The maids gossiped about Heifetz's despotic behaviour towards his wife. Whenever he came into a room she had to get up, they reported.

The Weizmanns were visited by a medley of American politicians, royalty from Scandinavia and elsewhere, Rothschilds and Hollywood stars such as Danny Kaye. Members of 'The Family' regularly drifted in and out, and I had a reunion with Richard Crossman, who was an intimate of the Weizmanns. The President particularly enjoyed the visit of Leo Amery, veteran Tory politician and friend of Winston Churchill. Amery was a life-long Zionist supporter. He brought along his son Julian, a contemporary of mine who was to make an interesting career in British politics. I noticed that he wore rather modish, pointed shoes of Italian make. While the two old men reminisced, Julian asked me sharp and pertinent questions about Israel's domestic affairs and the social mores of the young. With his Cartesian approach and cynical touch he seemed to me to have the mind of a French rather than a British politician. I took an instant liking to him.

Isaiah Berlin, of whom I was to see so much in the years to come, was a frequent visitor. Weizmann thought highly of him and tried to persuade him to enter the service of the State. He had used him as an intermediary during the Second World War when he was attached to the British Embassy in Washington, and the two men were close; they had much in common. Weizmann liked to take him for walks in the gardens in Rehovot. Isaiah and I used to stay up late, and when the others had retired we would regurgitate the events of the day. I fed him with gossip and enjoyed seeing the young Israel through his eyes. I always felt that he preferred to think of me in a Jewish role rather than on the social circuit. Indeed, he was one of the people who tried to persuade me to stay on in Israel.

Shortly after lunch the President would retire and would not reemerge before six o'clock. The Weizmanns spent many evenings alone playing gin rummy, or they would receive a never-ending cast of visitors from abroad. Vera Weizmann had few local friends – one often felt her heart was back in London, which she had always preferred to New York. The daughter of a regimental surgeon of the Tsarist Army from Rostov on Don, she was also qualified as a doctor. Her family belonged to that small segment of Russian Jewry that was enfranchised. There was only a handful of Jewish officers in imperial Russia, and her provenance left her with more than a touch of snobbery. She could be very patronizing, though she was sentimental as well as imperious. From the way she acted she might have been an English colonel's daughter. Strong-willed and domineering, she had a deep, booming voice, spoke with a heavy accent and chain-smoked through a long, elegant cigarette holder. The Russian habit of dropping the article turned her sentences into a string of nouns and verbs. She wore couture clothes, had formal manners, disliked folksy homeliness and winced when she heard Yiddish spoken – she regarded it as a language for plebs – though Weizmann loved the expressiveness of that language and made famous speeches in it. She was deferential towards the English upper classes and liked to be regaled with gossip about the Churchills, the Cavendishes and the Ormsby-Gores. She had, as most Jews do, a special foible for the Rothschilds, or the 'Rothchildren', as Dr Weizmann called them. But the ever-recurring leitmotif was the marital and extra-marital relations of the widely ramified 'Family', the codeword for the Marks, Sieff, Sacher, Laski and Blond clan that dominated Zionist Anglo-Jewry.

There were endless stories about Mrs Weizmann, about her sense of grandeur, her lack of knowledge of Jewish things and the way she was so impressed by Gentiles. There was an occasion when the new Soviet minister came to present his credentials, accompanied by a retinue of twelve diplomats and an equal number of officials from the Israeli foreign ministry. The Weizmanns gave a lunch at the pool which went on until teatime. Mrs Weizmann was in seventh heaven, speaking 'Tsarist' Russian, not Jewish Russian.

When we gathered for a postmortem at teatime, she enthused, 'Chaimchik, you know, these Russians are wonderful people, haven't changed at all. Ah, I had such a wonderful talk about Lermontov and Turgenev with the Russian diplomat, he was such a wonderful man.' Weizmann let her talk and urged her to describe him in greater detail. 'Ah, you would recognize him immediately,' she went on. 'He's got wonderful cheekbones and slit eyes and elegant bearing. He was the one dressed in striped suit like real gentleman.' At this point Weizmann pointed out that she had been talking to Mr Elyashiv, the head of the Russian section in the Israeli foreign office.

Mrs Weizmann invariably called her husband 'Chief' to others and Chaimchik when addressing him. They had met when they were both students in Geneva and had remained sweethearts for many years before they were officially engaged and eventually married. Since Weizmann was a Bohemian by nature, discursive and careless about dress and punctuality, Vera ruled her husband's life with an iron rod. One stern look and a hiss, 'Chaimchik', and she would call him to order. In Rehovot she tried to shield him from Zionist party politics and in-fighting, preferring to entertain grandees from abroad, which she did in a dignified, though somewhat stilted, way. But Zionist and Jewish leaders resented the aura of exclusivity which she built up around Weizmann.

She also kept him from his family. Weizmann had an elder

brother, Chilik, who had settled in Haifa. His son was Ezer Weizman, the founder of the Israeli air force, a distinguished Minister
of Defence (and since 1993 President of the State of Israel). That
part of the family was more or less banished from the house by
Vera, and young Ezer was too proud to push himself, although his
uncle was fond of him. Sometimes Ezer would fly very low over
Rehovot in a single engine aircraft, virtually blowing the roof off.
Mrs Weizmann was always furious, partly through jealousy and
partly through snobbery, but Weizmann chuckled.

Most of the time Weizmann fell in with her rigid regime, though
when she was not looking he would lapse into his old ways. He
had the caustic and self-mocking wit of the Russian intellectual
and could be both vindictive and cruel, dismissing people with one
crushing remark or delivering mordant parodies. Weizmann was at
the same time Bohemian and aristocratic, a Russian-Jewish Whig
– patriarchal, witty and sardonic. He was, as Isaiah Berlin has put
it in a brilliant essay, 'the first totally free Jew of the modern world'.
An autocrat and a leader, Weizmann's mood would shift from courteous attentiveness to intolerance and savage irony. He had his
traditional, ancestor-worshipping side, though he was an agnostic,
if not an atheist. He was at home with with kings and prime
ministers.

Weizmann's suits came from Savile Row, Hawes and Curtis were
his shirtmakers, his ties came from Sulka and his shoes from Lobb.
But he could also shuffle along in an old cardigan and he loved
ordinary people. Sitting in the garden in Rehovot, wearing dark
glasses because he was going blind, the old man used to have endless
conversations with his driver or the gardener. With his sense of the
bizarre, Weizmann also enjoyed the company of eccentrics, ghetto
figures, garrulous adventurers or mystical rabbis with long beards.
His favourite member of the cabinet was Rabbi Itze Meier Levin,
a figure straight out of *Fiddler on the Roof*, who represented the
Orthodox Aguda faction. He wore a kaftan and had a long beard
and a solemn expression, but would suddenly break into self-
mocking giggles. Trained in the Talmudic tradition of talking in
hyperboles and oblique allusions, he made Weizmann laugh. The
Chief was always in a good mood after a meeting with his Minister
for Social Welfare, and would tell me, 'You know, he's my favourite, he shaves under his beard.'

One day I joined them on a bench under the lime tree. As we sat talking, the Chief turned to the rabbi and asked him quizzically, 'Do you see the day coming when a great synod of rabbis will meet and bring our faith into the modern age?' Rabbi Meier raised both hands and his eyebrows in a gesture of perplexity. 'Before that happens this tree must learn to fly,' he quipped. Two seconds later he beamed and said, 'A synod, eh? A good idea. It could decide to stiffen the law of the Sabbath and make us pray more!'

I remembered this little episode many years later when reading an account of the preparations for the Vatican Council in 1963 when all the bishops of the Roman Church were asked to state their views on what, if anything, the Council should achieve. One ultra-conservative bishop sent a postcard with four lapidary Latin words: '*De Maria nunquam satis.*' (One can never say enough about the Virgin Mary.) Neither the bishop nor Rabbi Meier would relish this comparison, but I think there is much akin between the upper clergy of the two oldest branches of the family of monotheistic faith.

Weizmann was fortunate in having as his chief scientific assistant Ernst David Bergmann, an extraordinary young German biochemist who worked for his master with canine loyalty and demoniacal energy. In his few moments off he would run errands for Mrs Weizmann. Bergmann became an intimate of the couple, who regarded him as a substitute son. His father was a German Orthodox rabbi, but, though an atheist, Bergmann had a fanatical devotion to the Zionist State, believing, as Weizmann did, in the importance of science to the new Israel. He had a prodigious mind and drove himself ruthlessly, living on a diet of cigarettes and coffee while starving himself to the point where he almost had to be force-fed. He appealed to women and had, amongst others, a romance with Lorna, the widow of Orde Wingate, who, like her late husband, had the Bible-loving puritan's passion for Zion. It was Bergmann's infatuation with one of his assistants at the Institute, the wife of a prominent actor of the Habbima theatre in Tel Aviv, whom he later married, that later contributed to the rupture with Weizmann.

The Chief showed increasing distress as his protégé became involved in government work. He felt that the Institute was moving in the wrong direction under his influence and it pained him that Bergmann should allow himself to be lured by Ben-Gurion's plans to involve him in an atomic centre in the Negev desert. This crisis, which culminated in his resignation as Scientific Director, was building up during my year in Israel. It preyed on Weizmann's mind and affected his health. Almost every time I found myself alone with him, he would bring up the question of Bergmann's 'betrayal', irrespective of the context of our talks. It was a bitter blow to the old man.

Weizmann left domestic politics to a secretary, who prepared speeches for the various ceremonial occasions the President was asked to attend. His interests lay in foreign affairs, as did mine. My task was to liaise with foreign diplomats and draft speeches on world affairs, and to introduce new ambassadors and ministers to Weizmann when they presented their credentials, so I needed a morning suit. There was a wonderful Czech tailor in downtown Tel Aviv who had been a cutter in one of the finest establishments in Prague. I still wear the suit he made me on the few occasions when such formal attire is required.

During the week I worked in the presidential bungalow at the *kiryah* enclave in Tel Aviv, the de facto seat of government. The facilities were very primitive – Jerusalem was still contested internationally and only had skeletal government offices. With few exceptions the foreign missions and embassies were accredited in Tel Aviv, and most of the important ministries had their offices there, in Nissan huts or in houses that once belonged to the German Templar colony, a group of German settlers who had lived there before the First World War. At the outbreak of war they had been repatriated or taken prisoner. Their houses became the nucleus of the Israeli Government quarter, and were surrounded by barbed wire.

The sociological structure of the Government had a discernible pattern. The leadership, that is to say ministers and heads of department, tended to be Russian Jews; the middle rank and the administration were German Jews, who supplied system and efficiency; the dragoman class, on the lower rung, were Polish or Rumanian; and on the very bottom level were Sephardim, particularly Yemenites. Although they came from the most primitive part of the Arabian peninsula, the Yemenite Jews were alert and quick to learn. Minuscule, but beautifully formed, they made good soldiers, and skilled craftsmen.

My work centred around the *kiryah*. Once a week I visited the ceremonious presidential office in Jerusalem's new city near the

Mandelbaum gate, the divide between Israel and Jordan. I had a charming, matronly assistant, Aiga Shapira, who knew everything about protocol and briefed me on the intricacies and idiosyncrasies of emergent Israeli politics – she spared me many a faux pas. She was a cultured woman who came of good·Russian-Jewish intellectual stock and had excellent connections in the Zionist establishment. She had been a long-time companion of the scholar Schmarya Levin, a close friend of Weizmann's from their student days in Berlin and a champion of the Hebrew language who had been one of the great figures in Zionist cultural history. He had died by the time I met her and she shared a flat with her bachelor brother who was head of the Electricity Board.

The President's principal secretary specializing in home affairs was the mercurial Yigal Kimhi, an intelligent man of Oriental origin who looked like an affluent Oriental trader. He went his own way but never failed to cooperate when necessary. Relations with Major Arnon, the President's aide-de-camp and his Polish-born wife-cum-secretary who ran the household in Rehovot, were less smooth. Arnon was deeply unpopular, not least because of his peacock-like vanity. But he had the backing of Mrs Weizmann. As a matter of prestige she insisted he be given a rank higher than the prime minister's military aide. It fell to me to remonstrate with General Yadin, the reluctant chief of staff, that Arnon be promoted to the rank of lieutenant colonel. That was the occasion of my first meeting with the man who, together with his father Eliezer Sukenik, the Polish-born pioneering archaeologist, discovered the Dead Sea scrolls and later excavated Masada, where, in AD 73, 960 Jewish defenders killed themselves rather than fall into Roman hands. Yadin fought the battles of 1948 with maps based on the Bible. Using the Old Testament as his guide he worked out where the Philistines were defeated and deduced where a dried-up river might be which was mentioned in the Scriptures. He wrote copiously about his archaeological work and I published some of his books, including the internationally renowned *Masada*.

Among the friends I made at the foreign office was an eccentric old German-Jewish savant called Leo Kohn who came from Breslau and had a strong Silesian accent. He worked like a Chinese sage in a little pavilion belonging to the Ministry in that cluster of houses which had been part of the Templars' colony. There he sat, staring out of the window for hours on end, yet by the end of the day miraculously produced a sheaf of brilliant policy memoranda. I was lucky enough to be taken under his wing.

On Fridays I drove out to Rehovot in time for lunch, often accompanying the Foreign Minister, Moshe Sharett, who reported to the President once a week. I always sat in on their meetings. Sharett tried to act as a bridge between the 'White House' and Ben-Gurion. He came of Russian immigrant stock, and as a Palestinian Jew had served in the Turkish Army during the First World War. In the days before independence he had been head of the political department of the Jewish Agency and became one of the leaders of the Labour Party. Sharett had a shock of black hair and sported a Chaplinesque moustache. He was a gifted linguist. Didactic, pedantic and somewhat humourless, he spoke the English of a cultured Levantine, without hesitating or making a grammatical mistake, and his cadences were perfectly rounded off. He loved to hear himself talk. Sharett preferred his staff crowding into his office with an overflow squatting on the floor to the formality of meetings around a boardroom table. He was difficult to fathom, but he showed me nothing but kindness and I became devoted to him.

Sharett had a complicated relationship with Weizmann. Although a former disciple of his, he had sided with Ben-Gurion on the decisive issues leading to Weizmann's removal from the Zionist leadership in Basle. Neither man trusted him because each thought he tilted towards the other. Sharett always felt guilty towards Weizmann. He tried to mend his fences with him, but succeeded in doing so only partially; the Chief remained in two minds about him.

At their weekly meetings I often had to prevent the atmosphere from getting too sticky. Weizmann showed his ambivalence in subtle ways. When he felt well-disposed towards him he would affectionately call him Moshe. When he was testy he called him Moses. He was never openly hostile, but became sardonic. I began to read Weizmann's moods, and when I heard the codeword Moses I winced and knew we were in for a difficult time.

'Well, Moses, tell me, what's new in the world?'

Weizmann led Sharett on only to cut him down to size. The Foreign Minister rose to the bait every time, sometimes allowing himself to get flustered and tongue-tied.

'You know, Chief,' he once announced proudly, 'we had a major triumph last week. For the first time the United Nations coopted an Israeli delegate to a subcommittee. It shows we are making our mark in the international community.'

Weizmann commented sourly, 'What a triumph. It reminds me of the story of the bellboy in a Carlsbad hotel who wrote to his parents: "Dear Parents, I am making great progress. I am now allowed to serve those clients who never tip." '

On another occasion when the President was in one of his sarcastic moods, Sharett told him, 'Well, Chief, we now have diplomatic relations with thirty countries. That requires a great deal of correspondence and we have a hundred and fifty thousand words in cables a day.' To which Weizmann replied, 'Ah, you remind me of the two marriage brokers who were always busy, always rushing around sending each other telegrams. They invariably ended up with two bridegrooms or with two brides. So they never made a single match.' Nonetheless he seemed to look forward to Sharett's weekly *tour d'horizon* of Middle East and world affairs.

Weizmann's health was failing and his powers of concentration were erratic. There were moments when he could be rapier-sharp, and others when his mind wandered and his capacity for taking things in was very uneven. He had always been moody, but this trait was particularly noticeable in his final years when he was old and sick. I had to help him update his autobiography, *Trial and Error*, which had been published early in 1949. He was often bedridden and not really capable of working, so we just went through the motions. But Vera Weizmann always kept up the pretence. She would say, 'So glad you had good session with Chief.'

Weizmann knew he had no real power. He was frustrated by illness and old age and resented being a mere symbol. In his gloomier moods he would refer to himself as the 'Prisoner of Rehovot'. People in his entourage made matters worse by lamenting to his wife who would then nag him — 'Ben-Gurion doesn't consult you.' 'Ben-Gurion doesn't give you pride of place.' 'Ben-Gurion doesn't ask you to undertake big diplomatic missions abroad,' — when it was perfectly obvious that the doctors would advise against such arduous undertakings. At times he ignored the nagging, but then his bitterness would surface and he would snap at Sharett, 'I know what you want me to be: a Swiss president. That is what Ben-Gurion said when I took the job. I don't want to be a Swiss president. Why can't I be an American president?' Sharett always tried to appease him: 'But Chief, you have so much moral authority. After all, you are who you are!'

Ben-Gurion's attitude to Weizmann was ambivalent. He respected him as a scholar and man of the world; at the same time he looked on him as so many men of action look on intellectuals – he regarded him as a spectator, a compromiser who lacked incisiveness on important issues. Weizmann saw Ben-Gurion as an autodidact, a muddled thinker and militant rabble-rouser, but he also admired his toughness and his capacity to see through unpopular policies. Once, when we were discussing Ben-Gurion, he told me, 'You know, I couldn't have done what he did during the War of Independence. I couldn't have led a nation at war.' I think Weizmann was being too harsh on himself. He was nearly seventy-four years old and in bad health when he became head of state. Had he been younger in 1948, he would probably have been just as ruthless a national leader as Ben-Gurion.

Even so, there were times when Weizmann played a crucial role. His correspondence with Churchill did much to improve Anglo-Israeli relations at a time when the British Foreign Office showed a good deal of antipathy towards the new State. He had great moral authority, which he brought to bear in the Korean War by persuading the Israeli Government to toe the Western line.

For the first two years of statehood, Israel had remained neutral – French was the second official language because the Israelis wanted to break with the tradition of the British mandate. Besides, there was a feeling that the British had more sympathy with the Arabs, whilst the French began to show an affinity with the Israeli point of view when later, at the height of the Algerian crisis, President Nasser of Egypt, the arch enemy of the Jewish State, supported the National Liberation Front. The Soviet Union maintained friendly relations with Israel and was the first country to recognize the new state de jure, six hours before the Americans recognized it de facto at the United Nations. In the early days Moscow favoured Israel because the Arab world was then a group of feudal kingdoms in cahoots with the British, and it was Soviet policy to embarrass the British in the Middle East.

But the Korean war proved a watershed. Weizmann swayed events from his sickbed in Rehovot. He was furious when there was a hint that the cabinet wanted to remain neutral in the crucial UN vote – there was a principle at issue, and the President felt that

Israel had to take a stance, so he instructed me to summon a meeting of the inner cabinet. He was feverish but in full possession of his mental powers, and in a croaky voice delivered a sort of Gettysburg address to the ministers at his bedside, arguing that, 'We of all people must be on the side of the victims of aggression. Israel will be judged by moral standards.'

The Israeli Government voted with the Americans against the Chinese in Korea. Relations between Israel and the Communist world never recovered. But the break would have come sooner or later. The Soviets now realized that the emotional and financial ties with American Jewry had swayed Israel in America's favour and that neutrality was unsustainable, so when the various revolutions took place in the Arab world, the Soviets saw that they had a far bigger constituency there than in a pro-Western, capitalist Jewish State. The famous Slánsky show trial in Prague in 1952, where the Secretary-General of the Communist Party was condemned to death for 'Titoist and Zionist intrigues', had already indicated the way things were moving.

Weizmann took a strong line on human rights. I remember him intervening in a question regarding the treatment of Arabs. Philip Toynbee reported in the *Observer* that there had been some rough handling of Arab infiltrators on the Jordanian border. Weizmann summoned General Yadin to his sickbed and demanded that the Israeli frontier guard be disciplined. He lectured the chief of staff on how the Israelis of all nations had to attain higher standards on human rights than anyone else.

My job of liaising between Weizmann and the Government became routine after a while, not least because relations improved. Teddy Kollek, who was in charge of the American desk in the foreign ministry, and Sharett decided to put me in charge of a significant public relations campaign entitled 'Operation Jerusalem'.

When the United Nations had agreed on the partition of Palestine in November 1947, they had excluded Jerusalem from the Jewish State. At the time when I was in Israel the status of Jerusalem had still not been defined – it was partitioned between Israel and Jordan. The Old City had been lost to the Jordanians, and now the Jews, who had regarded Jerusalem as their capital since the days of David and Solomon, feared that they might also be deprived of the New City. At the United Nations, pressure was being exerted to turn Jerusalem into a separate entity under UN trusteeship, and in

January 1950 the UN Assembly adopted a resolution on the inter-nationalization of Jerusalem in a vote carried largely by a coalition of Arab–Latin-American–Catholic–Communist delegates. Obviously Israel was bitterly opposed to the separation of Jewish Jerusalem from the Jewish State, and Weizmann penned letters of protest to world leaders. The Government launched 'Operation Jerusalem' as a worldwide propaganda campaign to retain the New City. It allocated a budget of a million pounds to the campaign, a princely sum in those days, and I was entrusted with the coordination.

I set up a flying headquarters and hired a specialist staff to collaborate on a multimedia venture. We lobbied the press, arranged lecture programmes and exchange visits and issued a brief listing twenty-one arguments why the New City should remain part of Israel. We also published a beautiful book called *Jerusalem the Golden* in eight languages. All Israeli embassies and consulates were harnessed to the task. In New York, Gideon Rafael, one of the sharpest minds in the service, later to become ambassador in London during Harold Wilson's premiership, coordinated work in both the Americas. It was a heady experience which took up most of my time for six months.

There were plans for an ambitious festival for which we sadly never found the funds, but some of the ideas bore fruit years later. I brought Nicolas Nabokov together with Evzerov, the Israeli impresario of Russian descent who was full of gargantuan concepts, some of which came off thanks to his stubborn will. He raised the money for the Jerusalem Convention centre, a building which stands on the edge of the road which winds up from Tel Aviv and greets the visitor to Jerusalem. For years it was the most impressive modern edifice of that city until a new and imaginative building programme began under Teddy Kollek's mayoral rule. When we were still dreaming up grand schemes for a Jerusalem festival, Nicolas and I travelled to Naples to interview the director of the San Carlo opera house about a season of operas with biblical themes. Nicolas, who would have given anything to direct a great opera house or music festival, was enthusiastic about his suggestions. We telephoned Evzerov and Nicolas reeled off an exciting and adventurous programme ranging from the obvious to the obscure: Verdi's *Nabucco*, Rossini's *Moses in Egypt*, Halévy's *La Juive*, *Joseph* by Méhul and *The Queen of Sheba* by Karl Goldmark. When he added *Salome*, Evzerov bellowed from across the Mediterranean, 'You can't play Richard Strauss at a festival in Israel. That would be worse than Wagner.'

In early 1950 I was given an insight into the negotiations between the Israelis and Abdullah of Transjordan. These secret talks were conducted in the most bizarre manner. At sunset a group of Israeli leaders dressed in Bedouin clothes crossed the no-man's-land and made their way along a trail to Suneh, the royal winter palace. All through the night they discussed plans to make a separate peace between Jordan and Israel with Abdullah and his advisors. The agenda included a common currency, a customs union, a pact of non-aggression and a corridor through the West Bank 1.5 kilometres in width. It shows how close the two countries were to peace.

The cast of Israeli negotiators varied. It included Golda Meir, Reuven Shiloa, who had vetted me in Lausanne, and Moshe Dayan. More often than not Eliahu Sasson, a Sephardic Jew who had been head of the Arab department of the Jewish Agency, was also of the party. His first language was Turkish; in those days the Jordanian court spoke Turkish in preference to Arabic. These discussions were always informal – there was no protocol. In the course of a discussion the Jordanian monarch sometimes turned and whispered something in Turkish to one of his aides. He did not necessarily know that Sasson could understand, but since all parties were double-bluffing each other, some of the Israelis felt that he was using him to let their side know what he thought. Abdullah was very disrespectful of the other Arabs. His council was divided and pleaded, 'Your majesty, you are giving away so much to the Jews. What would our friends the Iraqis say?' Whereupon the Emir burst into a stream of florid curses about some of his fellow Arab rulers.

At dawn the delegation returned. On their way home they were debriefed in a house belonging to the military governor of Jerusalem. Secretaries would be waiting there ready to take dictation from them while the events of the night were still fresh. I was enlisted to collate the raw material of these proceedings and make an English language précis. The talks proceeded after I left Israel, but then came to an abrupt halt because the British did not want the Jews to make a peace treaty with Jordan lest it weaken King Farouk's position in Egypt. Hence Sir Alec Kirkbride, the British ambassador in Jordan, was far from helpful to these peace efforts. An agreement was never signed, and shortly afterwards the Emir was killed by an extremist in the mosque of El Axsa.

Through my friendship with Teddy Kollek and Reuven Shiloa, I became close to the Ben-Gurion entourage, though of course I was Weizmann's man. Teddy could easily have dismissed me as an outsider who could not even speak Hebrew, but he was warm without ever being patronizing. He saw me one day sweating in a wintery shirt. Next morning he sent me three silk shirts from his wardrobe. They were gifts from an American admirer of his which fitted me because we have similar frames. I still have his green silk shirt and wear it with pride.

Teddy drew me into many ad hoc meetings on the most diverse subjects and shielded me from Byzantine intrigues. He took me into the inner circle. The elite was made up of a group of people most of whom had been in the underground. They belonged to the Labour Party, not Irgun, the radical Zionist underground organization, which at one point was led by Menachem Begin. At that time I never came across such figures as Begin, who were the 'men behind the mountain'. They were isolated and in permanent opposition, rather like the Communist Party in France. Had Teddy Kollek left the stage in 1964 before he started a new career as mayor of Jerusalem, he would still have deserved his place in the history of Israel. He laid the foundations of a tourist industry and had a big share in the ambitious scientific and technical aid programme in Africa, on which he worked in close collaboration with Shimon Peres and Ehud Avriel.

The only one of Ben-Gurion's close aides I managed to smuggle into lunch at the White House was Ehud Avriel. He had been the first Israeli minister in Bucharest, and Weizmann's curiosity about what was going on in Romania prevailed over his resentment. Avriel and Teddy Kollek were like Castor and Pollux. They came from the same district of Vienna and had lived in the same kibbutz, Ein Gev, on the shore of Lake Tiberias. Both were pivotal figures in organizing the illegal immigration of Central European Jews. Ehud had sat face to face with Eichmann and rescued ten thousand Jewish children from his clutches. During the first Arab–Israeli War he did invaluable service as an arms procurer and Scarlet Pimpernel in the Balkans. He had left Vienna for Palestine in his teens to work in a kibbutz, changing his name from Überall to Avriel. An autodidact who had read widely and could recite Rilke, Goethe and

Schiller effortlessly, Ehud could have made a brilliant career but for his lack of organizational skills. He was a typical underground fighter, unable to reconcile this ability with that of the nimble technocrat in the way that Teddy could.

Avriel was convinced that Europe, and especially Germany, held the key to Israel's future, just as Reuvan Shiloa believed that the future lay with the United States. That sounds like a truism today, but just after the Second World War the US State Department was distinctly pro-Arab. General Marshall opposed the Jewish State and Roosevelt had given an undertaking to Ibn Saud that the Americans would not establish a Jewish State without the express approval of the Saudis. The friends of Israel in official Washington were few and far between. Avriel built up close relations with Conservative politicians in Germany, particularly the foreign minister, Heinrich von Brentano, and Baron Guttenberg, who was instrumental in the forging of the Grand Coalition of 1966. Ehud Avriel also shared my interest in winning support in the Catholic camp. Sadly, he died early of cancer.

Moshe Pearlman also belonged to this circle. He was a colourful figure who gave up a job in English journalism to emigrate to a kibbutz where he joined the Haganah. During the Second World War he had served as assistant press attaché at the British Embassy in Athens together with the cartoonist Osbert Lancaster. The only thing the two men had in common was a prominent moustache. For the rest they detested one another: each bore atavistic prejudices against the other. Moshe thought that Osbert was an inbred White's club anti-Semite, and Osbert regarded Moshe as a pushy and devious 'Hebrew'. Moshe was in fact a delightful character with a sunny disposition. In pre-State days he did some valuable work assembling arms and arranging transports of illegal immigrants for Haganah from HM Embassy's chancellery in Athens. When I met him he was running the Israeli Government press office. He was a brilliant communicator, probably the best army and government spokesman Israel has ever had. A devoted follower of Ben-Gurion and later of Dayan, and an intimate friend of Teddy Kollek, he became the Boswell of half of Israel's political leadership, helping them with or ghosting their memoirs.

In that early phase of statehood there was a feeling of constant improvisation. I learnt in that year in Israel what it means to build up a new country, and felt strongly reminded of that atmosphere when, after the collapse of Communism in Eastern Europe in 1989, I began to have dealings with Czechs, Hungarians and Poles. There were many parallel features. During that period of transition after the proclamation of the State, all kinds of people from outside, some self-serving, some sacrificial, offered their services, privately or with highfalutin titles like Economic Advisor to the Cabinet, or Personal Adviser to the Prime Minister. There were specialists to hand with practical advice as well as intellectual mercenaries and idealists trying to help. Flora Solomon's work in the immigration camps is a case in point.

Usually initiatives were taken in a haphazard way. I remember a group of us sitting together once and deciding that we needed the equivalent of the British Council to promote Israeli culture and coordinate the teaching of Hebrew abroad. Six or eight of us convened that evening at a vegetarian restaurant opposite the Dan Hotel in Tel Aviv, and there, over a meal of cheesecake, yoghurt and herring, we set up a new body and arranged to get it approved by the cabinet. The system was still very elastic. We were filled with a spirit of adventure and fired by a belief in the impossible.

Many young talents rose to new heights in those heady days. They were the golden boys of Israel. Eliahu Elath was in his thirties when he became Israel's first ambassador to the United States, having done yeoman work at the State Department and on Capitol Hill as the head of the Jewish Agency's Washington office in the gestation period leading up to the proclamation of the State. Abba Eban, still in his twenties, was so effective in putting Israel's case to the United Nations that he was made permanent representative there, before being rewarded with the ambassadorship in Washington. Probably one of the finest brains of his generation anywhere in politics, he shone as an orator; not, however, as a listener. Though much fêted abroad he never found a constituency in Israel wide enough to secure the highest office.

Yigael Yadin was only thirty-two when he became chief of staff, and Moshe Dayan, whom I got to know much better later, was already a hero in his early thirties, having defended Jerusalem against the Arab Legion, the toughest and best-equipped of the Arab armies, in the War of Independence. The most popular of all the young generals was Yigal Allon, who won the famous battle of the Faluja pocket against the Egyptians in 1948 and became an idol of the nation. He told the story of how he was sitting at a camp fire with two Egyptian field officers who had been taken prisoner. They were discussing the battle that had just taken place. Allon asked one of them, 'Why do you think you have lost the war?' The man answered, 'Because our officers are too fat and our soldiers are too thin. But one day we will beat you.' Turning to his fellow-officer who was sitting next to him smoking a pipe, he said, 'We will go home and make a revolution. We will unseat King Farouk.' Those two men were Nasser and Neguib.

Allon, with whom I made fast friends, appealed to the Chief because he saw in him the romantic Zionist. He belonged to that section of Israeli kibbutz elite which was drawn from old settler families, mainly of Russian origin, many of whom had worked in the Haganah. A number of public servants remained active members of kibbutzim on leave of absence, whilst their families continued living in the kibbutz. Some of them regarded their kibbutz background rather like the English gentry would their country estate. If they did not like what was going on at the centre of power they would return to their kibbutz and sell oranges or do administrative work and lead collectivist lives. The kibbutz and Haganah aristocracy formed the best element in the country. Only the elite made it into Palmach, the crack troop of the Haganah, which was commanded by Yigal Allon with Yitzak Rabin as his number two.

Then there was the old Zionist aristocracy, which counted the Gurs and the Ruppins among its leading families. Hadassah Samuel, the beautiful daughter-in-law of Herbert Samuel, was a Gur. Her father edited the first Hebrew dictionary. The Ruppins were German Jews. Their daughter married Yigael Yadin. The Schwartzes were among the grandest Israeli families because they had been in Palestine for several generations. Ruth Schwartz, the daughter of a respected lawyer in Jerusalem, married Moshe Dayan, and her sister married Ezer Weizman. I went to Ezer's wedding in 1950, where people sang South American sambas and rumbas with new Hebrew words and we danced in gay abandon. There were two parties, one of which was held in the grounds of the Ministry of Defence, hedged by barbed wire. At one point a crowd suddenly surged forward out of nowhere to join in the dancing. I recognized a number of faces from my Vienna schooldays, faces I had not seen since. We eyed each other uneasily. They were clearly spooks coming in from the cold. There was some winking and nodding between us but nothing more. The second wedding party was given by the bride's parents in their beautiful old Jerusalem home, and encompassed *tout Israel*.

The Herzogs also belonged to the elite. Isaac Herzog, the father of the former president, Chaim Herzog, had been Chief Rabbi of Ireland before becoming Chief Rabbi of Palestine and later of Israel. Once, when Isaiah Berlin was staying with the Weizmanns, Rabbi Herzog invited us to a Passover evening. Once the candles have burned down Jews are not allowed to light new candles after sunset or put on the light. It was a moonless night, and when the party broke up we all groped around in the dark to find our hats. Everybody grabbed the wrong one. Next day a despatch rider had to deliver a dozen or so hats to their rightful owners.

Rabbi Herzog played a crucial role as a mediator between synagogue and State. It was ironic that the first Jewish State for two thousand years should have an agnostic or even partly atheist Labour Government, but it had to work with the religious community for better or for worse. There were bizarre compromises. In order to get the religious vote, the Government had to make concessions on the most exacting rules of observance. Similarly, the religious faction had to stomach the mentality of the Labour regime, which, in their eyes, violated the Mosaic laws. Old Rabbi Herzog was an ombudsman between the parties. Three decades later his son Chaim, known as Vivian to his friends, was elected president against a three-line whip of the Begin supporters, thanks to the defection of some of the religious community who remembered what his father had done to make peace between the fighting factions.

Vivian had been a major in the Irish Guards. Good-looking in an Anglo-Irish sense, he had an attractive wife who came of a wealthy Russian-Jewish family which had lived in Alexandria for three generations. Her pretty sister Suzy was married to Abba Eban. Vivian had an illustrious career. A British officer in the Second World War, he was Director of Military Intelligence in the early years of the State and became the first military governor of Jerusalem immediately after the Six Day War. I visited him with Pamela Berry and the young Winston Churchill in the week after that war. We talked for hours on the roof terrace of the St George Hotel in East Jerusalem about the dramatic capture of the Old City by Israeli troops and the prospects that lay ahead. Vivian gained world prominence with his brilliant radio and television commentaries on the Yom Kippur War of 1973. His book, *The War of Atonement*, published by us in 1975, is an outstanding record of that campaign which had such a deep impact on the Israeli psyche. When he was ambassador to the United Nations in the mid-1970s he proved an effective debater.

Vivian and his wife Aura entertained beautifully in their Fifth Avenue apartment which was sandwiched between those of Jackie Onassis and 'Punch' Sulzberger, the owner of *The New York Times*. During his first official visit to England after he became president in 1983, I transformed the drawing room of my flat into a miniature banqueting hall with the help of the ingenious Diana Phipps, and entertained the presidential couple for a dinner attended by old and new faces. When Herzog paid a state visit to Bonn I mobilized some of my friends in the German press. My friend the magazine publisher, Hubert Burda, an ardent supporter of Israel, hosted a dinner at Schloss Brühl with about thirty German proprietors and editors where the President used his skills as a professional communicator to field frank questions on the sensitive topic of German-Israeli relations.

Vivian had a younger brother, Jacob, who might well have become prime minister one day but for Golda Meir. A devout but enlightened Jew, he was an ordained rabbi, though one would not have thought so on seeing him, for he was clean-shaven and conventionally dressed like an elegant Englishman. He spoke with a charming Irish lilt and had a wonderful sense of humour. Jacob was a polymath, equally well versed in secular and religious matters. In Jerusalem, where he lived, he had good personal contacts with the various religious communities, from the Catholics to the Abyssinians and the Copts. Ben-Gurion apointed him head of the interfaith department in the Ministry of Religious Affairs and made him one of his most trusted foreign policy advisors. Knowing that I spoke Italian and took an interest in the politics of the Catholic Church, Jacob invited me to attend important meetings with the Catholic clergy. We were more or less contemporaries and became firm friends. Jacob was appointed director-general of Prime Minister Eshkol's office during the '67 war, but he did not fare well under Golda Meir's premiership. She was not at ease with intellectuals and replaced him with Simcha Dinitz who made a name for himself as Israel's ambassador in Washington during the Nixon-Kissinger era.

Jacob gave me unusual insights into Jerusalem as a microcosm of world Christianity, explaining the subtle difference in the attitudes of Christian denominations to each other, to the Arabs, to the Jews, to Israel, to the world. He taught me how to speak to a Greek Orthodox, how to reassure an Abyssinian Christian, how to talk to Lutherans and above all what tone to strike with the Vatican. He also helped me with 'Operation Jerusalem'. Sadly, he died young of cancer, but we kept in touch until his death. I published a posthumous collection of his essays and articles under the title *The People That Dwell Alone*. It is a brilliant book.

My friendship with the Herzog brothers brought me incalculable benefits, one of which was to meet Professor Gershom Scholem, one of the world's leading experts on mysticism. An archetypal German-Jewish intellectual of the Weimar mould, his study was furnished in the German *Altvater* style. A polymath, kindly at times, irritable, benignly avuncular and sneering by turns, he wrote the standard work on the kabala and was respected by scholars of all denominations. Indeed, such was his reputation that he was given a state funeral when he died, and the traffic stopped for a few minutes as a gesture of mourning.

Intellectuals were held in high regard in Israel, but they were not the people who ran the country. In its early days the Hebrew university kept very much to itself. Weizmann, who had hoped it would have 'a centripetal force, attracting all that is noblest in Jewry throughout the world' when he laid the foundation stone in 1918, fell out of sympathy with it, not least because it was even more dovish than he. Its politics were not in accord with mainstream Zionism. Martin Buber's belief in a binational state where Jews and Arabs lived in symbiosis found fertile ground at the Hebrew university, as did the views of the American jurist Louis Brandeis, with whom Weizmann had clashed bitterly over the direction of the Zionist Organization.

With my omnivorous appetite for conviviality, I found it fascinating in a Proustian sense to watch the beginnings of a society and see cosmopolitan snobbism gradually impinge on the pioneering spirit. Very few patrician, worldly Jews settled in Palestine, and social life was rather austere, though not without adventure and frivolity. British Jews introduced touches of Kensington and Hampstead, while some of the richer Sephardic Jews tended to be more Francophile and echoed the spirit of Alexandria or Paris. But the British colonial past was the predominant influence.

Foreign diplomats caused something of a sensation, and the wives of industrialists and bankers would vie with each other to have the various dignitaries to dinner. The *chef de protocol* would come along beforehand to instruct the hostess in the nuances of '*placement*' and other social niceties. Wealth played a less important part than position and status in the Government. Of course there was a nouvelle société which gave big parties, led a loose life, ate pork and shellfish and drank expensive French cognac in spite of the austerity programme which made it illegal to import such things. I dubbed them the '*jeunesse d'orange*', because their money often came from citrus fruits. They were rather looked down on – just as in the Sweden of Gustavus Adolphus or Prussia in the eighteenth century the servant of the State ranked higher than the man of money.

This all changed later, particularly after Begin came to power in 1977 and the display of wealth became more ostentatious. But during my time there most people still lived on modest salaries, and parties were informal get-togethers after a meal with mainly non-alcoholic drinks and canapés, although they were called wine and cheese parties. I will always remember the warm summer evenings when we would sit on the roofs or in open-windowed apartments drinking Turkish coffee or tea from a glass in the Russian way, and talk endlessly about one subject: the future of Israel.

CHAPTER TWELVE

Publish and Nearly Be Damned

WHEN THE TIME CAME for me to return to London in September 1950, it was like the clock striking midnight at Cinderella's ball. I felt bound to the undertaking I had given to the Nicolsons that I would come back to publishing after a year's sabbatical, but I was loath to leave.

Many people tried to change my mind. The Weizmanns could not quite grasp why I would not stay on. They thought the job was still important, although Chaim's health had deteriorated to such an extent that his public duties were becoming necessarily less and less onerous. Sharett had appreciated my work on 'Operation Jerusalem' and offered me a permanent job in the foreign ministry. Tempting though it was, I did not allow myself to be swayed, but I promised to go on serving Israel's cause in whatever way I could. It is, I think, a promise I have kept.

In England I felt a curious mixture of a sense of homecoming and a need to find myself again. The year amid the Jewish pioneers had been a formative experience. I missed the sense of purpose and the intensity I had experienced in Israel, where we had all been almost monomaniacally absorbed by local issues, and found London conversation detached and diverse. By the spartan standards prevailing in Israel, postwar London seemed a Babylon of plenty and frivolity. I needed a period of ideological decompression, and had to relearn conventional small talk.

To add to my woe a love affair which had begun before I left for Israel came to an unhappy end. Marriage had been on the cards, but the object of my affection, an anglicized blonde of Austrian-Jewish origin, was still married to an English MP. By the time I left, the divorce had not come through, and in my absence she started another relationship. There was a failed attempt at reconciliation on my return, after which she went back to her new man. Feeling wretched, I threw myself into the publishing business.

From Israel I had kept in touch with all that went on at the firm as we gradually phased out *Contact* and established a general list under the imprint of Weidenfeld & Nicolson, and of course I had been there for the launch of our first list in November 1949. Foremost among the books we published that season were Mussolini's memoirs, which I had obtained through Raymond Klibanski, an academic who had been involved in wartime propaganda against Fascist Italy. Mussolini had written them in 1943 while he was held captive by General Badoglio, and they had come out in the Republic of Salò, but nobody in Britain knew about them. Our book did quite well.

We also published the memoirs of Hitler's Minister for the Economy, Hjalmar Schacht, under the title *Account Settled*. It was the first of many documentary books on Nazi Germany which we were to publish in the years to come. The other titles were *Truth Will Out*, an intellectual autobiography of Charlotte Haldane, the former wife of the Communist scientist J.B.S. Haldane, and a new translation of Goethe's *Truth and Fantasy*. The next two lists were a potpourri: *Stalin Means War* by Colonel Tokaev, one of the first Russian defectors, Alan Ross's *The Forties*, Giovanni Verga's *The House by the Medlar Tree*, Erich Kästner's *A Salzburg Comedy*, *Simpson* by Nigel's cousin Edward Sackville-West, and *Letters of Gustave Flaubert*, selected by Richard Rumbold, a friend of the Nicolson family who committed suicide years later. He was the nephew of the famous ambassador Sir Horace Rumbold, under whom Harold Nicolson had served in Berlin.

The publishing fraternity was largely dismissive of us. When we launched the first list, bets were made in the Savile club that Weidenfeld & Nicolson would not last more than a year. Victor Gollancz, Frederick Warburg and Hamish Hamilton were more hostile than most. Hamish Hamilton's dislike of me went beyond professional jealousy – after all, he was a highly successful publisher. An American by birth, he had set up in London as Harper's agent, helped by his close friendship with Cass Canfield, the head of Harper and the grand seigneur of American publishing. In the 1930s he had started his own firm and built up a very distinguished list. Through his American connections and his work for the American department of the Ministry of Information during the war, Hamish Hamilton had gained a virtual monopoly of the best American fiction and non-fiction, counting John Gunther, Walter Lippmann, Raymond Chandler and the bestselling James Thurber among his authors. Hamish Hamilton was also strong on French writers – he distributed Cyril Connolly's magazine *Horizon*, and his list very much reflected Cyril's Francophile taste. Hamilton was married to an Italian aristocrat, the Contessa Yvonne Franchetti. They lived in Hamilton Terrace, St John's Wood, where they entertained a wide circle in great style. I think Hamish Hamilton suspected me of competing with him in this technique of mixing work and social life, making authors feel that they had a hearth over and above the counting house in their publisher's office.

Others were more benevolent towards me. William Collins was friendly. So was Jonathan Cape, who gave me generous advice. He took Nigel and me out to lunch at Claridge's one day and told us, 'You must hang a framed notice above your desk stating that the only profits of a publisher are his economies.' Sir Stanley Unwin also offered pearls of wisdom. He pronounced, 'I can only give you one piece of advice. Any book on Mary Queen of Scots will always sell. No book on Latin America will ever sell. Beyond that you are on your own.' He was the chairman of the Publishers Association and felt he had to induct new members, but I was under no illusion that he would have been as friendly if I had gone to see him without Nigel. Allen Lane, the founder of Penguin, was most encouraging. He wrote us a letter saying ours was the best first list that he had ever seen. He probably had the ulterior motive of keeping us sweet to get favourable conditions for paperback rights, but he seemed genuinely impressed, though we could not boast any spectacular successes or books of outstanding importance until 1953, which was our *annus mirabilis*. Even when the firm had established itself I continued to be regarded as an outsider and never became a clubbable publisher. Feeling the cold, I avoided professional gatherings in London. Instead I cultivated foreign publishers and depended on a network of European and American houses which I built up over the years.

Nigel had held the fort while I was away, although he was already beginning to nurse a constituency in Leicester. He spent two-thirds of his time in the office, but he also had a fair amount of political work to do. He had always made it clear that politics was going to be his first priority, and when he won his Bournemouth seat in 1952 he phased out his active involvement with the firm, giving me the opportunity to buy his shares bit by bit and leaving himself with only a small holding.

Nigel and I worked well together. He accepted my position as head of the house and his as deputy. I bore the brunt of the business side, but we were equally involved in editorial matters. We occasionally had differences of opinion, but they never impinged on our friendship, which continues to this day. For years he remained a director of the company he had cofounded and was always at hand when I needed him. He continued to help us acquire a number of important books as well as letting us publish his own works, foremost among them *Portrait of a Marriage*, his moving account of his parents' unconventional conjugal life.

Publishing was still a gentleman's profession in the 1950s. Alongside the old family businesses there mushroomed small houses run by partnerships of dilettanti that were invariably undercapitalized. Many firms employed full-time editors or part-time readers of independent means who were prepared to work for a pittance. The Publishers Association was an oligarchy. Outsiders were unwelcome. To be a newcomer, and a foreigner to boot, who entertained ambitions of entering the main door of general literary publishing, was held to be an act of audacious folly. And yet writers, designers and discerning critics showed compassionate benevolence towards any pioneer, and Nigel and I received much encouragement.

During the war and in the immediate postwar period, the hunger for reading matter and a shortage of other consumer goods was such that it was not too difficult to make ends meet, even with small editions, provided you had a paper quota. Although very competitive, publishing had not yet become the high-risk business of today.

We were luckier than most young firms because we had more than one life belt. The Marks & Spencer contract for children's books that Israel Sieff had awarded us provided our fledgling company with its bread and butter. When that came to an end, I embarked on another venture through the good offices of the kindly Professor David Mitrany, a Rumanian sociologist whose study on political agrarian movements, *Marx against the Peasant*, was among the first books we published. Mitrany's optimistic writings on postwar economic possibilities and on the missionary role of multinational corporations won him a senior advisory position with Unilever. Thanks to him, Unilever awarded Weidenfeld & Nicolson a contract to edit and publish a sumptuous quarterly called *Progress*.

We also published a similar magazine, *Steel*, for the as then not yet nationalized British Steel Corporation. For this I employed the talented young illustrator, writer and designer Mark Boxer, who had recently been rusticated from Cambridge for his involvement with a much publicized 'blasphemous incident'. Without the yield from these sponsored publications we would never have been able to indulge any of our intellectual ambitions. They kept our heads above water and gave us a sounder financial base from which to woo other investors.

The real breakthrough for Weidenfeld & Nicolson came in 1953. It was the year we published Isaiah Berlin's *The Hedgehog and the Fox*, an intellectual landmark. Tito's memoirs, *Tito Speaks*, compiled by Vladimir Dedijer, was our first bestseller, and Rose Macaulay's *The Pleasure of Ruins* became another classic. Lali Horstmann's memoirs, *Nothing for Tears*, a deeply moving account of the final months of the war and the Russian occupation of Berlin, also did very well. I still think it is one of the best books of its kind.

The daughter of the distinguished banker Schwabach, Lali was an exceptionally sensitive and intelligent woman. Harold Nicolson had befriended her during his time as Counsellor of the British Embassy in Berlin in the late 1920s. She was married to the diplomat Freddie Horstmann, an art collector, whose considerable wealth derived from real estate and from the *General Anzeiger*, a Frankfurt newspaper owned by his family. Soon after Hitler came to power his wife's Jewish origins forced him to give up his diplomatic career, but throughout the Nazi period the Horstmanns kept a cosmopolitan salon in Berlin, even as the bombs fell. After the collapse of the Third Reich he was arrested and died of hunger in a Soviet detention camp in 1947. Lali moved to London, thinking herself very poor, although in fact she owned prime real estate in Frankfurt. She had also rescued some of her husband's magnificent treasures – china, silver and furniture – which she sold piecemeal to friends in America. I met her through the Nicolsons. She accompanied me on one of my first visits to Germany after the war and introduced me to a wide circle of friends.

In 1953, much to Hamish Hamilton's anger, we also published

two books by Cyril Connolly, who had been one of his star authors. The first was a collection of Cyril's essays called *Ideas and Places*, and the second was *The Golden Horizon*, a personal anthology of contributions to his monthly journal *Horizon*, which has become a collector's item.

1953 brought me two valuable assistants. After the first faltering steps, the firm was expanding, which meant we needed more staff. I was on the lookout for an editor who also had a head for business so that I could delegate some of the adminstrative and financial chores. That side of publishing has never been my forte – all my enthusiasm was directed at the quest for authors and ideas for new titles. Hugh Trevor-Roper recommended Nicolas Thompson, a former pupil of his and the grandson of Walter de la Mare. For seventeen years he was my closest associate, until he left to become managing director of Pitmans. He ended up as chairman of Heinemann. I was loath to see him go because he was probably the most congenial person I have ever worked with, but I could not match the terms offered him.

When Clarissa Churchill left the firm to marry Anthony Eden I needed an editorial associate to replace her. Among the people I asked whether they knew of any promising undergraduates were Elizabeth and Frank Pakenham. Without a moment's hesitation Elizabeth declared, 'I have the ideal candidate for you – my daughter, Antonia, who's just finishing at Oxford.' At first I gasped at this display of naked nepotism. But when a pretty, though plumpish, young undergraduate with a captivating blend of shyness and self-assurance came for an interview, I engaged her on the spot. She gave an impressive account of her qualifications in self-deprecating terms, and I was struck by her wide reading and intellectual curiosity.

Antonia Pakenham joined us in September 1953 on the same day as Nicolas Thompson. She soon became the life and soul of the firm, looking after both the *jeunes premiers* and the prima donnas among our authors with customary grace. She was quick to learn and showed great versatiliy. When Marks & Spencer asked us to produce new versions of children's classics for our series, Antonia wrote a full-length book on King Arthur and the knights of the Round Table, more or less at the drop of a hat. It was followed a year later by *Robin Hood*. These were her first steps to literary fame.

After her marriage to Hugh Fraser, the dashing Tory MP, she embarked on her first biography, *Mary Queen of Scots*, first published in 1969. It became a bestseller and sealed her success, making her a frequent butt of envy. She was already one of the most remarkable figures in London. Her passionate zest for life is combined with rigid self-discipline. With her subtle sense of irony and gift for narrative, she has the hallmarks of a born diarist. She has always said that she will not allow her journals to appear in her lifetime, but when they are eventually published they are bound to be a masterpiece.

It was a joy to get to know Hugh Fraser better, not least because I saw in him another ally in the championship of Israel. He became a great friend of Marcus Sieff and his father Israel, with whom both he and his legendary brother, Lord Lovat, shared business interests.

Shimi Lovat was known as the handsomest man in Britain. He was a dashing soldier who commanded one of the first commando brigades to land on the Normandy beaches on D-Day and was famous for having gone into battle in a kilt, preceded by his piper. His memoirs, *March Past*, which we published in 1978, sold extremely well. Lovat earned literary fame of another kind through Evelyn Waugh, whose commanding officer he became in the summer of 1943. Regarding him as 'a source of constant trouble' and 'a total misfit' from the Army's point of view, Lovat refused Waugh permission to join 'Operation Husky', the allied assault on Italy, and was instrumental in Waugh's departure from Combined Operations headquarters. Evelyn Waugh took revenge by vilifying him as an arriviste hairdresser in *Officers and Gentlemen*.

Hugh Fraser had a romantic view of life shot through with a tough streak of self-preserving business acumen. His declamatory style of conversation, his warmth and flamboyance, made him a most agreeable companion. Hugh was a friend of Woodrow Wyatt – they had been contemporaries at Oxford. In London the two of them out-boomed each other across the dinner table and the House of Commons.

Antonia adapted to the aristocratic, high Toryism Hugh represented, but her ambition and curiosity led her to extend her circle beyond these confines. As one of eight siblings and the mother of six children, her sense of family prevailed over all her other interests. Under her delicate direction Hugh embraced her friends. When Hugh and Antonia finally parted, the cohesive family ties did not suffer unduly because Harold Pinter, whom she then married, won the affection of Antonia's children. I felt very privileged to be among the first to be told by Antonia of her intention to marry Harold, just as I had been one of the first to learn of her engagement to Hugh Fraser years before. On both occasions she brought her intended to meet me, and on both occasions her men dominated the interview with probing questions about her. Harold was at his most Pinteresque, interrogating me about my first meeting with Antonia. He wanted to know every detail.

'Now, what was she wearing that day?' he asked. 'No, no,' he insisted, 'tell me precisely. What colour was her suit? How did she answer your questions? Was she confident? How exactly did she behave? Was she nervous? Was she brief or long-winded?' And so on.

Antonia changed her mode of life when she married Harold, and took a passionate interest in his work and method, in his circle, and in the many causes he espoused with such visceral passion. But she did not drop her close friends. A little band of her university contemporaries stuck together, confiding their triumphs and turmoils. Perhaps closest of all was Marigold Hunt, who married Paul Johnson. Although Paul's and Harold's politics represent a polarity of views they became good friends. Like her parents, Antonia was at her best in foul weather. In any crisis I could always rely on Frank, Elizabeth and Antonia for compassionate understanding and practical advice.

The English have a tradition of great literary families. I was fortunate in being closely associated with two of them, the Nicolsons and the Pakenhams. Their prolific output could at times have filled the list of any small publishing house; but not only that, Nigel Nicolson, Elizabeth Longford, Antonia Fraser and Thomas Pakenham have proved amongst our best and most successful authors.

I published Antonia's mother when she still wrote under the name of Elizabeth Pakenham. She had written a series of articles for the *Express* on bringing up children which I persuaded her to collect in a book called *Points for Parents*. I nagged her to write more, and some years later she produced a book about the Boer War. *The Jameson Raid* was excellent, as good as anything she has written since, but it had limited sales owing to lack of public interest. Elizabeth was disappointed that years of work should have fruited little more than a few prestigious reviews. I suggested that she take on a large and universally appealing biographical subject: Queen Victoria. She was aghast at the thought of such an ambitious project, but rose to the challenge. The book was enormously successful and established her as one of the major biographers of her generation.

On Antonia's recommendation, her fellow student Vanessa Jebb also came to work for Weidenfeld & Nicolson. Vanessa was beautiful, quietly witty and intelligent in an understated way. She was a shrewd observer of character, though she lacked self-confidence, largely, I think, as a result of having the two most self-assertive parents imaginable. In looks and posture her father, Gladwyn Jebb, was the quintessential British diplomat, a Lord Curzon reborn, who dominated a dinner table just as he did a conference room. Self-assured and faintly arrogant, he suffered no fools, asked no quarter and gave none. Her mother, Cynthia, was the archetypal Foreign Office wife, who relished her role as a social figure. Cultured, and with a voracious appetite for things worldly, she was beholden to the canons of conventional life.

When Vanessa accepted Hugh Thomas's proposal of marriage, Gladwyn, who knew that we were on friendly terms, asked me about Hugh's prospects. I had met him through Fred Warner, then one of his seniors at the Foreign Office where he worked for a while in a 'special' department. He struck me at once as an impressive, if somewhat eccentric, young man in his elegant, coloured shirts and large bow ties. He lived at Rose Cavendish's famous Cavendish Hotel, the haunt of high Bohemia for generations, and was befriended by Nancy Mitford. Fred Warner and his fellow diplomat Nicko Henderson praised him in the highest terms, but in the end he decided to become a full-time writer and academic rather than stick with the Foreign Office.

Hugh's remarkable career as a historian did not fail to impress his exacting and fastidious father-in-law. His books on the Spanish civil war and Cuba earned him a worldwide reputation, and he became a pioneer in the study of modern Europe at British universities. In the late 1960s and early '70s he assembled at his Graduate School of Contemporary European Studies at Reading University a distinguished group of younger historians such as Stuart Woolf, Robin Cecil, Geoffrey Warner and George Lehman. I published Hugh's shorter works on the Suez crisis and European unity, and

I value my friendship with him most highly. Every publisher has made misjudgements, and one that irks me to this day is that I turned down Hugh's first two novels. Eyre & Spottiswoode accepted his third and were richly rewarded with *The Spanish Civil War*, long acknowledged as a classic of modern history.

From the outset my interest as a publisher lay with history, politics, biography and ideas. Sometimes I thought first of the idea and then tried to match it up with an author. But I would just as often look for an idea to suit someone whom I felt had talent. My great passion is historians, especially those who scan a wide canvas and find links or distinctions between various cultures or civilizations. I am intrigued by the way an erudite person from one culture observes his counterparts in another, and love discussing Islam with a German Arabist or analysing the nuances of the Austro-Hungarian bureaucracy with a Frenchman.

My friendship with Victor-Lucien Tapié that venerable luminary of the Sorbonne, was founded in this way. He knew every street, every church and every palace in Warsaw, Prague and Vienna and would sing eighteenth-century Austrian ditties in the vernacular with a charming French accent. I love studying the distinctive characteristics of different nations and relating what I have read to my own observations and experiences. As a boy I shared my father's worship of Heinrich Heine and devoured that great satirist's descriptions of the German and French psyche. Later, Friedrich Sieburg's *Gott in Frankreich*, which held a German mirror up to the French, Salvador de Madariaga's *Englishmen, Frenchmen, Spaniards*, and Gustave Renier's hilarious anatomical dissection in *The English – Are They Human?*, were among the finest specimens of this genre.

I published Jean François Revel's *Pour l'Italie* about what he perceives to be the failings of a much-admired nation. We also boasted the bestseller *Major Thompson Lives in France* by Pierre Daninos, and I persuaded Luigi Barzini, the most cosmopolitan of Italian essayists and journalists of his day and author of *The Italians*, to write a similar work of epigrammatic reportage on *The Europeans*. He rose to the challenge, travelling through a dozen countries and dipping in to moods of the day in various capitals. It was to be his last book.

I was not ideally suited to nursing the artistic temperament of novelists and poets. I read fiction, but I did not trust my judgement.

In the early years of Weidenfeld & Nicolson I relied heavily on George Orwell's widow, Sonia, who acted as literary advisor. Sonia was a pretty, blowsy, reddish blonde, full of *joie de vivre* and generous to a fault. She was impulsive and quick to take sides. Her literary aspirations and her penchant for high Bohemia went hand in hand with a jolly-hockeystickish streak, a relic of the colonial upbringing she tried to reject. She was very secretive about her private life. During her time with us she had a romance with John Phillips, the famous *Life* photographer who made an international name for himself with his pictures of Tito's partisans, and who helped us get the Marshal's memoirs. Years later, during an intimate conversation about our past, Sonia burst out with the revelation that she had also had a whirlwind romance with Yigal Allon.

Sonia had been one of Cyril Connolly's assistants on *Horizon*, and the contacts she had built up there were invaluable to us. She introduced a number of outstanding authors to the firm, including Mary McCarthy, Sybille Bedford and Elizabeth Hardwick. We were also greatly helped by the demise of John Lehmann's publishing house.

A former Communist whose leanings were still leftish, Rosamond Lehmann's brother had become a central figure in English literary life through his editorship of Penguin 'New Writing'. John Lehmann was in fact a much more talented editor than he was a writer, and had persuaded a rich printer with a large paper quota to let him start his own imprint. In the short life of John Lehmann Ltd, some of the most promising names of the period appeared there. Lehmann was the first to publish Saul Bellow, Truman Capote, Carson McCullers, Gore Vidal and a host of English writers, many of whom he discovered and then fostered. Had his backer shown more imagination and endurance, and had John Lehmann had more business acumen (though he was by no means devoid of it), he might well have presided over the most significant literary imprint in the English-speaking world. But his backer let him down, John Lehmann Ltd disintegrated, and all the literary publishers of London scrambled for its authors.

Thanks to Sonia Orwell, Saul Bellow came to us. We published *The Adventures of Augie March*, one of the most important American novels of the postwar period, in 1954. It was praised by the critics and sold very well. Bellow often visited England and we were at one time quite close, though I found him too self-absorbed.

Mordantly witty when he wanted to be, he could also be self-pitying and irascible, particularly towards those who hurt his vanity. Whenever we met he seemed to be between wives or love affairs. During those bouts he sometimes behaved outrageously, thinking his distress excused everything. But he could also be manifestly charming. He was a difficult author, but Barley Alison, our editorial director, was slavishly devoted to him, and when she left to start her own imprint at Secker & Warburg, Saul Bellow went with her.

Barley was a popular Australian-born debutante who had been with Special Operations Executive (SOE), the organization which controlled sabotage, subversive activities and black propaganda in enemy-controlled countries during the Second World War. She was taken up by the Foreign Office and worked under Duff Cooper at the Paris Embassy. When she left the service in 1951, Duff Cooper wrote to her saying that he was glad to learn of her departure because the Foreign Office 'is no place for a pretty young woman'.

Barley had a heart of gold. She was slightly bossy and tended to be long-winded. Though not unattractive, she looked a little scraggy. She was the darling of her generation in the Foreign Office and had an outstanding war record, but she had problems passing exams, and the Foreign Office had to let her go. She had an excellent hand with fiction authors: Dan Jacobson and Vladimir Nabokov were amongst those she looked after. She also discovered Margaret Drabble, who sent in a manuscript of her first novel out of the blue with a stamped addressed envelope and a letter saying that she was drawn to us because we published Saul Bellow, whom she particularly admired. Barley read *A Summer Birdcage* overnight and declared it a masterpiece. It came out in 1963 to great acclaim.

When Sonia first introduced me to Mary McCarthy, she was married to the ultra-Wasp and waspish New York writer and schoolmaster Bowden Broadwater, who obviously revered his wife. I had heard a great deal about her from one of her former lovers, Philip Rahv, the burly ex-Trotskyite editor of the *Partisan Review* who appears in her fiction and never quite got over her. Mary was handsome and flirtatious. She knew how to use her sexual aura, but she also conquered with her acid wit and high spirits. Many men succumbed to her combative femininity and alluring looks. She had an insatiable appetite for high gossip and a gift for turning social chatter into brilliant literary improvisation spiked with sarcasm. Mary could be merciless in her judgements. For some years she spent her summer holidays near me in Bocca di Magra, where she stayed in the house of the Italian journalist Nicola Chiaromonte, a mentor of hers who had been one of the earliest left-wing critics of Moscow. We used to have running postmortems of the various literary parties on the Ligurian coast.

For all her curiosity about the beau monde, Mary was also a bluestocking among bluestockings, a passionate political debater and partisan of people and causes. She was the most loyal of friends, and enjoyed her role as confidante. I often unburdened myself to her. She had an intense friendship with Hannah Arendt and pounced like a tigress on Hannah's many critics, especially the Jewish ones, during the controversy over her reports of the Eichmann trial and her concept of the 'Banality of Evil'. Mary's devotion to Hannah Arendt was such that she spent years editing her papers after she died, neglecting her own work as a novelist. Her championship of Hannah Arendt, her involvement in the Vietnam war controversy and a wearing libel case brought against her by Lillian Hellman, whom she had described in a television interview as an overrated and dishonest writer, all had a destructive effect on her creativity. With her last husband Jim West, a steady and thoroughly honourable American diplomat, whom she married in 1961, she settled in Paris, and their apartment in the rue de Rennes was a regular port of call for me. I learnt from her biographer, Caroline Bingham, that at one point Mary had suffered a minor nervous breakdown in Florence and had woken one morning thinking she was me.

Mary McCarthy's early works were published in England by Heinemann. But when she submitted the manuscript of *A Charmed Life* to her editor there, he asked her to tone down a love scene between the heroine and her former husband, a thinly-veiled account of such an encounter between herself and her second husband Edmund Wilson. The obscenity threshold was very low in those days, and Heinemann considered it too risqué. Mary declined to alter anything. Instead, thanks to Sonia Orwell, she came to us.

In 1963 we were able to publish *The Group*, owing to similar circumstances. Mary's American publisher, Harcourt Brace, owned the firm of Hart-Davis in England, but Sir Rupert Hart-Davis turned it down for being too sexy. It was a bestseller and became one of our most successful books ever. I remember meeting Dwye Evans, the head of Heinemann, at the Booksellers' Conference before it appeared, and his saying to me rather condescendingly, 'I hear you've taken Mary's book. Great mistake, you know. It won't sell more than two thousand copies. Too American, too dirty.' In fact we sold more than two hundred thousand.

One of my priorities at Weidenfeld & Nicolson was to lay the foundation for a scholarly list over and above the fiction and general programme. In my pursuit of well-known academics I played two trump cards. One was to offer them more money than they could get from the university presses. As a back-up, I used the techique merchant bankers apply to public issues. That is to say I brought in international partners to whom I sold ideas on my constant travels to Europe and the United States.

The other incentive I used, for distinguished authors, was to invite them to contribute to an academic series. I knew that if I approached an Olympian with a request for his next big book he would, more likely than not, point out that he had a long-term commitment to another publisher. But if, instead, I went to him and said that we wanted him to contribute to the most important history of Europe in the twentieth century, or to a series on natural history, twentieth-century Europe, comparative government, a universal history of religion or a range of books on the emergent Asian-African countries, he had an alibi. He could put it to his publisher that this was outside the working arrangement and that he would return to the fold as soon as he had finished this special project. In many cases this led to a permanent connection, thus enabling us to build up an important history list. These were golden years of optimism and expansion in world publishing, and our financial risk was minimal because I sold each series internationally before I struck a deal.

The first series was the 'History of Civilisation'. My idea was to produce about forty titles, beginning with the cradle of history and leading up to the present, each of them written by an eminent historian. I wanted each book to be readable as well as authoritative, and at the same time reflect the views of a great mind. When I launched the project in 1957 I drew on the advice of Isaiah Berlin, Hugh Trevor-Roper and Sir Ronald Syme, the ancient historian once described as the greatest living Englishman. In fact he was a New Zealander.

Isaiah suggested that Maurice Bowra write about Greek civilization, and within less than a year Bowra handed in his manuscript for *The Greek Experience*, which was a great success and a wonderful send-off for the series. It was followed by Michael Grant's *The World of Rome*. Grant was at that time vice-chancellor of Belfast University. The Irish troubles had not yet flared up, but he told me one day that he had a feeling things would go badly in Ireland and that he did not envisage spending the rest of his life embroiled in the Irish question. Michael's great ambition was to become Master of Trinity College, Cambridge. He was short-listed, but he asked me whether, failing that, I thought he could make a living as a freelance historian. I swallowed hard and told him I would guarantee him a living. As a result, he bought a beautiful farmhouse near Lucca and has been closely associated with us ever since. It has been one of the happiest relationships I have had with any author, equalled only by Paul Johnson. Never a tiff, never a complaint, and no agents involved.

The third book was *The Medieval World* by the young Austrian historian, Friedrich Heer. My Oxford contacts had told me that there were two interesting historians of international standing for the late Middle Ages, Sidney Painter at Cornell, who was too old to write the book, and Friedrich Heer, on whom opinion was diametrically divided. Some regarded him not so much as a charlatan as a fantasist who lacked discipline. Others thought he was a genius.

I went to see him in Vienna and it was clear within half an hour of our meeting that we were going to be friends for life. With his broad face and finely chiselled bone structure, he looked like a young version of Martin Luther. He had slightly protruding eyes and a heavy build which masked his considerable height. He was a self-propelling rocket. His mind obviously raced ahead of his speech, and he talked at breakneck speed without finishing his sentences. He had a habit of creating obscure phrases, and you had to guess what he meant. He often broke into English, although his mastery of that language was far from complete. This resulted in the most extraordinary malapropisms. Every three minutes he would use the phrase, 'Don't fence me in,' without really knowing what it meant. But he was brilliant.

Heer suffered from persecution mania. He had had a traumatic experience during the war which he never defined. He was an unhappy man who drank a great deal and had a Spenglerian fear of the future. He invented strange incidents in his past in a way I also observed in André Malraux. It was not that he was lying or fantasising for the sake of it, but rather that he was providing missing links in an incomplete picture, like a restorer who takes artistic licence with an old fresco, filling in the odd line. He was deeply anti-Nazi, a left-wing Catholic and an early bridge-builder between East and West. In the worst period of the Cold War he maintained contacts with Czech, Hungarian and Polish intellectuals using his Church contacts, Cardinal Koenig in particular. In the 1950s he courageously gave a series of lectures in Vienna on 'The Catholic Roots of the Austrian Anti-Semite Hitler' which was deeply resented by some conservatives. Later he published *God's First Love*, probably one of the best histories of the tragic feud between Roman Catholicism and Judaism. It is a testimony to his desire for reconciliation between the two faiths, which he strove for all his life, enlisting the help of Cardinal Koenig, the ecumenically inclined Archbishop of Vienna, whom I first met through Friedrich Heer. *God's First Love* made a deep impression on the banker Sigmund Warburg, who asked me to arrange a meeting with the author. Warburg was fascinated by him. He used to take a private dining room at the Savoy and invite two or three guests from the world of business to listen to Heer ad lib, which he did with great gusto while consuming exquisite French white wine.

Heer had a following in Germany, but he became famous through the first book he wrote for us. In an unsigned review for the *Times Literary Supplement*, Arnold Toynbee praised it in most enthusiastic terms. In Austria the reverberations of *The Medieval World* were such that Vienna immediately awarded him a full professorship, lest a German university woo him away. We published about a dozen of his books, which read better in English because a deft translator had trimmed some of the stylistic weeds. Heer's *Medieval World* was not the only contribution to the 'History of Civilisation' series to become a classic. Others were J.H. Parry's *The Age of Reconnaissance*, Eric Hobsbawm's trilogy, *The Age of Revolution*, *The Age of Capital* and *The Age of Empire*, and Richard Pipes's *Russia under the Old Regime*.

The *succès d'estime* of our series of scholarly and well-written books on history, religion, natural history, literature and the visual arts encouraged me to expand into more specialist fields. Some of these books were among the finest we ever published but, alas, they did not sell well enough to break even. While the costs of manufacture, salaries and promotion escalated, the readership

failed to increase proportionately. I strove hard to match losses
incurred on serious books by opportunist publishing. Serious studies
had to be financed by the confessions of a royal courtier or a
fashionable formula novel by an American draft dodger. The life
of an independent publisher with ambitions of producing a distinguished international list entailing translation was becoming
increasingly difficult.

However, 1959 marked another milestone in the history of
Weidenfeld & Nicolson. This was the year we published *Lolita*,
which catapulted the firm from the literary pages of British papers
to headlines in the world press.

Vladimir Nabokov's novel had first come to the attention of the
wider world when Graham Greene recommended it in the Christmas issue of *The Sunday Times* as one of the three best books of
1955, thus sparking off a furious literary squabble in England. An
outraged John Gordon, editor of the *Sunday Express*, reacted by
denouncing *Lolita* as 'sheer unrestrained pornography'. Greene in
turn ridiculed him by forming a 'John Gordon Society', which proposed amongst other things that the purchasers of Scrabble pledge
not to use any words not included in the *Concise Oxford
Dictionary*.

Having failed to find a publisher in New York, Nabokov had
signed a contract with Olympia Press in Paris, a house run by
a somewhat picaresque figure called Maurice Girodias, who
specialized in erotic literature that had been outlawed in America
and England. Most of it was worthless, though, like his father Jack
Kahane, the publisher of Cyril Connolly's *The Rock Pool*, Lawrence
Durrell's *The Black Book* and Henry Miller's *Tropic of Cancer* and
Tropic of Capricorn, he also had a feeling for literature. *Lolita* had
immediately become a cult novel. Copies of the Olympia edition
were much sought after on the black market, and various American
firms now vied for the rights, put off, however, by Girodias'
demands for an unreasonably high royalty. Walter Minton of
Putnam was the only one willing to take him on and risk prosecution. He published the American edition in August 1958 to a
cacophony of praise and indignation. In some states the book was
withdrawn, but the American authorities refrained from banning it
and it soon reached the bestseller list.

I had read the novel when it was first published by the Olympia
Press and began negotiating with Minton before the Putnam edition

came out. But in England, where the obscenity laws were tougher, the situation was more precarious than in the United States. In September 1958 a court had imposed a £200 fine on a bookseller who tried to sell a copy of the Olympia Press edition to a plain-clothes policeman, and publishers risked going to prison for distributing a book which had been declared obscene by a British magistrate.

But now a new Obscene Publications Bill was going through Parliament. It laid down that a book be judged as a whole rather than by passages taken out of context, and it allowed the defence to call expert witnesses to testify to its literary merit. Most British publishers preferred to wait for the Bill to reach the statute book before committing themselves to *Lolita*. Of those who showed an interest, Nabokov inclined towards Bodley Head, of which Graham Greene was then a director, in gratitude for Greene's championship of the book. But Minton argued in our favour, mainly because he feared that Greene's ridiculing of John Gordon might still be resented by the powers that be. Though gruff and mercurial, Minton was a highly intelligent man with whom I worked closely for many years, until at the height of his career in publishing he sold his business and changed to the law.

We signed *Lolita* up in November 1958. Nabokov, who was then teaching at Cornell University, stipulated that not so much as a comma be changed. We also had to commit ourselves in writing to defending the book.

In the months preceding publication *Lolita* was the subject of fierce debate. In the face of public hostility, an impressive array of literary personalities registered their protest against the possibility of the book being banned in a letter to *The Times* which appeared on 23 January 1959. It read as follows:

> Sir, We are disturbed by the suggestion that it may yet prove impossible to have an English edition of Vladimir Nabokov's *Lolita*. Our opinions on the merit of the work differ widely, but we think that it would be deplorable if a book of considerable literary interest, which has been favourably received by distinguished critics and widely praised in serious and respectable periodicals were to be denied an appearance in this country. Prosecutions of genuine works of literature bring governments into disrepute and do nothing to encourage public morality. When today we read the proceedings against *Madame Bovary* or *Ulysses* –

works genuinely found shocking by many of their contemporaries
– it is Flaubert and Joyce whom we admire, not the Public
Prosecutors of the time. Let good sense spare us another such case.

The signatories were J.R. Ackerley, Walter Allen, A. Alvarez,
Isaiah Berlin, C.M. Bowra, Storm Jameson, Frank Kermode, Allen
Lane, Margaret Lane, Rosamond Lehmann, Compton Mackenzie,
Iris Murdoch, William Plomer, V.S. Pritchett, Alan Pryce-Jones,
Peter Quennell, Herbert Read, Stephen Spender, Philip Toynbee,
Bernard Wall and Angus Wilson.

'The battle for *Lolita* goes on,' I reported to Nabokov a few days
later. I was not to meet him until several weeks after this, on 1
March, when I called on him at the Chelsea Hotel in New York.
It was my first visit to that famous but rather gloomy place, and
as I arrived I saw a man in baggy tousers and a loose-fitting tweed
jacket over a white shirt standing by the elevator, a quizzical
expression on his face. This lean, stooping figure came and shook
me by the hand. Without saying a word he led me down a long
corridor and ushered me into his private room where a white-haired
woman sat upright in her chair with her back to the window,
reminding me of a Giacometti drawing. She put aside her knitting
and shot me a hostile glance. It was Véra Nabokov. The Nabokovs
had grown more and more suspicious of publishers as a result of
their acrimonious relations with Maurice Girodias, and it took a
while for them to warm to me. To break the ice I spoke about
Cambridge, where Nabokov had spent his student years, and
brought up mutual acquaintances. We then discussed ways of
launching *Lolita*. I wanted to delay publication until the Obscene
Publications Bill became law, and asked for a period of incubation,
but Nabokov was in a hurry to get the book out in England.

The prospect of prosecution loomed over us as the Obscenity
Bill went through its various stages in the House of Commons, and
there were plenty of people who warned us against taking *Lolita*
on. Our decision to go ahead led to a permanent estrangement
between Harold Nicolson and myself. Harold was fiercely opposed
to the publication of *Lolita*. He hated the novel and feared that it
would be a nail in the coffin of his son's political career, which had
already suffered from his opposition to Government policy in the
Suez affair and to capital punishment. Harold wrote to me saying
that Vita and he did not feel that the literary merits of *Lolita* in

any way justified 'the obscenity which underlies the whole book. Only one person in a million will feel that the book is really a moral or cautionary tale, or that it is anything but "corrupting" in the sense of the Obscene Publications Report. To the great mass of the public it will seem a salacious treatment of the worst sort of perversion, a vice in which an extreme form of lechery confronts the extremest innocence. It will be universally condemned, and will give your firm the reputation, not of a courageous and "advanced" firm of publishers, but as a firm which specialises in obscene books.' He urged me to give up the idea of publication which would 'prove an almost lethal blow to your reputation'.

Despite his difficulties and misgivings, Nigel stuck to us with self-sacrificial loyalty. He defended the book in a House of Commons debate, and stood firm when he came under heavy fire in his constituency. Pressure was brought to bear on him by his party. Edward Heath, who was then chief whip, implored Nigel to drop publication in the interests of political peace. He was not impressed by the formidable list of names who had signed the letter to *The Times*, and warned that the debate threated to turn the Obscene Publications Bill into a 'Lolita Bill'. Conservatives would vote against it if the Bill permitted publication of *Lolita*, and Labour would oppose it if it did not. A general election was looming and Heath feared the Party would be harmed. The Attorney General, Sir Reginald Manningham-Buller, later Lord Dilhorne, also warned Nigel off *Lolita*, jabbing a finger at him in the lobby outside the smoking room of the House of Commons as he stood talking to Harold Macmillan.

Nigel's problems with his staunchly conservative Bournemouth constituents helped keep *Lolita* in the news. In fact it contributed to his losing his seat. When the matter became a national controversy, Nigel proposed a postal ballot to Lord Hailsham, then chairman of the Conservative Party. He lost by ninety-one votes, and, having been effectively deselected, left Parliament at the general election later that year.

In the months preceding publication, the battle for *Lolita* raged unabated. The majority of newspapers were hostile, and Nigel Nicolson and I were vilified in the press. John Gordon made an issue of my private life in the *Sunday Express*. I was living in Fred Warner's rooms at Albany at the time, and it was like being in a glass cage. His rooms were easily accessible from the street, and reporters hung around outside at all hours, eager to find evidence of my depravity. One of them got me out of bed at 7.30 one morning – I staggered to the door in a plum-coloured dressing gown, the appearance of which was registered in minute detail by the chronicler. But our campaign also found some passionate champions over and above those who had signed the letter to *The Times*. Bernard Levin wrote a stirring defence of *Lolita* in the *Spectator*, and Roy Jenkins and Ian Gilmour were among those who showed their solidarity.

Our campaign was masterminded by Gerald Gardiner QC, the distinguished left-wing lawyer who later became Lord Chancellor of the Wilson Government. Gardiner looked rather like a Roman senator. He was tall, bald and gaunt and had a donnish manner. He believed passionately in the idea of free speech and proved a remarkable strategist. His tactic was to try to checkmate the Director of Public Prosecutions, for we had reason to believe that his department was itself uncertain as to what to do. The date of publication was set for 6 November. By 5 October, three weeks before we were due to send out review copies, we had had a handful of copies printed, and sent the Director of Public Prosecutions one copy with a letter, declaring our intention to publish it because we believed the novel to be of great literary merit, but stating that we did not want to break the law. He was to be given the opportunity to prosecute the firm for technically publishing *Lolita* before it reached the bookshops. We informed him that unless we heard from him by 26 October we would proceed with our plans. It was Nigel who had first proposed this idea of a test case based on a 'token publication'. We heard nothing from the department, and duly went ahead with our preparations, keeping the books in the warehouse until the last minute.

The Nabokovs arrived in England a few days before 6 November. We put them up at Brown's, and Vladimir spent most of his time receiving a select group of journalists and friends at his hotel. My friend Grace Radziwill was extremely helpful. She acted as a superior lady-in-waiting to the Nabokovs. As part of the campaign to win public opinion we had, even for that late hour, arranged for Nabokov to give a lecture at Cambridge. Before leaving New York he wrote to me, somewhat piqued that he was to speak at the invitation of the Slavonic Department: 'A lecture sponsored by the Department of English might conceivably serve your purpose in regard to the launching of "Lolita". I do not think that this purpose would be served by my appearing under the second-rate auspices of a fringe department.' He threatened to drop the lecture, saying that 'the present arrangement would hardly justify a trip to chilly Cambridge', and ended the letter with another pointed remark: 'Let me mention in passing that ordinarily I am a very expensive lecturer, though I had agreed to disregard this point for once when I envisaged my Cambridge appearance as part of your campaign rather than as an educational venture.' But in the end all was well.

We drove to Cambridge on 4 November in Grace's rented Rolls Royce, and Nabokov mounted the rostrum to deliver a lecture entitled 'Russian Classics, Censors, and Readers'. It was an amusing and learned survey of the battles of nineteenth-century Russian novelists with the censors which ended with the rhetorical question: 'Who today does not know such names as Pushkin, Lermontov, Turgenev, Chekhov? Who today knows the name of a single chief of police, or censor in St Petersburg?' Nabokov drew a standing ovation. Afterwards Noel Annan, ever a champion of libertarian causes, gave a splendid dinner at King's College of which he was then provost.

On the eve of publication, Weidenfeld & Nicolson held a reception for Nabokov at the Ritz, in London, which was attended by the cream of enlightened literary and political London. Among the guests were Igor Stravinsky and his wife, who had been brought along by the Berlins, and the press were out in full force. To begin with we were all very much on edge as our fate still hung in the balance. We expected the announcement that the Government intended to prosecute us for breaking the obscenity laws at any minute.

On the day of our reception at the Ritz, *Lolita* was, as we later learned, on the agenda of a cabinet subcommittee meeting which was attended by the Attorney General, Sir Reginald Manningham-Buller, and the Director of Public Prosecutions, Sir Theobald Matthew. The Home Secretary was represented by a junior minister, Sir Jocelyn Simon, a liberal Tory. During the launch party I was called to the telephone. At the other end of the line a voice belonging to an anonymous official from the Home Office said, 'This is highly irregular, but I'm a great supporter of your cause. You can go ahead. The DPP has decided not to prosecute.'

When I returned to the room in which the party was being held,

Nigel got onto a table to announce the news to general rejoicing. Véra Nabokov dabbed a tear with her white batiste handkerchief. The battle had been won. Coming, as it did, a year before the *Lady Chatterley's Lover* trial, *Lolita* was a breakthrough in the liberalization of the British obscenity laws and in the fortunes of Weidenfeld & Nicolson. The book sold well over two hundred thousand copies in hardback and put us on the map as an enterprising and daring firm.

My relationship with Nabokov deepened in the years to come, during which we published almost all his works. He was a hard taskmaster, taking a keen interest in publicity, presentation and sales, but he was never unfair. It took me a long time to gain Véra Nabokov's confidence. She was a distinguished woman of great charm whose whole life revolved around her husband. She managed his business affairs, found out about royalties, discussed the question of translations and acted as a domestic critic of everything he wrote. She was unquestioning in her loyalty to Nabokov and defended him like a tigress.

I used to make twice-yearly pilgrimages to the Palace Hotel in Montreux, where he and his wife lived simply but comfortably in a suite of rooms. The ritual was always the same. I would arrive at the hotel at around 12.30, announce my name at reception and wait for the Nabokovs to come down. First we would go to the bar for a drink, and then we would sit on the terrace over a long lunch. Then we might go for a walk in the park or up to their room for a *digestif*. Often we would be joined by Jane and Ledig Rowohlt, Nabokov's German publisher and translator. They lived nearby and were as close to the Nabokovs as anybody. At the end of my visit Nabokov always saw me into the taxi which took me back to the airport.

As we were sitting having a drink before lunch on one of my visits to Montreux in the late 1960s, an extraordinary thing happened to me. My right eye suddenly protruded out of its socket. Nabokov was horrified and amused at the same time. I was in a state of shock. He took me in a taxi to a White Russian female oculist, who recognized the condition and knew what to do, but her French was very poor and Nabokov spoke to her in Russian. The oculist was deaf and Nabokov had to shout to make himself understood. As she was dealing with my eye I heard him mutter in English, 'Blind publisher, deaf oculist, blind publisher, deaf oculist,' as though he were sketching a scene in a Nabokovian short story. The same thing had happened to me once before over breakfast with Sir Michael Blundell, a minister in the Kenyan Government before independence, whose books I published on Hugh Fraser's recommendation. The story made the rounds and is the origin of the Popeye joke in *Private Eye*. When I returned from Switzerland, Patrick Trevor-Roper, the oculist brother of Hugh, stitched my eyelid up to prevent it from happening again.

Nabokov did not see many people in Montreux. He reduced his social life to an absolute minimum so as to concentrate on his work. It was my impression that he liked to retain the freshness, the immediacy and the durability of human contact by restricting the frequency of it. He did not, as he once told me, want to clutter his mind. This accounted for his extraordinary memory. In his teasing and sardonic way he could give detailed descriptions of the mannerisms, the speech, the appearance of people he had met only briefly. Incidents and conversations which had taken place years before were still fresh in his mind.

Occasionally I orchestrated meetings between the Nabokovs and people who lived in the neighbourhood, such as the actor James Mason, who was having an affair with a friend of mine, Countess Vivi Crespi. She introduced Nabokov to Charlie Chaplin but he did not take to him, probably because of his left-wing sympathies. The Nabokovs were both fiercely anti-Communist. Their hatred was obsessive to the point of denying any form of achievement that emanated from the Soviet Union. I remember Nabokov freezing when my wife Sandra mentioned that we had just seen the Russian film of *War and Peace* and found it rather interesting. He asked Sandra how she could possibly be taken in by a film version of a great Russian classic which bore all the hallmarks of Soviet propaganda and the vulgarity that went with it. Although Nabokov was a liberal on questions of anti-Semitism, homosexuality and freedom of the individual, he would be inclined to side with a radical right-winger, provided the litmus test was anti-Communism. His long friendship with Jason Epstein, who had been at Doubleday before cofounding the *New York Review of Books*, cooled when Epstein became more politically committed. Nabokov disapproved of the *New York Review of Books* liberal school, and they thought of him as a reactionary.

Nabokov was serene, slightly aloof, cruelly observant, and

emphatic in his likes and dislikes. Even in conversation he was fastidious in his use of language, speaking rather like he wrote: a language full of subtle irony, hyperbole and stimulating analogies. We talked a great deal about contemporary literature, and between visits Nabokov would often send me sarcastic comments about our list. He had no time for Saul Bellow and looked on Mary McCarthy with amused tolerance. He was a great admirer of John Updike, who was not an author of mine, and he liked Henri de Montherlant, who was.

During our meetings we went through a regular repertoire of topics ranging from trivia about mutual friends – would Countess Crespi's liaison with James Mason end in marriage? – to memories of the *Lolita* affair, which he often reenacted. He always wanted to be brought up to date on the latest fracas between the Congress of Cultural Freedom, of which his cousin Nicolas was a cofounder, and its detractors. The breach with Edmund Wilson frequently came up. Nabokov fell out with him in 1965, after an intense friendship of more than two decades, over Wilson's vicious review of Nabokov's translation of *Eugene Onegin*. When the Nabokovs first met me, they thought I looked rather like Edmund Wilson, 'a mixture between Wilson and Churchill', Véra said.

Nabokov spent his days studying butterflies, reading, and playing chess. He played mostly against himself because he could not find anyone who was up to his standard. He read polemical literature about the Soviet Union, and reread the great Russian classics. He liked the aristocratic, Whiggish tradition of writing, and I found I could almost guess his pet hates. He was fond of Turgenev, Pushkin and Chekhov, and had ambivalent feelings about Tolstoy, whose greatness he did not deny, but whose soundness he would question. He hated Dostoevsky and had little love for Solzhenitsyn and his Dostoevsky-like appeal to pan-Slavist ideology. He used to say of him that he was 'just a barefooted priest'. But when Solzhenitsyn left the Soviet Union in February 1974, Nabokov wrote to him at once in Cologne, where he had been taken up by Heinrich Böll, congratulating him on his 'passage to the free world from our dreadful homeland' and suggesting a meeting. Solzhenitsyn, who then moved to Zürich for a while, wrote back saying that fate had brought them both to Switzerland. A date was arranged – Solzhenitsyn and his wife were to call on the Nabokovs at Montreux. They were ready at the appointed time, but the Solzhenitsyns never turned up. Days passed without word from them. Nabokov told me that he later heard that Solzhenitsyn had come to the Palace Hotel a little earlier than arranged, but that he could not bring himself to come in. The two writers never met.

CHAPTER THIRTEEN

One of 'The Family'

ALTHOUGH PUBLISHING filled my days, I found it hard to settle in after my return from Israel. Flora Solomon helped me find my feet again. She also smoothed ruffled feathers with President Weizmann and, more particularly, his wife, who had taken my departure as a personal slight. But we made it up at one of her private visits to London, when we spent a very agreeable evening of gossip and reminiscence together.

My friendship with the widely ramified Marks and Sieff clan grew ever closer after my return from Israel, and I became immersed in their world. I saw a great deal of the Sieffs, especially Marcus, then vying for the position of crown prince with Simon Marks's son-in-law, Dr Alec Lerner. Israel Sieff's younger brother Teddy, who in 1973 was the victim of a failed assassination attempt at the hand of a terrorist, who was assumed to be the notorious Carlos, had also become a friend. He tried to hide his shyness behind an aloof manner and could occasionally seem abrasive, but he was an exceptionally kind man who hero-worshipped his older brother and Simon Marks.

Teddy succeeded to the chairmanship after their deaths. He had married a charming, slighty fey woman, who was given to melancholy. They were temperamentally unsuited to one another, and the marriage was not happy. Though considerate, Teddy was not by nature communicative, and his wife, Maisie, became increasingly frustrated. She suffered from severe depression and committed suicide in the late autumn of 1951. They had two daughters. The younger was still at school but the elder, Jane, was studying at the Sorbonne. Teddy suggested I look her up when I next went to Paris.

On our first date I took her to *Don Giovanni*. Jane had a striking Etruscan profile rather like Jacqueline Picasso's in the drawings her husband made of her. Just turned twenty, she was refreshingly unspoilt and had a contagious enthusiasm for everything French, particularly contemporary painting and literature. I was immediately drawn to her and took her out several times in Paris. She came back to London to be with her father after her mother's death and we saw more and more of each other. Our courtship was brief and intense. In early December 1951 I proposed after dinner in my house in Chester Square. There was what seemed like an interminable pause, and in our embarrassment we both stared at the carved statue of St Francis of Assisi which I had bought at the Arcade Gallery only that week. Then we fell into each other's arms.

Jane's acceptance may well have been accelerated by her mother's death, which left her more prone to taking such a decisive step. She was a young and sheltered twenty, emotionally her age, while I was a rather old thirty-two. Therein probably lay one of the seeds of our ultimate estrangement.

I went to ask Jane's father for her hand in marriage. After enquiring into my circumstances, Teddy gave me a friendly nod. Lady Marks, her aunt, already a good friend and well-wisher, inspected my living quarters. Within a few days the 'nihil obstat' from the head of the Family percolated down to the junior branches, and a social chain reaction set in. Jane and I were fêted by all and sundry – there seemed to be a party every night. My parents were very much involved in all the preliminaries and had a warm relationship with Teddy Sieff. At Christmas I took Jane to stay with Henry and Shirley Anglesey at Plas Newydd. She was greatly appreciated there and seemed to enjoy herself. Raimund von Hofmannsthal, the family's arbiter of all things that lay outside the mainstream of British aristocratic life, showed his approval. 'It is as if you had found her in a superior convent school,' was his first comment.

The preparations for the wedding took up most of January. On the last day of that month we were married at the synagogue in St Petersburgh Place, Bayswater. Nigel Nicolson was my best man. It was a traditional ceremony, with the crushing of glass underfoot just before we were finally pronounced man and wife. Fred Warner, who was known for his conversational embroideries, told me he felt reminded of a Rembrandt painting. With their florid patriarchal faces the Sieff side did indeed look rather Rembrandtesque. The men wore top hats and morning coats, and many of the women were veiled. On my side there was a medley of sartorial moods. It was a clash of two worlds: Jewish patricians, manufacturing tycoons and courtiers of the Family faced a mixed group of Bohemians, radicals, friends from the BBC, Austrian refugees, debutantes and dandies. We held a reception at the Dorchester Hotel, with speeches and Palm Court music, before we set off for our honeymoon in Italy.

In Florence we called on Bernard Berenson on a breezy and sunny winter's day. I had an introduction from Count Umberto Morra, cultural counsellor at the Italian Embassy, who had been a tenant of mine in bachelor days. We went to Berenson's villa, I Tatti, for tea and were asked to stay on for dinner. The old man quizzed me about the London cultural scene. I had to parry malicious questions about Hamish Hamilton, then the most fashionable publisher in London. Yvonne Hamilton, Berenson's solicitous friend, was Florentine. She made many an attempt to be on passably friendly social terms with me, but her efforts met with her husband's stony objection. Later I learnt from Hugh Trevor-Roper that Berenson had given a warm account of our meeting to Hamish Hamilton, telling him that I had made a favourable impression – largely to feed his emergent professional rivalry.

Not long after our honeymoon, Jane and I went to stay with the art critic and collector Douglas Cooper. We were among the first guests at the Château de Castille, between Avignon and Nîmes, which Douglas and his young companion, John Richardson, had turned into one of the most quietly elegant domains I have ever seen. The walls were covered with the finest collection of Cubist and Surrealist pictures.

Douglas Cooper had only just emigrated from England, feeling that he had not been properly acknowledged there. He did not make allowance for his frightful temper – his reputation for not getting on with people probably cost him the directorship of the Tate Gallery. Having been passed over, he pursued all those who accepted the job with venom. I was present at the occasion in the Tate Gallery in 1954 when Cooper had his famous contretemps with the director Sir John Rothenstein. It reminded me of the gambling scene in *La Traviata*, when the whole of Paris is assembled, only in this case it was the whole of London and the whole of Paris which had come over for the opening of the great exhibition. Cooper followed Rothenstein around hissing in a loud stage whisper, 'Look at that little Jap.' Eventually Rothenstein turned and swiped him. Cooper's appointment to the Slade professorship of Fine Arts at Oxford a few years later was a form of compensation for the lack of recognition he had hitherto experienced in England.

Born of an English family which had emigrated to Australia and accumulated a great deal of wealth, Douglas was cosmopolitan and at the same time distinctly Anglo-Saxon. He had a histrionic talent for languages, though his accent was almost too perfect. He spoke the French of a cultivated Frenchman, and the German of a *Kunstforscher*. Even his English was rather mannered. His parents had given him a very European education and a large amount of pocket money to indulge his passion for collecting contemporary art. He specialized in Cubism, and cultivated Picasso, Juan Gris, Braque and Léger. In fact, when I visited the Château de Castille with Jane, Fernand Léger was also there with his Russian wife, whom he had only recently married. He had come to put the finishing touches on a large painting of circus acrobats which he had painted for Douglas. By combining research with personal contact, Douglas became a walking encyclopaedia of the artists' opus, so much so that they would sometimes ask him to verify their own work. More than once he was able to point out that a picture that had been sold at auction was a fake.

Douglas was flamboyant. He was fiercely and embarrassingly anti-monarchist and would refer to 'that Hanoverian bitch' or 'the terrible Huns on the throne'. During the war he gained a reputation in the Royal Air Force as a dreaded interrogator, and was flown out to various places like Malta and Cairo to interview the more truculent German airmen. By the time I met him he had got over the car accident which had changed his countenance. Earlier pictures show him as a rather demure and handsome young man, but he became a *monstre sacré*. He gained an enormous amount of weight and behaved like the Baron de Charlus. In keeping with the fashion of the day, he had a shrieking tone of conversation spiked with erudition and devastatingly malicious wit. He had a passionate and polemical turn of mind and took offence as easily as he gave it. For all his insensitivity he could be affectionate and kind. If you were on the right side of him he was a generous and thoughtful host who would defend you against any critics, but he was not a man to have as an enemy. I managed to avoid quarrels with him by listening to his stentorian judgements with a bland smile that reflected a sort of Gandhiesque pose of non-violent non-cooperation. He was not an easy person to deal with, but despite one tiff, the cause of which I cannot remember, our friendship persisted for more than twenty years. I benefited greatly from Douglas's advice on art books. A man of definite and intemperate views, he categorized writers on art either as great scholars or as charlatans. He was generous with ideas and introductions to authors. Under his guidance we published one of our most ambitious and successful art books entitled *The Great Private Collections*.

Douglas had many infatuations, ranging from rough trade to distinguished celebrities. But there can be no doubt that John Richardson was the love of his life. The son of a colonial official, John was educated at Westminster. After school he lived on his wits as a young man about town. He was taken up by Sacheverell Sitwell and Geoffrey Hobson, an Anglo-Irish collector and *bon vivant* who preceded Peter Wilson as head of Sotheby's. John learnt a great deal from Douglas. Had his mentor not been so possessive, the relationship might have lasted. On a trip Douglas eventually allowed him to make to America, John broke free from his restrictive embrace. During his liberating coast-to-coast tour, his rapid social success fascinated New York.

On the eve of his return to France, John attended a dinner party at the New York town house of Minnie and Jim Fosburgh. Minnie was the oldest of the three famous Cushing sisters and a former wife of Vincent Astor. Jim was a moderately gifted painter. A rather nervy and delicate man, he had problems with alcohol and his sexual identity. The other guests were Cecil Beaton, Loelia Westminster and myself. At the end of a pleasant and civilized evening, Cecil asked John to give us an account of his experiences in America. John rhapsodized about the unending opportunities for self-indulgence he had learnt about in the course of his stay. As he progressed with his pithy descriptions of erotic adventures in the beau monde, demi-monde and sous-monde of various cities in the United States, he became absorbed, as though in a trance. Jim Fosburgh's temples began to swell, and when John mentioned the subject of necrophilia, which he had been told about at second-hand, our host rose to his feet and stuttered, 'Get out of my house. I can barely take it, but it's my little woman I worry about ...' There followed a pantomime of speechless embarrassment. Loelia, unruffled, restored peace, and after a painful silence the atmosphere returned almost to normal.

The emancipating effect of John's American journey ruptured his relationship with Douglas. It all ended in acrimony and side-taking, with Douglas not speaking to anyone who spoke to Richardson. After the break-up John established himself on the New York intellectual and social stage, contributing distinguished pieces of art criticism to the *New York Review of Books* and advising collectors. He has become one of the foremost art critics, and as one of the wittiest raconteurs he is a coveted dinner partner. His Picasso biography justly earned him the membership of the British Academy and a Slade professorship at Oxford.

In those early years at the Château de Castille, the Douglas-Richardson partnership could not be faulted in terms of hospitality. John ran the house with great style, while Douglas presided as the expansive conversationalist. I spent two Whitsun holidays there during the bullfighting season, which Picasso attended with his colourful entourage. Like an Oriental despot, he always had at least half a dozen people in tow; they stayed at the Hotel Imperator in Nîmes but took their meals in Cooper's house. Picasso and Douglas vied with each other in mannered soliloquies while we sat listening in Louis XV fauteuils. One day we met in Arles for an early lunch before going on to the bullfight. Picasso's wife Jacqueline was of the party, so was his Basque barber who served as his window on the world. Picasso never read newspapers, but his barber would buy a Spanish refugee newspaper and, while shaving him, would regale him with the news of the day in the patois of his native region. Then there were the bullfighters, Dominguìn and Ordoñez, and someone from Kahnweiler, Picasso's dealer. A taxi driver was always in attendance. He was, in fact, Picasso's chauffeur, but because a chauffeur-driven limousine was hardly in keeping with his Communist sympathies, he kept a taxi instead.

We lunched out of doors, and in order to have a view of the arena we all sat on one side of the table with Picasso in the middle, like the twelve apostles at Leonardo's *Last Supper*. During the meal we watched as fleets of buses drew up beyond the hedge which separated the restaurant from the street and disgorged groups of aficionados from Spain. Most of them were young men in dark shirts with coloured scarves round their necks. The news that Picasso was in the restaurant spread like wildfire. He seemed to relish the gathering crowd gaping at him from a respectful distance. One particularly charming-looking Spanish student caught Picasso's eye, and he asked the waiter to bring him over. While we munched grapes and drank coffee, Picasso sat the young man down next to him and soon they were engaged in animated conversation. It transpired that he came from a place not far from where Picasso was born. He was studying medicine in reduced circumstances and had to support an aged mother and a tubercular sister. The young man told of his problems without a hint of supplication. Picasso listened attentively. He said nothing, but, reaching across the table he took the oversized menu and began drawing furiously on the back of it. Within twenty minutes he had signed and dated a bold tauromachian drawing. He handed it to the young man and said, 'Take this to Kahnweiler and ask for –' Picasso interrupted himself and asked, 'How much do you need to take you through college?' Somewhat taken aback, the student muttered a figure. Picasso instructed him to ask for no less than that. 'If Kahnweiler tries to give you less, refer him to me'. I was fascinated by this power to change a person's life with one gesture.

Douglas and John also took me to visit Braque and his rather small, canine-looking wife in their house in Paris. It was filled with his own ochre-toned canvases which radiated a sepia glow as dusk fell on that autumn day. We sat and listened to Douglas having an amiable bargaining session over a large oil painting. Though courteous, Braque was dour and taciturn. He had beady eyes and struck me as being very French. There was something old-worldish about him. He stood out among the artists I met with Douglas as the only one who held right-wing views.

After our marriage, Jane and I settled into the house at 11 Chester Square, the top floors of which I had originally rented from the Tory MP Ned Carson. His father, the barrister Edward Carson, had successfully represented the Marquess of Queensberry against Oscar Wilde but refused to accept the Crown's brief when criminal proceedings were started against him. It so happened that my parents lived in the house next door. My mother was a dab hand at finding bargains on the property market, and she sold the house at a profit some years later and moved to Lower Sloane Street, where she spent her final years.

Before Ned Carson I had shared the top maisonette with Woodrow Wyatt, who was then a young Labour MP and a rising star. He had been Sir Stafford Cripps's personal assistant on the Cabinet Mission to India in 1946 which had laid the foundations for

Independence. Although it was unpopular on the Left, Woodrow championed the cause of the Muslim leader, Jinnah. Before drawing attention to himself on the backbenches he had already made a name for himself in the media. The BBC cultivated talent in the Forces for actuality broadcasts, and Major Wyatt was called on to produce commentaries on India, on morale in the Army and on the postwar world. I used to bump into him in the BBC studios and the canteen. Woodrow knew Ned Carson, so when we discovered that we both needed digs we ended up in Chester Square. It was spacious rather than grand. The Carsons lived on the lower floors for a time while we had the upper maisonette.

When I married, my father-in-law bought the house in Chester Square for us, and when Jane left I bought it back from him at the same price as part of the divorce settlement.

Being married to Jane meant being married to the Family. It was close and clannish, and I liked this warmth and mutual dependence. There were certain rules to be observed. By convention a young couple was expected to give at least one cocktail party a year to which the wider Family was invited. Knowing that I knew nothing about wine, my father-in-law took charge of the wine cellar. Besides an eternal cycle of cocktail parties, adherence to the Sieff branch also entailed regular attendances at dinners and weekend parties. I built up an ever-widening circle and delighted in mixing the friends I acquired through publishing – intellectuals, writers and politicans – with members of the Marks & Spencer clan. It was a meeting of two worlds which both sides found intriguing. The Gargoyle Club continued, though it was no longer as central to all our lives as it had once been – after the war new horizons beckoned.

Driven by a desire to establish myself, I plunged Jane into a full life where work and conviviality danced a hectic round. The outside world may have mistaken for real, as it so often does, the trappings of wealth and security I displayed. But I was determined to be independent of Jane's relations. Unlike most of those who married in to the Family, I resisted pressure to enter the business. The Family showed me great kindness, but both Simon Marks and Teddy Sieff left me in no doubt that they would have preferred me to give up publishing and join them. Each of them in turn tried to bring me to reason in tense interviews. Simon warned me that I was foolish to start a firm 'at the highbrow end of the market' when he could offer me the prospect of a challenging and rewarding career. 'You have got one of the best brains in the Family,' he cried, 'and you want to publish books which only a few thousand people will read.' Nonetheless, they were quite proud when they heard of my early successes, and they enjoyed meeting some of the up-and-coming authors in our house.

Jane made valiant efforts to support me, and at first she seemed to take to her new life. We shared an interest in music and art, and she enjoyed the company of close friends like the Woodrow Wyatts and Sonia Orwell, who became one of her confidantes. Sonia joined us for an agreeable summer holiday in Lerici on the Ligurian coast, near Bocca di Magra where the Italian publisher Giulio Einaudi, an urbane Communist who was the son of Italy's president, Luigi Einaudi, presided over a literary colony. One of our neighbours was Marguerite Duras, at that time Sonia's closest friend, and not yet the literary star she was to become.

Our daughter was born on 2 June 1953, the day of the Queen's coronation. We named her Laura after my maternal grandmother, and gave her two middle names: Miriam, after her great-aunt Miriam Marks, and Elizabeth, in honour of our sovereign. I was beside myself with joy.

On that momentous day I went from the maternity clinic to Lady Marks's apartment in Grosvenor Square. Television sets had been installed in every room and excitable guests were milling around watching the ceremony and nibbling exquisite petits fours. Among them were Stanislas (Stas) and Grace Radziwill. They were a much talked-about couple in London and I was intrigued to meet them. Grace and I had an instant rapport, based on our Central European background. She had a Catholic Montenegrin mother and a Jewish Austro-Croat father who had made his fortune in shipping. She was highly intelligent and craved intellectual stimulation, but her social aspirations, heightened by the insecurity that comes from somehow still feeling a refugee, prevailed.

The Radziwills lived in grand style in Belgravia. When they gave dinner parties, Stas sat at one end of the table, a peasant prince, gruff and morose, with heavy eyebrows, an Adolphe Menjou moustache and a large handkerchief flowing from his breast pocket, and Grace at the other. The two of them would engage in a spirited dialogue loud enough to carry over the chatter of their guests. Often it would be about genealogy. Stas used his wife as a living *Almanac de Gotha*. He would boom across the table, 'Grace, this Lubomirska woman wants money. Says she's cousin. Is she cousin?' Grace would rattle off the ancestry in her distinctive Slav voice which was softened by a Franco-Italian accent.

Grace was vivacious, statuesque and conspicuously elegant. Conspicuous elegance of any kind was still a great rarity in London, where austerity psychologically outlasted the war and the rich were uneasy about displaying wealth. Grace introduced an element of French style and opulence to the London scene. The Radziwills entertained royally. In the summer they took grand country houses in foreign parts. I stayed with them in Lampedusa territory in Sicily. Their house parties were very cosmopolitan. They made friends with locals and imported grandees from France, Britain and America. Stas had a succession of affairs with fashionable women, which Grace tolerated with French complaisance. She managed to outlast them all until she found her match in Lee Bouvier, the beautiful, doe-eyed sister of Jackie Kennedy.

Lee was married to Michael Canfield, the adopted son of Cass Canfield, chairman of Harper. Michael never found his feet in publishing. While listlessly managing the Harper & Row sales office in London he became social secretary to Winthrop Aldrich, the American ambassador to the court of St James. The young Canfields were invited to Sicily, and the affair between Stas and Lee blossomed in the corridors of the Lanza palace. Grace asked me to intervene and I duly engaged Stas in a thankless conversation. He asked me what I thought of Lee, and I told him that she was an attractive girl but advised him not to leave Grace. He repeated all this to Lee. Since then we have not been on the best of terms.

The Canfields gave a New Year's Eve party in London six months later. After dancing cheek to cheek, they announced their separation at midnight. Grace was beside herself. She plunged into a life of restless travel, determined not to be outdone. After various adventures she married the Earl of Dudley, a post-Edwardian rake who owned a large estate outside London. I had an altercation with him once when he suddenly turned to me at dinner and declared, 'They tell me you are a Pinko. Is it true?' I rather sheepishly admitted that I was a supporter of the Labour Government. He seemed to be trembling with rage, but he regained his composure and was perfectly civil towards me for the rest of his life.

After Laura's birth I revelled in my first and, as it turned out, only year of conventional family life. Our daughter was smothered with parental and grandparental affection. But Jane needed more attention than I was capable of giving her, and I also failed to understand her need for privacy. Perhaps she underestimated the strains of building a publishing house with limited resources, but there is no doubt that I concentrated a disproportionate amount of my energies on work, travel and conviviality. We spent too little time together, and Jane felt neglected. At first she hid her growing disenchantment, but though she was reserved and reticent, she could speak her mind. Before long our estrangement grew markedly.

Jane felt she did not share enough of my life, and withdrew. All this was compounded by casual infidelities on my part which she was aware of despite my attempt at discretion. Yet I wanted the marriage to succeed, hoping that time, habit and a consolidation of my business life would improve our relationship. In retrospect I realize that I did not work hard enough at making the marriage work.

I felt things were going wrong in the spring of 1954 after I came back from a prolonged trip to New York. In the summer things came to a head, and Jane suggested that we separate. She was no longer in love with me, and had become attached to Cyrille Caën, a French student of psychology and the nephew of a friend of ours who was the cultural counsellor of the French Embassy. She told her father, who was very anxious that we should not give up. He talked her into spending the summer with me in a final effort to repair the marriage. We went to Cesenatico on the Adriatic coast and had a miserable time. It became clear that the marriage could not be mended. Jane wanted to leave. There followed weeks of numbing coexistence made all the more painful by superficial amity.

Sonia Orwell made her influence felt. She had a voyeuristic streak which her friends satisfied by confiding in her, so she was privy to the complexities of their intimate affairs. Her feminist side led her to assume that the man was always wrong, the woman exploited and the relationship doomed. Hers was either a mission of damage control or of cathartic change. Since we worked in the same office and she also saw a a great deal of Jane, Sonia had been quick to detect the first fissures. When the bonds became more frail, she was the first to suggest a cutting of the ropes. She was there throughout, concerned, compassionate and amusing.

One November night in 1954 we gave a party to celebrate the hundredth book on the Weidenfeld & Nicolson list. It was Peter

Quennell's *Baudelaire and the Symbolists*, the revised edition of a book first published in 1929, and Peter was the guest of honour. Evelyn Waugh, Randolph Churchill and Ian and Ann Fleming were among the guests, and Sonia Orwell helped Jane as hostess. There was much jollity, only slighty marred by a drunken Randolph Churchill smashing a valuable chair to smithereens. Next day, when I returned from the office, Jane had left with Laura. Within no time at all I received a handwritten letter from Isaiah Berlin. He commiserated but confessed that he was not surprised since our interests were too diverse.

I took the inevitable rather badly and tried to get custody of Laura. With hindsight I was unjustified, but I missed her terribly and was loath to see her move to Paris when her mother married Cyrille Caën. As the child of a broken marriage with parents living in different countries, her early years were far from easy. Laura was hopelessly spoilt by my mother and particularly attached to my father, who was, I think, a decisive influence on her. They used to talk about all kinds of things. He taught her Latin and some German and she developed a passion for classical languages. When she went to Oxford she opted for a degree in Classics.

Laura was an earnest child, inordinately ambitious academically, and intellectually mature, though in some respects young for her age. She was idealistic and romantic and obviously suffered from the rift between her parents, although her mother and stepfather gave her a great deal of warmth and love.

Fatherhood did not come naturally to me, and my efforts were further impeded by the logistics. I visited Laura in Paris as often as I could. We would meet for lunch, a few hours in the afternoon or occasionally an evening – a visit to the patisserie Rumpelmayer at the rue de Rivoli, which had the air of the Vienna cafés of my youth, or an excursion to the Jardin d'Acclimatisation, where for a panicky two hours I once lost Laura in the crowd, only to find her calmly reading a book of poetry on a bench near the exit. She must have been twelve then, but she already showed the composure I have always admired in her. It covers a passionate nature which occasionally surfaces.

When Laura was in her teens we tried an experiment. She came to live with me for a year and attended the Lycée Français in London. It was an unhappy time for her. I had just married Sandra Payson, whose younger daughter Averil was Laura's age. We lived in an enormous house where the two stepsisters had adjoining rooms. They became fast friends, and yet they were polar opposites. Averil was chic and mondaine, the product of American Wasp society; Laura was bookish and shy with a touch of the bluestocking. Neither really liked England very much then. Sandra tried hard to make Laura feel at home, but it all must have seemed unreal to her.

In the end Laura decided to sit her baccalauréat in France and passed with flying colours. Laura loved music, and her voice was sufficiently good for her singing teacher to plead with me not to send her to university but let her train as a singer. But she herself chose Classics at Oxford, changing to Ancient Iranian and Sanskrit after a year. My daughter has always shown great diplomatic skill in leading her own life, refusing to conform with my ideas of what she should do. Resolute, but always tactful and charming, she is a non-conformist rather than a rebel.

On her first day at Oxford Laura fell into conversation with an undergraduate in the queue for an opera performance at the Playhouse. He was a year older than her and was reading history at Oriel. They parted without exchanging addresses, but he sent messages to all the women's colleges asking the young girl in the queue to contact him. Laura responded. They were close throughout their studies and married shortly after they both graduated.

Christopher Barnett's first ambition was to be a history don; the grim vicissitudes of British academic life made that impossible. Instead he has carved for himself a distinguished career in secondary education. He started as head of the history department at Bradfield School College, Berkshire, and eventually became headmaster of Whitgift School in Croydon, an affluent public school founded in 1599 by John Whitgift, Archibishop of Canterbury. Laura and he have three sons, Benjamin, Rowan and Nathaniel, and a daughter, Clara.

Some of my fondest memories are of outings with Laura which included my parents. Together we went to Vienna and Salzburg, where Laura later spent some time learning German and taking singing lessons, living in an eccentric household of aristocratic intellectuals. We also went on a family trip to Venice and Israel, where she later returned to work on a kibbutz. She has shown a great attachment to my family, visiting old aunts and cousins and cultivating links which I myself had allowed to lapse. Though we have almost always been apart, I have a close relationship with my daughter. She has kept an intimate distance and shown a compassionate understanding of my turbulent life.

CHAPTER FOURTEEN

Near-Fatal Attraction

WHEN JANE LEFT, my dream of patriarchal family life was shattered. It had borne little relation to reality, but I refused to admit this until faced with the wreckage. Some people showed me great kindness during that gloomy winter.

Loelia, Duchess of Westminster, whom I had met through Grace Radziwill, invited me to join her for Christmas at Russborough, the palatial house of the South African financier and philanthropist Sir Alfred Beit and his wife Clementine, a cousin of Nancy Mitford. Whilst not exactly *terra incognita*, the grand country house circuit in Ireland, which was dominated by the three Guinness heiresses, had not until then been familiar territory. The Beits loved music, particularly opera (they backed the Wexford Opera Festival in Ireland), and worshipped beauty and talent. At Russborough they entertained lavishly amid their great paintings and fine furniture. They had a romantic reverence for stylized formality but also introduced fresh blood, mixing generations and bringing an international cast of guests together with Irish museum curators, academics, writers and artists.

Loelia Westminister's girlish enthusiasm and high spirits made her a sought-after hostess and guest. She was the third of the four wives of 'Bend'Or' Westminster, an eccentric who was both coarse and fastidious and who was reputed to have been the richest man in England, and she loved luxury and comfort. Her circle had a cosmopolitan flavour, at once Francophile and philo-American, with a conventional network of old families and grand Bohemians forming the backbone. She also embraced a wave of newly arrived postwar millionaires, beneficiaries of the building boom or merchant adventurers, and helped launch them into society. When Mr and Mrs Charles Clore gave their first big ball, she drew up the list and encouraged all those who were thought of as grand, chic or fashionable to accept. Noel Coward, with whom she often stayed in Jamaica, was a close friend and so were Ian and Ann Fleming – indeed the character of Miss Loelia Moneypenny in the James Bond novels is a jocular salute to her.

Loelia loved the ballet, the theatre and the opera and patronized young writers and artists. But she did not have a conventional salon of the kind her friends Ann Fleming and Pamela Berry were famous for. Loelia improvised great convivial occasions – a mass excursion to Paris for a masked ball or a tour of the great Irish castles – with a mixture of the old gratin and the new plutocracy. She was equally eclectic in her love life: among her admirers were the chief curator of Versailles, a director of the National Gallery and a young merchant banker. She had a heart of gold and was deeply loyal to those she cared for. 'In every garden,' she once told me, 'there must be a pond for lame ducks. You must look after your old friends.'

Loelia showed me great kindness and often gave me sound advice. In my early days as a publisher she helped me consolidate literary connections I had already forged for myself and introduced me to authors. She also brought me a new partner, Tony Marreco, a barrister who had been in the legal department of the British Control Commission in Germany in the assimilated rank of briga-dier general. With his devastating good looks he broke many a heart. Lali Horstmann, in whose Berlin flat he lived for a while, was beholden to him. At Loelia's suggestion Marrecco became a partner in Weidenfeld & Nicolson, selling out at a profit after about nine years. Loelia's own memoirs, *Grace and Favour*, a remarkably frank account of her miserable marriage to the Duke of Westminster which we published in 1961, were widely praised as a revealing social portrait of the age.

Sadly, the marriage of a close friend can often lead to estrange-ment. When Loelia unexpectedly decided in 1969 to accept Sir Martin Lindsay as her husband, our friendship faded. A former arctic explorer-soldier and long-time Conservative MP for Solihull, he was a trifle insensitive and rather dully knowledgeable. Even his wife's ebullient charm failed to sweep him along, and a number of her old friends stopped seeing her.

When my marriage broke down, Loelia told me, 'You must do two things: change your friends and move house.' I stayed in Chester Square, but she drew me into her world, and I drowned my sorrows further by immersing myself again in the beau monde I had begun to move in before I went to Israel. The house in Chester Square was far too big for me on my own, so I sublet the attic floor to Count Umberto Morra. Rumour had it that he was an illegitimate son of Victor Emanuel III. Though somewhat monastic by temperament, he was much loved in London. He did a great deal to promote Italian literature in England after the war and I met many Italian writers through him.

Alberto Moravia, whom I had first encountered in Wroclaw, came more than once to stay with him in Chester Square. I remember long and acrimonious late-night discussions about Israel: though he was more interested in girls than in talking about literature or politics, he was vehemently anti-Zionist. I visited him in Rome when he was married to Elsa Morante, and later on when he lived with Dacia Maraini, whom I published. Moravia was only one of several Italian writers I met in London. Another was Natalia Ginzburg, who lived here in the late 1950s when her husband, Gabriele Baldini, a professor of English literature, was director of the Italian Cultural Institute in Belgrave Square. Ignazio Silone was also a frequent visitor. I had a mild flirtation with his Irish wife, Derina. But of all the figures from the Italian intellectual sphere whom I came across in London, the one I knew best was the painter Renato Guttuso, whom I first met through Moura Budberg. Our paths crossed again in Wroclaw and I often saw him in Rome. He came to England on a number of occasions when he was painting Noel Annan's official portrait for King's College, Cambridge. We also had a common link with Douglas Cooper and the philosopher Richard Wollheim, then a close friend of mine.

Through Sonia Orwell, Cyril Connolly became very much part of my life during the Chester Square years. The stories of Cyril's coterie of adoring 'Horizon' girls, his intimates, associates and camp followers, have been perpetuated in *romans à clef* by Nancy Mitford, Evelyn Waugh and Anthony Powell. His magazine, *Horizon*, founded during the Phoney War and favourite reading in the rarefied cloisters of academe as well as in the services, has become almost legendary. He towered over the literary scene, holding court at the Gargoyle Club or the White Tower restaurant in Soho, a favourite meeting place of elegant Bohemia in Soho, whose Greek owner took a vicarious interest in the fortunes of his clientele.

At first Cyril looked on me with some suspicion. Although we shared friendships with Peter Quennell, Freddie Ayer, Clarissa Churchill and Janetta Jackson, a wayward beauty who had been the Egeria to many remarkable men, some of whom she wed, Cyril kept well out of my way. As the witty, capricious, and yet self-doubting editor of the most admired literary review of the decade, he did not relish the idea of *Contact*. Though he tried to dismiss it as a middlebrow experiment, he feared competition. Once, during the 1940s, he told Philip Toynbee half jestingly, 'One day I'm going to send my boys to smash your shop.' But our relations improved greatly after he closed down *Horizon* at the end of 1949, with his famous peroration: 'It is closing time in the gardens of the West and from now on an artist will be judged only by the resonance of his solitude or the quality of his despair.'

Cyril abandoned himself to this pessimistic vein, but though slothful and dispirited, he was still keen to keep some influence in the literary world. Sonia Orwell persuaded him that I might be a publisher worth backing, and he transferred his allegiance from Hamish Hamilton to us, becoming a literary mentor of the firm. He was sagacious but hard-hitting, alternating praise with cruel criticism. A Francophile who was widely read and travelled, Cyril approved of my quest for European authors and we began to see a great deal of each other, meeting once or twice a week when he came up to London from the country. Cyril could be somewhat patronizing, but on the whole he was affectionate and helpful, and he took great interest in my entertaining. He adored fantasizing about different aspects of ideal convivial occasions, from the guest list to the culinary offerings, and used his savage talent for mimicry to improvise imagined conversations at the table of the Goncourt bothers or a nineteenth-century Oxford gaudy, or to imitate the stilted postprandial banter at a ducal weekend. There was only one blemish in our friendship: his wife, Barbara Skelton, whom he had married in 1950, and I did not get on.

Our relations had started on the wrong foot. Barbara had been attached to the British Embassy in Cairo in 1942 where, to the discomfort of her employers, she had found favour with King Farouk. Fearing embarrassment, the British authorities had asked her to leave. One day Peter Quennell, with whom I was then sharing a house, announced rather sheepishly that an old friend of his would be coming to stay. She found herself at a loose end and he was taking her up, for old time's sake. In keeping with the strict code

Peter and I had established of not socializing without prior arrangement, I barely saw Barbara. We occasionally met when she was brewing tea late at night in the basement kitchen, and our casual exchanges were always cool. She would say to Peter, 'I don't know what you see in Weidenfeld,' and I did not take to her either. When our Irish housekeeper threatened to leave if Barbara stayed, it was Barbara who went.

Barbara Skelton came from a military family. Her father was invalided out of the Army, and her mother, by now a widow, had been a Gaiety Girl. Their daughter liked intellectuals. She was strikingly good-looking, with a honey-coloured complexion, reddish-blonde hair and slightly slit eyes. She had a slim figure and wore clothes with unstudied elegance. Her voice was unforgettably distinctive – there was melody in her speech, and a faintly accusatory and doubting tone in her questions. She had a gift for narrative and could be extremely funny. Barbara was a sceptic. She was hypercritical of people and unpredictable in her judgements. An intimiste who disliked large gatherings, she was quiet and aloof, though given to volcanic eruptions. There was a mixture of arrogance and dejection about her. She read a great deal, loved animals, painting and cooking, and despised convention. She wanted to be amused but it was not easy to attract her interest, and when men succeeded in doing so they felt they had scored a triumph.

It was soon after she left Park Village East that she took up with Cyril Connolly. Though he was addicted to her, he behaved ambivalently, and their marriage was known to be eccentric. They led semi-independent lives, spending long weekends together in Barbara's cottage in Kent, but in London often going their separate ways. Cyril stayed at White's or with friends, while Barbara used a service flat in Dalmeny Court, a dark apartment house in St James's. She hated most of his friends and they hated her. Barbara had her own coterie, and the two groups rarely converged. Sometimes she came with Cyril to dine in my house, and occasionally we met in other people's houses, but it was quite clear that she disapproved of me and more often than not she stayed away.

In the summer of 1953, while I was still married to Jane, Cyril and I embarked on a spree of the European music festivals at the invitation of René Podbielski, an entrepreneurial intellectual of Prussian-Polish descent who arranged public relations for the European Festivals Association. The climax of our tour was Bayreuth, recently reopened after the war. Cyril was a neophyte to Wagnerian opera and did not know German. I had to translate long passages of the *Ring des Nibelungen* to him, though he insisted on reading the German first. His response showed an extraordinary capacity for intuiting meanings of sounds.

One day, as we were basking in the sun in the Schlosspark overlooking Bayreuth and reading the libretto of *Siegfried* in preparation for the next performance, Cyril began to tell me about his marriage. Animated by the German wine, he spoke with disarming frankness of his unhappiness and Barbara's infidelities. In mock Wagnerian language he declaimed, 'Why is there no knight in shining armour, no Siegfried, no Siegmund, no Lohengrin to come and take her away from me?' He knew that I would not be that shining knight, as it was no secret that Barbara and I did not get on. Cyril begged me to tell him horrible things about Barbara. He said it made it easier for him to stomach the fact that she was in Rome with King Farouk.

Cyril's lament was interrupted by the arrival of the Pryce-Joneses, father and son. His wife having recently died, Alan Pryce-Jones was taking his son David on a literary grand tour of Europe. They had lunched with Max Beerbohm in Rapallo, stayed with Somerset Maugham in the south of France and visited Bernard Berenson at the Villa I Tatti in Florence. Young David, then still at Eton, was far from impressed by his father's friends and talked patronizingly of all the grand people they had visited. Father and son vied with each other in extravagant descriptions of their hosts' proclivities and peccadilloes, alternating between panegyrics and brutal satire, David capping Alan's stories with his far more outrageous versions. Cyril and I were impressed by David's self-assurance and his gift for blending narrative and fantasy. A few years later, when an undergraduate at Oxford, he was able to put these talents to other uses: he was summoned to the table of Maurice Bowra and other Oxford mandarins who demanded that he regale them with tales of undergraduate excesses.

Cyril was amused by that Bayreuth encounter, but it did not take his mind off his musings about Barbara for long. Throughout the week he identified with all the unhappy characters in the *Ring*, Siegmund in particular. For some time afterwards he signed himself 'Wehwalt' (Woe-wald) on postcards to me.

In early May 1955, John Sutro, a rich Oxford contemporary and lifelong friend of Evelyn Waugh and an old admirer of Barbara, asked me to the theatre with his wife. I arranged to take Antonia Pakenham to make up a foursome. We met at the Savoy for a drink, where Sutro revealed that his wife had dropped out and Barbara Connolly would be coming instead. Knowing of the froideur between us, he was slightly apologetic. When we left the theatre it was raining heavily. Barbara did not have a coat, so we stopped at Dalmeny Court on our way to dinner at Les Ambassadeurs. I got out of the taxi and saw her into the building. As she walked past she brushed against me in the narrow entrance. I suddenly felt very attracted to her. After dinner we all went on to the Milroy nightclub. By coincidence, Cyril was also there with a group of people. There was a jolly, back-slapping atmosphere on the dance floor, with Barbara teasing Cyril by saying of me, 'He dances rather well,' and Cyril replying, 'Yes, yes, you ought to get to know him better.' Barbara was animated; indeed, in her oblique way, she was coquettish. At the end of a pleasant evening I took Antonia back to her Chelsea basement and returned to my deserted conjugal home.

The next morning I was woken at 7.30 by the telephone. A husky voice at the other end said, 'George Weidenfeld?'

'Yes.'

'Do you have your diary handy? I suppose it's full of business meetings,' she said contemptuously.

Before I had a chance to answer, she asked, 'Do you want to have a drink before I go back to the cottage?'

'Yes. Shall we met before lunch at the Berkeley?'

'No. What are you doing for breakfast?'

Still somewhat taken aback, I admitted that I was free.

'Why don't you come over now?'

Within half an hour I arrived at Dalmeny Court where she had a small, dark suite consisting of a sitting room and bedroom. The curtains were drawn over the mock Gothic stained glass windows, and although it was a warm day, the apartment felt wintry. Barbara was wearing a fur-lined jacket over her pyjamas. She offered me breakfast and I asked for some tea. She ordered tea. I made my first advance, but she said, 'Wait for the tea.' As we sat waiting I made some banal remarks like, 'It's very like *sous les toits de Paris*.' She grunted disdainfully. The moment the waiter left the room, our love affair began. I left Barbara at about midday. I remember the sun blinding my eyes. As I walked down the street I heard an organ grinder. It felt like a scene from *Les Enfants du Paradis*.

Barbara spent the weekend in the country. We telephoned clandestinely and arranged to meet the following Monday. I cut short a lunch with Ann and Ian Fleming, one of their typical lunches with a mixture of lions and scions. Evelyn Waugh was there and was in one of his rare benign moods. When I left he shouted after me, 'Happy publishing.'

Barbara and I spent the afternoon together at my house. I had completely forgotten that Friedelind Wagner, the composer's rebellious granddaughter, was coming to discuss a literary project. Barbara hid upstairs while I dismissed Friedelind after the briefest of meetings. We met almost every day that week, and our relationship became very intense, but it was fraught with recriminations and dark moods, punctuated by brief, idyllic moments. The difficulty of communicating did not help, but John Sutro, who had been a rival of Cyril for Barbara's attentions and was opposed to the Connolly marriage from the outset, offered his services as *postillon d'amour*. Feliks Topolski, another of Barbara's admirers and confidants, also encouraged my suit – he too did not have good relations with Cyril. Barbara and I went on several furtive trips abroad. Once, when we were in Paris, Cyril tried to locate her by telephoning every hotel, but she knew a small place near the Place de la Concorde where we were left undisturbed. On another occasion, when Cyril was away, we spent the weekend in her cottage.

One July evening, about six weeks after we had started the affair, I was changing to go out to a late party given by Martha Gellhorn and her husband Tom Matthews a few houses along in Chester Square when the telephone rang. It was Barbara, saying she had to see me. She was speaking from a telephone box in a Soho restaurant where she had had a jealous scene with Cyril over dinner. Cyril crept up on her and she rang off. Twenty minutes later she arrived in a taxi and ran upstairs to my bedroom. Sobbing, she threw herself into my arms. Five minutes later disaster struck. The door opened and Cyril walked in. I had a temporary Spanish maid who spoke no English and he had simply pushed her aside. We froze as he stood in the doorway for the best part of a minute. Then he left. Cyril lost no time in telling Ann Fleming. Next day the news was all over London.

Ours was a passionate, heart-rending and hopeless relationship governed by alternating cycles of physical obsession, glimmers of hope, deep depression and profound guilt on both sides. While it lasted, it seemed like a suspension of normal life. I thought of nothing else. I knew no good could come of my relationship with Barbara, but it was an addiction which dwarfed everything else. I remember lunching in a hotel on the Boulevard Haussman in Paris with an Israeli friend and telling him I was at a loss as to what to do. At one point I made my excuses and went to find a telephone. In those days it was not possible to dial London direct. When my friend heard me give an English telephone number to the operator and guessed whom I might be ringing, he rushed up to urge me not to do so, nearly knocking me down in the process.

Friends, cynical onlookers and compassionate neutrals intrigued, polemicized and mediated. Some of Cyril's partisans, who included Stephen Spender, Sonia Orwell, Janetta Jackson and Robert Kee, devised strategies to make me desist. Stephen Spender took me to lunch at the Hungarian Czarda and warned me that if I pursued the affair I would suffer grievously as a publisher. Others were less censorious. Over lunch at Bertorelli's, Ben Nicolson, Freddie Ayer, Peter Vansittart and others went out of their way to say that they would not take sides. I have never forgotten that.

The summer of 1955 was very turbulent. Barbara went back to Cyril and we did not meet for a few weeks. But it was not long before we were reunited, and again there were tearful and bitter scenes, followed by periods of separation and renewed attempts to carry on in a carefree manner. There were times when Barbara wanted a conclusive break and I entreated her to stay, and there were other times when I got cold feet and asked for a breathing space. Whenever we escaped Cyril managed to find out where we were; often he was nearby, begging her to come back to him. In her maliciously teasing way Barbara must have sent him signals. It was psychological warfare. This unhappy state went on for more than a year of high drama, during which Cyril went ahead with divorce proceedings. Hamish Hamilton took great pleasure in calling at my office in person to say Cyril had instructed him to withdraw our contract with him. However, David Pryce-Jones effected a reconciliation between Cyril and myself and I saw him several times before his death.

By the late spring of 1956 it seemed as if it was all over and she would go back to Cyril once and for all. But some perverse compulsion drove us together again and in August we got married. The ceremony was a dismal affair, more like a wake than a wedding. We both felt a deep sense of doom. My parents were opposed to the match and did not come to the wedding. Even at the celebratory party Charles Clore gave for us the mood was subdued. No one seemed to think the marriage would last.

Our honeymoon was spent in Ischia, and once again Cyril Connolly was nearby, being consoled at the other end of the island by Maurice Bowra and W.H. Auden. Our conjugal life was a disaster from the outset. To my horror Barbara imported a cat to Chester Square and hired a drunken butler who took all my shirts with him when he left. She was disapproving of the company I kept and flaunted her boredom. When I gave dinner parties she would disappear in the middle, or turn up in tennis shoes. She only perked up when friends of hers were around, as when Graham Greene came to dinner and spent the whole evening telling highly technical ecclesiastical jokes. Barbara was a great dampener. She did not like my euphoric phases and made sarcastic comments when I dreamt of castles in the air, or on the ground for that matter.

In the autumn of 1956 I went to America on a prolonged business trip, leaving Barbara behind. After being cooped up in this distressing marriage I found the change of atmosphere and the warm welcome I received on the other side of the Atlantic gratifying. It was a relief to be catapulted into a different world. While I was there Caroline Blackwood, then already divorced from Lucian Freud, told me in an unguarded moment that Barbara had begun seeing Cyril again.

Cyril had a compulsive need for Barbara's company. In the early stages of our marriage he sometimes sat watching the house from a taxi in Chester Square. Barbara never denied her strong emotional link to Cyril and was deeply aware of the debt she owed him for having broadened her intellectual horizon. Saddened by the inadequacies of our marriage, she began to meet him again. Whilst I was in America they spent a weekend together in her cottage in Kent.

Not long after my return from America I consulted a lawyer. Mr Derek Clogg of Theodore Goddard spoke like Noel Coward and was the caricature of a naval officer. On his advice I employed a detective, who found evidence that Cyril had spent the weekend in Barbara's cottage. The local greengrocer, the postman and the gardener were all willing to testify. The people in the village said they had never been aware of Barbara remarrying and still referred to her as Mrs Connolly. On receiving this evidence Mr Clogg gave me the clipped command to leave the matrimonial home. I obeyed and divorce proceedings began. Barbara stayed on at Chester Square for a short time. She went back to Cyril, but it did not last. We met again in the early 1960s in London and New York, but have since lost touch. Our relationship had lasted twenty-two months from the onset of desire to separation.

CHAPTER FIFTEEN

Retracing the Third Reich

WHEN I FIRST VISITED the Frankfurt Book Fair in 1951, the German publishing trade was in a state of upheaval. I stayed in a small pension and made my way to the fair through the ruins. The city had been badly destroyed, transport was difficult and people were sleeping on the streets. Everyone looked grey, hungry and weary.

The fair had been going again for a few years, but it was still fairly primitive, though there was hope and ambition in the air. Like all other professions, German publishing houses were in a state of renewal. They had to think up ingenious ways of overcoming material deficiencies. Unable to get ordinary wood-free paper, Rowohlt published great works of world literature on rotary machines as newspapers. Other houses were bringing out first editions of important European and American authors banned by the Nazi regime. Some of the time-honoured publishers had been discredited because of Nazi connections, others were stuck behind the Iron Curtain. But a number of survivors of the grand old days of Weimar Germany were there – Jacob Hegner, old Ernst Rowohlt and his son Ledig, Peter Suhrkamp, and Joseph Witsch, the jovial bon viveur who published Heinrich Böll and Gottfried Fischer. The Fischer family were aloof to the point of seeming arrogant. So was the managing director of the firm, Dr Hirsch, a highly cultured man who acted as Hugo von Hofmannsthal's executor.

Since then the Frankfurt Book Fair has become an international stock exchange for the trade. For a publisher intent on working on an international scale, all roads converge there every year for a week in early October. In my experience of that event, which spans nearly half a century, a few figures stand out as symbols of continuity and distinctiveness. Perhaps the most remarkable of these was Heinrich Maria Ledig-Rowohlt, whose passion for books was informed by a mixture of adolescent enthusiasm, mature taste and commercial guile. Although he bellowed English poetry in sounds echoing the boulevards of Weimar Berlin, he had a magisterial sense of language which he brought to bear in his translations of Nabokov and other writers.

Ledig, as he was known to his friends, struck those who had a fixed idea of what they perceived to be the German stereotype as the most un-German German. He was a cosmopolitan who abhorred narrow patriotism, militarism and all that smacked of the philistine, reserving particular contempt for the 'grocer mentality' of many of his compatriots in publishing. He loved the bizarre, favoured rebels and condoned sexual licence in others. To me Ledig was the most typical and lovable representative of the Germany of protestant humanism, of the apostles of the enlightenment and the high-minded rowdies of *Sturm und Drang*. He might have been a drinking companion of Büchner, or commiserated with Heine. As a young man working for his father Ernst Rowohlt, the publisher of Tucholsky and Brecht, Ledig had been part of Weimar Berlin's Bohemia. After a war spent rather passively in the German Army on the Russian front, he helped his father revive the Rowohlt publishing house. While nursing young German talent, he also introduced the German public to the works of Sartre, Camus and Hemingway.

Ledig married a beautiful red-haired Englishwoman. Having grown up partly in France, where her father had been a director of Lloyd's International, she spoke with a distinct French accent which withstood even an Oxford education. Jane Rowohlt was a mixture of elitist elegance, profound shyness and hard common sense. She had a sharp critical judgement and worked discreetly but effectively at her husband's side.

Impeccably dressed in Savile Row suits, Ledig broke sartorial convention with his flamboyant ties and shirts. He was famous for a somersault party trick which he used to perform at private dinners or indeed in hotel lobbies. Equally at home with Nobel Prize winners and budding novelists, he regularly attended writers' gatherings the world over. He worshipped youth and beauty, and it was characteristic that he should side with the rebellious students in the stormy late 1960s.

Fixed in my mind is a scene one Sunday morning at the Hessischer Hof, the hotel opposite the Frankfurt fairground, where many notable publishers stay during the book fair. Daniel Cohn-Bendit, then one of the leading radicals of the student movement, had come to meet some publishers sympathetic to his cause. In a gesture part self-mocking, part genuine admiration, Ledig genuflected before the young rebel, his ever-present Havana cigar in his left hand and a red carnation torn from his buttonhole raised as an offering in his right.

To the end of his life he was always the first to arrive and the last to leave the lobby or the bar of the Hessischer Hof. He died in 1992 aged eighty-three after catching pneumonia in an air-conditioned railway carriage in India, where he had travelled to attend an international publishers' congress.

If Ledig Rowohlt represented the radical spirit of Weimar, Wolf Jobst Siedler, another remarkable figure in German postwar publishing, stood for Prussian humanism. He nurtured a whole generation of German historians, encouraging them to depart from the stilted professorial style which alienated the wider reading public. Tall, good-looking, pleasure-loving and at times even swashbuckling, Siedler, who had served a brief prison sentence under the Nazis, was a German conservative who had no time for the tendency to self-denigration common among the intellectuals of postwar Germany. He had an eye for art and was one of the first to condemn the failures of architects and town planners of the postwar years.

Besides the brassy mass entertainments in the ballrooms of the big hotels, the Frankfurt Book Fair featured some more discriminating events held on fixed days of that week. They were hosted by specific publishers, local figures or an out-of-town hostess who would put together a party with writers, politicians, bankers, the odd member of the Rhenish or Hessian nobility and whatever distinguished foreign guest happened to be in town to promote a book. Invitation to these occasions were highly sought after. Gabriele Henkel, the queen of German hostesses, made a regular appearance at the Frankfurt fair. She always managed to attract a select group of men and women of the moment.

In Düsseldorf, Gabriele and her husband Konrad, the longtime chairman of the Henkel detergent empire which includes Persil among its prime brands, received the political and cultural elite of Germany in their two houses, one in the inner city, the other on the outskirts. Gabriele perfected entertainment as an art; in fact her skill earned her a professorial chair in decorative arts. Her parties always had a theme. At a farewell dinner for the German President Walter Scheel she transformed her out-of-town guest house into a beautifully decorated railway station where the guests sat in carrri-ages. The motto of the evening was 'Grosser Bahnhof', an allusion to the days when foreign potentates used to arrive by train and be received by a royal host. At a dinner for a Middle Eastern celebrity, the place settings each had a minuscule hill of sand crowned with a flag bearing the guest's name. Gabriele had tireless enthusiasm for things new and fashionable. One of her intellectual mentors was the writer and critic Fritz Raddatz, a refugee from East Germany who worked for Rowohlt before joining the weekly newspaper *Die Zeit* in Hamburg, where he edited the cultural sec-tion for a number of years.

Experimental literature, literary criticsm and poetry – all genres which the more pragmatic publisher has learnt to shun – had a welcoming home in the publishing house Suhrkamp under the direc-tion of Siegfried Unseld. Robust in appearance and speech, auto-cratic in his dealings, he had a possessive, paternal relationship with his authors. He was one of the few publishers who succeeded in avoiding a compromise in standards, helped by a backlist of great authors and the firm's reputation, which dated from prewar times.

Over the years Frankfurt has become more and more inter-national. In the early postwar days one felt that foreign publishers were there on sufferance. They stood on the periphery, picking out the odd bargain or making an occasional deal. When I first went there, the Frankfurt Book Fair was more an opportunity for German booksellers to meet German publishers than for the sale of foreign rights. The booksellers looked a sorry lot in their frayed, prewar clothes or cheap new suits. I remember a group of them on a very hot September day in the courtyard of the fairground sitting cross-legged or kneeling on a red blanket they had spread on the ground, eating hunks of bread and boiled eggs flushed down with beer. They could not afford a restaurant.

As an Austrian-born Briton I was in a curious position. Some of the more patrician German publishers looked on me even more disdainfully than my British colleagues. Although it was in some ways easier to make deals because one spoke the same language and understood their mentality, many of them still preferred the old established British firms – this did not apply to the newer faces, with whom I worked very well.

The old liberal publishers of the Weimar period did not share my interest in contemporary history. They wanted to put the clock back to 1933 or before, whilst I had an unquenchable thirst for the details of daily life, for every shade of high life and low life during the Nazi period. I have always been passionately interested in the protagonists and humble witnesses of our time. Perhaps it is the passion of the historian manqué. During the war, as a BBC specialist in European and particularly German affairs, I became something of a walking card index of the Third Reich. The personalities enacting that ghoulish drama were, in a way, part of my life. All my knowledge had been derived from files, broadcasts, cuttings or books, but now that I was able to go to Germany I felt like an anthropologist who has spent a lifetime studying a remote African tribe in dusty volumes from a library shelf and is suddenly given a bursary to visit the object of his passion in its natural habitat. I was burning to know *'wie es eigentlich gewesen'* and used my profession as a means of satisfying my own curiosity, quite apart from the fact that I wanted to contribute to the British public's understanding of what had happened in Germany during those years. Publishing gave me a platform for seeking out eyewitnesses and protagonists wherever I went, though for obvious reasons Germany and Israel have always figured more prominently on the lists of Weidenfeld & Nicolson.

When I first travelled to Germany, the population was still numbed by the whole experience of Nazism. There was a general feeling of apathy, if not an aversion to dealing with the immediate past, until much later, when Joachim Fest's monumental Hitler biography helped spark off the debate about the Third Reich. In the aftermath of the war it was all too close to the bone for those who had lived through it, but we who had followed those events from the outside felt differently. In the course of my travels in postwar Germany I soon became aware how crude the picture we had of that country was. The canvas was painted in broad brushstrokes without any chiaroscuro. Through many conversations and observations I gradually formed a more detailed impression.

One of the people who helped give me new insights was Jean Rouvier, a Germanophile Frenchman who had a semi-diplomatic post as cultural attaché of the French Government in Munich. He spoke perfect German with a French accent, could recite great chunks of German poetry and was an amateur translator. I met him through Lali Horstmann. Rouvier was devoted to her, and although she rejected his advances he was always in attendance, even when she and Louise de Vilmorin spent tense weekends with Tony Marreco in Bavarian country houses or picturesque inns.

Rouvier was at the centre of a Francophile group in Munich which included Gerhard Heller and Horst Wiemer, two publishers who had both been in Paris during the German occupation. They crop up now and again in Ernst Jünger's diaries. An expert on French literature, Heller worked in the censor's office on the Champs Elysées, where he became a Schindler of endangered writers, earning himself a high reputation in Resistance circles. Horst Wiemer was seconded to the French publisher Hachette, which had been taken over by the Germans. He too was a great lover of French culture. At the end of the war he married Gaston Gallimard's secretary and went back to Beck Biederstein, where he had discovered Heimito von Doderer in the 1930s, while Heller worked first for Stahlberg and later for Ullstein. We used to meet regularly at the Wernicke Hof in Schwabing near Jean Rouvier's digs.

Lali Horstmann's world represented a microcosm of what was left of German society. She proved an ideal publishing scout. Not only did she have a wide range of contacts, but she could also be very persuasive. In those days many Germans were still reluctant to talk. German society had been cut off from the rest of Europe, and visitors from abroad were cautious about reestablishing contact lest they found themselves dealing with people who had a murky past in the Nazi Party. That all became more fudged with time. The Weizenbecks, who entertained whatever was left of café society in Munich, helped restore links with the international beau monde. Walter von Weizenbeck, 'Weizi' to his friends, worked for the insurance company Allianz. He was held in high regard in Munich because at enormous risk to himself he had used his position in the party to rescue Jews, including his wife Mimi, whose father had founded the *Prager Tagblatt*, one of the most important German-speaking newspapers in pre-Nazi days.

A number of Resistance figures, such as Ewald von Kleist, known as Pomorze, the Polish for Pomerania, because he came from there, or the Bavarian lawyer Josef Müller, always referred to as Ochsen

Sepp, moved in Lali's circle. Müller had been on Colonel Oster's staff in Admiral Canaris's military intelligence agency. A staunch Catholic, he was entrusted by the opposition to make use of his Vatican connections to establish a line of communication to the British Government through the Pope himself. Hans-Georg von Studnitz belonged to the same set. As an official in the press and information department of the Foreign Office, he had spent much of the war in Berlin. He was a German Scheherezade who kept me awake night after night with colourful tales about social life in the war-torn capital. No adventure seemed to have eluded his ear for gossip. In his characteristically *Junker*-like German he would give witty descriptions of the goings-on in Frau von Dirksen's famous salon, where Hitler was a frequent guest.

Studnitz had a wide repertoire of Horstmann stories. A particular favourite was his account of how Lali's husband Freddie played a practical joke on his guests by introducing a foreign party girl, whom he had dressed up and instructed like a latterday Professor Higgins as an aristocrat with some highfalutin title. One of his protégées was a Mexican beauty, Gloria. A grand German suitor fell for the ruse and ended up marrying her. She became Countess Fürstenberg, and later the pace-setting international socialite Mrs Loel Guinness. Apparently Freddie Horstmann also used to amuse himself by telling the women who came to his parties what colours to wear so as to match the china. I commissioned Studnitz to write a book called *While Berlin Burned*. In the hands of a truly gifted writer it could have been a masterpiece; nonetheless this account gives a flavour of that Berlin world.

On one of my early visits to Munich, Lali introduced me to Konstantin of Bavaria. He was a charming hedonist, an extrovert and a little florid. Like many members of former ruling houses, he had been exempted from military service early on in the war, Hitler being anxious to prevent any princelings from attracting undue popularity. When I met Konstantin he worked as a star reporter on *Kindler's Revue*. He was a talented raconteur and would give poignant accounts of the fates some people met in the wake of the war. He told a sad story about an Austrian refugee who joined the British Army and came to Rome in 1944 wearing the uniform of a major, was taken up by Roman society and made a member of the Caccia, an exclusive club, only to be dropped by the nobility and expelled from the Caccia once the Romans felt they were masters of their own house again. Unable to bear the humiliation any longer, the major, who had meanwhile become the representative of Rolls-Royce in Italy, killed himself in his hotel room. I commissioned Konstantin to write these stories up in a book called *After the Flood*, which, like a number of other foreign titles we published, was produced especially for the British market. Konstantin and I met regularly until he died in an air crash in 1969. He came to stay in Chester Square and I remember him being very smitten with Antonia Pakenham.

On one occasion Konstantin and I took another friend, Princess Herzeleide Biron, the daughter of the Kaiser's youngest son, to one of the earliest Salzburg festivals after the war. We went to a performance of *Don Giovanni*. It was Herzeleide's first visit to the opera. Next day, back in Munich, we lunched in a Biergarten with members of her family and various other blue-blooded Germans. Our visit to Salzburg came up in the conversation and one of the party exclaimed with utter incredulity, 'Herzeleide, whatever were you doing in Salzburg?'

'I went to see an opera.'

'An opera?'

'Yes.'

'What was it?'

'I can't remember what it was called.'

'Tell us about it.'

'Well, there was a man on the stage and he seemed to have a great deal of success with women. There were a lot of women he had jilted and they all shouted and screamed.'

The whole party collapsed in peals of laughter, but not at Herzeleide's touchingly simple account of the plot – the mere fact that somebody had been to the opera set them off.

Henriette von Schirach, the daughter of Hitler's photographer Heinrich Hoffmann, whose husband Baldur von Schirach, the former youth leader and later governor of Vienna, was then serving a twenty-year prison sentence in Spandau, also lived in Munich. I found her rather theatrical in the way that she played on pity and femininity. She came up to me, her Junoesque figure encased in a low-cut black dress, saying rather excitedly, 'How can you speak to me after all that has happened, how can I prove that I am also a human being?' She is known to have spoken out against the maltreatment of the Jews. On a visit to the Berghof, Hitler's retreat in Obersalzberg, she helped her husband try to draw Hitler's attention to the barbaric circumstances under which Jews were being deported. The only result was the couple's premature departure. Henriette von Schirach offered me her memoirs, but I did not take them. Some years later I also turned down Leni Riefenstahl. Albrecht Knaus could not understand why I would not publish a picture book about the 1936 Olympic Games in Berlin. 'After all,' he argued, 'they are masterly photographs.' But I felt that even a 'masterly' book about one of the great organizational feats of the Third Reich did not suit a Jewish publisher.

The first book I published on the Third Reich was a translation of Hjalmar Schacht's memoirs, *Account Settled*, which came out a year after the German original, *Abrechnung mit Hitler*. By a strange coincidence I met Schacht, who was acquitted of war crimes at the Nuremberg trials, about two years later. I spotted him on an aeroplane to Hamburg and introduced myself. We shared a taxi into town and ended up having dinner together. He had an old-world manner about him. But for a stand-up collar and tiepin, he was dressed à l'anglaise in a thick cream silk shirt with racing cuffs and a waistcoat, although it was summer.

I knew from other sources that, as head of the Reichsbank Schacht, he had opposed the Government's persecution of Jews, not least because of its detrimental effect on the German economy. Over dinner I asked him point blank about his attitude to the Jewish question. He was very knowledgeable about the activities of the Jewish Agency in Palestine in helping Jews transfer their money abroad, and told me that he had implored Goering to persuade Hitler to let the Jews leave for Palestine with all their chattels, minus a Reich tax of twenty-five per cent, thus enabling the Nazis to draw a line under the whole issue without giving up their racial theories. Schacht said he had argued for a form of positive apartheid under the motto, 'They don't get on with us, we don't get on with them, but they contributed to our economy and we contributed to their education, and since they are a bright, mercantile people we should use them as allies in the Middle East, where they could also prove useful in spreading German culture.' Schacht was full of regrets and keen to emphasize his resistance to the regime, as he had done in his memoirs.

I was helped in my pursuit of documentary material on the Third Reich by Hugh Trevor-Roper, who had dug witnesses out of the most obscure funkholes while researching his masterpiece of detective history, *The Last Days of Hitler*. One of his contacts was François Genoud, a French-Swiss lawyer who professed a deep historical interest in the Nazi regime. He was a curious figure, in his forties, intense and nervy with dark hair and slightly Mediterranean features. Genoud had established links with surviving Nazis or relatives of Hitler's henchmen, from whom he bought any document he could lay his hands on. He was a shrewd businessman who became something like a self-appointed executor of the Third Reich. We had endless discussions about the past, in the course of which he told me that he thought Hitler had made one fatal mistake: he should never have gone for the Jews. I always suspected this line to be a gambit.

I first met Genoud with Trevor-Roper at the Hotel Kléber in Paris not long after I married Jane. Her aunt, Lady Marks, was treating us to a weekend there and I had decided to combine it with business. I was rather secretive about the appointment, but the two women finally wormed out of me that I was meeting a distinguished Oxford historian and a strange figure who had access to important Nazi source material. Their curiosity was aroused, and they decided to take a good look. As I sat in the lobby, huddled together with Trevor-Roper and Genoud, Jane and her aunt walked past, pretending not to know us, but glowering at Trevor-Roper, whom they mistook for the Nazi sympathizer. He looked pronouncedly Nordic compared with the swarthy Genoud, who could have passed for a member of a Jewish or Arab underground movement.

The first book we did with Genoud was *Hitler's Table Talk*, edited by Trevor-Roper, which we published in 1953. The transcript we used came from Martin Bormann's family. His wife, Gerda, died in Merano in March 1946, less than a year after her husband's disappearance, but some of her papers found their way to Lausanne. The Bormann version is more complete than the text published by Henry Picker, one of the stenographers entrusted with taking down Hitler's musings. Picker's edition is based on his own copy, and anything Hitler said while he was off-duty is missing.

At my insistence, our publications of Nazi source material were prefaced and annotated by historians like Trevor-Roper and Alan Bullock so as to put them in perspective. Genoud agreed only grudgingly to this principle. He thought the texts should speak for themselves, whereas I was determined not to allow the Nazi leaders to have the last word. I have often been criticized for publishing these books, but I regard them as important historical documents which provide irrefutable evidence of the evils of the Nazi regime.

Alan Bullock's condemnatory introduction to *The Ribbentrop Memoirs* brought us a law suit from Ribbentrop's widow, but we won the case because the judge agreed that we had the right to publish a corrective commentary. I had bought the rights from an obscure firm in Germany run by a former propaganda ministry official. In the course of the negotiations I lunched with Frau von Ribbentrop in her rambling mansion in Wuppertal. She talked of her time in the German Embassy in London as though nothing had happened, and enquired in an insouciant way about the London social scene. She particularly wanted to know how the London-derrys had fared. They were great English Germanophiles with whom the Ribbentrops had been on close terms.

Another book we ferreted out of Genoud was the correspondence between Martin Bormann and his wife Gerda, the personification of the ideal Nazi woman, during the last two years of the war. Though scrappy and uneven, *The Bormann Letters*, also published with an introduction by Trevor-Roper, contain interesting details about life in Germany during the latter stages of the war, and give revealing insights into the personal relationships of the Nazi leadership. Bormann, ever the perfect bureaucrat, not only sent his wife's letters back home so that she could file them, but also included the love letters written to him by an actress, whose seduction he triumphantly reported to Gerda.

My final deal with Genoud was in 1962 over *The Early Goebbels Diaries*, which dealt with the period before Hitler seized power. A much fuller version came out via East Germany years later.

Genoud was not my only source. Through Hermann Langbein, a Polish Jew who became the head of the association of Auschwitz survivors in Vienna, I obtained the diaries of the camp commander, Rudolf Höss. We published *Commandant of Auschwitz* with an introduction by Lord Russell of Liverpool in 1959. All the royalties went to the victims of Auschwitz. I also bought Admiral Dönitz's memoirs. This time my contact man was the U-boat commander Wolfgang Frank, who wrote a book called *Der Seewolf*. He arranged a meeting with his former commander-in-chief in Hamburg, and we spent about two hours discussing the book. I asked Dönitz to write more about the twenty days after Hitler's death when he became Reich President and Supreme Commander.

Two or three years before Albert Speer was released from Spandau prison I wrote to his wife, expressing my interest in his memoirs. She received me in Heidelberg, but she was noncommittal. When the time came, I bought the memoirs from Ullstein, backed up by the *Daily Telegraph*, who acquired the serial rights. I first met Speer briefly with his German publisher Wolf Jobst Siedler at the Frankfurt Book Fair. We spoke about the possibility of him bringing more remarks about England into the English edition and we arranged another meeting with Lady Pamela Berry, who was married to the *Telegraph* proprietor, to discuss the serialization.

None of us particularly wanted to be seen dining in a restaurant, so I asked Gabriele Henkel, the wife of one of Germany's leading industrialists, to set up a small dinner with Speer, Lady Pamela and the diplomatic correspondent of the *Telegraph* at her house in Düsseldorf. Her husband, Konrad, was there and she also invited the writer Erich Kuby. Speer was inundated with questions, most of them fairly elementary. He answered in almost perfect English. As it grew late I noticed he was tiring and his English was deteriorating. We had just been offered Himmler's letters for publication and I had turned them down, but I wanted to hear what Speer had to say about him. During one of those intermezzos when people talk amongst each other, I turned to him and asked him quietly: 'Do explain to me, Professor Speer, the phenomenon of Heinrich Himmler. How is it that such a bigoted mediocrity could organize so vast an enterprise as he did in the final stages of the war when he was in charge of the whole German war effort and the economy?'

'Ah well,' Speer enthused, 'the man had a genius for choosing good people, he was a terrific manager.'

For an instant he had dropped his guard. Then he caught himself and added, 'But of course, he also had a satanic nature.' At one and the same time Speer revealed himself as the technocrat and the civilized European. It was a glimpse of the 'two souls dwell, alas!, in my breast' syndrome I have encountered again and again in Germans who, in one way or another, served the Nazi regime . . .

My attempt to publish a book on the German secret service during the war nearly broke the firm. The saga began in London when Moura Budberg introduced me to a friend of hers from prewar Berlin days, Dr Paul Leverkühn, a Christian Democrat member of the Bundestag and a well-known German laywer who had defended

Field Marshal von Manstein at his trial in Hamburg. Leverkühn spent many weeks in London in 1952 attending the negotiations for the settlement of Germany's foreign debt as a member of the delegation headed by the banker Hermann Josef Abs. During that time Leverkühn often came to dine at Chester Square. He was soft-spoken with a sense of irony, a discreet, family lawyer-type of man with an English pose characteristic of the Hanseatic patriciate. He still remembered the days of Rathenau and Balinn. I visited him at his home in Hamburg where we had a candlelit dinner. The household was run with military discipline.

One evening, during the London negotiations, Leverkühn brought Abs along for a late dinner. They arrived at Chester Square at about nine o'clock and we sat together until seven o'clock the following morning. I was riveted. Their tongues loosened by large quantities of white wine, Abs and Leverkühn began reminiscing about the war, when Abs had been a board member of the Deutsche Bank with a seat on the Reichbank advisory board, and Leverkühn had been in Intelligence. At times it seemed as though they had forgotten I was there. I remember Abs describing how Ribbentrop had summoned him in February 1945 to discuss his investments with him. He wanted to know where his capital would be safe from sequestration in the event of a German defeat, and whether he should send it to Switzerland or Sweden. Abs had to break it to him that it was too late for all that. To the last, Ribbentrop was convinced that his contacts with the British aristocracy and White-hall would save him. It was a poignant example of the curious naivety of the Nazi leadership.

Leverkühn had been in the Abwehr (counter-espionage) section of German Intelligence. He served as Chief of the Istanbul Station where Rashid Ali's failed attempt to rid Iraq of British influence convinced the Germans that they should increase intelligence activities in this part of the world. He was also responsible for reconnaissance in the Near and Middle East. It was clear from the way he talked about the Abwehr that Leverkühn wanted to put across the critical stance many of the senior officials recruited by Admiral Canaris, the head of German Military Intelligence, adopted towards the Nazi regime. He was keen to emphasize the distinction between the Abwehr and the activities of the Sicherheitsdienst, (SD), the secret service of the SS. So I asked Leverkühn to write a book about the Abwehr. He had no experience in writing, but agreed to have

a shot at it. However, he felt that he would need some key information which he knew one of Admiral Canaris's deputies in the
Abwehr, General Lahousen, the Chief of the Section for sabotage
and special duties behind the Russian lines, could provide. Leverkühn suggested we seek him out together.

We travelled to Hall in Tyrol where Lahousen, an Austrian who
had been taken over by German Intelligence after the Anschluss,
lived in modest circumstances. A pious Catholic who had never
been a Nazi sympathizer, Lahousen turned King's evidence at the
Nuremberg trial and helped nail a number of the accused. He
rejected Adenauer's offer of a leading position in the West German
Intelligence Service and withdrew to his village, a broken man, tall,
cadaverous and suffering from conflicts of conscience over his past.

We spent a long evening with him, in the course of which I asked
him how many of the German leadership knew about the plans
for the 'Final Solution' of the Jewish question. I will never forget
Lahousen's answer. Visibly moved, he said, 'Don't let anybody tell
you that we didn't know. Whatever you may hear now, all of us
in senior positions knew. I can tell you exactly how we found out.'

This is his story.

Late one night in the winter of 1940-41, he was sitting in the
Bendlerstrasse, the Army General Staff headquarters in Berlin, playing cards with Colonel Piekenbrok and Count Bentivegni, the heads
of the other two Abwehr sections. Suddenly the door opened and
Admiral Canaris, 'der Alte', the old man, as Lahousen called him,
stormed in, ashen and trembling with rage. He threw a document
onto the card table and said, 'Read this, Gentlemen.' It was the
copy of a memorandum from Heydrich to Himmler outlining plans
for the systematic extermination of the Jews, which Canaris had
secretly obtained from the SD. 'This is what we have been waiting
for,' he announced. He was convinced that the information gave
them moral grounds to break the personal oath of allegiance the
Wehrmacht had sworn to Hitler on 2 August 1934, the day of
Hindenburg's death. The others agreed. Together they resolved to
take immediate action. At Canaris's suggestion they flew to France
to see Field Marshal Keitel, Chief of Combined General Staff, who
was ensconced in one of the Loire châteaux, preparing for the Russian campaign. They arrived unannounced and were shown into a
large baronial hall.

Lahousen described what occurred next in graphic detail. It was cold and there was a large open fire at which Keitel sat, a great hulk of a man, warming his haunches. The portly Bavarian raised his eyebrows and enquired what he owed this visit to. Canaris said, 'Field Marshal, we have come to show you a document of the gravest importance.' Keitel took his glasses out of their case, put them on and studied the document slowly and carefully. In what seemed to Lahousen and the others like an eternity, he then took his glasses off and put them back in their case. They could see that he was deeply moved and they exchanged glances, thinking they had got Keitel on their side. But after a while he drew himself up again, straightened his tunic and said, 'Gentlemen, I have a good mind to institute disciplinary action against you. You have offended against the Führer Directive of 3 September 1939 which says that no officer may seek information on an operation outside his competence. That is all I have to say. Good morning, gentlemen.'

Still shuddering at the thought of that occasion, Lahousen told me, 'We were shattered. I remember Canaris turning to Piekenbrok and saying, "Piek, today we have lost the war."' They made a desultory attempt to enlist two other Field Marshals, Kluge and Rundstedt, but failed signally.

'So,' concluded Lahousen, 'don't let anyone tell you that the General Staff was ignorant of the Final Solution.'

When it came to discussing Leverkühn's project, Lahousen told us he would be unable to help. He had had enough, he wanted to blot it all out. Besides, he had allowed his diaries to be used by a fellow Austrian with whom he had shared a cell in Nuremberg while awaiting trial. Since Lahousen had no intention of writing his memoirs, he had signed away the rights to his cellmate Wilhelm Höttl, a young Austrian intelligence officer who joined the SD after the Anschluss, and who had been responsible for political espionage operations in the Balkans and later in Italy. He too was later acquitted at Nuremberg. We would have to address ourselves to Höttl for any Lahousen material.

So we contacted Höttl at his home in Alt-Aussee, the Alpine resort where a number of wanted Nazis briefly found refuge when the Third Reich collapsed and where it turned out Eichmann's wife had lived until she joined her fugitive husband in Argentina in 1952. Höttl came to meet us in the Hotel Vier Jahreszeiten in Munich, a glib, rather oily, plump man, not much older than myself. We asked him his conditions for releasing Lahousen from his obligation. Höttl had written a book about his Intelligence work which had been published a few years earlier under the pseudonym Walter Hagen by a small Austrian firm. If we agreed to bring out an English edition, Lahousen would be free to talk to Leverkühn. We made a contract, and in 1953 we published Höttl's book, *The Secret Front*. It contained some sensational material about Nazi operations in the Balkans, gave insights into the rivalry between various SS leaders, told of 'Operation Bernhard', the German secret service's attempt to overcome its financial difficulties by forging British currency, and revealed much that was new about Mussolini's rescue by the SS Captain Skorzeny and about German attempts to secure better conditions of surrender by convincing the Western powers of the so-called myth of redoubt in the final phase of the war.

In one chapter which dealt with Höttl's activities in Budapest, he mentioned a woman who, he claimed, had helped the Hungarian Security Services make contact with the Hungarian resistance movement. Höttl described Katerina Karady as a full-lipped brunette with dreams of becoming a great film star and aspirations to play a role in political society. She had worked in various Budapest nightclubs and distributed her favours fairly liberally amongst the local Army officers before being taken up by General Ujszassi, the Chief of the Hungarian Security Service. Her photograph was one of several that appeared on the cover of the book in a montage. *The Secret Front* had a considerable success in England. It was serialized in the *Evening Standard* and reviewed as an entertaining and useful source book.

Some time after publication I received a letter from a distinguished English law firm written on behalf of their client, a Mrs Katerina Vargas, Sao Paolo, Brazil. She was, the letter said, the wife of a respectable dental surgeon who had been caused great distress by false statements in *The Secret Front* portraying her as a woman of easy virtue and a spy. She had instructed her lawyers to sue for defamation. Enclosed were a number of documents to show the damages she had suffered as a result of Höttl's claims. Exhibit A was the cancellation of a contract with MGM; Exhibit B was a divorce petition from Dr Vargas; Exhibit C was a deportation order from Brazil, and so on. The lawyers also informed me that their client was seeking damages to the tune of £100 000 sterling. That was far beyond our means – it would have spelt the end of Weidenfeld & Nicolson. Our insurance only covered claims up to £5000.

My deputy Nicolas Thompson and I went to see a blasé young underwriter at Lloyd's. He sat there with his feet on the desk and said, 'My dear chap, this is an open and shut case. You can have your £5000, but you will have to find the other £95 000 yourself.'

Bankruptcy stared me in the face. I consulted Francis Mann, a German who became one of the great jurists of England, Honorary Professor of Law at Bonn University, the author of a text book on the legal aspects of money, and the man who saved Baron Heini Thyssen's fortune and intervened in the I.G. Farben affair and other de-Nazification law suits of the early postwar period. Francis was a studious, rather eccentric man of great talent to whom fees meant little, but interesting cases meant all. He told me in a heavy German accent, 'This case interests me.'

In order to be sure that Höttl would stand by his assertions we rang him up.

'Hallo, Herr Höttl? Hier spricht Dr Mann.'

'Jawohl, Dr Mann.' One could almost hear Höttl stand to attention. He said his honour was at stake and that he and his comrades could substantiate everything. Mann told him he would be sending him a list of his statements on Katerina. Alongside each of these statements Höttl was to add the names of witnesses. Within a fortnight he had came up with a number of names.

Mann and I set out on a fascinating journey to interview these survivors of the SD who were prepared to speak out for an old comrade, a number of them at considerable risk to their safety, for they were wanted men. Some came from abroad, from Spain or North Africa, where they lived under aliases, some crawled out of funkholes in Germany, some had gone into business, others had taken up their old profession, this time in the employ of the Federal German Government or with American or British Intelligence. Höttl had arranged for us to meet them in groups of three or four in various locations, each more picaresque than the last.

The official part took very little time. The witnesses signed their depositions stating all they knew about Katerina Karady. As soon as all that was over it was as though they were oblivious to the present. We plied them with sausages, beer and schnapps and they began talk about old times. Mann and I receded into the background. It was just like the *Tales* of Hoffmann – we sat there and watched as they reminisced.

I particularly remember one occasion in a suburban restaurant run by Yugoslavs or Turks. It had bead curtains and we sat in the back room with three or four of our witnesses, waiting for another man who was willing to testify. His former comrades all seemed rather nervous. As soon as he arrived it was clear that he had been one of their most prominent comrades. They had not seen him since the war, and they greeted him enthusiastically: 'Gosh, Delius!'

'Wagner is my name. Wagner,' he replied brusquely.

As before they lost themselves in their recollections. One of them said, 'Do you remember when we took those Jews from the concentration camp and dressed them in English uniforms. They were dropped in Palestine and they all escaped?' Suddenly, they remembered that that they were not among themselves. Realizing they might have gone too far one of them added, 'Of course, it was only human. Why should they come back?'

Armed with all these affidavits, Francis Mann presented the plaintiff's lawyers with our evidence and informed them that we would defend the case. Other than a demand to pay Mrs Vargas's costs which we passed on to Lloyd's, we heard nothing more of the matter.

The episode had a spin-off. When Höttl's book was published, the Israeli Government was still searching for Adolf Eichmann. Very little was known of his movements after the collapse of Germany, but *The Secret Front* contained a passage about Eichmann's escape. According to Höttl he returned briefly to Alt-Aussee and then survived for a few weeks on the run before being picked up by an American patrol. The sergeant failed to recognize his captive, although he gave his real name. It meant nothing to the American, and he wrote it down as Eckmann. Eichmann became Otto Eckmann, Lieutenant of the SS. He stayed in the prisoner-of-war camp for some time, making no attempt to escape. When his dreadful deeds were publicized through radio broadcasts of the proceedings at Nuremberg, Eichmann no longer felt safe, and fled. All trace of him was lost until 1959. I alerted Asher Ben Nathan to Höttl's account. As one of the Haganah emissaries despatched to Europe at the end of the war to help Jews escape to Palestine, Ben Nathan, who later became Israeli ambassador to Germany, spent years on Eichmann's trail.

Besides publishing source material I made it my business to find German historians of my generation. In those days the universities, especially the faculties of twentieth-century history and politics, presented an abysmal and arid picture. Their libraries had been cleansed by the Nazi inquisitors and were wanting in basic reading material. Academics were stunned by the traumatic experience of the Third Reich and discouraged by the apathy of a public wishing to forget or preferring to be enlightened by historians and eyewitnesses from the countries of the victors. An intellectual inferiority complex led to an exaggerated xenophilia. There was a passion for foreign writers which often went hand in hand with a savage belittling of the home-grown product. Senior academic posts could not be filled for lack of suitable candidates. And yet there were a number of younger scholars who began to write and research abroad and who on their return laid the foundations for a new school of German historiography. In the 1960s and '70s, Germans awoke from their collective amnesia and began a process of soul-searching about the origins and essence of the Third Reich. I felt it was important to transmit something of this discussion to the British public. Apart from personal curiosity, this was one of my main motives in seeking out professional historians and imaginative publicists. I acquired translation rights of important works and in some cases also commissioned Germans to write especially for a world public.

At Bonn University, Karl-Dietrich Bracher led a promising group of twentieth-century historians. We published *The German Dictatorship*, his comprehensive analysis of the circumstances leading up to and following the German path to catastrophe, and *The German Dilemma*, a collection of essays on the same theme. I have already mentioned Friedrich Heer of Vienna, who traced the murky Catholic roots of Nazism and showed great courage in defying the prevailing mood in his country, and Sebastian Haffner's masterly synthesis, *The Meaning of Hitler*.

Perhaps the most distinguished contribution came from Joachim Fest. His *The Face of the Third Reich*, the best group portrait of the Nazis leadership, was a prelude to *Hitler*, his enduring biography . A liberal conservative of staunchly anti-Nazi views, Joachim Fest not only succeeds in recounting Hitler's life in a brilliantly perceptive and analytical manner, he also explains the sinister, magnetic effect of the man and all the histrionic subtleties he perpetrated on the masses. As one of the editors-cum-publishers of the *Frankfurter Allgemeine Zeitung*, where he presided over the 'Feuilleton' for twenty years until his retirement in 1993, he wielded great influence on the German intellectual world. Invitations to his annual party on the Sunday evening of the Frankfurt Book Fair were much sought after, for he always assembled leading journalists, writers and politicians. Joachim Fest became a friend. We shared an interest in Richard Wagner and I respected his courage and his insight into European cultural history which he brought to bear as a valued participant of many of the conferences I organized. He hides a warm and compassionate nature behind a deceptively formal manner.

I also published Ernst Nolte's *The Three Faces of Fascism*, an attempt to compare the different brands of fascism – Mussolini's, Hitler's and similar currents in other countries. Nolte, a Professor of the Free University in Berlin, later became the focus of the embittered 'Historikerstreit', the 'Battle of the Historians', a controversy over the singularity of Nazi atrocities which broke out among German historians in 1986 and raged for many months. Charged with political and emotional overtones, this very public dispute led to harsh recriminations, with historians on the Left accusing their more conservative colleagues of attempting to minimize Hitler's crimes by equating them with those of Stalin. Nolte and others stood accused of minimizing the specificity of the Holocaust. Abroad, the dispute was seized on by critics as yet another example of how Germans were trying to play down their collective guilt. These issues were hotly debated at a conference I held at Leeds Castle in September 1987. Nolte has done some valuable historical spadework, but the bitter attacks he endured as a result of the 'Historikerstreit' made him more polemical. His strident professorial tone played into the hands of those who dubbed him a Revisionist. The 'later' Nolte held views that I found wholly unacceptable.

Ralf Dahrendorf was one of the outstanding figures of postwar German academe. Appointed Professor in Hamburg while still in his twenties, he was vice-chairman of the Founding Committee of the University of Konstanz which opened its doors in 1966, becoming its first Professor of Sociology and enhancing his reputation with writings which were hailed far beyond his own field. We published his *Democracy in Germany*, a work of Tocquevillian polish. In the late 1960s he embarked on a meteoric career in German politics as a member of the Free Democratic Party. He was Parliamentary Secretary of State in the Foreign Office and worked for the Commission of the European Community in Brussels, but in 1974 he abandoned politics for the directorship of the London School of Economics. Dahrendorf was an academic who moved easily between Germany and Britain. After a ten-year stint at the LSE he returned once again to Konstanz, but not for long. Since 1987 he has been Warden of St Antony's College, Oxford, whose founder William Deakin was another Weidenfeld & Nicolson author. We published his *Brutal Friendship*, an account of the relations between the Führer and the Duce. Building on Deakin's foundations, and consolidating the achievements of the outstanding wardenship of my old friend Raymond Carr, Dahrendorf has put his own stamp on the college and become a great figure in Oxford. He is probably one of the most brilliant minds in Europe today, a cool analyst and original conceptualizer, qualities which make him a first-rate chairman at conferences.

In my desire to understand German reaction to the Third Reich, I was also drawn to the novelists who made the war their main theme. It was a decade after the Great War before Erich Maria Remarque wrote *All Quiet on the Western Front*. There were no Remarques this time, although Theodore Plivier's *Stalingrad* would be my choice for a close second. I published Hans Hellmut Kirst's *Zero Eight Fifteen* trilogy which reflects the authentic whiff of the barrack and the officers' mess of the Wehrmacht. Willi Heinrich wrought deeper furrows with his realistic war novels. *The Willing Flesh* was the first of several of his books which figured on our list.

I relied on my friend Ledig Rowohlt's judgement on contemporary German fiction. His volatilely gifted literary editor Fritz Raddatz introduced me to Wolfgang Koeppen, whose *Death in Rome*, a haunting parable on Germany's repression of its Nazi past, we also published. Heinrich Böll, the Nobel laureate, was another of our authors. Böll and I had long discussions about Weimar literature, the attitude of the Christian Churches to the Holocaust, and pacifism. He wrote a poem for the *Festschrift* which was presented to me on the occasion of my fiftieth birthday. I was deeply touched by it.

In the 1960s and '70s the Weidenfeld & Nicolson list reflected my determined effort to convey Germany to the Anglo-Saxon reader. I felt that the stark, or at best fuzzy, picture Britain had of Germany needed to be cleared of cobwebs, and a justified revulsion against the ugly strain in German history at least partly balanced by compassionate understanding and recognition of the new, positive currents fostered by the Federal Republic.

My conviction in Germany's importance to Israel is reflected in my publishing activities. In the early 1960s a German publisher approached me about a book which the Conservative Bavarian politician Franz Josef Strauss was writing for the German market. Strauss was willing to work with a British journalist to turn the book into a more universal version suitable for other countries. It was to outline his geopolitical visions under the title *A Grand Design*. Strauss's support of Israel and his resolve to dampen anti-Semitic feelings within his own constituency of the German Right in Bavaria had always appealed to me, so I agreed to take the book. I commissioned Brian Connell, the veteran Bonn correspondent of the *Daily Telegraph*, to do the job. In the course of the preparations I went to see Strauss in Bonn and in Munich. I remember him telling me that from his youth he had been fascinated by the characters in the Bible. After that I met him at various receptions. He was little more than an acquaintance, but I was able to call on him in an hour of need.

In the spring of 1967, when the Arab countries were gearing up for war against Israel, there was a flurry of activity in the Jewish world. The Israelis were filled with fears as to whether they could meet the challenge. Although the war of 1948 had been brilliantly successful, as had the Blitzkrieg of the Suez campaign in 1956, Israel still only had a citizens' army. Would it withstand Nasser's Arab forces equipped with Soviet arms and vastly superior in number? Would the civilian population be able to survive gas attacks? Rumours of all kinds of dreadful eventualities circulated and we were all deeply concerned about the survival of the State. Whole task forces of influential Jews in England, Europe and America tried to rally support and persuade their various governments to lift the arms embargo in the Middle East. Abba Eban made a tour of the capitals of Europe and received nothing but oracular replies. De Gaulle famously warned the Israelis: '*Surtout ne soyez pas les premiers a tirer*' – above all don't fire the first shot.

Knowing that I had good relations with German politicians, a member of the Israeli Government asked if I could do anything to persuade the German Government to help supply gas masks, of which Germany had a huge surplus in store, to the civilian population. I duly went to Bonn and saw various politicians. The journalists Klaus Harpprecht and Werner Höfer, both of whom were very well-connected, helped me with introductions. The Social Democrats I called on were not particularly receptive to my pleas, but Franz Josef Strauss, then Minister of Finance, assured me that he would do anything he could, mocking the Social Democrats' unwillingness to help. 'The gentlemen of the other faculty,' he scoffed, 'only know how to celebrate dead Jews, they never want to do anything for the living.' He banged his fist on the table and said, 'If the gas masks aren't released I will send my Bavarians to Bonn.'

I later heard from Israeli sources that there had been a hiccup at Rome airport. Apparently the Italian Foreign Minister Amintore Fanfani tried to stop the transport, but Strauss intervened. According to the lurid version I was given, he threatened Fanfani with all kinds of reprisals, using strong language. Whatever may have passed between them, the gas masks arrived in Israel.

Another German politican on the Weidenfeld & Nicolson list was the great postwar chancellor Konrad Adenauer. Before publishing his memoirs, I went with Lady Pamela Berry and an editor from Plon, our French copublishers, to see him in Cernobbio, the Italian resort on Lake Como where he always spent his holidays. Since the others spoke no German, the old man took me aside and we walked in the garden for a while. Adenauer had a wonderful capacity for simplifying complex political issues. He did not like Mandarin talk, preferring to discuss politics on the level of *Kaffeeklatsch*. He was an inveterate joker, and told me with relish that he collected jokes about himself. There was the one about Nikita Khrushchev and 'your education minister, what was his name? It was some Lord? Yes, Eccles,' which he wanted to recount.

Khrushchev had asked Eccles whether he believed in the devil. Eccles had mumbled something about not believing in him literally, but that he did believe in good and evil. Khrushchev was not satisfied with the answer and asked again: 'Do you believe in the devil?' This time Eccles replied that, no, he didn't, to which Khrushchev said, 'I believe in the devil, and what is more I have met him in the shape of Dr Adenauer'.

For years I tried to persude Herbert von Karajan to write his memoirs. I knew his wife Eliette, and we also met through mutual friends like the Agnellis who were neighbours of the Karajans in

St Moritz. At one point he came close to saying he would do it, but eventually he opted for an authorized biography, provided we came up with an acceptable author. I suggested a number of names, but none of them appealed to him. He was deeply suspicious, saying there had been too many books about him which were either intellectually inferior or malicious and gossipy. One day he sent me a letter out of the blue enclosing a feature on the Boston Symphony Orchestra by Roger Vaughan, a name hitherto unknown to me. Karajan thought it the best article he had ever read on any orchestra. He had met Vaughan and found him agreeable. The two men shared a passion for sailing, and Karajan thought that they would work well together. I made a deal with Vaughan through his American agent. It turned out to be quite costly since it entailed several transatlantic trips and other expenses.

As work progressed the author began to signal to me that he was growing increasingly critical of his subject. The more research Vaughan did into Karajan's early career and his links with the Nazi Party, the less he was convinced by the conductor's own explanation that he was apolitical, that joining the party had meant nothing more to him than signing an income tax form. When the manuscript was delivered after about two years, Karajan was furious. He tried to suppress the book and I had to put forward the old argument about the limited powers of the publisher when it came to expressing views rather than contentious facts. In this case I was also able to point out that Karajan had, after all, chosen the author himself. In the end, the book did come out, but it created a certain froideur between Karajan and myself.

In the course of various discussions I had with him before this débâcle he became quite accessible. We talked at length about music, but he always struck me as the least intellectual musician I have ever met: he was a technocrat to the core, indeed this was the basis of his genius. On one occasion I went to Salzburg for a weekend out of season while Karajan was rehearsing and recording. His wife was away so he and I had several meals together. He would expand with great enthusiasm on the ins and outs of the latest recording systems, the positioning of the musicians to obtain the best possible effect, the impact of plywood on the sound, the split-second decisions of the conductor in adding a legato or rubato even if it was not in the score in order to achieve a balanced sound. He held forth on the size of opera stages, the acoustics of various concert halls, and the tonal qualities of Japanese and Korean singers as distinct from European voices. Karajan was rehearsing Verdi's *Don Carlos* at the time. I tried to draw him out on the content of the opera and the political influences on Verdi while writing it. When I began talking about how the composer changed the Austrians who were then occupying northern Italy into Spaniards, and made the rebellious men and women of Flanders stand for the Italian patriots of his day, Karajan gave me a glazed look. When I went on to talk about Church and State and the great duet between the Grand Inquisitor and King Philip, he could barely stifle a yawn.

After the first night of *Don Carlos*, which I attended with Karajan's daughter, we all drove off together. Karajan was in a valedictory mood. Sitting in the back of the Merccdes he said, 'That was my last *Don Carlos*'.

CHAPTER SIXTEEN

Making Friends in Europe

G.M. TREVELYAN'S DICTUM that those most involved in the turning points of history are the last to know when history really turns can be applied to any field, including publishing. But looking back over fifty years in the business I think one can distinguish four phases. I would describe them as the Age of Curiosity, the Age of Cosmopolitan Exuberance, the Age of Introspection and the Age of Muted Optimism.

In the wake of the war there was a tremendous hunger for knowledge, and countless bestsellers on history, archaeology, anthropology, psychoanalysis, political thought and religion were produced to satisfy it. In every field of knowledge the Anglo-Saxon experience, method and style set the trend in European publishing. The same was true of graphic presentation. The American style of book production, layout and typography became venerated models. Just as *Life*, *Colliers* and the *Saturday Evening Post* inspired European magazine production, so the bold and clean projection of word and image favoured by American designers helped create an international style of book production.

Conversely, Britons, Americans and Australians were eager to find out more about Continental Europe, where so many of them had risked their lives. Books on European history and speculative treatises on the future of each and every country became the order of the day.

In the defeated countries, indigenous literature took some time to get off the ground again, not least because it was up against the popular narrative talents of the English and French-speaking world. But the great themes of the recent past – Fascist oppression, the dilemma of collaboration, the hope and disillusionment of liberation – were expressed most pungently by such European writers as

Moravia, Sartre, Camus, Koestler and the authors of three classics which every historian of the period should read, for they are the most expressive testimonies of the lacerated soul of Europe: Curzio Malaparte's *Kaputt*, Virgil Gheorgiou's *Vingt-Cinquième Heure*, and Ernst von Salomon's *The Questionnaire*.

In all countries, victorious and vanquished alike, publishers were rebuilding their firms. New patterns and constellations developed, and new editorial personalities began to assert themselves with new ideas. Giants like Hachette in France, Elsevier in Holland, Mondadori in Italy were emerging. In Germany, Bertelsmann evolved from a modest family business to become a household name – it is now the largest publishing conglomerate in the world. The book club phenomenon, which had been born in Wilhelmine Germany from the concept of workers' education, spread to the new world in the form of America's Book of the Month Club, itself the creation of German émigrés. With membership running to millions, it opened new vistas and markets. The paperback revolution, initiated by Allen Lane's Penguin Books, was also well under way. Nonetheless, book publishing still flourished largely on a local, national level. The age of the multinational corporation had not yet dawned in the early 1950s.

But changes soon made themselves felt in English language publishing that were in many ways a reflection of the general decline of Britain as a world power. Until the war, British publishers had been in a dominant position. One need only read the memoirs of the leading British and American publishers of that time to realize what a one-way channel it was – the annual or biennial pilgrimage of Alfred and Blanche Knopf, Horace Liveright, generations of Scribners, Macraes and Lippincotts to Bloomsbury was the highlight of their professional calendar. This era lingered on until the late 1940s, but by the 1950s the relationship became that of equals, with British publishers playing the Greeks to America's Romans. America's home market already dwarfed that of the United Kingdom, but the Americans were not yet aware of their immense export potential and tended to leave the wider world to their colleagues in Britain.

However, in the late 1950s American houses grew conscious of their power and moved into the ascendancy. By then Frankfurt had established itself as the literary stock exchange, creating a spirit of internationalism which broke down the barriers of provincialism.

Through the Frankfurt Book Fair the knowledge of publishers, distributors and agents about their equivalents in other countries, and their understanding of each other's strengths and weaknesses, increased a hundredfold. Publishing houses throughout the world began to vie with one another to sell to and buy from their opposite numbers. The age of coproduction was born.

Major works of reference and art books require heavy investment in plant, text and illustration. Close collaboration with other publishers therefore became a necessity. Although cost reduction was of course the central motive, we were also driven by the desire to be cosmopolitan, to spread knowledge, share tastes, moods and intellectual attitudes. It was in this spirit that Weidenfeld & Nicolson devised the ambitious series on various aspects of cultural history which I have already described.

These international projects required some diplomacy. If, say, a book on *Great Military Battles* initiated in England and offered to a French colleague included a chapter on Waterloo, it had to be balanced by the description of a crushing British defeat. Many a promising project for the world market fell through because it offended the national sensibility of a prospective buyer. Some coproductions foundered on the parochialism of the initiator, others failed because the psychology and sociology of the reading public in the different countries had not been sufficiently understood. In this market, the extreme between the glittering prizes of success and the penalties for failure, which was generally largely due to conceptual faults, tends to be greater than in any other form of publishing. I can think of worldwide sales figures which read like the result of an Indian plebiscite – half a million here, a million there – but more often than not the international breakdown would look more like a variant of Leporello's famous list of his master's conquests in *Don Giovanni*: Italy 640, Germany 231, France 100, Turkey 91, and, even in America, only 1003.

The Prix Formentor, which lasted about a decade, was another offshoot of this phase of recklessly optimistic internationalism. The idea was born in the late 1950s over a lunch at the Frankfurt Book Fair. A number of publishers, including Gallimard, Einaudi, Barney Rosset of Grove Press, the Spanish firm Seix Barral, Rowohlt and myself, decided to found two new literary prizes. The Prix Formentor was named after the hotel in Majorca where the meetings were to be held, and the prize was to be awarded to a work of fiction

With Marella Agnelli, an effortless
perfectionist and friend of long
standing, and Dr Hubert Burda,
Munich multimedia publisher and
patron of literature.

Diplomat and novelist: Henry Kissinger and Edna
O'Brien at Chelsea Embankment.

Tuscan summers: Evangeline Bruce (*far left*) and Marietta Tree (*far right*), model joint
hostesses, flanking Lady (Mary) Henderson and myself.

Festive luncheon in London at Drue Heinz's house in July 1966. Sandra (*middle*) and her mother Joan Whitney Payson (*far right*), Lord Ampthill (*far left*) and my father at the window.

Barbara Walters, First Lady of American TV, and Malcolm Forbes, the publisher, in New York.

With Lally Weymouth, the foreign affairs columnist, who has the best political salon in New York.

President L. B. Johnson reminisces about the Six Day War at his Texan ranch, 1969.

Above: Knighted by the Queen. With Sandra and my mother outside Buckingham Palace, 1969.

From a 50th birthday book:

Left: drawing by Vladimir Nabokov
Below: poem by Paul Johnson

for young George

from old Vladimir

Congs!
(Ada, p.332)

Naboko
oux
g

from Paul Johnson

Prince of Publishers
And King of Hosts,
Firm Friend, Wise Counsellor,
Familiar of Distant Coasts.
The Profile of a Roman Emperor,
The Sense of Timing of a Klemperer,
The Shape (but not the Tastes) of Oscar Wilde,
The Rash Enthusiasms of a Child;
And yet withall, the Shrewdest Man Alive,
To Strike a Bargain, Make a Talent Thrive.
He mingles Young and old with Matchless Skill,
Their Wit and Happiness his Chiefest Thrill.
Space Forbids a Full Inventory
Of GEORGE's gifts, Matured though half a Century

Regulars at Cleve Lodge: a montage by
Diana Phipps.

TOP TABLE (*clockwise from far left*):
Lady Harlech, the French ambassador
Geoffroy de Courcel, Diana Phipps, Moshe
Dayan, Antonia Fraser, Jonathan Miller,
Martine de Courcel, Lord (Sheridan)
Dufferin, guest, Gore Vidal, Lady Rayne,
Richard Crossman, Evangeline Bruce,
Norman Mailer.

BOTTOM TABLE (*clockwise from far left*):
Gaia Servadio, Jayne Wrightsman,
Harold Wilson, Sandra, Roy Jenkins,
Lady (Kisty) Hesketh, myself, Lady Pamela
Berry, Sir John Foster, Lady Amabel
Lindsay, Thomas Balogh.

Right: An unpublished birthday sketch by
Cecil Beaton

With Moshe Dayan, soldier and author, in the 1970s.

With Teddy Kollek, Mayor of Jerusalem and my oldest Israeli friend.

Right: With Shimon Peres, the driving force behind Arab–Israeli peace today.

Below: President Chaim Herzog and his wife Aura with Drue Heinz (*right*).

Bush visits in London: George and Barbara Bush at the Dorchester in December 1993 with Annabelle and myself.

Below: Ann Getty and I discussing the Lisbon literary conference of the Wheatland Foundation with President Soares of Portugal, 1988.

Left: Sam Spiegel, film mogul and art collector, at his Barbados swimming pool.

With Pope John Paul II at Castel
Gandolfo, 1990. Professor Bernard
Lewis looks on.

Above: The inaugural meeting of
the Founders' Council of the
Europaeum, 1992. (*Seated, l. to r:*)
Maja Oetker; Lord Jenkins of
Hillhead, Chancellor of the University
of Oxford; His Serene Highness Prince
Hans Adam of Liechtenstein; Gräfin
Madeleine Douglas. (*Standing, l. to r:*)
Lord Weidenfeld; Professor Sir Richard
Southwood (then Vice-Chancellor of
the University of Oxford); Dr Gert-
Rudolf Flick; Sir Ronald Grierson.

Left: Rothschild anniversary in
Frankfurt: with German Chancellor
Helmut Kohl (*right*), Edmond de
Rothschild and Annabelle.

Jerusalem wedding November 1992. Annabelle and myself with Isaiah Berlin, Teddy Kollek, Professor Michael Sella of the Weizmann Institute and Shimon Peres.

Right: With Annabelle playing Scrabble on honeymoon on the Getty boat anchored at Barcelona during the Olympic Games, 1992.

Below: The next generation: my daughter Laura and her husband Dr Christopher Barnett with my grandchildren, (*l. to r:*) Clara, Nathaniel, Benjamin and Rowan.

from one of the twelve participating houses, all of which were committed to translating and publishing the winning novel. The second award, the Prix International de Littérature, was a sort of alternative Nobel Prize for Literature which paid tribute to the ensemble of an author's work. While the publishers named the winner of the Prix Formentor themselves, they appointed a jury with delegates from all the participating countries to award the Prix International de Littérature. Among those who received it were Jorge Luis Borges, Samuel Beckett, Carlo Emilio Gadda and Nathalie Sarraute. Vladimir Nabokov, whom I had nominated at the first meeting in Formentor, failed to get sufficient votes.

It was the Spaniards who had initiated the whole undertaking. Isolated from foreign literature by the Franco regime, they saw the Prix Formentor as a means of gaining international backing to break the oppressive censorship. Every publisher brought a delegation, and there would be a carefully worked-out programme of literary sessions lasting several days. The idea was to meet once a year in Formentor. The owner of the hotel was himself an amateur poet. He had a bar in his complex called *El club de los poetas* where we all used to convene. But the prize soon ran foul of the Franco police and we were not allowed to meet in Spain again. We were exiled first to Corfu; in another year, when I was president, we met in Salzburg, which the Left found too Baroque and Catholic for their taste.

The last meeting I attended was held in a hotel in St Raphael which was owned by Madame Florence Gould, a well-known collector. Mary McCarthy and Francis Wyndham were on the jury, as was John Gross, who brought his enchanting fiancée, Miriam. My friendship with both of them runs like a thread through the last thirty years. In their different ways they have been indispensable companions. John is a deeply civilized and compassionate observer of human frailty, a good-humoured sceptic who never forgets but almost always forgives. His conversation is punctuated by thumbnail sketches of people and events and has an epic quality. John is an encyclopaedist when it comes to English literature and his spectral knowledge of film and drama. One of the youngest dons of King's College, Cambridge, editor of the *Times Literary Supplement*, chief book reviewer of the *New York Times* and, more recently, theatre critic of the *Sunday Telegraph*, he savours the pleasure of describing and dissecting the social-cultural landscape in London and New

York. He is the ideal guest, a man of all seasons. John came to work at Weidenfeld & Nicolson as my deputy for a year, but he preferred the independence of being a writer to the febrile atmosphere of a publishing house. Our friendship surived even that experiment. John's *Rise and Fall of the Man of Letters*, a brilliant study of English literary life from 1800 to the 1930s which we published in 1969, was one of the best reviewed books and the most popular choice for Book of the Year that I can remember. His wife, Miriam Gross, the Jerusalem-born and Oxford educated daughter of a distinguished pair of German lawyers, is beautiful, witty and thoughtful. She is an outstanding interviewer and a distingushed literary editor who brooks no nonsense when it comes to style and clarity. Although uncompromising in her loyalty and decisive partisanship, she has never made an enemy.

The German delegation in St Raphael included the literary critic Hans Mayer and Gisela Elsner, whose grotesque novel *The Giant Dwarfs* had won the previous year. The Italian writer and critic Giorgio Manganelli gave a characteristically witty speech. His compatriots included Italo Calvino. The French fielded the experimental novelist Raymond Queneau, the author of *Zazie dans le Métro*; Dominique Aury, the mistress of Jean Paulhan and author of *Histoire d'O*, a key figure at Gallimard, and herself a powerful stirrer in French literary politics; and Michel Butor, a leading exponent of the *nouveau roman*. All the delegations were fairly nationalistic, none more so than the French, who tended to dominate the proceedings. Determined that an English-language book should win, Mary McCarthy overcame any personal reservations she had and pushed successfully for Saul Bellow's *Herzog*.

The French were forever changing the constitution, and what had originally attracted me as an enlightened publishing venture was transformed by an inner caucus from Gallimard, Einaudi and Seix Barral into too much of a platform for anti-Franco and pro-Communist activities for my liking. I became disenchanted with the political intrigues and withdrew. The others met once more in Tunis before it all petered out like many a great international scheme. But the Formentor experience yielded important insights and was a fruitful way of forging links. Twenty years later it served me as a role model for a series of ambitious conferences on world literature which I convened as Chairman of the Getty-backed Wheatland foundation.

In the 1960s, when European authors figured prominently on our list, cultivating French publishers was an essential part of my work. They were very much a world apart. Like their fellow countrymen in politics and diplomacy, they had their own ideas and had to be treated with kid gloves. In those days French publishing was Balzacian as far as day-to-day dealings were concerned, Proustian on the proprietorial level and Zolaesque when it came to the junior staff. Even the largest houses were family-owned until recently, when the pace of conglomeration accelerated. The senior partners usually had airy rooms decorated with beautiful *boiseries* and pictures in a *hôtel particulier* on the Left Bank, but the secretaries were installed in a rabbit warren behind the scenes where they worked in poor conditions, rather like the nineteenth-century seamstresses in Zola's novels. They would emerge from dark corridors lined with airless and overcrowded offices. I used to visit Paris regularly to work the *quartier*, going from publisher to publisher.

I struck up a particularly close relationship with Charles Orengo, the director-general of Plon, who had all the attributes of a minister of state at an eighteenth-century Italian court. His Latin features were marked by prominent cheekbones and he wore a beret over his crew cut. A Monegasque Catholic who had been in the Resistance, Orengo was fascinated by the human frailties of the mighty. He had a wonderful way of describing their machinations, punctuating his narrative with pauses and punch lines. Orengo was more of a power broker than an intellectual. Though he was well-read, prestige, politics, diplomacy and intrigue interested him more than anything else. There was always something conspiratorial about his conversation. He could turn the most banal office reshuffle or a tiff between Gallimard, Hachette and Plon, the three contenders for the leading role in French publishing, into a gripping yarn. Orengo was very well-connected. He had an extraordinary talent for making contacts and seemed to know everything that was going on in the most diverse milieus. I noticed he almost bowed visibly when mentioning important names. He used to give select but austere lunches and dinners for important clients in his flat in the rue Garancière next to Plon.

The firm belonged to the Bourdel family. Old Monsieur Bourdel was the chairman of the Syndicat des Éditeurs. He had two ravishing daughters. Colette, the elder, married first George Duhamel, a cabinet minister under Pompidou who died early of cancer, and later Claude Gallimard. The younger was married to a White Russian prince. Maurice Bourdel was a silent, grand seigneurial Frenchman and a skilled diplomat in the publishing field. Plon was a prestigious, conservative house which published many of the great and the good of France for over a century.

Orengo followed that tradition. We met in the early 1950s when I was competing for the war memoirs of General de Gaulle. I knew some of his entourage from the days when they had all been in London during the war, and, helped by Orengo, I used these connections as an entrée. Olivier Guichard, a Gaullist minister, reintroduced me to the General. I called on him at the Hotel Matignon in 1958 during the short period after the collapse of the Fourth Republic when he was Prime Minister before being elected President later that year. The office was very crowded. Georges Pompidou, then a part-time director-general of Banque Rothschild, had a kidney-shaped desk in the corridor. He negotiated some clauses in the contract with me in a tough businesslike way, as though we were dealing with international loans. Then I was ushered into a sumptuous antechamber where the Commandant Grandval, a naval aide-de-camp, made polite conversation for ten minutes before I was shown in to the General's office. He got up to greet me and made gracious reference to our meeting during the war.

We then discussed the translation which had been assigned to Richard Howard, a well-known American translator. De Gaulle was concerned that the text should sound English rather than American. Our conversation was in French, but he made it clear throughout that he had a command of other languages. He had just received the proofs of the Italian edition and asked me whether I had ever thought about the subtle difference between the word *considérer* in French, *considerare* in Italian and consider in English. He then launched into a disquisition about semantics. There was a touch of showiness, but also a genuine pleasure in musing about these nuances. '*Écoutez*,' he said at one point, 'sidewalk *n'est pas Anglais, c'est Américain, vous dites* pavement, *n'est ce pas?*'

I told him we wanted to publish the book to coincide with his state visit to England and asked whether there was the slightest chance that he might agree to a television interview. He answered rather haughtily, '*Le Général ne dit pas non.*' Throughout our conversation he alternated between *moi* and *le Général*, depending on the context. When talking about affairs of state he would refer to himself as *le Général*, but when making arrangements about proofs and other technical matters he spoke in the first person. After the book had come out in England I met him again at a gala given by Ambassador Beaumarchais on the occasion of his official visit to the Queen. He clasped my hand in both his hands and said, '*Merci, merci beaucoup.*'

De Gaulle's *War Memoirs*, which we published in 1959, was the first transaction I made with Plon. From then onwards Orengo and I worked on many projects hand in glove. Together we initiated books and series and jointly went on the hunt for important titles. We also copublished a number of Israeli books. On the fourth day of the Six Day War in 1967, I stopped for a night in Paris on the way to Israel to wait for a chartered flight. By then the victorious outcome for Israel was already manifest. Orengo gave a small dinner party for the Israeli ambassador Walter Eytan and his American wife Beatie, the daughter of my great friend Mrs Rae Schuster of Simon & Schuster. The most illustrious guest was Cardinal Tisserand, Dean of the Sacred College and, as it turned out, an eager supporter of Israel. Small, rotund, bearded and bald, and carrying a long-stemmed wine glass with great panache, he looked like a picture of Silenus in a Bacchanalia. He told us of his early adventures as a missionary in the Levant, and toasted the triumph of Israeli arms.

Orengo was a great friend of the writer Roger Peyrefitte. We had several dealings over a book which he decided in the end not to write, but he gave us lunch in his house, showed us his erotic library and regaled us with highly amusing gossip about the French Rothschilds. Orengo also introduced me to Marguerite Yourcenar. We published her book, *The Abyss*, in 1976. I took her and her constant companion to dinner at Le Mediterrané. She was aloof and taciturn.

Through Orengo I became involved with an entrepreneurial adventurer who claimed to be the Marquis de Acevedo. He came from Ecuador and worked as a freelance *chef de collection*, a figure peculiar to Continental publishing who acts as intermediary between publisher and author, who thinks up whole series of books and sells them to a publisher, finds the authors, supervises the project and is awarded a share of the profit. Some *chefs de collection*, like Guy Schoeller, the former husband of Françoise Sagan, did very well by bringing in ideas for one-volume encyclopaedias and other titles which became recurrent bestsellers. The French have a system called *vente a tempérament*. It involves door-to-door selling of collected editions of the classics as well as series like 'Les Prix Nobel', which consisted of one work by every winner of the Nobel Prize.

This was how the Marquis de Acevedo earned his keep. He presented us with an ambitious project entitled *L'histoire parallèle des Etats Unis et Russie*. André Maurois, whose *Ariel*, a romanticized life of Shelley, had been the first ever Penguin book, was to write the history of the United States, and Louis Aragon the complementary volume on the Soviet Union. Plon and Weidenfeld & Nicolson bought the world rights and sold the books all over the world for a considerable amount of money. Unfortunately neither of the authors met our expectations: they produced fairly feeble manuscripts. In the course of our dealings, Acevedo, Orengo and I gave dinner to André Maurois and Louis Aragon and their respective wives. Maurois was slightly tainted with the collaborationist brush. Being Jewish – he was really called Émile Herzog – he had spent the war in America but had sympathized with Pétain rather than de Gaulle. Aragon, on the other hand, had been a member of the Communist Party since the late 1920s and was an active member of the intellectual Resistance. He was married to Elsa Triolet, a well-known Russian-Jewish Communist writer in France, whose sister had been the mistress of the poet Vladimir Mayakovsky. It was amusing to observe Maurois and Aragon trying to outdo each other with courtesies and flatteries.

I had more dealings with Aragon and saw the two faces of a Soviet henchman. He had two domiciles. In the country he had a splendid house with Louis XVI and Régence furniture. The walls were covered with Cubist and Surrealist pictures. Aragon also had some first-rate Russian Constructivist works. The food was Russian too. We were given Armenian brandy and caviar. The house seemed to be teeming with servants: it was all very feudal. But in Paris Aragon worked on the fourth floor of a run-down building in a working-class district. When I visited him, the mulatto concierge looked me up and down suspiciously as if I was a contract killer. There were three flats on the fourth floor. The one on the left was marked Export-Import, the one on the right bore another business ensign. The middle flat had no nameplate. I rang the bell. The door opened to reveal Aragon sitting facing me in the anteroom, which was where he received Party comrades when playing the part of the austere Communist writer. He was deeply cynical about everything, including the Soviet Union. When I told him that I was going to Moscow with Moura Budberg, whom he knew well, he said, 'You're wasting your time. You won't find a single writer there who has a proper command of any language, let alone Russian.'

I also worked closely with Gallimard, the powerhouse of French literary publishing. It was a microcosm of the French intellectual scene. For years *le tout Paris* would meet at the Gallimard cocktail party in the courtyard of the rue Sébastien-Bottin. The jour-fixe on the first Thursday of the month was an institution famed well beyond the confines of Saint-Germain-des-Près. Gaston Gallimard, who had founded the firm in 1911, was without doubt one of the greatest publishers of this century. His first step had been to link up with the prestigious literary magazine *Nouvelle Revue Française*, which was launched in 1909 by a group of six young writers among whom André Gide was the oldest. *Nouvelle Revue Française* became an imprint of Gallimard, and over the years published a large number of the most distinguished French writers. Gallimard continued the nineteenth-century tradition of putting writers on the payroll. Instead of being given an advance on a book, budding authors would be awarded a salary deductible from royalties which most of them never earned, since only a small percentage made the grade. Gallimard owned a huge share of subsidiary rights which provided a steady income and enabled the firm to take gambles. With the revenue from the dramatic and film rights of stars like Proust, Saint-Exupéry, Sartre, Camus, Gide, Roger Martin du Gard and Éluard, Gallimard could afford to publish around forty, fifty or more first novels a year.

Although Gaston Gallimard remained active almost to the last, all my dealings were with his only son, Claude, who was gradually taking over the running of the business with his cousin, Michel. Claude and Michel were bitter rivals. Their dispute divided the firm into factions – the Left grouped around Michel, the more literary of the two cousins, while the Right tended to side with Claude. The infighting threatened to tear the company apart. But when Michel died tragically in January 1960 from injuries sustained in the car crash which also killed Albert Camus, Claude reigned supreme. With his white hair and red cheeks he looked like an Etruscan king. Shy and somewhat stooping, he was a cunning businessman who ran the company autocratically while giving the impression that he delegated power.

The house of Gallimard was politically diversified. The hard core was left of centre and had a distinct pro-Communist slant. But other currents were represented in the famous *comité de lecture*, the editorial board which had a decisive role in shaping the policy of the house. It comprised both in-house editors, most of whom were literary figures in their own right, and often distinguished figures who worked mainly from home, but would spend the odd day in the office. There were endless intrigues and cabals. It fell on Claude Gallimard to keep the balance, which he tried to do by playing one side off against the other.

An enduring friendship at Gallimard was that with Pierre Nora, the senior publisher of books on history, philosophy and the social sciences. He had an excellent mind and a deep understanding of contemporary currents in all the humanities. I find his cosmopolitan outlook a refreshing contrast to the entrenched insularity in certain British quarters and the more landlocked intellectual isolationism in America. But when the French are cosmopolitan they can be more so than anyone else.

Of a Jewish family, Pierre Nora has that attractive mixture of subtle irony, melancholy and ambivalence about the beau monde which he partly inhabits and partly shuns. His companion Gaby van Zuylen is one of my oldest and most reliable friends in Paris. For nearly thirty years, from the mid-1960s to the present, I always spent an autumn weekend as the guest of Gaby and her then husband, Teddy van Zuylen, at the Château de Haar in Haar Zuylen, near Amsterdam. It is one of the most enchanting places I know. Rebuilt in neo-Gothic style by the grandfather of the present incumbent on the grounds of a burnt-out castle belonging to the Flemish van Zuylens, it was paid for through the munificence of a French Rothschild whose daughter the baron had married.

Every September the castle is opened to an extraordinary group of French, British and American guests straddling many worlds and reflecting the catholic tastes of the van Zuylens. Writers, left-wing politicians, right-wing bankers and film directors rub shoulders with polo players, backgammon virtuosos and golf champions. Somehow it always works. The regulars included Jean d'Ormesson, to whom I feel temperamentally more akin than to any other Parisian literary figure, Jean-François Revel, Swifty Lazar, the legendary

Hollywood agent who dressed like a dandy and swore like Harry the Horse, Alexis Gregory, a cosmopolitan New York art publisher, Grace Dudley, and Yves Saint-Laurent and his muse, Lulu de la Falaise. Teddy's sister, Marie-Hélène, wife of Guy de Rothschild, the senior member of the French Rothschilds, was always there, surrounded by her favourites. She had a mini-court, presided over by the fastidiously elegant and quietly perceptive Alexis de Redé, who used to own the famous Hôtel Lambert where Guy and Marie-Hélène de Rothschild now live. Gaby van Zuylen was an imperturbable hostess, dispensing comfort and luxury without a touch of ostentation and arranging cease-fires between warring factions.

While Charles Orengo acted as my guide in the maze of French publishing and introduced me to a wide range of Establishment figures – from luminaries of the Conseil d'État and the Faubourg St Germain to the archiepiscopal residences – Pierre Nora and Gaby van Zuylen brought me into closer contact with a group of historians and writers. Among them was François Furet, the great historian of the French Revolution, who teaches at the Sorbonne and Chicago, and Emmanuel le Roy Ladurie, nicknamed *le Roi*, director of the Bibliothèque Nationale and author of *Montaillou*, that brilliant study of life in a medieval French village. He strikes me as being the Gallic version of Hugh Trevor-Roper – brilliantly fluent, effortlessly superior and subtly ironical. When he finds the company amusing he is the wittiest of companions. They also introduced me to Jean-François Revel, who was stigmatized by the Left as a doomsday prophet and cold warrior, and was laughed at in the 1980s because he predicted the end of the Western democracies when in fact it was Communism that collapsed. Since then this laughter has yielded to some nervous giggles. To my mind his robust mind, universal knowledge and mastery of polemical pamphleteering make him the French doppelgänger of Paul Johnson. Another regular was Ivan Nabokov, nephew of Vladimir and son of Nicolas, who was one of the best judges of foreign literature in French publishing. He inherited the Nabokovian wit, but has a gentleness and amused tolerance which the great Vladimir lacked.

I took pride in publishing an impressive group of French historians and political scientists, some of whom I commissioned directly, such as Raymond Aron, who was known to me from his wartime exile in London. I once had to give a talk in his honour at the Circle Interallié before awarding him the Bentinck Prize for important writings on Europe. As I had to speak in French I enlisted the help of Marie-Cygne James (now Lady Northbourne), who is the granddaughter of Paul Claudel. I have always found it useful to have a particular model in mind when speaking a foreign language, and in this case I tried to make my French diction more credible by imitating General de Gaulle.

We also published two great French women who leapt to prominence in literary as well as public life: Françoise Giroud and Edmonde Charles-Roux. Françoise Giroud, the co-founder and former editor-in-chief of the news magazine *L'Express*, was a practitioner of high journalism as well as being Minister for Women under President Giscard d'Estaing. I spent agreeable evenings with Madame Giroud and her companion, the lovably Anglophile publisher Alex Grall, with whom I worked on several joint ventures. Giroud's memoirs, *I Give You My Word*, came out in England in 1975. Edmonde Charles-Roux married Gaston Defferre, the mayor of Marseilles. She showed great understanding for the cause of Jewish-Catholic friendship. Her novel, *To Forget Palermo*, which was published in France in 1966, won the Prix Goncourt and even found an echo in insular England when the translation came out two years later. Edmonde Charles-Roux's brother, Jean, is a priest at St Etheldreda in the City of London.

One of the most powerful senior editors at Gallimard was Dionys Mascolo, a somewhat mysterious figure. He struck me as being a sphinx without a secret. Mascolo had joined the Resistance and was known by his employer to keep a revolver in his desk. After the Liberation when Gaston Gallimard, who had done a certain amount of jiggery-pokery with the Germans during the Occupation, stood accused of collaboration, he cited Mascolo among others as evidence for his good credentials. While Mascolo was a man of the Left, the young Right was represented by Roger Nimier, a talented novelist, whom Gaston Gallimard had taken a particular shine to. Nimier became editor of Céline, one of Gallimard's main authors. François Erval was entrusted with the German and Central European literature, and Michel Mohrt, a particular friend of mine, was the Anglo-Saxon expert. A French conservative of Breton origin, he was a highly cultured Anglophile. He had taught at an American university and spoke very precise and slightly stilted English. Mohrt's attractive wife Françoise, for many years the editor of French *Vogue*, was a gifted judge of literature as well as fashion.

Dionys Mascolo was married to Marguerite Duras, then at the beginning of her career as one of the most successful contemporary French novelists. They were friends of Sonia Orwell, and I first met them during the summer we holidayed together in Lerici just before my marriage to Jane broke up. The Mascolos were staying along the Ligurian coast in Bocca di Magra where there was a colony of Communist and Communisant French and Italian writers and publishers. One of the great literary prizes of Italy, the Premio Viareggio, was based in the region and various publishers had summer houses there. Count Bompiani had a palatial villa in Lerici, Alberto Mondadori lived in Camaiore, Giulio Einaudi lived in Bocca di Magra, and the Fischer publishing dynasty from Frankfurt had a house overlooking the Lucchesia. Three of the greatest sculptors of our age were virtual neighbours: Henry Moore, Marino Marini and Jacques Lipchitz. I came across them all there and remember particularly pleasant evenings with Marino Marini. I saw more of Lipchitz later with my good friend the collector Herman Elkon in New York who was an intimate of his and owned some of his finest work.

Italian publishing played a crucial part in my coproduction strategy. Realizing that for an Italian book to become known internationally it had to pass through the filter of English publishing, Italian publishers saw a firm like ours as a window to the world. But they also had much to contribute. They had large printing facilities, a great talent for graphics and huge picture libraries which they were anxious to marry with new texts, so they were always receptive to Anglo-Saxon ideas. With Alberto Mondadori we produced many illustrated art books of a superior kind, some of which were designed by Mark Boxer.

The Mondadori family history read like episodes from Homer. It was full of drama, intrigue and mayhem. Alberto Mondadori was one of two sons of the old Commendatore. While he was in charge of the publishing side of the business, his brother Giorgio looked after the newspapers, magazines and printing presses. The two of them fell out and Alberto started his own publishing house called Il Saggiatore, and built up a fine cultural list, including some of the great series we worked on together. As often as not Mondadori would do the printing for projects like *The History of Civilization*, *The World University Library* and endless archeological, art-historical and scientific series which we coproduced with other

companies. The various European publishers involved would convene in different places in London, Paris or Madrid, or in Alberto
Mondadori's country house in Camaiore.

Alberto had started out with grand visions and ambitions. He
collected modern art, was interested in philosophy and had a deep
respect for intellectuals. But it all ended in tears – Alberto over-
reached himself. He sank millions into his ailing firm, left his wife
Virginia, a voluptuous blonde with a predilection for gossip, for
one of his business aides and drank heavily. His health deteriorated
and he died a melancholy man.

Before his premature decline I spent at least a week or ten days
as Alberto's guest at Camaiore every summer. I was usually there
in the run-up to the Premio Viareggio, which aroused deep passions.
There was a constant coming and going of writers, publishers and
editors and I was riveted by the backstage wrangles. After the prize
had been awarded there were heated discussions about whether
the judges had allowed themselves to be swayed by subtle manipulation. Of course they usually had. The prize not only preoccupied
the Italian cultural world, it was also taken very seriously by
society and officialdom. The President of the Republic and the Prime
Minister were usually present, and the villas round about
resounded with tittle-tattle about the political and literary grandees
and their hangers-on. Signora Rèpaci, the wife of the writer
Leonida Rèpaci, was deemed particularly affected and arrogant, so
much so that a phrase was coined after her: people would say of
other women who were giving themselves airs that they were 'doing
a Rèpaci'.

One summer, poor old Goffredo Bellonci, the hen-pecked husband of Maria Bellonci, died while staying in the Mondadori house.
The couple had founded the Premio Strega, another prestigious
literary prize, in the late 1940s. He was a rather scholarly man,
while she wrote popular history books about the Renaissance. We
all had to pay our respects to the shrunken corpse which had been
laid out in a coffin; the whole literary world came to the funeral.
The widow, full of pathos, looked like Lucrezia Borgia after the
bloody demise of her second husband.

Maria Bellonci was one of our authors and I often saw her in
Rome, where she had an intellectual salon. We published her
biography of Lucrezia Borgia. Shorty before our edition appeared,
Simon Harcourt Smith, a swashbuckling English dilettante, pub-

lished *A Marriage in Ferrara*, another portrait of Lucrezia Borgia. A reviewer scanning the index found the largest entry to be that of a gentleman by the name of V. Anche. The author had obviously referred to Maria Bellonci's book and had found among the sources the Italian term *v. anche*, short for *vedi anche* which means 'see also'. A closer look revealed that Harcourt Smith had lifted several passages from Maria Bellonci's book and mistranslated them to boot. For instance, speaking of Cesare Borgia's sexual attractiveness, Harcout Smith had written that he attracted women to himself like iron attracts calamity. He obviously did not know that the Italian word *calamita* means magnet. The book had to be withdrawn and Signora Bellonci's book held centre stage.

As in Germany, Italy's young postwar historians slowly began to make their mark. They had suffered from the suffocating grip of Fascism and the dead hand of the philosopher and literary critic Benedetto Croce, who, with his aversion to positivist historiography, eschewed factual information and the portrayal of personalities in favour of broad generalizations and abstract concepts. After the war a new school emerged that was anxious to trace the origins of Fascism and analyse the strains of Italy's modern history. I met Leo Valiani and had interesting talks with Franco Venturi, the son of the famous art-historian Lionello Venturi. He wrote a history of Russian populism, a standard work, despite its Marxist influences, which we published.

My curiosity about Vatican politics and modern Church history brought me into contact with Carlo Falconi, a defrocked priest turned correspondent of the magazine *L'Espresso*, who wrote an anecdotal book on the Vatican. The most stimulating conversations I had on this subject were with Silvio Negro, the Vatican correspondent of the *Corriere della Sera*. He tried to explain to me the complex character of Eugenio Pacelli, Pius XII, that puzzling pontiff to whom Rolf Hochhuth meted out such harsh criticism in his sensational play, *The Deputy*, for favouring Nazism over Soviet Communism and failing to denounce the liquidation of Jews although the Vatican had ample information about the gas chambers. Negro told me that Pius XII was deeply sceptical about man's capacity to distinguish between good and evil, and was reluctant for the Church to fight a lethal war on two fronts. Communism, with its cradle-to-grave programme of human engineering, seemed more dangerous than Italian Fascism or National Socialism. Furthermore, Negro explained, Pacelli had an inferiority complex because he lacked pastoral experience. He spent most of his career as a diplomat, dealing with temporal matters and secular leaders, so when he was finally elevated to the Papacy he took it out on the External Affairs Department of the Vatican and deliberately failed to make his two assistants at the Secretariat of State, Tardini and Montini (the future Paul VI), cardinals.

I had negotiations with the Vatican regarding a series of books on Italian Renaissance art and met, among others, the rather mysterious German prelate Monsignor Kaas, a key figure in the Weimar Republic's Catholic Centre Party whose lack of robust opposition to the emergent Nazi movement was much criticized by the fighters for democracy. Journalistic gossips claimed that he was the head of the Church's secret service and that the Sacred Office for the Preservation of the Fabric of St Peter's that he held was a cover for a network of espionage behind the Iron Curtain. There were tales of a Collegium Russicum in southern Italy where Baltic priests were trained to parachute behind Communist lines. When I asked Monsignor Fallani what the Office for the Preservation of the Fabric of St Peter's did, he took me to the window overlooking St Peter's Square, raised his hand and pointed to the distant Tiber. 'Year after year,' he said, 'the foundations of this Basilica are being eroded by the floods of the river. It is this department's duty to see that the bedrock of our Church is reinforced. That is a noble task.'

In Rome I spent many an evening with the painter Renato Guttuso, who entertained lavishly in his palatial house. He was a genuine Communist idealist, warm-hearted and moderate in his views, but he set great store by his position in the Party. In my view his artistic development suffered from his willingness to conform with Russian social realism, although he claimed that his style sprang from deeply held convictions and was not imposed by Party ideology. Our relationship cooled after the Six Day War in 1967 when the Communist Party became ferociously anti-Israel.

Carlo Levi was another Communist friend of whom I saw less and less after 1967. Coming from an old Sephardic family in Rome, he had been an active Zionist and had even dedicated some of his writings to the State of Israel. He was related to Enzo Sereni, a hero of the Haganah who was parachuted into southern Italy from Palestine on a reconnaissance mission during the war. He was meant to report back on the condition of Jews in Italy, but the Germans captured him, and he was tortured and killed. His widow Ada belonged to Weizmann's inner circle and became a motherly friend of mine in Jerusalem.

The Mondadori coterie included the novelists Guido Piovene and Giorgio Bassani, some of whose books I also published. He was a close friend of Susanna (Suni) Agnelli, Gianni Agnelli's younger sister. She achieved prominence as mayor of the Argentario and Republican Deputy. At my suggestion she wrote a delightful memoir about growing up in Italy's most powerful dynasty. She begins her introduction to *We Always Wore Sailor Suits* by stating that when 'an English publisher' asked her to write a book she had not realized that he asked every woman he met the same question. In this case I was completely vindicated. The memoir was a bestseller.

My friendship with Suni's sister-in-law Marella Agnelli dates back to an evening in the late 1950s when Grace Radziwill and I were staying with Daisy Fellowes in Roquebrune. We were invited to dine at the Agnelli villa, La Leopolda, in Cap Ferrat, which had been built for King Leopold I of the Belgians, hence its name. A wonderful display of hurricane lamps lit the long approach from the outer gate to the house. It was a beautiful starless night. Up at the villa we were received by two breathtakingly beautiful women, Marella and the Parisian hostess Jacqueline de Ribes.

Marella and I struck up a friendship. Over the years we have established a pattern of regular meetings. I usually stayed with her in St Moritz but also in Rome, Turin and Villar Perosa, the Agnelli estate nearby. Marella's aristocratic features have often been described. I still think she is one of the greatest beauties I have ever set eyes on. Though she has a circle of devotees which never changes, she loves meeting new people. She has a maternal side which invites confidences and gives sound advice. Marella is also a woman of talent. Had she been forced to make her own living, she would have been a highly successful designer, but her husband never wanted her to be exposed to the hurly-burly of business life. Very much a personality in her own right, Marella has nevertheless subordinated her life to the brillant, capricious and mercurial personality of her husband.

A patron of the arts, a consummate diplomat and businessman, Gianni Agnelli, the legendary head of Fiat, has something of the Renaissance prince about him. It is true that he was late in seizing the reins, but when he did he immediately made his mark, ruling the company with a rod of iron. His extensive family stands in awe of him. Gianni has an excellent political brain. In his heyday he stood behind every twist and turn of Italian affairs: the so-called historic compromise between Christian Democrats and Communists during the 1970s was his brainchild. Though flattered when given the credit, he is careful not to take it. He has a short attention span and likes to keep his distance, shrouding his persona in an aura of mystery. The Duke of Beaufort, who owns the Marlborough Gallery in London, is one of Gianni's closest friends. They share a number of traits, such as the peculiar habit of wearing their wristwatch over the cuff, and it is difficult to decide who unconsciously imitates the other. Both men are insomniacs and call each other early in the morning to discuss the Stock Exchange, their friends and the latest scandal. Gianni has a good eye and indulges in unpredictable bouts of collecting. Each domicile has a different style. The art in the Agnelli house at St Moritz is distinctly, but not exclusively, early twentieth century – Nolde, Kirchner, Klimt and Schiele. There is Wiener Werkstätte furniture and exquisite lace. The house is approached through an underground tunnel studded with pictures which opens up onto a wonderful view of the valley. The flat in Rome is decorated with modern works of art – Bacons, Boteros and American paintings. The house in Turin has a staid, patrician character with its rather heavy eighteenth- and nineteenth-century furniture. In contrast Villar Perosa is light and elegant.

The Feltrinelli family have an estate not far from there. I met Giangiacomo Feltrinelli through his German-born wife Inge Schönthal, who is a pivotal figure in European literary circles. She started out as a paparazza – Hemingway was said to have been much taken by her when she went to photograph him. In the early 1950s she came to see me in Chester Square with an introduction from our mutual friend Ledig Rowohlt. I lost sight of her for some years until she reappeared again as Signora Feltrinelli.

Inge was the third of Giangiacomo's four wives, but it was she who took over the company on his death in 1972. His father, a marquis of Fascist creation, was one of Italy's richest industrialists and his mother the mistress of Curzio Malaparte. Giangiacomo had the bearing of a sportsman and looked like an Austrian cavalry officer with his bold moustache. I found him rather earnest and self-absorbed. A passionate supporter of the radical Left, he was able to draw on seemingly bottomless funds from the family timber and real estate fortune to finance his ambition to play a leading intellectual role. For all his revolutionary fervour he also had business acumen, and gave his company the appurtenances of a modern publishing house by starting the Libreria Feltrinelli, a chain of high-quality, supermarket-style bookshops which have since been copied all over the Continent.

As a publisher, Feltrinelli antagonized the profession by using his fortune to tear authors away from the established houses. His newly founded company scored two spectacular successes. It published Lampedusa's *The Leopard*, which had been rejected by several houses until Giorgio Bassani, who directed the Feltrinelli *Contemporanei* series, recognized the novel as the masterpiece that it is. Feltrinelli was also the first to bring out Boris Pasternak's *Doctor Zhivago*. On hearing that Pasternak had completed the novel, Feltrinelli's agent in Moscow had called on the author, secured the rights to the Western edition and smuggled the manuscript to Italy. But Pasternak was having difficulties with the Soviet authorities who insisted he abridge the text, and he asked Feltrinelli to defer publication. To Feltrinelli's fury Gallimard then obtained the revised version through a young Frenchwoman who worked for the Musée Tolstoi in Paris and had visited Pasternak in his datcha. The two publishers engaged in a race to get their respective versions out first. Feltrinelli won by a whisker.

Inge is the last great survivor of the international literary salonnières. Despite a keen nose for the sweet smell of success, she never neglects her old friends or punishes failure. Indeed, she is a byword of loyalty and warm-heartedness. Inge acted as a skilled social foil to her husband. In true Italian fashion their world straddled the Communist elite, the *haute Bohème* of artists and writers like Guttuso, Calvino and Bassani, and the aristocracy. We were all aware of Giangiacomo's revolutionary politics. In the early 1960s he had befriended Fidel Castro and dreamt of turning Sardinia into a second Cuba. Having distanced himself from the Communist Party after the Soviets sent their tanks to crush the Hungarian uprising, Giangiacomo devoted himself increasingly to anarchist left-wing groups and helped finance their underground activities. His violent death remains a mystery. He was torn apart by a bomb while apparently trying to blow up an overhead supply line at Segrate near Milan. His supporters prefer the theory that he was killed by right-wing extremists. But there can be no doubt that Feltrinelli was deeply involved with subversive circles. Once, when Marella Agnelli and I were dining at the Dutch Embassy in Paris, Georges Pompidou, who had been prime minister during the student revolt of 1968, expressed his surprise at our continuing friendship with Inge Feltrinelli. He told Marella who was sitting next to him that the French had proof positive that Giangiacomo had been the main financier of the Paris Évènements.

Since the late 1960s international publishing has undergone radical change. If one thinks of the reading public as a pyramid, then it would be fair to say that from the Middle Ages up to this century the intellectuals at the apex formed a close-knit cosmopolitan group, who had common standards of education and understood the same language. A student could start at the Sorbonne, proceed to Salamanca, Prague, Heidelberg and Oxford or vice versa. At the base of the pyramid the vast illiterate or subliterate public was isolated. Today, the pyramid is inverted. Television, travel and popular culture have brought the mass public more closely together and, paradoxically, the elites have grown more provincial. If one asked the members of a junior common room in Cambridge, England or Cambridge, Massachusetts thirty years ago to name ten modern writers in France, Germany and Italy they would have little trouble in coming up with appropriate examples. Today they would barely know one or two.

What have been the reasons for this impoverishment? No doubt the intense preoccupation of each country with its own affairs and changing economic circumstances have helped create a new cultural chauvinism at the upper end of the market. Vietnam made the United States become much more introspective. But publishing economics has also played its part. The recession following the oil crises of the 1970s hit most publishers hard and discouraged them from looking beyond their own frontiers. This was particularly marked in the English-language world where the decline of internationalism led to a dramatic reduction in the number of translations. European publishers are still far more open to the outside world than their Anglo-Saxon counterparts.

It is not always literary quality that makes for success. Curiosity often counts for more. If I now detect a muted optimism and a new brand of internationalism in world publishing, it is, I feel, because the political upheavals of recent times have created a new sense of concern and involvement. There is hope, but there is also anxiety and uncertainty, and these sentiments encourage the desire for knowledge on which our trade thrives.

CHAPTER SEVENTEEN

The Wilson Years

IN THE WAR YEARS the BBC canteens were always a hub of activity, even at midnight. They were the most useful meeting points for writers, journalists and politicians refreshing themselves before or after round-table discussions which were beamed by short wave to the Empire at all hours of the night. Because of the time difference between England and, say, the Far East, night duty was the order of the day for many of the overseas services, and it was not unusual to find George Orwell, Peter Quennell, Edmund Blunden, William Empson, Norman Collins and Cecil Day Lewis, all of them on the wartime BBC staff, in the same room as various distinguished Indian or African freedom fighters and young female announcers who later made careers in television.

Our jobs brought us into daily contact with governments in exile, spokesmen of resistance movements, British politicians, gurus and mavericks of every kind, all agonizing over the Allied war aims and the future shape of the world. The strains within the alliance were reflected in the heated political discussions in emigré circles. There were those on the Left who felt that the Russians were being slighted by their allies, and there were the committed anti-Communists who saw nothing but evil in the Soviet Union. Our political affiliations were conditioned by attitudes to world issues. Our interest in domestic affairs was always subsidiary to the broader canvas of Europe and the Middle East. In the heat of the moment we may have simplified issues, and the hectic schedule of producing, as I did, two, three, sometimes more commentaries a day, added to the tension.

Like so many of my generation, I was a *New Statesman* reader. Brilliantly edited by Kingsley Martin, the journal both accommodated and formed its public intellectually. The first half of the weekly was iconoclastic and imbued with a puritanical zeal for political reform. Its pundits uttered apocalyptic threats whilst at the same time promising a silver-lined future so long as their precepts were heeded. They steered a radical middle course between totalitarian Communism and rugged capitalism. In his weekly diary and leader column, the editor bared his personal doubts and dilemmas, often reaching preposterous conclusions, and his readers ended up condoning these idiosyncrasies because of the contagious passion of the exposition.

The second half of the magazine, devoted to cultural affairs, could not have been more different. Edited by Raymond Mortimer, a fastidious resident of the ivory tower, it was very elitist in its view of the arts. G.W. Stonier and V.S. Pritchett were the main literary critics, Edward Sackville-West and Desmond Shaw Taylor reviewed music, T.S. Worsley the stage, and Ben Nicolson was one of a thoughtful band of writers on art. None of them made any concessions to populist or 'middle-brow' taste. Like Connolly's *Horizon*, Mortimer's pages were decidedly Francophile. French Resistance writing figured more prominently than German underground offerings, though a mainly homosexual wing of the literary fraternity still felt nostalgic pangs for the dissolute life of pre-Hitler Berlin. But the Christian and conservative tone of the German opposition to Hitler was viewed with some wariness by the *New Statesman*.

I became part of the *New Statesman* circle, a sympathizer of the moderate Left, but not a member of the Labour Party. Like most European exiles, I had a deep respect for British democratic pragmatism and was convinced that if Britain so wanted it could take the lead in a future Europe. The Labour Left on the other hand had weary notions of a Europe dominated by conservative reactionaries, a vision of cold, clerical Fascists driven by fanatical anti-Communist ideology. They regarded the Foreign Office as a reactionary cabal, scheming to restore feudal monarchies and suppress progress. There was also within the Party a strong sentimental attachment to the Commonwealth, a commitment to a free India and the independence of Asian and African colonies, with a benign Britain holding loose reins and dispensing Fabian wisdom. This seemed to them a more desirable role for Britain than a revival of the Europe of Charlemagne. The appeal India had for figures like Attlee and Gaitskell was mirrored in the prodigious output of the Colonial Bureau of the Fabian Society. It clashed with the European panacea which the exiled French, Belgian or Scandinavian social democrats advocated with such energy.

Although there were grave doubts about Europe on both wings of the Labour Party, its views on the postwar order were broadly in keeping with my own. Jules Cambon, a distinguished French ambassador before the First World War, once said, 'In England politics is an atmosphere.' How right he was. In a country where political life is more consensual than politicians wish to admit, people are often drawn to one side or the other by subtle nuances. A foreigner coming to England tended to favour the Labour Party over the Tories because the mood and ethos of the Left seemed much more welcoming and sympathetic. Not only did Labour have many more Jewish MPs and municipal councillors, the Party also spoke out for the acceptance of refugees from Fascism, fought anti-Semitism more eloquently and repeatedly included pro-Zionist resolutions on its platform. At the annual May-Day parade, Zionist socialist groups marched proudly under the joint banner of the Star of David and the Red Flag. While it would be hard to find overt anti-Semitism in the Labour movement, the Tory Right and a good deal of the conservative rank and file had little sympathy for aliens or Jews. Of course this broad generalization gives undue credit to the Left and penalizes the Right. Nowhere was a genuine pro-Zionist spirit more warmly felt than in the circle of Winston Churchill, Leo Amery and Walter Elliott. Nor was there much enthusiasm for a Jewish Palestine among such Labour leaders as Ernest Bevin, although his lack of empathy for Jews and Zionist was largely due to the hostile influence of his pro-Arab counsellors at the Foreign Office. But the Labour Party, and especially the trade union movement, remained broadly in favour of a Jewish State.

Through my *New Statesman* connections and my friendship with Woodrow Wyatt, I was drawn into the mainstream of the young intellectuals of the Labour Party. Although these bonds grew closer later, after the war, when I shared a house with Woodrow who was then a junior minister in Attlee's Government, I established links with a number of Labour politicians at the BBC, many of whom I was introduced to by Richard Crossman. I also attended Fabian summer schools and conferences.

It was at one such event, on a hot summer's day towards the end of the war, that I first met Thomas Balogh, the Hungarian-born economist who became a close advisor to Harold Wilson. Harold Laski was making a rousing speech about the dangers of Fascism. A professor at the London School of Economics who had a signal influence on the Labour Party in opposition, he was a remarkable lecturer. His style ran the gamut from Gibbonesque phrases to Damon Runyonesque jokes. His vocal register was as spectral as his rhetorical style, piano, staccato, rising to a crescendo. Like most members of the Laski family he had a supercilious nasal inflection.

Balogh cut a flamboyant figure, dressed in a tiger-skin waistcoat, yellow shirt and Russian fur hat despite the summer heat. With his flowing white hair, young face and bushy black eyebrows he looked like a learned scribe at the court of Genghis Khan. We became close friends, and throughout the Wilson years I particularly enjoyed his running commentaries on British politics. Although conspiratorial in his demeanour and apocalyptic in his visions, he had a brilliant mind and a mordant sense of humour, heavily dosed with Hungarian cynicism. Twenty years later when he rehearsed his maiden speech in the House of Lords he proposed to open it thus: 'My Lords, this Chamber has heard many voices over the centuries, but I trust it has never heard anyone speak with an authentic Hungarian accent.' Balogh had deep disdain for civil servants and reserved much of his bile for Sir Eric (now Lord) Roll, a formidable Treasury knight of Central European-Jewish origin. 'Have you looked up Eric Roll in *Who's Who?*' he once asked me. 'Well, I'll save you the trouble. It says: "Born nowhere. Educated on the Continent".'

Early on in Wilson's first administration, Balogh and I helped persuade him to cast his vote for the establishment of Wolfson College in Oxford. Sir Isaac Wolfson, the puckish entrepreneur who built Great Universal Stores and became one of Britain's leading philanthropists, was thinking of setting up a postgraduate college which would not only enable young scientists and humanists to do research but would also provide much-needed places for retired dons who still had a contribution to make, but for whom their universities could not provide. Isaiah Berlin had been proposed as the first president, and Oxford as its venue. There was, however, one dissenting voice on the board of the Wolfson Foundation: Solly Zuckerman. A renowned expert on apes and monkeys, and a powerful organizer of scientific research who advised British governments in war and peace, he held great sway. Zuckerman spoke out against Oxford. I think he may have been partly motivated by jealousy of Isaiah, whom he regarded as having reached the apex of the social pyramid in Britain, access to which he felt had been denied him. Solly Zuckerman was an interesting example of a self-made struggler for recognition who failed to realize that he had in fact already been fully recognized.

Sir Isaac wavered in the face of such opposition. But he intimated that were the Prime Minister to 'pick up the telephone' to appeal to him in person to go ahead with the Oxford plan, he would do so. Having been briefed over the lunch hour by Isaiah in the Palm Court of the Ritz, Balogh and I talked to Wilson. Convinced by our proposition, the Prime Minister did indeed pick up the telephone. After a bantering introduction and a few words of warm praise for Sir Isaac's latest performance in the city, Wilson spoke in glowing terms about the future that such a foundation in Oxford held for the advancement of knowledge in Britain. Sir Isaac was convinced. Under Isaiah Berlin's stewardship, Wolfson College soon established a high reputation, so much so that a second Wolfson college was founded in Cambridge, thus ensuring that the name of its founder was honoured in both universities, an honour Wolfson shared with Jesus Christ and Mary Magdalene.

My closest friend in the Labour Party was Woodrow Wyatt. An activist and a covert romantic, he had that rare combination of a tendency to self-advertisement and integrity. His technique of engaging Winston Churchill from the backbenches during Question Time with a mixture of affability and irreverence ensured him press coverage, but when he stood out against the nationalization of the steel industry and criticized the militant tendencies of the trade union movement, he forfeited his chance of preferment and eventually left the Labour Party. Throughout the Thatcher years he was one of the lady's most ardent champions.

In the late 1940s, however, Woodrow was part of the Bevanite Keep Left Group which challenged the ruling party establishment and had the support of Richard Crossman, Konni Zilliacus, Ian Mikardo and Michael Foot, amongst others. Woodrow introduced me to Tom Driberg, the stormy petrel of the Left who won notoriety as a political gossip columnist. His links with Soviet Russia, the intelligence community, the homosexual scene and the Anglican Church were all part of his rainbow-like coverage of society. But at heart he was a fierce Jacobin. He would sup off the gold plates of the grandees only to mark them down for the guillotine. Eddie

Shackleton, the son of the explorer, was also part of Woodrow's world. A gregarious, self-mocking yet ambitious young politician who started on the Left, he moved steadily to the centre and then to the Right, holding high office, becoming a life peer and ending up as a Knight of the Garter. He admired Woodrow's wide-ranging talents which spanned literature as well as politics. Woodrow would have made a good publisher – at one time we considered going into partnership, but together with Hugh Gaitskell we became involved in another venture which never came off. Early in 1952 we discussed the possibility of buying the *Spectator* from Sir Angus Watson, who had made his money with tinned sardines. It was to become a Gaitskellite mouthpiece, financed by a number of rich Labour supporters, foremost among them Alan Sainsbury, then an active member of the Labour Party, though he joined the newly founded Social Democrats in 1981. I was asked to join the consortium of publishers, but the plan fell through, not least, I think, because Watson was reluctant to see the journal fall into the hands of outright socialists. He eventually sold it to the liberal Conservative intellectual Ian Gilmour.

Woodrow's career had its ups and downs, and what he once said about me defines him just as well: 'A frantic worrier, cushioned by optimism.' When he married his secretary, a temperamental girl of Russian-Jewish stock, I joined him on his honeymoon in Marseilles, where I remember dining on a giant bouillabaisse in the old port. When he married his third wife, the daughter of the Earl of Huntingdon, our friendship waned because Moorea and I never hit it off. But when Woodrow married Verushka, who is Hungarian, the Danubian link brought us together again and we restored our old camaraderie.

After publishing his *New Deal on Coal*, I saw little of Harold Wilson for a while. When he became Minister for Overseas Trade less than two years after his original appointment to the Ministry of Works, our paths crossed occasionally. One of his great passions was the British film industry. He liked to hobnob with colourful impresarios like Del Giudice and Alexander Korda, and he frequented the parties of Nicholas Davenport and his beautiful actress wife Olga who mixed the film world with the City, Bloomsbury and the social lions of Oxford.

Wilson much preferred assembling a group of ready listeners in a corner to working the room at a party. He had a schoolmasterly streak and easily fell into a lecturing tone, using his pipe, which was as much part of his image as the cigar was Churchill's, to underline a point. He loved flaunting his mastery of technical detail in the most diverse realms, astonishing the film moguls with his knowledge of attendance figures, production budgets and market shares, or civil servants with his grasp of their specialist field. Even as a thirty-year-old, Wilson had a partriarchal manner and a penchant for reminiscing. When he held forth in this vein he would intersperse anecdotes and general maxims with dazzling feats of memory. He had a habit of turning to his interlocutor, who might be an industrialist, and saying something like, 'Well, young man, I met you on the twenty-second of October, 1949, at the British Export jamboree in Huddersfield, and you were lecturing us about the merits of automation. That was what we called it then. We call it computer technology now.' And so on. Playing the game, someone invariably asked, 'How do you remember, Prime Minister?' And he would answer, 'Well, I'll tell you how. It was the day after the by-election which my friend John Parker just failed to win by three hundred and fifty votes.' As often as not Marcia Williams would correct him: 'Harold, you're wrong, it was six hundred and eighty,' and he would mutter, 'Ah well, the girl has a better brain than I have.' He delighted in folksy banter of this kind.

Wilson was neither *grand seigneurial* nor plebeian. He was a mixture of the provincial don and the technocrat, quintessentially North-Country, more puritanical than hedonistic, a strong pragmatist, a patriot and a monarchist. Oxford had left its mark on him – not the Brideshead Oxford one reads so much about, but the Oxford of scholarship boys who burnt the midnight oil rather than partying with the smart set.

After Wilson won the leadership battle in 1963, John Vaizey and the right-wing Labour MP Desmond Donnelly took me out to lunch. Vaizey had been the *enfant terrible* of the Labour Right, a moving spirit in university reform and a pioneer in the economics of education. Laid low by osteomyelitis in his childhood, about which he wrote a masterly memoir, *Scenes from an Institutional Life*, John was driven by a reforming zeal matched only by his impatience. As a young Oxford don he had attracted the attention of Labour notables like Tony Crosland and Hugh Gaitskell and became a partisan of George Brown, whose unsuccessful bid for the Party leadership he actively supported. He was excitable and irreverent, and although he could be frivolous, he was a brilliant social scientist and one of the most stimulating men I have known. John Vaizey probably did more to broaden higher education through the expansion of the universities than anyone else. He was rewarded with a peerage, and spoke eloquently in the House of Lords on the financing of state education.

Over lunch, Vaizey and Donnelly explained that Labour was keen to strengthen the intellectual debate within the Party. Knowing of my old ties with Wilson, they thought Weidenfeld & Nicolson might publish a series of books by the new Labour intelligentsia. George Brown had promised them a manuscript, and I suggested they approach Harold Wilson. George Brown never delivered, but Wilson contributed two books in 1964, the year he became Prime Minister: *Purpose in Politics*, a collection of his speeches and articles, and *The Relevance of British Socialism*, the extended version of an essay he had originally written for one of the year books of the *Encyclopaedia Britannica*.

That was my first direct involvement with Wilson since 1945. When he was Leader of the Opposition, and in the early stages of his tenure in Downing Street, my contact with him was mainly through Richard Crossman. Crossman, who saw himself as Wilson's talent scout, animator and man of ideas, had always argued that the Labour Party should bring in fresh talent to work alongside experienced politicians and civil servants. He wanted to build a circle of unofficial advisors who could feed the Prime Minister with ideas and enlarge his horizon. Because of my foreign contacts, Crossman, then Lord President of the Council, thought I might be useful, and so from the outset of Wilson's premiership I organized working breakfasts, lunches and dinners with visitors from abroad, mostly to brief members of the Government on Europe. When negotiations for Britain's entry into the European Economic Community began in earnest, Crossman invited me to be head of an informal committee to discuss ways of winning the backing of influential opinion on the Continent for our membership. The group included Hugh Thomas, John Vaizey, Mark Littman QC, an international lawyer who later became deputy chairman of British Steel, Sir Leon Bagrit, one of the pioneers of the computer revolution in Britain, and Thomas Balogh. We used to meet in the Lord President's office in Great Peter Street, though I sometimes widened the circle and entertained everyone at home. Crossman vascillated between a neutral and an adversarial stance on Europe. He could be very contrary and used to start off a meeting by saying, 'Now, convince me once again why I should be backing Europe.'

Later, most of our meetings took place in the Foreign Office rooms of whichever minister had the European portfolio, first Alun Chalfont, then George Thomson and Roy Hattersley. Alun was one of my most consistent champions. A professional soldier and a romantic poet, his Celtic temperament was combined with a strong intellect and a strategic sense that enabled him to navigate all kinds of bureaucratic currents. This made him an effective ally. His was one of Harold Wilson's more daring recruitments. Labour had promised to appoint a minister for disarmament, a thankless job since the Russians were then in their *niet, niet* mood. When Solly Zuckerman turned him down, the Prime Minister offered the job to Alun Gwynn-Jones, the defence correspondent of *The Times*, whose views on disarmament reflected his own. Overnight he became Lord Chalfont, changed from the Liberal to the Labour Party and moved from Printing House Square to Whitehall and Geneva, the seat of a permanent disarmament forum.

My involvement with the European information group eventually commended me to Wilson himself. But it was some time before I became part of his circle, and was entrusted with all manner of assignments particularly to do with Middle Eastern and European affairs and Anglo-American relations. My link with him grew much closer during the years of Opposition when Heath was in power. During Wilson's first administration my main links with the Party were George Brown, particularly in his Foreign Office days, Crossman and Chalfont. Brown was jealous of Wilson and distrustful of his circle, and felt apprehensive about Crossman, who had a not-so-secret yearning for the Foreign Office. Whatever else Crossman might have thought about Brown, he had a high regard for Brown's brain. He used to say that if Brown had won a scholarship to Oxford he would have achieved a double first, because he recognized the essentials of an argument more clearly than anyone else. Brown was touchy about his lack of formal education and, although intellectually curious, pretended to be 'low-brow'. At his request I arranged meetings with writers and academics, at which he would behave unpredictably. He could charm his audience with brilliant improvisation, or insult them one by one with wounding sarcasm. When his volcanic temperament was fuelled by alcohol, he tended

to be aggressive, litigious and downright rude. This made him a
plebeian doppelgänger of Randolph Churchill. Although he masterminded the United Nations Resolution 242 which was the basis of
all dialogue between Arabs and Jews in the Middle East, he became
an Arabist and tried to move the Labour Party away from its Zionist
stance. We had many rows over Israel. He would summon me to
the office and bellow, 'You must tell your Jewish friends that they
are going to lose all our sympathy and support if they go on like
this, my friend. Gamal [Nasser] means well and we could make
peace, if only I got some help from the other side.'

Wilson always thought he was surrounded by hostile forces conspiring against him. He was suspicious of the Establishment, the
Foreign Office and the security services. The small group of devotees, most of whom came from outside the civil service or the Party
hierarchy, was therefore specially important to him, though he
probably relied on some of them more than was good for him. He
had a subtle, devious mind, but at the same time could be naive.
He was not always a good judge of people. Underlying the at times
ruthlessly pragmatic exterior was a kindly disposition. He hated
making difficult personnel decisions and wherever possible he
would bypass a problem rather than pierce it with a lance, thereby
stockpiling difficulties for himself. He wanted to please, and sought
to turn enemies into neutrals and neutrals into allies, often at a
high cost to himself. As Prime Minister he was more anxious to
appease his critics or make inroads into the adversarial camp than
to stand behind his closest allies. Like Margaret Thatcher in her
later years, he thought they would always be there, ready to fight
his battles, and, like her, when it came to the crunch he was more
often than not disappointed by the doubters to whom he had given
preferment, thinking he had won them over.

The Wilsons led a frugal life. Harold was a man of simple tastes
who hated what he called the 'cocktail circuit', and was in turn not
well received by London society. The signet ring he wore on the
fourth rather than the little finger was a butt of derision at lunch
parties of snobbish ambassadresses or at the bar of Boodles. There
was no entertaining at Number Ten outside official business; it
was either a state function or sandwiches. Mary Wilson seldom
entertained in that austere flat upstairs in Number Ten; she sat
reading, or writing poetry, while her husband retreated downstairs
to read official papers. Although the Wilsons almost always spent

working weekends there, he enjoyed Chequers and used to take his private guests on conducted tours, proudly showing them prime-ministerial memorabilia. On hot summer days we would be invited to go down to the swimming pool which Walter Annenberg, that most munificent of American ambassadors, had donated after a visit. Wilson was not a swimmer – he liked standing at the shallow end and talking. There was an inscription along the inside which read: 'The construction of this pool was made possible by a generous gift to the Chequers Trustees from the Honourable Walter H. Annenberg to commemorate the visit to Chequers of the Honourable Richard M. Nixon, President of the United States of America on 24th of February 1969 and the presence of Her Majesty Queen Elizabeth the Second on 3rd October 1970.' Once, when we were standing there together, he pointed to the inscription and said, 'You know, this inscription is very useful to me. I always know where to stop, because the letter A in Annenberg is as far as non-swimmers can go.'

My meetings with Wilson tended to be informal. When there was an all-night session at the House of Commons, I would visit him in his room there, or he would ask to see me at Downing Street, mostly for no particular reason. Sometimes we had a sandwich lunch or an impromptu dinner in my house or at a restaurant. He wanted to know what was going on. Suspicious by nature, he saw politics as a war in which one had always to be on the alert, and his almost messianic self-confidence was undermined by an enduring suspicion that others were plotting his downfall. His constant forming and reforming of alliances would defy the notational skills of an experienced choreographer. When at one point he suspected Jim Callaghan of intriguing against him, he put all his friends on the alert. They were interrogated as to whom Jim had been consorting with and where. Callaghan's reported presence at a drinks party before Sunday lunch in the house of a musical noblewoman close to the royal family caused consternation at Number Ten and was interpreted as proof of a conspiracy to unseat the Prime Minister with the connivance of the Monarch. Nonetheless, Callaghan was Wilson's preferred choice for his succession.

In this bunker atmosphere, Wilson expected his friends to be his eyes and ears, his link to the world beyond Westminster and Whitehall. Although famed for the maxim that there must be creative tension in the Prime Minister's camp, he did not adhere to it himself. He was aware of rivalries, but tried to fudge them, thereby accentuating them. It was typical of him that he compartmentalized the confidants on whom he relied. In fact, he kept them apart, so that many of those who justly claimed to have been part of his circle never met each other.

Wilson was not unusual in surrounding himself with unofficial advisors, nor were his suspicions unique. Most leaders have tried to cushion themselves against perceived threats from the official machinery of government and in so doing have laid themselves open to manipulation by unscrupulous courtiers. In Wilson's case this tendency may have been compounded by another factor. In those days the Labour Party suffered from a disadvantage which has to some extent been eroded by social change. Unlike the Tories, who came from similar milieus, Labour lacked common social forums because of the different backgrounds of its members. Richard Crossman used to complain that, whereas a junior minister in the Conservative Government could meet the Prime Minister at his club, or at debutante parties, weddings and country-house weekends, and make his mark, aspiring Labour MPs were deprived of such opportunities. Similarly, where senior Tory ministers could huddle together in the corner of a dowager's drawing room or agree on some strategy in the men's room at White's, Labour notables had to do business on the telephone. During office hours that meant that a civil servant would invariably be listening in, ready to interject: 'Sorry, Minister, you've got that quite wrong.'

My dealings with Wilson were channelled through Marcia Williams, with whom I was in almost daily touch. Wilson would tell her that he wanted to see me, or I would ask her to pass on a message, or to say that there was somebody coming through London whom I felt he should meet. She was present at nearly all my meetings with Wilson. I did not get to know her until the latter half of Wilson's first premiership. Of course we had spoken on the telephone, but we first met by chance at a Jewish charity function held at the head office of Marks & Spencer in Baker Street. She had come with Gerald Kaufman, Wilson's trusted press officer. A tall, attractive woman with a well-structured face framed by a shock of ash blonde hair, she was both diffident and curious. I gave her potted biographies of some of the key guests at the party which amused her, and she observed the scene with a slightly ironical mien. This was the beginning of our friendship.

Marcia had a sharp brain and a strong grasp of politics in the raw. She sensed the mood of the electorate, was well briefed on all the candidates and could analyse the social problems and demographic complexities of every constituency in the land. She also proved to be a clever tactician with an intuitive ability to gain the advantage by putting herself into the shoes of an adversary. Having advanced from secretary and factotum to ever-present political aide, Marcia had made herself indispensable to Wilson. She was devoted, protective and shrewd. She could say things to Harold that nobody else dared say. He depended on her for objective advice, even though there were times when she, who suffered from the same bouts of persecution mania, fed his fears and clouded his vision. She was volatile and prone to emotional outbursts. One moment she was composed and coolly analytical, the next she could be shrill and strident. Her fiery temper was usually directed at those she trusted most. Marcia set high standards of friendship. Warm-hearted and generous, she was prepared to go to any lengths for her intimates and expected the same degree of loyalty in return. She could be trying, especially when under stress – there were many occasions when I felt the full brunt of her impetuous nature. Once, when I arranged a drinks party for some forty-odd friends of the Prime Minister and some American visitors, she took exception to one name on the guest list. She flew into a rage and insisted I disinvite him. Rather than incur the embarrassment of having to withdraw one invitation, I cancelled the whole party.

Marcia's closeness to Harold Wilson from the day she joined him in 1956 gave rise to rumours that they were lovers. In fact their relationship was that of avuncular friend to headstrong and emotional young ward. Wilson acted as father confessor. He was privy to most of her problems and emotional entanglements, often stepping in to smooth ruffled feathers. Just as she shared every problem Harold and his family might have and never shunned an errand on his behalf, he stood at her side in critical moments of her life. Mary Wilson trusted her completely – her problem was another one. She hated politics and regarded life at Number Ten as a temporary purgatory which had somehow to be endured; she yearned for privacy. Marcia's whole family, her parents, her brother Tony and her sister Peggy, were continually drafted into the service of the Wilsons. The Fields felt a kind of personal fealty, rather than political or ideological partisanship, for Harold. Underlying their deep sense of loyalty there were tensions and a certain degree of nagging, as in a soap opera family saga.

Though on one level she sided emotionally with the Labour Left, Marcia was a pragmatist like her master. She knew the limitations of power and the advantage of compromise. For all the Bevanite ideals which had drawn her to the Labour Party as a schoolgirl, she had a respect for respectability and a liking of tradition. She was very aware of her power, and, though friend and foe curried favour, she sometimes overestimated the lengths people would go to to earn patronage. She played on the baser instincts of sycophants the way a virtuoso plays a stringed instrument. It worked for a while, but in the end it backfired on her and her enemies took revenge for her excesses. They forgot the favours, the warmth and generosity and remembered only the capricious, irrational and stormy side of her complex character. As a temporary civil servant who liaised with the Labour Party, Marcia had a delicate role. She had many detractors, but she also had many supporters and admirers within the Whitehall machine and in Parliament.

Marcia's position was more subtle and less tangible than received wisdom has it. It was influence through attrition and power through devotion. Her apparent omnipotence made her a target of ill will and criticism. The press both hounded and flattered her. They gave her celebrity status on a par with film stars and royalty, but they also smeared her through innuendo and outright calumny. The breakdown of her marriage, the birth of her illegitimate twins, speculation about the nature of her relationship with Wilson and her reputed use of power provided Fleet Street with ready fodder. But she was also threatened closer to home. There were those in the Prime Minister's entourage who resented her easy access to him. Joe Haines, for many years Wilson's press secretary and speech writer, had at first worked amicably alongside her, but their relationship became uneasy. His adverse view of her was taken up by others in what began as an oral campaign of systematic deni-gration and has now been perpetuated in written accounts of the Wilson era. Haines, who rose from being the Saint Just of Fleet Street to occupying the executive suite at the Mirror Group head-quarters, becoming the hagiographer of Robert Maxwell, found a strong ally in Bernard Donoughue, the head of the Prime Minister's Policy Unit.

Arnold Goodman was also deeply antagonistic to Marcia.

Originally Gaitskell's lawyer, he first came to Wilson's attention in 1963, just after he became Leader of the Party. Goodman gradually assumed the role of legal advisor, confidant and troubleshooter extraordinary, a function which outlasted both Wilson's premiership and that of his successor Jim Callaghan, though Margaret Thatcher kept her distance. She acknowledged his remarkable talents as conciliator, lightning rod and power broker, but she identified him with the Liberal establishment, which she despised as much as it derided her. To one who, like Wilson, was wary of the world outside his familiar beat, Goodman seemed ubiquitously helpful.

Wilson's distrustful nature led him to heap responsibilities on a very small number of people whose loyalty he did not question. Goodman was one of the main beneficiaries of this tendency, amassing huge influence and becoming a fashionable figure. Like a Turkish grand vizier, he was entrusted with all manner of problems and was even sent on delicate diplomatic missions abroad. I found him a formidable friend of those he favoured, and a dangerous enemy of those of whom he disapproved. He would move mountains for his protégés whether they were clients or social friends, making his influence felt in every nook and cranny. He was more discreet about his dislikes but just as effective in barring their way.

Goodman and I had first met through Flora Solomon. Our paths crossed fairly frequently in the Anglo-Jewish world, in the realm of the arts, and peripherally in the Wilson circle. We never clashed openly, despite finding ourselves on opposite sides of an argument on half a dozen occasions, but I was bracketed as a close friend of Marcia and it was clear that there was no love lost between us. Marcia resented her exclusion from Wilson's private sessions with Goodman, and he in turn avoided her scrupulously. He saw her as an irritant, an irrational force which he failed to comprehend. But despite the inevitable tensions and rivalries, chroniclers of the Wilson regime have exaggerated the hothouse atmosphere of the political office.

My modest role in the Wilson entourage was that of unofficial go-between and networker. I arranged for him to meet German, French, Italian and American newspaper editors, publishers, politicians and businessmen. When one of his books was published in Germany, Gabriele Henkel hosted a dinner party for him in Düsseldorf, where luminaries from Bonn and industrialists from the

Ruhr mixed with intellectuals from Hamburg, Munich and Berlin. Wilson liked the idea of having emissaries who could explain the British dilemma over Europe to influential opinion-formers across the Channel, and enjoyed meeting distinguished foreigners informally, as he often did in my house.

London was blessed with some remarkable ambassadors during the decade of Britain's soul-searching over Europe. The gaunt and knightly Geoffroy de Courcel and his accomplished wife Martine, an elegant bluestocking who represented the best of the Left and Right Bank of Paris at Kensington Palace Gate, had a particularly difficult task. Her husband was one of de Gaulle's closest collaborators, and rigidly executed orders from the Elysée. Martine unruffled diplomatic feathers, and when de Gaulle pronounced his icy veto she gave little consolation lunches for jilted pro-Europeans. On the day after de Gaulle's veto on Britain's entry into the EEC, she took two Labour leaders and Lord (Roy) Thomson, owner of *The Times*, to the White Tower restaurant where, from a neighbouring table, I could hear her soothing the dejected trio.

Germany's discerning ambassador Herbert Blankenhorn was perhaps the best-informed envoy on the diplomatic turf. An Anglophile who was an intimate of Adenauer, he navigated between his master's Francophile and Atlantic inclinations.

I always had a romantic predilection for beautiful ambassadresses, especially when they combined elegance with a political bent. I saw in them the successors of the great salonnières who had held sway during the Congress of Vienna, soothing and swaying, animating and sometimes even entrapping the statesmen of the day with their wisdom and charm. No one fitted this image as well as Evangeline Bruce, the much-admired wife of David Bruce, that most distinguished of diplomats who was, from 1961 to 1969, American ambassador to London, and who did so much to strengthen America's bond with Europe. An American gentleman of the old school, David had served as ambassador to Paris and Bonn, where he had formed close friendships with Jean Monnet and Adenauer. He used his influence on Kennedy and Nixon to keep America's interest in Europe alive, and, a supporter of Britain's entry into Europe, also worked hard at bringing London, Paris and Bonn together in a triangle of friendship. David was on excellent terms with Tories and Socialists, and helped steer Wilson, Brown and Michael Stewart on a pro-American course. The Labour Government's understanding for the American dilemma over Vietnam was in part due to his efforts.

At Wingfield House, Evangeline mixed the young and talented from the arts world with politicians, financiers and other grandees whom the ambassador had to cultivate. Stunningly well-dressed and effortlessly distinctive, she displayed the same immaculate taste in compiling a guest list as she did in all other matters. With her subtle but unfailing talent for separating the sheep from the goats among the sprawling social herds of London, Evangeline picked people who stood out for their intelligence and wit. She was particularly receptive to budding writers and artists. At first Evangeline could seem aloof, but she would light up and join in enthusiastically if the conversation turned to a subject close to her heart, be it a historical anecdote from the age of Louis XV, a beautiful object in a current exhibition or the discovery of a new talent.

For more than ten successive summers Evangeline, by then a widow, and my friend Marietta Tree rented a delightful house in the Tuscan hills from the painter Teddy Millington-Drake. Roy and Jennifer Jenkins, Nicko and Mary Henderson and I were among the regulars they entertained there. Roy Jenkins first came into my life soon after the war, and over the years we overlapped in diverse social circles. We were introduced by Flora Solomon's son Peter Benenson, who, besides being a friend and neighbour of the Jenkinses, also stood as a Labour candidate in the East End of London. We had another link in Barley Alison, my long-time editorial colleague, with whom Roy was on good terms, and we shared a zest for transatlantic life. Although he made his mark as a European statesman, I believe he is intellectually more of an Atlanticist. Roy's understanding of American politics, his Whiggish charm and conversational skill made him a great favourite of the American Liberal establishment. I often saw him in Washington with Evangeline and in New York with Marietta Tree, Arthur Schlesinger, the historian of the New Deal, and Joe Alsop, who exuded New England in Britain and evoked Old England in Washington brownstones.

A champion of the reform of the censorship laws, Roy used his influence at Westminister to help in the battle for *Lolita*. He also chaired the launching at the Savoy Hotel of the World University Library. An eighty-volume academic series copublished by twelve foreign firms, it was the most ambitious enterprise Weidenfeld & Nicolson ever embarked on. I tried to woo Roy as an author, but he remained loyal to Collins, not least because his close friend Mark Bonham-Carter was a director there.

At times Roy could be affable, at others I found him reserved and wary. In the elegantly rustic atmosphere of Evangeline's and Marietta's Tuscan retreat he seemed more at ease. His conversation, ranging from politics to literature, was enriched by polished character sketches, mostly benign but sometimes spiced with subtle malice. With a finely tuned ear for the spoken as well as the written word, Roy phrases his sentences fastidiously, caressing the cadences and emphasizing them with a characteristic semi-circular movement of his left hand.

The Bruces were a hard act to follow, and the contrast between them and the Annenbergs, who succeeded to the Embassy, could not have been greater. They lacked the Bruces' savoir-faire, but after a shaky start and a certain amount of public ridicule over a television interview in which Walter talked brashly about refurbishing Wingfield House, the new couple eventually carved an important place for themselves. Whereas Bruce was at home among intellectuals, Annenberg preferred to cultivate the business community in London and in the provinces. He was one of the most effective and certainly the most munificent envoys America ever sent to Britain, making many anonymous gifts as well as public benefactions. His and the elegant Lee's recurring visits to London were hugely enjoyed by his friends.

Annenberg had a purposeful manner of pronouncing every syllable with equal weight and was an indefatigable storyteller. He had little regard for George Brown, and would wait for people to crowd around him before embarking on a story about a meeting where the Foreign Secretary made robust jibes at the American Government's handling of the European allies in the Vietnam war. Annenberg took pleasure in reporting that he had replied, 'What you need, Mr Brown, is a psychoanalyst.' The ambassador's audience would then play along by shrieking with laughter or gasping, depending on which reaction they felt was expected of them. Before they could adapt their facial expression Annenberg would continue, 'But that is nothing to what happened to me the other day at Downing Street . . .' He would then launch into another story. People would be afraid of stopping him, lest he try to top that by yet another anecdote.

At the beginning of his ambassadorial career, Annenberg had, understandably, little idea of who was who on the London scene. I remember standing with him in the corner of a drawing room at a very grand cocktail party when the elegant Madame de Courcel swept in on her way to the theatre. Annenberg turned to me and asked, 'Who's that dame?' I told him that she was the French ambassador's wife, and to complete the picture I proceeded to give him a brief rundown on her husband. Annenberg listened attentively as I pointed out Geoffroy de Courcel's friendship with de Gaulle and described the famous photograph depicting the General's arrival on English soil after the fall of France with a stylish young officer in tow. 'That was Baron de Courcel,' I explained. 'You can see how close he was to de Gaulle.' After a moment's reflection, Annenberg said, 'I see. He was onto a good thing and he knew it.'

Apart from drawing on my various connections, Marcia and the Prime Minister used me to bring to their attention men of outstanding ability who could be engaged in the battle for Britain's economic renewal. Being both pragmatic and broad-minded, Harold Wilson often chose candidates irrespective of their political affiliations. In fact, he was anxious to bring Conservatives into State-owned industries. In that area he did not think along narrow party lines, unlike Mrs Thatcher, who spurned those whom she did not consider 'one of us'. When Wilson was in urgent need of a chairman for the newly nationalized British Steel Corporation, he asked Tom Balogh to cast his eye around. He was looking for a fresh face which would be acceptable to the City. I suggested Lord Melchett, a bright and respected, if somewhat unconventional, merchant banker in his forties who had just been embroiled in a bitter boardroom struggle with the family bank, Hill Samuel, and was looking for something else to do. He agreed to have his name put forward. Since time was short he sent his curriculum vitae around to me by taxi. I passed it on to Balogh at Number Ten, and within less than a week the appointment was approved. Julian Melchett proved an excellent choice. He was open to innovation and recognized the need for improving relations between management and the workforce. As a Tory who had agreed to serve a nationalized industry, he was also a feather in Wilson's cap.

James Hanson and James Goldsmith, both of whom I introduced to Marcia and Wilson, also found favour, although they made no secret of the fact that they were Conservatives. Using his intimate knowledge of French business, Jimmy Goldsmith talked with unusual brilliance about ways of reviving small and medium-sized enterprises through new management techniques which concentrated on initiative. Wilson was fascinated. Not long before Wilson's resignation, Jimmy signalled that he might be willing to take full-time office for a year or two to organize the training of a new elite of managers in England. Wilson hoped his knighthood would be an incentive to him to stay there rather than go back to France. Hanson, another knight on the famous 'Lavender List', also impressed the Prime Minister with his entrepreneurial skill. A Yorkshireman like himself, Hanson shared Wilson's passion for Gilbert and Sullivan. He endeared himself to Wilson when the D'Oyly Carte Company found itself in one of its periodic financial crises and he fulfilled his request to help bail it out.

Once, when I gave a dinner for Mr and Mrs Henry Ford, my house was the setting for another informal meeting which proved useful to Wilson. Union trouble and the general economic climate was prompting Henry Ford to rethink the future of Ford Motors in Britain. He had no personal contact with the Labour Government, so I arranged a dinner to which I invited Harold Lever and Eric Varley, two economic ministers, Lord Balogh, by then Minister of State for Energy, Marcia Williams and Gerald Kaufman, and added a few friends from different worlds to ensure that it would seem like a social gathering rather than a board meeting. On the morning of the party Marcia telephoned to say that the Prime Minister would like to come in after dinner. He arrived at about ten o'clock and withdrew into my library with Henry Ford, where they remained closeted for well over an hour.

In his earlier days at the Board of Trade, and in Opposition when he was economic advisor to the timber group Montague L. Meyer, Wilson had had many dealings with the Soviet Union, and as Prime Minister he actively encouraged Anglo-Soviet trade. He prided himself on his good personal relations with Anastas Mikoyan, that great survivor from the Stalinist era who was trade negotiator when Wilson first met him and eventually became Head of State. Although he had never tarnished his record with a Communist or a fellow travelling past, Wilson had begun on the Left of the Labour Party, and, as one of those who, with Bevan and John Freeman, resigned from the Government in 1951 in protest against restrictions on health spending, he was identified with the left-wing challenge to the current leadership. While in power he moved further to the right and tried to hold the Party together by playing a subtle balancing act between Left and Right. But he was typecast as a left-winger. Nonetheless his outlook was Atlanticist. He was supportive of the United States over Vietnam, and of all the Labour prime ministers he took the least immoderate line on sanctions against South Africa.

Both Lyndon Johnson and Hubert Humphrey, with whom I had interesting talks about Wilson, regarded him as one of America's most loyal allies. I met Humphrey through Jacob Javits, the powerful Republican senator from New York who was one of the most influential members of the Foreign Affairs Committee of the Senate, and perhaps the most powerful Jewish spokesman in the United States. After Humphrey lost the presidential election in 1968, we both sat on the Advisory Board of the *Enyclopaedia Britannica*, which was then a partner in Weidenfeld & Nicolson. Humphrey was the the most popular American in the eyes of the Labour Party.

Harold Wilson enjoyed characterizing American politicians he had met. I remember him reminiscing with George Brown about the four presidential candidates for the 1968 election, each of whom visited Europe as part of their campaign. The first to call at Number Ten was the Democrat Hubert Humphrey, who came with one aide. Wilson and George Brown regarded him as a friend whose views were akin to their own. 'But,' said Wilson, 'he asked rather bland questions.' The next to come was Governor Rockefeller, who arrived with two aides. 'He was off-colour and didn't bother to ask any questions. When he left we shook our heads.' The third to come was Robert Kennedy. Wilson's verdict: 'He brought three aides, but I can only tell you that after three and a half hours my secretary murmured, "Senator Kennedy came at nine-thirty and left shortly before lunch. The meeting was marked by long silences punctuated by fatuous questions."' The last to come was Richard Nixon. 'We knew he stood for many things we didn't like,' Wilson went on. 'He came without an aide, opened two bulging briefcases, took out a yellow lawyer's notepad and a red pencil. He fired question after question at us. He was so well-informed he put us on our mettle. When he left George Brown and I agreed, "Not a nice man, but he'll make a great president".'

In March 1971, when Nixon was already well-established at the White House and we were about to publish Lyndon Johnson's memoirs, my wife Sandra and I went to stay at the LBJ ranch near

Dallas. On our arrival, Johnson saw me stare at six huge rocking chairs on the broad porch. He came out with the first of many Johnsonisms we were to hear over the next few days: 'I had those built when I left the White House. I said to Bird, I am going to sit on this porch for two years, doze and think, and then one day I will get up and get Walter Lippmann.' Knowing that Harold and Mary Wilson were due to visit the following weekend, I encouraged Johnson to talk about his recollections of dealings with the Wilson Government. Wilson had been deeply involved in the Anglo-Russian mediation efforts over Vietnam which climaxed in the famous night at Claridges in February 1967, when Kosygin, Wilson and George Brown met having been in touch with Hanoi and Washington respectively. LBJ smirked at the mention of that occasion. 'We could have done without his mediation,' he admitted. 'We had other things on our mind, and, damn it, so did Kosygin.' I showed my surprise, and Johnson said, 'You ask Arthur Goldberg to tell you what happened.'

Goldberg, the former ambassador to the United Nations, was staying with the Johnsons at the same time as we were. Our hosts gave a dinner that night for guests who included Orville Freeman, Minister of Agriculture under JFK and LBJ, and his wife, Arthur Krim, head of United Artists and a Johnson loyalist, Eppi Evron, Chargé d'Affaires at the Israeli Embassy during Johnson's presidency, and Eddie Marcus and his wife of the Nieman Marcus department store in Dallas and Houston.

When they all arrived there was not a car in sight, only helicopters and private jets. After dinner the men trooped off to the library and sat talking in deep armchairs around an oak table with huge decanters and massive humidors stocked with cigars handmade by Cuban exiles. I asked Goldberg to give his account. He told me how the Americans had monitored a call from Brezhnev to Kosygin in which there was talk of some trouble in the Politbureau and the Central Committee. It was all about the threat they were facing from the First Secretary of the Moscow Communist Party who was tabling a motion to unseat Brezhnev and Kosygin. 'In the end,' Goldberg said, 'they threw the First Secretary out, but whatever happened, believe me, their mind was not on Vietnam that night.'

Later, as if presiding over a Cabinet meeting, LBJ announced: 'Some of us haven't met since I left the White House. I want to go round the table and ask you people what you've been doing since, what you're doing now and how you see the future. Now, let's start with you, Orville. For the benefit of my British guest,' Johnson added, turning to me, 'I want to say that Orville Freeman was the goddamned best Minister of Agriculture we have had this century.'

'Well, Mr President . . .' Orville unconsciously stiffened and modulated his voice to catch the tone of the senior public servant reporting to his chief. One by one the guests replied as though they were addressing a president in Cabinet. Then Lady Bird appeared with an imperious summons for us to join the ladies again.

The next day, Sunday, after we had attended a Texan fiesta in San Antonio, LBJ took us on a whirlwind tour of the ranch in his jeep, chasing the deer and enthusing about his work as a farmer and real estate operator. Back in his library he opened up, roaming from one subject to the next without link or introduction and uttering terse and outspoken verdicts on events or personalities. Of Kennedy's assassination he said: 'I think I know who killed JFK. I can't prove it yet, but one day I will. Goddammit, I know it . . . It was Castro. You see, the Kennedy brothers liked playing cops and robbers, and when Bobby was Attorney-General he was responsible for the CIA and they sent people into Cuba to *git* Castro, but they failed and Castro *git* Jack Kennedy.' He continued to expand on his theory. 'I never could understand why Bobby tried to put some CIA people on the Warren Commission. I had Dick Helms here not long ago and I asked him point blank, but he refused to be drawn. Oswald was a Communist agent, he was in Cuba, he was in the Soviet Union. One day I will prove it.' I quizzed Johnson about the Six Day War which I felt he had not dealt with in sufficient depth in his book. 'Well,' he answered, 'I wish I could have written more. They made me take out quite a lot of things. The last day of the Six Day War was the worst day of my life.' He then gave me a blow-by-blow account. Johnson was woken at around three o'clock in the morning and told that the Soviet prime minister was on the hotline. He went down to his office and assembled his aides. McGeorge Bundy was there, so were Dean Rusk and Robert McNamara. While Kosygin was bellowing down the line, the teleprinter came through with the translation. Johnson said, 'I felt my guts coming up my throat.' There were three phrases which caused alarm: 'The Soviet Government has come to a decision . . .; It is of a military nature . . .; It will have catastrophic consequences . . .'

'There was silence in the room,' Johnson went on. 'McGeorge

tried to put a good face on the situation. Mind you, he's mighty smart. I used him a lot on detail, but not on judgement. Dean was always reliable and sound.'

He described how Bob McNamara was despatched to his room to telephone the Chief of Staff and find out where the Sixth Fleet was and how fast it could travel. 'Bob went out of the room and we sat there in silence, Bird came down and brought us some coffee.' Twenty minutes later McNamara reported that the Sixth Fleet was three hundred miles off the Syrian coast and that its normal speed, give or take a ten percent margin of error, was twenty-five knots an hour. Johnson quoted himself as having told McNamara, 'You go right back and tell the Fleet to sail right into the Russians' face, but normal speed, do you hear, normal speed.' After an agonizing two hours or so, a message came through saying that the Russians had backed off. As a postscript to this tale Johnson added, 'And I bet you, if Hubert Humphrey or McGovern had been sitting in my chair they would have been wetting their pants.'

On Monday morning the President came into my bedroom at about nine o'clock waving a copy of the *New York Times*. He burst out like a volley of quick fire, 'I am sure you want to read this goddamned Eastern newspaper. Could never do right by it. The Kennedys could never do wrong. When Jackie shoves a reporter on the sidewalk the *New York Times* writes: "Reporter shoves Mrs Kennedy". If I shove a reporter, they want to have me sent to a county gaol . . .' Without further ado he left the room.

Ever since Harold Wilson had risen to prominence, his less scrupulous opponents had tried to weave a net of calumny and disinformation around his links with the Russians, hinting at dual loyalties. His support of the United States, his staunch monarchism, his almost sentimental patriotism did not deter some of his detractors. They formed an incongruous alliance of extreme right-wingers in the British intelligence community, the CIA, where the highly-strung James Angleton led a subterranean chorus of denigration, the South African intelligence service BOSS, which hunted 'liberals' of every hue, and the KGB itself, which sought to destabilize any important non-Communist leader of the Left. In the final stages of the Wilson regime this intangible cloud of rumour, innuendo, stale jokes and lurid tales polluted the air. Some people in his entourage may have gone overboard in their suspicions of a smear campaign, but I had no doubt that something was afoot. There were mysterious break-ins at Wilson's private house in Buckinghamshire and at the offices of Arnold Goodman, and stories about agents, blackmail and compromising photographs began to circulate. Some of them seemed to originate in secret-service quarters. In the summer of 1975 at a lunch party in the country given by Michael Sacher, people with intelligence contacts regaled the other guests with talk of Harold Wilson, Marcia and the 'Russian connection'. Martin Gilbert, the historian, who was the host's son-in-law, was present. He felt indebted to Marcia for facilitating his research on Churchill in the Downing Street archives. Gilbert took notes under the table and telephoned Marcia at Downing Street. The story was corroborated by another source who alerted me to what had gone on. I informed Marcia. The Prime Minister discussed the matter with us over lunch in the House of Commons on the last day of Parliament before the summer recess. Members were behaving like schoolboys breaking up – there was a jolly atmosphere and people kept stopping at the Prime Minister's table to exchange pleasantries. But Wilson was in a sombre mood. He decided to summon the Head of MI5, Sir Michael Hanley, to confront him about the allegations point blank, to little effect.

One night in early February 1976 I had a call from Downing Street. There was an all-night session at the House of Commons, would I meet the Prime Minister in his room there at 10.30 p.m? He knew from Marcia that I was shortly to fly to New York and Washington, and wanted me to find out via our mutual friend Hubert Humphrey whether there was an intelligence cabal. 'I can't get any sense out of our own people,' he said. 'I want to know if the Americans are involved.' He dictated five questions about possible CIA activities in Britain which he wanted me to put to Humphrey. I still have the somewhat crumpled sheet of Downing Street paper on which I scribbled them.

I volunteered two other names I could approach on Wilson's behalf: Frank Church, the head of the Intelligence subcommittee of the Senate, and George Bush, who had just been appointed head of the CIA. George and Barbara Bush were friends of my wife Sandra, who had lived in Texas with her first husband, and we visited the Bushes when he was ambassador to the United Nations. I remember a particularly enjoyable supper à quatre at his apartment in the Waldorf Towers when we watched a special screening of Coppola's *The Godfather*, then a brand new film, a complimentary copy of which Bush had been sent. Wilson agreed that I should consult Church and Bush, provided I cleared it with Humphrey.

Next day I flew to New York. I saw Senator Humphrey on two occasions in Washington. At our first meeting I gave him a handwritten copy of Wilson's questions. He promised to talk to Senators Church and Mondale and instructed two of his aides to follow up various other sources. At our second meeting at the end of February, Humphrey gave me specific answers to each question. I was to assure Wilson that there was no official CIA policy aimed against members of the present British Government, nor were there operations sanctioned from above in this respect. Humphrey did not, however, exclude the possibility of activities by unauthorized 'hired hands' and low-level operatives who might cooperate with extreme right-wing elements in Britain or with emissaries of South Africa.

I was able to discharge my mission to George Bush at a private dinner party in his honour given by Mrs Mildred Hillmann, a political hostess in the realm of the United Nations who also had a large apartment at the Waldorf Towers. Bush talked openly about the problems he had to tackle in his new job, especially the need to restore the image of the Agency. When I had revealed the nature of my request, Bush told me to call him in Washington a few days later after he had made some inquiries. When I telephoned him, he confirmed what Humphrey had said. The records contained not the slightest blemish on Wilson's reputation. Bush said he was anxious to clear the air and give Wilson his personal assurance. He suggested a private visit to London en route for Pullach, where he was due to make his first inspection of German Intelligence headquarters. I reported back to Marcia on the open line, but we used code names. Bush was 'Gary Cooper' and Wilson 'the producer'. I said I had just been to see Gary Cooper and that he would like to come and see the producer again. When I told Marcia the date Bush had in mind, she shouted down the line, 'That's too late.' I did not know what she meant. 'Why is it too late?'

'Think, man, use your grey matter. It's got to be before that.'

I still did not understand.

'Never mind,' she said. 'Tell him it has to be earlier or not at all. That's all I can say.'

It was not until later that I discovered she meant the resignation date. Only a handful of people knew that it was to be his sixtieth birthday. Wilson had made his mind up long ago, but was very anxious to keep the decision secret, not least because he wanted to influence the succession. When news reached him that the date had been openly discussed at a London dinner party, he asked Lord Goodman if he had learnt how the story had leaked. Goodman had heard that it emanated from New York where I was said to have spread the word. Beside himself with rage, Wilson summoned Marcia and reproached her for my alleged indiscretion. She pointed out that I could not possibly have been the source; thankfully she had kept a note of our telephone conversation across the Atlantic. My inability to understand why the date Bush had suggested was no good proved that I was not in the know.

Long before Wilson announced his retirement, rumour had been rife, not least because he had often hinted to colleagues and friends that he would not stay the course, though he sent conflicting signals and nobody quite believed that he would go. But amid all the speculation there was already a valedictory feeling at the Downing Street Christmas party three months before he made his decision public. It was a cosy get-together of all the staff and a few close friends of the Wilsons. As well as celebrating Christmas we were saying farewell to Robert Armstrong, who was leaving his post as Principal Private Secretary to the Prime Minister. Armstrong was a good pianist, and he jollied us along by playing Christmas carols and Wilson's favourite ditties from Gilbert and Sullivan. All the while people were whispering in corners that this would be Harold's last Christmas in Downing Street.

Although I was not aware of the date, I knew some months beforehand that Wilson was planning to go. I remember going down to Chequers one weekend in the autumn and dining with Harold and Marcia. We had grouse, and I felt acutely embarrassed because I do not eat it. The subject of his resignation was discussed in general terms. Marcia was passionately opposed to it, and we both appealed to him to rethink his decision. All through the winter we argued every possible case to dissuade him. Wilson, who liked being oracular, always protested that he had not finally made up his mind.

On 10 March 1976, the eve of Harold Wilson's sixtieth birthday, I gave a party in his honour as I had done for some years. Since Marcia's birthday is only a day apart it was often a double celebration, confined to their families and a small circle of intimates. George Thomas, the long-time Speaker of the House of Commons (later Lord Tonypandy), Peter Shore, Tommy Balogh and Gerald Kaufman would usually be there. On this occasion James Callaghan, then Foreign Secretary, was included, somewhat to his puzzlement. There was a division in the House that night, and when it was time to vote, Wilson offered Callaghan a lift. As they were leaving, Callaghan turned to me and asked, 'Whose idea was it to ask me tonight?' Marcia was standing behind me in the doorway. She and I exchanged glances before she answered with perfect poise, 'We all wanted you here.' It was in the car on the way to the House of Commons that Wilson informed Callaghan of his decision to resign. The Cabinet was not to be told until six days later, but he wanted his chosen successor to have a head start in the leadership contest.

Despite all the rumours, the news of Wilson's resignation hit London like a thunderbolt. That week I spent many hours with Marcia and the Prime Minister. On 16 March, the day he made his announcement in the House, we suddenly found that nothing had been planned for the evening, so I arranged for my cook to rustle up dinner for the three of us. Marcia had agreed to go on television, and I took her to the studio. Afterwards we all met in my flat. The atmosphere was very tense. Harold was under great strain and Marcia was in a bad mood. She kept reproaching Wilson about the resignation: nothing would turn out as he imagined, had he not given any thought to the people who worked for him? He was embarrassed by the situation, and tried to change the subject. Then Marcia suddenly got up and stormed out of the flat, slamming the door behind her. Wilson's driver, Bill, was sent out onto the Embankment to get her back. Eventually she returned. There was a somewhat unconvincing reconciliation, and Harold and she left not long afterwards.

Shortly before eight o'clock the next morning the doorbell rang. It was Bill, the driver, saying that the Prime Minister had left his pipe behind. Like the little blackamoor in the *Rosenkavalier* who comes to retrieve the handkerchief dropped by the Marschallin and scurries off with his find as the orchestra plays the final chords, Bill took the pipe from the table where it still lay untouched amid the ashes of the previous night. Then the curtain went down on the Wilson era.

I have never been able to fathom the real motive for his premature departure from office, but I am certain that there was nothing sinister behind his decision. In his coquettish way he used to say that a younger man should have a go. Since Callaghan was his chosen successor, this cannot have been the reason. But there was some metal fatigue, and he may have given in to pressure from his wife who longed for him to leave office. The internecine struggles of the Labour Party cannot have been an incentive to stay, nor the mutinous trade unions or the general economic climate. I believe that Wilson did not intend the resignation to be a permanent departure from politics and that he thought he would be recalled, like Gladstone or de Gaulle. There was a feeling that he might think it wise to leave office temporarily, only to return as an elder statesman, possibly even to head a coalition government. When I went to thank him for my peerage, I told him that my joy was only tempered by the fact that I would not be able to serve him. He winked and said, 'Don't worry, I'll be back.'

The Wilsons were now forced to lead a frugal life. Special privileges granting research assistants, cars and drivers to former prime ministers were not introduced until after Wilson's resignation. He himself had shown little foresight in arranging his affairs. Whereas Ted Heath was well provided for, and other retired prime ministers had ample private means, Wilson depended on the income from his books and speaking engagements, which his deteriorating health prevented him from developing, to top up his modest pension. There was talk of a Foundation, but nothing materialized, not least because of an avowed disinclination among some of his circle to let Marcia play a part in such a constellation. Wilson might have liked the mastership of University College, Oxford, but in the end it was Lord Goodman who received that appointment.

Seldom has a prime minister had such a harsh press, nor a public image more tarnished by smear and innuendo, than Harold Wilson following his resignation. Most of the savage comment was based on ill-founded evidence, and his biographers have been less than generous. Although Philip Ziegler was given access to Wilson's papers, I cannot help feeling that he relies heavily on witnesses who were avowedly hostile to Wilson, and especially Marcia Falkender, and failed to interview others of equal weight who might have been more positive about them. Reading Arnold Goodman's memoirs I was taken aback by his critical assessment. At times he is caustic and condescending about the man who took him into his confidence and heaped him with special assignments and honours. It was thanks to this preferment that Goodman became an influential public figure. His portrayal of Wilson as a semi-educated philistine is unjust. Steeped in knowledge about statistics, economics and political history, Harold Wilson was a specialist rather than a man of wide learning, but he had a feeling approaching reverence for intellectuals. However one looks on his legacy, he made two towering contributions to British culture. To his immense pride he established the Open University, a landmark in the field of higher education, which enables adults with no formal qualifications to study at home; and he gave his Arts Minister Jennie Lee and the Arts Council, chaired by Arnold Goodman, a freer hand and, relative to the budgetary situation of the time, more generous resources than any British government before or since.

Lord Goodman's attack on the notorious 'Lavender List' echoes the hostile comment from the press and all sides of the political spectrum in Westminister. As ever, the media homed in on Marcia, who was said to have jotted down Wilson's original suggestions on her lavender-coloured notepaper and whose ennoblement two years earlier was still considered a sore point. But of the forty-two names on the list, most had made a valuable contribution to various realms of British public life and were no less distinguished than many of those honoured before or since. It was unfortunate that there were two people who attracted particular controversy: Sir Joseph Kagan, the Lithuanian-born manufacturer whose Gannex raincoats Wilson wore, and Eric Miller, a property developer who helped subsidize the Socialist International, which served the Prime Minister as a useful mantle for informal meetings with foreign leaders of the Left. Both men damaged Wilson's reputation. Kagan served a prison sentence for tax evasion, and Miller committed suicide in September 1977 following allegations of fraud. One or two other beneficiaries of Wilson's patronage were deemed eccentric, and some found it puzzling that a Labour politician, who had on occasion even expressed contempt for such baubles, should honour conspicuous free-marketeers like James Goldsmith. The unorthodox character of Wilson's resignation honours stemmed mainly from his wish to condense into this one list names which he might have spread over two or three years had he remained in office. He wanted to reward certain people whom he felt would be unlikely to be singled out by his successor. I remember him telling me once that he wanted to have an academic on the list. When the historians J.H. Plumb and

Asa Briggs were suggested, Wilson argued that both of them were destined to be honoured sooner or later, but that John Vaizey, who had undoubted merits, might not be chosen by a more conventional prime minister. So Vaizey was elevated to the House of Lords, where he became an active peer.

It has often been suggested that the carping about Wilson's resignation honours had anti-Semitic undertones. Be that as it may, the prominence of Jewish names on the list bears out Wilson's unselfconscious attitude to race. He was a libertarian, devoid of racial, religious or class prejudice. If he had a bias it was directed against worldly milieus rather than class. He would feel comfortable with a homespun duke, but ill at ease with a doctrinaire left-winger; he liked the Cartesian rather than the artist's mind. It never entered his head to think that he might have promoted a disproportionately high number of Jews or people of foreign birth. Whenever somebody put it to him that this was the case, he would reply, 'Good God, I don't count how many people around me wear double-breasted suits or have red hair.' And he really meant it. Mary Wilson and Marcia Williams felt the same way. Their unselfconscious liking for Jews stemmed partly from their own background, the sense of belonging to the disadvantaged and having to work hard to earn status in society. Wilson respected hard work and self-made people.

Wilson had always had strong links with the Jewish community in Britain. Through the Ministry for Overseas Trade, and later as President of the Board of Trade, he had come into contact with a number of refugees from central and Eastern Europe whose enterprise and buccaneering spirit impressed him. Successful businessmen like the Austrian trader Rudy Sternberg, the Hungarian-born metal broker Sigmund Sternberg and the Austrian-born chemical engineer Schon formed the Labour industrial phalanx of self-made men on which he leant. Wilson felt relaxed in their company, and some of them became personal friends.

I was staying in Scotland with Gaia and William Mostyn-Owen when Wilson's much-delayed resignation honours were published. My peerage met with a similar response in some quarters as my knighthood had done seven years earlier: I gather the chairman of Heinemann spilt his sherry on hearing the news at the Savile Club. It rankled the publishing fraternity that I should have been singled out. Mark Longman, who was then President of the Publishers Association, sent me the curtest of letters. It read as follows:

Dear George,
   It is customary for the President of the Publishers Association
to write, on behalf of the Council of the Association, when a member
is mentioned in the Honours List – hence this letter. I am sure that
all your fellow-publishers are aware of the hard work which you
have put in to attain your Knighthood and I send you this
recognition of your achievement.
   Yours,
   Mark

At one party in that summer of 1969 I was accosted by an imperious woman from the shires. I had never met her before, but she
came straight to the point: 'Why did you get a knighthood and not
Billy Collins? He deserves it much more.' But I took heart from the
many warm tributes I received. One of them came from Richard
Crossman, who sent a handwritten note on which he had crossed
out the Department of Health and Social Security letterhead:

Dear George,
   Many congratulations – I have put off writing for days and days
for a perverse reason – namely that I really wanted to see you a Life
Peer and for me therefore the news was a bit of a let down!!
   Nevertheless – as John Foster said when he joined SHAEF during
the war with the rank of Brigadier – 'one has to start somewhere'.
   And so, I regard this as a first instalment of recognition. Let's
hope we last long enough to enable the P.M. to complete the
operation.
   Love
   Dick Crossman

On the day of the Investiture, my mother and my wife Sandra
escorted me to Buckingham Palace where other recipients of the
Queen's Birthday Honours assembled with their close relations.
Miraculously, the morning coat that the Czech tailor in Jerusalem
had made twenty years earlier still fitted me. Sandra and my mother
joined the other guests in the Ballroom, where they were entertained
by a military band playing melodies from *South Pacific*, *Fiddler on
the Roof* and other popular musicals. It struck me that there were
no classical pieces. Meanwhile the honorees were ushered into a
special room, separated into groups, and instructed by uniformed
courtiers as to how and when to bow, walk backwards and kneel

before the Sovereign. Sir Eric Penn, who, as Comptroller of the Lord Chamberlain's Office, was responsible for protocol, oversaw the dress rehearsal. Toweringly handsome, with an immaculately trimmed black moustache, he looked like a figure straight out of *The Prisoner of Zenda.* The honorees were then presented to the Queen one by one. She was well briefed and gave us each about a minute of her time. After she had dubbed me with her sword on both shoulders, she remarked, 'I do admire the work of Cecil Beaton and his wonderful albums,' indicating that she knew me to be his publisher. I mumbled assent, bowed stiffly and walked backwards, rejoining my family at the bottom of the staircase. When we left the Palace and walked into the unusually warm sunlight, my first thought was one of regret: that my father, who had died recently, was not there.

Reception into the House of Lords is much more elaborate than the ceremony attendant on the knighthood, although it happens without a royal presence. Once the peerage has been announced, the first step is to find a proposer and a seconder. I chose the Earl of Longford and Lord Melchett, who had recently succeeded his father, my friend Julian, and was an able representative of the younger generation on the Labour benches. The formal introduction takes place immediately after lunch, and new peers are allowed to invite up to sixteen guests for a celebratory meal. My mother and Laura were there, as were the Longfords, Peter Melchett and his mother Sonia, one of my oldest friends. The party was made up by Nigel Nicolson, Diana Phipps, Evangeline Bruce, Fred Warner, Pamela Hartwell, my dear friend Herman Elkon, and the ever loyal and generous Jan Mitchell, both of whom came from New York. While the others remained at the table, Black Rod and Garter King at Arms, dressed in his tabard and carrying his staff, led me and my two proposers to the Robing Room and then to the empty Chamber for a dress rehearsal. The three of us were taken through the ritual: doffing our tricorn hats to the Woolsack, reading a declaration of loyalty, swearing by the Bible (the Old Testament in my case), and so on.

We rejoined the lunch party for a quick cup of coffee before adjourning to the Robing Room to wait for the Lord Chancellor's procession and the official opening of the session. Just as we prepared to march in after prayers there was a small crisis of protocol. The Earl of Longford prepared to lead, with myself in the middle and Lord Melchett at the tail. But Garter King of Arms pointed out that, although the Longford earldom went back a long time, it belonged to the Irish peerage and had only been acknowledged as a United Kingdom barony in 1945, whereas the Melchett title dated from 1928. So the order was reversed. Feeling both nervous and moved, I completed my ceremonial duties and took my seat on a backbench of the Chamber.

On being made a peer you are encouraged to see the Garter King of Arms to establish the name of your title and a coat of arms. Knowing very little about these matters, I took Diana Phipps with me to the meeting at the College of Heraldry. Coming from a long line of Bohemian aristocrats she was well versed in the historical and aesthetic aspects of armorial bearings. Since I lived in Chelsea I was allowed to add 'of Chelsea' to my name. Garter King of Arms asked me if there was anything in my family history or in my own life that I wanted to incorporate in the symbolic scheme. We decided on a number of disparate elements: the ramparts of Jerusalem and a wolf with a scroll in its mouth – an echo of the emblematic beast which has adorned the crest of my mother's family since the Middle Ages. They were to be flanked by two figures: a sage with a long beard in a flowing robe, and a young uniformed student with his sword in hand. I chose three words from a verse of Horace as the motto: *Arma cedant togae*. When I explained to my friend Valerie Wade that it meant that arms must yield to conciliation, she immediately translated it in her down-to-earth way as 'Everything is negotiable'.

CHAPTER EIGHTEEN

Manhattan Mosaic

OVER THE PAST forty-five years my work has taken me to America so frequently that I have come to regard it as a second home. To me as a European, America, especially New York, is Europe writ large. The streets of Manhattan are littered with touches of London, Paris and Berlin, or echoes of Italy and Greece.

Publishing entailed regular visits to New York and Boston, and my political interests led me to Washington at least twice a year. In the 1970s I had a close business association with Encyclopaedia Britannica which entailed four trips a year to Chicago, and in the 1980s, during my association with Ann Getty, I added San Francisco and Los Angeles to my American itinerary. Since Americans are the most spontaneously responsive of people, work and social life became inextricably entwined and I have made almost as many friends there as I have on this side of the Atlantic, evolving a seamless pattern of constant cooperation, reciprocal hospitality and, at times, sentimental attachment.

In my earliest encounters with American publishing I caught the autumnal glow of an age of enlightened despots – individuals who ran their companies, many of which were family-controlled, like dynasts. East Coast publishers liked to model themselves on the ideal of the English gentleman. Work done, they would indulge in the ceremonial of lunching with their British guests in places like the Twenty-One, the Colony, the Pavilion, the Brussels – Frenchified restaurants where the maître d' engages you in interminable discussions about the wine and the way the food is prepared with far more attention to detail than his Parisian original. Some publishers entertained at the Century or the Yale Club. When relations grew warmer they took you out to dinner and sometimes on to the Champagne Room of the El Morocco, which became a haunt of mine.

The first time I set foot in an American publishing office was in the autumn of 1950 when I visited Roger Straus, a forceful and promising beginner who had already made his mark with his Farrar Straus imprint. The pose of the bon viveur with a hint of the playboy was deceptive, for Roger was a passionate champion of literature who had a cosmopolitan outlook and a penchant for new European writing. I had just left the service of the Israeli government to return to Weidenfeld & Nicolson, but Moshe Sharett, the Foreign Minister, had asked me to take ten days off to sit in on the briefings of the Israeli delegation to the United Nations about the forthcoming debates on the status of Jerusalem. I combined this errand with making my first contacts with American editors. Through President Weizmann and Teddy Kollek I had introductions to a number of celebrities in New York, some of whom had visited Israel while I was there. This made it easier for me to meet heads of publishing houses who would normally take scant notice of a foreign newcomer.

Two of the less accessible and more fastidious of the enlightened despots were Alfred and Blanche Knopf. They worked as business partners but led separate lives and rarely entertained together. Blanche Knopf's beat was Continental Europe, with particular emphasis on France. She held court at the Ritz in London and Paris where she would see fashionable intellectuals like Sartre and Camus. In New York she cultivated museum curators, art critics and musicians as well as her authors. Alfred Knopf liked entertaining in his house in the country. In those days of rigid exchange controls and the assumed poverty of any British publisher, let alone a struggling beginner, his invitation would arrive with a train ticket to Purchase in upstate New York. I often went there for Sunday lunch. Knopf had a particular penchant for historians and built up one of the finest lists in that field. He could be crotchety and arrogant, which made occasional praise from him all the more heart-warming.

My idol and mentor was Cass Canfield, the Anglophile head of Harper and a great American gentleman, who backed my ideas and gave some of his best titles to me instead of selling them to established British publishers. Dinner at the Canfields' brownstone house was one of the highlights of my visits to New York. There one might meet opinion-formers such as John Gunther and Walter Lippmann, whom I got to know better through Mary McCarthy, and mandarins like John McCloy, Dean Acheson and Archibald MacLeish, the

Librarian of Congress. There would be a general conversation over dinner, and afterwards the regal Jane Canfield would sometimes whisk us all into limousines which took us downtown to a lecture club in an elegant house hired for the occasion. About a dozen or more similar dinner parties met up there, all in black tie. The assembled guests – a mixture of proud professional people, scions of old families, some of the *grandes dames* of New York and gangling debutantes – would then listen to an informal lecture. John Gunther might report on a recent trip to Eastern Europe, Luigi Barzini speculate about post-Fascist Italy, or there might be a talk about how the Maine countryside was changing. I remember one occasion when Alan Pryce-Jones tried to explain the differences in social manners and mores between New York, Paris and London. He bounced off some imaginative theories, but went on rather too long about his Rothschild connections. After the talk there would be dancing, and the evening would be over by midnight. It was all very Whartonian.

The Canfield fortune came from Chicago. They were a close-knit clan with unfathomable ramifications since many divorced ex-members and their offspring remained in the fold. Cass Canfield's elder son Cass, Jr., has been an active member of Harper since the late 1950s. Michael, the younger, was adopted and rumoured to be the illegitimate child of a member of the British royal family. After his first wife Lee Bouvier, Jackie Kennedy's sister, left him for Stas Radziwill, he married Laura Dudley, later Duchess of Marlborough.

When Michael Canfield was married to Lee and working for Harper in London, they were in great demand. While their parents belonged to the Roosevelt and Truman generation, the younger Canfields were very much in the Kennedy world. Once, when the young Jackie Kennedy was going through one of her marital crises during her husband's senatorial days, she came to stay with her sister in Belgravia. The Canfields gave a cocktail party for her which clashed with the annual reception of Lady Hulton, the wife of the magazine publisher. Nobody wanted to miss that, but some cognoscenti, thinking that Senator Kennedy might have a political future, were keen to make a mark with his wife. As a result a huge traffic jam built up outside the Canfield apartment house, as guests rushed in while their drivers waited to take them on to the grander Hulton event.

If the Knopfs stood for *bien-pensant* literary society and the Can-fields for the East Coast establishment, Max Schuster, the cofounder of Simon & Schuster, represented self-made talent and amiable hucksterism. It was through him that I first heard of the concept of 'marketing' in the book trade. Schuster rose from obscurity and started out in publishing with Dick Simon, a fellow graduate from Columbia. Their first great success was an anthology of crossword puzzles from the *The New York Times*. Behind a calm and decep-tively naive, almost other-worldly, manner, Max was far-sighted and uncannily perceptive. Although they are worlds apart, he reminded me of the eccentric Earl of Longford. His wife Rae, a *madame sans gêne* with a strong Brooklyn accent, mothered me.

The Schusters were warm and hospitable, and their house, an ornate fin de siècle building off Fifth Avenue which had belonged to the Pulitzers, became a home from home. Friends would stay on from lunch to tea, or come in for drinks and leave around midnight. There were film agents, Broadway stars, visiting relations and bankers with a literary bent. Somehow everybody was made to feel part of a big family. The cuisine was a mixture of homeliness and elegance. Menus ranged from fastidious French dishes to chopped liver and onions, but never a clam chowder or Virginia ham. I awoke the Schusters' interest in Italian Mannerist painting, and when Rae came to London I introduced her to my Austrian art dealer friend, Paul Wengraf. She bought a picture of an ascetic monk looking exultantly at a celestial apparition, but when she hung it in her house, her Jewish friends were so shocked that she had second thoughts about it.

Victor Weybright, the father of the American paperback revol-ution, was another friend and ally. I met him through Isaiah Berlin, whom he greatly revered. While doing his stint at the Office of War Information in London he was befriended by Allen Lane, the founder of Penguin Books, and after the war he became his Ameri-can agent. They soon parted company, and Victor set up his own paperback empire, the New American Library. He married a wealthy widow and became Master of Foxhounds in Maryland. Though passionately Anglophile, he was the archetypal American buccaneer. Small, red-faced and robust, Victor's enthusiasm was infectious. Without him many of the ambitious projects I initiated in the 1960s would never have got off the ground. Such was his confidence in me that we clinched many a major transaction over the telephone. I would ring him from London to announce: 'Victor, I've just been lunching with Professor Zaehner in Oxford and we want him to edit a twenty-volume history of religion.' I would then rattle off six or seven authors we had in mind and put it to him that we would need twenty advances of a thousand pounds each to go ahead with the series. Victor would ask me what would happen if some of the names did not agree, and I would assure him that I would find authors of comparable quality. Without further ado Victor would seal the deal with a confident: 'Done and done.'

Jason Epstein took Victor's pioneering efforts in paperback publishing one stage further. As a young editor at Doubleday he created the Anchor imprint and proved that there was a wide market for specialized books of high academic standards and esoteric content. Those very books might only have had a tiny print run in hardcover. Epstein profited from the spread of campus bookshops and the snob value of having erudite tomes on one's bookshelf, all of which coincided with the serious debate about America's role in the post-war world. Allen Lane showed great interest in Jason Epstein and started one of his long-distance love affairs, promising him a major job and the prospect of becoming his successor at Penguin. Jason was flown in for various meetings, but after a while Allen Lane ended his courtship and looked for more conventional solutions.

Jason continued to run Anchor Books, but he was unhappy with the somewhat unimaginative and impersonal direction of Doubleday and transferred to Random House, where he proved his inventive power by surprising the literary world with a new venture every few years. He started the Library of American Literature, which was inspired by the French Pléiade, that wonderful leather-bound edition of the classics. But his most important brainchild was probably the *New York Review of Books*, launched in 1962 during one of the coldest winters this century. The New York newspapers were on strike and book publishers had nowhere to place their advertisements to catch the Christmas market, nor could any of their titles be reviewed. Jason Epstein and his wife Barbara conceived the idea of a major literary journal devoted to book reviews which were to be longer and more fastidious than anything published in the daily or weekly press. They found a number of rich sponsors, Brooke Astor among them, to back the venture which was to fill the gap between *The New York Times*, whose inadequacy they had long bemoaned, and periodicals like the *Partisan Review*. Bob Silvers, then an editor at *Harpers Magazine*, left his job to become joint editor with Barbara Epstein. From the outset the *New York Review of Books* had the goodwill of the most illustrious American writers and intellectuals in the liberal camp such as Mary McCarthy and Norman Mailer, as well as a prestigious British contingent culled from the more fashionable Oxbridge and London dons.

The venture was an instant succès d'estime and became a financial success over the years. The Epsteins, who have since separated, and Bob Silvers remained major shareholders until they sold the paper for about five million dollars to a family-owned newspaper chain in Louisiana, who have conveniently stayed in the background while business at the *New York Review of Books* continues as before.

Bob Silvers was ideally suited for the job. After studying at the University of Chicago and the Sorbonne he had teamed up with the band of gifted Americans editing the *Paris Review*. Bob combined the editor's scent for unusual writing and new talent with an insatiable social curiosity and the adaptability of a chameleon. He liked the fashionable world, though his heart was with the Left. As editor of the *New York Review of Books* he courted Oxford and Cambridge dons and kept in touch with developments in the intellectual world of other European countries. His authors were paid American prices for reviews, which compared favourably with the measly fees meted out in Dickensian offices in Bloomsbury or on the Left Bank in Paris. All the time I have known Bob Silvers I have vacillated between feelings of genuine warmth and weariness. We often disagreed on politics. At times I thought him implacably partisan on the Cold War, Vietnam and the Middle East, but I have always respected his technical skill and fanatical dedication to maintaining the highest literary standards.

Jason Epstein is an even more complex character. One side of him is iconoclastic, another wants to be part of the American Establishment he has often decried. His likes and even more passionate dislikes often centre around politics. He disapproved of my friendship with Norman Podhoretz, the bête noire of the American Left and one of Israel's staunchest champions. Jason, who more or less grew up with Norman, never forgave him his defection from the Left. Norman wrote a book called *Making It*, a sort of non-fictional *Erziehungsroman* in which Jason Epstein was one of the heroes. But in the sequel, *Breaking It*, he rather cruelly described Jason's inconsistencies and his attraction to glamour, which did not square with his Saint Just-like criticism of Western society.

Jason was an admirer of Lally Weymouth, who played such an important part in my American life. She was a tall, striking American debutante visiting friends in London when I first met her. Her father, Philip Graham, was the much-admired publisher of the *Washington Post* and *Newsweek* and her mother, Katharine (Kay) Graham, was the daughter of Eugene Mayer, an international financier and founder of the World Bank before he turned to newspaper publishing. Kay Graham's mother was a great Washington hostess in the era of the New Deal, entertaining not only politicians but such intellectual giants as Thomas Mann and Walter Gropius, who had emigrated to the United States to escape Nazism.

Having been brought up in an intensely political milieu, Lally already took a keen interest in politics. Not long after I met her, she married a good-looking young architect who later worked with I.M. Pei. Inhibited by the image of the spoilt little rich girl, she yearned to do something intellectually and professionally worthwhile. These feelings were reinforced when her marriage broke up. But Katharine Graham, who ran the family newspaper empire after her husband's untimely death, was very sensitive to the suggestion of nepotism.

Lally had a sharp mind, a huge appetite for information and commitment, but she lacked self-confidence. I discerned in her an uncommon ability for persuading people to do the things she wanted, be it in connection with a charity event or some political cause, and I tried to steer her into the book world. Lally often reminds me of how I got her an appointment with Walter Minton, the head of Putnam, to discuss a collection of essays to commemorate the hundred-and-fiftieth anniversary of Thomas Jefferson's death. She had produced a list of contributors which included such distinguished historians as Henry Commager and Arthur Schlesinger. When I went to collect her I thought she was unsuitably dressed, so I advised her to 'dress down, but not too down'. She changed into a demure Chanel suit which she wore without any jewellery and came away with a contract for a twenty-five-thousand-dollar advance. I published the book simultaneously in England.

Lally did some more work for Putnam, talent-scouting and editing, but she had higher ambitions. I encouraged her interest in the intricacies of Middle Eastern politics, and we travelled to Israel together, where she met Moshe Dayan, Teddy Kollek and other leaders. She wrote up her impressions and thus launched her career in journalism. Lally soon made a name for herself and became one of the best-informed writers on foreign affairs. At the same time she kept the most impressive political salon in New York. In building parties around visiting statesmen and public figures from home and abroad she brings people together who might not normally meet. Her home has been the scene of many incidents which have made the news. It was there that Yitzhak Rabin and Arthur Schlesinger nearly came to blows over Nixon's policy on Vietnam.

Lally and Barbara Walters, another American mainstay, touched me to the core with a party for my seventieth birthday at Mortimers in New York to which they asked many of the people I like and admire most. Unbeknown to me they had dug up snapshots from different stages of my life and had them blown up to decorate the walls of the restaurant. Lally made loyalty a tenet of faith. If she heard someone four places away at a dinner table make an abusive remark about a friend, she would stop all conversation, wag her finger at the perpetrator, and take him to task regardless of his station.

When I first knew American publishing it was far less multicultural than it is today. In those days there were the Jewish houses, where one would be unlikely to find many Wasps, and then there were the predominantly Wasp houses, which could be criticized for the reverse. They did not exactly apply a house rule, but by habit and tradition they tended to employ people from their own circle who had been to the same schools and belonged to the same clubs. Simon & Schuster, Knopf and Random House were largely run by American Jews, though they employed the odd Wasp. Harper, Norton, Doubleday and the two Boston firms Houghton Mifflin and Little, Brown were on the whole Wasp, but Harper employed an exceptionally talented editor of Jewish origin, Simon Michael Bessie, who became a lifelong friend. I met him during the war in London where he worked in Psychological Warfare, attached to William Paley, the President of the American broadcasting company CBS, who in turn reported to Eisenhower. Bilingual in French and English, Bessie was well-connected. Besides being a member of Ivy League Clubs, he belonged to the Council for Foreign Relations, a good catchment area for political books and memoirs.

Bill Benton, a former Democrat Senator and the owner of the Encyclopaedia Britannica, which he had acquired from the University of Chicago after a singularly successful career in advertising, was another figure from the age of the enlightened despots. For all his contradictions, he was a liberal who believed in the dissemination of learning, a cause he pursued with evangelical zeal. Benton loved the glamour of public life and, having lost his seat in the Senate, tried to recreate something of the atmosphere of a cabinet meeting around the boardroom table in Chicago. Such luminaries as Hubert Humphrey, Clare Luce, Paul Hoffman, administrator of the Marshall Plan, and his wife Anna Rosenberg, a former Secretary of Labour, graced his councils. He also made friends with Harold Wilson when he was leader of the opposition, and was later a frequent guest at Downing Street.

I was introduced to Benton through Fred Praeger, an Austrian-born American publisher of books on current affairs who sold his business to Encyclopaedia Britannica, and Maurice Mitchell, then chief executive of EB, a man of great culture with a fine record of philanthropic and academic work. Benton bought a stake in Weidenfeld & Nicolson with an option to acquire the rest of the company after my retirement. For several years EB was a partner and I sat on the advisory board, enjoying the civilized *bonhomie* of the proceedings. During Benton's lifetime relations were excellent, but when he died the ties loosened and the partnership dissolved in the interests of both companies.

By the end of the 1950s the rule of the enlightened publishing despots had waned. They had tired, retired or died. As the book business expanded at home and abroad the curiosity and greed of conglomerates, bankers and investment analysts was roused and a wave of mergers swept through the publishing world, reaching a climax in the 1960s with infinite ownership changes and new configurations. The codewords of the next era were synergy, hardware, software and rationalization. This process has continued to the present with cyclical variations and occasional divestments and reinvestments.

I see this phase as the Age of the *Condottieri*, ambitious soldiers of fortune who ran large companies for absentee stockholders. Like the Italian *condottieri* in the age of Machiavelli they divided into 'lions' and 'foxes', the former seeking both power and the limelight, the latter being content with power, leaving the glory to highly visible editors or marketing geniuses who like having their names in the newspapers – at least for a time. But many a fox turned into a lion when he felt that his protégé had risen too high.

Bob Bernstein of Random House was an amiable *condottiere* who held such talent spotters as Joe Fox, Truman Capote's editor, and Jason Epstein on a long leash. Bernstein himself had various superiors: there was the mercurial Bennett Cerf, the impersonal collective leadership of NBC, and finally the shy but steely Si Newhouse who entered the publishing battlefield as France's Charles VIII had thrust forth into Renaissance Italy, capturing fortresses and city states, wreaking havoc but rallying gifted men in its wake. Harry Evans and Sonny Mehta, an inscrutable Brahmin who succeeded the legendary Robert Gottlieb as head of Knopf, were both Newhouse imports from England. Harry Evans had been editor of the *Sunday Times* and then *The Times*, where he came to blows with his new proprietor, Rupert Murdoch. With his quicksilvery temperament and journalistic talent he turned his feud into the autobiographical bestseller *Good Times Bad Times*.

Another towering figure was William Jovanovich, the son of a Montenegrin miner who turned the patrician Harcourt Brace into a media giant, grafting high-tech laboratories, zoos and amusement parks onto his literary and academic list and adding his own name to the imprint. A large, handsome man, Jovanovich had a European's reverence for high literature. He cosseted Kurt and Helen Wolff, venerable relics of Weimar publishing, and enabled them to continue their prestigious work within his empire. Jovanovich, with whom I had an uneasy relationship, struck me as being rather like one of those Illyrian guards in the entourage of an effete Roman emperor who craves power but is consumed by melancholy as soon as he attains it and revels in his unfulfilled longings. He fought a battle royal with the unscrupulous raider Robert Maxwell and destroyed his own empire in the process. My dealings with him centred around Mary McCarthy, whom he edited personally, and whose friendship with me he viewed with some misgiving.

When Max Schuster and his cofounders left Simon & Schuster it became part of Paramount and Hollywood but continued to make a distinct mark from its offices in the Rockefeller Center. The new management promoted a young Simon & Schuster insider, Dick Snyder, an awkward and insecure man who nonetheless rose to dazzling heights. Snyder had the nous to carry with him Michael

Korda, a nephew of Sir Alexander Korda, the wizard Hungarian impresario of the short-lived golden age of British cinema. Michael's father, Vincent, was an inspired art director.

The Kordas were hedonists, dreamers and cynics and Michael is no exception. After finishing his studies at Cambridge he volunteered to help Hungarian dissidents and fugitives when Russian tanks crushed the rebellion of 1956. He asked me for professional advice and I was much impressed by the young idealist who went to seek his fortune in New York. Within a year of training as an editorial bottle washer at Simon & Schuster, Max Schuster made him Secretary of the Editorial Board and assigned important authors to his care. I remember Max proudly rhapsodizing, 'The boy comes closest to being a genius in my experience.' I watched Michael shed his idealism and abandon himself to the cult of the golden calf rather than the literary muse, running up more solid bestsellers to his credit than anyone else in the business, but he always kept his cool judgement and never confused bestselling with best writing. He has written successful novels himself in which he has drawn with great panache on his experience in different worlds on both sides of the Atlantic. I figure in some of them, either by name or unmistakable description. We cooperated on many projects, among them the memoirs of Laurence Olivier, who had worked closely with his uncle Alexander.

Dick Snyder's twenty-year rule at Simon & Schuster came to an abrupt end in June 1994 after a multi-billion-dollar takeover bid by Viacom. Summoned by his new boss for an interview which according to some lasted two and according to others lasted five minutes, he was told to vacate his office by noon the following day. I was in New York the day it happened and saw the entire publishing world gasp, albeit with mixed emotions, because the *condottiere* Dick Snyder had himself given no quarter.

Peter Mayer, a stalwart viceroy rather than a power-driven *condottiere*, is head of Viking Penguin, part of a British family-controlled empire which straddles the Atlantic. An American of German-Jewish descent, he has preserved a yearning for good literature and lofty ideas, and maintains a Brechtian sense of irony or indeed of the absurd in a hectic life of trading and travel. Among the crosses, or more aptly crescents, he has had to bear was the decision to publish Salman Rushdie's *Satanic Verses*, an experience that added to the anguish of his tortured soul.

The enlightened despots and the *condottieri* had been men with charisma and some distinctive features, but the publishing conglomerates brought forth a different category of leader – grey, corporate men who were almost interchangeable. One could liken them to the mediaeval cathedral builders – anonymous artisans who performed useful tasks and sometimes produced some distinguished work. They were accounting or marketing men, bankers or former public servants. Like the cathedral builders, their names are forgotten, if indeed they were ever known. They ran McGraw-Hill and Macmillan, encyclopaedia and Bible sets, and vast primary school and college text factories, and while the end product was laudable, their names will scarcely be found in the indices of American history books.

As the publishing houses continually changed their shape and spirit and editors became less feudally beholden to their proprietors, the literary agent assumed more and more power, so much so that in the professional equation the author became the constant and the publisher the variation. The literary agent graduated from being a professional negotiator and debt-collector to being parent figure, psychoanalyst and editor. Some agents played that role nobly and responsibly, others turned into manipulators in a powerplay with the publisher. The explosion of the market, the burgeoning of multimedia activities and the nexus between New York, Boston, Hollywood and later Silicon Valley all spurred the agent on to acquire more skills and contacts. Mammoth agencies such as William Morris, MCA and later ICM began to dominate the field. A favourite friend in the agency world is Marvin Josephson, the head of ICM, a man of acute political judgement and a masterly trader. He handled Henry Kissinger's memoirs as well as the work of several leading Israeli politicians. Though he can be icily impassive, there is a warm heart pulsing for his political causes, and he has done a great deal for Israeli charities.

The age of the great one-man agent cum entrepreneur came to an end with the death of Irving 'Swifty' Lazar who died in Hollywood in 1993. He lived his legend with relish. Diminutive, bald and immaculately dressed, Swifty inhaled life, especially high life, with unbounded enthusiasm and sense of purpose. He cornered the market in autobiographies of Hollywood stars, often selling the project before their subject had thought of writing them. When he confronted the author with a seven-figure contract from several publishers who all thought the work was in progress, many of them were swayed and went ahead. Sometimes he failed to persuade them, but forgot to mention the fact to the unhappy publishers who had dutifully paid the first part of the advance and built the project into their financial projections.

For all his experience as a salesman, Swifty never bothered to look at the small print. Irwin Shaw, a stormy petrel but trusted client of his, was signed up for his novel *Rich Man, Poor Man*, which we published in Britain. Swifty made a spectacular deal with ABC Television, but neither he nor Irwin Shaw realized that they had conceded the right to use the characters of the novel in any sequel scripted by others. In the throes of completing a follow-up volume, *Beggarman, Thief*, which included many of the original characters, Irwin was startled when he switched on the television one night to see those same characters living through entirely different events in ABC's *Rich Man, Poor Man* mark II.

Swifty regularly came to Europe during the summer and winter seasons, and was a generous host in Hollywood, where his parties on the night of the Oscar ceremony became tradition. I met him frequently in the most diverse places, and each year in September we spent the same weekend at the van Zuylen château.

A most impressive trader in the American literary agency bazaar of today is Morton Janklow. Besides being a multimedia virtuoso, he still practises as a lawyer. Urbane and scrupulously honest, he collects Jean Dubuffet's paintings and has a passion for politics. He handled the memoirs of Nancy Reagan, which we launched with some aplomb in London as we had done those of Lady Bird Johnson a decade earlier. Not surprisingly, the more innocent and at times unconsciously indiscreet reminiscences of presidential wives tend to be more interesting and saleable than the bland revelations of their husbands. Lyndon Johnson's memoirs were a case in point: they fell flat because of their anaemic content.

Mort Janklow is greatly helped by his talented and worldly-wise wife Linda, a genuine Hollywood princess, since both her father and her stepfather were cine-moguls, and in Lynn Nesbit, Mort has a formidable associate who, in the best tradition of lady agents, is feminine and steely in equal proportions.

For a while Mort handled Arianna Stassinopoulos, the first woman, and foreign woman at that, to become President of the Cambridge Union. When I first knew her she had published a controversial tract attacking feminism and was looking for a topic after a brief lapse in popularity due to a less successful book. We arranged to have lunch to discuss possible subjects for a new book. The night before, I saw her at the opera. She was wearing a long white dress, which contrasted with her long, dark wavy hair, and a gold necklace. From a distance she looked like Maria Callas. 'You must write a life of Callas: you like opera, you look like her and you are Greek,' I told her as she sat down to lunch. I knew that with her driving ambition she would penetrate where others feared to tread. Arianna proved me right by writing an international bestseller on Callas. I accompanied her to New York just after the book came out and introduced her to many of my friends there, sensing that she would never return to Europe.

Arianna likes to tell people of a piece of advice I gave her and which she faithfully absorbed. I told her to woo the women of New York and react amicably but coolly to their husbands' advances. This is an elementary rule for all foreign women who wish to make their way in Manhattan, for America is a matriarchy. Arianna scored in New York society, followed her Callas biography with a successful book on Picasso and went to California, where Ann Getty introduced her to Michael Huffington, the scion of a dynasty of oilmen with political ambitions, whom she married in great style in New York. She has evangelical urges to propagate social and spiritual messages, and is now the power behind her husband's drive for high political office. For all her ambitions, she wishes other people well. At the outset of her career, a fellow student at Cambridge described her to me as an extra-terrestrial rocket with a built-in human heart of gold.

I have always been fortunate in finding friends who were accomplished catalysts, linking different strands of American political, literary and social life. Jean Stein started her career as a catalyst while still in her teens. Her father, Jules Stein, was a Central European eye doctor turned jazz band manager who became one of the most powerful international agents, head of MCA, Universal Pictures and a near billionaire. He used to say of his daughter that she would have been the best agent of them all had she been born a man.

Jules and Doris Stein commuted between Mayfair, Beverly Hills and Paris. They were part of the Marks and Sieff entourage and befriended me when I was married to Jane. Doris liked cosmopolitan society and had hopes of marrying Jean and her sister Susan to a French duke or a descendant of the Mayflower pilgrims. Jean rebelled by surrounding herself with a bustling circle of literati and talented artists, cultivating celebrities of the moment and discerning the stars of tomorrow with frenetic energy. She had a romance with Michael Hastings, the youngest of Britain's angry young men, and she was an intimate friend of Leonard and Felicia Bernstein. Through her parents she knew the Hollywood elite and had a much-publicized friendship with William Faulkner.

Even in adolescence Jean showed the compassion of an experienced adult when consoling me on the break-up of my first marriage and the travails of my courtship with Barbara Skelton. She used to send friends who were passing through London to see me. Among them were George Plimpton and James Jones, the young Tony Newley and the emerging Joan Collins, Gloria Steinem, who was just starting on her feminist crusade, and Mike Nichols, who once caricatured the hospitality lavished on my person by saying, 'Every minute of the hour, somebody somewhere gives a party for George Weidenfeld.'

Jean was accused of being the archetypal hostess of 'radical chic'. When she married William Vandenheuvel, a young lawyer active in the Democratic Party, she was at the epicentre of the Kennedy world and the earliest sponsor of Amanda and Carter Burdon, the original 'beautiful people'. Through her and others I got to know most of the Kennedys. I once took Patricia Lawford, one of the many siblings, to the opera to hear Verdi's rarely performed *Sicilian Vespers*. Having read the synopsis and sat through the first act, she turned to me and said, 'Now that we know how it's going to end, we might as well leave.'

Jackie Kennedy turned into a real professional when she became a publisher at Doubleday after the death of Onassis. She had a good eye for books on art and, always on the lookout for European subjects, occasionally visited London in search of new authors. I last saw her a few weeks before her death when we met for lunch to discuss commissioning a major biography of Napoleon from the English husband and wife team Artemis Cooper and Antony Beevor.

Another catalyst for young writers and artists who was equally at home in New York and on the West Coast was Marguerite Lamkin, who later married the British lawyer Mark Littman. She was a belle from Louisiana who profited from her classical southern accent by coaching northerners cast as southern women in Hollywood. Elizabeth Taylor was one of her pupils. Marguerite was a close friend of Tennessee Williams, who was so impressed by her histrionic talent that he promised to write a part for her if she took up acting as a profession.

Marguerite was famed for her lunches, where she mixed cult figures from the old South, new arrivals from England, Hollywood stars and shy young dilettantes. Above all she was appreciated for her surrealist way of telling a story in her idiosyncratic accent. Once, when I was renting an apartment from Afdera Fonda, the third wife of Henry Fonda, I invited Marguerite to a rather staid cocktail party in honour of an author who was a Jesuit priest. The janitor in that most respectable apartment block telephoned to announce that a Miss Lamkin was downstairs with half a dozen 'rather unusual-looking gentlemen'. Should he send them up? A colourful group in jeans and T-shirts appeared. They turned out to be Andy Warhol and some fellow artists, shepherded by Henry Geldzaehler, the mentor of the New York school of painters who turned out to be a not-too-distant cousin of mine. It was 1962 and their names were unknown to me then.

I had a similar experience in the late 1950s when I was living in Albany, once the most respectable bachelor chambers in London, as a tenant of Fred Warner while he was en poste in Moscow. I gave a party to which Tom Driberg brought the pugnacious Irish playwright Brendan Behan. He clearly did not like the company, and having taken a few long swigs of whisky he left, but not without first placing himself at the centre of the covered walk from which the various sets lead off, and giving a lusty rendering of a song so loud and so lewd that windows on all sides opened in a spontaneous burst of dismay. Next day I was carpeted by the dapper military gentleman who ran the chambers and issued with a stern warning. He followed up with a stern letter to my landlord in which he complained that I had entertained people 'of distinctly Bohemian appearance and loutish manners'. Apparently Princess Margaret had attended another party on the compound that evening, and my guest had seriously embarrassed the proceedings.

There were few places where one could feel the pulse of New York as strongly as in Benjamin Sonnenberg's mansion in Gramercy Park, which was decorated from top to bottom in mid-Victorian style with Edwardian touches here and there. Portraits of artists, writers and society figures filled the walls as they do in the Garrick Club, and there was polished brass and silver in profusion. Sonnenberg bluffed us all into thinking that he would leave this museum-like house and its contents to the City of New York, but in the end everything was sold at auction. I met Sonnenberg through Eileen Adler, Larry Adler's former wife, to whom I was greatly attracted before my marriage to Jane Sieff. Having been married to a successful entertainment artist, she was at home in the world of showbiz and American Bohemia. Over the years I came across many of the people I met through her in different settings.

Ben Sonnenberg had built a homogeneous personality out of a hundred affectations. Born in Russia, he grew up in poverty on the East Side. He came to the notice of Albert D. Lasker, the founder of modern advertising, who gave him a job. Sonnenberg then set up on his own and rose from being a humble press agent to becoming the master of grand hucksterism. He was a fixer who claimed to have invented the term 'public relations'. Sonnenberg behaved with circumspection. He looked after the public image of important clients, helping some to run for high office, getting their names into the newspapers when required, or seeing to it that even their most notorious peccadilloes were never mentioned by the gossip columnists.

Sonnenberg spoke with a long drawl which only occasionally betrayed a hint of Brooklynese. He sported a warrior's moustache, had a pot belly and looked like Beerbohm caricaturing himself. His striped shirts had a stiff white collar which he wore with a bow tie or an old fashioned narrow tie with a clip. He must have had dozens of identical Savile Row suits of Edwardian style. His wife, Hilda, lived a secluded life and only appeared at her husband's parties when close friends or family were there. I once lost my way in the maze of corridors and stumbled on her room, where she was lying in bed reading magazines.

Sonnenberg used to say that if he ever wrote an autobiography he would call it *Large Pedestals for Small Figures*. He loved advising promising young protégés on their careers, not least because it gave him a pretext for hearing himself talk, and he had a wonderfully methodical way of mapping out one's future. He made you feel as though you were his most urgent concern. Always full of wise-cracks, he used to chide me: 'The trouble with you, George, is that you take too much interest in the quality of the product and not enough in the profit.' He was concerned about my future because he had heard me described as a talented man. 'That is a very bad sign,' he said. 'Bobby Lehman [the founder of Lehman Brothers] used to say, "If I hear that a man is talented, I immediately close his account because it usually means he can't read a balance sheet".'

There are many legends about Ben Sonnenberg, and most of them are true. Having lived off expenses for years, he only made a fortune late in life. The story he told me went as follows: on a journey with his friend and most important client Robert Lehman, the two of them stopped at a country inn run by two elderly ladies who served homemade bread. Complimenting them on their baking, they suggested they turn themselves into a business. Out of this encounter grew a public company, Pepperidge Farm. Instead of a fee, Sonnenberg took shares and became a wealthy man.

It was impossible with Ben to distinguish between his cultivating people for their own sake or using them for some mysterious public relations campaign. My favourite Sonnenberg story concerns Lady Mary Dunn, the mother of Jacob Rothschild's wife, Serena. Mary Dunn had been to New York as a young debutante and had made many friends there. Years later, in late middle age, she told Sonnenberg of her regret at not being able to go back to New York. He immediately arranged a visit, put her up at the Waldorf Astoria and organized a whirl of social engagements with grand lunches, cocktail parties and dinners nearly every day. When the time came for her to leave, she felt unwell and postponed her return journey by a day. An hour after the scheduled departure, copies of the bills she had run up at the hotel arrived, all charged to Canada Dry. Unwittingly she had been used by Sonnenberg as part of a campaign to publicize the brand.

The apartment of the Republican Senator Jack Javits and his wife Marion was another home from home. Jack Javits was a man of demoniacal energy who stood centre stage in American politics for more than a quarter of a century. A high-ranking member of the Senate Foreign Relations Committee, he knew a great deal about Europe and was a wise supporter of Israel who could nonetheless be forceful in his criticism of some of Israel's policies.

The Javitses were a generous couple with a vast circle of friends. Marion enjoyed entertaining and added celebrities from screen and stage to foreign statesmen and royalty attending the United

Nations. You might dine there with Prince Sadruddin Khan, Shirley Maclaine, Gregory Peck and a Nobel Prize-winner in astrophysics. I often escorted Marion to parties when her husband was electioneering. To fit his busy schedule, Jack Javits used to wear a charcoal suit which he adapted to different occasions by putting on one of a number of ties he always kept to hand – a green tie for an Irish christening, a black tie for a charity dinner, a blue tie for a bar mitzvah or a more colourful specimen for a cocktail party in the Bohemian Village or Little Italy.

One of the New York friends on whom I could always depend was Jan Mitchell, a colourful, warm-hearted and self-effacing comrade-in-arms of Baltic origin and Swiss education. Whenever I faced a personal crisis or had to make an important decision I turned to Jan for succour and advice. When I first met him over thirty years ago, he owned a chain of restaurants with Luchows as its flagship. Famous for its authentic German cuisine, Luchows was a New York institution. It had an alcove in the big dining room which could seat up to thirty people. Jan always entertained there on Sunday nights. One could be sure to meet actors, journalists, writers, politicos and beautiful women at Jan's soirées. Luchows also had an upstairs room for private receptions which Jan often put at my disposal when I stayed in New York so that I could entertain authors or fellow publishers.

After he sold Luchows, Jan turned to other enterprises which he ran with a Midas touch, enabling him to be a most munificent philanthropist. I introduced him to Teddy Kollek, who helped him find his way back to Jewish life and was rewarded with the Mitchell Park in Jerusalem, wedged between the Old and the New City. He also donated his exquisite collection of pre-Columbian gold to the Metropolitan Museum, and at my instigation he founded the Mitchell Prize which is conferred on alternate years in New York and London on the author of the best art-historical book. A subsidiary prize was designed to help young art historians gain renown. The list of Mitchell Prize jurors and winners includes John Pope-Hennessy, Mayer Shapiro, Francis Haskell and Michael Jaffé and reads like a roll of honour of contemporary art history.

Another art collector and close companion was Herman Elkon, a restless globetrotter who retired early from his business to become a boulevardier of the old style. He loved art and music, and travelled incessantly to see new exhibitions and visit artists whose work he collected in their studios. Herman, my senior by a dozen years, was an eternal adolescent – pleasure-loving and enthusiastic – and yet a serious person.

The small but influential band of Anglophile Washingtonians was a wonderful boon for a regular visitor from Britain in the early 1950s. They made you feel you could ride on a carrier wave of goodwill, especially if you brought messages from shared friends who had spent the war years in Washington. Kay Halle's house in Georgetown was open to friends of the Churchill family, notably Randolph. She was also an admirer of Isaiah Berlin, who was seconded to the British Embassy by the Ministry of Information from 1942 until 1946, and John Foster, the brilliant lawyer whose many love affairs in wartime Washington and New York left an afterglow of romance.

Mrs 'Oatsy' Leiter's salon straddled Washington politics, grand life in the Bahamas and the circles of Ivar Bryce and Ian – but not Ann – Fleming. The preeminent Anglophile was the columnist Joe Alsop, who to my mind epitomized American 'high journalism' – a form which not only reports and analyses, but also influences decision-making. Joe Alsop was better informed on the goings-on at Westminster than many a Briton. His family background and his professional skill gave him access to presidents, secretaries of state and intelligence chiefs. He was on the embassy circuit and saw most important visitors to Washington. He wrote in a stentorian style, sure of his own judgement and courageous in his forecasts.

Joe was a European's idea of an American New Englander. When he spoke, he alternated clipped phrases and long drawls, echoing the mannerisms of his Oxford contemporaries, two of whom, Maurice Bowra and Isaiah Berlin, he held in particularly high esteem. He had a violent temper and was easily offended. I stayed as a guest in his elegant house where he entertained very much in the English style, and saw him at innumerable social occasions over three decades. Though born to be a bachelor, he was married for several years to Susan Mary Patten, who wrote several good biographies and published a rather touching selection of letters between herself and her great friend Marietta Tree. With her effusive cordiality, Susan Mary just managed to stop short of self-parody, but she had a wonderful way of drawing out her guests on the most self-revealing and indiscreet topics and was a gifted storyteller.

I could never have learned about American politics, met some of its protagonists or discovered a whole range of authors but for the generous friendship of the great Washington hostesses. Kay Halle introduced me to the French Nobel Prize-winning poet Alexis Léger, better known under his nom de guerre Saint-John Perse, a rather elegiac man who had been secretary-general of the prewar Quai d'Orsay and an opponent of de Gaulle. I remember him drawing a verbal pen portrait of the Vichy President Marshal Pétain that, while unconvincingly apologetic, was brilliantly lucid. Oatsy Leiter took me to political evenings where I met Alice Longworth, Theodore Roosevelt's daughter and undoubtedly the *grande dame* of Washington. Her nephew Archibald Roosevelt, whom I later urged to write his own life story, became a friend. He made a career in the CIA and became station head in London. Although he was suitably secretive, he could surprise one with the odd revelation about an Arab potentate or a Kurdish chieftain. Archibald's wife, Lucky, a lively Lebanese with a gusto for social life, became Nancy Reagan's chief of protocol and helped me launch her memoirs in London.

When I look back on Washington now and remember the kindnesses of good friends, I think of Evangeline Bruce, whose Georgetown house, where I nearly always stayed when visiting the capital, became a haven for her friends in Britain. There she entertained with the same tact and aplomb that had made her such a sought-after hostess at Wingfield House, mixing journalists, television stars and politicians young and old with a sprinkling of the diplomatic colony. Among the many friends we shared were Nicholas and Mary Henderson, the most appreciated ambassadorial couple in Washington, where they were posted from 1979-1982. Nicko knew how to cover the field, developing close links with both Republicans and Democrats and cultivating the younger generation. He was a talent-spotter and, unlike so many other ambassadors, liked to feel that the number two, three or twelve in his embassy had his share of contacts and recognition. Mary did the same with embassy wives. She was enterprising and full of imagination. During her reign in Washington she refurbished the residence by inviting leading British decorators to take charge of one room each. At the opening, admiring crowds were given a taste of the best of British ideas and materials in interior design.

The Hendersons were preceded by Peter and Margaret Jay, probably the youngest ambassadorial couple ever to serve in Washington. Margaret was the daughter of Prime Minister James Callaghan, and Peter the protégé of Foreign Minister David Owen. They focused almost exclusively on the Carter administration, making friends with the President's aides, members of his cabinet and the Liberal press. It was, I think, a calculated strategy, and it paid off: the Jays had a hotline to the White House. Their term was a grand time for left-of-centre visitors from London, and the embassy reflected a relaxed, egalitarian, 'swinging' Britain. At an embassy dinner one would find television stars and cult figures such as David Frost and Mark Boxer, young Oxford dons and London economists rather than old grandees or property millionaires.

Through my friendship with Lally Weymouth I got to know her mother, Kay Graham. She belongs to that generation of East Coast matriarchs which includes Evangeline Bruce, Susan Mary Alsop, Marietta Tree and Polly Fritchey. They were all brides together, all married remarkable men and led eventful lives. Great power was thrust upon Kay when her husband died and she was left in control of the newspaper empire. Though unprepared for this role she proved a highly successful proprietor. Shy and reticent by nature, she has a capacity to listen and sounds people out with an air of diffidence and quiet earnestness that is very occasionally punctuated by a sudden burst of passion. She probably considers herself a middle-of-the-road liberal, but although she opts for conservative methods in her business, her judgements and instincts betray glimmers of a youthful radicalism. I tried to reciprocate Kay's hospitality by entertaining her in London where she had a small circle of old friends including Isaiah Berlin, Edward Heath, Roy Jenkins and the Hartwell family. In the 1980s I accompanied Kay and her friend Meg Greenfield on a carefully orchestrated four-day trip to Germany, a country she barely knew. I set up a number of convivial occasions to enable her to meet influential Germans. In Frankfurt Joachim Fest, copublisher of the *Frankfurter Allgemeine Zeitung*, assembled a dozen leading journalists and political writers, in Düsseldorf Gabriele Henkel stage-managed a remarkable dinner with luminaries of the Rhine and Ruhr, and in Munich, our last port of call, Heidi Schoeller, a banker's wife with right-of-centre credentials, gathered an interesting group from the conservative camp, while Anneliese Friedmann, the publisher of the *Süddeutsche Zeitung*, invited a galaxy of liberal and socialist writers and politicians.

My visits to Washington enabled me to keep in touch with Irena Kirkland, whom I had befriended during my year in Israel when she and her twin sister Alena Lourie had just immigrated from Prague. Irena and her husband Lane Kirkland, that statesman of the American labour movement who did so much to help Solidarity in Poland, and who encouraged dissidents throughout the Communist world to build up a network of underground presses and political cells, became focal figures in Washington for all those who cared about the transition to democracy in Eastern Europe. Irena is a zealot, passionate in her views and in her friendships. Once you were in her good books she would defend you to the death. One of her closest friends is Nancy Kissinger, with whom she shares strength of character, combative loyalty to her husband and rigid views on world affairs.

I first met Henry Kissinger in London in the late 1950s when he was a young Harvard don who had already made a name for himself as a specialist in the new field of nuclear policy in world affairs. He was looking for support for his Harvard Summer School which became a nursery for budding European and American politicians and opinion-formers. It was Tangye Lean of the BBC who brought us together. Kissinger visited me at my house in Chester Square. He had just finished *A World Restored – The Congress of Vienna 1815*, his earliest and in some ways most programmatic thesis on world affairs. It was the first of a trilogy he planned to write on the maintenance of a hundred-year peace in Europe through a system of alliances based on a balance of power. The second volume was to be about Bismarck and the Berlin Congress of 1878, which convened the leading statesmen of the Europe and Turkey for negotiations on the Russian preponderance in the Balkans, and the final volume was to describe the way in which the guns of August 1914 shattered the peace system so laboriously established by Metternich, Talleyrand and Castlereagh. We published the first book in 1957. It had minuscule sales but a good press.

I lost sight of Henry Kissinger after that, but met him again when he entered the White House as President Nixon's National Security Advisor in 1969. I had been tipped off by his American publisher that he might be coming to the end of the Bismarck volume, but when we discussed it, he said, 'I am burning the manuscript. Even a few weeks near the centre of power have made me realize how much I still have to learn about how policy is really made.' This may have been an elegant excuse for not completing the book, but he was certainly cogent in illustrating his argument. In the years to come I saw a fair amount of him in various Washington and New York drawing rooms, particularly that of David and Evangeline Bruce, but it was only after he left office in 1976 that I got to know him better. We had close dealings over the two volumes of his *The White House Years*, which we published. He often dined in my house and was a magnetic draw for British friends and Continental visitors, who gladly made the journey from Paris, Rome, Munich or Bonn to meet him. I have always been much taken with Nancy whom I first met before her marriage when she worked for Governor Rockefeller. An attractive bluestocking, quietly elegant and well-informed, she had a special interest in the politics of the Vichy government in wartime France.

Power and glory have left their mark on the Kissingers. Having struggled to get to the top, Henry has a romantic, almost naive attraction to worldliness and glamour, and his hedonism escalated as he moved from academe and public service to the stratosphere of big business. His genius for conceptualizing political ideas, his sceptical, at times cynical, and always clinical approach to great issues and events make him the most formidable debater I know. He can be abrasive and intolerant, but I have hardly ever met an author who is so deeply disturbed by an adverse review, a personal criticism or even a doubting remark. The number of his detractors are legion, especially in the academic world where his former peers grudge him his greatness and question his authority as a scholar. This was particularly the case with *Diplomacy*, published 1993, which I found masterly. But perhaps his best writing is to be found in the descriptive portraits he paints in *The White House Years*, whether it be of the *grand-seigneurial* Chou En-lai or the petulantly mothering Golda Meir.

Henry Kissinger once told me in great detail about his first meeting with Richard Nixon. They were scheduled to spend forty minutes together, but in the event the meeting lasted several hours and resulted in Kissinger being offered a job notches higher than he had expected. His account reminds me of an episode I witnessed during the transition period between the election of Ronald Reagan in November 1980 and his inauguration the following January. It was at a dinner party given by Brooke Astor to introduce the Reagans to prominent New Yorkers. She invited Sir Fitzroy

Maclean, who happened to be in town, and me to a gathering teeming with bankers, museum directors and social and literary lions. Before dinner the men were asked to present themselves to the President Elect, and we all queued up in single file waiting to shake hands with him. The passage leading to the library where Reagan stood was so crowded that we were pressed tightly to each other. In front of me was Walter Wriston, chairman of Citicorp, who had been tipped by the press as a favoured candidate for the post of Secretary to the Treasury. When his turn came, Ronald Reagan shook him heartily by the hand and said, 'Walter, I'm so glad to meet you at last. We'll have a lot to talk about.' As it turned out, Wriston did not take the job, but I found it strange that the President of the United States had not even met the man whom he might have appointed to steer the finances of the nation. It struck me how differently politics work in Britain, where a prime minister forming his cabinet would know his Chancellor of the Exchequer extremely well.

Henry Kissinger has survived the loss of titular power better than any politician I can think of by remaining an oracle on international affairs and creating an impressive public platform for himself. He has kept his mystique. In 1983 I attended his sixtieth birthday party at the Pierre Hotel in New York which was arranged by his former graduate student Guido Goldman, now a Harvard professor and investment manager. As at the Congress of Vienna, speeches were followed by dancing. A number of subordinate celebrations were held in his honour all over Manhattan. John and Susan Gutfreund, then a much discussed and maligned couple, gave one such lunch.

There was more than a touch of perfectionism about Susan Gutfreund's horticultural approach to entertaining. I remember one occasion when she invited twenty-four guests to dinner after a private screening of a film on the life of Marcel Proust. She had transformed the dining room into an exotic garden. The flower arrangements dwarfed the table, and when the guests sat down they could hardly see who was opposite them. Stunned by his wife's creative imagination, John Gutfreund walked around the room as though in a trance.

Susan liked improvisation. She once asked some twenty or so guests to a surprise birthday party for her husband at Vaux-le-Viscomte, that marvel among the châteaux of France. Up to the very last minute, John Gutfreund, who had brought his aged mother from New York, thought that they would be having an intimate family dinner. Instead, Susan had laid on a lavish affair only slightly marred by an initial mishap. There was a transport strike in Paris that day, and the caterers, who had the keys, arrived after the first guests. The hostess had to complete her toilette in an improvised boudoir. But the evening, which culminated in a firework display to rival spectacles in Venice and Monte Carlo, was a great success.

Anxious to get to know the complex social scene, the British journalist Tina Brown, who was just starting on the dazzling career in America which led her to the editorship of *Vanity Fair* and later the *New Yorker*, asked me if I could take her to the Gutfreunds' celebration for Kissinger. The hostess gave her assent, and I escorted Tina Brown. When a somewhat satirical piece about this private party appeared in print I was blamed. Peace was only restored through the statesmanlike intervention of Jayne Wrightsman.

Kissinger's seventieth birthday also gave occasion for celebrations in New York and Europe. Gabriele Henkel transformed her house outside Düsseldorf for a party where the guests included President Richard von Weizsäcker, and in London Jacob Rothschild and Gianni Agnelli feted Henry Kissinger in Spencer House. Next day my wife Annabelle and I gave a small lunch where the husbands had to yield pride of place to Nancy Kissinger and Marella Agnelli. I often saw the Kissingers with their close friends Annette and Oscar de la Renta, who drew me into their cosmopolitan circle. Their public persona may seem grand but they are really a very private couple who cosset their friends.

The secret of successful intimacy often lies in a blend of shared interests, complementary temperaments and the absence of a romantic involvement. Diana Phipps has been my close friend and steady confidante for these reasons. By the time we met in New York in the early 1960s, she was already the widow of Harry Phipps, the scion of a well-known American family. Born Countess Sternberg, she comes from one of the oldest families of the Czech aristocracy. Her parents fled Czechoslovakia when the Communists took over after the war and settled in America, where she had a frugal child-hood. When she went to stay with relations she was struck by the stuffy atmosphere and Bourbon attitude of the Central European aristocrats who hankered after the past. It turned Diana into some-thing of a rebel. She developed a penchant for the unconventional and loved eccentrics. Though still very much an Austro-Czech aristocrat of the pre-First World War mould, she is at her happiest in the company of artists and writers. She has her devoted followers in New York, Vienna, London, and more recently in Prague and Castolovice, the beautiful ancestral palace which she recovered after the demise of Communism.

Diana is greatly admired for an understated elegance in her looks, her manner of entertaining and her taste, which were displayed in exemplary fashion when she and Evangeline Bruce gave a dinner party in her London house for my seventieth birthday. Besides going to great lengths to invite those who have been closest to me, they engaged Nigel Douglas, one of those rare British tenors versed in classical Viennese operetta, to sing from his sentimental repertoire after dinner. It was a nostalgic, warm and wonderful evening. Diana will always be remembered for the Opera Costume Ball she held in the country where her vast cousinage from the Continent mingled with her British friends. I was a member of the Royal Opera House Trust at the time and was lucky enough to find the gold uniform of Baron Scarpia, the villainous police chief in Puccini's *Tosca*, in the costume store. It had last been worn by Tito Gobbi.

In her various houses, both urban and rural, Diana has created an atmosphere of affordable luxury, an art on which she wrote an excellent book for us. She has little respect for material achievement and the values of the consumer society, and she shied from commercializing her considerable talents as a decorator. But she helped her friends, stapling fabrics, rehanging pictures or scanning country antique shops. Both of us suffer from mild insomnia, and we would spend hours on the telephone night after night, reviewing the scene, often breaking into Viennese dialect.

It was at a dinner party given by Diana early in 1966 that I met Sandra Payson. Among the guests that February evening in Diana's Bayswater house was a tall, imperious blonde with marvellous cheekbones who was introduced as Mrs Meyer. She was recently divorced and had moved to London with two teenage daughters. They were living in a furnished house in Durham Place, Chelsea. Sandra was different from other American women I knew. She was poised, yet she had an uncertainty about her. She was anxious to start a new life, but had little idea of where it would lead her. Sandra lived modestly, preferring to travel by bus rather than take a taxi.

It was not until we had been going out for a while that I discovered Sandra was the niece of John Hay Whitney, a former ambassador to the Court of St James's, and an heiress. The Whitneys were one of the wealthiest and most distinguished American families. When talking of her previous life Sandra gave me the impression of being imprisoned in a gilded cage. She felt crushed by her family, particularly her domineering mother, but was devoted to her somewhat rakish father. Charles Payson came from an old Maine family. He was nicknamed 'Charlie the Red Raper' because of his amorous adventures and his bibulous red face, which grew even redder when he became irate, as he often did. As a member of the America First Committee, which had extreme right-wing if not pro-Nazi sympathies, he had been kept under surveillance during the Second World War. Like the Duke of Buccleuch in England, Charlie Payson only escaped internment because of his connections. But he was strongly disapproved of by many people in New York society, including members of his wife's family.

Sandra's mother, Joan Whitney Payson, had an enormous girth and a forceful personality. She wore glasses and spoke in a nervous, at times high-pitched, voice. She was devoted to her husband and remained loyal to him despite his infidelities. Her great passion was the Mets, the New York baseball team which she owned. She and her brother, Jock Whitney, helped finance *Gone with the Wind* on a whim, quite expecting to lose the investment. Instead it broke all box office records. I think Joan gave the proceeds to charity.

Joan had been close to her brother Jock, the ambassador and proprietor of the *New York Herald Tribune*, but their respective spouses cast a shadow over their relationship. Jock was married to Betsy, one of the three Cushing sisters and a former wife of one of President Roosevelt's sons. Sombre and possessive, Betsy was like a figure out of a Theodore Dreiser novel. Her sister Babe Cushing had married William Paley, who was Jewish, and Charles Payson's anti-Semitism led to strained relations with her. Thus the Paysons were never seen at the Paleys and only seldom at the Whitneys. Unlike the Marks and Sieff clan where the younger generation stood in awe and admiration of the patriarchs and were involved in the family business, the Whitneys kept apart from one another. They liked to look across the hedge to see what the relations were up to, but they seldom cooperated. They were suspicious, and kept things close to their chest.

Joan Payson was a munificent woman and a keen collector, but for all her qualities she did little to encourage her five children to strike out on their own. Her eldest son, everyone's favourite, was killed in the last week of the Second World War. Diana Vreeland, who was one of Joan's oldest friends, told me that on learning that her son had died in battle she returned to the bridge table, finished the rubber without telling anybody, and then retired to her bedroom, where she stayed for the best part of a year. She was psychologically maimed, but she never showed her emotions. Grief made her even more crusty than she had been before.

Sandra was the eldest of three daughters. Her youngest sister married Vincent de Roulay, known as Page, a roisterous young businessman, active in Republican politics, who got himself appointed as American Ambassador to Jamaica under Nixon. The middle daughter, Payney, married a charming Southerner who was descended from an old Italian noble family and had a zest for hunting and travelling.

Sandra's first husband came from Long Island and worked in the family real estate company. For more than ten years they lived in Texas among the grand ranchers and oil clans of the state. Sandra's friendship with George and Barbara Bush dates from that time.

I loved Sandra's warmth and her rather brittle sense of humour, and felt challenged by her wish to break out of the closed society she had grown up in. Our romance grew rapidly in intensity. We travelled together to Paris, Vienna and Rome. By Easter we knew we wanted to get married, but that was only the beginning of a long odyssey: we knew that the Paysons would be difficult to win over. To brace ourselves for the confrontation with Sandra's family, we spent the Easter holiday in Montego Bay, where I rented a secluded house. It was run-down, but it had charm. In New York we decided to break the news first to a few friends and to Sandra's sisters before facing Joan Whitney Payson. Brooke Astor was among the first to be let in on the plot and was wholly supportive. Word soon got round. There was amazement and consternation. The gossip columns began to pick the story up. Leonard Lyons in the *New York Post* was the first to ask the question, 'How will Charlie Payson take to a Jewish son-in-law?' Apparently he was almost apoplectic when he heard that Sandra wanted to marry a Jew.

After Sandra had told her mother of our plans, it was arranged that I should meet her for tea at the St Regis Hotel. I arrived half an hour early and had a haircut. I later heard that Joan Payson had also arrived early in order to observe me. We discovered we had a mutual friend in Douglas Cooper, and that broke the ice. We talked about modern art, London life and New York friends, skirting around the subject that was uppermost in our minds. Eventually Mrs Payson said to me, 'You must come and see me sometime. I think Charlie would also like to meet you.' On returning home she told Sandra, 'You know, he's much more my type than yours.'

I met Mr and Mrs Payson the following week. We had lunch downtown in the Town House, a dark, thoroughly Wasp restaurant. I had heard that Charles Payson had a financial interest in an armament business, and having recently attended a conference on modern missiles and defence concepts, I was able to engage him in animated conversation on the topic. He was civil and attentive throughout the meal, ending the discourse by proposing a pact: Sandra and I were to separate for a six-month period of reflection, and if, at the end of that time, we were still of the same mind, there would be no objection to the marriage. Although Sandra was thirty-eight years old and the mother of three children, and I was forty-six, we agreed to comply, hoping to lie low, avoid publicity and then announce our decision to go ahead. Sandra once asked her mother why she was not yet reconciled to the match. She never mentioned my being Jewish. All she said was, 'We've heard he's a ladies' man.'

A war of nerves raged during the imposed interlude, with much lobbying in the Payson entourage. There were those who favoured the marriage and others who made it clear they thought it a misalliance. Rumours were planted and much mischief made, old love affairs of mine were dug up and held against me. It was all very tense. Irene Selznick and Diana Vreeland, who were both close to the family, supported the marriage. They were well-disposed towards me and thought Sandra might enjoy her new life. I had had professional dealings with both of them. Diana Vreeland, always on the lookout for new people, befriended me on my first visit to New York and we had a common friend in Cecil Beaton. In Irene Selznick, who was wholly acceptable to Wasp society, I found a fellow 'insider-outsider'. She and I traded the odd Jewish joke and shared observations.

Sandra was rattled by the volume of disapproval. Her sisters stood by her, particularly Payney and her Italian-American husband, who showed sympathy and a sense of European solidarity. When the sisters were all together, the conversation inevitably centred around family cabals and the trustees, who they felt were keeping them short. It was my first insight into the whole concept of American trusts, and I was struck by the parochialism of those financial advisors and crotchety lawyers. The man who looked after Sandra's money was nearly sixty, and yet he had never been outside the United States. When he came to our wedding I had to use my embassy contacts in London to get him a passport at the last moment.

Sandra managed to persuade her mother to lift the embargo on our marriage sooner. Mrs Payson gave an engagement party in New York for which the whole Whitney clan turned up; even Sandra's father made an appearance. The wedding took place in London on 31 July, six months after our first meeting. This time Charlie Payson did not attend. In fact, he rarely spoke to me for the best part of the marriage and he never accompanied his wife when she came to visit us, yet whenever we went to stay at their Manhasset home on Long Island he was icily correct. On one occasion when my mother-in-law visited my flat in London, she took exception to a Mannerist painting of a nude with a satyr stroking her mount of Venus, and asked me to sell it. I duly obeyed.

David and Evangeline Bruce gave a wedding party for us at the American Embassy. As the leaders of the American colony in London, the Bruces set the tone, and in displaying their friendship towards me and extending it to my wife by hosting the reception they poured oil on troubled waters. Later that evening Sir Leon and Lady Bagrit gave a dinner for us at their Hampstead home, which had previously belonged to the art historian Kenneth Clark. It was a shrine of beautiful paintings and early Italian bronzes.

Among the guests who flew in from abroad was Afdera Fonda, the third wife of Henry Fonda. She was a flamboyant Venetian countess who sprang to notoriety when she and her sister were portrayed in Hemingway's novel *Across the River and into the Trees*. When she was married to Henry Fonda in the 1960s, New York was at her feet, but she had a self-destructive urge which grated on the very people she loved. Henry Fonda wanted a quiet life, but night after night when he returned from the theatre exhausted he had to put up with a dozen or two boisterous young Italians

eating spaghetti on the stairs, lounging in the sitting room or dancing to the strains of the latest Brazilian samba. Peter Quennell and
I were once taken to the theatre by Afdera and then on to the
Twenty-One where we were joined by Fonda, who had been in the
play. He was drained. When his wife tried to explain to him who
Peter was and what he had written, Fonda exploded: 'Don't bring
me into the conversation,' he hissed, 'let me eat, for Christ's sake.'
Afdera had a heart of gold and was rather gullible. A London art
dealer asked her to take a parcel back to Italy for her lover, an
Italian painter. Sandra and I travelled to Rome on the same plane
as her the day after the wedding. At the airport her bag was searched
and the parcel was found to contain heroin. Poor Afdera was
arrested and sent to prison for a while.

During the first year of our marriage Sandra and I lived in rather
cramped circumstances in my bachelor flat in Eaton Square before
we moved to Cleve Lodge, a spacious Lutyens house in Hyde Park
Gate set in a private garden with its own tennis court. We bought
it at auction for fifty thousand pounds. The Markses had lived there
and so had the Hultons. Sandra tried very hard to attune to her
new life. She was diffident and could not quite make up her mind
about the role she wanted to play. But she had a lovable personality.
She was direct and honest, welcoming and touchingly anxious to
please.

Most of my friends reciprocated Sandra's warmth and did their
best to make her feel at home in London. With hindsight I overwhelmed her with social duties and a punishing travelling schedule.
It was not easy for her. My failure to devote enough attention to
her and communicate some ethnic nuances she cannot have known
with her Wasp background came glaringly to light at a dinner party
we gave on behalf of a Jewish charity in the early days of our
marriage. The Wolfsons, the Markses, the Sieffs and the Harold
Levers were among the guests. I forgot to discuss the menu beforehand and found to my horror that dinner consisted of coquilles
Saint-Jacques followed by Virginia ham and a pudding with crème
Chantilly, all of which offended against the three main canons of
the Kosher diet: no shellfish, no pork and no dairy products after
meat. Some of the guests left their plates untouched, others asked
shyly for a hard-boiled egg.

Various attempts were made to integrate me into Sandra's family.
We went to New York every two or three months and sometimes

spent weekends at the Payson home in Manhasset. The walls were decked with magnificent paintings by Manet, Monet, Corot and Picasso, and there was Van Gogh's famous *Irises*, bought by Mrs Payson in 1947 and sold at Sotheby's in 1987 for a record price of nearly fifty-four million dollars. But the house was comfortable as well as grand, filled with the most extraordinary mishmash of everything Mrs Payson liked most. A Renoir and a Degas might hang next to family photographs and other memorabilia. There were paintings of horses and pet dogs, baseball chalices and Oscars from *Gone with the Wind*.

Sundays were reserved for baseball. I once went with Mrs Payson to the Shea Stadium to watch the Mets. Her players had endeared themselves to the New Yorkers by always losing; in fact it was the only team I know which was cheered when it lost. I sat in the box with Mrs Payson, not understanding what the game was about. The crowd was ecstatic, there were shrieks of excitement, moments when everyone held their breath and then sighs of disappointment. It was all immensely bewildering, but my anthropological interest in the whole set-up made it fascinating for me.

On Christmas Eve the whole family gathered at Manhasset. Conversation rarely went beyond small talk. I cannot remember listening to any serious general conversation or an argument on current topics. If an attempt was made by a guest, it was politely discouraged. Nor did the older generation take a particular interest in the preoccupations of their children and grandchildren. I was very fond of Sandra's son, Blair, a handsome and intelligent young man, and found it strange that his grandmother never discussed his future with him. Instead there was talk of fast cars, gadgets from Hammacher Schlemmer and jolly jokes. They seemed to have no ambition for their children. I noticed that in many of the rich, old American families. East Coast or Texan, they had little faith in the prospects of their offspring and therefore took the view that everything must be done to protect them from themselves.

This attitude was very different from my experience of Jewish families, where sons were spurred on to emulate or even outdo the achievements of their elders. Legend has it that one of the great Anglo-Jewish traders of our time summoned his son when he was eighteen and said to him, 'You have been a sickly child, you have had no formal education, but you're bright. Here's a million pounds. If you come back to me in three years time having spent the million, you'll never see another penny from me. If you make good, you'll run my business.' The son came back with three million and became head of the enterprise. When I asked his father why he had trusted a youngster of eighteen with a million pounds, he said, 'It's cheap at the price. If it had turned out that he was a rotter I would have saved myself a few hundred million.' That attitude was unthinkable in the Whitney family. It seemed to me that their nonchalance crippled initiative and deprived the younger generation of any sense of responsibility.

Christmas mornings in Manhasset are vividly engraved on my memory. The family gathered in the suite of drawing rooms where a neat heap of presents had been piled high for each of them. They would all disappear behind the presents and while they investigated what was inside the wrapping the room would be as quiet as a church. The silence was punctuated by muted peals of laughter or exclamations of delight. Occasionally one might glimpse a blonde lock or the corner of a steel-blue eye through a gap in the wall of parcels. It was like the final scene in Wagner's *Rheingold* where the giants agree to accept the treasure hoard as a substitute for Freia, the Goddess of Youth and Beauty, whom Wotan had promised them as a reward for building Valhalla. The giants ask for a space as high and as wide as Freia to be filled with gold and watch intently as the hoard is piled up, but when the space is filled one of the giants, who has fallen in love with Freia, says he can still see the flashing light of her eye through a chink in the wall of gold. To Wotan's horror the other giants demand that the gap be stopped up with the Ring that the god wears on his finger.

The Long Island Wasp aristocracy to which the Paysons belonged spoke a language of their own, studded with terms borrowed from baseball, American football, golf or fishing. To anyone who was not familiar with the rules of these sports it was like listening to *Beowulf*. Anything intellectual was treated with deep suspicion in this circle, with the notable exception of some widely-travelled and well-read dowagers. Their houses reflected the optimism and ambition of the American century, but Europe was the inspiration behind the decor and handiwork of the Renaissance palaces, Baroque castles and Gothic turrets in Palm Beach or the 1920s and 1930s Long Island residences.

Sandra and I travelled a good deal and stayed with her friends in Spain and Mexico, Florida and Texas, as well as in upstate New

York. We also went to the Far East and had a memorable sojourn in India where we visited the Maharaja and Maharani of Jaipur for a weekend dominated by memories of the British Raj and the ethos of empire. We saw Angkor Vat just before the war in South East Asia spilled into Cambodia.

I remember an eccentric evening in Tokyo with Yukio Mishima, the Japanese novelist who lived and died as a samurai and kept a private band of armed bodyguards. He entertained us in what I took to be his private home but which in fact turned out to have been rented for the occasion. We met him through Ivan Morris, the distinguished Japanese scholar from Columbia University, who was a friend of Bud MacLennan, one of my staunchest collaborators at Weidenfeld & Nicolson. Mishima conversed in French. We spent the whole evening talking about a play he had written about the intellectual struggle for Hitler's heart and soul by two of his early comrades, Ernst Röhm, the leader of the Brown Shirts, and the more urbane and pragmatic Gregor Strasser, both of whom were liquidated on 30 June 1934 in the famous 'Night of the Long Knives'. Mishima recounted the plot: Röhm and Strasser argue their case. Sitting apart at one end of the stage is the sinister industrialist and politician Alfred Hugenberg who represents high finance. Hitler stands impassively in the background throughout until the very end, when he shoots Röhm and Strasser without warning, whereupon Hugenberg applauds heartily and says, 'That's my boy.'

Mishima went on soliloquizing about the dilemma of choosing between revolutionary modern ideas and the reinforcement of the ties of tradition. He wanted to convey his feelings about Japan, but stuck to the German scene.

Geography proved a great obstacle in my marriage to Sandra. She felt her children in America needed her, and wanted to spend more time with them. Her younger daughter lived with us for a while, but although she made friends she was a quintessentially American schoolgirl who missed the environment she had grown up in. Sandra and I tried hard to overcome the problem of rival pulls, but on reflection I was once again too involved with my work to give her the attention she needed, and we became more and more estranged. There was never a lack of affection or respect, but there were lengthening silences and distance developed between us. However, we were determined not to give up. After about five years of marriage we experimented with having different households in

London and New York, spending only part of the time together. In practice we were apart more than we were together. Cleve Lodge felt deserted. It was much too big for one resident, so we sold it and I bought a flat on Chelsea Embankment. Sandra had every intention of using it as her pied à terre, but we drifted further apart and in 1976, after ten years of marriage, we divorced amicably and have stayed on friendly terms.

In happier days Sandra and I used to stay regularly with Charles and Jayne Wrightsman in their house in Palm Beach during the winter, or on their boat in the summer. There was a group of other regulars which included Brooke Astor, Cecil Beaton, and Peter Wilson, the head of Sotheby's. Charles Wrightsman, a power in the oil business, was a fastidious host. Though spoilt in every way, his guests had to adhere to strict unwritten rules. One of them was not to socialize with anybody in the neighbourhood of whom he disapproved. He had his own list of 'acceptables' and a blacklist of people he would not see.

I continued to visit the Wrightsmans after my divorce from Sandra. On one occasion I flew down to Palm Beach with Lally Weymouth. Brooke Astor and Cecil Beaton were also in the party. At the airport we ran into Mary McFadden, the brilliant and eccentric fashion designer, who was then involved with a wealthy financier with a house in Palm Beach. A much older man who had a slightly controversial business reputation, he was shunned by our host. He was, however, an avid collector of contemporary art, and Mary McFadden urged us to come and see the collection. To Charles Wrightsman's great displeasure we went there for tea the following day and looked admiringly at the vast display of twentieth-century sculpture and painting. As we were sitting on the porch Cecil suddenly said, 'Mary, I hear your friend has a particular interest in erotica.' Her friend and she exchanged glances, and without further ado beckoned us to come downstairs where a dark corridor opened into a large eerie room with a dim light in the corner. As we approached we heard anguished cries of pain and thought something terrible had happened. It turned out that these noises came from the erotic artefacts and were recordings of Aborigines making love. There were further dark recesses to which only Cecil Beaton was allowed entry.

When Charles Wrightsman died after a long illness, during which he was devotedly nursed by his wife, Jayne became an active figure in her own right. A collector and generous benefactress, whose discriminating eye is famed in the art market, she is one of the most influential trustees of the Metropolitan Museum and entertains exquisitely in New York and London, widening her circle by inviting young writers and art historians to her small dinners and parties to the theatre or the opera.

My longest friendship with a transatlantic *grande dame* is that with Drue Heinz. Her late husband Jack Heinz of the great food empire was a much-loved figure. He could bubble with enthusiasm for new ideas and people, and was a shrewd judge of business and international politics. A friend of Prince Bernhard of the Netherlands, he was one of the earliest members of the Bilderberg group which brought together the Great and the Good for annual meetings in diverse places. Jack's zest for life was shared by Drue, and with her Irish temperament, energy and curiosity they made a formidable couple.

Drue is a munificent patron who has a particular love for literature. Among the many causes she supports and deals with in all their minutiae she published an ambitious literary magazine, *Antaeus*, and having bought Hawthornden Castle near Edinburgh, once the home of Sir Walter Scott, has revived and greatly enhanced the Hawthornden Literary Prize. Wherever she has lived she has surrounded herself with talented people.

It is rare for a friendship that has spanned more than two decades to have been unalloyed by vacillating moods or the slightest contretemps. I enjoy just such a relationship with Barbara Walters, the most beguiling yet down-to earth and dependable friend. We met when her career as a television interviewer was already in the ascendant at a dinner party given by Joan Whitney Payson before a grand gala at the Metropolitan Museum just across the road from the Paysons' triplex apartment. I sat next to Barbara. Dispensing with the usual social niceties, she turned to me with the professional questioner's mien and asked, 'Why did they make you a knight?' I uttered some embarrassed, self-deprecatory phrases and she made me answer more detailed questions about my life. We got on well and met frequently. I felt very drawn to Barbara, who succeeds in combining girlish naivety and grandmotherly wisdom, spontaneity and calculation within the same well-groomed frame. Besides being a virtuoso in the medium which made her famous, she is a great raconteuse, can sing and dance, and is a natural comedienne.

In 1973, Barbara joined a group of friends from London which included Miriam and John Gross and Nigel Ryan of Thames Television on a trip to Israel. Barbara interviewed Golda Meir and Moshe Dayan and made friends for life with his second wife. One memory of that autumn in Israel is of a magnificent concert given by Pablo Casals at the guest house built by Teddy Kollek's Jerusalem Foundation overlooking the gates of the Old City. Everybody felt confident, tourism was booming and no one had an inkling of the shattering events to come. Shimon Peres, then Minister of Transport in Golda Meir's government, said to me over luncheon. 'Do you realize we are now an industrial power? Our energy consumption rivals that of China, and we have the most effective army and air force between the straits of Messina and the sea of Japan.'

Barbara and I went on to Rome and Venice before returning to London on the Day of Atonement. I shall never forgot collecting her from the Connaught Hotel that October evening. As we emerged from the Connaught Hotel we saw the *Evening Standard* banner headline shouting 'War in the Middle East'.

CHAPTER NINETEEN

The Cause of a Lifetime

I HAVE ALWAYS FELT that an active Zionist has three roles: he is the guardian of Israel's security, an agent of Israel's prosperity and communicator of Israel's achievement. These three functions – especially the never-ceasing urge to explain and interpret the problems of Israel – have been central to my life for more than forty years. Looking back as a publisher, observer and occasional confidant of some of its leaders, I appreciate the wisdom of Henry Bergson's warning against the 'illusion of retrospective determinism'. To ascribe major turning points or catastrophes to inexorable laws of logic may be comforting, but it can be both wrong and dangerous. The opposite tendency, which exonerates opinions held or decisions taken in the past, is no more valid.

My involvement with Israel has been an absorbing, world-encompassing experience. During my many visits there I not only met Jews and non-Jews from every land and entered into friendships with admirable people – self-effacing idealists and charismatic figures – but wherever I went on my travels I came across like-minded people. I discovered a worldwide family of devoted activists who helped make one feel at home in the most unfamiliar places.

As a publisher I have tried to contribute to the understanding of Israel by producing books on biblical, archaeological, historical and current Israeli themes. I published the memoirs of Ben-Gurion, Golda Meir, Yigal Allon, Abba Eban, Moshe Dayan, Shimon Peres, Teddy Kollek, Yitzhak Shamir and Yitzhak Rabin as well as numerous biographies of international Jewish leaders. With Yigael Yadin's *Masada*, a serious text about the excavation of the last Jewish stronghold to fall to the Romans in AD 73, lavishly illustrated with original photography, Weidenfeld & Nicolson pioneered a genre of publishing which has since been widely adopted and adapted.

Another successful book of this kind was a history of Jerusalem written by Teddy Kollek in collaboration with the indefatigable Moshe Pearlman.

In the heady days after the Six Day War, I set up a branch of Weidenfeld & Nicolson in Jerusalem which published books in English and Hebrew. The office was run by a young British-born enthusiast, Asher Weill, and Chaim Herzog acted as deputy chairman. The main purpose was to draw on local talent for illustrated books on archaeology, history and the Bible. After five years, rising costs forced us to abandon the project, but we continued our programme of publishing titles on Israel and the Middle East from London. I commissioned gifted scholars from the Hebrew University of Jerusalem and the University of Tel Aviv to write not only of Jewish and Middle Eastern topics, but on subjects in which I thought they deserved worldwide recognition. Among them were Joshua Prawer, one of the great authorities on the Crusades, Walter Laqueur, historian of Germany and Eastern Europe, Shlomo Avineri, philosopher of the Enlightenment, and Zvi Yavetz, a disciple of Ronald Syme and historian of ancient Rome.

To my mind, Israel's history falls into distinct phases which reflect not only the defining events but societal changes and public moods. The first eight years from the proclamation of the State to the 'Hundred Hours to Suez' comprise one such phase. Exhilarating and precarious, austere and yet morally satisfying, this phase is inextricably linked with the personality of David Ben-Gurion, who embodied the ethos of the pioneering days. In Ben-Gurion's 'Age of Austerity', known as 'Zena', civil servants, soldiers and political and trade union leaders were the elite. The men of wealth in commerce, industry and finance only shared that status if they were politically involved and broadly in sympathy with the Labour-dominated coalition. Ben-Gurion was a law maker, military commander and mentor of a brood of 'young lions' on whom his influence persisted long after his death. Moshe Dayan, Shimon Peres and Teddy Kollek were three outstanding disciples.

Ben-Gurion commanded deep, sometimes almost canine loyalty. I was a friend of his closest aide, Nehemia Argov, who sacrificed personal happiness to his exacting duties. He committed suicide shortly after an assassination attempt against Ben-Gurion in October 1957, partly because he felt he had failed the Old Man. I had few direct dealings with Ben-Gurion during my Weizmann days, but after his retirement he received me on several occasions. The last time I saw him was when I took Evangeline Bruce on a trip to the Negev desert. Ben-Gurion lived in Sdeh Boker, a kibbutz in the heart of the Negev, and we called on him there. He was not in the best of form and he drew a rather sombre picture of the Middle East, bellowing Cassandra-like visions in staccato sentences.

In the early years, British Jews of influence and wealth played a dominant part because Britain was still the most influential country in that area. The Markses and Sieffs were relied on for contacts with Westminster, Whitehall and the press. Marcus Sieff remained the most respected and effective figure in the Anglo-Jewish community until well into the 1970s. After Menachem Begin became prime minister in 1977, his influence waned, not least because Marcus was a man of compromise, out of sympathy with the policy of settling Jews on the West Bank. By then a new generation of Anglo-Jewish activists was emerging, the most effective being Sir Trevor Chinn, a dynamic businessman with a flair for politics and a gift for reconciling feuding factions. But none have succeeded as admirably as Marcus, the ultimate Jewish patrician, in bringing the interests of Israel and Great Britain to a common denominator. He and I worked closely together. I tried to introduce interesting new figures in Israeli politics or culture to people of influence in London, and found breakfast parties an effective format.

We take America's support for Israel so much for granted today that we forget that it was not always so. For the first fifteen years the State Department and the White House maintained at best an even-handed, more often a critical, attitude towards the Jewish State. When Britain's influence declined dramatically as a result of the Suez campaign, Israel was isolated. But Nasser's involvement in the Algerian rebellion against France awakened French interest in Israel, an interest which was reinforced by comradeship in arms in Suez, and joint intelligence operations against Nasser's subversive activities throughout the Arab world. Ben-Gurion was able to exclaim, 'At last we have a friend – France.' Eisenhower's administration took an unforgiving line on the Anglo–Franco–Israeli collusion.

Despite official ambivalence in Washington, American Jewry came increasingly to support Israel with money, enthusiasm and mass tourism. American Jews made massive contributions to institutes of higher learning, notably the Weizmann Institute, the Hebrew University and the new but rapidly expanding University of Tel Aviv.

In the 1950s and '60s I devoted time and energy to helping in the university and cultural sectors. I was elected to the Board of Governors of the Weizmann Institute, and worked closely with the redoubtable Meyer Weisgal, finding supporters, and publishing literature on the Institute conference proceedings. One of my tasks was to introduce Meyer Weisgal and his collaborators in Europe to potential donors. We shared many friends, Charles Clore and members of the Wolfson family among them. Sir Isaac Wolfson, the founder of the family fortune and one of the most brilliant merchants of the century, often entertained me in London and in the Californian-style house he built on the grounds of the Weizmann Institute. His son Leonard, later Lord Wolfson, was a young man when we first met. He held his own against his ebullient father, whose flair and genius he inherited, though he had a different temperament. His diffidence was misleading. Though wary, Leonard was decisive and punctilious.

My favourite project has been the Ben-Gurion University of Beersheba in the Negev desert, Israel's third university. Ben-Gurion always believed that Israel's fate was bound up with the colonization of the Negev desert, which amounts to almost forty per cent of Israeli territory but has attracted less than ten per cent of the population. His motto was, 'Either we conquer the desert – or it will conquer us.' He always thought that the south was to Israel what the west was to the United States – the country of tomorrow, and he demonstrated his faith by building himself a house on the Sdeh Boker kibbutz. That was where he retired to, and where he died. He is buried at Sdeh Boker next to his wife.

In ancient times, indeed right up to the Byzantine period, the Negev was a granary, but the many Islamic wars and conquests ravaged the land and the desert took hold. Incorporated into the borders of the new State in 1947 at the insistence of Weizmann, who succeeded in convincing Truman to lend his weight to Israel's claim to that territory, the Negev has attracted many Jews from Arab countries and from the Soviet Union. It is strategically important as a highway between Egypt and the heartland of Israel. In a peaceful Middle East, the region would be one of the great arterial links between the northern and southern tiers of the Arab world.

The biblical Beersheba, which gave sanctuary to Abraham the Patri-arch, lies five kilometres east of the present city. When I first visited Israel Beersheba was a staging post for Bedouins, the dwelling of a few hundred idealistic Jewish settlers and a marketplace. Today it has 115,000 inhabitants and stands as a rare example of good town planning. It boasts many impressive modern buildings, a theatre, and, thanks to Russian immigrants, an excellent symphony orchestra. But its special pride is the university, which grew out of a centre for desert research and aspires to be 'a little Oxford, Cambridge or Heidelberg in the Negev'. Ben-Gurion laid the foundation stone in 1965. Besides engineering and Jewish studies, the initial strengths of the university were tropical medicine, thanks to its first president, Moshe Pryves. The vicinity of Dimona, the site of Israel's nuclear reactor, brought many eminent scientists into its orbit.

Pinhas Sapir, Golda Meir's Minister of Finance, who was reputed to run the economy from a small black notebook, and Shimon Peres, who was also in the cabinet, visited me in London and asked me to become chairman of the new group of Friends of Ben-Gurion University. I was delighted, not least because of a sentimental attachment going back to my earliest days as a refugee in England when I was befriended by Theodore Zissiu, who had devoted every-thing to his romantic obsession with developing the Negev. I set up a committee and recruited a band of helpers. The philanthropist Abraham-Curiel and his wife, whose daughter lectured at the uni-versity, gave generous support. My friend Clarissa, Countess of Avon, Anthony Eden's widow, who had become a staunch advocate of Israel and showed her solidarity wherever possible, joined the committee. She was motivated mainly by conviction, but there was also an element of piety, for Anthony Eden had drawn from Suez the lesson that Israel was the stablest factor in the Middle East and needed all the help it could get. It was not easy to raise funds for yet another centre of excellence and I was fortunate in meeting Hyman Kreitman. He was married to one of the two daughters of Sir John Cohen, the founder of Tesco, the giant British food chain. The other daughter, Dame Shirley Porter, the Thatcherite leader of Westminster City Council, was married to Leslie Porter, who was committed to Tel Aviv University. Hyman was looking for a fulfil-ling cause. Profiting from a change of guard at Tesco and a degree of healthy philanthropic competitiveness within the family, I per-suaded him to visit Beersheba and look around the campus. He returned full of enthusiasm and has been its most munificent supporter ever since.

Having worked with a number of distinguished presidents and rectors of the university, I also had a hand in recruiting its present head, Avishai Bravermann, an Israeli-born scientist who worked at the World Bank in Washington on the problems of water resources in the Middle East. I first met him in 1989 at a conference which I convened in Lausanne on the economic possibilities in the Middle East after a settlement between Jews and Arabs – a hypothetical theme which yielded surprisingly constructive discussions, for the tone was less shrill and stereotyped than previous gatherings of this kind had led one to expect. The conference at the Beau-Rivage, that old fashioned Grand Hotel where the Lausanne Peace Treaty with Turkey was signed in 1923, might have been a dress rehearsal for the multilateral negotiations for peace in the Middle East that have since been held in Washington, Cairo, Rome and elsewhere. Among the participants was Faisal Husseini, then scarcely known, but now a leading voice in the Palestinian movement.

The Suez War of 1956 was an incisive event in Israel's history, as it was in world affairs. For Britain it proved yet another milestone on the path of decolonization, and in France it coincided with the rapid worsening of the Algerian crisis. But in Israel the extraordinary performance of the defence forces, which made military history, strengthened morale. It also made the reputation of a number of commanders. Once again the name Dayan shone bright, and Ariel Sharon and Yitzhak Rabin became household names.

I had a strong publishing involvement with that war. Through Pamela Berry, who was married to Michael Berry, later Lord Hartwell, the proprietor of the *Daily Telegraph*, I had formed a special relationship with the newly established *Sunday Telegraph*. I had met Pamela briefly in the early 1950s with Loelia Westminster, but we did not strike up a rapport until later. In fact our friendship sprang from a feud. In December 1956 I published a book on the Soviet spy, Guy Burgess, by Tom Driberg, who had spent several weeks in Moscow that summer interviewing his old friend. *Guy Burgess: A Portrait with a Background* caused quite a stir at the time. In contained a passage which claimed that Michael Berry, a contemporary of Burgess's at Eton, had offered him the job of diplomatic correspondent of the *Daily Telegraph* only days before his defection to Moscow. It was probably wishful thinking on Burgess's part. Anyhow, Michael Berry emphatically denied the allegation and was so incensed about its publication that he broke off all business relations with us. For about a year none of our books were reviewed in the *Daily Telegraph*. The froideur continued for some time, but peace was eventually restored thanks to the Duchess of Westminster. We all happened to find ourselves in the south of France at the same time, and she brought the Berrys and me together at a dinner party. It was not long after the *Sunday Telegraph* was founded. As part of the strategy to establish the new title, Michael Berry asked me to suggest major political biographies suitable for serialization. This was an exciting task, not least because it gave me a powerful base for obtaining material with the financial backing of a national newspaper. Michael also encouraged me to seek out potential authors and create book projects, many of which became joint ventures of the *Telegraph*, Weidenfeld & Nicolson and various foreign publishers and newspapers.

Pamela Berry became involved in these projects. She also proved an excellent scout. She and I made many trips together in pursuit of our various schemes. A dozen or so remarkable books by eyewitnesses of contemporary history sprang from our association.

As the daughter of the conservative Lord Chancellor F.E. Smith, politics had been part of Pamela's life from her earliest childhood. She presided over the last real political salon in London. Although a true blue conservative, she had a particular fondness for Labour intellectuals. She liked dons and accomplished artists and performers, and also made forays into the world of fashion, but her heart was in politics and serious journalism. Unlike the wives of other press lords, who treated even the senior staff of their newspapers as glorified office boys, Pamela Berry had a healthy respect for talented writers and enjoyed furthering their careers. At her lunch parties, where the guests were chosen for their wit, their conversational powers or their momentary news value, she would place a young columnist or a new leader writer next to a senior cabinet minister. I remember one occasion when, instead of telling a protégé that she had put him in a privileged position, she turned to R.A. Butler and announced, 'Now, Rab, I have a treat for you. I have put you next to Perry Worsthorne, one of our most brilliant young writers.'

Pamela Berry looked on journalists rather as the Americans do

– as important figures on the political chessboard. Her style of entertaining was reminiscent of that of Katharine Graham of the *Washington Post* and the Sulzbergers of *The New York Times*, who would rank senior columnists as highly as a cabinet minister in the seating plan. In fact Kay Graham was a close friend of Lady Pamela, as were two other American women, Evangeline Bruce and Susan Mary Alsop, the wife of the columnist Joe Alsop.

The Berrys had been very pro-Suez and blamed Eden's loss of nerve for the fiasco. There was not much love lost between the Berrys and the Edens. At that time many of the details surrounding the collusion between Britain, France and Israel had not emerged. There was a conspiracy of silence between all the leading survivors of the secret meeting at Sèvres from 22–24 October 1956 when the three parties worked out a joint plan of action. Both Berrys were keen to get to the bottom of the story, spurred on by the thought of a journalistic scoop. Pamela and I set out to interview most of the surviving protagonists of the Suez affair and urge them to publish their reminiscences. We visited Guy Mollet, the French prime minister of the day. Over a large entrecôte he told us that he had given his word not to reveal anything about the Sèvres confer-ence, but he consoled us with an account of a conversation he had had with General de Gaulle whom he had visited in his retreat at Colombey-les-deux-Églises some time after Suez. The two men were walking around the garden and Mollet asked the General point-blank what he thought of his role in the crisis. De Gaulle stopped dead amid the rose hedges and said, 'Mollet, you were a good patriot and a sound statesman, but you committed a cardinal error: you should never, never, definitely never have submitted yourself to a British command.' Mollet introduced us to his Defence Minister, Bourgès-Manoury, who was equally unforthcoming, and we also saw Abel Thomas, an Intelligence chief. The British Foreign Secre-tary Selwyn Lloyd, ever the discreet Establishment politician, gave nothing away.

In Israel our quest took us to Ben-Gurion, who simply said, 'The British, the British, what do you expect of them?' and then changed the subject. Shimon Peres, who had been director-general of the Defence Ministry, was more forthcoming. In his first autobiographi-cal work, which we published in 1967, he was quite revealing about the Sèvres meeting, but by that time a good deal had percolated to the public. The fullest account appeared even later, in 1976, in

Moshe Dayan's book, *The Story of My Life*. When Pam and I had asked him about Sèvres years earlier he had given a particularly graphic description of the conference. He was more disdainful of the aura of hypocrisy when with us than he was to be in print. I will never forget his portrayal of Selwyn Lloyd, who clearly viewed the collusion with Israel with distaste. Dayan said he had reminded him of a crotchety country solicitor who, confronted by clients with an amateurish plan of tax evasion, takes his glasses off, cleans them with his handkerchief, puts them on the desk, folds his hands and declares: 'You'll never get away with this tax fraud, but if you insist I'll show you a way round it.'

My friendship with Dayan dates back to the period between the Suez War and the Yom Kippur War in 1973. It was prompted by his daughter Yael, for whom I have great affection and respect. I met her on the steps of the Dan Hotel in Tel Aviv on a swelteringly hot day shortly after the Suez War. She was with her mother, Ruth, a dedicated social worker with strong sympathies for her Arab neighbours. On being introduced, Yael nodded curtly and quipped, 'You know, you shouldn't wear shorts, they are very unbecoming.' She was in her late teens and had recently done her military service. Before I returned to London she gave me the manuscript of her first novel, a frank and fresh account of army life seen by a girl conscript. Mistrusting my judgement on fiction, I gave it to Barley Alison. Within twenty-four hours I received an enthusiastic report. *New Face in a Mirror* came out in 1959. It was copublished in the United States and many European countries and became a best seller. Yael was hailed as the Françoise Sagan of Israel.

Yael had a difficult relationship with her father. It dominated her life, and her attempt to escape from him drove her to many peregrinations. However, she developed a distinctive personality and has become an effective speaker for Israel in the United States and Europe. Yael married a senior Army officer and was elected as a Labour member of Knesset. She espoused unpopular causes such as homosexual and lesbian rights. As a campaigner for the recognition of the PLO she was one of the first Israeli politicians to seek out Yasser Arafat in Tunis.

For most of the time I knew Dayan he was Minister of Defence or Chief of Staff. We sometimes had lunch at a discreet restaurant in the suburbs of Tel Aviv. Dayan would arrive preceded and followed by armed guards on motorcycles. The head waiter always knew his order, and we would launch straight into a two-point agenda: first publishing, then Israel's geopolitical situation. At these meetings Dayan was brief and businesslike. He never spoke about money in connection with the books he wrote for me. These matters were referred to Moshe Pearlman, his collaborator and translator. I remember a family outing to the cinema on a Saturday night when an exhausted Dayan fell asleep during the Western, and I remember many visits to his house in Zahallah, that secluded settlement near Tel Aviv which is mostly inhabited by former officers and civil servants. The house was like an archaeological museum, its court-yard filled with Canaanite statues and urns. Archaeology was Dayan's passion. From an early age he had collected antiquities dug from the multilayered soil of Israel. He had taught himself a great deal about the subject and was adept at piecing together fragments.

It is difficult to describe Dayan's charisma. He had great natural charm: even his aloofness was strangely appealing. He attracted the loyalty of other men like a magnet and always came first in popu-larity polls, but the highest office was denied him because he had a disregard for the nitty-gritty of politics. He was not good at small talk and showed his boredom openly, but when a subject interested him he became animated, even loquacious. Dayan relaxed in the company of women, which gave him the reputation of a Don Juan. Stories about his antics were probably much exaggerated. He had a long liaison with a married woman who eventually became his second wife and made him very happy. Rachel Dayan, a serene and elegant blonde, was a calming influence. She could hardly have differed more from the passionate and zealously independent Ruth.

Dayan was born and bred in the Middle East and had a deep feeling for its land and peoples. His supporters thought him the most likely Israeli politician to conclude that 'Peace of the Brave' of which many Zionists and some Arabs dreamt. Dayan respected the Arabs and understood their psyche. Even before 1967, when he was given command of the occupied territories, he had friendly relations with Arab mayors and notables. I met members of the Arab community at his house, and Ruth Dayan took me to Gaza to have lunch with Arab families which her parents, a distinguished professional couple of the pioneering generation, had known in earlier days. It must not be forgotten that besides Begin, Dayan was the main Israeli protagonist of the Camp David accord which was signed in 1979.

One of the received ideas amongst students of the Arab–Israeli conflict is that Zionism underrated the problems Jewish immigration posed for the Arabs in Palestine. The allegation is largely true, for neither Theodor Herzl nor Weizmann nor Ben-Gurion understood the depth of Arab, let alone Palestinian, feeling. In fact the word Palestinian, connoting an inhabitant of Arab Palestine, was unknown in the Jewish vocabulary until very late in the day, although Jews and Arabs alike had held Palestinian passports under the British mandate. In the 1960s Golda Meir denied the existence of a Palestinian nation, and as late as 1977 Begin would interrupt an interlocutor who asked how he got on with the Palestinians by saying, 'What do you mean? I am a Palestinian – a Palestinian Jew. Our neighbours are Palestinian Arabs.' Behind this terminological misunderstanding lies a deeper argument to which Arabs unwittingly contributed.

Traditional Zionist reasoning runs thus: most of the Arab world from North Africa to the Indian Ocean, from the Nile to the Tigris and to the Persian border, was directly or indirectly subject to Ottoman rule. It was governed by Turkish officials and often arbitrarily subdivided into provinces or districts – *vilayets* ruled by a vali or governor. There was little Arab self-rule or national consciousness until the break-up of the Ottoman Empire. The notion of an Arab revolt was a myth, the myth of T.E. Lawrence, for it was the British who freed the Arabs. When the maps were redrawn after the First and Second World Wars, twenty-odd sovereign states emerged in an area with untold mineral resources covering territory the size of Europe from the Atlantic to the Urals and, if one includes the Saudi-Arabian desert, the largest part of Australasia. By contrast, the Jews, who had been promised a homeland in the territory bounded by the British mandate on both sides of the Jordan, ended up with a state the size of Wales; even during the years from 1967 to 1979 when Israel occupied the Sinai peninsula it was no larger than Scotland.

Arab nationalism developed piecemeal in the twentieth century. It prided itself on shared aspirations and regarded itself as one nation. Gamal Nasser not only preached but also practised Arab unity. Under his presidency Egypt and Syria merged in 1958 to form the United Arab Republic. It only lasted a few years, but there were many treaties of unity and there was much talk of temporary fusions of states in the Arab region. Vigorous propaganda led the

Israelis to believe that they had to reckon with a vastly superior opponent. The Arab population on the West Bank and in Gaza only gradually developed its own identity and formed a resistance movement, the Palestine Liberation Organization. Violence and terror crystallized a Palestinian identity and established it in the minds of Arabs and Jews alike.

In the decade between Suez and the Six Day War, Israel consolidated many of the economic and social achievements of the early years. The older generation, Ben-Gurion, Levy Eshkol and Pinhas Sapir, were still at the helm, but new men like Dayan, Allon and Shimon Peres had come to the fore. For me the election of Teddy Kollek, my closest friend in Israel and one of the people I most admire, as Mayor of Jerusalem in 1965 was a signal event. Teddy embodies the best of the Viennese temperament. His flexibility and charm have made him Jewry's greatest apostle to the Gentiles. His strength of will, his sincerity and fairness are impressive, and it is impossible to resist his gentle persuasiveness. If there is one person who exemplifies that spirit of improvisation which I believe to be one of the great qualities of Israel, it is he.

When Teddy succeeded the burly and pugnacious American-born Gershon Agron, the Jewish city comprised only the new Jerusalem, the former suburbs to the north and west divided from the Old City by barbed wire and a no-man's-land of weeds and rubbish. Yet even that new Jerusalem was multicultured. The various strands of religious Jewry lived alongside Armenians, Copts, Melchites, Greek Orthodoxes and Protestants. In spite of all the munificence from abroad, Jerusalem was a poor city. Housing for the growing population was modest and the official buildings were provincial in style.

Teddy set about turning the city into a metropolis with frenetic energy. He set up a committee of Israelis and Jewish and non-Jewish well-wishers from all over the world to advise him on replanning. As a member of the International Jerusalem Committee and of the Jerusalem Foundation I was able to watch Teddy carry out his ambitious projects from close quarters. Our committees met at regular intervals; their scope widened when Jerusalem was united under a single administration after the Six Day War. Distinguished architects such as the American Louis Kahn and the Italian Bruno Zevi, and political scientists and urbanists from South America, Germany, France, Switzerland and Britain gathered together with their Israeli counterparts to discuss the problems of a growing modern city and how best to tackle the excavation and preservation of Jerusalem's great past. The Jerusalem Foundation was involved in projects ranging from the restoration of the ancient Jewish quarter, the venerable City Gates and the mediaeval citadel to crèches for Arab children, Arab-Israeli playgrounds or a football stadium. The area which had been a no-man's-land was transformed into a park donated by my friend Jan Mitchell.

One of the wonders of new Jerusalem is the Jerusalem Museum which Teddy created from a blueprint, collecting funds with indefatigable zeal. Much of the workload was borne by Ruth Cheshin, the scion of an old Jerusalem family. Her acerbic charm and common sense blended with Teddy's winning manner which was only rarely marred by volcanic eruptions of irascibility. The museum, which houses Jewish antiquities alongside old masters, European furniture and treasures of the ancient Middle East, won international fame for the Dead Sea Scrolls, whose discovery by Yigael Yadin and his father Professor Sukenik has contributed so much to our understanding of the transition between ancient Judaism and early Christianity. Another of Teddy's benefactors was Vivien Duffield, Charles Clore's philanthropic daughter, who financed the Turner Wing of the Tate Gallery in London. In Jerusalem she established a museum of the city's history in the old Citadel and, as a gift to young Jerusalemites, built an impressive football stadium.

Teddy Kollek was a great inspiration to the Rothschild family. As founders of one of the oldest Jewish settlements in Palestine, they were involved in the Zionist adventure from the outset. They brought their talents and complex characteristics to bear in the service of the cause, though many of them were ambivalent about its political as distinct from its cultural and charitable aims – it is interesting to look at that unique clan with its long tradition of philanthropy through the prism of its commitment to Israel. In France, the great Baron Edmond was the target of Theodor Herzl's entreaties and the butt of his sarcasm. While Herzl regarded him as a rich dilettante, Weizmann saw him as a 'very wise old man, but a terribly *meshugener* [crazy] fish' and won his support for a Hebrew University.

In England the Rothschilds remained aloof at first, sharing the scepticism, if not downright hostility, of the old established Anglo-

Jewish families towards a movement that struck them as politically explosive and Utopian. They felt more at home with the gradualist approach of the moderate Zionists who seemed content with building up farming colonies and tilling the land 'acre by acre, ox by ox', as Chaim Weizmann had put it. But when in 1917 Weizmann wrung from the British government the promise to establish a Jewish national home in Palestine, the famous Declaration was written in the form of a letter addressed by Balfour, the Foreign Secretary, to Lord Walter Rothschild.

The most committed Zionist sympathizer of the family in that generation was James ('Jimmy') de Rothschild, Baron Edmond's son. Having served in the British army and married into an Anglo-Jewish family of Sephardic origin, James settled in England and became a Liberal MP. He lived in palatial splendour in St James's Place and Waddesdon Manor in Buckinghamshire, which was built in the style of a Loire château by his great-uncle, Baron Ferdinand, and filled with magnificent works of art. James and his young wife Dorothy (Dollie) Pinto were fervent Zionists and endowed some of the most important cultural and educational institutions in British-ruled Palestine. I met James de Rothschild while I worked with President Weizmann. A gaunt, towering figure who wore an eye-glass and was slightly hard of hearing, he had a *grand-seigneurial* manner and could be curt and friendly at the same time. He wanted to hear gossip from the Weizmann court and was particularly interested in the nuances of the political differences between the Israeli President, the Prime Minister and the Foreign Minister.

James de Rothschild died in 1957. His widow Dollie, whom I got to know better after his death, was the strongest personality among the Rothschilds. Weizmann had recognized her qualities when she was a young bride of twenty. He became her mentor and she his confidante. She was small and resolute, a rustic *grande dame*, who epitomized the Anglo-Jewish squirearchy and had a quiet but firm grip over whatever she did. Pamela Hartwell, who was one of her admirers, called her 'The King of the Jews' because she enjoyed deep respect not only from within her family but throughout the community. She took an active interest in the extensive work of the Rothschild charitable foundation in Israel and supported many Jewish causes in Britain. Israel's image in the British press, the recurrent waves of anti-Semitism in its various manifestations, was a particular concern of hers, especially after the 1967 wars when so many people, notably on the Left, distanced themselves from Israel.

As part of her effort to improve Anglo-Israeli relations, Dollie Rothschild held regular afternoon meetings with concerned Jews and non-Jews in the dining room of her London house to discuss the repercussions of events in either country and think of ways to ward off any unpleasantness. Terence Prittie, the writer and long-standing foreign correspondent of the *Manchester Guardian* acted as the first secretary of the group, which over the years included Marcus Sieff, Leon Bagrit, Sigmund Warburg, Lord Goodman, Isaiah Berlin, two former British ambassadors to Israel, the historians Martin Gilbert and Hugh Thomas, and the writer David Pryce-Jones. The younger Rothschilds were represented by Evelyn and Jacob.

Although they shared certain family characteristics, there could be no more diverse temperaments than these two cousins who were destined to run the family business and further the Rothschild charitable causes. Evelyn, the elder cousin, was the controlling shareholder of the N.M. Rothschild Bank in which his father Anthony had been the senior partner. As the son and heir of Lord (Victor) Rothschild, Jacob was handicapped by the fact that his father had chosen to be a scientist rather than a banker: the parental milieus of the two cousins were very different. Evelyn had had a conventional upbringing – he went to Harrow and Cambridge and was an athlete and country gentleman. Though Jacob was similarly educated (Eton and Oxford), his parents were unconventional – his father had been part of the Cambridge circle that included Anthony Blunt and other Apostles, while his mother came from a family at the epicentre of the Bloomsbury group.

A profoundly competitive streak in his make-up spurred Jacob to make his mark both intellectually and as a businessman. I first met him when he was an undergraduate. Over the years I got to know him better and found him a fascinating, complex character torn between conformism and non-conformism. A desire to be acknowledged by the City, grand Bohemia, the upper reaches of the aristocracy, court society and the brash new billionaires on both sides of the Atlantic testifies to his omnivorous curiosity and ambition. His personal taste straddles the traditional and the new, and he has inherited the Rothschilds' eye for beautiful things.

Jacob's interest in Jewish causes greatly intensified after 1989 when he became the main beneficiary of Dollie Rothschild's will and took on the stewardship of the Rothschild Foundation in Israel. Not long afterwards his father died, Jacob became the 4th Lord Rothschild and therewith took on what is generally recognized as being the preeminent role among British Jews. He continued Dollie's tea parties and lent Spencer House, the palace in St James's that he leased from the Princess of Wales's family and restored to its Palladian splendour, for many Jewish charitable functions. Jacob combines a strain of Rothschild melancholia and innate caution with a robust capacity for epicurean self-indulgence. His successful chairmanship of the National Gallery and his personal interests have distinguished him as one of the foremost patrons of the arts.

Evelyn came into his own as a merchant banker when Jacob left the family business. He is probably more introverted and more reserved than his younger cousin, but when he takes up a cause such as the Haifa Technion, Israel's centre of technological excellence, he does so with single-minded persistence. He hides a kindly nature and a sensitivity to other people's feelings under a crust of aloofness, even arrogance.

One of the last great moments of Teddy Kollek's regime in Jerusalem was the opening of the new building for the Supreme Court which was funded by the Rothschild foundation. Jacob Rothschild presided over an illustrious international gathering which had flown in for the event. Revered by citizens from both the Arab and Jewish communities, Teddy Kollek had been reelected to the mayorship of Jerusalem time and again, regardless of whether the national vote went Right or Left. His eightieth birthday in May 1991 which was attended by well-wishers from all over the world was a moving tribute to his achievements. It was also a decisive event in my life, for it was there, on the terrace of the Mishkenot Sha'ananim, the guest house of the Jerusalem Foundation with its dazzling view of the Old City, that I met Annabelle Whitestone. A tall, strikingly beautiful blue-eyed woman with a cascade of shining blonde hair caught my attention when she smiled at me at a buffet lunch.

Annabelle Whitestone comes from a British naval family and had a convent school education. She left England aged barely twenty to work as a concert agent in Madrid where she looked after an impressive roster of musicians, many of whom have remained good friends. She became particularly attached to the Polish-born pianist Artur Rubinstein. They fell in love, he left his wife and Annabelle lived with him for several happy years until his death in 1982. Rubinstein was a frequent visitor to Jerusalem, where he gave master classes and made generous donations to the School of Music. In fact I had met Annabelle with Rubinstein a dozen or so years earlier when Teddy Kollek took the three of us out to dinner.

Over lunch on the terrace of the Mishkenot Sha'ananim we had a wonderfully animated talk – about music, Jerusalem, our past lives and mutual friends. I was immediately struck by Annabelle's sense of humour and her gift of mimicry, so accurate but never cruel. In fact, I loved everything about her and instinctively felt that I knew her well. A line from one of Lewis Namier's essays sprang to mind: 'In a drop of dew there can be seen the colour of the sun.' I asked Annabelle to join me for dinner with another of Teddy's guests, my friend Hubert Burda, the German magazine and news-paper publisher and a warm supporter of Israeli cultural causes. Annabelle and I stayed up talking in the bar of the King David Hotel to the languid strains of a pianist, who was obviously a recent Russian immigrant. Next morning I had to return to London, but I could not get Annabelle out of my mind. The following weekend I went to see her in her charming flat in Lutry near Lausanne. I took Annabelle to Vienna, retracing the steps of my childhood. Next she visited me in London, we went to Salzburg and Bayreuth and saw each other continually thereafter. In spite of my earlier failures I had never given up hope that I would one day find the ideal wife, and by the end of the year I thought the time had come to propose. I asked rather pompously, 'Do you think we should regularize our situation?' Annabelle nodded assent. Without any prompting on my part she decided to convert to the Jewish faith. Even the most censorious among the myriad people I introduced her to during our months of courtship fell for her natural charm.

On the eve of our wedding I gave a stag party at the Garrick Club which included some special guests from abroad: Teddy Kollek, who was giving the bride away, and Cardinal Koenig from Vienna symbolized the ecumenical spirit, Karl Schwarzenberg came from Prague and Krzysztof Michalski from Vienna, Hubert Burda and Stefan Sattler from Munich and Joachim Fest from Frankfurt. Among those who spoke was Peter Bauer, the Hungarian-born economist whom I have known since my days in the BBC Monitoring Service and who has always been a critical but loyal friend. Peter was educated at Cambridge where he later taught economics.

He acted as advisor to Weidenfeld & Nicolson and introduced the economists Richard Lipsey and A.R. Prest. Peter was a lone voice in the 1950s and '60s when he first started arguing his case against development aid for the Third World. His unfashionable stance drew violent protests from fellow economists, but he was eventually rewarded with a peerage by Margaret Thatcher. A master of irony, especially when portraying his fellow economists, Peter might well have coined the phrase that foreign aid is all about taking money from poor people in rich countries and giving it to rich people in poor countries, but although he denies authorship, he agrees it is an apt description of his analysis.

Only family and a few very close friends were present when we were married at the Chelsea Registry Office on Bastille Day, 1992. Drue Heinz gave a splendid lunch party in her Mayfair house on that gloriously hot fourteenth of July. Annabelle and I invited a larger gathering of friends, colleagues and authors to drinks at the National Portrait Gallery later that day, and to round off the celebrations Gert-Rudolf and Donatella Flick, who have become very close friends, hosted a wonderful dinner where Teddy Kollek joined in a sing-along of fraternity songs from my student days.

Five months later we celebrated a religious marriage in Jerusalem with the traditional accoutrements of the wedding canopy, the crushing of glass and some folksy Jewish dancing. Shimon Peres and Isaiah Berlin, Teddy Kollek and Michael Sella, a former head of the Weizmann Institute of Science, stood at the four corners of the canopy.

After a record twenty-eight years in which he transformed Jerusalem, Teddy Kollek suffered defeat in 1993. It spelt the end of an era. Some of Teddy's friends had tried in vain to dissuade him from standing for reelection and had supported him with a heavy heart. Annabelle and I arrived in Jerusalem on polling day. Teddy showed remarkable resilience in the face of his bitter disappointment. We who knew him had no doubt that he would continue to work as a great ambassador-at-large for his city as it prepared to celebrate the three-thousandth anniversary of King David's ascent to the throne in the year 1996.

General Smuts, the great South-African soldier-statesman, defined the best kind of propaganda as that which paints a picture of a cause, a country or a movement in a way that excites admiration and is at the same time truthful. That has been the line I have taken on the Jewish State. I have always tried to reconcile my own views with my commitment to the democratic consensus which I regard as covering the whole spectrum of Israeli politics except for the extremes on the Right and Left. That has been my attitude to all Israeli governments, all of which I have had dealings with in one way or another.

I first met Golda Meir briefly in 1950 when, as Minister for Employment and Social Security in Ben-Gurion's cabinet, she was charged with the absorption of the first waves of immigrants who were streaming into Israel from Europe. They were given temporary accommodation in improvised shanty units which were so primitive and overcrowded that some of the wretched newcomers compared them to the displaced persons' camps in liberated Europe. Flora Solomon, who was then helping Golda Meir in her efforts to improve conditions in these complexes, accompanied her to a meeting with Ben-Gurion and a small group of officials from other government departments. I was there representing the President's office. Backed by Golda, Flora pleaded with the Prime Minister to slow down the pace of immigration and concentrate energies on creating more durable homes for those who had already arrived. 'B-G,' she asked, 'have you seen how bad things are there?' Ben-Gurion resolutely shook his head. 'I know what you are saying, but I won't allow myself to go and see because I can't afford to falter in my resolve. We need to take in as many homeless Jews as is humanly possible – or impossible. That's the priority. The rest will follow, you will see.' He was, of course, proved right.

I saw more of Golda when she was Foreign Minister and after she became Israel's first woman prime minister in 1969. She was a curious amalgam of qualities. In some ways the archetypal union boss in the mould of Ernest Bevin, she combined the no-nonsense single-mindedness of Margaret Thatcher and a mordant sense of humour with a certain Russian-Jewish folksiness. Despite a grand-motherly touch, she was a steely woman with an indomitable will, but she had a subtle way of appealing to the filial longings of her male interlocutors. She was reluctant to write her autobiography, but spurred on by her family she finally relented. In the course of my dealings with her I experienced a whole range of moods: arrogance, self-doubt – which was never convincing – and homeliness.

My friend Rinna Samuel, public relations officer at the Weizmann Institute and at that time married to a distinguished biochemist who was the grandson of Herbert Samuel, agreed to work with Golda on her autobiography. Rinna had a hard time pinning her down. Many an appointment was broken, and those recording sessions which did take place often began with a violent outburst from Golda, who would exclaim, 'I need this book like a hole in my head. I hate indiscretion, I hate memoirs. Why don't you go away and find another subject?' And Rinna would be curtly dismissed. But by some extraordinary combination of diligent research and intuition she produced a manuscript which was so authentic and touching that it became an international bestseller. It was published after Golda's retirement from office. She was fêted in Paris, London and New York and her life story was televised and made into a musical.

I used to go and see Golda in her small house in Tel Aviv. She would brew me a cup of tea and then launch into fascinating monologues about Israel's ubiquitous enemies and her frail friends, chain-smoking all the while. She had a comic touch and would mimic some of the international leaders she had met, savaging them with her caustic tongue. Her stories about the Yom Kippur War always included a paean for the resolute Richard Nixon, of whom she said, 'He was the best friend we ever had, his word could always be trusted.' She was more guarded and slightly patronizing about Henry Kissinger, and contemptuous of 'the Europeans', though she was appreciative of Harold Wilson's friendliness towards Israel. Once – it must have been shortly before her resignation in 1974 – I called on her at the recently built prime minister's office. Golda caught me eyeing an object more in keeping with the office of a British colonial governor: a large stuffed tiger which looked as though it were ready to pounce. 'That's a present from the Kurdish leader Barzani,' she said with a mixture of irony and pride. Then, raising her voice and wagging a finger at me, she launched into a tirade: 'Tell your friend Harold Wilson that if he is so concerned about human rights, the British should do more for the wretched Kurds in Iraq.' Her government had been dropping arms to the Kurds by night, and she was incensed at the lack of support from the West. A relief map of the Middle East showing tiny Israel surrounded by inimical states had pride of place on the wall of Golda's new office. Pointing to it, she raised her eyes to the ceiling, shook her head and muttered, 'What a neighbourhood to live in.'

Golda could be harsh, even vindictive. As a loyalist of the Labour

Party who dominated the caucus in Tel Aviv, she never forgave those who split from the Party, and always held it against Dayan, Peres and Teddy Kollek that they had joined forces with Ben-Gurion to set up the Rafi Party. Although she worked with some of them in various constellations, and indeed valued their qualities, she never condoned what she considered to be a betrayal. Her most trusted colleague was Yigal Allon, that kindly but shrewd dreamer, who was Deputy Prime Minister and Foreign Minister. He had grown in stature since the early days when I first knew him. During the first new wave of Russian immigration there was a heady moment when he took me to the airport to greet a group of Georgian Jews. We shook hands with bearded grandfathers in colourful oriental garb, sturdy men with fiery moustaches. I particularly remember a graceful, dark-haired girl with gazelle eyes carrying a cello case as her baby brothers clung to her quilted skirt.

The three-week-long war sparked off by the surprise Arab attack on the afternoon of the Day of Atonement, the holiest day in the Jewish calendar, in October 1973 was undoubtedly the most traumatic experience of Golda Meir's career. While the Six Day War represented a high point of military triumphalism, national self-perception reached a low point with the Yom Kippur War six years later. It strengthened Palestinian resistance and intensified pressure from international public opinion to make a compromise peace. In Israel, which had until then been ruled continuously by a Labour-dominated government, there were increasing doubts about the quality of leadership. Why had the country been inadequately prepared for the Syrian and Egyptian attack? The nation's doubts were compounded by a succession of scandals, and one could sense a yearning for change. Dayan lost much of his aura of invincibility, and although Golda Meir came out as the 'strongest man in the cabinet', her reputation suffered too, and she left not long afterwards to be succeeded by Yitzhak Rabin, the first *sabra* prime minister. As ambassador to Washington he had been absent during the Yom Kippur War and could not be blamed for the military disaster in the early stages. His Labour government had a tough stand. Its record was marred by the bitter feud between the Prime Minister and his Minister of Defence, Shimon Peres, who was Rabin's rival for the party leadership. It was tragic that these two statesmen should have been pitted against each other by fate.

I have always admired Rabin's analytical mind and his integrity.

I first knew him when he was posted in Washington, where his wife Leah was liked for her vivacious intelligence, a blend of her native East Prussia with a Tel-Avivian brand of humour. The Rabins were particularly successful with the Republican establishment. At a dinner party at Lally Weymouth's house in New York, the ambassador was fiercely attacked by Arthur Schlesinger, the intellectual standard bearer of Franklin Roosevelt's brand of Liberalism, for defending President Nixon's policy on Vietnam. 'You are more Republican than the President,' cried the outraged historian. A heated dialogue ensued during which the other guests held their breath. Rabin is famed for not wasting time on empty courtesies. When, after a long and tiring session at the White House, President Carter suggested that his guest might like to say hello to his daughter, Amy, Rabin is said to have declined curtly: 'I don't want to see Amy. I must make an early start tomorrow.' The story, true or apocryphal, is in stark contrast to one describing a similar situation which was related to me by Lady Bird Johnson. When her husband received the jovial Israeli premier Levy Eshkol for serious and at times tense talks, their grandchild sometimes came into the Oval Office. Eshkol would take the child into his arms, tweak its nose and whisper Yiddish terms of endearment which the Texan matron said sounded to her like 'Kuchinoo, Muchinoo'.

Rabin is very much a general's general. Over the years I have asked experts in several countries how they rated the various military leaders of Israel. Field Marshal Carver, the one-time Chief of Britain's Armed Forces, reserved a special place for Dayan among the 'Apostles of Mobility'. Two West Point generals enthused about Ariel Sharon, citing his crossing of the Suez Canal in the Yom Kippur War which turned the earlier Israeli defeat into victory. But according to the straw poll I have taken among Israeli critics, the supreme accolade belongs to Yitzhak Rabin. During the War of Independence a mixed band of ill-trained and badly equipped men, supported by a few buccaneers from various Allied armies and underground cells, fought for their existence with their backs to the sea and won. Rabin was their commander. During the Suez campaign of 1956, the so-called War of One Hundred Hours, there was much more cohesion and expertise, but victory was again determined by the daredevil initiatives of tank commanders and pilots. Rabin was Chief of Staff at the time. I remember lunching with a British general who also wrote on defence matters for one of the

Sunday newspapers. He said to me, 'You know, these Israeli tank commanders are pretty good, but they take desperate chances. They break from the pack and rush into enemy lines without cover of artillery, not to speak of infantry. Pretty foolhardy.' I told him that I had spoken to one of those tank commanders only a week before and had put the same point to him. He had answered quite calmly, 'But I was not alone. I had behind me the massed ranks of the Armies of the Night: Auschwitz, Treblinka, Buchenwald.'

It was in the eleven years between 1956 and 1967 that the Israeli Defence Force was built into the efficient precision instrument it has become. Credit is due to a team of leaders: Ezer Weizman, the architect of the Israeli Air Force, Moshe Dayan, with his pragmatic ingenuity, a number of leaders of the Tank Weapon, and gifted army educationalists who welded a culturally diversified medley of recruits into a unified force. But the most outstanding figure is that of Rabin, who performed his tasks as Chief of Operations and Chief of Staff with method and dogged determination, sparing no one, least of all himself.

The contrast between Yitzhak Rabin and Shimon Peres is great, yet their talents are complementary, and despite the implacable bitterness between them there have been times when they have sunk their differences. Peres is given to swings of mood, though optimism is predominant. An inspiring orator, he is in love with words, so much so that he can be intoxicated by an intellectual phrase and sometimes bends reality for a felicitous mode of expression. While Rabin makes tactical alliances and works with a structured team of officials, Peres favours a close-knit band of intimate collaborators. Rabin has assistants, Peres has disciples, not unlike Ben-Gurion and his 'young lions'.

As Foreign Minister during the long drawn-out peace process, which reached a climax when PLO-chief Arafat and Rabin shook hands on the lawn of the White House in September 1993, Peres benefited greatly from the talents of his two close aides, Deputy Foreign Minister Jossi Beilin and the Director-General of the Foreign Ministry, Uri Savir. They are both political risk-takers who have attracted a certain amount of jealousy. Beilin was a young lecturer at the Hebrew University of Jerusalem when he was pointed out to me as one of the best minds in the Labour Party, then in opposition. He wrote a book for us, *Government in Israel*, about the evolution of governmental structures in the new State. In a quiet, slightly whimsical manner he exudes courage and originality. Beilin is more effective with small groups of intellectuals and the politically sophisticated than he is as a public speaker. There is a good deal of suppressed fire in his make-up, but nonetheless logical argument is his forte. He has always adopted a conciliatory line on the Arab-Israeli conflict and deserves the greatest credit for initiating the Norwegian connection which led to the historic handshake in Washington. Beilin flies kites for his master by articulating daring ideas. 'What Beilin thinks today, the government will think tomorrow and the public a day later,' one of his critics once told me. The suave and charming Uri Savir, who began his career in the New York Consulate General, has become one of Israel's most consummate diplomats. He made a rapid transition from a young man dazzled by the bright lights of the world stage to a leading actor with a critical, even cynical capacity for unravelling a plot. I have worked with both of them in pursuit of the cause which has become increasingly important to Israel: rapprochement with Europe and reconciliation with the new Germany. On several occasions when Shimon and his two aides visited London, I arranged private briefings over breakfast or lunch where they could talk to leading journalists, politicians, academics or businessmen on or off the record. The trio was invariably effective and in their different ways impressed even the most hardened doubters.

The victory of the Likud Party under Menachem Begin in the 1977 election sent shock waves through the Jewish world. There had always been a strong conservative and nationalist opposition – the Likud Block, with the Herut (Freedom) Party, descendants of Jabotinsky, Irgun Zvai Leumi and the Stern Gang at its core; but these groups were regarded as the counter-establishment to the Zionist Labour establishment that had been dominant from the beginning. Their activists kept clannishly to themselves, just as their supporters in the Diaspora worked in worlds of their own. In my days in Israel it was unthinkable to be seen lunching with any of them, so great was the split between establishment and counter-establishment. The more militant stance of Begin's government, its determined expansion of Jewish settlements on the West Bank and in Gaza alienated a large proportion of liberal opinion. In Britain, for instance, the banker Sir Sigmund Warburg resigned from the board of various Israeli cultural institutions in protest, and even such loyalists as Marcus Sieff and Evelyn Rothschild made their unease known. But gradually Begin's integrity and his stature as a leader were recognized, even though many critics abhorred his policies. He accepted me despite my Weizmann connections and my friendship with the old Israeli establishment. When we first met he said to me, 'I don't care what your politics are, as long as you are a proud Jew.' My juvenile association with the Brit Trumpeldor and mutual Vienna acquaintances helped.

Early in his premiership, Begin telephoned me in London. He was with Professor Nethanyahu, the father of Yoni Nethanyahu, the hero of the Entebbe raid in July 1976. He was looking for someone to write the authorized life of his son and wondered if I could help. The professor, a scholar of mediaeval Spanish history who had at one time been political secretary to Vladimir Jabotinsky, duly called on me in London and asked me to introduce him to a number of potential biographers. On balance, he said he would prefer a non-Jew because he felt the story of his son, who commanded and died in the rescue operation, had a symbolic message for all mankind. Among the names I put forward was that of Max Hastings, who had written excellent reports on the Yom Kippur War for the *Evening Standard* extolling the heroism of the Israeli forces. He set out to write the life of the hero of Entebbe, but after a reasonably friendly start, relations between Hastings and the Nethanyahu family, especially Yoni's brother Benjamin (Bibi), now leader of the Likud opposition, soured. Hastings grew disenchanted with his subject and Bibi, a strong-willed zealot, became suspicious and hostile. Both Hastings and the Nethanyahu family felt let down, and each side complained about the other. The result was a book that pleased neither. I was in the unenviable position of being blamed by both sides, and while the episode did not prevent me from getting very friendly with Bibi Nethanyahu, it led to somewhat glacial relations between myself and Hastings, who went on to become editor of the *Daily Telegraph*

Though most of my friends in Israeli politics were in the Labour opposition, I had no difficulty in helping the Begin and Shamir governments wherever I could, for I have always believed that ours must be a broad church and that there must be room for Weizmann and Jabotinsky, for Ben-Gurion and Begin, for Dayan and Sharon in our Hall of Fame. The tough and inflexible attitude of the government made it all the more necessary to explain Israel's underlying anxieties to decision-makers and opinion-formers abroad. In New

York drawing rooms it was unfashionable to speak up for Likud policies, and in London the Labour Party and the trade unions passed one anti-Israel resolution after another. I spoke regularly on the Middle East in the House of Lords, to little avail, since only a small band of peers shared my views. Although Margaret Thatcher and her foreign policy advisor Charles Powell were distinctly sympathetic, there was still much opposition in Whitehall, where the 'Camel Corps' of Arabists at the Foreign Office set the tone. It is true that their serried ranks were thinning, largely because disillusionment had set in which led to a 'plague on both your houses' attitude towards the Arab-Israeli conflict. Nonetheless the 'Camel Corps' was still a formidable phalanx. In her memoirs, Margaret Thatcher says the Foreign Office perceived Israel as a pariah nation. But the Jewish State also had genuine friends among the staff, some of whom even prejudiced their prospects of advancement through their unequivocal support. In between the extremes there were two strata of Foreign Office functionaries – those who were genuinely even-handed, not having spent their most impressionable years serving in an Arab country, and those who were inclined to bestow furtive favours and whisper encouragement while presenting a cool façade. They reminded me of Heinrich Heine's couplet about the Berlin bourgeois who implores his socially unacceptable mistress not to acknowledge him if they happen to meet on the city's most fashionable avenue: 'Greet me not Unter den Linden!'

During his time as Foreign Secretary and Leader of the Lords in the early 1980s, Lord Carrington of course attended all debates on foreign affairs. He was often accused of bias against Israel, just as he has been mistakenly cast as the archetypal Tory aristocrat. I have always found him an open-minded observer of the manners and mores of other nations. The very fact that he was abroad on an official visit to Israel when news reached London on 31 March 1982 that the Argentine fleet was en route for the Falkland Islands testifies to his commitment. Politics apart, he struck up a rapport with Ariel Sharon, a fellow soldier and enthusiastic farmer, during that lightning visit to Israel. I spent a most agreeable weekend with Peter and Iona Carrington in Brussels when he was head of Nato, and admired the ease with which he got on with the military and civilian top brass of the alliance.

I met Yitzhak Shamir, as I had done Begin, through Yehuda Avner, the suave Manchester-born Israeli ambassador who was posted to London in 1983 and proved a most effective intermediary. Avner was a particular favourite of Prime Minister Begin, although he did not have any right-wing credentials. Begin and, even more so, Shamir were extremely wary about negotiations with the Palestinians, but both recognized that they had to make an attempt at peace sooner or later. Their attitude resembled that of an atheist embarking on a pilgrimage to Lourdes knowing that the hoped-for miracle of healing a cancer had a million-to-one chance of happening.

Shamir grew into his office. Over his long premiership he became less distant and suspicious in his manner. As an author he was a most forbearing client, and I have always been struck by his integrity. I dealt with him through his lawyer, Dan Meridor, who was appointed Minister of Justice when Shamir became Prime Minister and is probably the best mind in the Likud Party. It is an open secret that Shamir did not get on with his American and British interlocutors. He had more of a rapport with the Russians and felt he could speak to them quite openly. Once, when we were discussing the coup against Boris Yeltsin in August 1991, he surprised me by finding warm words for Rutskoi, the leader of the conspiracy. Shamir thought that the Western press had over-simplified the issues and demonized the middle-of-the-road faction who had despaired of Yeltsin's fitful political style.

The great changes in Eastern Europe during the Gorbachev years were of seminal importance to the Jewish people. With the crumbling of the Berlin Wall, the notion of European Jewry was brought to life again after five decades of suppression. Although frail and fearful after having been partly driven underground, several million Jews in the former Soviet Union or its zone of influence regained access to the Jewish communities of Western Europe. Once again there was a family of Jewish communities from Manchester to Minsk and from Berlin to Baku.

The collapse of the Soviet Empire also meant the lessening of a hostile influence in the Middle East. Syria and Iraq lost their main political ally and arms supplier. This helped to open the 'road to Damascus' in a literal sense, and led to the Washington accord of 1993 which, however hazardous the process of implementation may be, is of historic significance: for the first time Israel's immediate neighbours have conceded her right to exist. These achievements are rounded off by the Holy See recognizing that the 'wandering

Jew' has a right to sovereign rule in part of the Holy Land. Although considerable progress had been made in the doctrinal debate as a result of the Vatican Council's work in the mid-1960s, diplomatic recognition put a solemn end to a bitter feud. 'Perfidious Jewry' now became, in the Pope's own words, 'the elder brother of the Church'.

I regard the establishment of the Jewish State as one of the great miracles of the twentieth century, if not of all history. It is the 'Miracle of the Twelve Hundred Days' because that was the time that lay between the day when Auschwitz emitted the last fumes of death and the day when Yigael Allon reached the Suez Canal in the War of Independence and asked Ben-Gurion, 'What shall I do next?' The passage from total humiliation and near-extinction to the triumphant reassertion of strength and patriotism represents the vindication of a dream which I am proud to have witnessed.

CHAPTER TWENTY

Building Bridges

A MAIDEN SPEECH, I was told, when I took my seat on the Labour benches of the House of Lords in the latter half of 1976, must not exceed thirteen minutes or be too controversial. Having decided to make international affairs, particularly the Middle East and Europe, my subject, I picked a fairly anodyne topic of voluntary youth services in Europe and the need for education in a transnational spirit, and was acknowledged with the customary 'Hear, Hear' attendant on the maiden speaker. Such is the courtesy shown to a novice that a noble Lord speaking before him might get up and apologize for not being able to stay for the maiden speech, but tell the House that he was sure that the peer would make 'a most notable and impressive contribution and be heard often in the future'. I received a number of congratulatory notes from colleagues and strangers, including some charming lines from Roy Jenkins who noticed that I had introduced a Wagnerian theme when I compared the Bundesbank to the Nibelungs sitting on the Rhinegold. The House of Lords was altogether a friendly and welcoming place. Lady Llewellyn Davies, the government Chief Whip, was like a benign headmistress, and Lord Goronwy Roberts, the equally amiable Welsh front bench spokesman on Foreign Affairs, was always available for avuncular advice. Grey Gowrie, the Conservative Leader of the Lords, a versatile politician, literary critic and art connoisseur, went out of his way to guide me through the labyrinthine ways of the Lords.

I took infinite trouble with two longer speeches, each lasting nearly half an hour. One dealt with East–West relations and their impact on the Middle East and the other was in a debate on Foreign Office reform based on the controversial Berrill report which had been commissioned as a result of a Downing Street Think Tank

Inquiry. The report lashed out against the style and ethos of the Foreign Service which it typecast rather oddly as being too middle class. It argued that too much was spent on formal entertainment, that the embassies, notably the Paris embassy, were too grand and that since prime ministers and foreign secretaries dealt with all diplomatic issues, our missions abroad should concentrate on promoting Britain's trade interests. Like many others I was deeply critical of the report because I hold the view that but for the less than even-handed treatment of Israel, the intellectual calibre and integrity of the British Foreign Service is second to none, that it is underfunded rather than extravagant and that it is unfairly exposed to the gibes of the populist press. Mystified by the label 'middle-class' I asked, 'is middle class meant as a term of opprobrium? Is this meant as a patrician slap from above or a plebeian kick from below?' Peter Jay, then ambassador in Washington, sent an approving letter and a former head of the Foreign Office stood me my first drink at the Bishop's Bar. After my contribution on East–West relations in a debate following the Queen's Speech, George Brown, the ennobled former Foreign Secretary, bellowed at me, 'the first half of your speech on Russia was first class, the second half on the bloody Jews and Arabs was utter rubbish.'

My allegiance to the Labour Party was badly shaken by its internal turbulences, the growing influence of the left wing, its anti-European policies and a notable shift both in the Parliamentary Party and in the Trade Union movement from a sympathetic to an increasingly critical, if not outright hostile attitude to Israel. This trend was compounded by the election of Begin's Likud Party which made it more difficult for Israel's supporters to enlist the sympathies of the British Left. When Margaret Thatcher became Prime Minister in 1979 she gave unmistakable signs of friendship towards Israel and showed an understanding of its predicaments and needs.

As long as Harold Wilson was Leader of the Party I felt loyalty bound to stay within its ranks. When the 'Gang of Four', Roy Jenkins, Shirley Williams, David Owen and William Rodgers, all of whom I knew and respected, left Labour early in 1981 and formed the Social Democratic Party, I threw in my lot with them in the heady days when we all thought we could change the face of British politics. Since there were rather few of us on the SDP benches I added Broadcasting and the Arts to my brief, but continued to speak on foreign affairs, sometimes clashing with Lord

Kennet, once a junior Labour minister turned committed Social Democrat. Although an old friend as well as being a Weidenfeld & Nicolson author, he stood up for the Arab cause and was more critical of Reagan's America than I was prepared to be. I attended party conferences in Derby and Buxton and formed the Social Democrat Friends of Israel with the Duke of Devonshire, who had moved from the Tory benches, as President.

My relations with Andrew Devonshire were not affected by the rift between myself and his wife's family over David Pryce-Jones's biography of her sister Unity Mitford. The Mitford family won notoriety for the sympathies some of its members had with the Nazis, ranging from amused benevolence on the part of the parents, Lord and Lady Redesdale, to the partisan attachment of their daughter Diana and her husband Oswald Mosley and, in Unity's case, fanatical devotion to Hitler. David wanted to write the book. Since he spoke German and knew the nuances of that particular strand of Germanophilia among the British upper class, he seemed the ideal author. When word got around that he was working on the book, pressure was brought to bear on us by friends of the Mitford sisters to abandon the project. It began subtly and rose to a crescendo of threats and accusations suggesting that David was betraying his class and I my adopted country. Lord Lambton, whose hospitality I had often enjoyed, issued a stern warning couched in terms more sorrowful than angry, while Ann Fleming urged me not to open old wounds and hinted that I would be putting my social position at risk. Late one night my old friend, the effervescent and talented Lindy Marchioness of Dufferin and Ava, rang me in a perturbed state. She was staying in a country house where the assembled party felt that I should desist from a project which would cause so much unhappiness to Unity's sisters. 'After what we've all done for you, this is quite unworthy of you, George', she said. The idea that I should stop a serious work of biography dealing with an unhappy episode of recent history which illustrates how there were those in Britain who not only appeased, but openly embraced Nazi Germany, made me very angry. There was no question of my giving in. When the book came out both David and I received hate mail and ugly telephone calls. Anthony Lambton blasted me with ill-tempered abuse in an article he wrote for the *Spectator*. He also circulated manuscript copies of a novel he had written in which the villain is a young German Jew who works as tutor to a Bavarian prince during the Nazi regime. Detested by his pupil, the tutor worms his way into the affections of the lady of the house who protects him against Goebbels, who had met the Jewish tutor at a family lunch and obviously disliked him, enables him to emigrate to England where he makes a career and marries. The book ends with the couple being killed in a bomb attack by Palestinian terrorists. The tutor and his wife are thinly disguised parodies of Grace Dudley and myself. The novel was never published.

The fate of that great experiment in breaking the mould of British politics by establishing a Third Party is well known. The incompatibility of David Owen with Roy Jenkins and David Steel tore the movement asunder. When it came to making a choice between merging with David Steel's Liberals or carrying on under the SDP banner, I opted for the SDP and David Owen. It was not an easy choice, for I had known Roy Jenkins far better than I did the embattled Dr Owen. But I had a strong sense of loyalty to the Social Democrat label which harked back to my youth in Vienna. Besides, I felt uneasy about the Liberal front bench and the ambience among the grass roots. The Liberal foreign affairs and defence spokesman, Christopher Mayhew, a formidable orator, was to me the Arab Lobby personified, but though we crossed swords in debates on the Middle East, our personal relations were never unfriendly. Shortly after the historic handshake between Rabin and Arafat on the lawn of the White House we debated the subject at Winchester College in what seemed to me a courteous and conciliatory spirit.

The mutual antipathy of Jenkins and Owen is, in my view, one of the most tragic factors of postwar British politics, for both of them are outstanding figures of the 'militant middle'. In all my dealings with Jenkins I have always found him friendly, but aloof, helpful and wary at the same time. Our paths have crossed in various spheres, not least because we share many friends. In contrast, David Owen and I had had few points of contact on a personal level. I was attracted by his candour. He often came alone for breakfast or drinks and spoke openly about his hopes and fears. In hindsight he could have mended the rift and emerged as the leader of a powerful centre block in British politics but for his streak of unbending self-absorption.

When the SDP disintegrated, I moved to the cross-benches in the

House of Lords and have never regretted my choice, for it gave me the freedom to endorse or attack both government and opposition policies and champion my causes as an Independent. I continued to work for Anglo–Israeli friendship by chairing an All Party House of Lords Group of Friends of Israel and liaised with Marcus Sieff, whose wife Lily shared his deep political commitment. The esteem in which he was held was expressed by James Callaghan when he offered Marcus the Embassy in Tel Aviv, a position he refused. Margaret Thatcher also looked to Marcus for advice. Besides Marcus, the activist with whom I have become most involved in recent years is Sir Trevor Chinn, a forceful, almost obsessively devoted communal leader, animator, fund raiser and sophisticated lobbyist.

We worked in close association with the Israeli Embassy, whose various heads of mission in the Thatcher and post-Thatcher era have been proof of the high calibre of Israel's Foreign Service. Shlomo Argov was an excellent communicator. The attempt on his life outside the Dorchester Hotel in June 1982, which left him a permanent invalid, sparked the ignition for Begin's military drive into Lebanon. I saw Argov the very morning of the shooting and then, weeks later, sat at his bedside in Jerusalem's Hadassah Hospital. His successor, Yehuda Avner, had Begin's ear and was very helpful to me in maintaining friendly relations with the Likud government in spite of differences on policy. Avner was followed by Yoav Biran, a more retiring man, but a meticulous reporter who won respect in Whitehall. Since Moshe Raviv served twice in London before becoming ambassador in 1993 I have had the closest relations with him. A self-effacing, discreet professional, Raviv is an eloquent advocate of the peace process. In 1994 he arranged for me to lead a delegation of four peers to Israel. They were the lively and pugnacious Lady O'Cathain, the head of the Barbican Centre in London, the fiery Lord Morris of Castle Morris, a former principal of St David's University College in Lampeter who used to chair the Museums and Galleries Commission, and my old friend the philospher Anthony Quinton, a former President of Trinity College, Oxford, who steered the board of the British Library through stormy times. We not only met the Israeli leaders Rabin, Peres and Teddy Kollek but also the formidable PLO-spokeswoman Hannan Ashrawi and three other Palestinian notables. The group delivered a positive report, though they expressed some disappointment in the rather one-sidedly pro-Arab attitude of the British Consul General in East Jerusalem, who admittedly has one of the most sensitive assignments of any diplomat.

As a cross-bencher in Thatcherite Britain it was easy for me to support some government policies while distancing myself from others. I admired the Prime Minister's dynamic will for change, her unshakeable faith in the Western alliance, her resolute stand against Communism and was moved by her genuine sympathy with Jews and the State of Israel. She felt deeply about Russian Jews and spoke to me warmly about the memoirs of Anatoly Sharanksi, which we had published and whom she had met. But on Europe, on her ungenenerous attitude towards the arts and education, especially the universities, I found myself very much in opposition. Although I met Margaret Thatcher on innumerable occasions, our conversations never lasted more than a few minutes, but I knew a good many of her close entourage. Charles Powell, her influential foreign affairs advisor, became a valued friend who was always ready to help in any way he could. He has a first rate intellect and is a brilliant debater, a skill he has displayed at conferences I organized. Undeterred by finding himself in a minority of one on European issues, he puts his case more eloquently than anyone else in that camp. While Charles is reserved and punctilious, his Italian wife Carla is an elemental force. Outspoken, uninhibited and often unconsciously funny, she is a generous hostess with a gift for assembling the most colourful and unlikely mixture of guests around her table and making the mixture work.

Throughout the Thatcher years Edward Heath was obsessed with the person and the policies of the woman who had ousted him from the party leadership. This veritable *odium theologicum* dominated his conversation. One year when I was staying with the film producer Sam Spiegel in Barbados, we discovered that Heath was hibernating alone at the nearby Sandy Lane Hotel. We invited him over and he struck up a friendship with Sam, spending the rest of the holiday with him. No cue was too irrelevant for him to bring Margaret Thatcher into the conversation. When our host complained that the postal services in the Caribbean were inefficient, Heath would cry, 'you wait, and it will be even worse in England under *her*.' When Marietta Tree, who was also staying, was called to the telephone and returned to report that Roy Jenkins would be coming to New York the following weekend, Heath snapped, 'he'd better stay at home and not leave Margaret Thatcher without an opposition.'

Sam Spiegel was a protean figure who straddled a dozen worlds and combined within himself the sentimental Polish Jew of Habsburg coinage, an intellectual and artist manqué, the tough deal maker, inspired impresario and cinema mogul. He was a universal uncle, though to women, whose threshold of amorous susceptibility he probed as a matter of course, he was more of a Svengali. A provider of lavish hospitality on land and sea, he coralled friends, acquaintances and near strangers from every segment of his multifaceted life. When he was cruising on his yacht Sam used to stay in port for long periods. He made the most bizarre local contacts. It might be the owner of a bar in St. Tropez who played for high stakes at gin rummy and was known as 'the Japanese' because he wore a kimono day and night. In Monte Carlo or Palma de Majorca an elderly lady might come aboard, bringing a starlet for an audition. For all his libertinage and hedonism, Sam Spiegel was generous to talented young people and charitable causes. He left his valuable collection of Impressionist and twentieth-century masters to the Israel Museum in Jerusalem in memory of the members of his family who had perished in the Holocaust.

The twin causes of reconciliation between Jews and Christians, especially the Roman Catholic Church, and between Jews and Germans have preoccupied me for many years. My interest was spurred by travels and conversations in Europe during the first decade after the war, when I tried to understand the many conflicting experiences and emotions which the Nazi years had left me with. The bitter memories of childhood, forced emigration, rejection and the grief and horror over the Holocaust made it difficult to be balanced and avoid wholesale condemnation of what I perceived to be the two mainsprings of anti-Semitism: the Catholic Church and Germany. A growing awareness of their sufferings from tyranny and bigotry, the dilemmas of daily life under totalitarian rule and contacts with Catholics and Germans anxious to promote friendship with the Jews swayed my judgement. Furthermore, the emergence of Israel as the home for the Wandering Jew had brought a psychological change in creating a sound basis for a new relationship. In Vienna the historian Friedrich Heer and the publisher Fritz Molden intro-

duced me to Catholic writers and journalists who had worked in
the resistance against Hitler or, in the case of the younger ones,
stood up for inter-faith friendship and a new beginning. Under
Pope John XXIII those currents within the Church which favoured
theological and political change and found their expression in the
Vatican Council were personified by Cardinal Koenig, Archbishop
of Vienna and a wise and inspiring bridge builder.

When the Waldheim affair burst into the open in the 1980s it
threw an adverse light on Austria's failure to admit the degree to
which its people had condoned Hitler and its wholly inadequate
compensation of the victims of Nazism. I had several discussions
with the Austrian Chancellor Franz Vranitzky, the Foreign Minister
Alois Mock and the Minister of Higher Education, Erhard Busek,
a cultured and humane Catholic of progressive views, who was
particularly eager to repair the damage. One of the suggestions I
made was to bring together leading Christian and Jewish thinkers,
lay and religious, for discussions on how public opinion could be
made more aware of the changes initiated by the Second Vatican
Council of the 1960s. What could be done to make news of this
progress percolate to the Tyrolean priest, the Irish school teacher
or the Spanish parish journalist? The Austrian government agreed
to allow me to organize a conference on the theme of 'Jews and
Christians in a Pluralistic World' in the Vienna Hofburg with Cardinal Koenig as the co-convenor. I prepared it in close cooperation
with Sir Sigmund Sternberg, the Anglo-Jewish businessman who,
as chairman of the International Council of Christians and Jews,
has devoted his life to ecumenical causes with stubborn single-
mindedness. He enlisted the help of a number of American and
European clergy, Lord Coggan, the former Archbishop of Canterbury among them. I invited the Islamic scholar Bernard Lewis and
Conor Cruise O'Brien, the brilliant Irish writer and political commentator.

Cardinal Koenig referred me to Krzysztof Michalski, director of
the Institute for Human Sciences in Vienna, which bore the organiz-
ational burden. A former philosphy don at Warsaw University,
Michalski had come to the attention of his fellow philosopher Karol
Wojtyla, later Pope John Paul II, with his translation of some of
Martin Heidegger's writings into Polish. Michalski drew on his
excellent contacts with intellectuals from Central and Eastern
Europe to set up a Viennese institute of advanced studies in the

early 1980s, encouraged by the Pope and helped by Monsignor Jozef Tischner, a Catholic priest and professor of philosophy in Cracow, who also worked on the history of the theatre and the nexus between drama and religion. In a clergy riven by doctrinal and political feuds, Tischner, an old friend of the Pope, preserved an independent and thoroughly ecumenical line. The purpose of Michalski's institute was to enable philosophers, political scientists, and historians from Eastern Europe, mostly dissidents, to meet Western colleagues, conduct research and hold conferences and seminars. Some of the early associates such as Bronislav Geremek and Adam Michnik became prominent leaders in the struggle against Communism in Poland.

One of the institute's most interesting activities was to organize occasional seminars at the Pope's summer residence in Castel Gandolfo outside Rome. In August 1990 I was first invited to take part in one such conference on political and philosophical questions related to the major currents of our time, and four years later I was there once again. The group of about two dozen participants, sometimes extended by guests from the Vatican or the odd member of Rome's 'black aristocracy' who drop in and listen quietly, convenes around a table in a rather bare room adorned only by a terracotta bust of John XXIII and one or two religious paintings. There is an aura of calm austerity. Clad in a white soutane with a gold crucifix around his neck, the Pope sits impassively at a small table set apart. But when mingling with his guests during the coffee break he makes pertinent comments which show that he has followed the proceedings attentively. The Pope invites participants to lunch and dinner in groups of six or eight. When it came to my turn, at the 1990 meeting, I lunched with a group that included the lively and witty Cardinal Poupard of Toulouse, whose assignments in the curia are in the field of communication. We were served simple and good Central European fare. Before lunch the nuns who look after the Pope offered us vodka and pretzels. The meal itself consisted of a first course of charcuterie followed by a hefty portion of Wienerschnitzel and an assortment of cheese, but there was no coffee. My neighbour, a high dignitary from the curia, must have noticed a certain sense of deprivation, for he whispered: 'Our pontiff has offered pretzels and vodka, but no coffee. Paul VI would have offered coffee, but no pretzels or vodka.'

In that summer of 1990 Poland was in a state of high tension.

The Solidarity movement had to decide whether or not to enter the government and was split on the isssue. Geremek and Michnik, two of the most eminent voices within the movement, were at Castel Gandolfo and must have discreetly sought the Pope's advice. It was also the summer when the feud over a temporary convent for Carmelite nuns on the grounds of the former extermination camp at Auschwitz flared up into a passionate dispute between the Polish Catholic clergy and Jewish opinion world wide, threatening to undo much good work between Christians and Jews. The Polish Church under its Primate Cardinal Glemp brooked no interference from abroad. Feelings were running high and at one point American–Jewish activists dressed as concentration camp inmates demonstrated outside the parameters of Auschwitz. Two participants at the Castel Gandolfo conference, Prince Karl von Schwarzenberg, who was working closely with Vaclav Havel and Bernard Lewis, both old friends of mine, urged the Polish contingent to use all their influence to settle the dispute. A solution was finally found: the Carmelite nuns were to move beyond the Auschwitz complex, which the Jews wanted to keep untouched as a constant memorial to the Holocaust, and German bishops promised to erect a memorial to the dead at a respectful distance from the scene of carnage. The question then arose as to who in the Jewish camp should be the recipient of this message from the Polish Church, for the Vatican had not yet recognized the State of Israel. After some discussions in London it was decided to send a letter to the International Council of Christians and Jews in answer to a forthright but courteous letter its chairman, Sir Sigmund Sternberg had written to Cardinal Glemp, pointing out the profound Jewish objections to the convent on theological as well psychological grounds.

The patient efforts of those who were intent on achieving closer relations between the two faiths were often encumbered by apathy and bigoted hostility. But they bore fruit when in December 1993 the Vatican and Israel agreed to exchange ambassadors. The normalization of relations between the Holy See and the Jewish State, formalized by an accord signed in June 1994, was as important in the secular field as the series of positive theological changes which came about in the years of John XXIII and Paul VI. On my second visit to Castel Gandolfo in August 1994 the Pope acknowledged with satisfaction the improvement of Jewish–Catholic relations and had warm words for the continuity of the Jewish people's collective memory throughout its long history. Although he showed the strain of his recent illness he was full of plans for future travels and expressed the hope that he would one day visit Jerusalem.

The gradual thaw in relations between Christians and Jews was matched by events elsewhere. The advent of Gorbachev and the impact of Glasnost and Perestroika on the peoples and governments of Communist Europe, the resurfacing of old political patterns and ideas, moved me deeply and spurred me to travel widely in those countries. I visited Russia during the twilight period of the old regime. My friendship with Krzysztof Michalski brought me into close contact with outstanding leaders of the Polish resistance and in Prague Karl Schwarzenberg and Diana Phipps introduced me to the circle around the playwright turned president, Vaclav Havel. In September 1991 I accompanied Olga Havel and Diana to Jerusalem, where the president's wife wanted to study Israel's system of voluntary work, especially in the field of health. Karl Schwarzenberg, who moved from Austria to his native land, had actively supported Czech dissidents for years. I once visited him at his ancestral castle in Franconia where a whole wing was given over to a printing and publishing office for the Czech underground. When Havel became the first democratic president of Czechoslovakia after forty-one years of Communism, Prince Schwarzenberg worked as his 'Chancellor', the ancient Bohemian title for the chief-of-staff to a ruling figure.

The 'velvet revolution' in Prague was in full swing when I dined with Diana Phipps and some of the leading spirits of the new regime in a traditional tavern at the foot of the hill leading to Haradçany Castle, the seat of government. The heady air of liberation was marred by a cloud of uncertainty and the mood was a strange mixture of ebullience and moroseness. A youthful minister said to me wistfully: 'I have a hundred-and-fifty senior civil servants in my department and I know that half of them have worked and probably still work for the KGB, but I don't know which half.' He continued: 'They are all trained people. If I have to start all over again, where do I find new young professionals?' He spoke with bitterness about the sorry state of the universities, where some of the best teachers had been banned and forced to become window-cleaners, garage hands and shop keepers. In those disciplines of the humanities which had been contaminated by Marxist–Leninist directives, there was nobody to train a new generation of public servants or business managers. In Warsaw and in Budapest I heard similar, albeit less shrill, complaints. Amid a a furious controversy over the influence of the secret police in universities, the Humboldt University in East Berlin and many another venerable alma mater of the former German Democratic Republic were faced with the same moral dilemma as to how far the purges should go. I heard many tales from lecturers and students which all threw a glaring light on the arid academic and intellectual scene.

In London I discussed my experiences with Sir Ronald Grierson, a friend and confidant with invaluable contacts in the world of philanthropy who was for more than twenty-five years a director of Weidenfeld & Nicolson. When he was Chairman of the South Bank in London, he had invited me to serve on his board and I had seen at first hand how he operated as an almost miraculously successful fund-raiser. Ronnie had recently become involved with the Campaign for Oxford, an initiative launched to secure the financial future of the University. I proposed an idea to him which we developed and then presented to Lord Jenkins, the Chancellor of the University, having first tried it on the outgoing Vice-Chancellor, Sir Patrick Neill. We had in mind an Institute of European Studies at Oxford, where graduate students from Eastern and Western Europe would be trained for positions of leadership in law, politics, diplomacy, public administration and business in a pan-European spirit, drawing on the tutorial system of that great humanist university and creating new resources. The institute was to be the first of an open-ended network of like-minded centres of learning in other European countries aimed at helping to ease the transition from an authoritarian to a civil society in former Communist countries. I suggested the name *Europaeum* for this network.

Oxford accepted the idea and proceeded to set up the Institute with unexpected speed and genuine enthusiasm. Under the leadership of the new Vice-Chancellor, Sir Richard Southwood, an eminent scientist and subtle university diplomat, a framework was set up in Oxford supported by a board of management combining academics, benefactors and volunteers and chaired by Hans-Adam, reigning Prince of Liechtenstein. The Chancellor and the Vice-Chancellor represented the apex of the University, Sir Claus Moser,

then Warden of Wadham College and a versatile enthusiast straddling the worlds of education and music, the political scientist Peter
Pulzer, and John Woodhouse, who holds the Chair of Italian Literature, completed the academic component. Ronald Grierson and I
were also co-opted, so was my friend Gert-Rudolf Flick, one of the
first benefactors. He established a Chair for European Thought
combining philosophy, politics and culture from the Enlightenment
to the present – an innovation at Oxford. John Burrow, joint editor
of the Yale History of Europe, became the first incumbent. Sir Isaiah
Berlin's sage advice on filling this particular post, as indeed on the
whole direction of the Europaeum, was invaluable. Our frequent
lunches in the most diverse ethnic eating places in Soho, where we
were sometimes joined by his wife, the lovably distinguished Aline,
and Annabelle, were as productive as they were entertaining.

The Oxford Institute of European Studies admitted its first students in 1992. It has two streams of teaching: a law centre specializing in European Community Law and a multi-disciplinary centre
for social sciences, history, the environment and politics. Two new
degrees, the Magister juris and the Magister philosophae and the
necessary professorial posts were established. Jack Hayward, Dean
of Social Studies at Hull University and a Fellow of the British
Academy, became the first Professorial Director and was particularly involved with the M. Phil course. I took great pleasure in
funding a Visiting Professorship of Comparative European Literature, which was awarded to George Steiner, whose work spans the
worlds of literature, history and philosophy. Born into an Austro-
Czech milieu, educated in France, Britain and the United States, he
seemed an ideal choice. I have heard him speak brilliantly in four
languages and I believe he reads another four with ease. The
Weidenfeld Visiting Professorship is anchored at St Anne's College,
whose Principal Ruth Deech is also of Austrian origin; in fact, in
my student days in Vienna I had known her father who later wrote
a thoughtful biography of Theodor Herzl, the founder of Zionism.
As one who was unable to finish his studies because of Hitler's
annexation of Austria, the Honorary Master's Degree awarded to
me by Oxford and the Honorary Fellowships to which I was elected
by two colleges, St Peter's and St Anne's, probably mean more to
me than any honours I have received.

Our next step in the Europaeum was to build up the network.
The University of Leiden, which aleady had close links with Oxford,

was the first to sign up. The instant response of the Leiden teaching body was matched by the enthusiasm of the graduate student body, one of whose members, Prince Constantine, second son of the Queen of the Netherlands – plain Mr von Orange to his fellow students – played an important part in arranging the first student conference of the Europaeum in the summer of 1994. The second partner to join was the University of Bonn which enjoys a particularly high reputation in the fields of politial science and contemporary history. The Rector Magnificus, Max Huber, a physicist, showed singular drive and zeal in cementing the link with Oxford. German leaders were particularly receptive to the Europaeum idea and helped open doors. Bologna University has also joined the venture and others are sure to follow. Beyond the inner circle of old-established universities affiliations with an outer circle of academic institutes are envisaged. If more exchanges, seminars and ever closer personal contact can bring about an *esprit de corps* among those who might occupy positions of leadership in the various countries involved, the Europaeum will have made a contribution to the 'deepening' and 'widening' of Europe. Jean Monnet is reported to have said shortly before his death that were he to embark on the European enterprise all over again he would begin with culture and education rather than with coal and steel. Whatever the authenticity of that remark, the advent of a new generation of Europeans who can achieve understanding and compassion through knowledge must be the loftiest of ideals.

In some respects my involvement with Oxford and the Europaeum is a continuation of what I tried to achieve with the journal *Contact* all those years ago, for I have always been committed to strengthening the cultural ties within Europe. In the maelstrom of events following the collapse of Communism, which opened up so many possibilities, Germany has been the central focus. How would the two newly unified Germanies fit into a changing Europe? On the many visits I paid to Dresden, Leipzig, Weimar, Berlin – not to mention the cities in the former West – I listened attentively to the seemingly endless discussions about Germany's identity and role and felt the pulse of public opinion. The first attempt to bring German and non-German academics and publicists together to focus on the German condition at the conference on the Historikerstreit, which the Wheatland Foundation held at Leeds Castle, Kent in September 1987, proved so successful that I decided to repeat the format. Since then I have convened an annual Berlin Colloquium with the patronage of Hubert Burda, the Axel Springer Foundation and the trust set up by Martin Landau, a British businessman who has been a friend for over thirty years.

As a Jew, a British citizen and a European I became convinced that friendship with the new Germany and a fair appraisal of its success in establishing a fully functioning democracy after the traumas of the Hitler years was a key issue. Initially I had shared the unease of so many of my fellow fugitives from Nazi rule when they first set foot on their native soil. It took me many trips and countless heart-searching talks to come to terms with my feelings, but I was increasingly impressed by the deep change, especially among the younger generation. When I was awarded the German Order of Merit on the occasion of my seventieth birthday I took my eldest grandson Benjamin, then aged ten, to the presentation ceremony at the German Embassy. I wanted him to hear the ambassador, Baron Hermann von Richthofen, talk reassuringly about his country's resolve to reforge links so cruelly broken by Hitler.

On 28 November 1989 Helmut Kohl made a speech setting out a ten-point plan for German unification. Abroad some reacted with stunned disbelief, others were outright hostile. Believing that a united Germany would play a major role in building bridges between West and East I published an article in *The Times* some weeks later, which was reprinted in the German Sunday newspaper *Welt am Sonntag*, welcoming the Chancellor's speech. The first and last paragraphs express my feelings:

'The colourful presence of the Royal Welch Fusiliers, with their regimental goat, Billy, at the opening of the Brandenburg Gate on December 22 was a much more positive endorsement of German unity than the sweet-sour ambiguities from the chancelleries of Europe, including, of course, Downing Street.

'By the middle of the 1990s the Federal Republic, barring unforeseen events, will have completed half a century of a civil society built by enlightened men. If, then, unity were to crown this achievement, moderation must be seen to triumph. After the First World War, had Britain and France shown a fraction of the compassionate understanding to such moderate men as Rathenau, Stresemann or

Brüning which they later lavished on Papen, Ribbentrop and Hitler, we might have been spared a Third Reich and a Second World War. Those who still have a nightmarish vision of a Fourth Reich might banish their fears and put their trust in the enduring continuity of the moral standards set by such human pragmatists as Adenauer and Heuss, Brandt and Weizsäcker, and in the younger generation of Germans of goodwill.'

Shortly afterwards I received a letter from Chancellor Kohl expressing his thanks. Through Hermann von Richthofen, an indefatigable bridge-builder, I was invited to lunch with Kohl at the so-called Chancellor's Bungalow, the Bonn equivalent of 10 Downing Street, in July 1990. I had met him briefly in March of that year at the Königswinter Conference in Cambridge where Sir Oliver Wright, a former ambassador to Bonn, had acted as a buffer between Kohl and Margaret Thatcher at the formal dinner to celebrate the fortieth anniversary of the annual Anglo-German meeting. None failed to notice that the British Prime Minister and the German Chancellor had barely exchanged a word throughout the meal. Relations between them were never simple. They were marked by an amalgam of suspicion, antagonism and prejudice on her side, and irritation tinged with a sense of spurned love on his. These traits came out in the banter preceding the speeches they both made in Cambridge. When Mrs Thatcher observed that the Chancellor always spread his white napkin circumspectly around his waist, he rejoined that this was a white flag – a symbol of surrender to her.

Helmut Kohl received me with outstretched hand in a small anteroom where we chatted for a while before sitting down to a simple lunch. He put me at ease by asking me about my schooldays in Austria, we touched on the Waldheim affair and discussed mutual acquaintances in an atmosphere that was modest and informal. Kohl was a jovial host, both relaxed and concentrated. It was clear from his conversation that he is a voracious reader who keeps up to date with books of political biography and current affairs. He is proud of his training as a historian and fond of drawing analogies with previous events in European history. We soon came to the crux of our discussion: relations between Germany and European Jewry. Kohl told me of a number of initiatives under his aegis: the Jewish Museum in Berlin, the Martin Buber House near Frankfurt, the growing number of academic chairs on Jewish affairs in German universities and the reparations the newly unified country was making on behalf of the GDR, which had persistently refused to acknowledge any guilt in the persecution of the Jews under Hitler. He spoke with deep emotion about the need to strengthen the bond and referred to Jewry's vast contribution to German culture, science and the arts. It struck me forcefully that independently of any feeling of collective responsibility, shame or guilt about Germany's Nazi past, Kohl had a genuine desire to bring back something of that creative force of the Jewish *Bildungsbürgertum* (cultured bourgeoisie), a term he used several times. He was stung by critical comment, notably from Jewish leaders in America, and made it clear that he welcomed my idea of an occasional dialogue between independent Jewish personalities, drawn mainly from European countries, chaired by him or other political leaders of the new Germany. I explained my thesis that there was once again a concatenation of fate between Jews and Germans. The crumbling of the Berlin wall and the unification of Germany had created a vast clearing, ending the division between East and West so that East European Jewry could now be rebuilt as one of the three pillars on which the Jewish people stand: Israel, American Jewry and the Jews of Europe. Moreover, I continued, Germany was destined to play a constructive role, upholding human rights and leading the fight against anti-Semitism in the eastern half of Europe where there were still two or three million Jews. Kohl agreed wholeheartedly. I have vivid memories of Kohl expostulating his attitude to France and emphasizing how he wanted the new Germany to be deeply anchored in the European Community and closely linked to France. To illustrate his point he got up and rather dramatically drew open the curtains. Pointing to the Rhine a few hundred metres away he said, 'Whatever happens, whether we move from Bonn to Berlin or stay here, the Rhine is, and will remain, the chief river and not the frontier of Germany. It flows between France and us.' It was fascinating to hear the Chancellor tell of how the French needed to be treated differently. 'When I speak to any head of government, I speak as an equal', he said, 'but when I speak to Mitterrand, I always make it clear that I, a mere Chancellor of Germany, am speaking to the President of the French Republic.'

As a result of our lunch he asked Horst Teltschik, his former foreign affairs advisor who had been present at all the vital meetings with Gorbachev and Bush, Mitterrand and Thatcher during the unification process and who had recently left government service to become head of the well-endowed Bertelsmann Foundation, to organize the German–Jewish dialogue we had discussed. The first meeting was chaired by Helmut Kohl at the Chancellery in the week after the Gulf War. Teltschik had chosen the German participants and I had put together a handful of representatives of European Jewry ranging from Lord Rothschild to the Paris lawyer and Auschwitz survivor Samuel Pisar. We had an animated dinner that lasted four and half hours.

I reported back to the Israeli Embassy on these discussions and also talked to Shamir about them, remonstrating that Kohl's Ten Point Plan on German re-unification gave no cause for concern. I was invited to present my case at a conference of Israeli ambassadors and information officers, including those designated to take up posts in the newly established embassies in Central and Eastern Europe, which was held in Geneva. With cooperation from both sides there has been a notable upswing in relations between Germany and Israel.

The first discussion group chaired by Helmut Kohl set the pattern for future meetings. They begin with an informal dinner followed by a day's meetings where members of of the German government such as the Minister for Home Affairs and the Minister for Justice, ministers from the Länder and representatives of all political parties openly discuss topics ranging from the neo-Nazis, xenophobia and immigration to attitudes to the Arab-Israeli conflict. Richard von Weizsäcker presided at one gathering in Berlin, and further meetings have been chaired by his successor Roman Herzog, then President of the German Constitutional Court, and Rita Süssmuth, President of the Bundestag. Among the Jewish participants who have attended in their personal capacities have been Sir Leon Brittan, Lord Justice Woolf, Peter Pulzer, Sir Claus Moser and Lord Mishcon from Britain, Ernst Kramer of the Axel Springer Foundation, a champion of German–Jewish relations, the sociologist Dominique Schnapper, the surgeon Adolphe Steg and Baron Eric de Rothschild from Paris, the Lord Chief Justice of Denmark, the journalist Arrigo Levi from Rome, the Israeli writer Amos Oz and Israel's former Foreign Office chief David Kimche, and from the United States the historians Richard Pipes and Fritz Stern, Lloyd Cutler who became one of President Clinton's chief aides and Martin Peretz, publisher of the Washington-based weekly *New Republic*. The small but remarkable post-war German–Jewish community was represented by its leader Ignaz Bubis, who has won the respect of the wider German public with his fearless, yet sensitive performance. Stefan Sattler, who has devoted much of his life to rekindling friendship between Jews and Germans, and Josef Joffe, one of Germany's leading political journalists, have helped me set up these meetings. Liz Mohn, whose husband heads the Bertelsmann concern, and the professor of political science Werner Weidenfeld, a namesake, but no relation, who is Teltschik's successor at the Bertelsmann Foundation and also advises the German government, take an active part. Russian, Latvian, Czech and Bulgarian speakers introduced new voices from the East, thus rounding off a truly global assembly. On each occasion both sides came away with distinct impressions: the Germans appreciated the wide spectrum of Jewish concerns and the Jewish contingent was impressed by the German desire to deepen relations. The dialogue continues.

Helmut Kohl showed his commitment once again when in February 1994 he took part in a moving celebration at the Jewish Museum in Frankfurt, formerly a house belonging to the Rothschild family, to mark the two hundred and fiftieth anniversary of the birth of Meyer Amschel, the founder of the dynasty. In front of a large gathering of the Rothschild clan from London, Paris and New York, many of whom had come to Germany for the first time since the Holocaust, the Chancellor paid tribute to the great debt of gratitude Germany owed to Jewish enterprise and cultural achievement. During the evening Charlotte de Rothschild of the English branch sang songs specially composed for various nineteenth century Rothschild ladies by Rossini, Chopin, Liszt and Meyerbeer.

All these pursuits were of course contiguous to my publishing life which saw great changes in the late 1970s. It began when I visited San Francisco in the spring of 1978 and was taken to a dinner at the Gordon Gettys. I had known Gordon's father John Paul and at his suggestion I had published the first major catalogue of the museum he founded in Malibu. At that time Claus von Bulow was his secretary and man of affairs. The Getty house in the top of Pacific Heights is a stately, Italianate building filled with exquisite eighteenth-century furniture and with a breathtaking view over the bay. On that occasion there must have been eighty to a hundred guests – out of town musical celebrities, European royalty and San Francisco society. There was music and dancing and the mood was one of festive elegance. I sat next to the hostess, Ann, at dinner and we soon found a common interest in opera. Music is the focus of the Gettys' lives. Gordon is a composer who would be more widely appreciated were it not for the Getty name, which has been more of a hindrance than a help. He has an encyclopaedic knowledge of recorded music and his record library is formidable. The Gettys are patrons of the San Francisco and Metropolitan Operas, they support orchestras and young singers and visit festivals throughout America and Europe.

On that first evening I struck up an immediate rapport with Gordon and Ann and they soon became part of my life. I dimly remembered meeting them as a very young couple at his father's house in London. John Paul Getty was estranged from his sons and Gordon had to make his own way. Ann's charm, modesty and tact were instrumental in effecting a rapprochement with the rather tyrannical patriarch. Having led relatively simple lives they assumed their new position within the Getty Trust and all the trappings of great wealth with a sense of proportion and sobriety. With his curly hair and spectacles Gordon reminded me of Franz Schubert, despite his huge frame. Earnest, thoughtful and mild-mannered, he abhors small-talk and gossip. He prefers to talk about broad issues or specific details and can hold forth with passion when a subject captivates him. Besides music he is interested in economics, abstract and applied, in fact, he has a shrewd business sense. It was he who questioned the management of Getty Oil and started an investigation, triggering a chain-reaction which ultimately led to the sale of the company. He eschews large administrations and takes decisions on who should benefit from his philanthropy personally, rather than employing legions of advisors and bureaucrats. Gordon is scrupulous in separating his philanthropy from his work as a serious composer. Many a scheming fund-raiser hoped to flatter his vanity by proposing to put on his works, only to be turned down.

Ann has a passion for learning. She likes the academic temperament and prefers the company of those who she feels can teach her something. On the whole the Gettys have avoided the danger run by the very rich of assembling byzantine courtiers. Instead Ann has a sorority of women friends of different ages and backgrounds, mostly San Franciscans, with whom she shares a variety of activities.

Anxious to find a mission in life, Ann wanted to make a working contribution to the causes she espoused. Early in our friendship we developed the idea of a foundation that would organize conferences on the performing arts, enabling artists, administrators and critics to pool their thoughts. Out of this was born the Wheatland Foundation, named after Ann's birthplace in California.

Our first venture was a symposium in Venice on the future of opera where the theme of 'producer power' was hotly debated, followed by another in Jerusalem on the future of the orchestra. In its short life-span the Wheatland Foundation also funded translations into English of contemporary works of fiction and poetry and sponsored an ambitious programme of conferences on world literature along similar lines as the Formentor Prize of a quarter of a century earlier. We convened novelists, poets, critics and publishers from all parts of the world to discuss the current literary output and monitor the moods and preoccupations of writers. Just as at the Formentor meetings the differing nuances in the appraisal of other nations' intellectual and emotional concerns were often surprising. We were fortunate in finding an able director in Rose Marie Morse, an American-educated Croatian with linguistic skills, a warm and winning personality and an almost missionary enthusiasm for writers, whom I had known since the 1960s when she was a young editor at McGraw-Hill. Among the regulars, Roberto Calasso, the Italian publisher, critic and author of the bestselling high-brow novel *The Marriage of Cadmus and Harmony*, who is a messenger of transnational literature, was particularly helpful.

The first of these literary conferences, held at the Library of Congress in April 1987, was remarkable in that it was the first time that exiled Russian writers sat on the same platform as writers from inside the Soviet Union. Although Gorbachev was already in power Glasnost was still in its infancy and Rose Marie had to use all her skill to persuade the Soviet Embassy in Washington to allow the meeting to go ahead. It was moving to see the exiles Joeseph Brodsky and Andrei Siniavsky embrace the novelist Andrei Bitov and the poet Oleg Chuknosev, just arrived from Moscow. The following year we held our conference at the Portuguese Versailles, the splendid Palace of Queluz, thanks to President Soares whom I had known in the Wilson days, when he was a frequent visitor at meetings of European social democrat leaders. Once again events in Eastern Europe provided a fiery backcloth to the discussions. The novelist

Tatiana Tolstoya, who combined mild Russian nationalism and cosmopolitan allure, sparked off a heated debate between the Russians and the Eastern Europeans about their respective priorities in the struggle for freedom. The Russians seemed to think, somewhat patronizingly, that if a civil society were restored in the Soviet Union, the Czechs and Poles, Hungarians and Balts would find that they would have no serious problems in their lands. Salman Rushdie, hot-foot from having signed a seven-figure dollar contract for the as yet unpublished *Satanic Verses*, delivered an impassioned attack on Margaret Thatcher's 'police state', consoling, as it were, his Eastern European colleagues with the thought that freedom of speech was not as self-evident in the capitalist West as they might think.

In the neo-Baroque Congress Hall of the Hungarian Academy of Science in Budapest, the scene of the third in this series of conferences, we received a sadly salutary reminder of how wide the gulf was between Arab doves and Israeli ultra-doves. After a plea from the dovish Israeli author Amos Elon for Arab and Israeli writers to seize an initiative for reconciliation, the even more dovish Israeli novelist Yoram Kaniuk, who had brought upon himself the opprobrium of the Shamir regime, began to develop this idea even more passionately. He had hardly begun speaking when Arab writers from Egypt, Qatar and Morocco demonstratively left the conference hall. Kaniuk shook his head disconsolately. Four Wheatland conferees, Octavio Paz, Joseph Brodsky, Derek Walcott and Nadine Gordimer, later received the Nobel Prize for Literature. I would like to think that these gatherings made at least a small contribution to international literary exchange and helped some writers, especially those from lands far removed from the main centres of publishing, to find outlets for their work.

Ann had always shown a special interest in literature and in publishing. She was not only thinking of a role for herself, but also of a possible career for her eldest son Peter, who had a creative imagination and was a voracious reader. I was in my sixties then and had been concerned about the succession at Weidenfeld & Nicolson for some time. I wanted to secure the future of the imprint and, if at all possible, preserve its independence, rather than merge with a large conglomerate. The idea of a partnership with Ann Getty, who would eventually be succeeded by her son, was tempting, especially since it also opened possibilities of publishing in New York. We discussed a partnership at leisure over several years and in 1985 we reached an agreement whereby Ann was to acquire a large minority stake in Weidenfeld & Nicolson London with a view to buying me out when I retired. In the interim I would go on running the British firm and help in establishing an American publishing house. We looked for a suitable small firm with a literary tradition and found it in Grove Press, a pioneer of avant garde literature in the United States. It was run by Barney Rosset, the publisher of Henry Miller, William Burroughs, Bertolt Brecht, Jean Genet, Samuel Beckett and Harold Pinter. I had had business dealings and friendly relations with Barney for as long as I could remember. He is one of the legends of the postwar cultural scene. He made a foray into the experimental film scene with *I am Curious, Yellow* and broke lances against censorship. An uncompromising fighter for his beliefs, he has a rugged, anarchic strain and can be litigious when roused. Barney agreed to sell his business to Ann and continue to run it for a few years. We also set up a Weidenfeld & Nicolson imprint in New York to reflect the spirit of the London list with its blend of biography, memoirs and that grey area between the academic and general markets. We hired Dan Green, a senior executive from Simon & Schuster, John Herman, an editor from the same firm, Aaron Asher, an experienced publisher from the Harper stable, Connie Sayre, a marketing expert and Juliet Nicolson, Nigel's daughter, who had made her mark in British publishing as a subsidiary rights executive.

It would have made sense to merge the two imprints, but there were some delicate reasons why this could not be done, for it would have meant a clash of publishing 'cultures' and Barney Rosset and the senior staff might not have acquiesced. Ann was sensitive to suspicions of bloodletting and eager to avoid provoking angry protests from Grove's literary constituency. Although we maintained the two imprints in different houses, relations with Barney deteriorated and it came to a parting of the ways. The New York literati were up in arms. They picketed the offices and wrote letters of protest to the *New York Times*, suggesting that the oil lobby was destroying the last bastion of the literary avant-garde. As a result Grove Press continued largely autonomously under the direction of Fred Jordan, a fellow Austrian with a wide range of literary contacts in Europe and a knack for discovering unknown talent.

Although I was chairman of the New York company, London

remained my anchor and, having underestimated the difficulty of operating effectively on both sides of the Atlantic, I urged Ann to engage an American publisher emeritus with sound financial judgement. Instead she chose to delegate financial responsibility to a lawyer and financial advisor in Washington, who was already laden with work for the Getty family. He also liaised between the London and New York managements and Ann herself, who could not devote all her time to publishing, for San Francisco was her home and besides her family commitments she also had increasing civic responsibilities in her state. She was nonetheless active in helping us recruit authors.

In the heady days of change Ann and I made several trips to Moscow and visited Prague and Warsaw accompanied by Rose Marie Morse. The shock of seeing the full horror of Stalinism confirmed that even the Soviet Union's sternest critics in the West had not plumbed the depths of the material and spiritual desolation of the country, a fact which hit me when we called on Colonel General Volgokonov, head of the Military History Archives at the Soviet Ministry of Defence and author of a Stalin biography for which we bought the rights. Volgokonov sat there in his uniform, surrounded by aides, the very image of a Soviet general. The Communist Party was still intact and he wore the insignia of the State. He talked volubly about the dictator and I asked him diffidently if Robert Conquest, the distinguished British Sovietologist, who also published a book on Stalin for us, had exaggerated the number of victims of the Terror. 'Exaggerated? He grossly underestimated them.' From the bottom drawer of his desk Volgokonov pulled out a grubby copy of a hand-written letter. It was a plea for clemency from one of Stalin's comrades in the civil war who had written from prison during the great purges, invoking old memories. Across the letter Stalin had scrawled: 'Shoot the dog'.

My favourite Russian recruit to our list was Arkady Vaksberg, who gave me the most honest insight into the trials and crosses of a Russian intellectual and Jew by describing his relations with the *nomenklatura* without false heroics or intemperate denunciations. A lawyer by training, he wrote for the *Literaturnaya Gazeta* and produced two books for us. One was a portrait of the sinister Andrei Vyshinsky, a renegade member of the petite noblesse who as chief prosecutor of the show trials became Stalin's most vicious handyman. The other was an investigation of the new Russian mafia, a book which broke new ground. The poet Andrey Voznesensky, whose amorous escapades were almost as well known as his lyrical work, took us under his wing, arranging lunches and dinners at the Writers' Union and in Moscow apartments and rural datchas. In July 1988 we also attended the first international art auction in Moscow. Under the blinding arc lights of the world's television companies in a huge room of the Sovincentr, Sotheby's, the largest auctioneer of the capitalist world, offered the work of avant-garde and contemporary Soviet artists to a bevy of collectors and dealers from the West. It was at the height of the boom in the world art market and at a low point of the Soviet economy. Hundreds of Russians stood and watched open-mouthed, dazzled by the five and six figure dollar bids.

My travels with Ann also took me to the Far East and South America. Under the aegis of Henry Keswick, head of Jardine Matheson, the international trading giant with roots in China and Hong Kong, we met politicians and businessmen in the colony. Henry's wife, Tessa, a beauty with a good head for politics, was with us and so was the top interior designer John Stefanides, another author and friend. A highlight of the trip was a visit to Burma which I found as beautiful as I found it eerily alien. We were entertained by the British ambassador Martin Morland, a cousin of Henry, who introduced us to Aung San Suu Kyi, the symbol of democratic resistance to the military regime who was put under house arrest shortly afterwards and later received the Nobel Prize. She was there with her husband Michael Aris, the Oxford Tibetologist. On an excursion to the north-west of the country we met Saw Sai Mong, another opposition leader whose uncle rules one of Burma's largest provinces. Through some inexplicable mix-up we arrived at a house whose owner had not expected us, but showed no flicker of surprise. He spoke perfect English and was suave and hospitable. After half an hour, when we had exchanged courtesies and exhausted general topics, it was clear that our host was not only not the man we sought, but his bitterest political enemy. Despite being related, the two men had had no contact for many years. Our host winced; however, mustering all his self-control, he telephoned his enemy and arranged for us to be collected. Saw Sai Mong was an hour's drive away and so, by now, was our driver. As we left, Henry Keswick deftly removed the bottle of whisky which we had brought as a gift and presented it to the real Saw Sai Mong.

Ann and I travelled to Argentina to see President Alfonsin and recruit writers and critics for our Wheatland Conferences. To this end I visited Brazil, where my friend Ira von Fürstenberg, Gianni Agnelli's niece, introduced me to many people she knew from when she had lived there. Ira is ebullient and beautiful. Fluent in six languages, she can entertain a stuffy banker or product of the École Normale as effectively as she can a polo champion or a disc jockey. We spent a day with Jorge Amado, the Brazilian writer, whom I had first met at the Wroclaw Congress and whose *Dona Flor* is, I think, one of the most exquisite novels we ever published.

Although Weidenfeld & Nicolson and Grove Press produced some excellent books, Arthur Miller's memoirs *Timebends*, Harold Pinter's novel *The Dwarfs* and new works by Robert Ford and Milan Kundera among them, the venture did not flourish. After four years Grove Press, having merged with Weidenfeld & Nicolson Inc., was offered for sale and eventually merged with Atlantic Monthly Press, another small and reputable literary imprint, which was re-named Atlantic Grove. Ann threw herself into research on pre-history and anthropology at Berkeley where she found a congenial circle of friends. She retained her connections with the British company and only severed them when I sold the firm to Anthony Cheetham and his partners. My friendship with Gordon and Ann survived. When Annabelle and I married in the summer of 1992 we spent part of our honeymoon on a boat the Gettys had chartered and, anchored in Barcelona harbour, we disembarked to watch the Olympic Games. On the first anniversary of our marriage we went cruising again with the Gettys, this time along the Anatolian coast of Turkey in the company of the Berkeley philosopher John Searle and other distinguished academics from that university.

On 23 October 1991 I learned through the publishing bush telegraph that Anthony Cheetham had been asked to resign as chief executive of Random Century, the British arm of America's mighty Random House, that same morning over breakfast at the Connaught Hotel. Having founded Century, taken over Hutchinson and then sold his company for a huge sum to Random House, which had meanwhile incorporated Jonathan Cape and Chatto, Cheetham had been in control of one of the largest agglomerations of publishing imprints in Britain. But there was a clash of temperament between him and his American masters which led to a sudden and acrimonious parting. I had known Cheetham from his earliest days in the trade, indeed we once had a joint paperback venture which we called Contact, reviving memories of pioneer days. Weidenfeld & Nicolson had also published his *Life and Times of Richard III* as part of our series on the Kings and Queens of England. Strongwilled and ever ready to fight his corner, he struck me as being withdrawn and private behind his worldly and charming manner. I admired his business acumen and his blend of commercial flair, gusto for innovation and reverence for good literature. When I heard of his dismissal it occurred to me that, still only in his forties, he might want to strike out on his own once again. I telephoned him to commiserate and asked him to breakfast the next morning. We met and after two hours shook hands on a deal. Within a matter of weeks Cheetham produced an impressive business plan for an enlarged company. He proposed to buy Weidenfeld & Nicolson in partnership with his wife Rosie, a highly skilled editor of fiction, and Peter Roche, his financial and managerial alter ego, leaving me as chairman of the imprint with a small share. In addition I was to be executive director of a new publishing group financed by Cheetham and investors from the City.

In June 1992 the new Orion Group was formed with Weidenfeld & Nicolson as the main imprint for non-fiction and a list of literary novels. The group also encompassed Dent and the Everyman Library which we had acquired in the 1980s. An old imprint, Phoenix House, was revived for new writing and almost immediately came up with a bestseller: Vikram Seth's monumental *A Suitable Boy*, and a new imprint, Orion Books, was created, combining popular publishing in hardcover and mass paperbacks. That resource was central to the whole concept, because the absence of a paperback outlet can prove a severe handicap for any major general publishing operation in the current scene. I felt that this was the best possible solution for the future of the firm, far preferable to my selling to a large publishing combine where our imprint would be just one of many and swingeing cuts might be the order of the day. I was also encouraged by the prospect that I would at last have more time to concentrate on causes outside the publishing sphere, while continuing with what I am happiest doing – matching authors with ideas – for as long as my energy prevails. I have made my offices at Orion House in the heart of London's theatre land and a few steps away from English National Opera and the National Portrait Gallery, on whose boards I sit, my base of operation, content in the knowledge that the imprint which Nigel Nicolson and I created would continue under a new band of enthusiasts.

Looking back on the years which had brought me to that point, I often think of the literally thousands of books we have published. It would of course be impossible, even invidious to single out individual titles from so many which have in their various ways been of significance to our firm and therefore in my life. After all, we have successfully published books which cross a spectrum from Richard Lipsey's long dominant textbook *An Introduction to Positive Economics* to the cult *Henry Root Letters*; from the works of Booker Prize-winners like J. G. Farrell to those of sporting heroes like Sir Matt Busby with whom, I am told, I managed to keep my end up in a discussion about the influences of prewar Central European football styles. It has been my good fortune that quite a few of our authors became valued friends. Paul Johnson holds a special place in my affection. His versatility and energy have never ceased to amaze me, whether as a prolific journalist and political commentator or as the author of magisterial books on such ambitious themes as the history of the Jews, of Christianity and of 'The Modern World'.

Edna O'Brien too has been a friend of many years. Like her novels and short stories, she is passionate and poetic, forthright but full of humour. Edna is overwhelmingly generous in spirit – one of nature's givers, whether speaking at a literary lunch, which she hates, or sparkling at a dinner party.

In publishing the path to success – or failure – can be a labyrinthine minefield or a short dirt track and once in a while every publisher gets stuck in the mud. High on my litany of failures was our attempt to get Mick Jagger's memoirs. Having put together a consortium of international publishers offering a handsome seven figure deal I signed him up with the help of Prince Rupert Loewenstein, a friend and one time business associate, who managed his financial affairs. Jagger chose John Ryle, a music journalist, as his literary amanuensis. Judging by his style, his temperament and his passion for the subject we all thought he would be the ideal associate. The vicissitudes of the courtship experienced by both Ryle and myself were bizarre and have induced a form of selective amnesia in me. All I can remember is a haze of exasperated telephone calls, emergency conferences, anxious reminders from the

consortium of publishers and hasty trips to various Jagger residences. In the end the project came to nothing, but Jagger honour-
ably repaid the advance.

Out of the large number of political memoirs I recall particular
satisfaction at publishing those of Cardinal Mindszenty, the Hungarian prelate who defied the Communists and stayed at the American embassy for fifteen years before he was allowed to leave in
1971. He died four years later in Vienna. We obtained the book
against worldwide competition through a personal contact of Hans-
Heinrich Coudenhove, a friend and cherished colleague of our firm,
whose uncle, Count Coudenhove-Kalergi was the founder of the
Paneuropa Movement in the 1920s.

Whenever I am asked to name one book that was an unexpected
world-wide success, I think of J.D.Watson's *The Double Helix* –
the story of how the genetic code was broken. In 1962 James Watson received the Nobel Prize for Medicine for his discoveries. His
achievements, and those of Francis Crick, whom we also published
later, are well known, but the story of how the book came about
needs re-telling. It began in the late 1960s when I received a call
from Thomas Wilson, head of the Harvard University Press and
dean of American academic publishing. He was not one for many
words. 'I've got something important for you. Please don't ask any
questions, just come over.' Next morning I flew to Boston and
called on Wilson. He closed the door and said in an emphatic stage
whisper: 'The syndics of the Harvard Press have seen fit to reject
a manuscript of epochal importance.' He gave me the gist of Jim
Watson's book and impressed on me that it ought to be published
internationally by a circuit of important publishers. 'I want you to
have it and handle it worldwide.' With Wilson's approval we
assigned the American rights to the emerging Atheneum imprint,
co-founded by my friend Mike Bessie. The book, published in 1968,
came out in twenty languages and was serialized by the *Sunday
Times* and great newspapers all over the world. *The Double Helix*
is now a classic.

In my quest for memoirs, biographies and contemporary history,
a close relationship with the press was of paramount importance.
The Sunday newspapers in Britain always had an appetite for pre-
published extracts, for which they often paid large sums of money
in the hope that they would drive the circulation up. Since I preferred to take the initiative and approach authors myself rather

than wait for manuscripts to come in via agents, I relied on the support of proprietors and editors such as Stuart Steven, who when editor of the *Mail on Sunday* was my partner in many major book projects, and Andrew Neil during his ten-year tenure at the *Sunday Times*. In many cases agents were co-operative and allowed me to make a combined serial and book publishing offer, entrusting negotiations with the newspaper to me. In other cases they insisted on handling the matter themselves. These negotiations have increasingly taken the form of an auction, but I have always preferred to deal with one potential buyer at a time. This experience gave me a certain insight into the conduct and character of the sultans and grand viziers of Fleet Street and Docklands.

Some of these relationships started in acrimony and ended harmoniously. Tom Driberg, the controversial left-wing Labour MP, notorious libertine and suspect in unresolved intelligence scandals, was the cause of an incident between myself and Lord Beaverbrook, the legendary proprietor of the *Express*. Driberg had a love-hate relationship with Beaverbrook who was known to have sacked him for his political views, but to everyone's amazement he was asked to write the authorized biography. We signed Driberg up and the book was underwritten by Express Newspapers. At first everything went smoothly. Driberg visited the old man at his country retreat and in Jamaica, but halfway through his researches whispers reached Beaverbrook that his biographer had fallen out of love with his subject and was preparing a hostile book. The Beaver, as he was known, at first subtly and then more obviously changed tune. Instead of offering lavish hospitality in the Caribbean he kept Driberg at arm's length and subjected him to wily social tortures, some of which Daisy Fellowes, a frequent guest of Beaverbrook, described to me. Tom would be put up in a second-class hotel rather than in the house; he would be asked to come at midday and made to wait for his Lordship on the terrace in the glaring sun; they would have a desultory talk and Driberg might or might not be offered a drink; the butler would ask his master, 'Will there be ten for lunch today?' to which Beaverbrook would reply, 'No, we shall be nine', making it clear that Driberg had to find his repast elsewhere.

When the manuscript finally arrived the family were aghast. Beaverbrook, who had managed to obtain the proofs after something of a tussle with us, sent them back with an enormous number of margin notes. I found it fascinating to see where his sensitivities lay. He seemed indifferent to accusations of unfair business practices and political intrigue, but any mention, however harmless, of women such as Lady Jean Norton, were queried with a view to excision and he exploded over the telephone over Driberg's account of his relations with Mountbatten and of his role in the unhappy Dieppe raid during the Second World War. Beaverbrook's son, Max Aitken, asked for an interview. We met at the Reform Club and then walked up and down Pall Mall. He urged me not publish the book which he said was 'both bad and libellous' and offered financial compensation. Naturally I declined, and after protracted negotiation between the lawyers, in which a few alterations were made by mutual consent, the book was published – and serialized in the *Daily Express* with a caption stating that the newspaper prided itself on publishing extracts from a book which, though biased and unfair, should not be withheld from the reader. It was made quite clear that the book should be considered as a betrayal of trust of a great public figure by a thankless scribe.

Thankfully, I was able to patch up relations with the Aitken family just as I did with the Berrys when Driberg landed me in trouble a second time over his book on Guy Burgess. Michael Berry was one of the most honourable men I have met. Taciturn, even melancholy, he spoke in a brisk, clipped manner and was always quick to make a decision. I valued my friendship with him and his wife, Pamela, highly and it meant a great deal to me that I was asked to write her obituary for the *Sunday Telegraph*. One of Pamela's last acts of friendship was to introduce me to John Mills and Laurence Olivier, both of whose memoirs I published in the 1980s thanks to her. John Mills was as charming off screen as he is on screen, modest, helpful and appreciative. Laurence Olivier, on the other hand, was beguilingly complicated, veering from bouts of self-doubt as a writer to Olympian self-assurance. In one of his more diffident moments he felt he needed a collaborator and so Mark Amory was engaged. One of the few remaining young throwbacks of a prewar British man of letters, Amory was knowledgeable about the theatre. He taped Olivier's narrative, but then the great man decided he wanted to write the book himself in longhand, and so he did, dispensing with Mark's services, but not with his company, for he had him around constantly.

It is well known that Robert Maxwell wrought havoc in many

people's lives and mine was no exception. I first met him during my fledgling years as a publisher when he was head of Simpkin Marshall, one of the largest book wholesalers. They folded owing us £20 000 which we could ill afford to lose. During the weeks and months before Maxwell came clean about his insolvency he made discreet soundings among his creditors to ascertain that no one was going to precipitate a public scandal. Far from suspecting the reason for his sudden interest in our business relationship, I agreed to have lunch with him in a Czech restaurant near Marble Arch, where I tried to sell him more and more books. Disguising his relief at my naivety he said, 'George, I'm going to build you up into a big publisher and give you more business than you can handle!' Satisfied that he could strike me off the danger list, he rose to leave in the middle of the meal, not without shouting to the waiter to give me pudding and coffee and put it on his bill. We lost our money. During Maxwell's years as a Labour MP we met occasionally but it was not until much later, when, after first denying his Jewishness, he re-emerged as a vociferous patron of Jewish causes in Israel, that I ran into him more often. For the sake of the cause I became quite friendly with him and his French wife who, though not Jewish herself, is dedicated in her commitment to the memory of the Holocaust. I went to birthday parties at Headington Hall, the mansion Maxwell leased from Oxford County Council, and marvelled at his stage-managed appearances and departures by helicopter. I witnessed embarrassing scenes in his penthouse office in Holborn, where his guests sat on uncomfortably low sofas while he towered over them on an oversized stool. Every few minutes his telephone would ring and after a hushed exchange he would apologize for having to make a quick exit to speak to the Russian Prime Minister or some other Eastern potentate. On one occasion half the cabinet of Bulgaria was waiting in the ante-room. Most painful of all was the sight of Peter Jay, former Ambassador of Her Britannic Majesty in Washington and now his amanuensis, slinking in, grey-faced, to take instructions from Maxwell.

Lord Thomson of Fleet, the burly Canadian who bought the *Sunday Times* and then, in 1966, *The Times*, was perhaps the first newspaper proprietor who unashamedly avowed that his line was the bottom line. In my view it was he who started the process whereby newspapers follow the requirements of the market and the trend of reader interest rather than setting the agenda. When discussing a project with him he always had his ready reckoner at hand. Denis Hamilton, his faithful aide, was as good as his word. He backed me up at a merciless auction for Henry Kissinger's White House memoirs and through dramatic serialization helped make James Watson's *Double Helix* the worldwide success it became. But the most creative collaboration I had with the *Sunday Times* was in the period of Harold Evans's editorship, when the paper already belonged to Rupert Murdoch. Harry was a engaging mixture of starry-eyed adolescent from the north of England, social missionary and professional perfectionist. He worked wonders with copy and could turn turgid raw material into rhapsodic prose. He left Murdoch's employ after one of the most spectacular editor–proprietor duels in Fleet Street.

I have never found Rupert Murdoch the vindictive autocrat he has sometimes been described as. He never seemed to mind that we published and re-published *Good Times, Bad Times*, Harold Evans's passionate *j'accuse* against him. He strikes me as having that touch of ruthlessness in business mingled with sentimental attachment to old friends which is the attribute of many an absolute monarch. I came very close to persuading him to publish his own memoirs. Ann Getty and I happened to be present at a small dinner in Sydney given for Rupert and his wife Anna by Neville Wran, a former Premier of New South Wales. The Murdochs arrived an hour late flushed with excitement. 'This has been an important day in my life', Rupert announced. 'I have re-acquired my father's newspaper business in Australia; I have bought the *South China Morning Post* in Hong Kong and I have just been told over the telephone that I have beaten the unions at Wapping.' I urged him to make this day the opening chapter of his memoirs. He was taken aback, thought for a moment and then said, 'Talk to me in a few months' time.' When I met him again at Kay Graham's in Washington half a year later I reminded him of our conversation. We lunched shortly afterwards in London and he signed a contract for his memoirs. Random House, New York, offered a million dollars for the American rights and we were backed by the *Sunday Telegraph*. But Murdoch's initial enthusiasm waned when he was hit by a calamitous downturn in his affairs and after some months I received a lapidary telegram calling the whole thing off.

The newest of the international press tycoons to arrive in Britain is the Canadian Catholic Conrad Black, who made a spectacular entry when, still in his mid-forties, he bought the *Daily* and *Sunday Telegraph* from Lord Hartwell, provoking emotional reactions in the Hartwell circle and indeed the British Establishment. Who was this colonial intruder, this rugged frontiersman who stops at the threshold of a crowded room and eyes it hesitantly, if not with suspicion, before entering? I first met him at Jayne Wrightsman's dinner table in New York and was prepared to have my prejudices confirmed, but was pleasantly surprised when he drew me into a corner and embarked on a discourse about de Gaulle's literary style, quoting passages from his memoirs and from one of his early works, *Le Fil de l'Épée.* I learnt that Black had himself written a magisterial biography of the French-Canadian Premier Duplessis and had collected a considerable library of historical and political biography. Indeed he was the most learned of press lords while still bearing the marks of the company raider and deal maker. Conrad married the Canadian journalist Barbara Amiel, a dear friend of mine who made a meteoric career with her polemical columns. Her sharp mind and stylish pen are matched by stunning looks and a becoming self-mocking modesty. Theirs was a quick courtship. They married shortly after Annabelle and I. We went to their intimate wedding dinner where the Thatchers, the Duchess of York, Miriam Gross, the Metcalfes, Jacob Rothschild and David Frost were among the guests. When I joined the board of Hollinger Inc., the Toronto-based parent company of Conrad Black's British titles, I discovered part of his strength. He has assembled a team of dynamic fellow executives, some of them comrades in arms from his earliest days, who lend the whole enterprise a distinctive *esprit de corps.* Conrad and Barbara Black, both passionately interested in politics, may well prove to be the most dynamic press couple since Henry and Clare Luce of *Time Life* fame.

In my own career I found the recent transition from a proprietorial to a consultative role centred on ideas and projects rather than management a relief rather than a trauma. I came to enjoy my new position all the more when Ion Trewin, whom I had tried unsuccessfully to win for our firm in the past, joined Weidenfeld & Nicolson as publishing director under the Orion banner, thus ensuring continuity. From the outset Weidenfeld & Nicolson has benefited from remarkable editorial talent: Sonia Orwell, Antonia Fraser, Barley Alison all made their mark in the early years. Nicolas Thompson's contribution to the academic list was invaluable and

Tony Godwin, a former bookseller and Penguin editorial star, had a charismatic touch with authors and even agents. Robin Denniston spent a fruitful period as Deputy Chairman and dedicated editor of such authors as Elizabeth Longford, Frances Donaldson and Thomas Pakenham among many others. And John Curtis, quiet, reliable, but full of original ideas, ran the editorial department, handling art books, biography and fiction with an equally sure touch in the 1970s and '80s.

We gave Ed Victor his first job in publishing. An American at Cambridge who went through various stages of fashionable rebellion, Victor left us to found an exotic magazine and then helped Tom Maschler run Jonathan Cape. A visit to India provoked cathartic change. He met an American lawyer, married and set up as an agent. Today he is unique in Britain as a transatlantic dealmaker, and though twice as tall as Swifty Lazar, he is of equal stature as a worldly, exuberant impresario.

It would be wrong of me not to acknowledge that my relationships with British literary agents were often far from easy. This was because my publishing style was most effective when I acted as an agent myself, selling rights in our books to American and foreign language publishers and to proprietors and editors of national newspapers for serialization. Matching authors to ideas and ideas to authors meant, in many instances, generating large advances for them by pre-selling the rights myself.

There are of course British agents with whom I established the best of relationships. Our star authors Elizabeth Longford and Antonia Fraser were both represented by Graham Watson of Curtis Brown, a quiet literary man whose neatly trimmed beard adds to his air of scholarly distinction. A shrewd businessman, he also had an understated but on occasion devastating sense of gossipy humour. Another star author, Nigel Nicolson, was represented by Diana Crawford who later became Diana Baring. Clever, attractive and outgoing, Diana was a frequent guest at my parties. With Michael Sissons, one of the most powerful and creative agents I have known, I enjoyed periods of harmonious and productive collaboration. We had spells of acrimony which ended in reconciliation. Indeed, a list of friendly or helpful agents could go on, but not for too long.

Relations with my fellow British publishers were also more distant than might have been expected. Some regarded me as an outsider, others as a rival. I never saw myself as part of the British publishing Establishment, nor did I seek to belong to it, not being in this context group minded or drawn towards committee work. While my own preoccupations were a restless searching for authors, books and wider contacts, there was a publishing industry whose leaders operated in fields in which I played little or no part. I did not for example participate in the activities of our professional body, the Publishers Association. It was not that I regarded such activities as unimportant – indeed they related to matters central to all of us in the trade. Thus the Association lobbied long and hard against the extension of VAT to books; it supported the Net Book Agreement which forbids discounting by booksellers; it encouraged the enforcement of laws against pirated editions which, produced mainly in the Third World, deprived the originating publishers of their rates and authors of their royalties; it fought successfully against illegal photocopying of works still in copyright. It also defended against many challenges that last legacy of imperialism, the 'exclusive market' for British books which means that for all their power and riches American publishers forgo the right to export their editions to the British Commonwealth as constituted in 1947, together with prewar 'dependencies', such as Jordan, Iraq, Egypt and even Israel as part of the former Palestine. Today this almost papal division of the world is not observed as rigidly as before, not least because of the revolution which has seen American houses like Random House, Harpers and Simon and Schuster establish themselves as British publishers as well.

My outsider status may have been reinforced by one other factor – namely that my permanent quest for purchases of rights in the books we published did not include my fellow British publishers. This applied even to paperback rights. In the postwar years nearly all the famous names – John Murray, Chatto & Windus, Cape, The Bodley Head, Eyre & Spottiswoode, Michael Joseph, Hamish Hamilton, Secker & Warburg – were essentially hardback publishers. Only a few, like Collins, had an interest in publishing paperbacks. There was something elitist, almost snobbish, in the way paperback companies were dismissed as 'reprint houses', for the notion of paperbacks originating their own titles was only in infancy. Nothing could be in more marked contrast with the position today. Now the paperback potential of a book – particularly in the age of large retail chains with enormous buying power, airport bookstalls, film and television tie-ins – is more likely than not to dictate the profile of a publisher's list.

Two highly gifted publishers who worked with me later made it on their own. Colin Haycraft, a brilliant classical scholar and athlete who edited our World University Library in the 1960s, left to revive the old, distinguished Duckworth imprint and Colin Webb, an inventive virtuoso of the coffee-table book, set up Pavilion Books. Michael Dover, whose tact and bedside manner with his authors has made him a great reputation, still runs the art book department of Weidenfeld & Nicolson. I feel a special debt to Christopher Falkus, who in terms of ten years and four years, interrupted by the tenure of a temptingly senior job at Methuen, was my principal lieutenant. Our relations were tense and difficult at times and our temperaments not always congenial, but I owe him a great debt of gratitude. He was imaginative, decisive and sensible, often much more sensible than I was. Equally at home in the senior common room and on the cricket field, his versatility was remarkable. Christopher, a devoted friend of Antonia and Harold Pinter, brought Olivia Manning and Marina Warner to the firm among many other authors and organized compendious illustrated reference books in association with *Newsweek* and Book Club Associates. He also oversaw a sumptuous volume on Westminster Abbey commissioned by Walter Annenberg.

We were well served in other respects. A distinguished lineage of publicists included Jeremy Hadfield and if our firm never had a crisis in printing quality or disastrous delays in production it is due initially to Keith Lilley and then to Richard Hussey. Twenty years old when he arrived, Richard became one of the best book production directors in the business and still holds the reins magnificently. Alan Miles was financial director for over a quarter of a century, a dedicated professional who retired with the advent of Orion as did the most loyal of all collaborators and a lifelong friend, Bud MacLennan. Impeccably dressed, pretty and elegant, Bud, who was for many years in charge of foreign rights, started as an agent at Curtis Brown and sold me the first *Private Eye Annual*. She introduced the founding trio of outrageous iconoclasts – Richard Ingrams, Christopher Booker and William Rushton – and we drank to the health of a journal which waged a merciless guerrilla war against a multitude of targets – myself among them – and which was to have a formative effect on British publishing.

Ariadne's thread through the maze of my work and personal life has been provided by my personal assistant and friend Pat Kinsman who, ever loyal yet never uncritical, steered me through many a dangerous current.

Having traversed half a century of book publishing, I feel we have come to the end of a distinct era. Even before the new century begins, changes at least as vast as those of Gutenberg's revolution have occurred in the world of communication. These changes will radically alter means of production and channels of distribution and vary the role of the writer, editor and publisher. Yet works of the imagination, fiction, poetry and drama, works of creative thought, interpretative insight and original scholarship, will be as crucial as before. They will be needed as the indispensable matrices of multimedia use. Already new works of reference are being transferred from book to disk. Like actors in an evergreen classic, writer and publisher will adapt costume and scenery to the exigencies of a changing *Zeitgeist*. They will continue to create and serve an ever-widening world without barriers.

*   *   *

Nigel Nicolson once told me that his father considered a year in which he had not made a new friend a lost year. I have been lucky in finding new friends throughout my life and the last few years are no exception. Above all, they brought me Annabelle. I love my married life and the companionship of one who shares my interests. One proof of an enjoyable relationship is having an overabundance rather than a shortage of subjects to talk about, and we keep each other up until all hours. Annabelle's love of music and knowledge, greater than mine, makes pilgrimages to Salzburg, Bayreuth and Pesaro, Rossini's birthplace, even more stimulating. She helps me with my work for English National Opera and she has made fast friends with authors, colleagues and fellow partisans of different causes – and their wives. In an ever more active life there are new challenges and much work to be done, but I feel I can do it with some confidence for, having known contentment, obsession and the distress of divorce, I have at last found happiness.

INDEX